THE MACMILLAN ILLUSTRATED ENCYCLOPEDIA OF
DINOSAURS
AND PREHISTORIC ANIMALS

THE MACMILLAN
ILLUSTRATED ENCYCLOPEDIA OF
DINOSAURS
AND PREHISTORIC ANIMALS
A VISUAL WHO'S WHO OF
PREHISTORIC LIFE

Dougal Dixon, Barry Cox, R.J.G. Savage, Brian Gardiner
Foreword by Dr. Malcolm C. McKenna

MACMILLAN PUBLISHING COMPANY
NEW YORK

A Marshall Edition
This book was conceived, edited and designed by
Marshall Editions Limited
170 Piccadilly
London W1V 9DD

Copyright © 1988 by
Marshall Editions Limited.

First published in the USA in 1988 by
Macmillan Publishing Company,
a division of Macmillan, Inc.

Macmillan Publishing Company
866 Third Avenue
New York, NY 10022
Collier Macmillan Canada, Inc.

Library of Congress Cataloging-in-Publication Data
Dixon, Dougal.
  Macmillan illustrated encyclopedia of dinosaurs and prehistoric animals.

  Includes index.
  1. Vertebrates, Fossil. I. Macmillan Publishing Company. II. Title.
QE841.D588 1988 566 88–1800

ISBN 0-02-580191-0

Macmillan books are available at special discounts for bulk purchases for sales promotions, premiums, fund-raising, or educational use. For details contact:
    Special Sales Director
    Macmillan Publishing Company
    866 Third Avenue
    New York, NY 10022

10 9 8 7 6 5 4 3 2 1

Printed in Italy

Consultant Editor: **Professor Barry Cox** Department of Biology, King's College, London

CONSULTANTS:
Fishes: **Professor Brian Gardiner**
Professor of Vertebrate Paleontology, King's College, London
Contribution: Introduction to fishes (*pp. 18–21*).

Amphibians and Reptiles: **Professor Barry Cox**
Contribution: Introduction to amphibians (*pp. 46–49*), reptiles (*pp. 58–61*), ruling reptiles (*pp. 90–93*), birds (*pp. 170–173*) and mammal-like reptiles (*pp. 182–185*).

Birds: **Dr. Colin Harrison**
Former Principal Scientific Officer, Sub-Department of Ornithology, British Museum (Natural History), London
Contribution: Text on birds (*pp. 174–181*).

Mammals: **Professor R. J. G. Savage**
Department of Geology, University of Bristol
Contribution: Introduction to mammals (*pp. 194–197*).

The publishers would like to thank C. G. Sibley *et al.* for their kind permission to base the chart on pp. 170–171 on their recent work on bird evolution. This is published in full in: Sibley, C. G., Ahlquist, J. E., and Monroe, B. L. Jr. (1988) *A classification of the living birds of the world based on DNA-DNA hybridization studies. Auk*, 105 (op. 3).

Maps p. 11 based on material from Cox, C. B., and Moore, P. D. (1985) *Biogeography*. Blackwell Scientific Publications Limited.
Archaeopteryx fossil p. 15 (top) from Colbert, E. H. (1980) *Evolution of the Vertebrates*. John Wiley, New York.

Index by Richard Raper and Stewart Ulyott of Indexing Specialists, Hove.

Editor	**Carole C. Devaney**
Deputy Editor	**Philip Boys**
Mammals Editor	**Jonathan Elphick**
Art Director	**John Bigg**
Art Assistant	**Jonathan Bigg**
Researcher	**Jazz Wilson**
Managing Editor	**Ruth Binney**
Production	**Barry Baker**
	Janice Storr

ARTISTS:
Colin Newman Fishes (*pp. 22–43*) and Amphibians (*pp. 50–55*)

Steve Kirk Reptiles (*pp. 62–167, 186–191*) and Mammals (*pp. 238–239*)

Malcolm Ellis Birds (*pp. 174–179*)

Graham Allen Mammals (*pp. 198–203, 210–235, 246–251, 258–263, 282–283*)

Andrew Robinson Mammals (*pp. 242–243, 254–255, 270–279*)

Andrew Wheatcroft Mammals (*pp. 286–295*)

Steve Holden Mammals (*pp. 206–207, 238–239, 266–267*)

Grundy & Northedge Evolutionary charts (*pp. 8–9, 46–47, 58–59, 90–91, 170–171, 182–183, 194–195*)

Vana Haggerty Additional illustrations (*pp. 11–17, 20–21, 48–49, 60–61, 92–93, 172–173, 184–185, 196–197*)

Contents

Foreword

If any proof were needed that the study of prehistoric life is more than a matter of "old bones," then this book provides it in ample measure. For here is a natural history of times past, featuring real creatures that lived, breathed, reproduced — then died forever. That they could be brought back to life in such convincing form is a credit to the painstaking scientific detective work of a team of paleontologists, writers and artists.

In embarking on this project, the first decision was which animals to select. The mighty and ever-popular dinosaurs were obvious candidates for inclusion in the portrait gallery of past life, but to recreate a truly comprehensive collection of prehistoric animals it was vital to add to them not only their reptile relatives but also representatives of all the other major groups of vertebrates, or animals with backbones. The result is a fascinating catalog of creatures, which includes the fishes of the past, many of them heavily armored with bony scales; the first amphibians, pioneers of life on land; the

ancient masters of the air, in the form of flying reptiles and the first birds and bats; and the mammals that were our predecessors, from mammoths and sabertooths to the early apes and hominids.

The reconstructions were then made through a combination of the knowledge of the paleontologists and the skills of the artists. The resulting creatures may look fantastic, but they are by no means the creations of the imagination. All have been drawn and painted according to the strictest of scientific principles. In recreating each animal the artists have held faithfully to the fossil record — which sometimes contains not merely bones and teeth but also impressions of skin, hair, feathers and even footprints millions of years old.

From study of fossils and of animal anatomy, plus detailed observations of the appearance and behavior of modern creatures, the artists have been able to "clothe" the skeleton of each animal, and make realistic reconstructions of physical features, posture and coloration. The results are surprising

and fascinating, both in the similarities to familiar modern creatures, and the obvious differences.

Life began on Earth several billion years ago. The first fishes, the most ancient of the creatures in this book, appeared about 500 million years ago. The dinosaurs and other reptiles began their rule some 225 million years ago, a domination which lasted for another 150 million years. By comparison, we humans branched away from other primates a mere 5 million years ago.

Such vast expanses of time are hard for the human mind to grasp, but it is only possible to make a meaningful study of life in prehistoric eras by considering time in these broad sweeps. The reasons for this are twofold. First, although evolution can proceed rapidly, it usually progresses relatively slowly. The changes that take place in the bodies of animals from generation to generation are generally minute, so it can be hundreds, thousands or even millions of years before differences become discernible in the fossil record. Second, the history of animal life on Earth must be considered hand in hand with the climatic and geological forces which have molded the planet over the millennia. These forces exert their impact over huge periods of time.

Although we humans are relative newcomers on Earth, we have done much to change its face. Not least, we have been instrumental in causing the extinction or near-extinction of many animals and plants. So as you marvel at the wonders of the life in the past it might be as well to remember that many of the animals with whom we share our planet might be confined, in future generations, to the pages of a book such as this. Animals past and present are part of our heritage as Earth dwellers. This book pays them tribute.

Malcolm C. McKenna
Fisk Curator of Paleontology
American Museum of Natural History

Introduction

The solar system, which includes the Earth, is about 4.6 billion years old. The earliest traces of life on our planet are microscopic fossils of blue-green algae and bacteria that are found in rocks some 3.5 billion years old (*opposite*).

The atmosphere of the ancient Earth contained no oxygen. Like most modern green plants, the early algae produced oxygen, but this would have quickly disappeared because it combined readily with various elements and compounds in the Earth's crust. Not until about 1.5 billion years ago was there enough free oxygen available for animals to use to keep themselves alive.

The tracks and burrows of sea-dwelling animals, nearly 1 billion years old, are known. Animals with external skeletons in the form of shells appeared about 600 million years ago, in the Precambrian Era.

Fossil animals contained in Cambrian rocks include worms, corals, sponges, mollusks, brachiopods and jointed-limbed trilobites. Most of these fed either by digesting mud or by filtering tiny organisms out of the seawater. In the succeeding Ordovician period a variety of predatory animals, such as sea urchins and starfish, appeared.

The oldest fossils of vertebrates, the animals with backbones to which this book is devoted, were jawless fish. The fossil remains of the most ancient vertebrate, *Arandaspis* (*see p. 24*), come from marine Ordovician rocks in Australia, more than 500 million years old.

Life on land
Colonization of the land began in the Devonian, when the first insects and many different plants, similar to ferns and club mosses, appeared. By the Late Devonian, some of these plants had evolved into the first trees, up to 82 ft/25 m high.

The major units of geological time are the eras, starting with the Precambrian. Each era is further subdivided into periods and epochs. The dates on the chart indicate the time at which each unit of time is thought to have begun.

The arrows show in broad outline the evolution of the vertebrates, and the links that are thought to exist between the major groups. Notes on the evolution of plants and invertebrates indicate other trends. For instance, the rise of the mammals in the Cretaceous can be seen to coincide with the burgeoning of flowering plants.

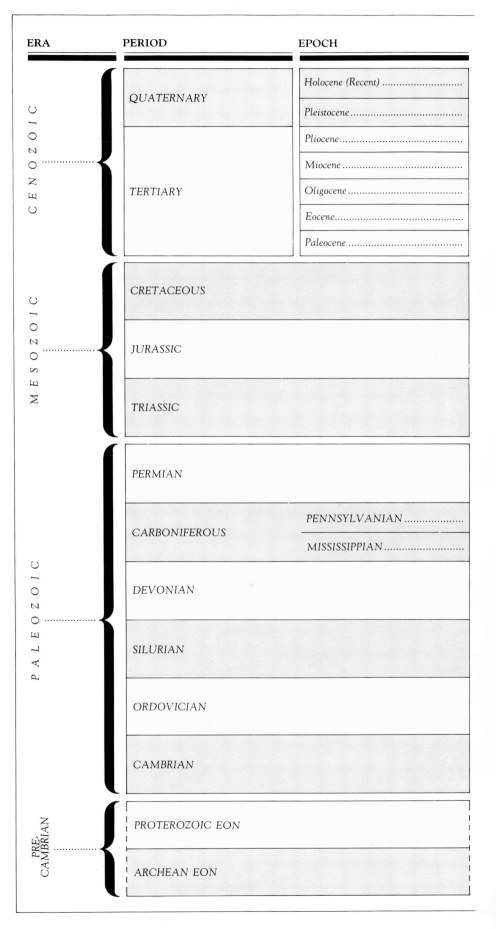

ERA	PERIOD	EPOCH
CENOZOIC	QUATERNARY	Holocene (Recent) ....
		Pleistocene ....
	TERTIARY	Pliocene ....
		Miocene ....
		Oligocene ....
		Eocene ....
		Paleocene ....
MESOZOIC	CRETACEOUS	
	JURASSIC	
	TRIASSIC	
PALEOZOIC	PERMIAN	
	CARBONIFEROUS	PENNSYLVANIAN ....
		MISSISSIPPIAN ....
	DEVONIAN	
	SILURIAN	
	ORDOVICIAN	
	CAMBRIAN	
PRE-CAMBRIAN	PROTEROZOIC EON	
	ARCHEAN EON	

EVOLUTION OF VERTEBRATES (backboned animals)

EVOLUTION OF PLANTS AND INVERTEBRATES

JAWLESS FISHES

CARTILAGINOUS FISHES

BONY FISHES

AMPHIBIANS

TURTLES AND TORTOISES

SNAKES AND LIZARDS

CROCODILES

DINOSAURS

BIRDS

MAMMALS

MAMMAL-LIKE REPTILES

REPTILES

Plants and invertebrates similar to today's groups.

Burgeoning of flowering plants, including grasses and other non-woody types. Also, formation of vast forests in tropical and temperate zones. Radiation of modern bivalves and gastropods. Invertebrate groups similar to modern types.

First flowering plants (angiosperms), including beech, fig and magnolia. Pollinating insects diversify. Ammonites and belemnites extinct. Brachiopods decline.

Abundance of cycads, ferns and conifers. Abundance of ammonites and belemnites. Brachiopods common. Diversification of mollusks and echinoderms.

Horsetails, ferns, ginkgos and conifers dominant land vegetation. Appearance of cycads. Extinction of seed ferns. Heyday of ammonites. Appearance of modern corals.

Abundance of ferns, conifers and seed ferns. Decline of horsetails. *Glossopteris* flora in Gondwanaland. Radiation of insects. Extinction of trilobites and other marine groups.

Giant club mosses and horsetail ferns abound. First gymnosperms (ginkgos, yew, conifers). First flying insects. Decline of trilobites and brachiopods. Graptolites become extinct.

First ferns appear, initially leafless and rootless, eventually treelike (tree ferns). First true seed plants (seed ferns). First ammonites, crabs, spiders, mites and insects (non-flying).

First land plants. Calcareous algae abundant in seas. Profusion of marine invertebrates. Appearance and radiation of eurypterids (sea scorpions). Decline of graptolites.

Simple and reef-building algae. Heyday of graptolites. Abundance of trilobites, brachiopods, gastropods, crinoids, corals, echinoids, bryozoans and cephalopods.

First green and red algae. Trilobites abound in shallow seas. Many shelled brachiopods, gastropods, bivalves; also crinoids, graptolites, sponges and segmented worms.

First multicellular, soft-bodied animals, which looked like worms, jellyfish and seapens, appeared toward end of Eon.

First single-celled organisms appeared toward end of Archean Eon, including the first bacteria and blue-green algae.

Introduction

The leaves and débris of land plants produced the first deposits rich in organic remains. When mixed with rainwater, these formed muds, which provided a habitat for the first freshwater communities of creatures. Many types of fish lived here, and at the end of the Devonian their descendants, the amphibians, first crawled out of the water, and for a time led a largely land-based existence.

By the Late Carboniferous (Pennsylvanian), different floras had evolved. A lush, swampy tropical rain forest covered much of North America and Europe, and was inhabited by a variety of fishes, amphibians and the first reptiles.

During the Permian period, reptiles gradually came to dominate the land, and ousted the amphibians. Herbivorous reptiles became common in the Late Permian, and, in turn, provided an opportunity for the evolution of large, carnivorous reptiles that preyed on them.

At this time, and into the Triassic, the continents of the world were united in one huge landmass called Pangaea (see p. 11). Land-living creatures could spread anywhere in this vast area. However, many parts of that landmass were far from the sea and its rain-providing clouds, and these areas became arid. Many older types of plant became extinct during this time, and were replaced by the seed ferns, ginkgos and many new types of conifers.

This was the type of arid scene, with its changing flora, that witnessed the long reign of the ruling reptiles, starting in the Triassic and culminating at the end of the Cretaceous. The mammals arrived in the Late Triassic, but did not take center stage until the Tertiary, when the dinosaurs, and most of their kin, had bowed out. The first birds appeared in the Late Jurassic.

The modern plant world began in the Early Cretaceous, when the first flowering plants (angiosperms) evolved. Hand in hand with this came a great diversification of insect pollinators. So by Early Tertiary times, the world was dominated, as it is today, by flowering plants, birds and mammals on land, and by advanced types of bony and cartilaginous fishes in the waters.

The geography of life
The geography of yesterday's world was very different from that of today. The way in which ancient and modern animals are distributed can be explained by the discovery that the Earth's surface is divided into moving sections, or "plates."

The force that powers these movements — which are still happening — originates in the heat of the Earth's core. In some areas, upward currents move this heat so that it is just below the crust of the Earth. There, the current spreads out sideways, and cools before returning toward the core. If this upward current lies below a continent, it can split the continent into diverging fragments. Between these, new oceanic crust is formed. Elsewhere, old oceanic crust disappears down a system of great trenches that lies around the edge of the Pacific Ocean.

Sometimes, these movements — known as continental drift or plate tectonics — caused existing continents to split into pieces, or else to become fused together (see opposite). This process, together with encroachments or retreats of the sea, lead to progressive changes in the world's geography.

In the Devonian period, between 408 and 360 million years ago, North America and Europe were part of the single continent "Euramerica," since the North Atlantic Ocean did not exist at that time. Fossils of the first land vertebrates — the early amphibians and reptiles — have been found almost exclusively on that continent, which suggests that they may have evolved there. Only during the Carboniferous period did Euramerica become attached to the great southern continent of Gondwanaland, made up of what is today South America, Africa, Antarctica, Australia and India.

The early amphibians and reptiles did not penetrate into Gondwanaland until it became united to Euramerica in the Late Permian. By the Triassic all the major land areas of the world were united into the single supercontinent of Pangaea.

Toward the end of the Triassic, or at the beginning of the Jurassic, Pangaea started to split up. While oceans developed between the continents, shallow seaways spread across them during the Cretaceous. By the Late Cretaceous, there were 2 landmasses in the northern hemisphere, which contained different faunas of dinosaurs (see p. 93) and mammals, as well as different plants. At the same time, Gondwanaland was breaking up also. By the middle of the Cretaceous, India had already split away and started its long journey northward. Our familiar, present-day geography appeared only after Africa had joined Europe in the Miocene, as recently as 20 million years ago, and the Panama Isthmus had linked North and South America in the Pliocene.

By chance, the separation of the continents took place after modern types of mammal had started to spread through the world. As a result, each continent came to have its own typical fauna of mammals, which had evolved within that landmass.

The fossil record
The evidence of life in these prehistoric eras comes from a unique "history book." This is the record of the rocks, in which is inscribed in fossil form a picture of life in times past.

A fossil is any trace of an ancient form of life. Most animals or plants live and die without leaving any permanent evidence of their existence. But, occasionally, the conditions are suitable for organisms to become fossilized.

When an animal dies, the soft parts of its body normally decay quickly or are eaten by other animals. The hard parts, too, may be gnawed away and broken up. But if the animal's body is buried in soft sediments — such as mud at the bottom of a stream or lake, or fine sand on the seabed — it may be protected from attack by other animals. Though the soft parts will probably decay, the skeleton or the teeth may remain. It is now, potentially, a fossil.

Several events can now turn the skeleton into a true fossil (see pp. 12–13). First, sediments continue to be laid down, and the layers (strata) of mud or sand become consolidated and harder. The water that continues to seep through the sediments contains minerals, which then cement the particles of sand or mud into solid rock. And those minerals also percolate through the skeleton itself, and gradually replace the material of the bones themselves. This often happens in such a way that the detailed microscopic structure of the original bone is still visible, unchanged.

Sometimes, after the skeleton has become entombed, it may be completely dissolved away by the percolating waters, leaving a cavity. If this cavity then becomes filled with a mineral deposit, this may form a natural cast of the original bone (see p. 13).

Possibly the most unchanged and perfect fossil bones are those from Pleistocene mammals and birds entombed in the tar pits of Rancho La Brea in Los Angeles. Here, tar seeped to the surface and formed deep pools. After rainfall, the water would lie on top of the tar, and attracted animals such as mammoths and ground sloths to drink. They would then become mired in the sticky tar and gradually sink into it. Before they disappeared forever, their carcasses attracted predatory direwolves, sabertooth cats and scavenging vultures, all of which also became trapped and died. All of their bones are perfectly preserved in

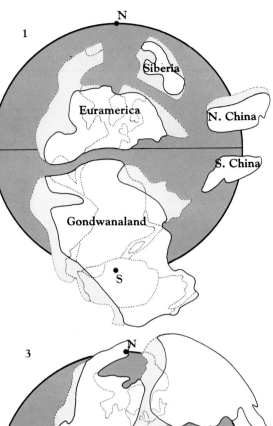

THE WORLD'S CHANGING FACE

The series of globes shows how the face of the Earth has changed over the millennia. In these maps, areas at the "back" of the globe have been folded out. Dotted lines indicate the coastlines of the modern continents; shallow seas are shaded light gray, deep seas in dark gray.

1 In the Late Carboniferous to Early Permian, there were 2 great continents, Euramerica in the north and Gondwanaland in the south. Three other land masses were the forerunners of eventual Asia. Euramerica was the exclusive home of early amphibians and reptiles.

2 By the Late Permian, all the world's continents were united into one huge landmass called Pangaea. At this time, early amphibians and reptiles penetrated into Gondwanaland, and spread into Asia.

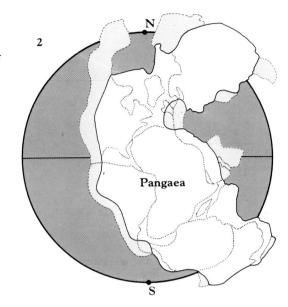

3 Pangaea started to split up so that, by the Mid-Jurassic, seaways spread down the eastern coast of Africa. The fledgling Atlantic appeared as North America started to separate from Europe.

4 In the Early Cretaceous sea had spread around Africa's southern tip. North and South America split apart at this time. Seaways spread northward to separate Europe from Asia. India had split away from Gondwanaland and begun its long journey northward.

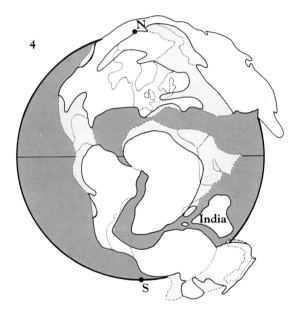

5 By the Late Cretaceous, there were 2 landmasses in the northern hemisphere. One, "Asiamerica," included Asia and western North America. The other, "Euramerica," comprised Europe and eastern North America. These 2 continents contained different faunas of dinosaurs and mammals, as well as different plants.

6 By the Eocene, the modern continents had nearly taken shape. India had nearly completed its northward journey and Australia and Antarctica had split from the tip of South America. Each continent came to have its own fauna of mammals.

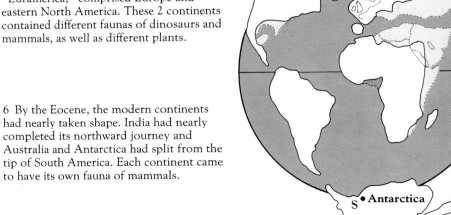

11

Introduction

the tar, and need only to be washed in petrol to extract and clean them.

An even more complete fauna and flora, dating from Middle Eocene times, is found at Messel in southern Germany. Dead animals and plants were swept into a deep lake in a subtropical forest. Each year a thick growth of algae sank to the bottom of the lake and covered them. As a result, the bones and hair of a complete fauna of early mammals — including bats, horses, anteaters and rodents — are preserved, together with their stomach contents and even the skeletons of unborn young. Crocodiles, snakes, frogs, insects, fruits, flowers and leaves are also preserved in this 50 million-year-old time capsule.

Traces of the soft parts of animals can very occasionally be seen as markings on the rocks. For example, it is known that ichthyosaurs, preserved in the fine shales of Holzmaden in southern Germany, had a fin on their backs and sharklike tail fins because, although these structures contained no bony skeleton, an outline of the body exists as a stain in the rock (see p. 80).

The fine limestones of Solnhofen in southern Germany have preserved detailed impressions of the plumage of *Archaeopteryx*, the link between reptiles and birds (see p. 176). Similar impressions show that at least one type of pterosaur may have had a covering of hair (see p. 105).

Fossil footprints are another type of impression. Dinosaur tracks, formed in soft ground which dried and hardened before new layers of sediment covered them up, remain in this permanent, compacted surface. Other traces of the existence of ancient animals are their fossilized droppings, or coprolites.

Which rocks contain fossils?
Because fossils are most commonly formed when an animal's skeleton is entombed within sediments that are being deposited, fossils are thus most likely to be discovered in sedimentary rocks, which are laid down in layers and composed of either mineral or organic matter. Fossils are not usually found in igneous rocks, such as granites and basalts, which pour hot and molten from the earth's interior. Nor are they present in metamorphic rocks, such as marble, which have been transformed by great heat and pressure.

The oldest sedimentary rocks were laid down about 350 million years ago, and vary widely in the size of mineral particles they contain. Fossils are rarely found in rocks in which the "particles" are bolders or pebbles, since the bones are crushed or ground up as the rocks are deposited.

Many fossils have been found in finer-grained sandstones. For example, in Silurian and Devonian times, between 440 and 345 million years ago, a thick belt of Old Red Sandstone was deposited across northeastern North America and northwestern Europe, before those areas had moved apart to form the Atlantic Ocean. These sandstones contain a rich fauna of Devonian freshwater and marine fishes.

Rocks made up of even finer particles, the clays and shales, are common; they form about 60 percent of all sedimentary rocks. As mud dries, it loses its organic débris, and becomes compacted. It first becomes a soft clay, and then either a hard shale, which readily breaks into flat pieces, or mudstone, which breaks up randomly. Clays laid down in the Eocene, about 50 million years ago, have preserved many fossils around both London and Paris.

In contrast with sandstone rocks, limestones and dolomites are not mineral in origin, but are made up mainly of calcium carbonate, or calcium magnesium carbonate, which has been produced by marine animals or plants. The hard shells of many mollusks and of sea urchins and their relatives, the hard bases secreted by reef-building corals, and the cell walls encasing some algae — all these materials are made of solid calcium carbonate. This becomes broken into minute fragments, and is the major constituent of such organic sedimentary rocks.

Chalk is one such rock, and is composed almost entirely of the shells of tiny, marine planktonic organisms. Thick deposits of chalk, laid down in the Late Cretaceous (between 70 and 65 million years ago) in southeastern England, France and central North America, contain the remains of many marine fishes, reptiles and birds.

Peats and coals also have their origins in organic matter, but are formed from the remains of dead land plants. The plant material originally accumulated in

FOSSILIZATION OF AN ICHTHYOSAUR

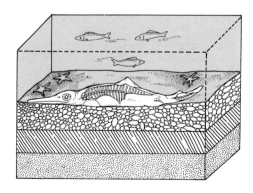

Any animal is most likely to be fossilized if it is buried in soft sediments, like the ichthyosaur body illustrated here in fine sand on the sea bed. The flesh decays, but the bony parts — skull, teeth and skeleton — do not.

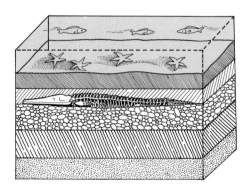

Layers of sediment pile up on top of the bony remnants. Minerals from the sea water percolate through the skeleton and become deposited in the bones, filling any spaces between them. They gradually replace the material of the bones.

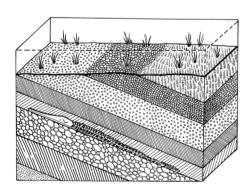

The fossilized skeleton is compressed and distorted by the addition of more layers of sediment and by movements of the land. Here the rock has been pushed upward so that the strata have become tilted and are exposed as dry land.

coastal swamps (rather like the Everglades of Florida today), or in inland basins. They first formed peats, some of which later dried and became compressed into solid coal. The Carboniferous coal belts of eastern North America and of Europe are examples of these, and contain the fossils of many fishes, early amphibians and early reptiles.

Finding fossils
Paleontologists must search for fossils in areas where the appropriate rocks are exposed. That is easiest in the deserts, where many hundreds of square miles of rock may be on view.

The rocks can also be seen in the mountains or hills, where they are not covered by sediments, or in cliffs that may be exposed as the result of earthquakes, the action of rivers or streams, or quarrying by humans.

Although it is not difficult to find rocks which may contain fossils, it is much more difficult to locate the fossils themselves. The rocks of the more densely populated areas of North America and Europe are now fairly well explored, although surprising discoveries can still be made (such as *Baryonyx*, see p. 113). In search of new finds, paleontologists have turned their attention to other parts of the world, particularly to arid regions where rocks are eroding over wide areas.

But paleontologists do not merely go in search of any fossil. Rather they try to answer very specific questions — for example, "What land-living vertebrates

METHODS OF FOSSILIZATION
When bones themselves are not fossilized, a fossil animal can be found in the form of a cast (*top*), or a mold (*below*). A mold is created when an entombed animal is dissolved away, leaving behind a cavity. Usually, the mold is of the hard parts of the body. Where these cover the outside of a creature, as in the bony fish illustrated, the whole body shape can be discerned. A cast is formed when a mold becomes filled with a mineral deposit. In such circumstances, no traces remain of internal body structure.

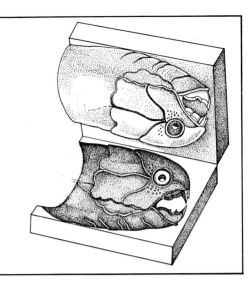

inhabited Australia during the Early Cretaceous?" Such questions lead them, in turn, to study geological maps to find out where suitable, accessible rocks can be found. Even then, the costs of an expedition are so high that this would normally be undertaken only if some promising remains had already been found there.

Once "on location," the scientists can begin to search for fossils. There is no magical method by which these can be found. Long hours tramping across the exposed rocks under a hot sun, and returning, usually empty-handed, to a fairly spartan camp normally precede any discovery. Rocks are searched methodically, layer by layer, or area by

area. Usually, all that the paleontologist finds at first is a piece, or pieces, of bone, projecting from the ground or the side of a cliff.

The hard work then begins. The overlying rock must be taken away to reveal the fossil skeleton, often by cutting the fossil into pieces. The bones then have to be covered with moistened tissue paper and then with a layer of sacking (burlap) soaked in plaster-of-Paris. When this dries and hardens, it protects the fossil during its long, and often rough, ride back to the museum.

Paleontologists must not neglect their record-keeping. Each specimen must be given a number, painted onto it, and a precise note kept of where it was found. This is necessary because later analysis of such information may show, for example, that some animals occur in different rock strata, and thus belong to different communities (*see p. 14*).

Extracting and dating fossils
Once the fossils have arrived back in the laboratory of the museum or university, the plaster jacket is removed, and the fossil bone extracted from its rocky home. Sometimes, this can be done with a hammer and chisel or, on smaller specimens, with sharp, steel needles. But when possible, scientists use chemicals to dissolve away the mineral cement that binds together the particles of sediment. This process can reveal beautifully preserved, 3-D skulls, showing as much detail as those of recently-dead modern animals.

Whatever method is used, the fossil bone is usually badly cracked after its many millions of years in the ground, and must be strengthened by impregnating it with solutions of plastics.

There are both relative and absolute methods of establishing the age of fos-

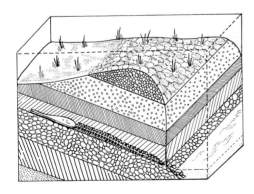

The forces of erosion wear away the land surface. The eroding action of a stream has created a sheer cliff face (*right*). As a result, the tail of the ichthyosaur is beginning to be exposed and bones drop into the bed of the stream.

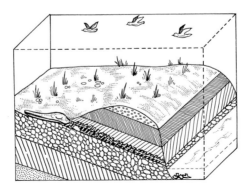

With further erosion, more of the ichthyosaur tail becomes visible. The fossil skull can also be seen, again due to erosive forces wearing away the surface of the land. A paleontologist who discovered these would be prompted to search for the complete skeleton.

Introduction

sils. The relative method depends on 2 facts. First, because sediments are deposited successively, one on top of the other, paleontologists can often establish that one organism lived at a later time than another simply because it is found in rocks that lie higher in the rock sequence of a particular area.

The second fact is that no group of animals or plants lives forever. So within any such sequence, a new group may appear, persist through a number of strata, and then disappear without trace. Some groups evolved early in geological history, some later; some existed for a long time before they became extinct, while others had only a brief span before they were replaced by competitors. So, each unit of geological time is characterized by a unique assemblage of animals or plants (*see p. 14*).

A vast amount of information about many groups of fossil plants and animals has been obtained from different rock strata all over the world. But much work had to be undertaken by early paleontologists and geologists before even the major subdivisions of geological time — into the different eras, periods and epochs (*see pp. 8–9*) — were established and accepted.

The absolute method of dating or aging a fossil establishes its age in "millions of years." It relies upon the fact that some rocks contain radioactive minerals, which were incorporated in the rocks when they were originally deposited. These minerals change, or "decay," into other substances at a rate that can be measured. For example, the rate of decay of the radioactive mineral uranium-235 into lead-207 is such that half of it has turned into lead-207 in 713 million years. So, by studying the relative amounts of uranium-235 and lead-207 in a rock, it is possible to calculate how long the mineral has been decaying, and when the rock was deposited.

Each radioactive date can then be inserted into the chart of relative ages already established for fossil-containing rock strata, to provide the final series of absolute dates quoted throughout this book.

Reconstructing fossil animals

It is rare to find complete fossil skeletons of land-living animals, which means that paleontologists often have to reconstruct the missing portions. This may be straightforward if another specimen of the same type, or a closely related type, is already known, or if the missing part is quite trivial, such as part of the vertebral column.

For example, all the duckbilled dinosaurs (the hadrosaurs, *see pp. 146–153*) have skeletons that are similar from the head down. So, if the skull of a new type of duckbill were to be found, it would be reasonable to assume that the rest of the animal was similar to its relatives. But if a headless duckbill were discovered, it might be impossible to decide which of the various, very different duckbilled skulls originally adorned it, or whether it belonged to a new genus or species.

Similarly, if a very unusual, partial skeleton is found, it may be difficult or impossible to restore the rest of it. For example, paleontologists discovered a large and extraordinary pair of dinosaur forelimbs in the Gobi Desert in 1965. Each forelimb alone was 8 ft/2.4 m long. But paleontologists are still unsure what the remainder of this dinosaur (which was named *Deinocheirus*) might have looked like (*see p. 109*). And if only the skull of the strange dinosaur *Baryonyx* had been discovered in 1986, it would not have been possible to predict the structure of the rest of its skeleton (*see p. 113*).

Paleontologists have to be cautious in these matters of reconstruction, for

their suggestions are carefully evaluated by their colleagues around the world. Paleontologists are as pleased as members of any other profession to have the opportunity to put a colleague right publicly!

Once a specimen is ready for complete restoration, the bones can be fitted together to reveal the proportions and posture of the extinct animal. From the shapes and sizes of the bones themselves, deductions can be made about how the animal lived. Long bones in the lower limbs, for example, suggest a fast-running creature, while short, powerful limb bones may well have belonged to a burrower.

The bones often show projections, depressions or roughened areas indicating where muscles may have been attached. These can be compared with the bones of similar, related living animals, so that an accurate picture can be deduced of the way the creature was clothed with flesh.

Further information on an animal's way of life comes from its teeth. Does it have the sharp, cutting and rending teeth of a carnivore; the little, sharp teeth of an insectivore; the simple, pointed teeth of a fish-eater; or the blunt, grinding teeth of a herbivore? This information tells much about how an animal existed.

Restoration and naming

The really difficult task in reconstructing the appearance of an extinct animal is to work out what its body covering was like, and what color it was. Fish, and some amphibians and reptiles, had bony scales, which are frequently preserved. Birds have feathers, and most mammals have hair. But there is no way of being certain about the body covering of such reptiles as the great dinosaurs or the mammal-like reptiles. All the experts can do is to use their knowledge of living animals (such as elephants) to suggest that larger animals, like the great dinosaurs, did not need any insulation to keep them warm, since their main problem was to get rid of the heat inevitably produced as they exercised their great bodies.

Paleontologists also deduce the color and patterning of fossil creatures from studying their living relatives. Thus, some are colored to match their environment and blend unseen into their background. In smaller animals, that coloration is usually variations of a single color, often shades of brown or green, depending on the surroundings.

When a fossil has been found, the investigating paleontologist will eventually have to decide whether it is another specimen of a fossil that has already

RECORD OF THE ROCKS

When rocks consist of a number of layers, each deposited after the other, the fossils they contain give important clues to the diversity of creatures that lived when each layer was formed, and to their relative age. The rock illustrated contains 8 strata (A–H), of which A is the oldest, H the youngest. Found within the layers are 5 different fossils, each with a different range in time. The distribution of the fossils is unique to each layer and is said to define its stratigraphy. Thus layer A contains only fossil 5, layer H only fossil 1. All 5 fossils are found only in layer E.

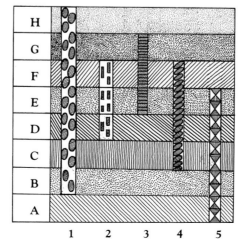

been described and named, or whether it is new to science. If it is new, then its place within the known array of animals has to be ascertained, by comparing its features with those of other fossils, down to genus or species level (*see p. 17*).

Paleontologists rely on an assessment of the degree of difference between 2 fossils when classifying and naming them. If the differences are trivial, or of size alone, or involve characteristics that could have had a sexual function, then the specimens may both belong to the same species. If the differences are greater than that, but the specimens are basically similar, then it is reasonable to interpret them as 2 closely related species. So, a new species of the genus *Anatosaurus* might be called *Anatosaurus edmontoni*, to distinguish it from *Anatosaurus annectens*.

If the differences between 2 fossil specimens are greater, and perhaps suggest that, for instance, the creatures fed on different types of plant or lived in different environments, then the new specimen will instead be recognized as a new genus, just as *Anatosaurus* was recognized in 1942 as a new genus different from *Hadrosaurus*.

So, every organism has a double name. In this example, the generic name is *Anatosaurus*, and the species name is *annectens* — just as one might have a family name, such as Smith, and a forename, such as John or Mary.

The paleontologist is free to choose a name for the new animal, but it is normal to choose a name that has the form of a Latin or Greek word or words. Often, the name reflects some aspect of the animal's structure or presumed habits or origin. So, *Oviraptor* was given that name because it means "egg thief", which is thought to have been its diet and habit.

Sometimes, it becomes clear that different parts of a single genus or species have been independently recognized and named as a new type by 2 scientists. The rule of priority then applies — the earliest name is the one accepted. So, for example, although the name *Brontosaurus* was given to a skeleton of a great dinosaur by Marsh in 1879, it was later realized that a pelvis belonging to the same type of dinosaur had been named *Apatosaurus* by him in 1877. All scientists now refer to this dinosaur as *Apatosaurus* (*see p. 132*).

The creatures in this book
Today, about 9000 different genera of fossil vertebrate are recognized — in round figures, about 2500 fishes, 400 amphibians, 1500 reptiles, 1000 birds and 3500 mammals.

In choosing fossils for description

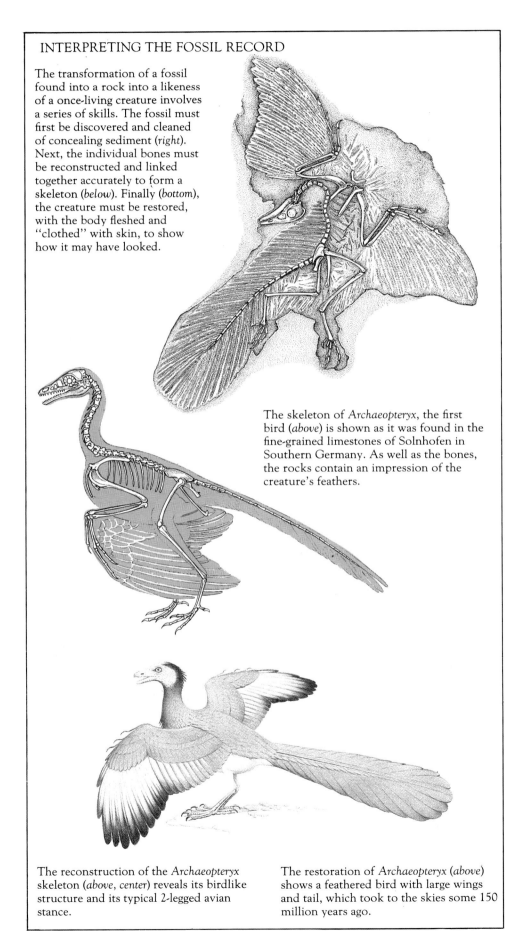

INTERPRETING THE FOSSIL RECORD

The transformation of a fossil found into a rock into a likeness of a once-living creature involves a series of skills. The fossil must first be discovered and cleaned of concealing sediment (*right*). Next, the individual bones must be reconstructed and linked together accurately to form a skeleton (*below*). Finally (*bottom*), the creature must be restored, with the body fleshed and "clothed" with skin, to show how it may have looked.

The skeleton of *Archaeopteryx*, the first bird (*above*) is shown as it was found in the fine-grained limestones of Solnhofen in Southern Germany. As well as the bones, the rocks contain an impression of the creature's feathers.

The reconstruction of the *Archaeopteryx* skeleton (*above, center*) reveals its birdlike structure and its typical 2-legged avian stance.

The restoration of *Archaeopteryx* (*above*) shows a feathered bird with large wings and tail, which took to the skies some 150 million years ago.

Introduction

and illustration, several principles have been used. As far as possible, they provide a reasonable sample of the diversity of each group. They show interesting features of anatomy and adaptation, and their remains are complete enough to allow an accurate restoration. At the same time, care has been taken to illustrate those that have been important to the history of paleontology, such as *Iguanodon* and *Megalosaurus*, and those that generations of both adults and children alike have found romantic and fascinating, such as *Tyrannosaurus* and *Stegosaurus*.

In this book, the scientific names of the animals or groups have been translated where it is helpful to do so. Also to make the book more "user-friendly," such terms as "megalosaurs" are used when referring to the classification groups, rather than the more formal "megalosaurids" or "Megalosauridae."

To make the story as complete as possible, each major group of vertebrates is introduced by its evolutionary history. This is also graphically depicted in a chart, their span in time and their relationship to each other.

The description of individual animals on the following pages is preceded by

the headings TIME, LOCATION and SIZE. TIME is based on geological time scale, and refers to the age of the rocks in which the fossilized animal was found, and therefore when it lived. LOCALITY refers to the continent and country or state where the fossil was discovered, and therefore where the animal lived. SIZE refers generally to the total length of the animal, from the tip of its snout to the tip of its tail, if it had one. Sometimes, where relevant, the animal's height is also given as well as or instead of its length. Specimens of animals can vary greatly in size, so the measurements are often an average of the fossil finds.

Paleontology and evolution

Though many of the philosophers of Ancient Greece, such as Herodotus, realized that fossils were the remains of once-living creatures, this knowledge was forgotten during the Dark Ages. For a long time, fossils were thought merely to be one manifestation of a mysterious tendency for stony objects to appear spontaneously, like pearls in oysters.

In 1667, Niels Stensen, a biologist from Copenhagen studying in Florence, realized the true nature of fossils when he saw that objects called "tongue

stones" were identical to the teeth of living sharks. Stensen suggested that the tongue stones were teeth that had become encased in sediments which had later hardened, and this explanation was soon accepted for many fossils that looked like parts of living organisms.

But it was much harder to accept in this way the remains of such creatures as ammonites, which did not correspond to any living creature. For the idea that any once-living thing could have become extinct suggested that part of God's original creation must have been imperfect — an idea that was quite unacceptable to many Christians in those days. Another problem was that these objects looked as though they must have been marine animals, yet they were often found in rocks high in the mountains of Europe.

One solution was to suggest that these animals were not really extinct, but that their living relatives had not yet been found, since the world was still only partly known. And that seemed to be true in at least some cases, as, for example, when the living deep-sea nautilus (similar to an ammonite) was found.

The reality of extinction was finally proved in 1796 by Georges Cuvier, a

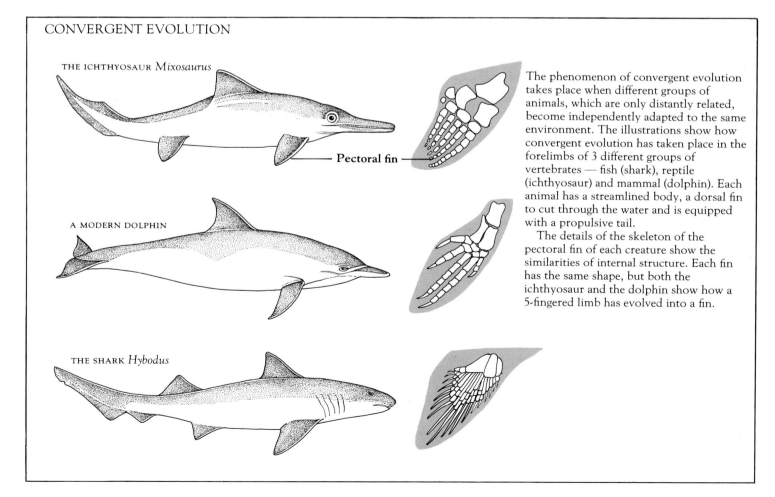

CONVERGENT EVOLUTION

THE ICHTHYOSAUR *Mixosaurus*

Pectoral fin

A MODERN DOLPHIN

THE SHARK *Hybodus*

The phenomenon of convergent evolution takes place when different groups of animals, which are only distantly related, become independently adapted to the same environment. The illustrations show how convergent evolution has taken place in the forelimbs of 3 different groups of vertebrates — fish (shark), reptile (ichthyosaur) and mammal (dolphin). Each animal has a streamlined body, a dorsal fin to cut through the water and is equipped with a propulsive tail.

The details of the skeleton of the pectoral fin of each creature show the similarities of internal structure. Each fin has the same shape, but both the ichthyosaur and the dolphin show how a 5-fingered limb has evolved into a fin.

French anatomist and biologist. Cuvier had been sent some drawings of the recently discovered fossil of a giant ground sloth, *Megatherium*, of South America. He showed by means of comparative anatomy that it was similar in structure to the living tree sloths. But he also realized that there was little chance that such an enormous, browsing creature could still be alive but undetected, even in the great forests of South America.

Cuvier's colleague at the National Museum of Natural History in Paris, Jean-Baptiste Lamarck, disagreed with Cuvier's belief in extinction. He argued that one type of animal had simply changed or evolved into another, and that organisms have some inbuilt tendency gradually to improve themselves.

Cuvier continued his work on fossils, especially those found around Paris. There, he found that below the beds that contained mammoths and fossil rhinoceroses lay other beds with a fauna of more archaic mammals, such as the early horse, *Palaeotherium*. Below these, in turn, lay the great chalk beds with a fauna of even earlier creatures, such as the giant marine lizards, or mosasaurs (*see p.* 88), but there were no mammals.

Cuvier explained this arrangement of fossils in discrete layers by suggesting that sudden changes had led to the extinction of many creatures. But the record of the rocks also showed an unexpected regularity. The oldest rocks contained only fishes. Amphibians and reptiles appeared later, when the great marine reptiles of the chalk were dominant. Mammals were the last to appear. It really looked as though there had been a progression of vertebrate life, with gradual improvements taking place as Lamarck had suggested.

It was in this climate of scientific opinion that Charles Darwin climbed aboard the survey ship HMS *Beagle* in 1831, at the beginning of an around-the-world voyage. Darwin was particularly impressed by 2 discoveries that he made during the course of the 5-year trip. The first was the finding of a variety of fossil mammals in South America — including ground sloths, the giant armadillo-like *Megalonyx*, and a relative of the living llama. The fact that these extinct animals were found on the same continent as their living relatives was, Darwin thought, readily explained if there was an evolutionary relationship between them.

In the Galapagos Islands of the Pacific Darwin found that each island bore related species of bird and tortoise, but that those of each island were distinct and different from those of the other islands. This suggested that evolution had taken place separately on each island.

It was these "biogeographical" observations that led Darwin to wonder what might cause species to gradually change. After years of study, Darwin realized that the key lay in the fact that those individuals best adapted to their environment are most likely to survive and pass on their characteristics to their offspring.

Darwin refused to make this idea of "evolution by natural selection" known to the world at large until he had amassed a wealth of supporting data from many areas of biology. Even when he did publish his theory in 1859, a furious debate arose within the scientific community and beyond.

Though paleontologists gradually filled the gaps in the evolutionary record (which at first had seemed to diminish it as a major support for evolution) the chief weakness in Darwin's theory was not any lack of evidence that evolution had taken place, but rather a lack of understanding of *how* the characteristics of an organism were controlled, and how they were passed on from one generation to another. That gap in our knowledge was filled early in the 20th century, with the discovery of the genetic basis of inheritance.

So, nowadays, although they argue about the details of what controls the rates or pattern of evolution, almost all biologists accept that extinction and evolution have taken place, and that Darwinian natural selection is the major mechanism underlying them. There is nothing in this that necessarily contradicts a belief in God or even in Divine intervention, for the record in the rocks could be interpreted as a testament to the way in which God chose to create the natural world.

HOW ANIMALS ARE CLASSIFIED

Animals are classified in groups of decreasing diversity. The smallest unit of classification is the species. Species that share several common characteristics are grouped together into genera, genera into families, and so on. The largest group, the animal kingdom, embraces animals of all kinds, including trilobites and other creatures without backbones. The diagram shows the classification of the imperial mammoth (*Mammuthus imperator*).

Mammuthus imperator (imperial mammoth)
Mammuthus primigenius (wooly mammoth)
Elephas falconeri (dwarf elephant)
Moeritherium (early elephant)
Alphadon (mammal)
Tyrannosaurus (reptile)
Trilobite (invertebrate)

KINGDOM ANIMALIA (animals)

PHYLUM VERTEBRATA (animals with backbones)

CLASS MAMMALIA (vertebrates with hair and mammary glands)

ORDER PROBOSCIDEA (mammals with a trunk or proboscis)

FAMILY ELEPHANTIDAE (elephant family)

GENUS *Mammuthus* (mammoth)

SPECIES *Mammuthus imperator* (imperial mammoth)

Fishes: The first vertebrates

Fishes are all those freeliving, cold-blooded, water-dwelling creatures which breathe with gills and swim with fins. They all have a backbone, although it may not necessarily be made of bone, and the brain is encased within a protective box, the cranium. These last 2 features classify them as members of the Vertebrata (animals with a backbone) and the Craniata (vertebrates with a cranium). It also distinguishes them from all other invertebrate, acraniate creatures — from sea urchins, worms and snails, squids, corals and sponges — which have neither backbone nor cranium.

On the basis of this definition, several vertebrate animals could be confused with fishes. For example, the adults of some amphibians breathe with gills, but they have distinct limbs. Again, all marine mammals, such as whales, dolphins and seals, swim with fins, but they have lungs, not gills, and they are warm-blooded.

The story of vertebrate evolution started, paleontologists surmise, in the seas of the Cambrian period, when jawless, toothless, soft-bodied fishlike creatures wriggled through the water, sucking up microscopic food particles. Only after tough, non-decaying bone was developed — initially as a scaly outer covering and later within the body — did fossils form and become preserved in the rocks. And only then could paleontologists take up the story with any certainty.

The earliest traces of bony scales are found in rocks of the Late Cambrian period, and the first recognizable vertebrate fish has been found in Australian rocks of Early Ordovician age. So, the first chapter in the vertebrate evolution starts with the ancient *Aradaspis*, a fish about 6in/15cm long with no jaws, no teeth and no fins other than a tail (*see p. 22, 24*). It did, however, have gills and

Lampreys, and their relatives the hagfishes, are the sole survivors of the first fishes to evolve, the jawless agnathans. One of their members, possibly an osteostracan, gave rise to all the jawed fishes. The Devonian period was the "Age of Fishes," when many of the groups evolved and flourished. The cartilaginous chondrichthyes include the dominant predators of today's seas, the sharks. The bony fishes (osteichthyes) evolved into 2 groups. The ray-finned actinopterygians include the modern teleosts. And the lobe-finned sarcopterygians were the ancestors of the first land animals. (*For key to silhouettes, see p. 312.*)

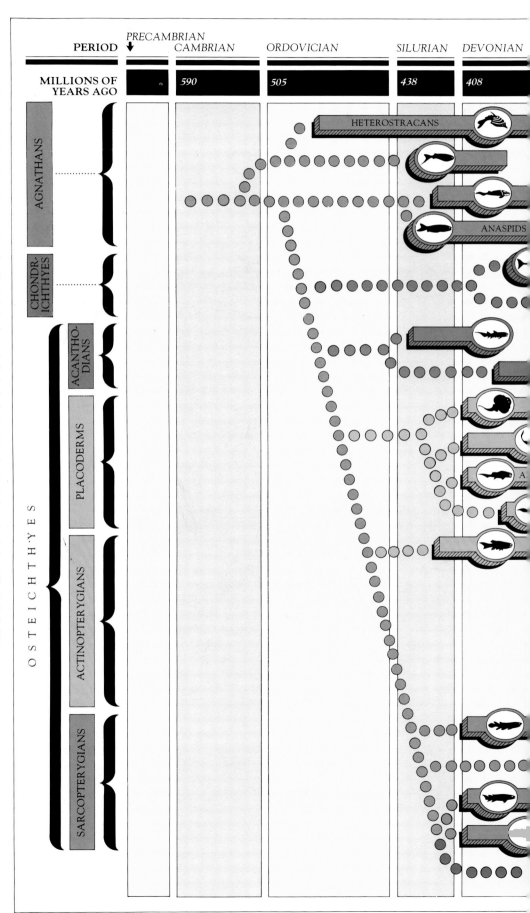

Solid bars show the known fossil record of a group. Dotted lines denote the possible evolutionary relationships between groups.

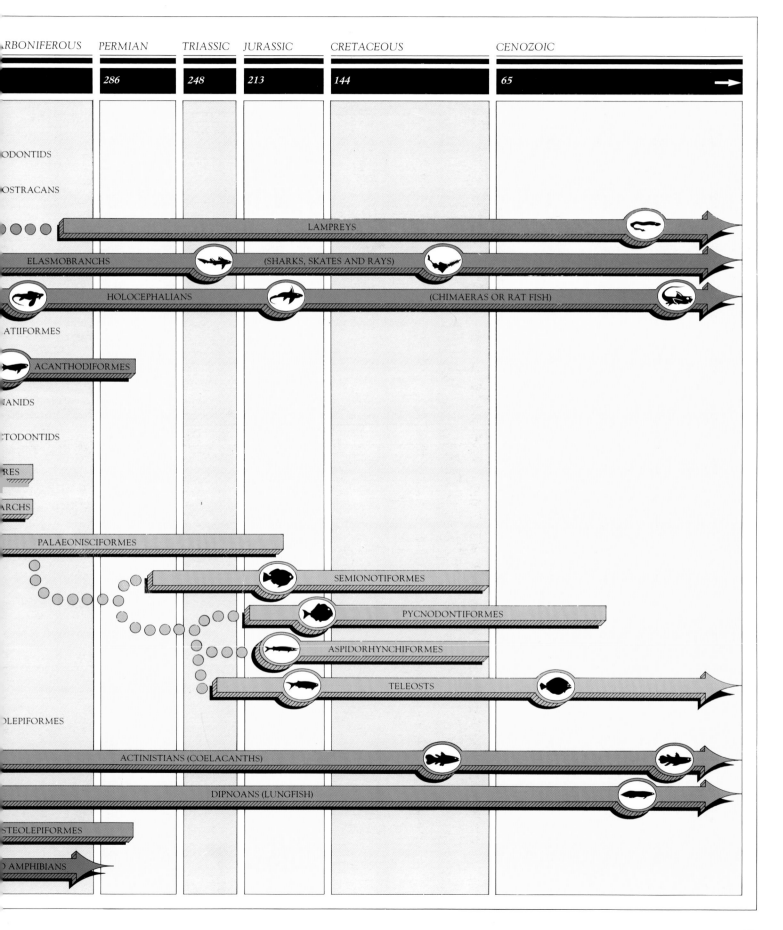

CARBONIFEROUS | PERMIAN | TRIASSIC | JURASSIC | CRETACEOUS | CENOZOIC

286 248 213 144 65

ODONTIDS

OSTRACANS

LAMPREYS

ELASMOBRANCHS (SHARKS, SKATES AND RAYS)

HOLOCEPHALIANS (CHIMAERAS OR RAT FISH)

ATIIFORMES

ACANTHODIFORMES

NANIDS

CTODONTIDS

RES

ARCHS

PALAEONISCIFORMES

SEMIONOTIFORMES

PYCNODONTIFORMES

ASPIDORHYNCHIFORMES

TELEOSTS

OLEPIFORMES

ACTINISTIANS (COELACANTHS)

DIPNOANS (LUNGFISH)

STEOLEPIFORMES

AMPHIBIANS

Fishes: The first vertebrates

a stiffening rod of cartilaginous material (the notochord) that served as a backbone.

By the end of the Ordovician, many types of jawless fishes (agnathans) had evolved. They had developed primitive fins, to propel and stabilize themselves in the water. Their boneless bodies were encased in great shields of bone set in the skin of the head and upper back, or by thick, overlapping scales. These were the ostracoderms, or "shell-skinned" fishes. Amazingly, descendants of these ancient, jawless fishes survive today in the form of the lampreys and hagfishes.

The jaws that revolutionized life
From among the jawless fishes came the ancestor of the jawed vertebrates. The first fishes with jaws and teeth (*see p. 20*) evolved in the Early Silurian, some 80 million years after the jawless fishes had appeared. These were the spiny sharks (acanthodians, *see pp. 30, 32*). Not only did they have bone outside their bodies (in the form of fin spines); they also had "dermal" bone, set in the skin. This took the form of plates covering the gill openings and lower shoulder area. And, more importantly, these fishes had bone developed inside their bodies, laid down as a thin film over the cartilage that made up the braincase and "backbone."

With the evolution of biting jaws, the lives of fishes changed. They no longer had to rely for sustenance on minute animals in the plankton or food particles in the bottom mud. They could actively pursue prey, seize it in their jaws and manipulate it between their teeth. They could become larger, colonize fresh habitats and specialize in particular lifestyles and diets.

Jaws were the evolutionary innovation that led the fishes out of their experimental phase in the Silurian into their explosive diversification during the Devonian, some 400 million years ago. They evolved along 2 lines. One group retained the cartilaginous skele-

ANATOMY OF A SHARK

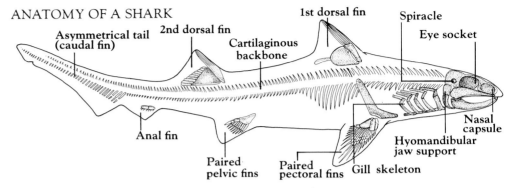

A shark is a typical fish. It has an anal fin and paired pectoral and pelvic fins on the ventral, or under, surface; 2 dorsal fins on the back; and a caudal or tail fin, in which the upper lobe is often longer than the lower lobe. All the fins are supported by stiff rays. A shark's "backbone" is made of calcium-impregnated cartilage with a thin layer of bone. In bony fishes bone replaces cartilage.

ton of their ancestors, and this line led to the chondrichthyans — the sharks, skates and rays, and their relatives the chimaeras or ratfishes (*see pp. 26–29*). Early on in their evolution, sharks succeeded in becoming the dominant predators in the sea, and have remained so to this day.

Bone replaced the cartilage in the skeleton of the other line of fishes — the osteichthyans (*see pp. 34–45*). Two distinct types of bony fishes evolved from a common ancestor — the ray-finned fishes (actinopterygians, (*see pp. 34–39*) and the lobe-finned fishes (sarcopterygians, (*see pp. 42–45*).

The most successful vertebrates
The ray-finned fishes evolved into the most successful group of fishes — the modern teleosts (*see pp. 36–39*). In addition, the 21,000 living species make the teleosts also the most successful of *all* living vertebrate groups in terms of abundance. (For comparison, there are about 4000 living species of mammal, 8600 species of bird, 4000 species of reptile and 2500 species of amphibian.)

In terms of diversity of form and lifestyle, teleosts surpass all other water-

dwelling creatures (both freshwater and marine, vertebrate and invertebrate). They range from fast-moving predators, such as barracuda and marlin, to sluggish bottom-dwellers, such as stargazers and flatfish; from typical "fishy" shapes, like mackerel and perch, to weird and wonderful forms like the seahorse, ocean sunfish and lionfish; from the very surface of the ocean, such as the Alantic flying fish, to its very depths, such as the deep-sea angler fishes.

Modern teleosts are at the top of an evolutionary ladder which proceeded in a series of steps from one group of ray-finned fishes to another (*see pp.18–19*). This progression started in the Late Silurian, with the appearance of the paleoniscids. Their heavy scales, inflexible fins and asymmetrical tails gave way to the thinner scales of the neopterygians, with their flexible jaws and near-symmetrical tails. These fishes were replaced in turn by the teleosts, with even thinner scales, symmetrical tails and highly mobile jaws and fins.

Herringlike teleosts were the first to evolve. Then the group advanced in 2 major evolutionary bursts. The first occurred in about the middle of the

EVOLUTION OF JAWS

The first fishes had neither jaws nor teeth. Their gills, behind the mouth, were supported by a series of arches made of cartilage, between which were the gill slits. Jaws probably evolved from the 1st gill arch on either side, which folded over and joined in the midline to form the upper and lower jaws. Teeth were developed from the skin that lined the mouth. The 2nd gill arch (hyomandibular) moved to support the jaws from behind, and ligaments attached them to the braincase. The 1st gill slits became tiny holes, or spiracles.

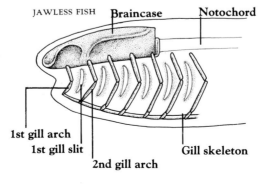

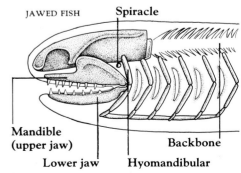

Cretaceous period, when the salmon/ trout group appeared. The second, and final, burst came in the Late Cretaceous/Early Tertiary period, when the highly advanced perchlike forms evolved. These make up some 40 percent of the teleosts species of today.

The close of the Mesozoic Era, about 65 million years ago, saw the rise of the teleosts in the waters of the world and also the rise of the mammals on the land. Major changes were occurring at this time in the world's flora and fauna. Fish-eating reptiles, such as the plesiosaurs, ichthyosaurs and mosasaurs, had become extinct. The dinosaurs disappeared from the face of the land, and the pterosaurs vanished from the skies. Many types of small planktonic organisms in the seas disappeared without trace.

These extinctions seem to have been the signal for the teleosts and the mammals to enter their final explosive phase of evolution, and develop into the creatures that dominate the waters and the land today.

The ancestors of land animals
It may seem strange to describe the evolution of the world's most successful vertebrates — the bony ray-finned teleosts — as an evolutionary sideshow. But this, in fact, is what it was, since in the overall story of the evolution of life the ray-finned fishes were a dead-end. Their bony cousins, the lobe-finned fishes — an unspectacular assemblage by comparison — proved to be in the mainstream of evolution.

One of the members of the lobe-finned group provided the ancestor of the first land animals, the amphibians. This transition was accomplished relatively quickly in their evolution; the first lobe-finned fishes appeared in the Early Devonian, and by the end of that period, some 20 million years later, the amphibians had set foot on dry land.

The lobe-finned ancestor may have been an osteolepiform or a dipnoan (lungfish); paleontologists are not in agreement on this point, a fact which is reflected in the 3-pronged arrangement of the evolutionary lines at the base of the chart on pp. 18–19.

General trends among fishes
There are some general trends that can be seen in the evolution of fishes, all of which led to fishes that were better adapted to finding, seizing and chewing prey, and to detecting and avoiding predators.

The earliest fishes, the ostracoderms, were protected by a heavy bony armor, developed as a platelike head shield, and thick, square-shaped body scales. Such

EVOLUTION OF LUNGS AND SWIM BLADDER

PRIMITIVE BONY FISH (palaeoniscid)

Lungs

LOBE-FINNED FISH (dipnoan)

Air sacs

Swim bladder

RAY-FINNED FISH (teleost)

The earliest bony fishes (the palaeoniscids), with thick, heavy scales, had paired air sacs connected to the gut. These could be inflated with air to buoy the fish up in the water. As evolution progressed, the bony fishes split into 2 lines. The lungfish developed air-breathing lungs (while retaining gills), their tissues infolded to increase oxygen uptake. The teleosts, the majority of today's fishes, developed a swim bladder above the throat, to control buoyancy. In the most advanced teleosts, the swim bladder is disconnected from the throat, and is able to secrete and absorb its own gases.

a covering would have made swimming an energy-expensive process, and many of these fishes lived and fed on the seabed. The upper lobe of their tails was often longer than the lower lobe, which tended to drive the body down in the water, a useful feature for a bottom-feeder.

Other ostracoderms developed "fins" in the form of various spines, flaps and projections, which acted as hydrodynamic aids. These, combined with the enlarged lower lobe of the tail, which tended to drive the fish up in the water, meant that such fishes could swim and feed among the plankton in the surface waters. (The ostracoderms illustrated on pp. 22–23 are arranged according to the depth at which they lived in the water.)

The general trend among bony fishes was to develop smaller, thinner scales of a rounded, more hydrodynamic shape. At the same time, the tail fin became symmetrical, with lobes of equal size, so keeping the fish on a straight course. Paired fins developed at the front of the body (the pectorals) and towards the rear (the pelvics); these not only stabilized the fish, but also worked like built-in oars, allowing it to change direction as it moved.

Accompanying these changes in the shape of the tail and the weight and extent of scales, bony fishes were also developing a more efficient means of controlling their position in the water. Even the earliest bony fishes had paired air sacs on the underside of their body (*above*). By pumping gases in or out of these sacs, the fish could change its level in the water.

In the ray-finned fishes, the air sacs evolved into a single swim bladder, placed above the throat; in most teleosts, it remains connected to the throat, but in the advanced perchlike forms the connection is broken, and the swim bladder functions independently as a sophisticated buoyancy device, secreting and absorbing its own gas.

In the lungfishes, the air sacs evolved into proper air-breathing lungs connected to the blood system, as they are in land-living animals. The walls of the lungs became highly convoluted to increase the uptake of oxygen. Living lungfishes, as well as having gills, can breathe air, and the African species can even exist for long periods out of water, curled up in a burrow in the muddy riverbank.

Feeding and breathing go together in the bony ray-finned fishes. The general trend was for their jaws to become more mobile and flexible, allowing them to be pursed together to form a tube. At the same time, the gill chambers behind the jaws became expandable, so that more water could flow through them. This increased the uptake of oxygen, and so increased the fish's activity. Since the tubular jaws acted in conjunction with the expandable gills chambers, this resulted in prey being sucked or drawn toward the fish, rather than the fish having to engulf it at close quarters. Watch a goldfish or any aquarium fish feed, and this method can be seen in action.

Jawless fishes

DORYASPIS

BOREASPIS

ARANDAPSIS

JAMOYTIUS

DREPANASPIS

DARTMUTHIA

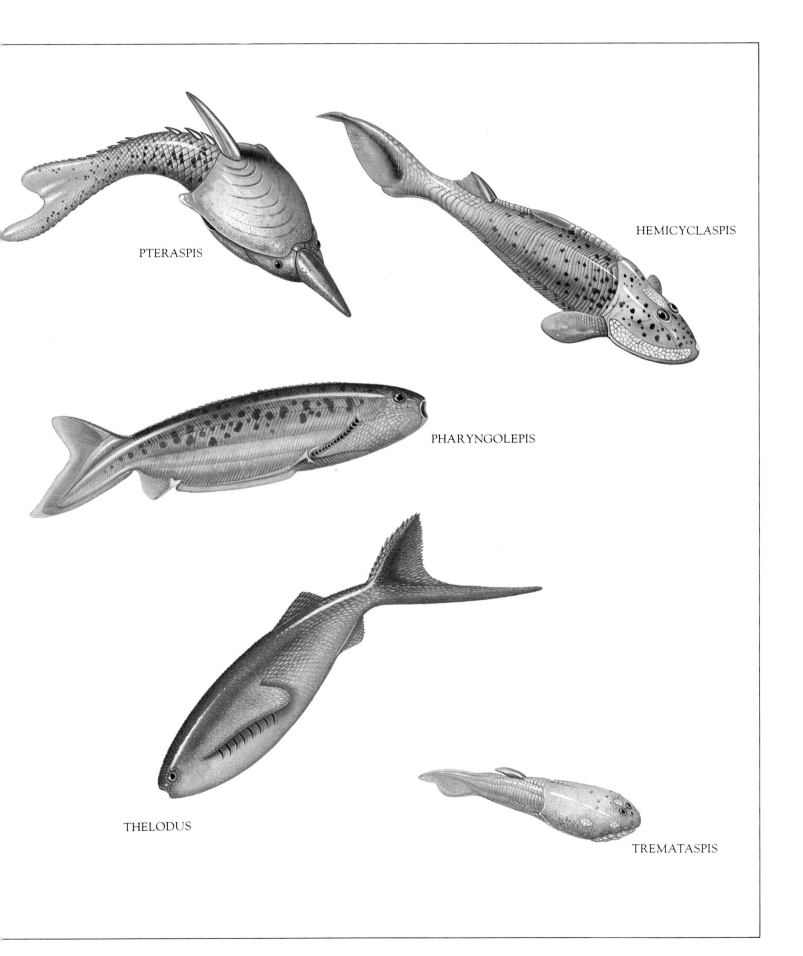

PTERASPIS

HEMICYCLASPIS

PHARYNGOLEPIS

THELODUS

TREMATASPIS

Jawless fishes

CLASS AGNATHA

The first vertebrates to evolve were the agnathans, or "jawless fishes." Their traces are found in rocks of the Late Cambrian period, more than 520 million years old. These first fishes had no jaws in which to seize and manipulate prey. Nor did they have paired fins, to stabilize their bodies in the water. Catching prey and eating it therefore presented problems; consequently, these fishes were all small (rarely more than 1 ft/30 cm long), and restricted to either sucking up microscopic food particles from the mud of the seabed, or feeding on plankton in the surface waters.

Agnathans had no bone in their bodies. The internal skeleton was made entirely of gristle or cartilage. Unlike bone, this material decays. So the only way that paleontologists know these ancient fishes existed is because their bodies had an "overcoat" of bone. This consisted of a large bony shield that covered the head, and small bony scales that covered the body. This armor plating was the only protection these small, jawless fishes had against attack by the large, predatory sea scorpions that also lived in these Paleozoic seas.

The bony armor has been preserved in the rocks, and gives the fossil agnathans their collective name of ostracoderms, meaning "shell-skins." Despite their lack of jaws, ostracoderms dominated the seas and freshwaters of the northern hemisphere for about 130 million years, from Early Ordovician to Late Devonian times. Two distinct lines evolved (*see pp. 18–19*) — the pteraspidomorphs (the heterostracans and thelodontids), and cephalaspidomorphs (the osteostracans and anaspids).

Only 2 types of agnathan survive today. Neither has the bony armor of their ancestors, and both are highly specialized, mainly marine fishes — the wormlike, scavenging hagfishes and the eel-like, parasitic lampreys.

ORDER HETEROSTRACI

The heterostracans were the first fishes, and the earliest vertebrates, to evolve. The oldest undisputed remains date from the Early Ordovician, some 500 million years ago (*below*). These fishes were the most abundant and diverse of all the agnathans. They reached their peak during Late Silurian and Early Devonian times, when a variety of marine forms evolved, from mud-eating bottom-dwellers to free-swimming plankton-feeders. Later, they invaded freshwaters. All had the characteristic bony head shield, which could grow throughout the life of the fish.

NAME: *Arandaspis*
TIME: **Early Ordovician**
LOCALITY: **Australia (Northern Territory)**
SIZE: **possibly 6in/15 cm long**

In 1959, fossils of 4 distinct types of fish were discovered south of Alice Springs, in the heart of the Australian continent. They were entombed in marine sandstones, laid down in a shallow sea about 500 million years ago. It was not until the late 1960s that these remains were recognized as belonging to the earliest-known vertebrates.

The name of *Arandaspis* was given to the best-preserved specimens. This was coined to celebrate the aboriginal Aranda tribe of the area, and to reflect the fish's bony head covering — in Greek *aspis* means "shield."

Arandaspis had a streamlined, deep-bodied shape. With no fins to stabilize it, it would have swum in an erratic, tadpolelike style. Its lower body was covered in oblique rows of small bony scales, each shaped like a cowrie shell, and decorated with pointed tubercles, which must have given the skin a rough, abrasive texture, like that of a shark.

The front of the body was encased in a head shield, made from 2 large plates of thin bone — a deep, rounded ventral (underside) plate and a flatter dorsal (topside) plate. There were openings for the eyes, nostrils and the single pair of gill apertures on either side. Deep grooves in the shield marked the position of the lateral line canals — the organs in a fish that sense vibrations.

Arandaspis' jawless mouth was on the underside of its head, suggesting that it may have fed on or near the seabed. Like other heterostracans, there were probably small, movable plates inside its mouth equipped with ridges of dentine. These could have formed a flexible pair of "lips," capable of scooping or sucking up particles of food from the mud.

NAME: *Pteraspis*
TIME: **Early Devonian**
LOCALITY: **Europe (UK and Belgium)**
SIZE: **8 in/20 cm long**

Pteraspis is typical of the pteraspid family of heterostracans, which became very numerous and diverse during the Late Silurian and Early Devonian. Although it lacked paired fins, *Pteraspis* was a powerful swimmer, to judge by several hydrodynamic features of its body. Stability was provided by bony outgrowths from the back of the head shield — a large spine acted as a kind of dorsal fin, while 2 rigid "wings" or keels functioned as pectoral hydrofoils.

The long, flexible tail was also hydrodynamic, with the lower lobe elongated to provide lift at the front of the body

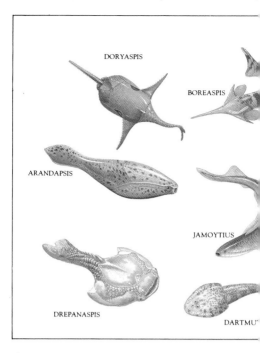

during swimming. Additional lift was provided by the elongated snout, which was drawn out into a bladelike "rostrum," below which the mouth opened.

Paleontologists think that *Pteraspis* and its relatives fed in mid-water or near the surface of the sea, among the shoals of planktonic, shrimplike crustaceans.

NAME: *Doryaspis*
TIME: **Early Devonian**
LOCALITY: **Spitsbergen**
SIZE: **6 in/15 cm long**

This pteraspid (also called *Lyktaspis*) had a much longer snout or rostrum than that of its relatives. There were bony spines set along its length (rather like the "saw" of a modern sawfish), and the mouth opened above, rather than below, the rostrum. This strange appendage must have had a hydrodynamic function, since the shape of *Doryaspis* suggests it was an active swimmer, probably feeding on plankton.

An additional function of the rostrum among pteraspids could have been to stir up the bottom mud or sand, to root out crustacean prey.

Doryaspis had unusually long, lateral keels growing from the back of the head shield. Their leading edges were armed with toothlike spines. These may have acted as gliding planes, and together with the rostrum and downturned tail, would have elevated the front of the body during swimming.

NAME: *Drepanaspis*
TIME: **Early Devonian**
LOCALITY: **Europe (Germany)**
SIZE: **1 ft/30 cm long**

A number of heterostracans, such as *Drepanaspis*, were well-adapted bottom-dwellers, scavenging in the mud of the seabed for food. The front of the body was broad and flattened, and the eyes were set wide on either side of the upturned mouth.

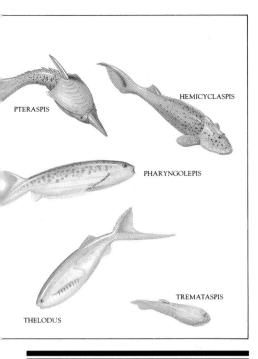

PTERASPIS

HEMICYCLASPIS

PHARYNGOLEPIS

TREMATASPIS

THELODUS

ORDER THELODONTIDA

The thelodontids were small jawless fishes, related to the heterostracans, although they did not have head shields. Only the tiny bony scales that covered their bodies remain to testify to their existence during Late Silurian and Early Devonian times.

NAME: *Thelodus*
TIME: **Late Silurian**
LOCALITY: **Worldwide**
SIZE: **7 in/18 cm long**
The mouth of this small thelodontid was on the underside of its flattened head, which suggests that it fed on the seabed. But it could obviously swim well also. The lower lobe of the tail was elongated, and fins were developed for stability — a dorsal and an anal fin at the rear, and 2 pectoral flaps at the front.

ORDER OSTEOSTRACI

The osteostracans (also called the cephalaspids, meaning ''head shields'') appeared in the Late Silurian, about 80 million years after the earliest heterostracan fishes. They evolved in the sea, and then colonized freshwaters.

The osteostracans were flattened bottom-dwellers that sucked up food particles from the seabed through a rounded mouth on the underside of the head. The head shield was made of a single plate of undivided bone, which did not grow during the fish's adult life (unlike the individual bony head plates of the heterostracans).

Evidently, osteostracans were also good swimmers, since many of them had a dorsal fin, paired scale-covered flaps where the pectoral fins are normally found, and a strong, upturned tail.

The anatomy of osteostracans is well known because of a unique develop-

ment among these jawless fishes. Bone was laid down *inside* the body, in a thin layer over the cartilage of the skeleton. From this fossilized bone, the detailed structure of the brain, gills, mouth and even individual nerves and blood vessels can be traced.

Another innovation was the concentrated patches of sensory organs developed on both sides, and on top, of the head. These organs were richly supplied with nerves, and must have detected water-borne vibrations. Alternatively, they could have been electric organs.

NAME: *Tremataspis*
TIME: **Late Silurian**
LOCALITY: **Europe (Estonia)**
SIZE: **4 in/10 cm long**
This early osteostracan had the typical flattened body and ventral mouth of a bottom-dweller. Its eyes and single nostril were on top of the head, near the midline. It fed by sucking up tiny food particles from the seabed, using the gill muscles in the throat as a suction pump.

The bony head shield extended halfway along the body. Since it was made of one piece of bone, it is unlikely that it became larger as the animal grew. Paleontologists think that osteostracans had an unarmored larva, and that the bony shield developed only when the fish was full-grown.

NAME: *Dartmuthia*
TIME: **Late Silurian**
LOCALITY: **Europe (Estonia)**
SIZE: **4 in/10 cm long**
The broad head shield is the only part of *Dartmuthia* that is known. It was a bottom-feeder, with a round, sucking mouth on the underside of the head, like its contemporary *Tremataspis* (*above*). There was a small dorsal fin halfway along its back, and the pressure-sensitive organs were well developed on its head and behind the eyes.

NAME: *Hemicyclaspis*
TIME: **Early Devonian**
LOCALITY: **Europe (England)**
SIZE: **5 in/13 cm long**
This osteostracan was a more powerful swimmer, and could maneuver itself better in the water, than either of its bottom-dwelling relatives *Tremataspis* or *Dartmuthia* (*above*). A dorsal fin stabilized the body, while a pair of scale-covered flaps, like pectoral fins, provided uplift and kept it on course.

The corners of the head shield were drawn out into keel-like cutwaters. And the enlarged upper lobe of the tail produced lift at the rear of the body, so keeping the fish's head down while it sucked up food from the seabed.

NAME: *Boreaspis*
TIME: **Early Devonian**
LOCALITY: **Spitsbergen**
SIZE: **5 in/13 cm long**
At least 14 species of *Boreaspis* are known from sandstones laid down in the lagoons of Spitsbergen during the Early Devonian. They differ in the width of their triangular-shaped head shields, and in the length of the bony spine that grew out from the cheek area on either side. The snout was elongated in all species into a bladelike rostrum. Beside its hydrodynamic function, the rostrum was probably used to probe for prey on the muddy lagoon floor.

ORDER ANASPIDA

The anaspids lacked the heavy head shields of other armored agnathans. Covered in thin scales, their bodies were slender and flexible, with stabilizing fins. Numerous in the seas of Late Silurian Europe and North America, these active swimmers later invaded rivers and lakes during the Devonian, and survived to the end of that period. They are the likely ancestors of the modern lampreys.

NAME: *Jamoytius*
TIME: **Late Silurian**
LOCALITY: **Europe (Scotland)**
SIZE: **11 in/27 cm long**
Named for the English paleontologist J. A. Moy-Thomas, the marine *Jamoytius* had a narrow, tubular shape, with a long fin on its back, a pair of lateral fins running along its flanks and a small anal fin. Uplift was produced by the strongly downturned tail.

Jamoytius had a round, suckerlike mouth, and it was probably a parasite like its living descendant, the marine lamprey. This jawless fish attaches itself to other fishes, rasps away their flesh and then sucks their blood.

NAME: *Pharyngolepis*
TIME: **Late Silurian**
LOCALITY: **Europe (Norway)**
SIZE: **4 in/10 cm long**
This anaspid must have been an awkward, inefficient swimmer, since it lacked the basic stabilizing fins of other fishes. A row of crested scales ran along its back, and a pair of bony spines projected from the pectoral area. There was a well-developed anal fin, and the tail was downturned. But none of these features would have stabilized this fish's deep body in the water.

Pharyngolepis' feeding method was probably to plow through the bottom sediment, head-first, scooping up tiny food particles in its rounded mouth.

Cartilaginous fishes

ISCHYODUS

DELTOPTYCHIUS

HYBODUS

XENACANTHUS

COBELODUS

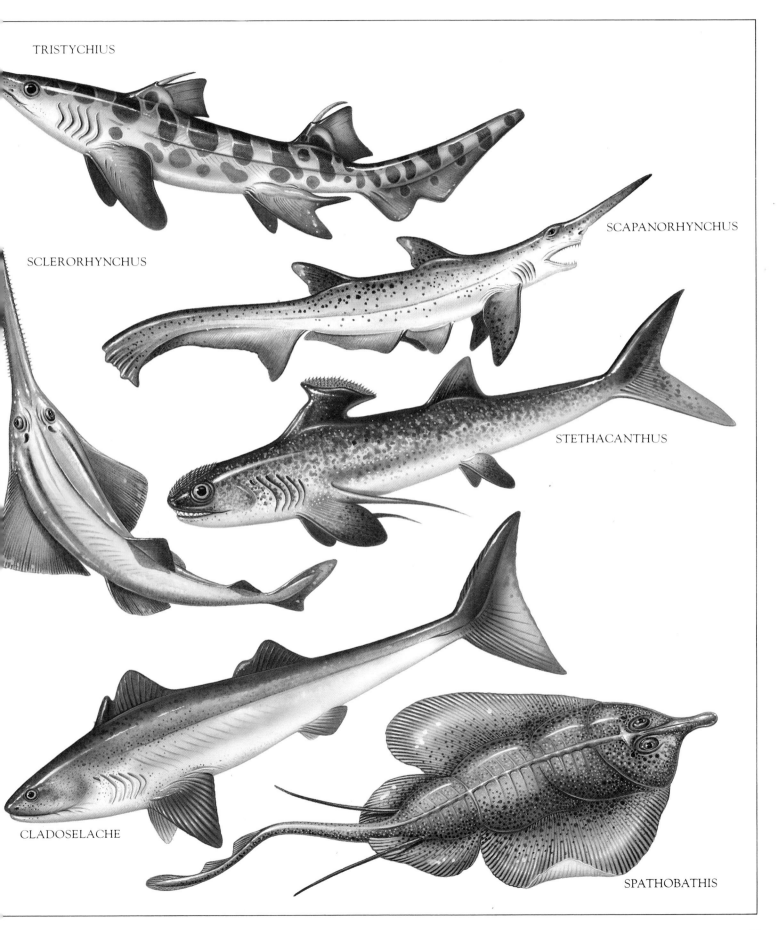

TRISTYCHIUS

SCAPANORHYNCHUS

SCLERORHYNCHUS

STETHACANTHUS

CLADOSELACHE

SPATHOBATHIS

Cartilaginous fishes

CLASS CHONDRICHTHYES

What could be more evocative of "jaws" than sharks? In fact, sharks and their relatives — the skates and rays, and the chimaeras or ratfishes — were among the earliest vertebrates to develop jaws and bony teeth (see p. 20).

These jawed fishes also share another feature. All have skeletons made entirely of gristle or cartilage, which unites them as the chondrichthyans, or cartilaginous fishes. (Agnathans also have cartilaginous skeletons, but they, of course, have no jaws.) The skeleton is "calcified," or strengthened by prismatic granules of calcium carbonate deposited in the outer layers of the cartilage. These granules are arranged in an unmistakable mosaic pattern, unique to these cartilaginous fishes. Finally, a thin layer of bone covers the cartilage.

Cartilaginous fishes share other characteristics. For example, their fins are paired, and stiffened by horny rays of cartilage. The pelvic fins in males are modified into penislike "claspers," to aid in the transfer of sperm during copulation — a feature unique to these cartilaginous fishes. The skin bristles with tiny, teethlike scales, which give it a rough texture like sandpaper. (In fact, 19th-century cabinet-makers used shark skin, called "shagreen," to give a smooth finish to the wood.) Like the teeth, the body scales are constantly replaced throughout the fish's life.

Two main groups of cartilaginous fishes evolved from a common ancestor during the Early Devonian period, some 400 million years ago (see pp. 18–19). Representatives of both groups — the elasmobranchs and the holocephalians — survive today, distinguished by their teeth and quite different feeding habits.

SUBCLASS ELASMOBRANCHI

The elasmobranchs — sharks, dogfishes, skates and rays — evolved from a common ancestor during the Early Devonian, some 400 million years ago. Sharks have changed little over this vast span of time. They diversified into many forms during the Carboniferous, and after a period of decline, underwent a second burst of evolution in the Jurassic, when most of the modern groups appeared. Then, as now, sharks were the dominant predators in the seas, ousting other creatures that attempted a marine, fish-eating lifestyle — reptiles such as the ichthyosaurs and plesiosaurs.

The skates, rays and sawfish evolved in the Early Jurassic, some 200 million years after the sharks. They are essentially sharks that have become flattened for a life on the seabed.

NAME: *Cladoselache*
TIME: Late Devonian
LOCALITY: North America (Ohio)
SIZE: up to 6 ft/1.8 m

Remains of shark scales are known from the Late Silurian and teeth from the Early Devonian. But it is only in the Late Devonian that recognizable specimens are found. *Cladoselache* has been remarkably well fossilized in the Cleveland shales of Ohio, USA. The fleshy outline of its body has been imprinted in the rocks, and even traces of its skin, muscles and kidneys.

Cladoselache had a streamlined, torpedo-shaped body, with 2 equal-sized dorsal fins; a pair of large pectoral fins; a pair of smaller pelvic fins; a large tail shaped like a half-moon, with equal lobes, and a pair of horizontal keels at its base. Its head was blunt, its eyes large and 5 to 7 gill slits opened behind its toothed jaws.

Superficially, the description of this ancient shark, that cruised the open seas 400 million years ago, is strikingly similar to that of a modern oceanic shark, such as the infamous Great White. The main differences are that the modern shark has a pointed snout, a high first dorsal fin, a tail in which the upper lobe is considerably longer than the lower lobe, and an additional fin — the anal fin.

Like many early sharks, *Cladoselache* had a spine in front of each dorsal fin. The spines were made of toothlike dentine and probably skin-covered during life, since they are not coated in the protective layer of enamel seen in later sharks. Another unusual feature of *Cladoselache* is the lack of scales on its body. The only scales were concentrated round the eyes and along the margins of the fins.

Besides being a powerful swimmer, *Cladoselache* was obviously a formidable carnivore. Its mouth was filled with sharp, pointed teeth, each with a long central cusp or projection, flanked by several smaller cusps. The seas of the Late Devonian teemed with prey — squid, crustaceans, small jawless fishes, and early bony fishes.

NAME: *Stethacanthus*
TIME: Late Devonian to Late Carboniferous
LOCALITY: Europe (Scotland) and North America (Illinois, Iowa, Montana and Ohio)
SIZE: 2 ft 4 in/70 cm long

The remarkable feature of this early shark was the strange adaptation of the first dorsal fin. It was anvil- or T-shaped, and the flat, upper surface bristled with teethlike denticles. The top of the head was also covered with denticles.

Some paleontologists speculate that these structures were part of a threat display to others of its kind, maybe giving the impression of an enormous pair of jaws. Another theory suggests that these toothy patches were connected with sexual display, perhaps forming some sort of mating device.

NAME: *Cobelodus*
TIME: Middle to Late Carboniferous
LOCALITY: North America (Illinois and Iowa)
SIZE: up to 6 ft 6 in/2 m long

This strange-looking shark had a bulbous snout and a humpbacked profile, with only one dorsal fin on its back, set far to the rear, above the pelvic fins. It also had remarkably large eyes, which could suggest that it hunted in deep, dark waters for crustaceans and squid.

One of the cartilaginous rays that supported the pectoral fin was drawn out on each side into a whiplash, about 1 ft/30 cm long. These appendages were obviously movable, since they were jointed along their length.

NAME: *Xenacanthus*
TIME: Late Devonian to Middle Permian
LOCALITY: Worldwide
SIZE: 2 ft 5 in/75 cm long

Early in their evolution, a group of sharks invaded freshwater, spreading into rivers and lakes all over the world. These xenacanthids were specialized fishes and highly successful, since they existed from Early Devonian times to the end of the Triassic — a span of almost 150 million years.

Xenacanthus was a typical member. A thick spine grew out from the back of its skull. The dorsal fin formed a continuous ribbon along the length of the back, right around the tail, and joined up with the anal fin — like the arrangement seen in the modern Australian

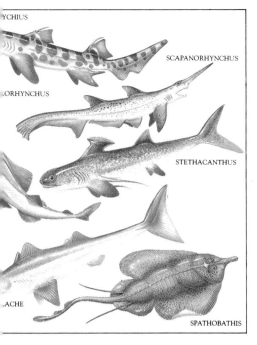

YCHIUS

SCAPANORHYNCHUS

ORHYNCHUS

STETHACANTHUS

ACHE

SPATHOBATHIS

lungfish or the conger eel. It probably swam like these modern fishes, with sinuous movements of its long, streamlined body. Paired pectoral and pelvic fins stabilized it from below.

The dentition of these freshwater sharks was also unusual; each tooth was V-shaped, and formed of 2 prominent cusps. Shrimplike crustaceans were probably the chief prey, as well as the thick-scaled bony fishes, the paleoniscids (see p. 36).

NAME: *Tristychius*
TIME: **Early Carboniferous**
LOCALITY: **Europe (Scotland)**
SIZE: **2 ft/60 cm long**
Superficially, *Tristychius* looked like a modern dogfish. It was a hybodontoid shark; this group was to dominate the seas from Carboniferous times to the end of the Cretaceous — a reign of almost 300 million years. Some fine tuning occurred in their structure, but essentially sharks had "got it right" some 40 million years earlier.

Like all its relatives, *Tristychius* had a pair of large spines in front of each dorsal fin. The pectoral and pelvic fins had much narrower bases, and were therefore more flexible swimming appendages, than the broad-based, rigid fins of earlier sharks, such as *Cladoselache*. The upper lobe of the tail had developed into the powerful, propulsive, upturned fin seen in modern oceanic sharks.

NAME: *Hybodus*
TIME: **Late Permian to Late Cretaceous**
LOCALITY: **Worldwide**
SIZE: **6 ft 6 in/2 m long**
Hybodus was one of the most common, widespread and long-lived types of fossil shark. It looked essentially like a modern Blue shark, although only half its size and with a blunter snout.

It had two types of teeth in its powerful jaws, suggesting a varied diet. Pointed teeth at the front seized and pierced its fish prey, while the blunt, low-crowned teeth at the back crushed their bones, and also the hard shells of bottom-living snails, sea urchins, crustaceans and shellfish.

Hybodus and its relatives gained (and their descendants have retained) a reproductive advantage over other fishes. Part of the pelvic fins in the male shark were modified into erectile, penislike organs, called "claspers" (seen in the illustration of *Hybodus* on p. 26). These were inserted into the female during copulation, and sperm was transferred directly into her body — a superior method of fertilizing eggs than the wasteful shedding of sperm into the open sea practised by most bony fishes.

NAME: *Scapanorhynchus*
TIME: **Early to Late Cretaceous**
LOCALITY: **Worldwide**
SIZE: **20 in/50 cm long**
A final burst of evolution among the elasmobranchs in Late Jurassic times led to the modern sharks, skates and rays — the neoselachians, or "new sharks."

Several improvements had been made to their skeletons. For example, the cartilaginous "backbone" was strongly impregnated with calcium (calcified) to resist the powerful forces produced by lateral flexure of the body during swimming. The bones of the upper jaw articulated with the braincase by a movable joint, allowing the jaws to be opened wide, and even to be protruded beyond the skull so that large chunks of flesh could be gouged from their prey. Finally, the brain and its sensory areas became larger, especially the lobes associated with smell.

Scapanorhynchus was an early, but not a typical, neoselachian. It had a greatly elongated snout, and its teeth were all of the biting/tearing kind, suitable for fish-eating.

NAME: *Spathobathis*
TIME: **Late Jurassic**
LOCALITY: **Europe (France and Germany)**
SIZE: **20 in/50 cm long**
Of the elasmobranch skates, rays and sawfishes, the rays were the first to evolve. *Spathobathis* is the earliest-known ray, and is strikingly similar to the modern Guitar or Banjo fish of Atlantic waters off North America.

Its body was essentially like that of a shark, but broad and flattened for a life on the seabed. The eyes and spiracles (for water intake) were repositioned on top of the head, and the mouth and gill slits were on the underside. The pair of

pectoral fins were expanded into great "wings" for swimming.

The teeth of this ancient ray were also broad and flattened and formed effective shellfish-crushers. Its elongated snout probed the seabed for prey.

NAME: *Sclerorhynchus*
TIME: **Late Cretaceous**
LOCALITY: **Africa (Morocco), Asia (Lebanon) and North America (Texas)**
SIZE: **3 ft 3 in/1 m long**
The skates had evolved from the rays by Early Cretaceous times. *Sclerorhynchus* was an early type of skate, though it looked more like a modern sawfish. Flapping its pectoral "wings," this flattened fish "flew" just above the seabed, probing and sifting the mud with its long, toothy snout for hidden shrimps, shellfish and bony flatfish.

SUBCLASS HOLOCEPHALI

The second major group of cartilaginous fishes are the holocephalians, or chimaeras — commonly known as rabbit- or ratfishes. They appeared in the Early Carboniferous, and looked essentially like modern chimaeras, the males complete with penislike claspers. Today, 25 species live in the oceans of the world, usually swimming in deep water and feeding on the seabed.

NAME: *Deltoptychius*
TIME: **Early to Late Carboniferous**
LOCALITY: **Europe (Ireland and Scotland)**
SIZE: **18 in/45 cm long**
This early ratfish had practically all the features of its modern descendants. It swam by flexing the long body and whiplash tail from side to side, and gliding on its outstretched, winglike pectoral fins. Its large eyes enabled it to see better in the ocean depths, while large dental plates (rather than individual teeth) crushed shellfish.

NAME: *Ischyodus*
TIME: **Middle Jurassic to Paleocene**
LOCALITY: **Europe (England, France and Germany) and New Zealand**
SIZE: **5 ft/1.5 m long**
Ischyodus, more than 150 million years old, was practically identical in size and shape to *Chimaera monstrosa*, the modern ratfish found in the depths of the Atlantic and Mediterranean. It had the same large eyes, pursed lips, tall dorsal fin, fanlike pectorals and whiplash tail of its living relative. It even had a similar spine in front of the dorsal fin, which in the living species is connected to a venom gland, and used for defense.

Spiny sharks and armored fishes

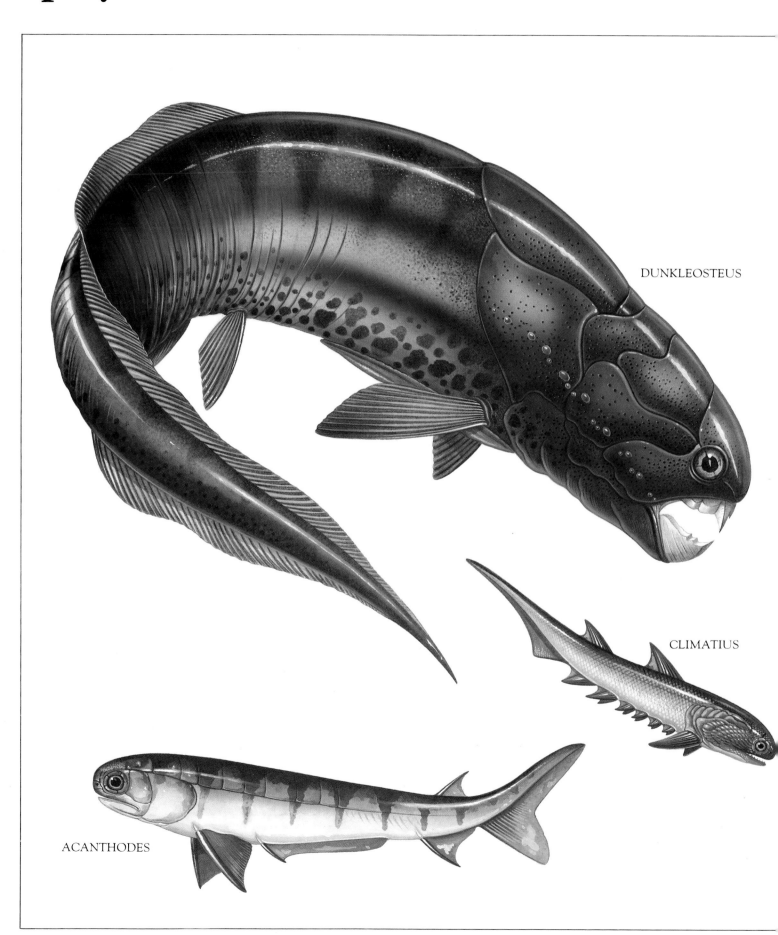

DUNKLEOSTEUS

CLIMATIUS

ACANTHODES

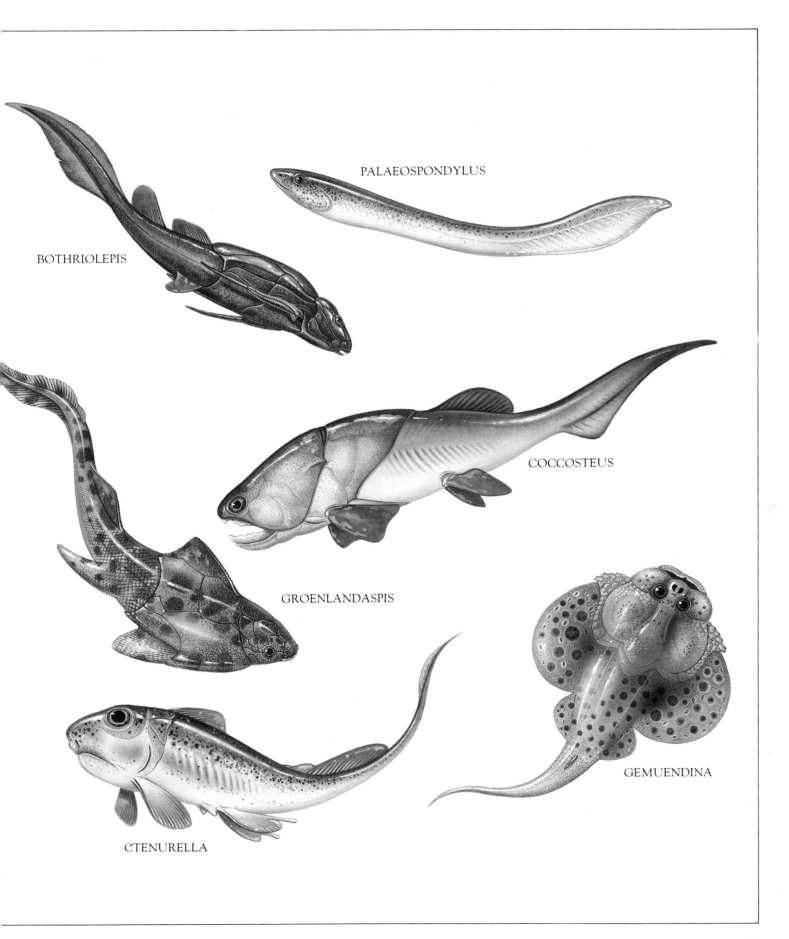

PALAEOSPONDYLUS

BOTHRIOLEPIS

COCCOSTEUS

GROENLANDASPIS

GEMUENDINA

CTENURELLA

Spiny sharks and armored fishes

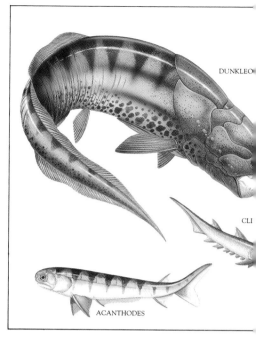

DUNKLEO
CLI
ACANTHODES

CLASS ACANTHODII

The acanthodians — commonly known as the "spiny sharks" — are the earliest-known vertebrates with jaws. These structures are presumed to have evolved from the first gill arch of some ancestral jawless fish which had a gill skeleton made of pieces of jointed cartilage (see p. 20).

The popular name "spiny sharks" is really a misnomer for these early jawed fishes. The name was coined because they were generally shark-shaped, with a streamlined body, paired fins and a strongly upturned tail; stout bony spines supported all the fins except the tail — hence, "spiny sharks."

In fact, acanthodians were a much earlier group of fishes than sharks. They evolved in the sea at the beginning of the Silurian period, some 50 million years before the first sharks appeared (see pp. 26–29). Later the acanthodians colonized freshwaters, and thrived in the rivers and lakes during the Devonian and in the coal swamps of the Carboniferous. But the first bony fishes were already showing their potential to dominate the waters of the world, and their competition proved too much for the spiny sharks, which died out in the Permian.

Many paleontologists consider that the acanthodians were close to the ancestors of the bony fishes. Although their internal skeletons were made of cartilage, a bonelike material had developed in the skins of these fishes, in the form of closely fitting scales. Some scales were greatly enlarged, and formed a bony covering on top of the head and over the lower shoulder girdle. Others formed a bony flap over the gill openings (the operculum in later bony fishes).

NAME: *Climatius*
TIME: **Late Silurian to Early Devonian**
LOCALITY: **Europe (UK) and North America (Canada)**
SIZE: **3 in/7.5 cm long**

The name "spiny shark" seems particularly appropriate for this fish. Its tiny body was crowded with spines and fins. Two large dorsal fins rose from the back, each supported in front by a stout bony spine, superficially embedded in the skin. There was a large anal fin and spine at the back, and a pair of large pectoral fins with spines at the front.

The underside of *Climatius'* body bristled with spines, but no fins. There was a pair of pelvic spines and 4 pairs of belly spines.

Climatius was obviously an active swimmer, to judge by its stabilizing fins and the powerful, sharklike tail, with its large, upturned upper lobe. Like many other acanthodians, it had no teeth in its upper jaw, but there were whorls of small teeth in the lower jaw, continually replaced as they were being worn — another sharklike feature. Its large eyes suggest that sight was the chief sense used for locating prey, and it probably fed on crustaceans and fish fry in mid-water and at the surface.

Its swimming agility and the tight-fitting armor of bony scales must have protected *Climatius* from attack by larger fish and predatory invertebrates, such as squid. The 15 fin spines that arrayed its body were its chief defense, making it extremely awkward to swallow.

NAME: *Acanthodes*
TIME: **Early Carboniferous to Early Permian**
LOCALITY: **Australia (Victoria), Europe (Czechoslovakia, England, Germany, Scotland and Spain) and North America (Illinois, Kansas, Pennsylvania and West Virginia)**
SIZE: **1 ft/30 cm long**

Acanthodes was a member of the last group of spiny sharks to evolve. They had no teeth in their jaws, but the gills were equipped with long bony "rakers" made of toothlike spikes. *Acanthodes* and its relatives were probably filter-feeders, sieving tiny, planktonic animals through their gills.

Like all later acanthodians, *Acanthodes* was larger than its earlier relatives; some members of its group reached lengths of over 6 ft 6 in/2m. *Acanthodes* was also less spiny than earlier forms. Its paired pectoral fins still had stout spines, as did the large anal fin. But there was only one spiny dorsal fin, set far back near the tail, and the pair of the ribbonlike pelvic fins that ran along the belly each had a single spine. Thus, *Acanthodes* only had 6 fin spines on its body, compared with the 15 spines of its prickly relative, *Climatius* (above).

CLASS PLACODERMI

The placoderms, or "flat-plated skins," were a strange assemblage of heavily armored jawed fishes. Several large, interlocking plates formed a bony head shield, while another series of plates encased the front part of the body in a trunk shield. The rest of the body was usually naked, with no scaly covering.

The placoderms represent a specialized offshoot from the main evolutionary line leading to the bony fishes (see pp. 18–19). A comparatively short-lived group, they first appeared in the Early Devonian and had died out by the Early Carboniferous.

Many placoderms spent their lives on the seabed, their flattened bodies weighed down with heavy bony armor. Others had less armor and became swimmers in the open sea. The jaws of all these fishes were equipped with broad dental plates, rather than individual teeth, for crushing hard-shelled prey.

Representatives from the 4 main groups of placoderm (rhenanids, ptyctodontids, arthrodires and antiarchs) are described.

NAME: *Gemuendina*
TIME: **Early Devonian**
LOCALITY: **Europe (Germany)**
SIZE: **1 ft/30 cm long**

The rounded, flattened body of this early bottom-dwelling placoderm (of the rhenanid order) was remarkably like that of a modern ray. Its pectoral fins were drawn out into winglike lobes on either side of the body, and the eyes and nostrils were repositioned on top of the head.

These features were duplicated about 260 million years later in an unrelated group of fishes — the rays and skates that dwelt on the seabed from Jurassic times onward (see p. 29). Here is an excellent example of convergent evolution — in which unrelated creatures adopt the same structure, and often the same habits, in response to a similar environment and lifestyle (see p. 16).

Gemuendina did not have the heavy armor of its later relatives. A mosaic of small bony plates covered its body, decorated with sharp, defensive denticles; a few large plates were developed above and below the head. This placoderm also lacked the characteristic tooth plates of its later relatives. Instead, the jaws were equipped with star-

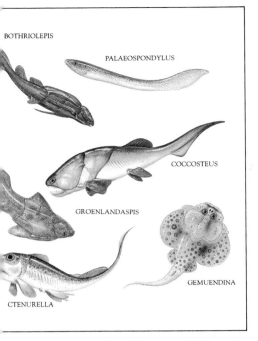

BOTHRIOLEPIS

PALAEOSPONDYLUS

COCCOSTEUS

GROENLANDASPIS

GEMUENDINA

CTENURELLA

shaped tubercles, which acted like teeth; the jaws could be protruded out of the mouth to pick up sea urchins and shell-fish from the seabed, which were then crushed between the teethlike tubercles.

NAME: *Ctenurella*
TIME: **Late Devonian**
LOCALITY: **Australia (Western Australia), and Europe (Germany)**
SIZE: **5 in/13 cm long**
Ctenurella was a small, naked placoderm (one of the ptyctodontids). Its only armor was developed on top of its head and in a band around the shoulder girdle. It had 2 dorsal fins, one upright and the other long and low. Large, paired pectoral and pelvic fins stabilized it from below, and the tail tapered to a whiplash.

This small placoderm had crushing tooth plates in its jaws, the upper bones of which were firmly fused to the brain-case. It fed on the seabed, grinding up shellfish and sea urchins. It could obvi-ously swim also, to judge by its hydro-dynamic shape and paired fins.

Here again is an example of converg-ent evolution. As with the raylike rhena-nids (*above*), *Ctenurella* and its relatives had evolved a body design that was to endure in a later group of cartilaginous fishes — the chimaeras or ratfishes (*see p. 29*). These placoderms even had the penislike claspers developed in the males of the cartilaginous group.

NAME: *Groenlandaspis*
TIME: **Late Devonian**
LOCALITY: **Antarctica (South Victoria Land), Australia (New South Wales), Europe (England, Ireland and Turkey) and Greenland**
SIZE: **3 in/7.5 cm long**
This tiny armored fish, found in sites literally poles apart, was a member of the most abundant and diverse group of placoderms — the arthrodires, or

"jointed-necked" fishes. They account for 60 percent of all known placoderms.

Groenlandaspis was a flattened bottom-dweller, crushing mollusks and crustaceans between its tooth plates. Since the lower jaw could not be dropped while the fish was lying flat on the seabed, this fish, like most of its relatives, evolved an ingenious hinge system to allow them to open their jaws wide to engulf large prey. The head shield was hinged to the trunk shield by a pair of ball-and-socket joints set high up on either side of the body. These hinges allowed the head to be tilted up and back, while the lower jaw dropped and the gaping mouth moved forward to seize the prey.

NAME: *Coccosteus*
TIME: **Middle to Late Devonian**
LOCALITY: **Europe (Scotland and USSR) and North America (Ohio)**
SIZE: **16 in/40 cm long**
Coccosteus was a fast-moving hunter and scavenger of the seabed. Its smooth, streamlined body (devoid of scales), paired fins, upturned tail and stabilizing dorsal fin made it a powerful swimmer.

It must also have been an aggressive carnivore, due to improvements in the jointing system of its neck. Not only were the head and trunk shields hinged externally, as in *Groenlandaspis* (*above*); an internal joint had also developed between the neck vertebrae and the back of the skull, enabling *Coccosteus* to tilt its head back farther. Thus, it could attain an even wider gape than its rela-tive. Its jaws were also longer, so extend-ing its predatory range.

Another advantage of this jointed-neck system was that the up-and-down movement of the head would help to pump water through the gill arches, which were expanded when the mouth was opened. *Coccosteus* probably supplemented its diet by swallowing great mouthfuls of mud; the organic matter contained in it was digested and the remainder expelled as faeces.

NAME: *Dunkleosteus*
TIME: **Late Devonian**
LOCALITY: **Africa (Morocco), Europe (Belgium and Poland) and North America (California, Ohio, Pennsylvania and Tennessee)**
SIZE: **11 ft 6 in/3.5 m long**
Some arthrodires grew to an enormous size, and may even have competed for fish prey with contemporary sharks such as *Cladoselache* (*see p. 28*). *Dun-kleosteus* was the giant of the group, with a skull over 2 ft/65 cm long. Some of its relatives, such as *Dinichthys* and *Titan-ichthys*, rivalled it in size, at 7ft/2.1 m and 11 ft/3.4 m respectively.

The bony trunk shield in *Dunkleosteus* stopped short of the pectoral fins, so freeing them for better control of steer-ing and braking maneuvers. Sinuous movements of the smooth, scaleless body and the long, eel-like tail would have swept this great creature through the sea in search of its fish prey.

The jointed neck and hinged body shields endowed *Dunkleosteus* with a slow, powerful bite. Having caught its victim, the great dental plates got to work, with the fanglike picks at the front of the jaws holding and piercing the prey, while the sharp-edged, cutting pavements at the back macerated it.

NAME: *Bothriolepis*
TIME: **Late Devonian**
LOCALITY: **Worldwide**
SIZE: **1 ft/30 cm long**
Bothriolepis was a member of the most heavily armored group of placoderms, the antiarchs. These fishes shared a com-mon ancestor with the arthrodires (*above*), and like many of them, were flattened bottom-dwellers — although antiarchs lived in freshwaters. The head was protected by a short bony shield, which hinged onto a long trunk shield.

The pectoral fins of *Bothriolepis* and its relatives were reduced to a pair of bony-plated spines, which could have played no role in swimming. They ar-ticulated with the front edge of the trunk shield via a complex hinge. A joint halfway along their length suggests that they could have been bent, and used like stilts to carry their heavy owner over the river bed. The upturned tail would have produced lift at the rear of the body, keeping the fish's head down while it scavenged in the bottom mud or sand for food particles.

NAME: *Palaeospondylus*
TIME: **Middle Devonian**
LOCALITY: **Europe (Scotland)**
SIZE: **2 in/6 cm long**
This tiny creature has vexed paleontolo-gists ever since its discovery in 1890. Hundreds of specimens have been found at the one Scottish locality. All consisted of a long "backbone" with spines at one end, presumably support-ing a tail fin, and a strangely shaped skull at the other end. This creature had no obvious jaws and no paired fins.

Over the years, it has been interpre-ted as a jawless agnathan, a naked placo-derm, a type of ratfish or even a lungfish. Some have even suggested that it repre-sents the tadpole larva of an amphibian. To add to the enigma, paleontologists cannot determine whether the skeleton is made of calcified cartilage or of bone.

Primitive ray-finned fishes

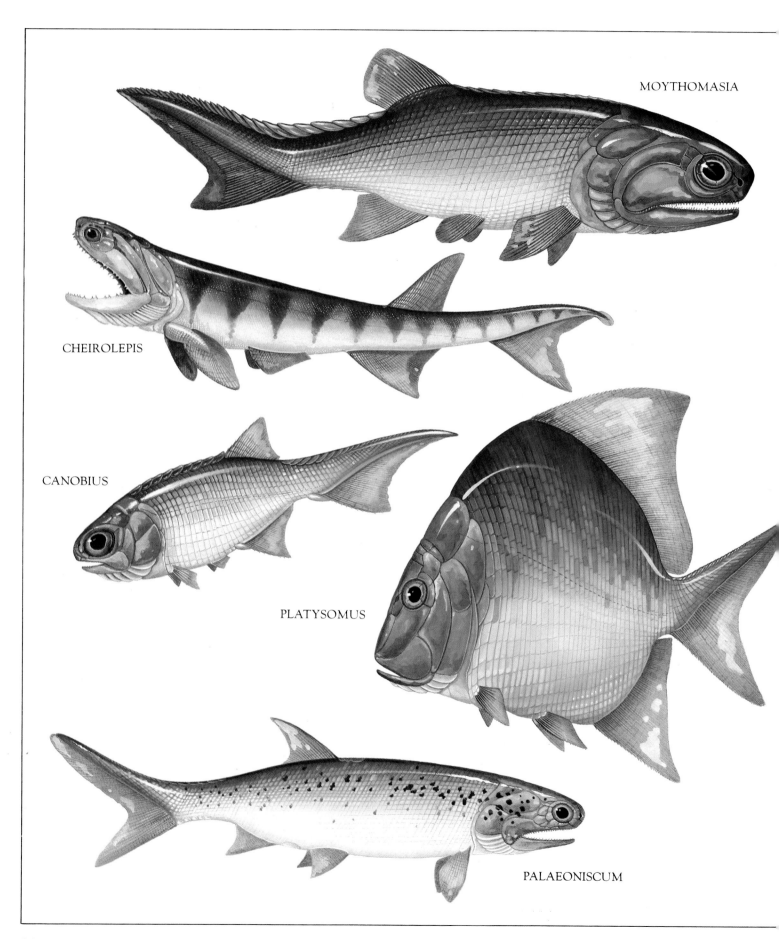

MOYTHOMASIA

CHEIROLEPIS

CANOBIUS

PLATYSOMUS

PALAEONISCUM

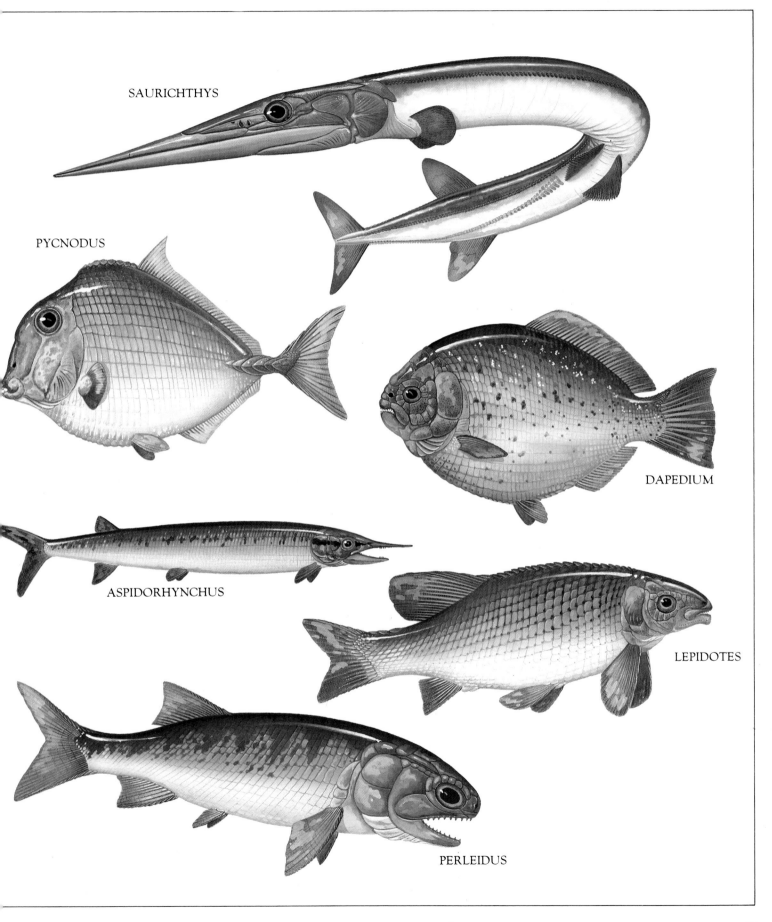

SAURICHTHYS

PYCNODUS

DAPEDIUM

ASPIDORHYNCHUS

LEPIDOTES

PERLEIDUS

Primitive ray-finned fishes

CLASS OSTEICHTHYES

In terms of abundance and diversity, the "bony fishes," or osteichthyans, are the success story of vertebrate evolution. There are more than 20,000 modern species known to dwell in the freshwaters and seas of the world.

Bony fishes account for half of the total number of *all* living vertebrates. In a sense, the bony fishes are also the most successful group of vertebrates, since their descendants inherited the lands of the world in the form of the amphibians, reptiles, birds and mammals.

All osteichthyans, ancient and modern, are characterized by an internal skeleton which is completely "ossified," or made of bone. The process of ossification (the replacement of cartilage by bone) happened suddenly in their evolution. It was preceeded by the laying down of a thin film of bone over the cartilages that made up the skull and "backbone" in the agnathans and cartilaginous fishes.

Ossification was taken a step farther in the spiny sharks, or acanthodians, which had also developed large bony plates set in the skin. These covered the gill arches and shoulder girdles, just as they did in later bony fishes. This feature, together with several others, has led paleontologists to believe that spiny sharks were close to the ancestry of the bony fishes.

Two major groups (or subclasses) of bony fishes evolved some 400 million years ago. They are distinguished by the arrangement of the bony skeleton that supports their fins. The "ray-finned" fishes, or actinopterygians (*below*), include the majority of today's bony fishes, the teleosts (*see pp. 38–41*). And the "lobe-finned" fishes, or sarcopterygians (*see pp. 42–45*), provided the ancestors of the first land animals.

SUBCLASS ACTINOPTERYGII

The ray-finned actinopterygians were the earliest bony fishes to appear. A great diversity, first of marine and then of freshwater types, evolved some 400 million years ago. Today, this ancient group lives on in the vast and varied assemblage of modern teleosts, as well as in the much rarer representatives — the sturgeons, paddlefishes, bowfin, garpike and birchirs.

The characteristic feature of all the actinopterygians, both fossil and modern, is the skeleton of parallel bony rays that supports and stiffens each fin — hence the name, "ray-finned" fishes. In early actinopterygians the fins were quite immovable; in later, more advanced forms the fins became more flexible, culminating in the highly mobile fins

that characterize modern bony fishes.

In conjunction with these fin changes, other improvements were made as the actinopterygians evolved toward modern teleosts. A swim bladder developed from the paired air sacs of earlier fishes, and enabled the fish to control its buoyancy (*see p.21*). The heavy body scales were replaced by a lighter, more flexible scaly covering. And the tail became symmetrical, with lobes of equal length, to provide an even, propulsive thrust.

The classification of bony fishes is extremely complex, with several dozen orders involved; 5 of these have been selected here to illustrate the evolution of the group (*see pp. 18–19*).

The palaeoniscids were the earliest ray-finned fishes to appear, in the seas of the Late Silurian, more than 400 million years ago. They evolved rapidly, and many groups invaded freshwaters. Toward the end of the Paleozoic Era, these early fishes (sometimes grouped as the chondrosteans) diversified into many new types (the neopterygians, *see p. 37*), from which arose the teleosts.

The typical features of the early ray-finned fishes were thick bony scales which articulated with each other; a single dorsal fin to the rear of the body; and an asymmetric, sharklike tail.

NAME: *Cheirolepis*
TIME: **Middle to Late Devonian**
LOCALITY: **Europe (Scotland) and North America (Canada)**
SIZE: **up to 22 in/55 cm long**

Cheirolepis was a fast-moving freshwater predator and one of the largest members of the palaeoniscids, the first ray-finned fishes to evolve (*above*).

Its streamlined body was encased in a heavy coat of small, rectangular (rhomboid) scales, arranged in diagonal rows — just like those of the spiny sharks. (The scales were covered with a unique type of enamel called ganoine, which gives the palaeoniscids their collective name of "ganoid" fishes.) A row of large scales stiffened the top side of the tail's elongated upper lobe, enhancing its powerful flexing movements during swimming. These scales were a unique feature of all early ray-finned fishes.

The upturned tail tended to drive the fish downward in the water. So to counteract this, the paired pectoral and pelvic fins on the underside functioned as hydrofoils, elevating the body at the front. Stability was provided by the large dorsal and anal fins.

Like all palaeoniscids, *Cheirolepis* had large eyes, and probably hunted by sight. Its jaws were equipped with many sharp teeth, and could be opened wide to engulf prey two-thirds its own length.

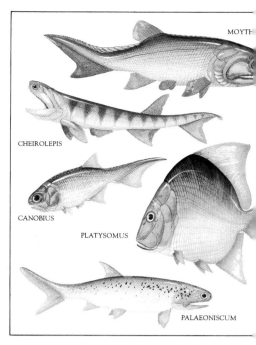

NAME: *Moythomasia*
TIME: **Middle to Late Devonian**
LOCALITY: **Australia (Western Australia) and Europe (Germany)**
SIZE: **3½ in/9 cm long**

The palaeoniscids evolved into a great variety of forms during the Devonian, and became the most abundant and diverse of freshwater fishes in the Late Paleozoic.

Although a contemporary of *Cheirolepis* (*above*), *Moythomasia* had evolved a new type of ganoid scale, unique to the early ray-finned fishes. A peg on the top edge of each scale fitted into a socket on the bottom edge of the scale above. So all the body scales articulated with each other, to form a flexible, and protective, coat of jointed armor.

NAME: *Canobius*
TIME: **Early Carboniferous**
LOCALITY: **Europe (Scotland)**
SIZE: **3 in/7 cm long**

A new development had occurred in the skull of this tiny fish. The cheek bones and the hyomandibular bones, which attached the upper jaws to the braincase (*see p. 21*), both became upright. So, the jaws were suspended vertically beneath the braincase (rather than obliquely as in other palaeoniscids). This new arrangement allowed the mouth to be opened wider, while at the same time the gill chambers behind the jaws were greatly expanded.

This innovation affected both respiration and feeding. As the mouth was opened wide, a greater volume of water passed over the gills. More oxygen could be absorbed from the water, which in turn led to increased activity.

Canobius could also exploit a rich source of food. Tiny planktonic creatures were carried into its gaping mouth in the surge of incoming water, and were caught on the minute teeth that lined its jaws and gills.

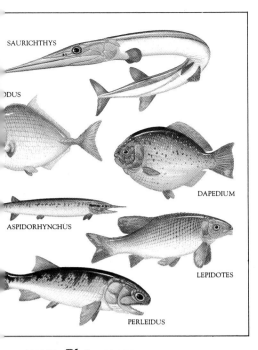

SAURICHTHYS

...DUS

DAPEDIUM

ASPIDORHYNCHUS

LEPIDOTES

PERLEIDUS

NAME: *Platysomus*
TIME: Early Carboniferous to Late Permian
LOCALITY: **Worldwide**
SIZE: **7 in/18 cm long**

One family of palaeoniscids became disk-shaped — rather like such modern teleosts as the reef-dwelling blue tang or the Amazon discus fish. *Platysomus* lived in both freshwater and the sea.

Its deep body was fringed toward the rear by the elongated dorsal and anal fins. The pectoral and pelvic fins were tiny. *Platysomus* must have sculled along, bending its body from side to side in a slow swimming action. A fairly straight course could have been maintained, since the tail was deeply forked and symmetrical, although the main propulsive force still came from the tail's upper lobe which was stiffened by rows of stout, interlocking scales.

Like *Canobius* (*above*), the jaws of *Platysomus* were suspended vertically from its braincase, giving it the advantage of a wide gape and bulging gill chambers when the mouth was open. *Platysomus* probably also ate plankton.

NAME: *Palaeoniscum*
TIME: Late Permian
LOCALITY: **Europe (England and Germany), Greenland and North America (USA)**
SIZE: **up to 1 ft/30 cm long**

Torpedo-shaped, with a high dorsal fin and powerful, deeply forked tail, *Palaeoniscum* was built for speed. It must have been a ferocious predator of other freshwater bony fishes. Its jaws were set with numerous sharp teeth, which were constantly being replaced.

Like all the early ray-finned fishes, *Palaeoniscum* had a pair of air sacs connected to the throat, which could be inflated to act as a primitive buoyancy device (*see p. 21*).

NAME: *Saurichthys*
TIME: Early to Middle Triassic
LOCALITY: **Worldwide**
SIZE: **up to 3 ft 3 in/1 m long**

The long, narrow body of this freshwater palaeoniscid is reminiscent of that of the modern pike. Similarly, its dorsal and anal fins were placed well back on the body, near the equal-lobed tail.

Saurichthys probably also behaved like a modern pike. It may have lurked among the water weeds, or lain still on the river bed, seizing passing fishes in its toothed jaws. These were elongated into a long beak, almost a third of the body length, which greatly extended the fish's predatory range. The symmetrical placing of its fins, together with a great reduction in its bony coat of scales, also made *Saurichthys* a powerful swimmer.

NAME: *Perleidus*
TIME: Early to Middle Triassic
LOCALITY: **Worldwide**
SIZE: **6 in/15 cm long**

Perleidus and its relatives evolved from the palaeoniscids, and survived during the 35 million years of the Triassic period. They were all freshwater predators with strong, toothed jaws, which could be opened wide due to their vertical suspension from the braincase.

A notable feature of this group was the flexibility of their dorsal and anal fins. This was made possible by a reduction in the number of bony rays within each fin, a thickening of the bases of those that remained, and an alignment with their bony supports within the body. Such mobile fins, together with an almost symmetrical tail, allowed greater swimming maneuverability.

NAME: *Lepidotes*
TIME: Late Triassic to Early Cretaceous
LOCALITY: **Worldwide**
SIZE: **1 ft/30 cm long**

Toward the end of the Paleozoic Era, many new types of ray-finned fishes evolved from the marine palaeoniscids. Grouped together as the neopterygians, these fishes show many of the features developed in the modern bony fishes, which descended from this group.

Lepidotes (a member of the semionotids, *see pp. 18–19*) had evolved a new jaw mechanism, which allowed it to feed differently from earlier fishes. Its upper jaw bones were shortened and freed of their connection to the cheek bones, to which they had formerly been fused. This new mobility allowed the mouth to be formed into a tube, and prey could be sucked from a distance toward the fish, rather than engulfed at close quarters as early fishes had done.

NAME: *Dapedium*
TIME: Late Triassic to Early Jurassic
LOCALITY: **Asia (India) and Europe (England)**
SIZE: **14 in/35 cm long**

The deep, round body of *Dapedium* (another member of the semionotids) was stabilized by long dorsal and anal fins at the rear. Its body was covered in heavy, protective scales with a thick outer layer of enamel.

Dapedium had long, peglike teeth in its short jaws and crushing teeth on its palate. These, combined with its body shape, suggest that it was a molluskeater, weaving slowly through the coral reefs of the Early Mesozoic seas.

NAME: *Pycnodus*
TIME: Middle Cretaceous to Middle Eocene
LOCALITY: **Asia (India) and Europe (Belgium, England and Italy)**
SIZE: **5 in/12 cm long**

Although belonging to a later group (the pycodontids), *Pycnodus* had evolved the same deep-bodied shape and grinding teeth as *Dapedium* (*above*), probably in response to living in the same type of environment — calm reef waters — and eating similar food — hard-shelled mollusks, corals and sea urchins.

NAME: *Aspidorhynchus*
TIME: Middle Jurassic to Late Cretaceous
LOCALITY: **Antarctica and Europe (England, France and Germany)**
SIZE: **2 ft/60 cm long**

Superficially, *Aspidorhynchus* looked like the modern gar, or garpike (*Lepisosteus*) of North America, although there is no evolutionary relationship between them. Like it, *Aspidorhynchus* must have been a ferocious predator. Its elongated body, protected by thick scales, was perfectly adapted for fast swimming. The symmetrical tail propelled it, the dorsal and anal fins stabilized it, and the paired pectoral and pelvic fins kept it on course. The jaws were studded with sharp, pointed teeth, and the upper jaw was elongated into a toothless guard.

Aspidorhynchus and its relatives (the aspidorhynchids, *see pp. 18–19*) are closely related to the modern teleosts (*see pp. 38–41*), and most probably shared a common ancestry with them. Only a single species of aspidorhynchid survives today — the bowfin, *Amia calva*, of North American freshwaters.

Modern ray-finned fishes

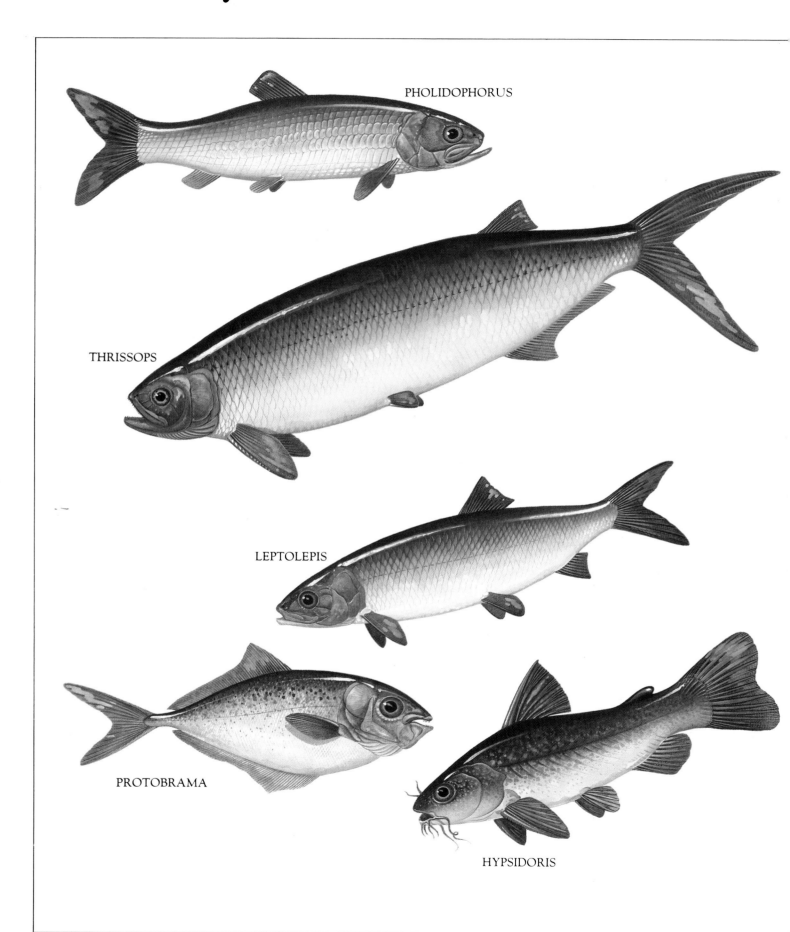

PHOLIDOPHORUS

THRISSOPS

LEPTOLEPIS

PROTOBRAMA

HYPSIDORIS

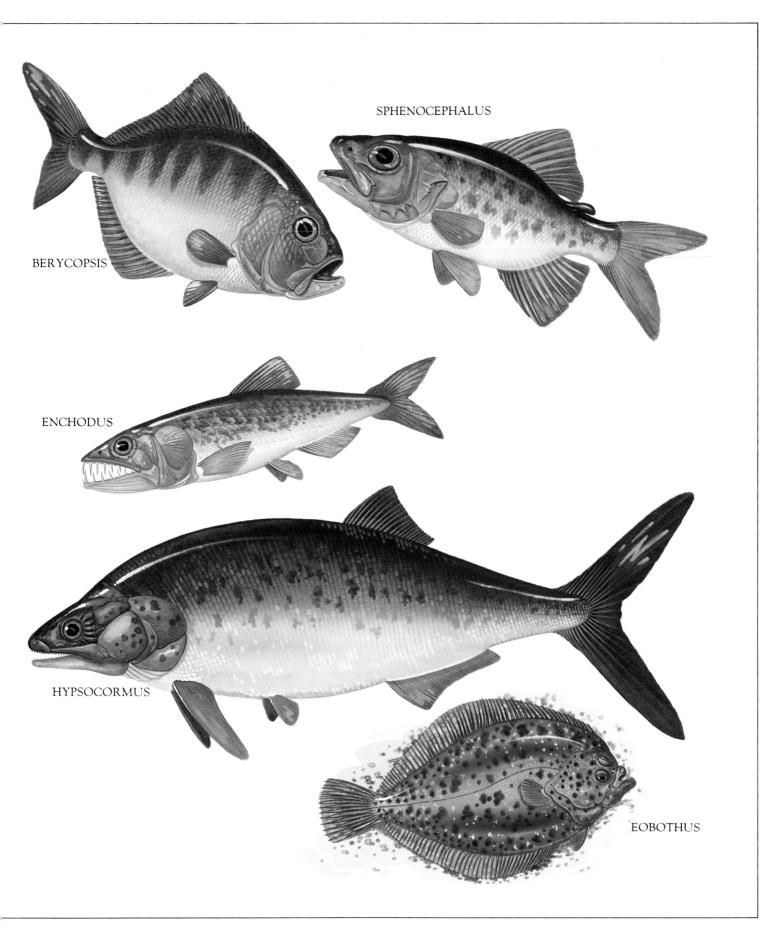

SPHENOCEPHALUS

BERYCOPSIS

ENCHODUS

HYPSOCORMUS

EOBOTHUS

Modern ray-finned fishes

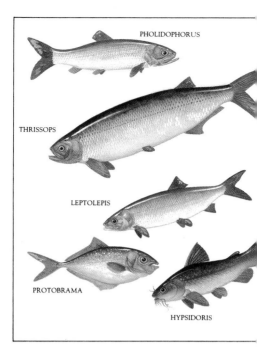

ORDER TELEOSTEI

By the close of the Mesozoic Era, some 65 million years ago, the teleosts were well established as the dominant bony fishes in the seas, lakes and rivers of the world.

The teleosts had evolved more than 150 million years before the end of the Mesozoic. They first appeared in the seas of the Late Triassic, some 220 million years ago. Initially, they were small herring-type fishes, with symmetrical tails and flexible jaws, rather like advanced neopterygians such as *Aspidorhynchus* (*see p. 37*). But in the middle of the Cretaceous period, the teleosts underwent an explosive phase in their evolution, which resulted in more advanced fishes like the modern salmon and trout. These diversified rapidly, and by Late Cretaceous/Early Tertiary times, a second evolutionary burst gave rise to the highly advanced teleosts of today — the spiny-rayed, perchlike fishes (*see p. 41*).

NAME: *Hypsocormus*
TIME: Middle to Late Jurassic
LOCALITY: Europe (England and Germany)
SIZE: up to 3 ft 3 in/1 m long

The dividing line between the advanced neopterygians (*see p. 37*) and the primitive teleosts is unclear. *Hypsocormus* was a fast-swimming, fish-eating predator, which could have belonged to either group since it had both primitive and advanced features.

For example, it had the heavy, "old-fashioned" body armor of its palaeoniscid ancestors — thick, enamel-covered, rectangular (rhomboid) scales. But the scales were comparatively smaller and allowed greater flexibility during swimming.

Its tail was symmetrical and half-moon-shaped, superficially like that of a modern mackerel, although there were many more bony fin rays supporting the lobes of the tail than in modern teleosts.

Its fins, too, were arranged differently on the body. Besides the long anal fin, there was only one dorsal fin. The extra-large pectoral fins were placed low on either side (rather than high up on the flanks, behind the gills, as in more advanced bony fishes). And the pelvic fins were unusually small and placed halfway down the belly.

Hypsocormus did, however, have fairly advanced jaws. They were flexible and mobile, and well equipped with muscle-attachment points to ensure a powerful bite. The upper and lower jaw bones were long, and equipped with teeth along their length.

NAME: *Pholidophorus*
TIME: Middle Triassic to Late Jurassic
LOCALITY: Africa (Kenya and Tanzania), Europe (England, Germany, Italy and USSR) and South America (Argentina)
SIZE: 16 in/40 cm long

Pholidophorus is one of the earliest-known undisputed teleosts to appear in the sea. Superficially, it looked like a modern herring, with a symmetrical tail, a single dorsal fin halfway along its back, paired pectoral and pelvic fins on the underside, and an anal fin toward the tail. With large eyes and flexible jaws, equipped with small, rounded teeth, it was obviously a fast-moving, predatory fish, probably feeding on crustaceans in the plankton. Some specimens have also been found with the remains of other bony fishes in their stomachs.

Despite their "modern" appearance, *Pholidophorus* and its relatives were primitive bony fishes, betrayed by 2 main features. Their bodies were encased in the heavy, enameled scales of the earlier "ganoid" fishes, the palaeoniscids (*see p. 36*). And their "backbones" were only made of bone in places. Their successors, the leptolepids (*below*), were the first teleosts to have a backbone made entirely of bone.

NAME: *Leptolepis*
TIME: Middle Triassic to Early Cretaceous
LOCALITY: Africa (Tanzania), Australia (New South Wales), Europe (Austria, England, France and Germany) and North America (Nevada)
SIZE: 1 ft/30 cm long

Leptolepis and its relatives were herring-type fishes, like the pholidophorids (*above*). But unlike them, the leptolepids lived and moved in shoals, gaining safety in numbers as they fed on plankton in the surface waters. This gregarious lifestyle is deduced from the many fossil finds in which hundreds of these fishes have been preserved in the same slab of rock.

The leptolepids were also more advanced than the pholidophorids in 2 important respects. First, their skeletons were made entirely of bone, and second, their bodies were covered in thin, rounded scales with no enamel coat.

Both these developments aided swimming. The backbone formed a strong, yet flexible, rod to resist the pressures created by the S-shaped bending of the body during swimming. The thin scales reduced the fish's weight, and their rounded shape made the body more hydrodynamic.

NAME: *Thrissops*
TIME: Late Jurassic to Late Cretaceous
LOCALITY: Europe (England, France and Germany)
SIZE: 2 ft/60 cm long

Thrissops was a streamlined predator that hunted others of its own kind in the warm, shallow seas of the Late Mesozoic, some 140 million years ago. Its tail was deeply cleft into 2 equal lobes, which may have increased its speed. The pelvic fins were tiny, and could have played little part in stabilizing the fish's deep body in the water. Perhaps to compensate for this, the anal fin formed a long fringe on the underside.

Thrissops was small in comparison with some of its relatives, such as *Xiphactinus* (formerly called *Portheus*). This fossil fish grew to a length of 13 ft/4 m — as large as any shark that cruised Cretaceous seas. One specimen is preserved with a 6 ft/1.8 m bony fish intact within its stomach.

A modern group of freshwater fishes may be the sole survivors of *Thrissops* and its relatives. These modern fishes are called the "bony tongues" (grouped in the Order Osteoglossomorpha) because of the tooth plates embedded in their stout tongues. The tongue shears against the teeth on the palate, so holding and crushing prey.

The huge bony-tongued pirarucu (*Arapaima gigas*) of today's South American rivers is the world's largest-known freshwater fish. It reaches a length of 13 ft/4 m and a weight of some 440 lbs/200 kg.

NAME: *Protobrama*
TIME: Late Cretaceous
LOCALITY: Asia (Lebanon)
SIZE: 6 in/15 cm long

This small relative of *Thrissops* (*above*) had lost its pelvic fins. Its deep body was fringed toward the rear by a long dorsal and anal fin, in front of the deeply

SPHENOCEPHALUS

EOBOTHUS

forked tail. The pectoral fins were placed high on the flanks, greatly improving its maneuverability.

The size of this fish and its body shape suggest that it may have been a reef-dweller, nipping in and out of the coral formations after prey.

NAME: *Enchodus*
TIME: **Late Cretaceous to Paleocene**
LOCALITY: **Worldwide**
SIZE: **7 in/18 cm long**
At the very end of the Cretaceous and during the Early Tertiary, a second burst of evolution led to the advanced bony fishes. Salmon and trout are survivors of this evolutionary phase, and from their ancestors descended all the modern types of teleost.

Enchodus was one of these early, salmonlike teleosts. Its large head and big eyes, together with the lightweight, streamlined body, suggests an agile predator of the open seas. The scales were reduced to a band along each flank; the pelvic fins were set well back on the belly, directly beneath the large, stabilizing dorsal fin; and the pectoral fins were mounted higher on the flanks, giving greater control of steering and braking.

The remarkable feature of *Enchodus*, however, was its mouthful of greatly elongated teeth, which were slightly recurved and interlocked when the jaws were closed to form an effective trap. *Enchodus* probably preyed on plankton-eating fishes in the surface waters.

NAME: *Hypsidoris*
TIME: **Eocene**
LOCALITY: **North America (Wyoming)**
SIZE: **8 in/20 cm long**
Early in the Tertiary, a group of fishes (called the Ostariophysi) diverged from the main teleost line, and became specialized for life in freshwaters, though some groups later returned to the sea.

Today, more than 6000 species survive, including the carp, minnow, goldfish, loach, piranha and catfish.

Hypsidoris was strikingly similar to a modern catfish. It lived in the subtropical rivers and lakes of western North America some 50 million years ago. Many excellent specimens have been preserved in the Green River deposits of Wyoming, laid down in the Eocene.

The structure of *Hypsidoris'* backbone indicates that it had the acute hearing (especially of high-frequency sounds) characteristic of all living ostariophysid fishes.

This sensitivity to sound is due to a unique specialization of the vertebrae at the front of the backbone in these fishes. The vertebrae are modified into a chain of small, movable bones, which transmit vibrations picked up by the swim bladder (which acts as a hydrophone and resonator) to the inner ear. There, they are interpreted by the brain as either potential prey or approaching predator.

These sound-transmitting bones in fishes are called the Weberian ossicles, and serve a similar function to the hammer-anvil-stirrup chain in the middle ear of mammals (see p. 185).

Like its modern relatives, *Hypsidoris* had a stout spine at the front edge of each pectoral fin. These spines were defensive, and could be erected by powerful muscles in times of need. Prey was located, or danger sensed, by its acute hearing (*above*) — a valuable asset in the often dark and murky waters of the sediment-laden rivers in which it lived.

Having homed in on the potential prey, its edibility was assessed at closer quarters by the long, sensory filaments surrounding the catfish's mouth. These "feelers" were sensitive to touch and to chemical substances in the water. Fish were *Hypsidoris'* chief prey, but crayfish and other bottom-dwellers were also detected by the trailing feelers.

NAME: *Sphenocephalus*
TIME: **Late Cretaceous**
LOCALITY: **Europe (England and Italy)**
SIZE: **8 in/20 cm long**
Two groups of advanced teleosts arose from the ancestral salmon/trout group. These were the cod/haddock-type fishes (the paracanthopterygians) and the spiny-rayed, perchlike fishes (the acanthopterygians, *below*).

Sphenocephalus seems to have been intermediate in structure between the 2 groups. In fact, it looks remarkably like the living freshwater "trout-perch" of North America, so called because it has both primitive-trout and advanced-perch characteristics.

Besides its rather large head, the distinctive feature of *Sphenocephalus* was that its pelvic fins had moved forward to lie beneath the pectoral fins, which were placed high on the sides of its body. The arrangement of these paired fins greatly enhanced the fish's maneuverability. In the modern cod group, the pelvic fins are actually in front of the pectorals.

NAME: *Berycopsis*
TIME: **Late Cretaceous**
LOCALITY: **Europe (England)**
SIZE: **14 in/35 cm long**
Berycopsis was one of the earliest spiny-rayed teleosts (the acanthopterygians) to appear. Today, this group, with an evolutionary history of some 70 million years, is the most successful and varied of all bony fishes, accounting for 40 percent of living species. They range from barracuda and swordfish, to perch, tropical reef fish, flatfish and seahorses.

Berycopsis had all the typical features of the group. The first fin ray in the dorsal and anal fin was enlarged into a stout spine, which could be erected for defense (hence the name of the group, "spiny-rayed" fishes). Its pectoral fins were placed high on the side of the body, to better control steering and braking; the pelvic fins had moved forward, to counterbalance the pectorals. *Berycopsis'* body had a lightweight coat of thin, rounded scales, their surfaces made abrasive by tiny, comblike teeth. And its swim bladder was no longer connected to the throat, and the fish relied on the bladder's own gas-secreting and absorbing glands to make it neutrally buoyant.

NAME: *Eobothus*
TIME: **Middle Eocene**
LOCALITY: **Asia (China) and Europe (England and France)**
SIZE: **4 in/10 cm long**
As evolutionary "late-comers," the flat-fishes, such as *Eobothus*, filled one of the few remaining niches left among the spiny-rayed fish group. They became specialized for living and feeding on the seabed. Unlike the rays and skates, which became flattened from top to bottom, the flatfish became compressed from side to side. The most obvious indication of this lateral compression is the presence of both eyes on one side of the head, since the eye on the underside had to migrate onto the top side.

As in all flatfish, *Eobothus'* dorsal and anal fins formed an almost-continuous fringe around its oval-shaped body. By undulating these fins, the fish glided over the seabed. Modern plaice, sole, turbot, halibut, and flounder are the living relatives of *Eobothus*.

Fleshy-lobed fishes

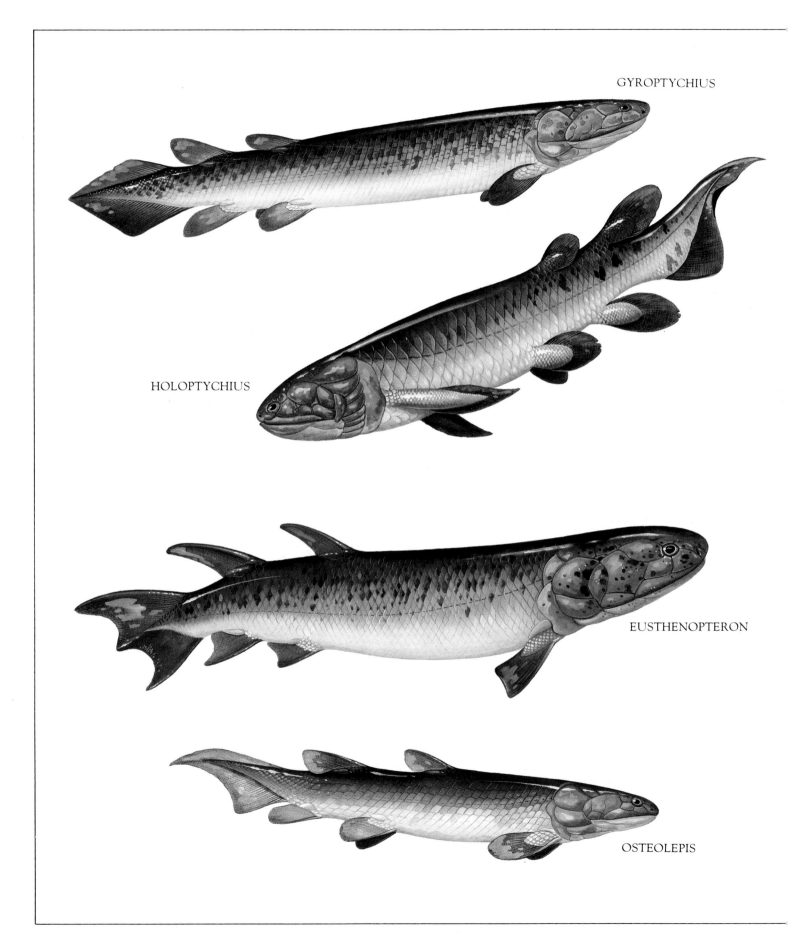

GYROPTYCHIUS

HOLOPTYCHIUS

EUSTHENOPTERON

OSTEOLEPIS

DIPTERUS

GRIPHOGNATHUS

DIPNORHYNCHUS

MACROPOMA

STRUNIUS

Lobe-finned fishes

SUBCLASS SARCOPTERYGII

In the Early Devonian, about 390 million years ago, the first lobe-finned fishes (sarcopterygians) appeared in the sea. Only 7 species survive today — a single species of coelacanth and 6 species of lungfish (see p. 45). Some 10 million years before this, the first ray-finned fishes (actinopterygians, see p. 36) had evolved, and the 21,000 species alive today testify to their success.

Both these types of fishes are bony fishes (osteichthyans); both have an internal skeleton of bone and an external skeleton of bony scales. But their fins differ fundamentally.

The fins of actinopterygians are supported by numerous stiff, parallel bony rays (hence the common name for the group, "ray-finned" fishes). There are no muscles within the fins; they are moved by muscles within the body.

In contrast, the paired pectoral and pelvic fins of sarcopterygians consist of long, fleshy, muscular lobes (hence the common name for the group, "lobe-finned" fishes). Each lobe is supported by a central core of individual bones, which articulate with each other. The first bone of the series articulates with a sturdy shoulder (pectoral) or a hip (pelvic) girdle. Most of the bones can be directly related to the bones that make up the limbs of land animals (see p. 49).

The rounded tip of each lobed fin is stiffened by bony rays, which fan out from the bony skeleton above. Muscles within each lobe can move the fin rays independently of one another.

The structure of these muscular, lobed fins was of great evolutionary importance, because some member of the lobe-finned group of fishes (and paleontologists still hotly debate *which* member, see p. 48) was to evolve into the first amphibian (see p. 52).

The lobe-finned fishes are grouped into 2 major types, both with living, though exceedingly rare, representatives. First, there are the extinct rhipidistians (the Porolepiformes and the Osteolepiformes, see pp. 18–19) and the related coelacanths, or actinistians, today represented by a single marine species. These 2 groups are classed as the crossopterygians. The second major group of lobe-finned fishes are the lungfishes, or dipnoans.

ORDER ONYCHODONTIDA

The onychodontids were an odd group of Devonian rhipidistians. They were undoubtedly lobe-finned fishes, possibly the most primitive of the group, and yet they did not have the characteristic muscular, lobed fins.

NAME: *Strunius*
TIME: Late Devonian
LOCALITY: Europe (Germany)
SIZE: 4 in/10 cm long

Strunius had a short body, compressed from side to side, and covered in large, rounded bony scales. It had the characteristic jointed skull that is unique to both the rhipidistians and the coelacanths (but not the lungfishes). This design evolved as an adaptation to increase the bite-power of the jaws. The chief prey of the day were the palaeoniscid ray-finned fishes, which were covered in thick bony scales (see p. 36).

The bones on the roof of *Strunius'* skull were divided across the midline by a deep joint, which separated the bony skull into front and back portions. The braincase, fused to the skull roof, was presumably similarly jointed, and a large muscle probably connected both halves. (This is the arrangement seen in *Eusthenopteron* and coelacanths, *below*.) When this muscle contracted, it pulled the front half of the skull downward, and the teeth were sunk into the prey.

The arrangement of the fins on *Strunius'* body was like that of all other rhipidistians, in fact of all other lobe-finned fishes. There were 2 dorsal fins on its back, set near the tail, and paired pectoral and pelvic fins, plus a single anal fin, on its underside. The tail was 3-pronged, with 2 equal lobes on either side of a central axis. The fins were not the usual muscular lobes; they were stiffened by numerous bony rays, like those of the ray-finned fishes.

ORDER POROLEPIFORMES

The porolepiforms, like the onychodontids (*above*), were rhipidistians that existed only during the Devonian period. But, unlike their contemporaries, the porolepiformes had developed the muscular, lobed fins typical of the sarcopterygians. They also had the unique jointed skull, as described for *Strunius*.

NAME: *Gyroptychius*
TIME: Middle Devonian
LOCALITY: Europe (Scotland)
SIZE: 1 ft/30 cm long

Gyroptychius was a fast-moving, long-bodied predator in Devonian rivers, with small eyes and a keen sense of smell. Like other porolepiforms, it had short jaws. This actually enhanced the bite-power of the jaws.

Gyroptychius had fleshy, muscular fins, all of which, except for the pectorals, were concentrated at the rear of the body. This increased the propulsive force of the arrow-shaped tail.

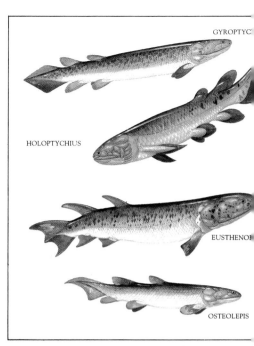

NAME: *Holoptychius*
TIME: Late Devonian
LOCALITY: Worldwide
SIZE: 20 in/50 cm long

Holoptychius was a deep-bodied, streamlined fish, with a lightweight covering of thin, rounded scales. It was a voracious predator of other bony fishes. Like all its rhipidistian relatives, it had fanglike teeth arranged around the margin of its palate, and numerous smaller, pointed teeth lined both jaws. Prey would have been held fast between the teeth, then swallowed whole.

Holoptychius had an asymmetrical tail. The powerful thrust produced by its upper lobe would have tended to drive *Holoptychius* down in the water. To compensate for this, the muscular pectoral fins were extra-long and mounted high on the flanks. They acted as hydrofoils; their slightest movement out to the sides would have elevated the front of the body, and counteracted the downthrust produced by the tail. They also stabilized the fish and steered a course by their concerted movements.

ORDER OSTEOLEPIFORMES

The osteolepiforms were the longest-lived group of rhipidistian fishes. They appeared in the Early Devonian and died out during the Early Permian, a span of some 130 million years. Many paleontologists are convinced that these rhipidistians were the ancestors of the amphibians (see p. 48).

NAME: *Osteolepis*
TIME: Middle Devonian
LOCALITY: Antarctica, Asia (India and Iran) and Europe (Latvian SSR and Scotland)
SIZE: 8 in/20 cm long

This early member of the osteolepiforms was encased in thick, square

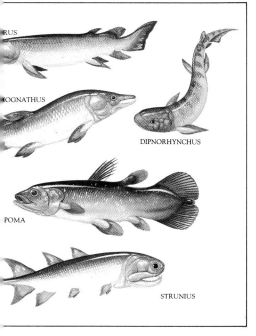

RUS

OGNATHUS

DIPNORHYNCHUS

POMA

STRUNIUS

scales, which must have weighted its body in freshwater. A thin layer of bony and spongy tissue (called cosmine) covered the scales and the bones of the head. This outer coat of cosmine was vitally important to *Osteolepis* and other early lobe-finned fishes, since through it ran tiny canals connected to sensory cells deeper in the skin. The canals opened on the surface as tiny pores.

Thus, the whole surface of the body was alive with sense cells, which probably detected vibrations in the water (made by potential prey or predators) and maybe chemical substances also.

NAME: *Eusthenopteron*
TIME: **Late Devonian**
LOCALITY: **Europe (Scotland and USSR) and North America (Canada)**
SIZE: **up to 4 ft/1.2 m long**
This large osteolepiform rhipidistian fish is considered by most paleontologists to be the direct ancestor of the amphibians. The pyramidal arrangement of the bones in its paired fins is strikingly similar to the arrangement of the limb bones in land animals (*see p. 49*). In addition, the structure of its backbone, the pattern of the skull bones and the complex, labyrinthine folding of the enamel inside each tooth all bear a remarkable resemblance to these features in the first amphibians (*see p. 52*).

Eusthenopteron was a long-bodied, predatory fish with a powerful 3-pronged tail, consisting of 2 equal-sized lobes on either side of the bony axis of the vertebral column. Its pectoral fins were well forward on the body, and articulated with the shoulder girdle, which in turn articulated with the back of the skull. The pelvic fins were well to the rear, as were the 2 dorsal and anal fins.

ORDER ACTINISTIA
The actinistians, or coelacanths, have a long evolutionary history, longer in fact than anyone thought. They arose in the Middle Devonian and the last fossils found come from Late Cretaceous rocks, some 70 million years old.

Then, in 1938, a living coelacanth was caught in the deep waters of the trench that separates Madagascar from southern Africa. The people of the nearby Comoro Islands had known of this fish for generations, but it was new to science. The term "living fossil" was awarded to *Latimeria chalumnae*, the only surviving species of a group that evolved over 380 million years ago.

NAME: *Macropoma*
TIME: **Late Cretaceous**
LOCALITY: **Europe (Czechoslovakia and England)**
SIZE: **22 in/55 cm long**
Macropoma was only about one-sixth the length of its living relative, *Latimeria*, but in all other respects the two fishes, separated in time by almost 70 million years, are remarkably similar.

Macropoma had a short, deep body and a bulbous, 3-lobed tail — a design characteristic of coelacanths. The only teeth in its mouth were concentrated at the front, but the hinge joint in the skull (the same arrangement as in the rhipidistians) ensured that the jaws could be opened wide and closed forcefully on prey. Its pectoral fins were set high on the flanks, to aid maneuverability, and the pelvic fins were placed midway along the belly. The first of the dorsal fins was sail-like and supported internally by long bony rays; the other fins were fleshy, muscular lobes.

The living coelacanth is one of the few bony fishes that give birth to live young. Whether this was the case among its ancient relatives is not known, but discoveries of fossil coelacanths in Niger and Brazil may shed light on their breeding habits.

ORDER DIPNOI
The dipnoans, or lungfishes, arose in Early Devonian times and survive to this day in the form of 3 genera of highly specialized freshwater fishes — the Australian lungfish (*Neoceratodus*), the African lungfish (*Protopterus*) and the South American lungfish (*Lepidosiren*). The African and South American fishes live in tropical areas subject to drought. When the waters get low or become stagnant, the fish changes from its normal gill-breathing method to breathing air at the surface. Air is taken in

through the external nostrils, placed low on either side of the mouth; then it passes directly to the internal nostrils on the roof of the mouth and into the 2 lungs (only 1 in the Australian species) connected to the throat on the underside (*see p. 21*). Fossil lungfishes also had internal nostrils, so they too could breathe air in times of necessity.

Fossil lungfishes, like some modern species, could survive out of water during the dry season by "hibernating" in watertight burrows in the mud, linked by tiny air vents to the surface.

NAME: *Dipnorhynchus*
TIME: **Early to Middle Devonian**
LOCALITY: **Australia (Western Australia) and Europe (Germany)**
SIZE: **3 ft/90 cm long**
Even the earliest lungfishes were quite different to other lobe-finned fishes. For example, *Dipnorhynchus'* skull and braincase did not have the hinge joint that divided the skulls of coelacanths and rhipidistians into 2 parts. Its skull was a solid bony box, like that of the first land animals, the amphibians. This early lungfish had also lost its cheek teeth; these were replaced by a crushing surface of teethlike "blisters" on the palate and lower jaw. The palate was fused to the braincase (as in land animals).

NAME: *Dipterus*
TIME: **Middle to Late Devonian**
LOCALITY: **Europe (Germany and Scotland)**
SIZE: **14 in/35 cm long**
The raised blisters that acted as teeth in *Dipnorhynchus* (*above*) had been replaced by a pair of large, fan-shaped tooth plates on the palate and on the lower jaws of *Dipterus*. This type of dentition was to remain practically unchanged over the next 380 million years.

The arrangement of the fins, however, has changed. The 2 dorsal fins of *Dipterus*, together with the tail fin and anal fin, have merged in modern species.

NAME: *Griphognathus*
TIME: **Late Devonian**
LOCALITY: **Australia (Western Australia) and Europe (Germany)**
SIZE: **2 ft/60 cm long**
By the end of the Devonian, various specialized types of lungfish had evolved. *Griphognathus* had an elongated snout, and small, teethlike denticles, capped with enamel, studded its palate and lower jaws. Like all its relatives, this lungfish was covered in large, overlapping, rounded scales, and the tail was asymmetrical.

Amphibians: Invaders of the land

The modern newts and salamanders, frogs and toads are the survivors of the amphibians that first ventured out on land some 370 million years ago. Their pioneering land effort was not a total success, however, since amphibians must still return to water to breed. It was their descendants, the reptiles, that truly conquered the land.

The very word *amphibia* defines the essential quality of these animals, for it means "both lives." It refers to their ability to live in 2 worlds — the world of water that their fish ancestors still inhabit, and the world of land that their descendants, the reptiles, inherited.

The young amphibian larva that emerges from the egg is adapted to life in water — it has gills and a swimming tail. Later, there is a fairly rapid change in structure (a metamorphosis), when the larva loses these features, and replaces them with lungs and stronger limbs to adapt it to life on land.

There are several reasons for believing that the fossil amphibians of the Paleozoic Era passed through a similar aquatic larval stage of development. In some cases, small specimens have been found in which traces of the gills have been preserved, and a series of progressively larger forms link them to an adult with no trace of gills.

In other cases, such as *Seymouria* (*see p. 53*), the head of young specimens still shows traces of canals in which were located the sensory, lateral-line organs (inherited from their fish ancestors) that could only have been used in the aquatic environment of a larval stage.

Finally, some living amphibians, such as the mudpuppy of North America, have returned to a wholly aquatic life, retaining into adulthood the gills that previously only the larva had possessed. This is true also of some of the Paleozoic amphibians, such as *Gerrothorax* with its 3 pairs of feathery gills (*see p. 53*).

Amphibians colonized the land during Late Devonian times. Several groups of large amphibians (labyrinthodonts) dominated the land during the Late Carboniferous and Early Permian. At the same time, smaller snake- and salamanderlike amphibians (lepospondyls) evolved. Only 2 groups of amphibians survive today — frogs and toads, and newts and salamanders.

Paleontologists can, as yet, establish few linkages between the various groups of fossil amphibians. (*For key to silhouettes, see p. 312.*)

PERIOD	DEVONIAN	CARBONIFEROUS
MILLIONS OF YEARS AGO	408	360

LEPOSPONDYLS

LABYRINTHODONTS

ANTHRACOSAURS

TEMNOSPONDYLS

NECTRIDEAN

AISTOPODS

ERYOPIDS

COLOSTEIDS

ICHTHYOSTEGALIANS

Solid bars show the known fossil record of a group. Dotted lines denote the possible evolutionary relationships between groups.

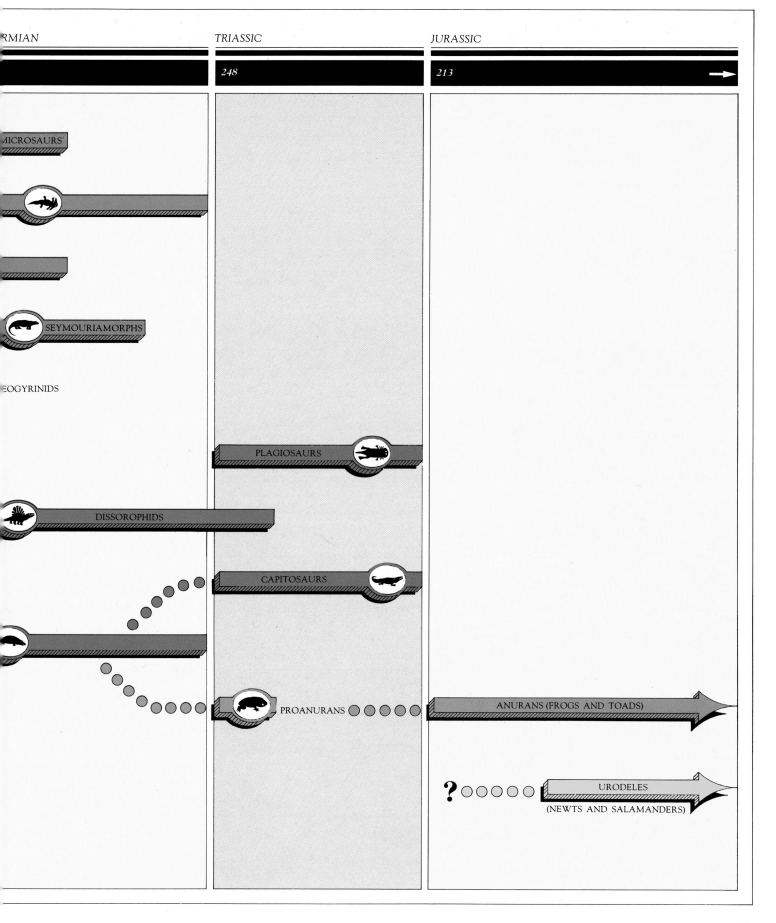

RMIAN

TRIASSIC

JURASSIC

248

213

MICROSAURS

SEYMOURIAMORPHS

EOGYRINIDS

PLAGIOSAURS

DISSOROPHIDS

CAPITOSAURS

PROANURANS

ANURANS (FROGS AND TOADS)

? URODELES

(NEWTS AND SALAMANDERS)

Amphibians: Invaders of the land

The problems of breathing on land

Although one of the most obvious characteristics of living amphibians is their moist skins, this is, in fact, one of the ways in which they differ most markedly from their Paleozoic ancestors.

Modern amphibians supplement their normal respiratory exchange through the lungs by breathing through their moist skins. But this, in turn, limits their size and way of life.

Many Paleozoic amphibians had scales or armor covering their bodies, and many of them grew to a great size. Both these facts suggest that early amphibians had not evolved the skin-respiration system of their living descendants. Those ancient amphibians that did emerge from the water to live on land must, therefore, have had an impermeable, leathery or scaly skin, to prevent water loss. Such a covering would have made them rather slow and cumbersome.

A controversial lineage

Paleontologists agree that the amphibians must have evolved from one of the 3 groups of lobe-finned fishes (see pp. 18–19). These are the lungfish or dipnoans, which survive today; the coelacanths or actinistians, also living; or the extinct rhipidistians (the porolepiformes/osteolepiformes).

The muscles and bony axis of the paired fleshy fins of these fishes provide a structure that could easily have evolved into the limbs of an early amphibian (see p. 49). Similarly, there seems little doubt that these fishes possessed lungs like those of amphibians. Living lungfish, for example, have them, and a similar structure (though single) is present in the living coelacanths (see p. 21). It is, therefore, likely that the extinct rhipidistians also had lungs.

Furthermore, both the lungfish and the rhipidistians have openings in the palate of their mouths that are similar to the internal nostrils of amphibians.

Most paleontologists consider that amphibians evolved from the rhipidistian fishes, based on the remarkable similarity in the pattern of bones in their skulls and fins/limbs. Other paleontologists, however, believe that the lungfish were ancestral to the amphibians, since the development of the lungs, nostrils and limbs of living lungfish is strikingly similar to those of living amphibians.

An evolutionary opportunity

Whatever may have been the group from which the amphibians evolved, the interesting question is why did they leave their ancestral waters to brave the land, with its greater range of temperature and the dangers of desiccation? At one time, it was thought that this evolutionary change had taken place in an environment liable to seasonal drought. Then, there would have been considerable advantage for any fish that could leave its drying-up pond or stream, and travel overland in search of another that might still contain water.

The current theory suggests that it was more likely the pressure of predation in the waters themselves that drove the first fish ashore. With their lungs and stout, muscular fins, young lobe-finned fishes might well have moved out of the water and up the river bank, to escape larger, predatory fishes. Once on land, they would have found a rich source of food in the insects, worms, snails and other invertebrates that lived in the mud and moist vegetation. Here lay the opportunity that evoked the crucial evolutionary changes that produced the first amphibians.

The Paleozoic amphibians, extinct for over 200 million years, are divided into 2 main groups, The larger forms are known as the labyrinthodonts (divided into the temnospondyls and the anthracosaurs), and the smaller forms are known as the lepospondyls. Only a selection of the 34 families of temnospondyl, 16 families of anthracosaur, and 20 families of lepospondyl are described between pages 50 and 57.

Since the early stages of amphibian evolution in the Carboniferous period is poorly known, paleontologists are not certain how these groups relate to each other, or even the relationships within each group. This gap in knowledge is reflected in the evolutionary chart for the amphibians (see pp. 46–47), in which few lineage lines are shown compared to other evolutionary charts throughout the book.

Radiation of the amphibians

The earliest amphibian, *Ichthyostega*, was found in rocks of Late Devonian age in Greenland. At that time — some 370 million years ago — Greenland was part of a Euramerican continent that lay near the equator, and stretched from today's western North America to eastern Europe (see pp. 12–13).

A remarkable feature of the distribution of these early amphibians, and of their relatives, the reptiles, is that until the middle of the Permian period (about 100 million years later), nearly every one of them has been found only on this former Euramerican continent. This strongly suggests that this continent was the homebase in which they first evolved and diversified. Only after the middle of the Permian — when Asia and the southern landmass of Gondwanaland had become attached to Euramerica to form the supercontinent of Pangaea — did the amphibians and reptiles spread throughout the world.

In the Early Carboniferous (Mississippian) times that followed the

THE EARLIEST AMPHIBIAN (*Ichthyostega*)

Labels: Tail fin; Strong vertebral column; Eye; Pelvic girdle (hip); Hindlimb; Thick overlapping ribs; Forelimb; Pectoral girdle (shoulder); Nostril

The earliest-known land animal was the amphibian *Ichthyostega*. It was a strongly built creature, with 4 sturdy legs, supported by massive limb girdles at the shoulder and hip. Like its fish ancestors, this creature had a tail fin and the remnants of bony scales, set in the skin of its belly and tail. But unlike a fish, *Ichthyostega* had developed a short neck, and its backbone and ribs were greatly thickened, so that it could support itself and move around on land.

FROM FLESHY-LOBED FIN TO FORELEG

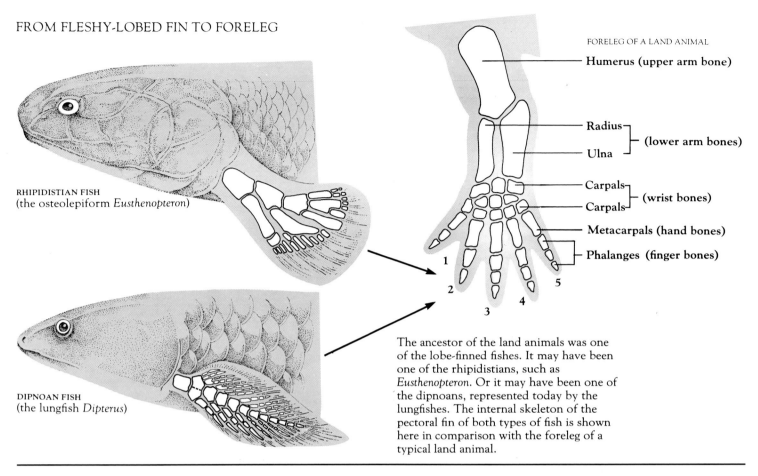

RHIPIDISTIAN FISH
(the osteolepiform *Eusthenopteron*)

DIPNOAN FISH
(the lungfish *Dipterus*)

FORELEG OF A LAND ANIMAL

Humerus (upper arm bone)

Radius ⎤ **(lower arm bones)**
Ulna ⎦

Carpals ⎤ **(wrist bones)**
Carpals ⎦

Metacarpals (hand bones)

Phalanges (finger bones)

1 2 3 4 5

The ancestor of the land animals was one of the lobe-finned fishes. It may have been one of the rhipidistians, such as *Eusthenopteron*. Or it may have been one of the dipnoans, represented today by the lungfishes. The internal skeleton of the pectoral fin of both types of fish is shown here in comparison with the foreleg of a typical land animal.

Devonian, there was an increase in diversity of the Paleozoic amphibians. Twenty genera are known from that time, belonging to 14 families, and including both types of labyrinthodont, as well as the limbless, aïstopod lepospondyls. Nearly all of these amphibians were aquatic or semi-aquatic.

In the Late Carboniferous (Pennsylvanian), much of the Euramerican continent was covered by low-lying, tropical swamplands. From these swamps rose tall coniferous trees, 49–130ft/15–40m tall, and tree ferns up to 25ft/7.5m tall. Seed ferns and other smaller plants abounded.

A variety of insects, spiders, millipedes and centipedes lived in the rich leaf litter that covered the forest floor. A giant dragonflylike insect, *Meganeura*, with a wingspan of up to 2 ft 5 in/76 cm, flew among the trees, while a giant centipedelike arthropod, *Arthropleura*, up to 6 ft 6 in/2 m long, fed on the leaf litter. The thick accumulations of leaves eventually formed the rich coal deposits that have long been mined in eastern North America, Britain and central Europe.

The lakes and streams of this Late Carboniferous landscape abounded with a variety of fishes, providing the amphibians with a rich food source.

The total known amphibian fauna of the Late Carboniferous is made up of over 70 genera, in 34 families, and representing all of the Paleozoic orders.

In the succeeding Permian period, the Paleozoic amphibians reached their greatest diversity, with nearly 100 genera known, belonging to 40 families. However, an interesting change occurred within the amphibian fauna during the 40-odd million years of the Permian.

The amphibians of the Early Permian are known best from the Red Beds of Texas. These seem to have been laid down in a flood-plain or delta environment, similar to that around the Mississippi River today. The amphibians shared this environment with the pelycosaurs, early types of mammal-like reptile (*see pp. 186, 188*).

At this time, the amphibians made a decisive shift to the land. About 60 percent of the labyrinthodonts were terrestrial, another 15 percent were semi-terrestrial, and only 25 percent were exclusively aquatic.

This, however, was to be the peak of achievement for the amphibians in their conquest of the land. The Late Permian Karroo Beds of southern Africa reveal an amphibian fauna in which terrestrial and aquatic types of labyrinthodont are now equal in diversity, and most of the

terrestrial forms have a protective body armor. This dramatic turnabout was due to the rise of the therapsids, the later mammal-like reptiles (*see pp. 187–193*); they had clearly ousted the amphibians from most of their recently acquired, land-based niches.

Demise of the ancient amphibians

The Triassic period saw the final exclusion of the ancient amphibians from the land. Although over 80 genera are known, these belong to only 15 families, and all are temnospondyl labyrinthodonts. Almost without exception, they were aquatic, but some were of considerable size. The largest known amphibian, *Parotosuchus*, from southern Africa, was probably over 13ft/4m long.

The long existence of the labyrinthodonts was now almost over. Only 2 genera are known in the Jurassic period, one in Australia and the other in China. By this time, the ancestors of today's moist-skinned amphibians had already appeared. The first frog, *Triadobatrachus*, is known from the Early Triassic of Madagascar; bones of the first urodele (the group to which modern newts and salamanders belong) are found in Jurassic rocks. The other order of modern amphibians, the caecilians, are almost unknown in the fossil record.

Labyrinthodonts

GREERERPETON

ERYOPS

ICHTHYOSTEGA

CRASSIGYRINUS

PLATYHYSTRIX

CACOPS

PARACYCLOTOSAURUS

PELTOBATRACHUS

SEYMOURIA

GERROTHORAX

EOGYRINUS

Labyrinthodonts

SUBCLASS LABYRINTHODONTIA

The labyrinthodonts were the first group of amphibians — in fact, the first group of vertebrates — to colonize dry land. Their experiment lasted for over 160 million years, from the Late Devonian to the Early Jurassic. It could be considered a partial success, since in their heyday during the Early Permian, some 60 percent of labyrinthodonts were fully adapted land-living, insect-ivorous animals. Thereafter they declined until, by the end of the Triassic, they were all but extinct.

The labyrinthodonts are so called for the structure of their conical teeth. In section, the enamel that covers each tooth is infolded into a complex, laby-rinthine, or mazelike, pattern. This is strikingly similar to the teeth of the rhipidistian lobe-finned fishes (see pp. 42–45). This fact, along with several other skeletal features, has led many paleontologists to speculate that the ancestors of the amphibians lies among these bony fishes (see p. 48).

There are 2 distinct orders of labyrin-thodont — the temnospondyls and an-thracosaurs (below). A third order con-tains the ichthyostegalians, the first am-phibians, which some paleontologists believe were early members of the temnospondyls.

ORDER ICHTHYOSTEGALIA

The ichthyostegalians are the earliest-known amphibians and the first labyrin-thodonts to evolve. Their remains have been found only in eastern Greenland in rocks of Late Devonian age.

NAME: *Ichthyostega*
TIME: **Late Devonian**
LOCALITY: **Greenland**
SIZE: **3 ft 3 in/1 m long**
Ichthyostega is the earliest well-known amphibian. It was a large, semi-aquatic animal, larger than any of its fish ances-tors, with a long, deep body and a heavy skull of solid bone (see p. 48). Its 4 limbs, each with 5 toes, splayed out from the sides of its body. To remind it of its fish ancestry, a long fin ran the length of the tail, and bony scales covered the belly and tail.

This creature would never have strayed far from water. On land, it moved with an awkward, sprawling gait that swung its body from side to side. However, it was in its element in water, where the heavy body was buoyed up, and the strong, finned tail could propel it along with ease after its fish prey, abundant in these Late Devonian streams and ponds.

Besides the limbs, *Ichthyostega* dif-fered from a fish in having the cheek region and the roof of the skull solidly fused together, unlike their looser ar-rangement in fish. Its head was no longer connected to the shoulder girdle, and a short neck had developed. This was useful now that it was spending more time on land; it did not need to be so streamlined as a fish, and it could also turn its head around to look for prey or predators.

To support its body on land, *Ichthyostega*'s backbone was strength-ened along its length by long, broad ribs which overlapped each other. They formed a large, barrel-shaped rib cage, which supported and protected the vital organs — the heart, lungs and digestive organs. The rib cage was so solid that it probably could not be expanded and contracted for breathing — the method used by later land animals. *Ichthyostega* and its relatives probably breathed by lowering the floor of the mouth to draw air in, and raising it to pump air down the windpipe into the lungs.

Ichthyostega had a wide mouth, equipped with many small, conical teeth. The palate was also studded with teeth, some of them long and fanglike — another feature of rhipidistian fishes.

ORDER UNCERTAIN

The remains of about 5 genera of Car-boniferous amphibian have been found in Europe and North America. Although they can be grouped into families, they do not fit into any of the known orders.

NAME: *Crassigyrinus*
TIME: **Early Carboniferous**
LOCALITY: **Europe (Scotland)**
SIZE: **6 ft 6 in/2 m long**
Crassigyrinus was a strange-looking crea-ture, even for an early amphibian. It had a fishlike body tapering into a long tail, with tiny finlike limbs. Its head was about 1 ft/30 cm long, and the teeth-filled jaws could open wide, to judge by their hinge point far back on the skull. Its eyes were particularly large, and set close together.

These unusual features suggest that *Crassigyrinus* had already lost the use of its limbs, and had reverted to an aquatic life. Its teeth are those of a fish-eater, and the streamlined body indicate a fast-moving predator. The large size of the eyes could suggest that it hunted in the dark, murky waters of the Carbonifer-ous swamps, swimming eel-style be-tween the vegetation after its prey.

ORDER TEMNOSPONDYLI

The temnospondyls evolved at the end of the Early Carboniferous period (Late Mississippian), about 330 million years ago. Over the following 120 million years, they developed into many varied, often very large, terrestrial forms. But with the rise of the terrestrial mammal-like reptiles in the early Permian, the temnospondyls were forced back to the damp places from whence they came (see p. 49).

They were extinct by the Early Jur-assic times, but not before some of their members had given rise to the ancestors of today's frogs and toads (see pp. 46–47). Representatives of the main families are described below.

NAME: *Greererpeton*
TIME: **Early Carboniferous**
LOCALITY: **North America (West Virginia)**
SIZE: **5 ft/1.5 m long**
The colosteids, as represented by *Greererpeton*, evolved as the first land-living temnospondyls. But it seems they reverted soon after to a fully aquatic life. Their body shape was ideal for moving through water with sinuous, eel-style undulations. The low, flat head, about 7 in/18 cm long, was carried on a short neck, connected to a greatly elongated body (made up of about 40 back ver-tebrae, about twice the usual number) and ending in a long, finned tail. The legs were short, each with 5 spreading toes for steering and braking.

Open grooves along the sides of *Greererpeton*'s skull are a telltale sign of its fish ancestry. These grooves mark the position in life of the sensory lateral line canals, which could detect water-borne vibrations. The ear structure of this water-dweller was poorly developed, unlike that of land-living amphibians.

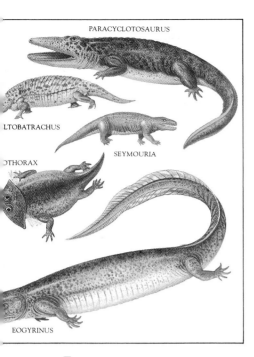

PARACYCLOTOSAURUS

LTOBATRACHUS

SEYMOURIA

OTHORAX

EOGYRINUS

NAME: *Eryops*
TIME: Late Carboniferous to Early Permian
LOCALITY: North America (New Mexico, Oklahoma and Texas)
SIZE: 6 ft 6 in/2 m long
This large, semi-aquatic creature was a member of the successful eryopid family, whose members thrived from Late Carboniferous (Pennsylvanian) times to the end of the Permian. Its thick-set body and large head was supported by sturdy limbs. Bony plates covered its back, perhaps to brace the muscles and help support the heavy body on land.

Eryops probably fed in water, since the position of the jaw hinge indicates that the mouth could not have been opened on land without lifting the heavy head clear of the ground.

NAME: *Cacops*
TIME: Early Permian
LOCALITY: North America (Texas)
SIZE: 16 in/40 cm long
Cacops was a member of the dissorophids. This diverse family of temnospondyls arose slightly later than the eryopids (*above*), and became extinct after them, in the Early Triassic. Many members of this family were fully adapted land-living amphibians. Their heyday came in the Early Permian, when the climate in Euramerica changed from the warm, humid conditions of the Carboniferous to the more arid conditions of the Permian.

Cacops and its relatives, along with some of the eryopids, were quick to adapt to this drier climate. *Cacops* is regarded as the amphibian best adapted to life on land. To protect itself, bony plates covered its body, and a row of thick armor ran down the backbone. Its legs were well-adapted for walking on land, and were almost reptilelike in their structure. There was a broad opening (the otic notch) behind each eye. In life,

this was covered by a taut membrane which acted as an eardrum to detect airborne sounds.

NAME: *Platyhystrix*
TIME: Early Permian
LOCALITY: North America (Texas)
SIZE: 3 ft 3 in/1 ft long
Platyhystrix was more heavily armored than its close relative, *Cacops* (*above*). It had a more pronounced covering of armor plates on its back to protect itself against predators. Certain carnivorous pelycosaurs, such as the sphenacodont *Dimetrodon*, lived in the same area, and would have preyed on *Platyhystrix* and its terrestrial relatives (*see pp. 186, 188*).

Platyhystrix also had a spectacular "sail" on its back, made of tall spines that grew up from the vertebrae. Blood-rich skin may have covered the whole structure. The contemporary pelycosaurs, *Dimetrodon* and *Edaphosaurus*, also had great sails, which are believed to have helped these cold-blooded reptiles to regulate their body temperature. Such a device would also have proved useful for such cold-blooded amphibians as *Platyhystrix*.

NAME: *Peltobatrachus*
TIME: Late Permian
LOCALITY: Africa (Tanzania)
SIZE: 2 ft 3 in/70 cm long
Peltobatrachus was a slow-moving, fully terrestrial amphibian, its body enclosed in an armadillo-type armor, for protection against the fierce carnivores of the day — the gorgonopsian therapsids with their great canine teeth (*see pp. 187, 189*).

The bony armor-plating was arranged in broad shields over the shoulders and behind the hips, and in close-fitting bands across the body. The teeth of this amphibian have not been found, but it probably ate insects, worms and snails, just as armadillos do today.

NAME: *Paracyclotosaurus*
TIME: Late Triassic
LOCALITY: Australia (Queensland)
SIZE: 7 ft 5 in/2.3 m long
By Triassic times, 2 groups of mammal-like reptiles, the dicynodonts and cynodonts (*see pp. 190–193*), dominated the land. *Paracyclotosaurus*, and other amphibians of the capitosaur family, had been forced to return to the water. A general adaptation among these Triassic water-dwellers was toward a general flattening of the body.

The great head of the bulky *Paracyclotosaurus* was flat-topped and almost 2 ft/60 cm long. Its flatness meant that the point of articulation with the neck was almost on the same plane as the jaw hinge. As a result, the mouth could be opened easily by raising the head.

NAME: *Gerrothorax*
TIME: Late Triassic
LOCALITY: Europe (Sweden)
SIZE: 3 ft 3 in/1 m long
The general trend toward flattening the body reached its climax among the plagiosaurs, such as *Gerrothorax*. This large amphibian probably lay quite still on the stream or lake bed, camouflaged among the sand and pebbles, and watching for fish with its upwardly directed eyes. It may even have attracted prey with a fleshy, brightly colored lure dangling inside its open mouth. Once the prey was within easy reach, *Gerrothorax* would have swiftly closed its gaping jaws, trapping the victim.

Gerrothorax could live permanently in water because it still retained the 3 pairs of feathery gills that it possessed as a larva. So, this ancient creature clearly proves that fossil amphibians, like their modern counterparts, went through an aquatic, gill-breathing, larval stage before developing into a 4-legged, lung-breathing adult.

ORDER ANTHRACOSAURIA
The anthracosaurs (also known as batrachosaurs) were labyrinthodonts that arose during the Carboniferous and survived until the middle of the Permian. They were not so numerous or diverse as the temnospondyls (*above*), but among their members were the ancestors of the reptiles.

NAME: *Eogyrinus*
TIME: Late Carboniferous
LOCALITY: Europe (England)
SIZE: 15 ft/4.6 m long
Eogyrinus was a long-bodied aquatic predator, probably living an alligator-type life in the deltas and swamps of the Carboniferous coal forests. It swam after its fish prey using powerful strokes of the long tail, its body stabilized by the tall, fishlike dorsal fin on its back.

NAME: *Seymouria*
TIME: Early Permian
LOCALITY: North America (Texas)
SIZE: 2 ft/60 cm long
Excellent specimens of this seymouriamorph were found in the Red Beds of Texas. It was a well-adapted land-dweller, with many reptilian features (such as the joint between its head and neck, and the structure of its hip and shoulder girdles).

In fact, *Seymouria* was originally thought to be an early reptile, until fossilized juveniles were found. Their skulls clearly showed the marks of fish-like, lateral line canals, whose only function is to detect water-borne vibrations.

Lepospondyls

KERATERPETON

PANTYLUS

MICROBRACHIS

OPHIDERPETON

DIADECTES

PHLEGETHONTIA

VIERAELLA

KARAURUS

PALAEOBATRACHUS

TRIADOBATRACHUS

DIPLOCAULUS

Lepospondyls

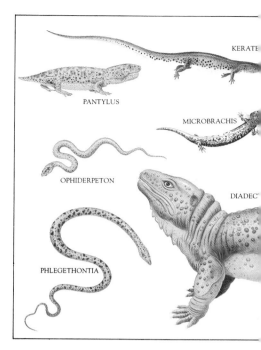

SUBCLASS LEPOSPONDYLI

Contemporary with the large, bulky labyrinthodonts (*see pp. 50–53*) were a group of smaller, insectivorous amphibians, grouped together as the lepospondyls. (The anatomical feature that unites them is the structure of their vertebrae.) These amphibians evolved in the Carboniferous period, and survived until the end of the Permian.

During this span of some 100 million years, a variety of small lepospondyls evolved, which tended to look like salamanders or snakes. They can be grouped into 3 major orders — the aïstopods, nectrideans and microsaurs (*see pp. 46–47*).

ORDER AISTOPODA

The earliest group of lepospondyls, the aïstopods, were, interestingly, the most specialized of all amphibians. They first appeared in the Early Carboniferous (Mississippian) — about 20 million years after the first amphibians, the ichthyostegalians, had set foot on land (*see p. 52*). Presumably the aïstopods evolved from a 4-legged ancestor, but almost immediately they lost their legs, and became snakelike, burrowing amphibians.

Obviously, this specialized way of life had its advantages, since the aïstopods were a long-lived group, surviving for almost 80 million years, until the middle of the Permian period.

NAME: *Ophiderpeton*
TIME: **Late Carboniferous**
LOCALITY: **Europe (Czechoslovakia) and North America (Ohio)**
SIZE: **28 in/70 cm long**
About 230 vertebrae made up the elongated body of this snakelike aïstopod. There is no trace of limbs or limb girdles within the skeleton. The eyes were quite large, and placed well forward on the skull, which was about 6 in/15 cm long. The structure of the skull was similar to that of a primitive labyrinthodont, although paleontologists can find no definite connection between these 2 groups.

Ophiderpeton must have led the life of a burrower. Certainly, this lifestyle would have paid dividends during the Late Carboniferous, when vast amounts of rotting vegetation were accumulating on the forest floor and in the swamps — the coal beds of today. All kinds of insects, worms, centipedes, snails and other invertebrates would have lived and fed on this débris, and provided the burrowing aïstopods with a rich source of food.

NAME: *Phlegethontia*
TIME: **Late Carboniferous to Early Permian**
LOCALITY: **Europe (Czechoslovakia) and North America (Ohio)**
SIZE: **3 ft 3 in/1 m long**
Although *Phlegethontia* had the same snakelike body as that of *Ophiderpeton* (*above*), and presumably led a similar burrowing life, its skull was quite different in structure. Large openings, separated by narrow bones, made it a lightweight structure (fenestrated like that of a modern snake).

ORDER NECTRIDEA

The nectrideans were 4-legged amphibians, newtlike in appearance and with long, flattened tails for swimming. Exclusively aquatic in lifestyle, they evolved during the Late Carboniferous, and survived until the end of the Permian.

Early nectrideans had a skull structure very like that of a labyrinthodont. Their limbs were well developed, with 5 toes on each. The later members of the group tended to have small forelimbs, and a toe had been lost from each. The snout also became greatly elongated in some of the later nectrideans.

NAME: *Keraterpeton*
TIME: **Late Carboniferous**
LOCALITY: **Europe (Czechoslovakia) and North America (Ohio)**
SIZE: **1 ft/30 cm long**
The tail of *Keraterpeton* was more than twice the length of its body and head combined. It was flattened sideways, and would have provided the propulsive force that pushed the animal through the murky waters of the coal swamps in which it lived. The 5-toed hindlegs were longer than the 4-toed forelegs. The skull was short and rounded, with the eyes far forward.

Although its body was long and slender, *Keraterpeton* had no more trunk vertebrae than usual (15–26 on average), unlike other long-bodied amphibians, such as the anthracosaur *Eogyrinus* which had some 40 vertebrae in front of the hips (*see pp. 51, 53*).

NAME: *Diplocaulus*
TIME: **Early to Late Permian**
LOCALITY: **North America (Texas)**
SIZE: **3 ft 3 in/1 m long**
Diplocaulus had a flattened, triangular-shaped head, like a boomerang. Two of the bones at the back of the skull had become greatly elongated on each side to form the points of the triangle. The body was short, and the limbs weak. Its tail, too, was quite short, unlike that of

other nectrideans, which has led some paleontologists to think that this amphibian swam by using up-and-down undulations of its flattened body.

Diplocaulus may have lived on the bottom of ponds and streams. The "wings" on either side of the head may have acted like hydrofoils, allowing the animal to swim above the river bed facing into the current. Alternatively, perhaps the odd shape of the head made *Diplocaulus* awkward to swallow, and so acted as a deterrent to such local predators as the thick-set, semi-aquatic labyrinthodont *Eryops* (*see pp. 50, 52*).

ORDER MICROSAURIA

The microsaurs, or "small lizards," were the most varied group of lepospondyls, with terrestrial types that lived like lizards, burrowing types with legs, and aquatic types that kept their larval gills into adult life. All microsaurs had small legs and short tails.

The group evolved late in the Carboniferous period, and survived into the Early Permian. They may have been the ancestors of the newts and salamanders.

NAME: *Microbrachis*
TIME: **Late Carboniferous**
LOCALITY: **Europe (Czechoslovakia)**
SIZE: **6 in/15 cm long**
This tiny microsaur had the typically elongated body of an aquatic animal, made up of more than 40 vertebrae. Its legs were tiny, and played no part in swimming. This was achieved by sideways undulations of the body and slender tail. This amphibian probably fed on small shrimplike invertebrates in the freshwater plankton.

Microbrachis was a Peter Pan among the lepospondyls, since the adult retained the 3 pairs of feathery gills it had

as a larva. This phenomenon is called paedomorphosis, and is seen in several modern salamanders, such as the cave-dwelling olm of Europe and the North American mudpuppy. The Mexican axolotl goes one step further; it also retains the tadpole tail of its youth.

NAME: *Pantylus*
TIME: **Early Permian**
LOCALITY: **North America (Texas)**
SIZE: **10 in/25 cm long**
A great head on a small, scaly body characterized this microsaur. It was a well-adapted land animal, moving about on short, sturdy limbs. It probably lived like a modern lizard, scuttling about after insects and other small invertebrates, which were crushed by the numerous large, blunt teeth.

ORDER ANURA
Modern frogs and toads are grouped together as anurans. As adults, they are the most specialized of all vertebrates, with the shortest backbones in the animal kingdom and powerful jumping legs not known in any other creature.

It is not surprising, therefore, that an anuran must undergo a profound transformation, or metamorphosis, to change from the limbless, herbivorous, swimming larval tadpole with a long tail, to the jumping, insectivorous, tailless, bulging-eyed adult.

Paleontologists are fairly certain that today's frogs and toads arose from among the land-living, temnospondyl labyrinthodonts, possibly from eryopid-types (see p. 52).

The first amphibian with any resemblance to a modern frog dates from Early Triassic times (below).

NAME: *Triadobatrachus*
TIME: **Early Triassic**
LOCALITY: **Madagascar**
SIZE: **4 in/10 cm long**
This tiny, froglike creature lived about 240 million years ago. The structure of its hips suggests that it swam by kicking out with its short hindlegs. This vigorous motion may have evolved over millions of years into the characteristic jumping action of modern frogs.

Triadobatrachus' skull is strikingly similar to that of a modern frog (a latticework of fine bones, separated by large openings). It could obviously hear well on land, since the bony parts of the ear were well developed, and there was a broad tympanum or eardrum on either side to pick up air-borne sounds.

Triadobatrachus had a relatively short body (made up of 14 back vertebrae) when compared with a primitive amphibian (with 24 vertebrae). But it had a long body when compared with a modern frog, which has only 5 to 9 back vertebrae, giving it the shortest backbone of all vertebrate animals. It also had a short tail, made up of 6 vertebrae, which is totally lost in modern anurans.

Triadobatrachus, therefore, represents an intermediate stage in the evolution of the anurans. It is sufficiently different from its modern descendants, the frogs and toads, to be placed in a distinct order (Proanura) and family of its own.

NAME: *Vieraella*
TIME: **Early Jurassic**
LOCALITY: **South America (Argentina)**
SIZE: **just over 1 in/3 cm long**
After *Triadobatrachus*, there is a frustrating gap of about 30 million years in the fossil record. Then, the first true frogs appear in the Early Jurassic.

Vieraella is the oldest-known frog. Its anatomy is essentially that of a modern frog, with the characteristic latticework skull, long hip girdle (shaped like a 3-pronged fork) and long jumping legs.

NAME: *Palaeobatrachus*
TIME: **Eocene to Miocene**
LOCALITY: **Europe (Belgium and France) and North America (Montana and Wyoming)**
SIZE: **4 in/10 cm long**
An offshoot from the main line of frog evolution, *Palaeobatrachus* has been preserved in large numbers in the freshwater sediments of Early Tertiary Europe. Even its tadpoles have been fossilized. It probably looked and behaved like a modern African clawed toad (*Xenopus laevis*). It was an adept swimmer, as fast as any fish, with a streamlined body and powerful, webbed feet.

ORDER URODELA
Newts and salamanders, grouped together as urodeles, first appeared in Late Jurassic times. Their modern descendants are the least specialized of living amphibians. Unlike frogs and toads, they do not undergo a complicated metamorphosis, since the larvae and adults live similar lives; both are long-tailed, swimming insectivores.

The ancestors of the urodeles remain a mystery. They may have had a common ancestor with the anurans (which are suspected to have descended from the temnospondyl labyrinthodonts, see p. 52). Or they may have arisen from among the lepospondyl microsaurs (see p. 56). But no linking fossils have yet been found.

NAME: *Karaurus*
TIME: **Late Jurassic**
LOCALITY: **Asia (Kazakhstan SSR)**
SIZE: **8 in/20 cm long**
Salamanders seem to have changed little over the known 150 million years of their evolution. The structure of the oldest-known salamander, *Karaurus*, is practically the same as that of modern forms. Its lifestyle was presumably similar, also — a good swimmer and a voracious predator of snails, worms, crustaceans and insects.

ORDER UNCERTAIN
A number of fossil animals show a mixture of amphibian and reptilian features, and are therefore difficult to classify in either group. Paleontologists generally agree that such animals were probably specialized land amphibians.

NAME: *Diadectes*
TIME: **Early Permian**
LOCALITY: **North America (Texas)**
SIZE: **10 ft/3 m long**
This creature was one of the bulkiest land animals alive in Early Permian times. Its skeleton was like that of a reptile, and well adapted to life on land. But certain features of the skull prove that it was not a member of that group.

Diadectes had a specialized skull, with a secondary bony palate (a feature found in advanced reptiles, see p. 185), though this was only partially developed. It had stout grinding teeth in its short, strong jaws.

It is possible that *Diadectes* ate shellfish, but its bulky body suggests that it ate plants. If so, it was the first amphibian herbivore, and lived at the same time as the first reptilian herbivore, *Edaphosaurus* (see p. 189).

Reptiles: Conquerors of the land

Within the unfolding history of the vertebrates, each new group has been hallmarked by some new feature, or number of features, that allowed it either to survive more efficiently in the environment of its ancestors, and thus to replace them, or to move on and conquer new environments.

The egg that revolutionized life

Below a certain minimum size, a tiny vertebrate would find life on land impossible. Its weight would be too great for its frail limbs to bear or propel, and it would rapidly lose its body moisture and dry out. Amphibians solve this problem by dividing growth into 2 phases. The egg first develops into an aquatic larva; this feeds and grows into a miniature adult, which then leaves the water and emerges onto land.

Reptiles, however, have found an alternative solution. The evolution of a shelled egg was the innovation that allowed the reptiles to quit the watery home of their amphibian ancestors, and to step out on land, fully equipped for terrestrial life. Henceforth, they could dispense with the aquatic larval phase that was, and still is, obligatory for amphibians.

A reptile's egg is similar to that of a bird, except that the shell is usually leathery and not hard, and the egg contains less-watery albumen. The shell has 2 main functions. It protects the developing embryo from drying out, and it protects it from predators. Safe within its egg, the developing reptile can sustain a longer period of growth; it emerges only when it has reached a size at which it is already competent to survive on land.

The reptiles evolved from the amphibians during the Late Carboniferous. The anapsid reptiles were the first to appear, and are represented today by the turtles and tortoises. The anapsids gave rise to the synapsid reptiles, the ancestors of the mammals, and to the diapsid reptiles, including the modern sphenodonts, lizards and snakes.

Many groups of reptile have become extinct, including the great marine reptiles, the ichthyosaurs and plesiosaurs. One of the diapsid groups, the protorosaurs, gave rise to the dinosaurs and the other ruling reptiles. (For key to silhouettes, see p. 312.)

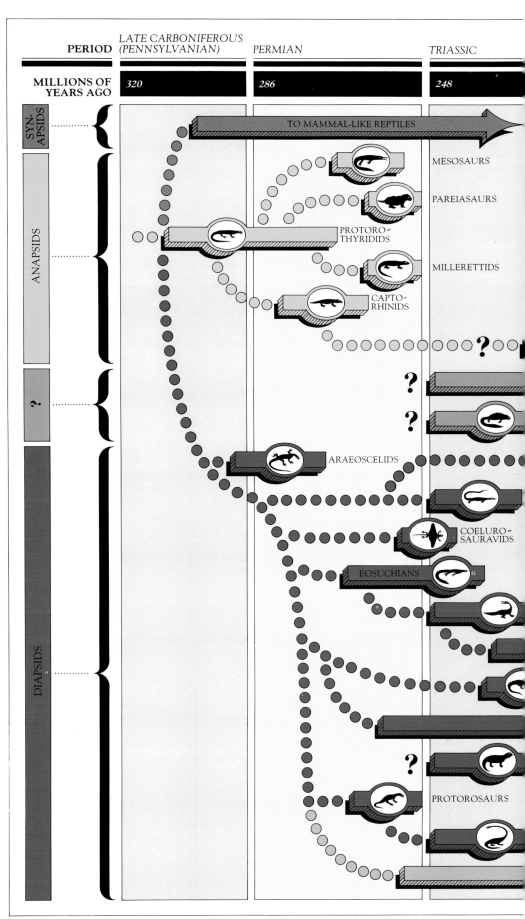

Solid bars show the known fossil record of a group. Dotted lines denote the possible evolutionary relationships between groups.

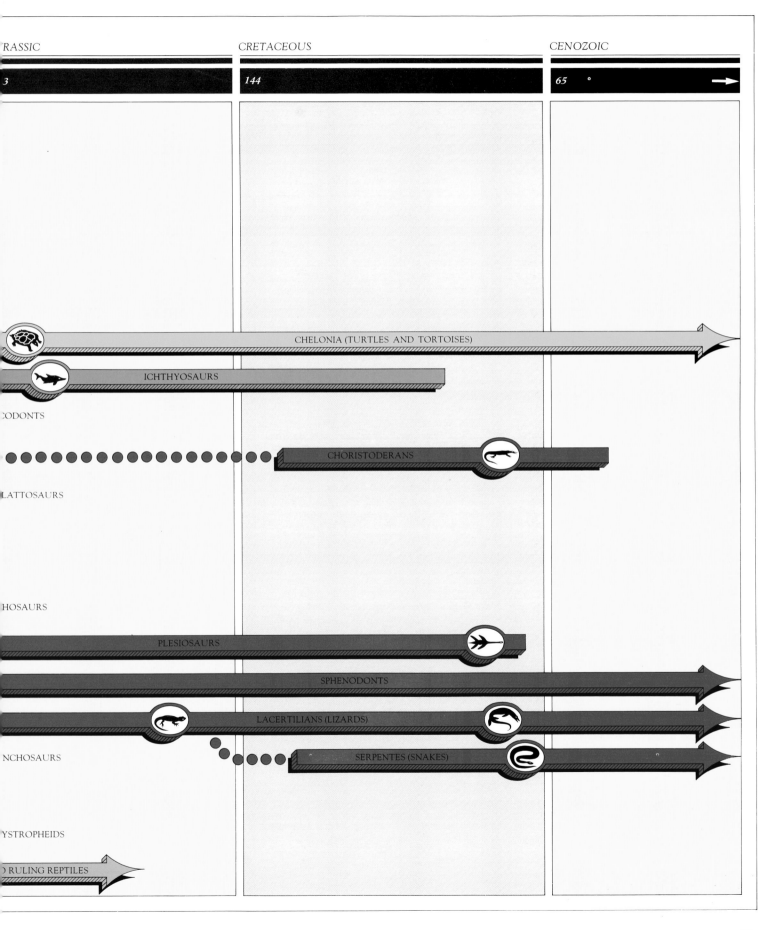

RASSIC

CRETACEOUS

CENOZOIC

3

144

65

CHELONIA (TURTLES AND TORTOISES)

ICHTHYOSAURS

CODONTS

CHORISTODERANS

LATTOSAURS

HOSAURS

PLESIOSAURS

SPHENODONTS

LACERTILIANS (LIZARDS)

NCHOSAURS

SERPENTES (SNAKES)

YSTROPHEIDS

RULING REPTILES

Reptiles: Conquerors of the land

The egg's shell inevitably cuts off the developing reptile from the surrounding world. The embryo must, therefore, be self-sufficient throughout its term of development. This is achieved by a food source, the yolk, and a series of ingenious membranes — the amnion, allantois and chorion — that transform the egg into an independent, life-support unit.

The eggs of all modern reptiles show exactly the same pattern of membranes, and biologists are confident that a single, ancestral group of original reptiles possessed this new, complicated type of "amniotic" egg (*right*), and that all later groups of vertebrates evolved from this basal stock.

Land adaptations for adult reptiles

Although protection of the developing embryo from drying out was a great step forward in the conquest of the land, 2 other innovations were necessary before that conquest was complete. First, reptiles had to be protected from desiccation after they emerged from the egg. This was achieved by evolving a horny layer that covered their scales or armor, making them impermeable to water loss.

Second, in order to remain active, reptiles had to develop a more efficient breathing method than that of their amphibian ancestors. Amphibians ventilate their lungs by means of a throat-pump, which forces air into the lungs. Reptiles developed a new system, in which the rib cage was expanded and contracted, resulting in air being sucked into the lungs, and then expelled. The capacity of this system was limited only by the volume of the lungs, not merely by the volume of the mouth.

However, even with all these adaptations, living reptiles are still, like amphibians, limited in one respect. They are "cold-blooded" — that is, they obtain nearly all of their energy from the heat of the sun. When the weather or climate becomes cooler, their body temperature is lowered, and they become inactive. The physiology of reptiles is, therefore, geared to a low and varying body temperature, and they cannot sustain prolonged periods of activity.

In contrast, "warm-blooded" birds and mammals obtain their energy from

THE AMNIOTIC EGG

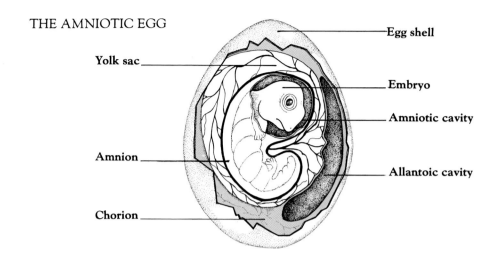

Egg shell
Yolk sac
Embryo
Amniotic cavity
Amnion
Allantoic cavity
Chorion

There are 4 membranes inside the shelled egg of a reptile — the amnion, chorion, allantois and yolk sac. Each plays a particular role to enable the embryo — in this case a turtle — to develop to maturity within its protective egg, independent of its surroundings.

The developing embryo is suspended in a fluid-filled cavity surrounded by the amnion. It receives nourishment from the surrounding yolk sac through blood vessels connected to its gut. Waste products are excreted into the allantoic cavity. Oxygen enters the egg via the chorion, which lies just beneath the egg's porous shell.

their food, and have a high, constant body temperature, independent of their surroundings, which allows them to sustain a high rate of activity for much longer periods. Paleontologists are currently debating whether dinosaurs were cold- or warm-blooded (*see p. 93*).

Like their amphibian ancestors, and the fish before them, reptiles move by lateral flexure of their bodies (*below*). The upper parts of a reptile's limbs project laterally from the body, since the length of each stride depends on the distance across the body from one knee or elbow joint to the other. The feet are also angled somewhat to the side, to resist the lateral forces produced by this type of movement. The toes have to be of different lengths if they are to leave the ground at the same time, so that the weight of the body is shared evenly between them.

As a result of all these adaptations, both structural and physiological, reptiles were able to colonize the land to the full, living even in the hottest deserts. The peak of their evolutionary development was reached in the form of the

great dinosaurs, which grew to sizes that even their successors, the mammals, were unable to rival.

Radiation of the reptiles

The reptiles evolved from the amphibians some time in the Late Carboniferous (Pennsylvanian) period. The earliest-known reptile is *Hylonomus* (*see p. 64*), preserved in the Late Carboniferous rocks of Nova Scotia. These rocks are about 300 million years old — some 60 million years after the first amphibian *Ichthyostega* crawled out of the water to form the spearhead for the invasion of the land (*see p. 52*).

From *Hylonomus*, many different types of reptile evolved. Like the early amphibians, all of the early reptiles seem to have been confined to the ancient continent of Euramerica (*see p. 49*). Fortunately for paleontologists, most of these different lineages of reptile can be distinguished by the pattern of openings in the skull (*see p. 61*).

In addition to skull structure, evidence for the interrelationships of reptiles can be seen in the structure of

HOW A REPTILE MOVES

The legs of a typical reptile, such as a lizard, are splayed out to the side of its body. This results in a sprawling gait, with the whole body being twisted from side to side at each step. Here the backbone and limb girdles are emphasized to illustrate this bending of the body.

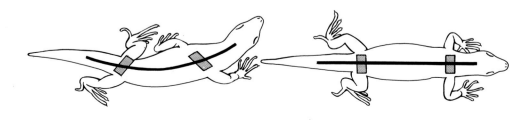

their ankles and major blood vessels. In some reptiles, one of the ankle bones is hooked, and provides extra leverage for one of the foot muscles (just as our projecting heel bone provides leverage for the Achilles tendon). This type of ankle is found in all lizards and chelonians (including modern turtles and tortoises), as well as in the "ruling reptile" lineage — the crocodiles, dinosaurs and their relatives.

The living representatives of all these groups also have an unusual arrangement of the major blood vessels near the heart. These twist around one another in a spiral fashion.

For all these reasons — skulls, ankles and blood vessels — paleontologists are confident that these groups of reptile are closely related to each other.

Skull patterns

In the earliest reptiles, as in their amphibian ancestors, the skull was a box of bone, without any openings except for those of the eyes and nostrils. The muscles of the jaws were attached to the underside of the bony roof of the skull.

In most later reptiles, the weight of the skull was reduced by the development of areas in which the bone was replaced by a sheet of elastic, tendonlike material. This material decays, but the areas in which it was located appear in a fossilized skull as holes (called temporal openings) between the bones. These openings not only serve to lighten the skull, but also provide additional attachment points to which the jaw muscles can attach, thereby increasing the bite-power of the jaws.

The presence or absence of these temporal openings in the skull form the basis for grouping reptiles into major groups or subclasses (*above right*).

The earliest reptiles (such as *Hylonomus* and other protorothyridids, and mesosaurs) had no temporal openings, and their skulls are called *anapsid*. The chelonians (today represented by turtles, tortoises and terrapins) also lack openings in their skulls, and so they, too, are placed in the anapsids, although it is not certain from which group of early reptiles they evolved.

The ruling reptiles — including the thecodontians and their descendants,

TYPES OF SKULLS

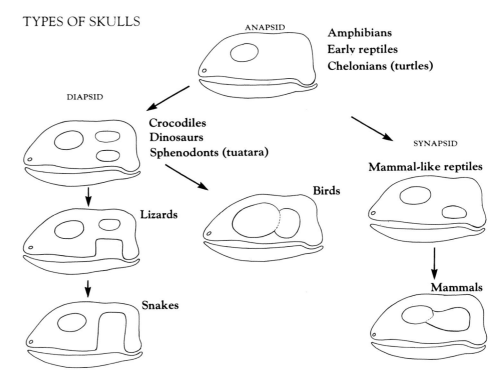

Amphibians
Early reptiles
Chelonians (turtles)

Crocodiles
Dinosaurs
Sphenodonts (tuatara)

Lizards

Birds

Mammal-like reptiles

Snakes

Mammals

Three main types of skull evolved among reptiles, with a trend toward reducing the amount of bone and replacing it with tendonlike material to which the jaw muscles could attach. The most primitive reptiles, the anapsids, had no openings in their skulls, which resulted in weak jaws.

The anapsids gave rise to 2 major groups. The diapsid reptiles had a pair of openings behind each eye. In lizards the openings became larger, enabling the jaws

to open wider, while the snakes have an even wider gape, with the openings merging together. The birds evolved a variation of the dinosaur's diapsid skull, with a very large opening behind each eye.

The mammal-like reptiles evolved synapsid skulls, with a single opening set low on either side. Their descendants, the mammals, enlarged the single opening, which helped to increase the bite-power of their jaws.

the dinosaurs, pterosaurs and crocodiles — have *diapsid* skulls, with 2 pairs of openings behind the eyes on each side. The primitive lizards, the sphenodonts (today represented by the sole surviving member, the tuatara), also have a diapsid skull. Later lizards have made the skull even lighter and more flexible, by losing the bar of bone below the lower opening on each side. Snakes have taken this tendency even further, by dispensing with the bar of bone between the upper and lower openings.

Other groups are not so easily defined. The extinct marine reptiles, the nothosaurs and plesiosaurs, for

example, developed a skull pattern (sometimes called *euryapsid*) similar to that of most lizards. These groups would also seem to have evolved from diapsid ancestors.

Two other groups of extinct marine reptiles, the ichthyosaurs and placodonts, also have a euryapsid type of skull. But these animals are very different from one another and from the plesiosaurs. Each group may have evolved from diapsids, but there is no evidence to detail their precise lines of ancestry. A similar uncertainty surrounds the origin of the diapsid, herbivorous rhynchosaurs, also extinct.

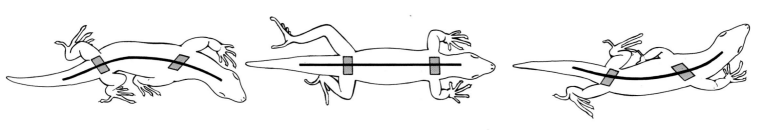

Early reptiles

HYLONOMUS

LABIDOSAURUS

MILLERETTA

MESOSAURUS

HYPSOGNATHUS

PAREIASAURUS

ELGINIA

SCUTOSAURUS

Early reptiles

SUBCLASS ANAPSIDA

The earliest, most primitive reptiles, the anapsids, all shared a common characteristic — the skull was a heavy, solid box of bone, with no openings apart from the sockets for the eyes and nostrils (*see pp. 60–61*). The muscles that controlled the jaws were confined within this bony box; this limited their size and length, which meant that the mouth could not be opened wide or closed with any force.

In later, more advanced reptiles, openings developed in the skull that allowed for an increase in the efficiency of the jaws. Such "diapsid" reptiles and their descendants had greater bite-power, and could open their jaws wider to tackle larger prey (*see pp. 82–85*).

Only one order of anapsid reptiles survive today — the chelonians, or turtles and tortoises (*see pp. 66–69*). The other 2 orders of primitive reptiles, the captorhinids and the mesosaurs, became extinct over 250 million years ago (*below*).

ORDER CAPTORHINIDA

The captorhinids (sometimes called the cotylosaurs) are the earliest and most primitive of reptiles. They evolved from the amphibians during the Late Carboniferous period, some 300 million years ago, but were all extinct by the end of the Triassic, about 90 million years later. From among their members came 2 major evolutionary lines — one led to the mammals, and the other to the ruling reptiles (*see pp. 58–59*).

FAMILY PROTOROTHYRIDIDAE

Members of this family are the earliest-known reptiles. They first appeared in the Late Carboniferous period, and survived into Mid-Permian times, a span of some 50 million years. The protorothyridids were the basal stock from which many specialized groups evolved, including the ruling reptiles — the dinosaurs, crocodiles and flying pterosaurs (*see pp. 90–93*).

NAME: *Hylonomus*
TIME: **Late Carboniferous**
LOCALITY: **North America (Nova Scotia)**
SIZE: **8 in/20 cm long**
Hylonomus is the earliest-known, fully-adapted terrestrial vertebrate — a milestone in the evolution of life on land. In appearance and lifestyle, it closely resembled a modern lizard.

This small creature probably ate insects and other invertebrates, crushing them with its conical teeth. Though the

teeth were simple and unspecialized, some of the front ones were longer than the rest — a feature usually found in the more advanced reptiles.

Hylonomus was preserved in the coal beds of Nova Scotia in an unusual way. Giant, treelike club mosses flourished in swampy areas during Late Carboniferous times. Periodic flooding buried their lower trunks in deep layers of mud and rotting leaf litter, which caused the trees to die and their interiors to rot away. This left deep, cylindrical cavities in the ground, which would have filled up with decaying debris. Insects and other invertebrates would have been attracted there, and these in turn would have attracted *Hylonomus*. It would have been unable to escape from the deep, vertical-sided cavities, and its remains were eventually fossilized there.

FAMILY CAPTORHINIDAE

This successful group of primitive reptiles ranged throughout the Permian period, surviving for almost 40 million years before becoming extinct. They lived in Africa, Asia, India and North America.

Primitive though the captorhinids were, they were more advanced than their protorothyridid ancestors (*above*). Their skulls were much stronger, with the braincase now firmly attached to the skull roof and cheeks, and the multiple rows of teeth in their jaws could deal with tough plants or hard-shelled animals.

NAME: *Labidosaurus*
TIME: **Early Permian**
LOCALITY: **North America (Texas)**
SIZE: **2 ft 5 in/75 cm long**
This primitive, heavily built reptile was a squat animal with a large head and short tail. Its shape suggests that it was fully at home on land.

A typical captorhinid, *Labidosaurus* had several rows of teeth in the jaws, all functional at the same time. This was an improvement on its ancestors, the protorothyridids, which had only a single row of small conical teeth in their jaws. The rows in *Labidosaurus*' mouth provided a broad surface on which shelled invertebrates, such as insects and snails, could be crushed, or tough plant material ground down.

FAMILY PROCOLOPHONIDAE

This family ranged throughout the world from Late Permian times to the end of the Triassic. Early members were small and lightly built. They were probably quite agile, and crushed insects and

other invertebrates with the many, small, peglike teeth in their jaws.

Later members, however, from the Mid-Triassic onward, were larger creatures with a very different dentition. Their broad cheek teeth suggest that they ate plants. Strange, bony spikes grew outward from the sides of their skulls, presumably as a means of defense for these heavy, slow-moving herbivores.

NAME: *Hypsognathus*
TIME: **Late Triassic**
LOCALITY: **North America (New Jersey)**
SIZE: **13 in/33 cm long**
One of the later members of the family, *Hypsognathus* had many features that indicate it was a plant-eater. It had a wide, squat body, which suggests that it was not an agile animal. Its broad cheek teeth were suitable for grinding up tough plant material. And an array of spikes around its head were probably for defense against predators, such as the contemporary carnivorous dinosaurs, the podokesaurs (*see p. 108*).

FAMILY PAREIASAURIDAE

The pareiasaurs were the largest of the early, primitive reptiles, reaching lengths of 10 ft/3 m. They were massively built herbivores, supported on sturdy limbs, which in later members tended to be placed beneath the body so that the animals could walk more upright, rather than sprawl.

The pareiasaurs appeared in southern Africa during the Mid-Permian, and had spread to Europe and Asia in large numbers by the end of that period when they became extinct.

PAREIASAURUS

ELGINIA

SCUTOSAURUS

NAME: *Pareiasaurus*
TIME: **Middle Permian**
LOCALITY: **Southern and eastern Africa, and eastern Europe**
SIZE: **8 ft/2.5 m long**
This massive, squat animal was a typical pareiasaur. Its back was protected by bony plates embedded in the skin. Its legs were thick and strong, and splayed out to the sides in typical reptilian fashion, to support the huge body, with its enormously thickened backbone.

The skull, too, was heavy and solid, studded with spikes and warty lumps. The teeth were small and leaf-shaped, with serrated edges to deal with the tough plant fiber that *Pareiasaurus* ate. Even the palate was equipped with teeth to help grind down the food.

NAME: *Scutosaurus*
TIME: **Late Permian**
LOCALITY: **Europe (USSR)**
SIZE: **8 ft/2.5 m long**
The typical features of the pareiasaur family — massive body, spiked head and bony armor — were developed to an extreme in *Scutosaurus*. This later member of the family had also developed a more upright gait than its relatives. Its legs were drawn in, and held more directly beneath the body to support its great weight. This trend was to be perfected among the later ruling reptiles, the dinosaurs (*see pp. 106–169*).

The presence of such large plant-eaters as *Pareiasaurus* and *Scutosaurus* in eastern Europe during Permian times could suggest that the climate in that region was warm and stable at the time, since these heavy, slow-moving reptiles could neither migrate away from cold conditions nor hibernate through the winter months.

NAME: *Elginia*
TIME: **Late Permian**
LOCALITY: **Europe (Scotland)**
SIZE: **2 ft/60 cm long**
One of the last of the pareiasaurs, *Elginia* was also one of the smallest. Its head was decorated with the head spikes typical of the family, but they were developed into an incredible array on *Elginia*'s small skull. Their purpose was probably more for display than for defense — perhaps this little reptile shook its head about to threaten a rival male or to attract a female.

FAMILY MILLERETTIDAE
The millerettids were a family of anapsid reptiles with a pair of openings in the skull behind the eyes. This may sound like a contradiction, since the anapsids are that group of reptiles with no openings in their skulls, apart from the eyes and nostrils.

In the case of the millerettids, other features of the skull place them firmly in the anapsid group. Most likely, they represent a specialized side branch of the main reptilian tree, and evolved these openings independently.

Millerettids were all small insectivores that lived from the Middle to Late Permian in southern Africa. So far, their remains have not been found elsewhere.

NAME: *Milleretta*
TIME: **Late Permian**
LOCALITY: **South Africa**
SIZE: **2 ft/60 cm long**
This small, lizardlike creature was agile enough to chase after insects. Because of the pair of openings in its skull, some paleontologists used to hold the theory, now disproved, that *Milleretta*, or a closely related member of its family, may have been ancestral to the more advanced group of reptiles, the diapsids, which had 2 pairs of openings on either side of the skull (*see pp. 60–61*). This group includes nearly all the modern reptiles and the extinct dinosaurs and pterosaurs.

However, the earliest-known diapsid, the araeoscelid *Petrolacosaurus* (*see p. 84*), dates from the Late Carboniferous period — more than 40 million years before the millerettids evolved.

ORDER MESOSAURIA
The mesosaurs were early aquatic reptiles, the first group to return to the water since their ancestors had adopted a land-living existence. They appeared at the beginning of the Permian period, and died out relatively soon after. Their remains have only been found in the southern hemisphere.

FAMILY MESOSAURIDAE
This is the only family of mesosaurs. Its members were all fully aquatic, swimming by means of a long, broad tail and long hindlegs, and steering with the forelimbs. They probably sieved plankton from the water through the fine, pointed teeth in their elongated jaws.

NAME: *Mesosaurus*
TIME: **Early Permian**
LOCALITY: **Southern Africa and South America (Brazil)**
SIZE: **up to 3 ft 3 in/1 m long**
This small creature was the first reptile to revert to a water-dwelling existence. It possessed many adaptations to an aquatic life. Its long tail was flattened from side to side, and there may have been a fin running along its length, top and bottom. Its hindlegs were long, and the elongated footbones were splayed and probably webbed. The forelegs were shorter, but also with broad, webbed feet. Thus, the tail and hindlegs propelled the animal forward, while the forelegs kept it on course.

Mesosaurus could evidently bend easily from side to side, as seen in the flexible structure of the backbone, though it could not twist its body. The ribs were greatly thickened — an aquatic adaptation also seen in the modern sirenians, or sea cows.

Mesosaurus' head was long and narrow, with the nostrils placed high on its snout near the eyes. It had only to break the surface of the water to breathe and to see. An impressive array of long, delicate teeth armed the elongated jaws. Each tooth fitted into its own socket — a feature of meat-eating animals. Yet the teeth would have been too fine for capturing prey. Instead, they probably formed a kind of sieve through which small shrimplike animals were filtered from the water — similar to how a modern flamingo feeds with its comb-like bill.

The evolutionary importance of *Mesosaurus* does not derive from its aquatic adaptations, but from its geographical distribution. Because its remains have been found in both southern Africa and eastern South America, this distribution was one of the earliest pieces of biological evidence for continental drift or plate tectonics (*see pp. 10–11*). Such an animal could not possibly have swum across the South Atlantic; the only explanation, therefore, for its peculiar distribution is that these 2 southern continents had not yet split apart when *Mesosaurus* was alive.

Turtles, tortoises and terrapins

PROGANOCHELYS

STUPENDEMYS

TESTUDO

MEIOLANIA

ARCHELON

PALEOTRIONYX

Turtles, tortoises and terrapins

PROGANOCHELYS

STUPENDEMYS

TESTUDO

ORDER CHELONIA

Turtles, tortoises and terrapins are the only surviving members of this ancient group of reptiles, the chelonians. They differ from all other reptiles in having their bodies, except for the head, tail and legs, enclosed within a shell, above and below. Many of them can pull their heads and legs into the shell for total protection.

Even the earliest chelonians, dating from the Late Triassic, had a shell; in fact, today's turtles and tortoises have hardly changed since those times, over 200 million years ago.

Like other anapsids (*see pp. 62–65*), chelonians have solidly roofed skulls, with no openings in them save for the eyes and nostrils. They are classified for convenience in the anapsid order, but some paleontologists believe that their anatomy is so specialized, and their lifestyle so different from that of other reptiles, that they should be put in a subclass (Testudinata) of their own.

There are 2 distinct suborders of chelonian, which include the 230 species of living turtles, tortoises and terrapins. They are distinguished by the way in which the animal retracts its head into its shell — either by bending the neck sideways (Pleurodira) or by bending it back vertically (Cryptodira). The members of a third suborder (Proganochelydia) are all now extinct, but they were the ancestors of the chelonian group (*below*).

SUBORDER PROGANOCHELYDIA

The proganochelids were land-living, tortoiselike reptiles with shells encasing their bodies. They began to evolve in Late Triassic times, some 215 million years ago, and were most probably the stock from which today's land tortoises and aquatic turtles arose. But the ancestry of the proganochelids themselves is not known. Most paleontologists believe it to lie among one of the early groups of anapsid reptiles, perhaps the captorhinids (*see pp. 62–65*).

FAMILY PROGANOCHELYIDAE

Most of the early tortoises belong to this family, and date from the Late Triassic period. The best-preserved skeletons have been found in Germany, although others have come from Southeast Asia, North America and southern Africa. Many of the characteristic features seen in modern tortoises were developed at this early stage in their evolution.

NAME: *Proganochelys*
TIME: **Late Triassic**
LOCALITY: **Europe (Germany)**
SIZE: **3 ft 3 in/1 m long**

This is the most primitive chelonian known, but the typical tortoise shape and structure were already well established. In fact, *Proganochelys* was remarkably similar to a modern land-living tortoise, except that it could not retract its head or legs into its shell.

The body of this ancient tortoise was short and broad, with only 10 elongated vertebrae making up the backbone. This is also a feature of modern chelonians, and, except for frogs, gives them the shortest backbones among vertebrate animals. *Proganochelys'* short neck (made up of only 8 vertebrae) and head were armed with bony knobs.

Proganochelys had a broad, domed shell (known as the carapace) covering its back, and flat, bony plates (the plastron) protected its underside. About 60 plates of various sizes made up the shell, and they were solidly fused to the underlying vertebrae and ribs. Their arrangement was essentially the same as that found in the shells of modern turtles and tortoises. Unlike its modern relatives, however, *Proganochelys* had a number of extra plates around the margin of its shell. These projected outward, and gave the legs some protection.

In life, the shell would have been completely sealed over with plates of smooth horn — the beautiful "tortoise shell" from which combs and other ornaments are made. (The horn itself does not fossilize, but marks on the bones indicate its presence.)

The only teeth in *Proganochelys'* mouth were on its palate. Otherwise, it had the typical toothless, horny beak characteristic of modern tortoises. Like them, *Proganochelys* probably spent most its time cropping low-growing vegetation.

SUBORDER PLEURODIRA

A few members of this group of aquatic chelonians survive today, and are known as the "side-neck" turtles, because of their peculiar method of retracting their head inside their shells. This is done with a sideways-flexing of the short neck, and is made possible by the jointing system between the vertebrae.

Pleurodires date from Jurassic times, and were once abundant in the rivers and lakes of the world. Today, only 49 species survive, grouped in 2 families — the Pelomedusidae (*below*) and the Chelidae. All are restricted to the freshwaters of the southern continents.

FAMILY PELOMEDUSIDAE

These aquatic turtles were the most prolific of all the pleurodires during Late Cretaceous and Early Tertiary times. There are only 19 living species — in the rivers and lakes of tropical Africa, Madagascar and South America.

NAME: *Stupendemys*
TIME: **Early Pliocene**
LOCALITY: **South America (Venezuela)**
SIZE: **6 ft 6 in/2 m long**

This turtle, extinct for some 3 million years, was a giant among the pleurodires; in fact, it was the largest freshwater turtle that has ever existed. None of its modern relatives come close to it in size — the largest living species is the Arrau Turtle of the Orinoco and Amazon rivers of South America (*Podocnemis expansa*), and it only grows up to 2 ft 6 in/75 cm in length.

The heavy shell that covered *Stupendemys'* back was immensely broad and over 6 ft/1.8 m long. Its weight would have allowed the animal to stay submerged for fairly long periods, while it cropped the prodigious quantities of weeds needed to fuel its body.

SUBORDER CRYPTODIRA

The cryptodires were the most successful group of chelonians, and survive to this day — most modern turtles and tortoises belong to this group. Many of them can retract their heads into the shell by lowering the neck and pulling it back vertically.

As a group, the cryptodires evolved along with their pleurodire cousins during Jurassic times. But by the end of that period they had become enormously diverse, and replaced the pleurodires in the seas, rivers and lakes of the world. New forms developed on land.

MEIOLANIA

ARCHELON

PALEOTRIONYX

FAMILY MEIOLANIIDAE

The land tortoises of this family appeared in the Late Cretaceous period, and only became extinct relatively recently — in the Pleistocene, less than 2 million years ago. Although unable to retract their heads into their shells, they were well protected in other ways.

NAME: *Meiolania*
TIME: **Pleistocene**
LOCALITY: **Australia (Queensland, New Caledonia and Lord Howe Island)**
SIZE: **8 ft/2.5 m long**

Apart from its great size, the most remarkable feature of this well-armored tortoise was the flamboyant ornamentation on its head. It was surmounted by great spikes, two of which stuck out on either side, giving the head an overall width of some 2 ft/60 cm. Their presence makes it highly unlikely that *Meiolania* could have withdrawn its head into the shell in times of attack. However, the shell protected the back, and the tail was encased in rings of bony armor, and ended in a spiked club.

FAMILY TESTUDINIDAE

Modern land tortoises belong to this family, the most successful of the cryptodires. They appeared in modern form during the Eocene, some 50 million years ago, and have remained practically unchanged since then.

All tortoises have high, domed shells to accommodate the capacious gut needed to digest their plant food. The shell also offers complete protection, since the animal can withdraw its head and elephantine legs inside.

NAME: *Testudo atlas*
TIME: **Pleistocene**
LOCALITY: **Asia (India)**
SIZE: **up to 8 ft/2.5 m long**

The extinct *Testudo atlas* was the largest land tortoise ever to have existed. Sometimes it is called *Colossochelys*, meaning "colossal shell." It weighed about $4\frac{1}{2}$ US tons/4 tonnes. The elephantine legs sprawled out at the sides of its body in typical reptilian fashion, and supported the massive shell carried on its back. Cushioned pads on the soles of its compact feet spread the weight evenly over the 5, heavy-nailed toes of each foot — like the arrangement seen in modern elephants.

Testudo atlas probably fed exclusively on plants, as do most of its modern relatives (though some are known to eat slugs and worms as well). It would have spent its time cropping leaves with its sharp, toothless beak without fear of being attacked. If a predator, such as one of the saber-toothed cats, did try, *T. atlas* would have simply pulled its head and legs into its shell, and presented a solid, bony box, impossible to shift or turn over.

The modern counterpart of this extinct tortoise, in terms of size and weight, is the Galapagos giant tortoise, *Geochelone elephantopus*. But this animal is only 4 ft/1.2 m long — half the length of *T. atlas* — and weighs a mere 500 lb/225 kg.

FAMILY PROTOSTEGIDAE

The protostegids numbered among their members some of the most spectacular sea turtles that ever lived. All are now extinct, but they thrived during the Late Cretaceous.

By that time, the protostegids had developed the 2 main features that distinguish all sea turtles from their land and river-based relatives. First, since there were fewer predators in the sea, they did not need such heavy armor on their backs, and so the shell was reduced to a much lighter structure, which also made them more maneuverable. Second, the toes of the front and back limbs were greatly elongated, and modified into broad flippers for swimming.

Today, only 7 species of sea turtle survive, grouped in 2 families. All are endangered due to man's interference with their habitats, especially the nesting beaches. The green turtle and the great leatherback turtle, both of warm seas, are the most familiar members. No sea turtle, either extinct or modern, can retract its head or legs into the shell.

NAME: *Archelon*
TIME: **Late Cretaceous**
LOCALITY: **North America (Kansas and South Dakota)**
SIZE: **12 ft/3.7 m long**

This giant turtle of the Cretaceous seas did not have the heavy, many-plated shell characteristic of its land and freshwater relatives. Instead, the shell of *Archelon* was reduced to a framework of transverse struts, made from the bony ribs that grew out from its backbone. Most probably, the ribs were covered by a thick coat of rubbery skin (as seen in the modern leatherback turtle), rather than by the usual plates of horn.

The limbs of this ancient sea turtle were transformed into massive paddles that would have cleaved the water in powerful, vertical strokes — the method is comparable to the underwater flight of penguins, which propel themselves along by flapping their wings. The front flippers of *Archelon* were well developed, and would have provided the main propulsive force.

Like the modern leatherback turtle, *Archelon* probably fed on a diet of jellyfish, whose soft bodies were easily dealt with by the reptile's weak jaws and toothless beak.

FAMILY TRIONYCHIDAE

This family of soft-shelled turtles first appeared, along with the sea turtles, in the Late Jurassic period. They were an early group of specialized cryptodires, and a relatively successful one, since over 30 species survive today, in the freshwaters of North America, Africa and Asia.

The shells of trionychids are low and rounded, and have lost the horny covering that usually protects the underlying bony plates. Instead, a layer of soft, leathery skin covers the shell, hence the name of the family.

NAME: *Palaeotrionyx*
TIME: **Paleocene**
LOCALITY: **Western North America**
SIZE: **18 in/45 cm long**

This extinct, freshwater turtle was a specialized cryptodire. Unlike most of its relatives it had a long, mobile neck; only 3 toes on each foot; and a skin-covered shell, rather than the usual coat of horny plates.

Palaeotrionyx was probably similar in appearance and lifestyle to its living cousins, the soft-shelled turtles (*Trionyx* species) of North America and Africa. Like them, it was probably omnivorous, using its sharp beak to crop water weeds and snap up insects, mollusks, crayfish and even small fish.

Placodonts and nothosaurs

PLACOCHELYS

HENODUS

LARIOSAURUS

CLAUDIOSAURUS

CERESIOSAURUS

PISTOSAURUS

NOTHOSAURUS

PLACODUS

Placodonts and nothosaurs

MARINE REPTILES

During the Mesozoic Era, several groups of reptiles returned to the sea, and became adapted to a marine life. The ichthyosaurs, or "fish lizards," and the long-necked plesiosaurs were the most successful groups, and they dominated the seas of the world for more than 100 million years.

The relationship of these marine reptiles to other reptilian orders, and even to each other, is still unclear. But they are sufficiently alike in one respect to be grouped together conveniently. Their common feature is a pair of openings in the skull, behind the eyes and below the cheekbones.

There are 4 distinct types of marine reptile, each showing varying degrees of adaptation to the marine environment. The least specialized were the placodonts of the Triassic (*below*). The nothosaurs, also of the Triassic, were more adapted to aquatic life (*below*), and their relatives, the plesiosaurs, ranged the open seas throughout Jurassic and Cretaceous times (*see pp. 74–77*). The ichthyosaurs shared the Jurassic seas with the plesiosaurs, and were the most specialized group of marine reptiles (*see pp. 78–81*).

ORDER PLACODONTIA

The placodonts were the least specialized swimmers among the marine reptiles. They appeared and disappeared in the Triassic period, and during this span of some 35 million years, many types evolved. But they never became fully adapted to life in the open seas. They were confined to the shallow, coastal waters of the Tethys Sea, which existed at the time between the northern landmass of Laurasia and the southern landmass of Gondwanaland (*see pp. 10–11*). Many types had turtlelike shells protecting their backs and undersides.

FAMILY PLACODONTIDAE

This group of semi-aquatic reptiles were equally at home walking along the seashore or swimming in the coastal shallows. Both areas provided them with rich feeding grounds for their preferred diet of shellfish, which were crushed between the broad teeth.

NAME: *Placodus*
TIME: **Early to Middle Triassic**
LOCALITY: **Europe (Alps)**
SIZE: **6 ft 6 in/2 m long**
The skull of *Placodus* shows that this reptile was a specialized feeder. Its teeth were fully adapted to a shellfish diet. An array of blunt teeth protruded at the front of the jaws, and were used to pluck

shellfish — bivalves and brachiopods — off the rocks. The back teeth were broad and flat, for crushing the shells (hence the name of the family, Placodontidae, meaning "flat-plate tooth.") Even the palate was covered with large, crushing teeth.

This formidable battery of teeth was powered by massive jaw muscles, which could extend through the pair of openings on each side of the skull to give the jaws great bite-power.

Some modern sharks (such as the Port Jackson shark, *Heterodontus portusjacksoni*) that eat such hard-shelled animals as mollusks, crustaceans and sea urchins have the same kind of specialized teeth. So similar are they that when the teeth of *Placodus* were first found, paleontologists thought that they belonged to ancient sharks.

Placodus was hardly modified at all for an aquatic lifestyle. Its body was stocky, its neck short, and its limbs sprawled out to the sides like those of early, land-living reptiles. Its only swimming aids were the webs of skin between the 5 toes of each foot, and the long, slender tail, which was flattened from side to side, and may have had a fin along its length.

Like all placodonts, the underside of *Placodus'* body was protected by a strong armor of belly ribs. A row of bony knobs was raised above the backbone, and provided some protection for this otherwise defenseless animal. Body armor was developed to a much greater extent in later placodonts (*below*).

FAMILY CYAMODONTIDAE

This group of placodonts had developed turtlelike shells on their backs. They evolved in the Mid-Triassic and survived to the end of that period.

These shelled placodonts assumed a more completely aquatic lifestyle than *Placodus* (*above*), and began to look and behave like modern turtles, although they were unrelated — a phenomenon known as convergent evolution.

NAME: *Placochelys*
TIME: **Middle to Late Triassic**
LOCALITY: **Europe (Germany)**
SIZE: **3 ft/90 cm long**
This small reptile was well adapted to an aquatic life. The slender body of *Placodus* had been replaced by a broad, flat, turtlelike body in *Placochelys*. A tight mosaic of knobby plates covered its back, forming a protective body armor. Its tail was short, and its limbs elongated into paddles for swimming.

Its head, however, was that of a specialized shellfish-eater. It had lost the protruding front teeth seen in *Placodus*.

In their place was a horny, toothless beak, but this was still strong enough to pluck shellfish off rocks. Like *Placodus*, strong muscles worked the jaws, which were equipped with broad, crushing teeth along the sides and on the palate.

FAMILY HENODONTIDAE

These armored placodonts evolved in the Late Triassic period. The similarity to turtles, first developed among the cyamodonts (*above*), was brought to an extreme in members of this family. They had developed a great, bony shell that covered their backs and undersides, and they had lost most of their teeth, replacing them with a horny beak like that of a modern turtle.

NAME: *Henodus*
TIME: **Late Triassic**
LOCALITY: **Europe (Germany)**
SIZE: **3 ft 3 in/1 m long**
The body of *Henodus* was as broad as it was long — the same shape as that of a modern turtle. Its back and belly were covered in an irregular mosaic of many-sided, bony plates. These formed a defensive shell to protect it from attack by other marine reptiles in the Triassic seas, such as the ichthyosaurs.

Many more plates made up the shell of *Henodus* than are present in the shell of a modern turtle. But as in a modern turtle, the shell was completely covered by plates of horn.

Henodus' head was peculiarly square and boxlike. There were no teeth in its jaws; instead, there was probably a horny beak, like that of a modern turtle, which could be used effectively to both dislodge and crush shells.

CERESIOSAURUS

PISTOSAURUS

...OSAURUS

PLACODUS

ORDER UNCERTAIN

The claudiosaurs were marine reptiles that evolved in the Late Permian period. Their classification is uncertain, but they may represent a transition group between the land-living eosuchian reptiles (see p. 85) and the later, more advanced aquatic reptiles, the nothosaurs and their relatives, the plesiosaurs.

Only one genus of claudiosaur has been found to date — a semi-aquatic, lizardlike animal named *Claudiosaurus*, which is placed in its own family, the Claudiosauridae (below).

NAME: *Claudiosaurus*
TIME: **Late Permian**
LOCALITY: **Madagascar**
SIZE: **2 ft/60 cm long**
Claudiosaurus was a long-necked, lizard-like animal, whose lifestyle could be compared to that of the modern marine iguana. *Claudiosaurus* probably spent much of its time resting on rocky beaches, warming up its body so that it could go foraging. It would have fed underwater, poking its long, flexible neck and small head in among the seaweeds to find suitable animals and plants. When it swam, its fore- and hindlegs would have been folded against the body to give a more streamlined shape, and offer less resistance to the water. The main propulsive force came from sideways-undulations of the rear body and long, narrow tail.

There was quite a lot of cartilage in the skeleton of *Claudiosaurus*. This suggests that the animal relied on the buoyancy of the water to give it support. Also, the breast bone, or sternum, was neither well developed nor ossified, as it is in true terrestrial animals, where it braces the ribs apart on the underside of the body as an adaptation to walking. The sternum in *Claudiosaurus*, therefore, suggests that its limbs were not well adapted for moving on land.

ORDER NOTHOSAURIA

Nothosaurs were streamlined, fish-eating marine reptiles. Their necks, bodies and tails were long, their feet were webbed, and they had many sharp teeth in the narrow jaws. Their forelegs were much sturdier than their hindlegs, which suggests that they were more actively used for propulsion.

Like the placodonts, nothosaurs evolved and died out during the Triassic period. Some paleontologists believe that they may be a halfway stage between the land-living reptiles and the aquatic plesiosaurs. However, certain features in the palate and shoulder girdles show that the nothosaurs were not the direct ancestors of the plesiosaurs, rather an offshoot of their ancestors.

FAMILY NOTHOSAURIDAE

There are several families of nothosaurs, but the best-known representatives belong to the family Nothosauridae. They have been found in the marine sediments of Europe and Asia, dating from the Early to Late Triassic.

NAME: *Nothosaurus*
TIME: **Early to Late Triassic**
LOCALITY: **Asia (China, Israel and USSR), Europe (Germany, Netherlands and Switzerland) and North Africa**
SIZE: **10 ft/3 m long**
This typical nothosaur probably lived as modern seals do, fishing at sea and resting-up on land. It possessed few specific adaptations to an aquatic way of life. The feet had 5 long toes, and several well-preserved specimens show that these were webbed. The body, neck and tail were all long and flexible. The length of the spines on the vertebrae of the tail suggest that it probably carried a fin to help in swimming.

The jaws of *Nothosaurus* presented a formidable fish trap — long and slim, with sharp, interlocking teeth.

NAME: *Lariosaurus*
TIME: **Middle Triassic**
LOCALITY: **Europe (Spain)**
SIZE: **2 ft/60 cm long**
Lariosaurus was one of the smaller nothosaurs, though not the smallest — some of them were only 8 in/20 cm long. It possessed a number of primitive features, including a short neck and short toes. The webs of skin between the toes would therefore have been small in area, and not much use for swimming. This reptile probably spent much of its time walking about on the seashore or paddling around in the coastal shallows, feeding on small fishes and shrimps.

NAME: *Ceresiosaurus*
TIME: **Middle Triassic**
LOCALITY: **Europe**
SIZE: **13 ft/4 m long**
The toes of *Ceresiosaurus* were much longer than those of most other nothosaurs. In fact, the animal exhibited the phenomenon of hyperphalangy, in which the number of bones (phalanges) in each toe is increased. Longer toes mean longer feet, and *Ceresiosaurus* had 2 pairs of paddlelike flippers. These would have been efficient swimming organs, and anticipated the great, oar-like limbs of the advanced swimmers of the Jurassic period, the plesiosaurs (see pp. 74–77).

Ceresiosaurus swam by undulating its long, sinuous body and tail from side to side. The bones of the forelegs were more massive than those of the hindlegs, suggesting that the front flippers played more of a role in swimming, maybe for effective steering and braking.

FAMILY PISTOSAURIDAE

The close relationship of the nothosaurs and plesiosaurs is revealed in the sole member of this family. Most of the skeleton of *Pistosaurus* is that of a typical nothosaur, but the skull has many plesiosaur features.

NAME: *Pistosaurus*
TIME: **Middle Triassic**
LOCALITY: **Europe (France and Germany)**
SIZE: **10 ft/3 m long**
This marine reptile may represent an intermediate stage between the nothosaurs and the plesiosaurs, since it possessed features from both groups. Its plesiosaur-type head still had the palate of a nothosaur. And its nothosaur-type body still had the stiff backbone typical of the plesiosaurs, which meant that most of the propulsion came from the paddlelike limbs. This was in contrast to the swimming method of the nothosaurs and other earlier marine reptiles, where lateral undulations of the body and tail were the chief propulsive force.

Pistosaurus had a mouthful of sharp, pointed teeth. It would have been an efficient fish-eater — a way of life shared by both the nothosaurs and the plesiosaurs.

Marine reptiles

PLESIOSAURUS

KRONOSAURUS

ELASMOSAURUS

PELONEUSTES

MACROPLATA

CRYPTOCLIDUS

LIOPLEURODON

MURAENOSAURUS

Marine reptiles

ORDER PLESIOSAURIA

The great ocean-going reptiles of the Mesozoic Era were the plesiosaurs. Some of these marine creatures were huge — up to 46 ft/14 m long. They had been adapted for life in the sea by transforming the limbs into long, narrow flippers. Instead of there being only 5 or fewer bones in each finger or toe, there were up to 10 in each. They had sturdy, deep bodies and short tails.

At one time, paleontologists thought that plesiosaurians used their flippers like great oars — moving the limbs backward and forward to row through the water. A more recent theory suggests that the flippers were moved in great vertical strokes, like the wings of a bird, and that plesiosaurs "flew" along, beating their limbs in slow, steady rhythm. The flippers were shaped like hydrofoils, with rounded leading edges and tapering rear ends. Their shape is comparable to the wings of modern penguins or the flippers of sea turtles, both of which swim in a kind of "subaqueous flight."

The specialized limbs of plesiosaurs required modifications in the limb girdles, and their structure was unique to this group of marine reptiles. The collar bones and 2 of the 3 hip bones were massive, and formed broad plates on the underside of the body. The powerful muscles that operated the limbs were attached to these great, bony plates.

A dense series of belly ribs connected the bones of the shoulder and hip girdles on the underside. This made the short body more rigid, and provided a strong, solid arrangement against which the great flippers could work.

The belly ribs would also have protected the animal when it had to leave the water to lay its eggs. Just as modern sea turtles have a belly armor of bony plates, so the belly ribs of plesiosaurs would have protected their undersides as they dragged themselves ashore and crawled laboriously up the beach, pushing their bodies along with the flippers.

There is no evidence to show that the plesiosaurs gave birth to live young, as the ichthyosaurs did (see pp. 8–81). It is likely that they laid their eggs in nests dug out of the sand, just as sea turtles do today. Plesiosaurs would probably have been even more clumsy on land than turtles because of their long necks. They would have been highly vulnerable to attack by predators at such times, as would their young once they hatched from the egg and began the long trek down the beach to the sea.

The ancestry of the plesiosaurs is not known. Paleontologists used to think that they had evolved directly from one of the well-known nothosaurs. But a more likely candidate is now recognized in the Mid-Triassic reptile Pistosaurus (see p. 73), whose structure seems to be intermediate between the 2 groups. It had the body of a nothosaur and the skull of a plesiosaur.

There were two major groups (or superfamilies) of plesiosaurian, which differed in the lengths of their necks and in their feeding habits. The plesiosaurs had long necks and short heads, and fed on smaller sea creatures. The pliosaurs had short necks and large heads to enable them to bite and swallow larger prey. So the 2 groups probably did not compete, although they shared the same seas for many millions of years with one another and with their cousins the ichthyosaurs or "fish lizards" (see pp. 78–82). Both the plesiosaurs and the pliosaurs survived to the end of the Cretaceous period.

SUPERFAMILY PLESIOSAUROIDEA

The early members of this group of long-necked marine reptiles were the basal stock from which all other plesiosaurs developed. The group first appeared in Early Jurassic times, and flourished throughout that period. One family, the elasmosaurs (below), continued to the very end of the Cretaceous period, and were the last of the group to survive.

The general trend among the various families of plesiosaur was toward the development of longer necks and limbs. This reached an extreme in later members of the group, some of which had necks as long as their bodies and tails combined, and huge, paddlelike flippers that would have swept them inexorably through the water. The forelimbs of these plesiosaurs were always somewhat larger than the hindlimbs.

The plesiosauroids fed on modest-sized fishes and squid. Their long necks enabled them to raise their head high above the surface of the sea and scan the waves in search of traces of their prey.

NAME: *Plesiosaurus*
TIME: **Early Jurassic**
LOCALITY: **Europe (England and Germany)**
SIZE: **7 ft 6 in/2.3 m long**
Plesiosaurs seem to have changed little during their 135 million years of evolution. The earliest member of the group, Plesiosaurus, had already developed all the main structural features that characterize these marine reptiles.

There were several species of the genus Plesiosaurus. P. macrocephalus, for example, illustrated on p. 74, had a larger head than most species, but in other respects its structure sets the pattern for all its relatives.

A plesiosaur was built for maneuverability, rather than speed. Its fish-hunting habits would have required quite precise movements. For example, a forward stroke by the flippers on one side of the body, coupled with a backward stroke by the flippers on the other side, would have turned the animal's short body almost on the spot. Its long neck could then dart out swiftly to catch fast-swimming prey.

NAME: *Cryptoclidus*
TIME: **Late Jurassic**
LOCALITY: **Europe (England)**
SIZE: **13 ft/4 m long**
Crytopclidus and other members of its family retained the same moderately long neck proportions as Plesiosaurus. But they evolved a large number of very sharply pointed curved teeth which intermeshed when the jaws were closed. This arrangement formed a fine trap for holding very small fishes or shrimps.

Like other Late Jurassic plesiosaurs, Cryptoclidus had perfected the transformation of the limbs into flippers by greatly increasing the number of bones in each of the 5 digits to produce a long, flexible paddle.

NAME: *Muraenosaurus*
TIME: **Late Jurassic**
LOCALITY: **Europe (England and France)**
SIZE: **20 ft/6 m long**
The most successful family of plesiosaurs were the elasmosaurs, of which Muraenosaurus is an early member. They evolved in the middle of the Jurassic period and survived to the end of the Cretaceous. Elasmosaurs had the longest necks of all plesiosaurs.

The neck of Muraenosaurus was as long as its body and tail combined and

CRYPTOCLIDUS

PLEURODON

MURAENOSAURUS

was supported by 44 vertebrae. The head, perched at the end of this crane-like neck, was tiny — only about one-sixteenth of the total body length.

The typically short, stiff plesiosaur body had become quite stout and inflexible in *Muraenosaurus*. This rigidity would have helped to make the flippers more effective propulsion organs.

NAME: *Elasmosaurus*
TIME: Late Cretaceous
LOCALITY: Asia (Japan) and North America (Kansas)
SIZE: 46 ft/14 m long

"Snakes threaded through the bodies of turtles" — this description of the long-necked plesiosaurs was coined by Dean Conybeare, a nineteenth-century English paleontologist who did much of the initial work on these marine reptiles.

Conybeare's description is more than vindicated in *Elasmosaurus*, which was the longest member of the elasmosaur family, and, in fact, the longest-known plesiosaur. More than half of its total length was neck — 26 ft/8 m out of a total of 46 ft/14 m.

The length of *Elasmosaurus'* neck was due to a great number of vertebrae, 71 in all — many more than in the earliest plesiosaurs, which had about 28 neck vertebrae.

This long structure would have enabled *Elasmosaurus* to curl its neck around sideways, making almost 2 full circles on either side of its body. It would have been only half as flexible in the vertical plane. However, had *Elasmosaurus* swung its neck around underwater while swimming, it would have met with great resistance from the water.

Some paleontologists suggest, therefore, that the habit of such long-necked reptiles was to paddle along on the surface, their necks held clear of the water. When fish or other prey were

spotted from this vantage point, the long neck was plunged into the sea, and the prey snapped up. The modern anhinga, or snake bird, has a long neck, and hunts in much the same way.

SUPERFAMILY PLIOSAUROIDEA

The pliosaurs first appeared in the Early Jurassic, alongside their ancestors, the plesiosauroids. The pliosaurs became the tigers of the Mesozoic seas, chasing and overpowering the large sea-creatures such as sharks, large squid, ichthyosaurs and even their relatives, the plesiosauroids. To do this, they evolved a large head with very strong teeth and jaws, powered by huge jaw muscles. Some pliosaurs had heads almost 10 ft/3 m long. Their bodies were streamlined for speed by progressively shortening the neck. Some had as few as 13 vertebrae, compared to at least 28 in the shortest-necked plesiosaur. They also became larger, in order to tackle even larger prey.

NAME: *Macroplata*
TIME: Early Jurassic
LOCALITY: Europe (England)
SIZE: 15 ft/4.5 m long

This early pliosaur had a slender crocodilelike skull which was only a little larger proportionally than that of early plesiosaurs. And it still had quite a long neck, with 29 slightly shortened vertebrae, which was fully twice the length of its head.

As in the plesiosaurs, the pliosaurs progressively improved the limbs into powerful paddles, with a great increase in the number of bones in the digits. But the hindlimb, not the forelimb, became the larger, implying a difference in the use of the limbs in the 2 groups.

NAME: *Peloneustes*
TIME: Late Jurassic
LOCALITY: Europe (England and USSR)
SIZE: 10 ft/3 m long

Although smaller than *Macroplata*, this Late Jurassic pliosaur shows an advance in the trend to increase the size of the head and to shorten the neck. It had only about 20 neck vertebrae, so that the large head was almost equal to it in length.

With this more steamlined shape, *Peloneustes* was able to swim rapidly after its fast-moving prey, such as squid, cuttlefish and ammonites. The long head of *Peloneustes* gave it the reach that its short neck did not allow. Its teeth were adapted for its specialized diet: they were fewer and less sharp than

those of the fish-eating plesiosaurs, and better for catching soft-bodied squid and crushing the hard shells of ammonites.

The stomach contents have been preserved in some of the pliosaurs found. The bulk of the undigested mass consisted of hooks from the suckers that cover the feeding arms of cephalopods.

NAME: *Liopleurodon*
TIME: Late Jurassic
LOCALITY: Europe (England, France, Germany and USSR)
SIZE: 39 ft/12 m long

This large pliosaur was typical of the later members of the family. It was whalelike in appearance, with a heavy head, short, thick neck and a streamlined body. From the structure of the limb girdles, it is evident that this pliosaur was extremely maneuverable in the water, and could swim at all depths.

The front flippers were used in an up-and-down motion, like those of the plesiosaurs. The strong downward stroke would have pushed water to the rear, so propelling the animal forward. On the recovery stroke, the flippers would have been lifted up automatically by the passage of water over their hydrodynamic shape.

The hind flippers would have thrust back against the water in a powerful kicking motion, and then been turned, to offer the least resistance to the water on the recovery stroke.

This combination of movements would have made for efficient, fast long-distance swimming. This, in turn, enabled the pliosaur to sustain the chase after its fast-moving cephalopod prey.

NAME: *Kronosaurus*
TIME: Early Cretaceous
LOCALITY: Australia (Queensland)
SIZE: 42 ft/12.8 m long

The Australian *Kronosaurus* is the largest-known pliosaur. Its skull was flat-topped and massively long, measuring 9 ft/2.7 m — almost a quarter of the total body length, and therefore substantially larger and more powerful than that of the greatest carnivorous dinosaur, *Tyrannosaurus* (see pp. 118–121).

Throughout the Triassic and Jurassic periods, the modern continent of Australia had been dry land, but in the early part of the Cretaceous, the seas flooded in to submerge many areas. The environment was warm and the seas shallow, and these conditions would have supported large populations of fish and their cephalopod predators. *Kronosaurus* and other short-necked pliosaurs were highly maneuverable swimmers, and they would have found rich feeding grounds in these shallow seas.

Marine reptiles

CYMBOSPONDYLUS

MIXOSAURUS

SHONISAURUS

ICHTHYOSAURUS

STENOPTERYGIUS

OPHTHALMOSAURUS

TEMNODONTOSAURUS

EURHINOSAURUS

Marine reptiles

ORDER ICHTHYOSAURIA

The ichthyosaurs were the most specialized of marine reptiles. Their name means "fish lizards," and describes them well, since they ate fish, and were shaped like fish (though, of course, they were air-breathing reptiles). In fact, their overall body shape was like that of a modern mackerel or tuna — a highly streamlined form that allows these living fish to reach swimming speeds of over 25 mph/40 kmph.

Unlike their contemporaries, the plesiosaurs (see pp. 74–77), ichthyosaurs did not rely on their paddlelike flippers for swimming. Instead, they developed a fishlike tail, whose lateral movements provided the main propulsive force, just like the tail of a modern shark or tuna.

So fully adapted were the ichthyosaurs to a marine life that they could no longer come ashore to lay eggs, as did the sea turtles and plesiosaurs. Ichthyosaurs gave birth to live young at sea. In fact, some of the most remarkable of fossil finds show adult female ichthyosaurs with young babies just emerging from their bodies — preserved forever in the process of birth.

As a group, the ichthyosaurs occupied the ecological niche of today's dolphins. They were wide-ranging and highly successful for about 100 million years. They cruised the open seas of the world from Early Triassic times, and reached their peak of diversity in the Jurassic. Thereafter, they declined until, by the mid-Cretaceous, they were all but extinct. Their demise could be related to competition from the advanced sharks, which had evolved into their modern form by this time, and were the dominant carnivores of the Late Mesozoic seas (see pp. 26–29).

The origin of the ichthyosaurs is not known. The only certainty is the fact that they descended from some terrestrial group of reptiles, rather than evolving from one of the known types of aquatic reptile.

FAMILY SHASTASAURIDAE

The shastasaurs were among the earliest ichthyosaurs to appear, in Mid-Triassic deposits mainly from North America. (Older types are known from Japan and China, dating from the Early Triassic.) At this early stage of their evolution they moved in an eel-like fashion. But by the end of the Triassic period, they had assumed the fish shape characteristic of the ichthyosaur group and swam like modern fishes.

NAME: *Cymbospondylus*
TIME: **Middle Triassic**
LOCALITY: **North America (Nevada)**
SIZE: **33 ft/10 m long**

This large ichthyosaur was one of the least fishlike of the group. The body and tail made up most of its length. There was no fin on its back nor on its tail, features that were to develop in later ichthyosaurs. However, it did have the typical long, beaklike jaws, armed with pointed teeth — the sign of a fish-eater.

The limbs of *Cymbospondylus* were short, and looked more like the fins of fish than the paddles of later ichthyosaurs. They would not have been effective for swimming, so they were probably used to control steering and braking. The main propulsive force must, therefore, have come from lateral undulations of the long body.

NAME: *Shonisaurus*
TIME: **Late Triassic**
LOCALITY: **North America (Nevada)**
SIZE: **49 ft/15 m long**

Shonisaurus is the largest-known ichthyosaur, and the only almost-complete skeleton known from Late Triassic rocks. It had developed the fishlike shape characteristic of the group. Its enormous length was divided approximately into equal thirds — the head and neck, the body, and the tail.

The backbone of *Shonisaurus*, too, had started to show a typical feature of later ichthyosaurs — it bent downward into the lower lobe of the fishlike tail.

It seems likely that *Shonisaurus* was an independent, specialized offshoot from the main line of ichthyosaurs. It had a number of structural peculiarities. For example, its jaws were greatly elongated, and had teeth only at the front. Its limbs were also extended into extra-long, narrow paddles. This was not a typical feature of the ichthyosaurs. Not only was the length of the paddles unusual, but also the fact that they were of equal size — the front pair in most ichthyosaurs was longer than the hind pair.

FAMILY MIXOSAURIDAE

The mixosaurs had developed a stabilizing fin on the back (like the dorsal fin of a fish) — a swimming aid present in all later ichthyosaurs. But they did not have the typical fishlike tail, with 2 equal lobes, that made their later relatives such powerful swimmers.

In mixosaurs, the end of the backbone was not bent sharply down into the tail, as it was in later ichthyosaurs; instead, the vertebrae were extended upward, probably to support a low fin on top of the tail.

NAME: *Mixosaurus*
TIME: **Middle Triassic**
LOCALITY: **Asia (China and Timor, Indonesia), Europe (Alps), North America (Alaska, Canadian Arctic and Nevada) and Spitsbergen**
SIZE: **3 ft 3 in/1 m long**

Mixosaurus seems to have been intermediate in appearance between the early, primitive ichthyosaurs, as exemplified by *Cymbospondylus* (above), and the later, more advanced types. For example, *Mixosaurus* had a fishlike body with a dorsal fin on its back, and probably also the beginnings of a fin on the top of its tail.

Its limbs were transformed into short paddles, the front pair being longer than the hind pair. Each paddle consisted of 5 toes, which were greatly elongated by the addition of many small bones (hyperphalangy). The long, narrow jaws were equipped with sharp teeth, adapted for catching and eating fish.

FAMILY ICHTHYOSAURIDAE

The typical fish lizards belong to this large family, which flourished throughout the Jurassic period and into the Cretaceous. They are known from some remarkably well-preserved specimens, which show them to be highly specialized marine animals.

The ichthyosaurs had developed a streamlined body, torpedo-shaped, with a stabilizing dorsal fin on the back; short, paired paddles for steering; and a strong, fishlike tail with 2 equal lobes for swimming. Ball-and-socket joints between the tail vertebrae allowed for powerful strokes from side to side. The tail, together with the great flexibility of the backbone, propelled the animal rapidly through the water — the swimming method used by modern, fast-moving fishes.

TERYGIUS

OPHTHALMOSAURUS

TEMNODONTOSAURUS

EURHINOSAURUS

NAME: *Ichthyosaurus*
TIME: Early Jurassic to Early Cretaceous
LOCALITY: Europe (England and Germany), Greenland and North America (Alberta)
SIZE: up to 6 ft 6 in/2 m long

Ichthyosaurus is one of the best-known prehistoric animals, since a graphic record of its remains are preserved in the shales of southern Germany, near Holzmaden. These rocks were laid down in shallow waters during the Early Jurassic.

Several hundred complete skeletons of *Ichthyosaurus* have been found, their bones still articulating with each other. The tiny bones of their young were also found inside the bodies of several adults. This — combined with some specimens where the young is preserved actually emerging from the body of the adult (tail-first, as in modern whales) — shows without a doubt that these marine reptiles gave birth to live young at sea.

The find in Germany also yielded a unique picture of how the animals looked in life. A thin film of carbon had been laid down around many of the specimens, outlining the exact shape of their bodies when the flesh was still on the bones. The characteristic features of a typical ichthyosaur can be clearly seen — the high dorsal fin on the back; the half-moon shape of the tail (caudal) fin, with the backbone angled down sharply into its lower lobe; and the short, hydrofoil-shaped paddles that enclosed the greatly elongated toes of the limbs, the front pair longer than the hind pair.

The nostrils of *Ichthyosaurus* were set far back on its snout near the eyes, so the animal only had to break the surface of the water to breathe. The bones of the ear were massive, and probably transmitted vibrations from the water to the inner ear, so that the direction of potential prey could be judged. But *Ichthy-*

osaurus' main sense for locating its prey would have been sight — its eyes were large and, most probably, extremely sensitive.

Even fossil droppings (called coprolites) and stomach contents of these marine reptiles have been preserved in the rocks. They confirm that fish constituted the bulk of the diet, but that cephalopods were also eaten, such as the straight-shelled belemnites.

The remains of pigment cells have also been preserved, and analysis of these suggests that the smooth, thick skin of *Ichthyosaurus* was a dark reddish-brown color in life.

NAME: *Ophthalmosaurus*
TIME: Late Jurassic
LOCALITY: Europe (England and France), North America (Western USA and Canadian Arctic) and South America (Argentina)
SIZE: 11 ft 6 in/3.5 m long

Ophthalmosaurus was even more streamlined than its contemporary, *Ichthyosaurus* (*above*). Its body was shaped almost like a teardrop — massive and rounded at the front, and tapering toward the rear to culminate in the great, half-moon-shaped caudal fin. Its front limbs were much more developed than the hindlimbs, indicating that the front paddles did most of the steering and stabilizing work, with the tail propelling the body from the rear.

The most remarkable feature of *Ophthalmosaurus* was its huge eyes. Their sockets are about 4 in/10 cm in diameter, and occupy almost the whole depth of the skull on each side. A ring of bony plates (sclerotic ring) surrounded each eyeball, to prevent the soft tissues from collapsing under the external water pressure, and to help with focusing. (The eyes of all ichthyosaurs had these sclerotic rings, but they are particularly noticeable in *Ophthalmosaurus*.)

The super-large eyes of this ichthyosaur suggest that it was a night-feeder. It probably hunted close to the surface, feeding on squid, which in turn were feeding on the plankton-eating fish.

FAMILY STENOPTERYGIIDAE

During the Jurassic period, 2 distinct types of ichthyosaur evolved, differing in the shape of their paddlelike limbs.

Ichthyosaurus and members of its family (*above*) had short, broad paddles, with more toes than the normal 5 — sometimes up to 9 toes in each limb.

The stenopterygiids, in contrast, had longer, narrow paddles, each made up of 5 toes but with an increased number of bones in each toe.

NAME: *Stenopterygius*
TIME: Early to Middle Jurassic
LOCALITY: Europe (England and Germany)
SIZE: 10 ft/3 m long

The remarkable find of ichthyosaur skeletons near Holzmaden in southern Germany includes well-preserved specimens of *Stenopterygius*. Many of the adults have the bones of unborn young preserved within their bodies.

Stenopterygius was similar in overall build to *Ichthyosaurus*, but it had a smaller head and the narrow paddles characteristic of its family. Five toes made up each paddle, but there were many more bones than the normal average of 4 in each toe, so giving the paddles their long, narrow shape.

FAMILY LEPTOPTERYGIIDAE

This family contains the last surviving members of the ichthyosaurs before they became extinct at the base of the Late Cretaceous. Like the earlier stenopterygiids (*above*), the leptopterygiids had narrow paddles, with a great number of bones in each of the 5 toes.

NAME: *Temnodontosaurus*
TIME: Early Jurassic
LOCALITY: Europe (England and Germany)
SIZE: 30 ft/9 m long

This great creature (sometimes known as *Leptopterygius*) must have cruised the warm waters of the shallow Jurassic seas, its movements finely controlled by the long, narrow paddles at the front of its body. Propelled forward by its great tail, it would have hunted large squid and ammonites.

NAME: *Eurhinosaurus*
TIME: Early Jurassic
LOCALITY: Europe (Germany)
SIZE: 6 ft 6 in/2 m long

This was an extraordinary-looking ichthyosaur, unlike any other known member of the group. Its upper jaw was twice the length of its lower jaw, giving it the appearance of a modern sawfish. Teeth stuck out sideways along the length of this bladelike projection.

The function of this strange structure is not known for certain, just as the purpose of the saw of the modern sawfish also remains somewhat mysterious. *Eurhinosaurus* could have used it to probe around in the sand or mud of the seabed, or among seaweeds and rocks, to flush out flatfish, shrimps or octopus. Perhaps it was also swung rapidly from side to side as *Eurhinosaurus* swam through a shoal of fish, stunning and wounding them as it passed.

Early diapsids

ARAEOSCELIS

HOVASAURUS

THADEOSAURUS

PETROLACOSAURUS

COELUROSAURAVUS

CHAMPSOSAURUS

ASKEPTOSAURUS

PLEUROSAURUS

PLANOCEPHALOSAURUS

Early diapsids

SUBCLASS DIAPSIDA

Most modern reptiles belong to the diapsids, an ancient group that first appeared in Late Carboniferous times, more than 300 million years ago. The skulls of these animals are distinctive because they have a pair of openings on either side of the skull behind the eye (*see p. 61*).

The muscles of the jaws are attached to ligaments that stretch across these holes, and endow their owners with stronger jaws, which can be opened wide and closed forcefully to deal with large prey.

The diapsids are not only an ancient group. They are also an important group in evolutionary terms, because from them came the ancestors of most modern reptiles (lizards, snakes and tuataras), and the ancestors of the ruling reptiles (the extinct dinosaurs and pterosaurs, and the modern crocodiles).

ORDER ARAEOSCELIDA

The earliest and most primitive of the diapsid reptiles were the small, lizard-like araeoscelids, with long necks and slim running legs. Only about 4 genera are known, classed in 2 families. They date from the Late Carboniferous period to the middle of the Permian — a time span of less than 40 million years.

NAME: *Petrolacosaurus*
TIME: **Late Carboniferous**
LOCALITY: **North America (Kansas)**
SIZE: **16 in/40 cm long**
The earliest-known diapsid reptile, with the characteristic pair of openings on either side of its skull, looked much like a modern lizard, but with longer legs and a tail as long as its body and head combined.

Petrolacosaurus probably behaved like a modern lizard, also. It would have been an active hunter, chasing around after insects and other small invertebrates. Its home was the dry, upland areas of what is now Kansas, above the swampy marshes where coal was forming during the Late Carboniferous (Pennsylvanian) period.

The jaws of this early reptile were equipped with many sharp, pointed teeth, including an upper pair of canines. This arrangement is reminiscent of that of *Hylonomus*, the most primitive reptile known (*see p. 64*). Despite the newly evolved openings in its diapsid skull, the jaws of *Petrolacosaurus* were not very strong. The openings probably served to lighten the skull, rather than to provide attachment points for the jaw muscles — their function in later diapsids.

NAME: *Araeoscelis*
TIME: **Early Permian**
LOCALITY: **North America (Texas)**
SIZE: **2 ft/60 cm long**
Araeoscelis was the closest relative of *Petrolacosaurus* (*above*), although it lived several million years later. Both animals were similar in appearance — lizardlike creatures, with long running legs, long necks and small heads.

The teeth of *Araeoscelis*, however, were different to those of its earlier relative, and indicate that it may have been a more specialized feeder. Instead of sharp, pointed teeth, *Araeoscelis* had fairly massive, blunt, conical teeth. These would have been ideal for crushing the tough chitinous covering of insects such as beetles.

Associated with this specialized diet was a structural change in the skull of *Araeoscelis*. One of the 2 pairs of openings in its otherwise-typical diapsid skull had been closed over with bone. This was probably an adaptation to strengthen the skull, so that the animal could develop a more powerful bite to deal with its tougher food.

ORDER UNCERTAIN

There is no fossil record of diapsid reptiles during the Mid-Permian period. So far, no traces have been found to indicate the course of their evolution during this time. However, in the Late Permian a number of specialized groups appear, which cannot be related to each other with any certainty.

The Coelurosauravidae family is one such specialized group (*below*), with only a few members known from Madagascar and Europe.

NAME: *Coelurosauravus*
TIME: **Late Permian**
LOCALITY: **Madagascar**
SIZE: **16 in/40 cm long**
This early reptile was highly adapted for gliding through the air, and probably looked similar to the modern lizard known as the flying dragon, *Draco volans*, of Southeast Asia.

The ribs of *Coelurosauravus* were greatly elongated on each side of its short body. Flaps of skin would have connected the ribs, to form a pair of "wings" with a total span of about 1 ft/30 cm. This reptile probably lived in forests, like the modern flying dragon, and glided from tree to tree, feeding on insects. Its legs would have been held out from its body as it glided, its feet spread wide to offer resistance to the air, and hence slow its descent.

The skull of *Coelurosauravus* was considerably lighter than that of other early

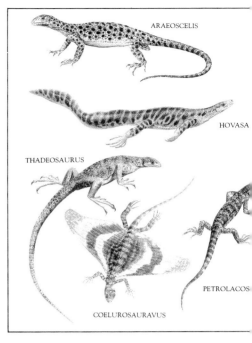

diapsids. The openings for the eyes were huge, and there was a wide frill developed from the bones at the back of its head, presumably to make it more aerodynamic.

ORDER THALATTOSAURIA

The thalattosaurs were another specialized group of early diapsid reptiles that lived during the Triassic period. They were adapted to a marine way of life, probably spending most of their time at sea, and only coming ashore to lay their eggs.

The few thalattosaurs known from Europe and western North America are classed in 3 families, the Askeptosauridae being the best known.

NAME: *Askeptosaurus*
TIME: **Middle Triassic**
LOCALITY: **Europe (Switzerland)**
SIZE: **6 ft 6 in/2 m long**
As with many animals adapted to an aquatic life, the neck and body of *Askeptosaurus* were long and slim. Its tail was greatly elongated, almost ribbon-like, and accounted for about half the body length. Sinuous movements of the body and tail would have propelled the animal, eel-style, through the water. Its feet, too, would have helped in swimming — they were broad and webbed, and probably used to control steering and braking.

Askeptosaurus had long jaws, armed with many sharp teeth. It probably dived deep after its fish prey. This is deduced from 2 features; its eyes were large, for seeing in the ocean's twilight zone, and they were strengthened by a ring of bony plates, to prevent the eyeballs collapsing under the water pressure at depth.

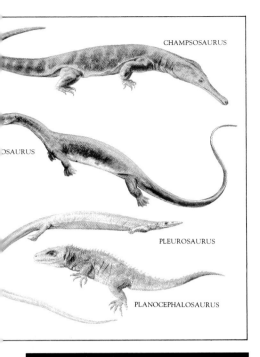

CHAMPSOSAURUS

OSAURUS

PLEUROSAURUS

PLANOCEPHALOSAURUS

ORDER CHORISTODERA

A strange assemblage of crocodilelike reptiles diverged from the main diapsid line during the Early Cretaceous period, some 140 million years ago. The Choristodera lived in the freshwaters of North America, Europe and eastern Asia until well into the Tertiary period — becoming extinct during the Eocene epoch, some 50 million years ago.

NAME: *Champsosaurus*
TIME: **Late Cretaceous to Eocene**
LOCALITY: **Europe (Belgium and France) and North America (Alberta, Montana, New Mexico and Wyoming)**
SIZE: **5 ft/1.5 m long**
With its long, narrow jaws, filled with fine, pointed teeth, *Champsosaurus* could easily have been mistaken for the modern gavial of India, a close relative of the crocodile. However, although both animals are diapsid reptiles, they are not closely related to each other. Their similarity is explained by the phenomenon of convergent evolution, in which adaptation to life in a particular environment leads unrelated animals to adopt the same body shape, and often the same behavior.

Champsosaurus lived in the rivers and swamps of Europe and western North America throughout the Late Cretaceous and Early Tertiary periods. It probably swam by lateral undulations of its sinuous body and tail, holding its legs tight against the flanks for a more streamlined effect — the same swimming method seen in modern crocodiles and marine iguanas.

This reptile was a fish-eater with extremely powerful jaws, judging by the great width of the skull behind the eyes, which would have provided a large area to which jaw muscles could attach.

ORDER EOSUCHIA

The lizardlike eosuchians are thought to be close to the ancestry of the later, advanced diapsid reptiles, many of which survive today in the form of snakes and lizards (*see p. 86–89*).

Eosuchians first appeared in Late Permian times, and continued until the middle of the Triassic. They are grouped into 4 families, all of whose members were apparently confined to southern and eastern Africa, and Madagascar. The family Tangasauridae contains 2 representative members (*below*).

NAME: *Thadeosaurus*
TIME: **Late Permian**
LOCALITY: **Madagascar**
SIZE: **2 ft/60 cm long**
The tremendously long tail of the land-living *Thadeosaurus* measured about 16 in/40 cm — making up two-thirds of the animal's total length. The 5 clawed toes of each foot were greatly elongated, and so arranged that the longer toes were on the outside. This had the advantage of allowing most of the toes to remain in contact with the ground as the foot was lifted, and so give a strong push off the surface with each step taken. The sternum, or breast bone, was massively developed, to help increase the stride of the forelegs.

NAME: *Hovasaurus*
TIME: **Late Permian**
LOCALITY: **Madagascar**
SIZE: **20 in/50 cm long**
The most striking feature of this aquatic lizardlike reptile was its tail. Not only was it twice the length of the rest of the body; it was also deep and flattened from side to side. Each of the tail vertebrae was extended above and below the midline. The result was a tail that formed a broad, stiff paddle, allowing *Hovasaurus* to swim efficiently.

Another unusual feature of *Hovasaurus* is the mass of pebbles found in the abdominal cavities of most of the specimens recovered. Evidently, these reptiles swallowed stones as ballast, to help them sink quickly in the water when diving for their fish prey, or to keep them submerged when feeding.

SUPERORDER LEPIDOSAURIA

The evolutionary line leading to the surviving lepidosaurs — the 6000 species of modern snakes and lizards — arose from an eosuchian-type ancestor some time during the Late Permian period. A third group of lepidosaurs, the sphenodonts, did not meet with such success (*below*).

ORDER SPHENODONTA

The sphenodonts (sometimes called the rhynchocephalids) are an ancient group of lepidosaur reptiles. They are an offshoot from the main evolutionary line of diapsids leading to the true lizards and snakes.

Once a diverse group, sphenodonts appeared in the Late Triassic, over 200 million years ago, and many families evolved during the subsequent Jurassic period. Thereafter, their members began to decline, perhaps due to competition from the true lizards, which were well established at that stage.

Today, the sole surviving member of the whole sphenodont order is the tuatara, *Sphenodon punctatus*, found only in New Zealand.

NAME: *Planocephalosaurus*
TIME: **Late Triassic**
LOCALITY: **Europe (England)**
SIZE: **8 in/20 cm long**
This lizardlike animal, with a large head and long legs, was among the earliest of the sphenodonts to evolve. Its skeleton is almost identical to that of the modern tuatara of New Zealand. But its skull is primitive in having the teeth fused to the jaw bones, rather than attached to grooves in the jaw bones as they are in advanced lizards.

The teeth of *Planocephalosaurus* were strong, and its jaws could have delivered a powerful bite. It would have snapped up insects, and crushed them between the teeth, supplementing its diet with worms and snails, and probably the occasional small lizard.

NAME: *Pleurosaurus*
TIME: **Late Jurassic to Early Cretaceous**
LOCALITY: **Europe (Germany)**
SIZE: **2 ft/60 cm long**
Pleurosaurus was a member of the aquatic pleurosaur family. This group of specialized sphenodonts first evolved on land, and then returned to the water during Early Jurassic times, possibly because there was too much competition among reptiles on the land.

The only specific aquatic adaptation among the pleurosaurs seems to have been a great elongation of the body — up to 57 vertebrae in some types, about twice the typical sphenodont number.

Snakelike movements of the long, sinuous body and tail moved *Pleurosaurus* rapidly through the water. Its nostrils were set far back on its snout, near the eyes. Its legs were much shorter than those of land-living sphenodonts, and played no role in swimming.

Snakes and lizards

PLATECARPUS

PLOTOSAURUS

MEGALANIA

TANYSTROPHEUS

HYPERODAPEDON

PACHYRHACHIS

PROTOROSAURUS

ARDEOSAURUS

KUEHNEOSAURUS

Snakes and lizards

ORDER SQUAMATA

The most successful group of reptiles today comprises the lizards and snakes. There are some 6000 species of walkers, gliders, crawlers, swimmers, climbers and burrowers, living in every continent of the world except Antarctica. They are descended from an ancient lineage of diapsid reptiles, most probably the lizardlike eosuchians, stretching back over 250 million years, to Late Permian times (see pp. 82–85).

The other living reptiles — the turtles, tortoises and crocodiles — evolved along quite different lines (see pp. 58–59, 90–91).

The chief feature that distinguishes the lizards and snakes from all other diapsid reptiles (including their closest relatives, the sphenodonts, see p. 85), is the great flexibility and power of their jaws. Two structural changes brought this about. First was the loss of the lower arch of bone that enclosed the lower pair of openings in the skull. This gave more room for larger muscles to develop to operate the jaws. Second, a movable hinge joint developed within the skull, which provided even more flexibility in the movements of the jaws.

SUBORDER LACERTILIA

Lizards are a much more ancient group than the snakes. The earliest-known lizards were small insectivores that lived in southern Africa during Late Permian times. Few fossils remain to trace the course of their evolution during the first half of the Mesozoic Era. However, at the end of the Jurassic period the group seems to have undergone a burst of evolution, and primitive members of all the major modern groups had suddenly appeared — including geckos, skinks, iguanas, blindworms and monitors.

Besides the changes in the skull that produced more efficient jaws (above), other structural changes gave lizards better hearing and better articulating surfaces in the joints of their limbs for improved walking. All these features combined to make lizards fast, efficient hunters, able to deal with comparatively large prey, such as other reptiles.

FAMILY KUEHNEOSAURIDAE

Members of this family are among the earliest-known lizards. Early though they were, they had a specialized lifestyle — that of gliding through the air on outstretched, winglike membranes.

NAME: *Kuehneosaurus*
TIME: **Late Triassic**
LOCALITY: **Europe (England)**
SIZE: **26 in/65 cm long**

This was a long-legged lizard that could glide through the air on a pair of membranous "wings." These projected out from each side of its body, between the front and hindlimbs, and spanned more than 1 ft/30 cm.

The greatly elongated ribs formed the framework for the skin-covered gliding membranes. This was exactly the same arrangement developed by an earlier type of diapsid reptile — the gliding *Coelurosauravus* (see pp. 82, 84). And the same pattern occurs in a living lizard — the flying dragon, *Draco volans*, of Southeast Asia. This modern forest-dweller, only 8 in/20 cm long, can glide on similar skin flaps to those of the extinct *Kuehneosaurus* — a single glide can cover up to 200 ft/60 m, losing only 6 ft 6 in/2 m in height over that distance. Its ribs are movable, and so it can fold its wings against the body when at rest.

FAMILY ARDEOSAURIDAE

The geckos were among the earliest of the modern groups of lizard to appear, in the Late Jurassic period. The only surviving family, the Gekkonidae, evolved relatively recently — in the Late Eocene, some 40 million years ago. It contains more than 670 species, which have spread throughout the warm tropical zones of the world.

NAME: *Ardeosaurus*
TIME: **Late Jurassic**
LOCALITY: **Europe (Germany)**
SIZE: **8 in/20 cm long**

This early gecko had the flattened head and large eyes typical of its modern relatives. Like them, it was probably a night-hunter, agile enough to snap up insects, spiders and smaller lizards with its powerful jaws. Whether it had the "friction pads" of today's geckos is not known; these are specialized scales under the toes which enable the animal to climb up smooth, vertical surfaces.

FAMILY VARANIDAE

The monitors were, and still are, the largest of all land lizards. They appeared in the Late Cretaceous period, more than 80 million years ago, and have changed little since. They were large, heavy animals, agile for their size, and active hunters, seeking out their prey with the long, forked tongue that acts as an organ of smell. Modern representatives include the giant Komodo dragon.

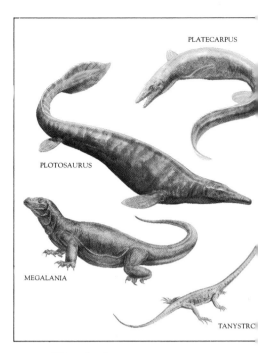

NAME: *Megalania*
TIME: **Pleistocene**
LOCALITY: **Australia (Queensland)**
SIZE: **up to 26 ft/8 m long**

This monitor lizard was much larger and maybe weighed 4 times as much as its living relative, the Komodo dragon, *Varanus komodensis*, of Indonesia. Although the Komodo dragon is the giant of modern lizards — with some individuals growing up to 10 ft/3 m long, and weighing some 360 lb/163 kg — it is small in comparison to some of its extinct relatives.

Megalania hunted on the plains of Australia less than 2 million years ago, ambushing the large marsupials, such as kangaroos, that grazed there (see pp. 202–205). It would have torn away great chunks of flesh with its powerful jaws and long, sharp teeth, serrated along their edges.

FAMILY MOSASAURIDAE

The mosasaurs were a successful, though short-lived, offshoot from the monitor lizard group. They were fully adapted to a marine life, living in inshore waters during the Late Cretaceous period. Some of them were giants.

NAME: *Platecarpus*
TIME: **Late Cretaceous**
LOCALITY: **Europe (Belgium) and North America (Alabama, Colorado, Kansas and Mississippi)**
SIZE: **14 ft/4.3 m long**

Many specimens of this marine lizard have been found in the chalk deposits of Kansas, laid down in the warm, shallow seas that covered much of North America during Late Cretaceous times.

Platecarpus swam in these waters some 75 million years ago. Its tail was as long as its body, and judging from the vertebrae, it was flattened from side to

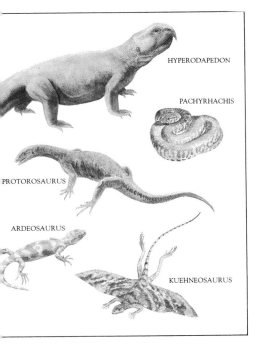

HYPERODAPEDON

PACHYRHACHIS

PROTOROSAURUS

ARDEOSAURUS

KUEHNEOSAURUS

side, and probably had a broad, vertical fin running along its length, above and below. Snakelike undulations of the long, sinuous body, combined with the finned tail, would have propelled *Platecarpus* forward, while the short legs and broad, webbed feet steered.

This marine lizard would have eaten fish and soft-bodied cephalopods, snapping them up in its long, pointed jaws, equipped with many sharp, conical teeth. But it could also have tackled the most abundant cephalopods around at the time — the ammonites, whose soft bodies were enclosed within a hard, coiled shell. Evidence for this comes from a number of fossilized shells of these creatures, scored by a similar pattern of V-shaped tooth marks as that of the mosasaurs. The shells seem to have been bitten about a dozen times from different angles, in attempts to crack them open and get at the flesh inside.

NAME: *Plotosaurus*
TIME: Late Cretaceous
LOCALITY: North America (Kansas)
SIZE: 33 ft/10 m long
Found in the same North American chalk deposits as *Platecarpus* (above), *Plotosaurus* was a giant among mosasaurs. About 50 vertebrae made up its body and neck, with at least the same number again making up the long tail. The rear part of its tail was expanded into a vertical fin, which must have helped to move the great body of this marine lizard through the water.

Its limbs were developed into short flippers, with the front pair longer than the hind pair due to a greater number of bones in each one. (This hyperphalangid condition was also developed in many other marine reptiles.) Impressions preserved in the chalk near the bones of the limbs suggest that *Plotosaurus* was covered in a scaly skin, like that of a modern snake.

SUBORDER SERPENTES

Modern snakes developed relatively recently, during the Miocene epoch some 20 million years ago. But snakes have a longer evolutionary history than this. The oldest-known snake is more than 80 million years old, and comes from Late Cretaceous rocks in South America. Already, it shows many of the features of the modern groups.

These features include the elongation of the body (in some snakes more than 450 vertebrae); loss of the limbs; loss of the bony arches above the 2 lower openings in the skull, which allows the development of more powerful jaw muscles; and even greater flexibility of the jaw hinges than seen in lizards, to give a wider gape for swallowing prey whole.

Paleontologists differ on the ancestry of snakes. Some say they evolved from a type of burrowing lizard, while others say they arose from an aquatic, monitor-type lizard, such as *Pachyrhachis* (below).

NAME: *Pachyrhachis*
TIME: Early Cretaceous
LOCALITY: Asia (Israel)
SIZE: 3 ft 3 in/1 m long
The aquatic reptile *Pachyrhachis* had the long body of a snake and the large head of a monitor lizard. The limbs and shoulder girdles had disappeared, but there were still traces of the hip bones. The ribs were broad, as in many water-dwelling animals, and evidently *Pachyrhachis* swam by snakelike undulations of its flexible backbone.

Pachyrhachis is considered by some paleontologists to be close to the ancestry of the whole snake group.

INFRACLASS ARCHOSAUROMORPHA

The ruling reptiles, or archosaurs, constitute a spectacular assemblage of reptiles — the dinosaurs, pterosaurs and crocodiles (see pp. 90–169). They arose from a group of primitive diapsid reptiles, the archosauromorphs (meaning "ruling reptile types") in the Late Permian period — quite a different evolutionary line from the lizards/snakes.

Most archosauromorphs were well-adapted land animals, with their long legs placed more directly under the body than in other reptiles. Associated with this change in stance were improvements in the feet, particularly in the articulation of the ankle joints and flexibility of the "big toes."

The carnivorous protorosaurs are the earliest-known members of this group, ancestral to the ruling reptiles. The plant-eating rhynchosaurs are a later group that thrived in the Mid-Triassic.

NAME: *Protorosaurus*
TIME: Late Permian
LOCALITY: Europe (Germany)
SIZE: up to 6 ft 6 in/2 m long
This lizard-type reptile is the earliest-known archosauromorph. It lived in the deserts of Europe toward the end of the Permian period. Its long legs were tucked in under its body, allowing it to chase after fast-moving prey — mainly insects. Its neck was made up of 7 large and greatly elongated vertebrae.

NAME: *Tanystropheus*
TIME: Middle Triassic
LOCALITY: Asia (Israel) and Europe (Germany and Switzerland)
SIZE: 10 ft/3 m long
The long necks characteristic of the protorosaurs reached an extreme in this member of the group. *Tanystropheus'* neck was longer than its body and tail combined. Yet, only 10 vertebrae made up the neck — only 3 more than in *Protorosaurus* (above) — but each bone was greatly elongated. In fact, when these neck bones were first discovered, they were thought to be leg bones.

So bizarre is *Tanystropheus'* shape that some paleontologists believe it must have lived in water to support its long neck. But it shows no specific adaptations to an aquatic life. Perhaps it lived on the shoreline, dipping its head into the water after fish or shellfish, and crushing them with its peglike teeth.

NAME: *Hyperodapedon*
TIME: Late Triassic
LOCALITY: Asia (India) and Europe (Scotland)
SIZE: 4 ft/1.3 m long
Hyperodapedon was a member of the rhynchosaur group of early reptiles. They were all heavy, barrel-shaped plant-eaters, which thrived from the Middle to Late Triassic. They were the most abundant reptiles of the day, especially in South America and Africa.

The success, though short-lived, of *Hyperodapedon* and its rhynchosaur relatives can be attributed to their teeth. There were 2 broad tooth plates on each side of the upper jaw. Each plate contained several rows of teeth, and a groove ran down the middle. The 2 single tooth rows of the lower jaws fitted into this groove when the mouth was closed, to give a chopping action.

Rhynchosaurs would have feasted on seed ferns, everywhere abundant during the Triassic. But these plants died out at the end of that period, and were replaced by conifers. The rhynchosaurs died out, too, and their herbivorous niche was taken by the newly evolved, plant-eating dinosaurs. The "Age of Ruling Reptiles" had begun.

Dinosaurs and their kin

The dinosaurs and their kin — the crocodiles and flying pterosaurs — dominated the air, land and waters of the earth during the Mesozoic Era. This "Age of the Ruling Reptiles" began more than 200 million years ago, and ended some 65 million years ago. During this span of almost 140 million years, some of nature's most awesome beasts evolved — carnivorous dinosaurs standing 20 ft/6 m tall, plant-eating dinosaurs some 85 ft/26 m long, and pterosaurs with a wingspan of some 40 ft/12.2 m. The sole surviving members of this great assemblage of "ruling reptiles" (the archosaurs) are today's crocodiles, with an evolutionary history stretching back some 230 million years.

The first step in the evolution of the ruling reptiles was taken in the Late Permian period, some 250 million years ago. A new line of small, diapsid reptiles evolved, called the protorosuchians (*see p. 89*). From them radiated a variety of reptiles called the thecodontians (*see pp. 94–97*). They thrived during the subsequent Triassic period, and some of their members became progressively more skilled at walking upright on 2 legs. The dinosaurs (*see pp. 106–169*) arose from such a stock of 2-legged thecodontians, called the ornithosuchians. The crocodiles (*see pp. 98–101*) descended from the same line, and probably also the flying pterosaurs (*see pp. 102–105*).

Dinosaurs: Past masters of the world
The first-recorded dinosaur bones were found in the rocks of southern England, and belonged to the giant carnivore *Megalosaurus* (*see p. 116*) and the giant herbivore *Iguanodon* (*see p. 144*). They were described to the scientific community in 1824 and 1825. More than a decade was to pass before it was realized that they were representatives of a totally different, and totally extinct, group of reptiles. It was Sir Richard Owen, the

The "Age of the Ruling Reptiles" spanned the Jurassic and Cretaceous periods, when the great dinosaurs dominated the land, the pterosaurs ruled the skies, and the crocodiles flourished in the seas and rivers. The ancestor of all these reptiles was a small, 2-legged thecodontian, one of the ornithosuchians.

With the exception of the crocodiles, all these ruling reptiles, great and small, had perished by the end of the Cretaceous period — the close of the Mesozoic Era. The birds probably evolved from among the lizard-hipped (saurischian) dinosaurs. (*For key to silhouettes, see p. 312.*)

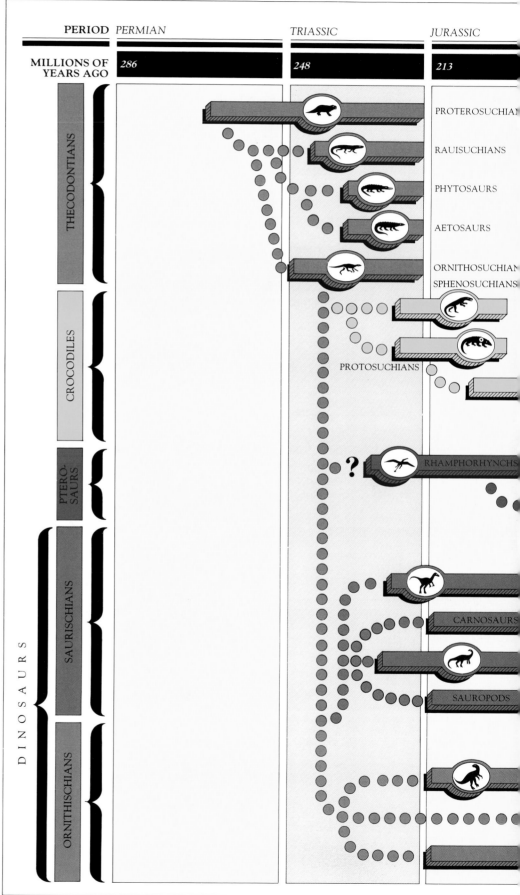

Solid bars show the known fossil record of a group. Dotted lines denote the possible evolutionary relationships between groups.

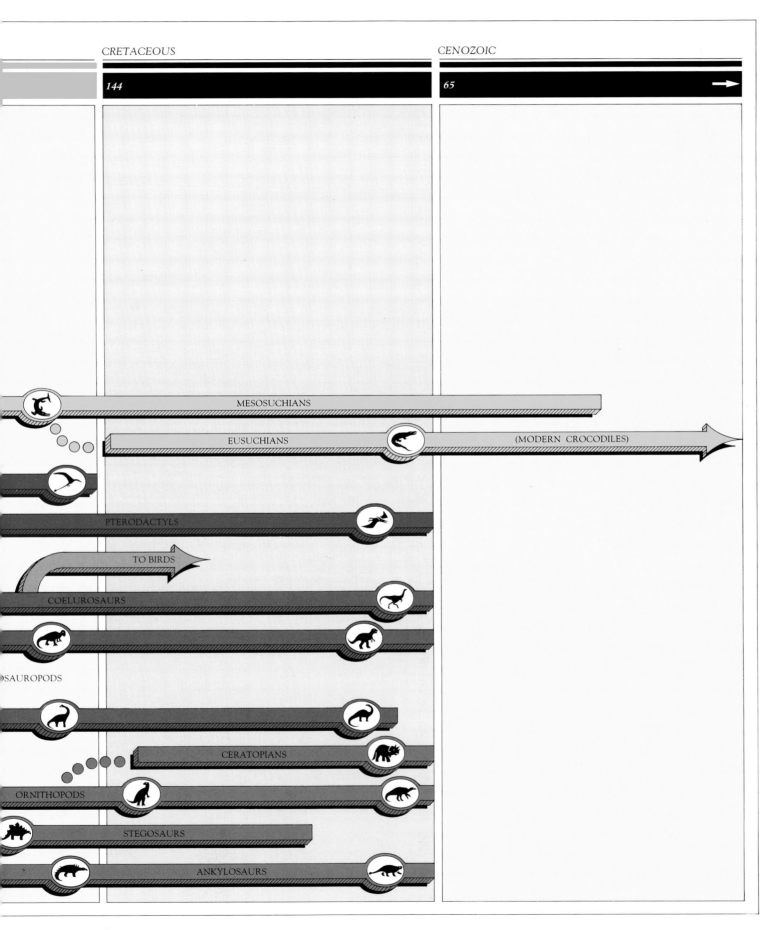

CRETACEOUS

CENOZOIC

144

65

MESOSUCHIANS

EUSUCHIANS

(MODERN CROCODILES)

PTERODACTYLS

TO BIRDS

COELUROSAURS

SAUROPODS

CERATOPIANS

ORNITHOPODS

STEGOSAURS

ANKYLOSAURS

Dinosaurs and their kin

great English anatomist who founded the British Museum of Natural History, who made this discovery and who, in 1841, coined the name *Dinosauria* for them, meaning "terrible lizards."

Over the next half-century, many dinosaurs were discovered in Europe and North America. Various systems of classification were proposed for them, but it was not until 1887 that another English anatomist, Harry Seeley, recognized that there were 2 distinct types of hip girdle or pelvis (*see p. 92*). In some dinosaurs, the pelvis was of a normal reptilian build, so Seeley called this group the Saurischia, or "lizard-hipped" dinosaurs. In others, the pelvis resembled that of modern birds, and so he called them the Ornithischia, or "bird-hipped" dinosaurs.

Both groups may have evolved independently from the thecodontians, but it is also quite possible that the "bird-hipped" dinosaurs evolved from an early member of the "lizard-hipped" group.

Dinosaur finds
The first traces of dinosaurs in North America were found in the Triassic rocks of the Connecticut Valley as early as 1835. These traces did not consist of bones; they were footprints, recording the passage of some great, 2-legged creatures that walked the earth 220 million years ago. Edward Hitchcock, Professor of Theology and Geology, and later President, in Amherst College in Massachusetts, described the footprints in 1848; he concluded that enormous birds had made these trackways.

The first description of dinosaur bones from North America did not come until 1856, when Dr Joseph Leidy of the Academy of Natural Science in Philadelphia described some dinosaur teeth from Montana. Two years later, he described the first skeleton of a North American dinosaur, which he named *Hadrosaurus* (*see p. 148*).

An immense wealth of dinosaurs was soon to be revealed in the American Mid-West, among the great Jurassic and Cretaceous deposits laid down over 65 million years ago. The driving force for their discovery lay in the rivalry between 2 wealthy men from the eastern States — both leading, and competing, paleontologists. The first was Othniel Charles Marsh of Yale University, financed by his philanthropist uncle, George Peabody, who was a merchant and importer. The second was Edward Drinker Cope of the Academy of Natural Science in Philadelphia, whose father was a wealthy shipowner.

The first great bones of dinosaurs that lived in the Late Jurassic, some 150

DINOSAUR HIPS

LIZARD-HIPPED DINOSAUR
(the saurischian *Ceratosaurus*)

Ilium
Pubis — Pelvic girdle
Ischium

BIRD-HIPPED DINOSAUR
(the ornithischian *Lesothosaurus*)

Pelvic girdle
Ilium   Ischium
Pubis

Pre-pubic process

When dinosaurs evolved an upright, 2-legged posture, they had to evolve a new attachment site for the muscles that swung the powerful hindlimbs forward. Lizard-hipped dinosaurs (*top*) evolved a downward and forward extension of the pubis bone to which the muscles attached. In bird-hipped dinosaurs (*right*) the muscles were attached to either a forward extension of the ilium, or, in later types, to a new "pre-pubic" extension of the pubis.

million years ago, were discovered in 1877 in the Morrison Formation of Colorado, and later in Wyoming. Samples found their way to both Marsh and Cope, and the "dinosaur wars" began. Rival teams of fossil hunters went west, bent on acquiring the biggest and the best dinosaurs for their masters. Marsh financed 6 years of excavation at Como Bluff in Wyoming, where many tons of bones were prised from the rocks. Cope, too, sent parties of collectors to that region, as well as to localities in Colorado.

From these Late Jurassic sites, many now-famous dinosaurs were described by both men, including *Allosaurus* and *Ceratosaurus* (*see p. 117*), *Camarasaurus* (*see p. 129*), *Diplodocus* and *Apatosaurus* (popularly known as *Brontosaurus*, *see p. 132*), *Camptosaurus* (*see p. 144*) and *Stegosaurus* (*see p. 156*).

However, the richest treasure house of dinosaurs was found preserved in the Late Cretaceous rocks of Montana and Colorado. These rocks were laid down toward the end of the Mesozoic Era,

between 100 and 65 million years ago. Here again, it is due to the rivalry between Marsh and Cope that many long-dead creatures were discovered, among them *Ornithomimus* (*see p. 109*), *Nodosaurus* (*see p. 160*) and *Triceratops* (*see p. 168*).

Canada, too, has contributed its share of dinosaurs to the museums of the world (*see p. 306*). The Late Cretaceous deposits of Red Deer River Valley, Alberta, were discovered and explored cooperatively by parties from both the American Museum of Natural History in New York, and from the National Museum of Canada and the Royal Ontario Museum.

The Red Deer rocks yielded a rich variety of dinosaurs, especially during the years 1910 to 1917, among them the carnosaur *Albertosaurus* (*see p. 120*), the duckbilled dinosaur *Corythosaurus* (*see p. 152*) and the horned ceratopian *Styracosaurus* (*see p. 168*).

Another area rich in dinosaur remains was discovered in the Gobi Desert of Outer Mongolia, central Asia. It

was first explored by parties from the American Museum of Natural History during the years 1922 to 1925. Ironically, it was the search for fossil humans, rather than fossil reptiles, that led to the exploration of the region.

This ancient dinosaur graveyard yielded an array of Late Cretaceous beasts, including *Protoceratops*, the ancestor of the North American horned dinosaurs, together with its nests and eggs (see p.165). Other finds included the saurischian dinosaurs *Oviraptor* (one specimen preserved with a clutch of *Protoceratops'* eggs, see p.112), *Velociraptor* and *Saurornithoides* (see p.113).

Dinosaurs have been found in South America, Africa, Australia and even New Zealand. But, as yet, the southern hemisphere has not produced any dinosaur faunas of comparable richness to those of the northern hemisphere.

Perhaps the most famous locality is Tendaguru in Tanzania, East Africa, where a wealth of Late Jurassic dinosaurs was found, similar to those of the Morrison Formation in the western USA.

Another African site, discovered in 1987 in Niger, south of the Sahara, promises to yield rich dinosaur remains. Initial work has unearthed the bones of *Camarasaurus*, one of the giant, plant-eating sauropods (see p.129).

A worldwide distribution

Although the dinosaurs of the southern hemisphere are less well known than those of the north, there is little doubt that, in reality, they were just as diverse. Both "lizard-" and "bird-hipped" dinosaurs evolved in the Triassic, when all the continents of the world were still joined together in one super-landmass called Pangaea (see pp.10–11). Any land animal, including dinosaurs, could have spread throughout the world.

The continents were still interconnected throughout the Jurassic, and it was not until the Late Cretaceous that there is evidence of different, isolated dinosaur faunas. By then, there were 2 separate areas of land in the northern hemisphere — Euramerica and Asiamerica (see pp.10–11). For some reason, many new types of Late Cretaceous dinosaur evolved in Asiamerica. The hadrosaurs, ornithomimids, saurornithoids, tyrannosaurs and protoceratopids all started life on that continent. As a result, more "old-fashioned" types of dinosaur, such as the iguanodonts, persisted for longer in Euramerica, removed from the competition of their new relatives.

About 300 genera of dinosaur have so far been described, of which about 55 percent are "lizard-hipped" saurischians, and the rest are "bird-hipped" ornithischians. Only 7 percent of the known dinosaurs come from Triassic rocks (nearly all are saurischians), and 28 percent from Jurassic rocks. The remaining 65 percent come from Cretaceous rocks, and three-quarters of these have been found only in the Late Cretaceous.

It is significant that at the end of the Cretaceous, the flowering plants underwent an explosive evolution, diversifying into many new types which adapted to niches all over the world. This new source of food may well have led to the evolution of new types of dinosaur.

Warm-blooded dinosaurs?

For many years, biologists assumed that dinosaurs, like their living reptilian relatives and the ancestral amphibians, were cold-blooded, or ectothermal. But recently it has been suggested that they may have been warm-blooded, or endothermal, like modern birds and mammals.

Cold-blooded animals rely on the sun as their main source of heat and energy. Warm-blooded animals, in contrast, rely on energy derived from their food. Living warm-blooded animals maintain a high body temperature (on average, between 97–106°F/36–41°C), and therefore use energy at a high rate — about 12 times the rate of a living cold-blooded animal. Even if a dinosaur such as *Brachiosaurus* had eaten 24-hours a day, it could not have produced enough energy to fuel its massive body at such a rate.

Paleontologists believe that dinosaurs had a lower body temperature than modern warm-blooded animals. Since they lacked an insulating covering of hair or feathers (which allows modern warm-blooded animals to keep warm when the environmental temperature drops), dinosaurs must have relied on the environmental temperature remaining relatively stable. This would have made them vulnerable to any major climatic change, and it may have been such a reliance that led to their extinction, and replacement by the less vulnerable, well-insulated, furry mammals.

Mass-extinction of the dinosaurs

The disappearance of the dinosaurs worldwide at the end of the Mesozoic Era is the best-known mass-extinction event of the prehistoric world. But other extinctions took place at or about the same time. The flying pterosaurs, and also the marine ichthyosaurs, plesiosaurs and mosasaurs, all disappeared at or near the end of the Cretaceous. And several marine invertebrate groups suffered the same fate — ammonites, certain bivalves and many tiny organisms of the plankton.

Since modern methods of dating rocks is only accurate to within a few hundreds of thousands of years (see p.13), it is difficult to be certain whether the terrestrial and marine extinctions of the Cretaceous took place at the same time. It seems that the vertebrate extinctions happened gradually. For example, the ichthyosaurs became extinct before the end of the Cretaceous. Also, the plesiosaurs, pterosaurs and dinosaurs may have been becoming less common toward the end of that period. These facts suggest that some gradual change in the environment was taking place worldwide, rather than the popular notion of a sudden cataclysmic event that wiped out huge numbers of creatures.

Sea levels dropped comparatively rapidly during the Late Cretaceous. As a result, the average air temperature dropped, and the climate became more variable worldwide. This could have been the cause of the gradual decline of the pterosaurs and dinosaurs, especially if the dinosaurs' method of regulating their body temperature depended partly on the equability of the environment.

In contrast, the extinction of many types of microscopic marine invertebrates seems to have happened suddenly and simultaneously, at the end of the Cretaceous. They disappeared at precisely the time that the rocks show an abnormally high concentration of a number of normally rare metals, such as iridium, osmium and rhodium. This enriched layer has been found in some 50 different localities, ranging from North America and Europe to New Zealand, and in deep-sea sediments of the Pacific.

The American geologists Luis and Walter Alvarez pointed out that these rare metals are present in the same proportions as in meteorites. They suggest that an enormous meteorite, some 6 ml/10 km in diameter, hit our planet at the end of the Cretaceous period, some 65 million years ago. The impact would have thrown up a mass of débris, which would have darkened the skies for many years, affecting plant life. This could well have caused climatic changes that led to the mass-extinction of both the marine plankton and the terrestrial vertebrates, which were already on the decline.

If the meteorite had impacted in areas of calcium carbonate (as in the Cretaceous seabed) great amounts of carbon dioxide would have been released into the atmosphere. This could have increased the average temperature worldwide so much that dinosaurs, which relied on a warm, steady, climate, may have expired of heat.

Early ruling reptiles

LAGOSUCHUS

LONGISQUAMA

EUPARKERIA

CHASMATOSAURUS

STAGONOLEPIS

DESMATOSUCHUS

TICINOSUCHUS

RUTIODON

ORNITHOSUCHUS

ERYTHROSUCHUS

Early ruling reptiles

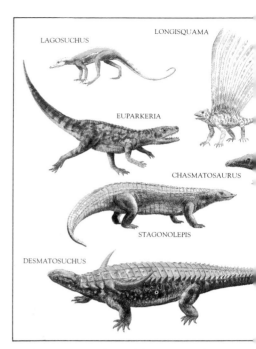

SUPERORDER ARCHOSAURIA

The archosaurs were the most spectacular group of "ruling reptiles." They dominated life in the Mesozoic Era, reigning for more than 180 million years. Flying reptiles, the pterosaurs, ruled the skies (see pp. 102–105); dinosaurs ruled the lands (see pp. 106–169); and crocodiles — the only surviving archosaurs — invaded the seas and freshwaters (see pp. 98–101).

These diverse creatures all shared a common feature — a diapsid skull, with 2 openings behind each eye (see p. 61).

ORDER THECODONTIA

The earliest archosaurs were the thecodontians. They first appeared in the Late Permian, more than 250 million years ago. They evolved rapidly into many forms during the Triassic, and became extinct by the end of that period. Their evolutionary history was brief (less than 40 million years) but successful, for from the thecodontians arose the ancestors of the 3 groups of ruling reptile — the dinosaurs, pterosaurs and crocodiles (see pp. 90–91).

The thecodontians are grouped into 5 suborders (below). Members show a general trend toward a more upright stance, with the hindlimbs especially being progressively brought in from their former, sprawling position to be oriented more directly beneath the body. This trend was perfected in the ornithosuchians, which could walk upright on 2 legs. The ancestor of the dinosaurs lies among their members (see p. 97).

SUBORDER PROTEROSUCHIA

The proterosuchians were the earliest thecodontians to appear, and are known from Late Permian times in Russia. Some were aquatic, crocodilelike animals, while others were fully adapted land-dwellers. They spread throughout the world during the Triassic, and died out at the end of that period. All the other thecodontian groups may have descended from them.

NAME: **Chasmatosaurus**
TIME: **Early Triassic**
LOCALITY: **Africa (South Africa) and Asia (China)**
SIZE: **6 ft 6 in/2 m long**
Chasmatosaurus (formerly named Proterosuchus) is the earliest well-known thecodontian. It looked rather like a modern crocodile, and probably behaved in much the same way. Its robust limbs, each with 5 toes, were angled out horizontally from the body, resulting in a sprawling, lizardlike gait.

Although Chasmatosaurus could walk on land, it probably spent most of its time in rivers, swimming after its fish prey using sinuous movements of the long tail and body. Its jaws were well equipped with sharp, backwardly curved teeth, each set in a shallow socket; the upper jaw turned down sharply at its tip. There were also teeth on the palate — a primitive feature, lost in later thecodontians.

NAME: **Erythrosuchus**
TIME: **Early Triassic**
LOCALITY: **Africa (South Africa)**
SIZE: **15 ft/4.5 m long**
Erythrosuchus and other members of its family were the largest, land-living predators worldwide during the Early and Mid-Triassic period. Some of them reached a length of 16 ft/5 m. Their predation must have exerted a profound, selective pressure on the evolution of other terrestrial reptiles. For example, several new types of thecodontian with protective body armor appeared at around this time, such as the phytosaurs and aetosaurs (below).

Erythrosuchus had a large head, up to 3 ft 3 in/1 m long, and powerful jaws filled with sharp, conical teeth. Its legs were held rather more directly beneath its bulky body than those of the sprawling Chasmatosaurus (above), suggesting that this active predator could move more effectively on land.

SUBORDER RAUISUCHIA

This group of crocodilelike thecodontians were large, carnivorous land-dwellers, some of them growing up to 20 ft/6 m long. They evolved in the Mid-Triassic and survived to the end of that period. They are known from the Americas, East Africa and western Europe.

Not only were the hindlimbs of rauisuchians held more directly beneath the body, but an effective ankle joint had been developed, together with a heel that enhanced the leverage and flexure of the feet during walking.

NAME: **Ticinosuchus**
TIME: **Middle Triassic**
LOCALITY: **Europe (Switzerland)**
SIZE: **10 ft/3 m long**
The back of this medium-sized rauisuchian was lightly armored, with a double row of small, bony plates; the long tail was also armored, above and below. From the structure of the hips, and the ball-and-socket joints with which the thigh bones (femurs) connect, paleontologists can tell that the hindlegs of Ticinosuchus' were held almost directly beneath its body, unlike their sprawling position in earlier thecodontians.

In addition, the ankle joints of Ticinosuchus and other rauisuchians had become adapted for walking on land, and part of one of the foot bones had developed into a heel. This was an important innovation, since a strong tendon (the equivalent of our Achilles tendon) could attach to the heel, and serve as a lever to flex the foot.

Until the development of the heel, it had been the fifth, or outer, foot bone (metatarsal), together with the long fifth toe, that helped to lever the foot off the ground. Animals with heels could afford to reduce the length of the fifth toe. In some, it was lost completely; in others, it was shortened so that it did not reach the ground at all.

SUBORDER PHYTOSAURIA

The phytosaurs were aquatic carnivores that are known only from the Late Triassic. With heavily armored, crocodilelike bodies, up to 16 ft/5 m long, they were the dominant predators in rivers of the northern hemisphere.

Phytosaurs represent a classic case of parallel evolution with the true crocodiles; both types of reptile are descended from the same ancestral thecodontian stock, and each assumed independently the same general structure in response to the same way of life.

NAME: **Rutiodon**
TIME: **Late Triassic**
LOCALITY: **Europe (Germany and Switzerland) and North America (Arizona, New Mexico, North Carolina and Texas)**
SIZE: **10 ft/3 m long**
Rutiodon was a typical phytosaur, its back, flanks and tail armored with bony plates. It had a long snout like a modern gavial (a crocodile found only in Indian rivers), and jaws filled with sharp teeth,

ideal for fish-eating. It probably also ate other reptiles, since their remains have been found preserved in the body cavities of some phytosaurs.

Rutiodon and its relatives bore a striking resemblance to modern crocodiles. However, the immediate feature that distinguishes them is the position of the nostrils. In phytosaurs, they were elevated on a bony bump far back near the eyes, while in modern crocodiles they are at the tip of the snout.

SUBORDER AETOSAURIA

Unlike all their thecodontian relatives, the aetosaurs were plant-eaters, with small, leaf-shaped teeth and deep, bulky bodies encased in a heavy, bony armor. Looking like short-snouted crocodiles, aetosaurs were an offshoot from the main thecodontian line, and are known only from the Late Triassic of Europe and North and South America.

NAME: **Stagonolepis**
TIME: **Late Triassic**
LOCALITY: **Europe (Scotland)**
SIZE: **10 ft/3 m long**
The deep body of *Stagonolepis* is typical of the herbivorous aetosaurs, and was developed to accommodate the longer intestines needed to digest plant food. A slow-moving browser, *Stagonolepis* also needed its heavy body armor to protect itself from attack by its agile, carnivorous, thecodontian relatives.

Stagonolepis had a small head for its size, a length of only 10 in/25 cm out of a total of some 10 ft/3 m. It had no teeth at the front of its foreshortened jaws, but the peglike teeth at the back would have dealt effectively with tough plants such as horsetails, ferns and the newly evolved cycads. The snout was flattened and almost piglike, a good shape for rooting about in the undergrowth.

NAME: **Desmatosuchus**
TIME: **Late Triassic**
LOCALITY: **North America (Texas)**
SIZE: **16 ft/5 m long**
This large North American aetosaur had particularly heavy armor encasing its body. Great quadrangular plates covered its back and tail and part of its belly, while long spines, up to 18 in/45 cm long, projected sideways from its shoulders. It had the small head, piglike snout and weak, peglike teeth characteristic of the plant-eating aetosaurs.

SUBORDER ORNITHOSUCHIA

Paleontologists regard the ornithosuchians as ideal intermediaries between the 4-legged thecodontians and the 2-legged dinosaurs. One family in particular, the Lagosuchidae, is considered to contain the likely ancestors of the dinosaurs (*below*).

Ornithosuchians probably descended directly from some type of proterosuchian, the earliest-known group of ruling reptiles, during the Late Permian (*see p. 96*). They became extinct at the end of the Triassic, but not before they had produced the ancestral dinosaur stock (*see pp. 90–91*).

NAME: **Euparkeria**
TIME: **Early Triassic**
LOCALITY: **Africa (South Africa)**
SIZE: **up to 2 ft/60 cm long**
The powerful hindlegs and long tail that had evolved in the ancestral thecodontians gave rise to a new stance in their descendants, the ornithosuchians.

Euparkeria was an early member of this group. It was a small, slimly built creature, with a light armor of bony plates running down the center of its back and tail. The hindlegs were longer than the forelegs, by about one-third. Although it spent most of its time on all-fours, this thecodontian was capable of rising up on 2 legs to run away from danger. Its long tail, making up about half the body length, would have been stretched out behind to balance it at the hips as it ran.

This 2-legged (bipedal) stance was to become the norm among the carnivorous dinosaurs that made their first appearance at the end of the Triassic (*see pp. 106–109*).

Euparkeria's skull was large, but its weight was reduced by several wide openings between the bones. Its teeth were well suited to a carnivorous diet — long and sharp, curved slightly backward and serrated along the edges.

NAME: **Ornithosuchus**
TIME: **Late Triassic**
LOCALITY: **Europe (Scotland)**
SIZE: **13 ft/4 m long**
At one time, *Ornithosuchus* was regarded by some paleontologists as a primitive dinosaur. However, it is now thought of as a highly advanced thecodontian, and from it, or a closely related animal, arose the theropod dinosaurs.

Ornithosuchus' stance was certainly dinosaurlike — its hindlegs were held vertically beneath its body, allowing it to walk upright, although moving on all-fours was probably its usual habit.

The primitive features of *Ornithosuchus* include a double row of bony plates down its back; a short, broad pelvis, which was attached to the backbone by a weak arrangement of only 3 vertebrae; and 5 toes on each hindfoot. However, its skull is advanced, and strikingly similar to that of the large theropods, such as *Tyrannosaurus*.

NAME: **Lagosuchus**
TIME: **Middle Triassic**
LOCALITY: **South America (Argentina)**
SIZE: **1 ft/30 cm long**
Members of the family Lagosuchidae are the most dinosaurlike of all the thecodontians known. *Lagosuchus* itself is considered as the most likely ancestor of the dinosaurs. This is based mainly on the structure of its hip bones, ankle joints and long, slim hindlegs, in which the shin bones are almost twice the length of the thigh bones — a feature of running animals, and particularly well seen in the bipedal dinosaurs.

In addition, *Lagosuchus* has been cited as a possible ancestor of the pterosaurs, the flying reptiles which also appeared in Late Triassic times (*see pp. 102–105*).

NAME: **Longisquama**
TIME: **Early Triassic**
LOCALITY: **Asia (Turkestan)**
SIZE: **6 in/15 cm long**
A curious, lizardlike creature, *Longisquama* was a tiny thecodontian. It cannot be placed in any of the known suborders or families of the group. Its body was covered in overlapping, keeled scales. A remarkable row of tall scales, stiff and V-shaped in cross-section, rose from the back. Their function is unknown. They could have been display structures, either for attracting a mate or for warning away rivals. Other suggestions are that they could have been used for gliding through the air, or as heat-exchange devices; they may even have been an early stage in the evolution of feathers.

Crocodiles

TERRESTRISUCHUS

GRACILISUCHUS

PROTOSUCHUS

BERNISSARTIA

METRIORHYNCHUS

TELEOSAURUS

DEINOSUCHUS

PRISTICHAMPSUS

Crocodiles

ORDER CROCODYLIA

The crocodiles can be regarded as the most successful of the archosaurs or ruling reptiles, since they are the only representatives of that group alive today. They have changed little from their prehistoric relatives, which appeared in Mid-Triassic times, some 230 million years ago. In fact, crocodiles have been remarkably consistent in structure throughout their evolution.

The crocodiles most probably evolved from an ornithosuchian-type of thecodontian (see pp. 90–91). Although modern crocodiles are more at home in water than on land, they evolved as small, terrestrial carnivores, capable of running upright on their long, slim hindlegs, unlike the short, sprawling limbs of their modern, semi-aquatic relatives.

All crocodiles, even the earliest ones, have long, low massive skulls, built to resist the pressures created by the powerful snapping-shut of their elongated jaws. The muscles attach far back on the skull, allowing the jaws to be opened wide to deal with large prey. A secondary palate of bone separates the mouth from the nasal passages, allowing the animal to eat and breathe at the same time — a particularly useful feature for water-dwellers.

SUBORDER SPHENOSUCHIA

The sphenosuchians are the earliest-known crocodiles, making their appearance in the middle of the Triassic period. So similar are they to the lightly built ornithosuchians that they were long regarded as belonging to that group of thecodontians (see p. 97). These early crocodiles were built for a life on land.

NAME: *Gracilisuchus*
TIME: Middle Triassic
LOCALITY: South America (Argentina)
SIZE: 1 ft/30 cm long

This tiny creature is so unlike a modern crocodile that it was classified with the ornithosuchians until the early 1980s. Like them, it had a lightly built body and a disproportionally large head, and it could run erect on its slim hindlegs, balanced by the long, straight tail. However, the structure of *Gracilisuchus'* skull, neck vertebrae and ankle joints place it firmly among the crocodiles.

Gracilisuchus was a well-adapted land animal, protected by a double row of bony plates that interlocked down the length of its backbone, to the tip of the tail. It probably chased after small lizards on its long hindlegs, despatching them in its powerful jaws, with their sharp, recurved teeth.

NAME: *Terrestrisuchus*
TIME: Late Triassic
LOCALITY: Europe (Wales)
SIZE: 20 in/50 cm long

Terrestrisuchus was smaller and much more delicately built than *Gracilisuchus* (above). Its body was also shorter, with extremely long, slim limbs and greatly elongated footbones in the hindlegs. The tail was almost twice the length of the body and head combined. Its head was more crocodilelike — longer and lower — than its earlier relative.

From its light build — almost like that of a greyhound, although it was completely unrelated to that mammal — it seems that *Terrestrisuchus* must have sprinted over the dry landscape of Late Triassic Europe, snapping up insects and small lizards in its elongated jaws. It probably ran mostly on 4 legs, but could easily have risen upright to move even faster.

SUBORDER PROTOSUCHIA

Although their skulls were slightly more crocodilelike in appearance, the protosuchians were still long-legged land-dwellers like the sphenosuchians (above). They lived all over the world during the early part of the Jurassic period. Some members may have developed a secondary palate that separated the mouth from the nasal passages, but it could only have been made of a fleshy membrane as yet, since there is no sign of the solid bony palate developed in later crocodiles.

NAME: *Protosuchus*
TIME: Early Jurassic
LOCALITY: North America (Arizona)
SIZE: 3 ft 3 in/1 m long

Protosuchus was obviously a terrestrial crocodile, since it has been found in rocks that also yielded the remains of dinosaurs. It would have shared its North American homeland with such carnivorous dinosaurs as the agile, 2-legged coelurosaurs (see pp. 106–109) and the newly evolved carnosaurs (see pp. 114–117).

The skull of *Protosuchus* was more crocodilelike in appearance than that of the earlier sphenosuchians. The short jaws broadened out at the base of the snout into a fairly wide area at the back of the skull. This provided a large surface to which the jaw muscles could attach, thereby increasing the gape of the jaws and the force with which they could be closed.

Among the sharp teeth, there was a pair of long caninelike teeth at the front of the lower jaw, which fitted into a notch on either side of the upper jaw

TERRESTRISUCHUS

GRACILISUCHUS

PROTOSU

BERNIS

when the mouth was closed.

This tooth arrangement is characteristic of modern crocodiles. Alligators also have lower canines, but they fit into bony pits in the upper jaw.

SUBORDER MESOSUCHIA

Most of the fossil crocodiles belong to this group. They evolved in the Early Jurassic, most probably from the protosuchians (above), and continued well into the Tertiary period. The last known mesosuchian dates from the relatively recent Miocene epoch, some 15 million years ago.

There are approximately 70 genera of mesosuchian known, grouped into about 16 families. Most of them were either fully adapted land-dwellers, like their predecessors, or semi-aquatic in their habits.

One terrestrial family, the sebecids, lived in South America during the Early Tertiary period. Their fanglike teeth were serrated along the edges and compressed into long blades, similar to the teeth of the large carnosaur dinosaurs. This has led some paleontologists to speculate that these crocodiles were the dominant predators of the day, since no large, carnivorous mammal had reached the island continent of South America at the time.

Only 4 families of mesosuchian adopted a permanently aquatic lifestyle. The teleosaurs and metriorhynchs (below) are the best known. They shared the seas of the world with the ichthyosaurs and plesiosaurs throughout the Jurassic period and into the Cretaceous.

METRIORHYNCHUS

URUS

DEINOSUCHUS

PRISTICHAMPSUS

NAME: *Teleosaurus*
TIME: Early Jurassic
LOCALITY: Europe (France)
SIZE: 10 ft/3 m long

Teleosaurus was a member of one of the 4 families of mesosuchian crocodiles that adopted the sea as their home. It probably looked similar to the modern gavial of India's northern rivers.

The body of this ancient marine crocodile was long and slim, its back heavily armored like that of a modern crocodile. Its jaws were tremendously narrow and elongated, in comparison with those of its land-living relatives, and lined with many sharp teeth. These interlocked when the mouth was closed, to form an ideal trap for catching slippery fish or squid.

The forelegs were particularly short — only half the length of the hindlegs — and were probably held flat against the flanks during swimming to reduce drag. Sinuous movements of the long body and tail would have moved *Teleosaurus* rapidly through the water, just like a modern aquatic lizard.

NAME: *Metriorhynchus*
TIME: Middle to Late Jurassic
LOCALITY: Europe (England and France) and South America (Chile)
SIZE: 10 ft/3 m long

Metriorhynchus and other members of its family were the most specialized of the aquatic crocodiles. They had dispensed with the heavy back armor of their relatives, since such protection was unnecessary in the sea, and also its loss made them more maneuverable. Their limbs were transformed into paddlelike flippers, the hind pair longer than the front pair. And their tails had developed a large, fishlike fin for swimming, supported by the sharply downturned tip of the backbone. Exactly the same adaptations were developed independently by the ichthyosaurs (see pp. 78–81).

Geosaurus was another member of the metriorhynch family, found in Late Jurassic and Early Cretaceous sediments in South America and Europe. It was about the same length as its relative *Metriorhynchus*, but even more streamlined in shape. One excellent specimen of *Geosaurus* from southern Germany was outlined by a fine film of carbon, showing the shape of the fleshy limbs in life. The front flippers were considerably shorter than the hind pair, and the tail fin was particularly large. The tip of the backbone bent even more sharply into the lower lobe than did the backbone of *Metriorhynchus*.

NAME: *Bernissartia*
TIME: Early Cretaceous
LOCALITY: Europe (Belgium and England)
SIZE: 2 ft/60 cm long

This mesosuchian was tiny in comparison with its relatives. It lived along the shores of the shallow Wealden Lake that stretched from southeast England into Belgium during Early Cretaceous times, some 130 million years ago.

Bernissartia led a semi-aquatic life, judging by the 2 types of teeth in its jaws. Those at the front were long and pointed, as if for catching fish, while those at the back were broad and flat, as if for crushing shellfish, or even the bones of dead animals.

SUBORDER EUSUCHIA

This group comprises the true crocodiles, including the 21 living species of modern crocodile, the 7 species of alligator and caiman, and the single species of gavial. Crocodiles and alligators appeared in their modern forms in the Late Cretaceous. But their ancestors evolved at least 80 million years before that, in the Late Jurassic. They probably descended from among the semi-aquatic mesosuchians.

The eusuchians were once a much more abundant and widespread group than they are today. They lived in the swamps, rivers and lakes of the late Mesozoic Era. They were contemporaries of the great dinosaurs, and most probably preyed on them when they strayed too close to the water's edge.

Sturdy, well-armored bodies, massive heads, powerful jaws and meat-shearing teeth — these weapons of the crocodile would have been used to overpower even a large dinosaur. Once it had been dragged into the water, the crocodile could have held it under in a vicelike grip; the secondary bony palate allowed the crocodile to open its mouth without inhaling water and flooding its lungs.

NAME: *Deinosuchus*
TIME: Late Cretaceous
LOCALITY: North America (Texas)
SIZE: possibly 49 ft/15 m long

Only the skull of this immense crocodile has been found. It measured more than 6 ft 6 in/2 m in length. Assuming *Deinosuchus* had the same body proportions as those of other crocodiles, its overall length is judged to be just under 50 ft/15.2 m. The name *Deinosuchus* reflects this size; it means "terrible crocodile". Sometimes it is called *Phobosuchus*, meaning "horror crocodile."

Deinosuchus lived in the swamps of Texas toward the end of the Cretaceous period. It probably ambushed passing dinosaurs, lying very still and grabbing its prey in the same way as the modern Nile crocodile seizes mammals and birds that come to the water's edge to drink. It probably swallowed stones, like its modern counterparts, which remained in the stomach to act as stabilizing ballast in the water.

Some paleontologists, however, dispute this lifestyle. They suggest that *Deinosuchus* was a smaller, short-bodied, long-legged predator that lived on land. Until more of the skeleton is found, the way of life of this giant crocodile will remain uncertain.

Gigantic crocodiles were not confined to the Mesozoic. *Rhamphosuchus* was a gavial from the Pliocene deposits of India. Only part of its jawbone is known, but it is estimated that this creature may have been the same size as *Deinosuchus*.

NAME: *Pristichampsus*
TIME: Eocene
LOCALITY: Europe (Germany) and North America (Wyoming)
SIZE: 10 ft/3 m long

A number of heavily armored eusuchians lived on land during the Tertiary period. *Pristichampsus* was typical of these terrestrial crocodiles. It had long running legs, and its feet had hooves instead of claws. It fed on the abundant mammals that had recently evolved, and that had replaced the dinosaurs throughout the world.

Pristichampsus had sharp teeth, flattened from side to side and with saw-edges, like steak knives. Such teeth were almost identical to those of the largest carnivorous dinosaurs, such as *Tyrannosaurus* or *Albertosaurus*. So, when isolated teeth of *Pristichampsus* were found in Tertiary deposits, paleontologists at first thought they belonged to such theropod dinosaurs, and mistakenly took them as evidence that these great creatures had survived into Tertiary times.

Flying reptiles

EUDIMORPHODON

DIMORPHODON

RHAMPHORHYNCHUS

SORDES

ANUROGNATHUS

SCAPHOGNATHUS

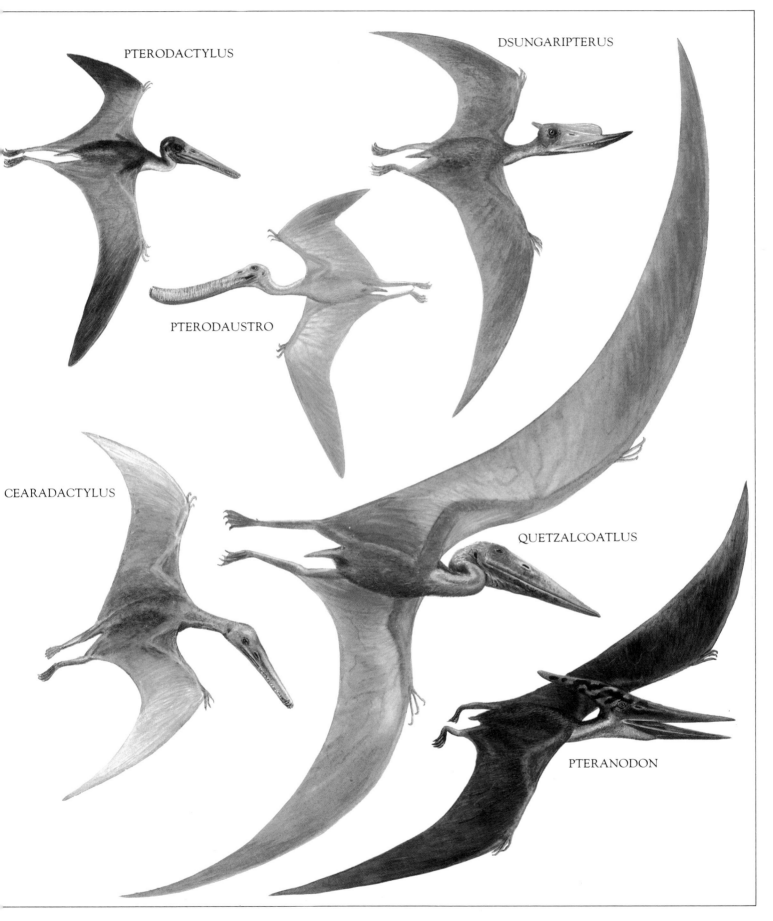

PTERODACTYLUS

DSUNGARIPTERUS

PTERODAUSTRO

CEARADACTYLUS

QUETZALCOATLUS

PTERANODON

Flying reptiles

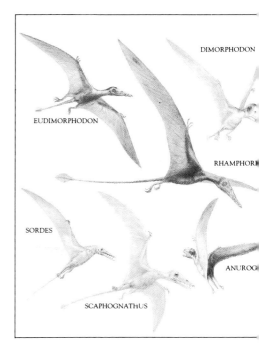

ORDER PTEROSAURIA

The first group of vertebrates to take to the air as a way of life were the pterosaurs. These flying reptiles flew on "wings" made of skin, which were attached along the length of the greatly elongated, fourth fingers of each hand, and rejoined the body at thigh-level.

These flying reptiles evolved in Late Triassic times, some 70 million years before the first-known bird, *Archaeopteryx*, appeared (*see p. 176*). They thrived throughout the Jurassic and early part of the Cretaceous, diversifying into many forms, among them the largest flying creatures of all time. Then the group began to decline, its last members becoming extinct at the end of the Mesozoic Era. Pterosaur remains have been found all over the world, except in Antarctica, mostly in marine deposits.

There are 2 suborders of pterosaur (*below*). The earliest and most primitive types are the rhamphorhynchs; the later types include the more familiar flying reptiles — the pterodactyls.

SUBORDER RHAMPHORHYNCHOIDEA

The earliest-known pterosaurs were already advanced flyers by the Late Triassic period, some 190 million years ago. They flourished worldwide until the end of the Jurassic, when they became extinct.

NAME: *Eudimorphodon*
TIME: **Late Triassic**
LOCALITY: **Europe (Italy)**
SIZE: **2 ft 5 in/75 cm wingspan**

Eudimorphodon is well known from remains preserved in marine rocks of northern Italy. It was a typical rhamphorhynch, with a short neck and a bony tail, which made up about half the animal's length of 2ft 4in/70cm. The head was large but lightweight, owing to the 2 pairs of openings in its diapsid skull (*see p. 61*).

The membranous flaps of skin that made up *Eudimorphodon*'s wings were attached to the enormously elongated fourth finger of each hand. This finger was composed of 4 extra-long finger bones (phalanges), and was attached to the wrist by an elongated hand bone (metacarpal). The wings joined the body on each side at the thighs. Another small flying membrane ran from the bones of each wrist to the base of the neck.

Eudimorphodon was evidently an active flyer, capable of flapping its wings like a modern bird. The sternum, or breastbone, was developed into a broad, flattened plate, to which the powerful flight muscles attached, although the

keel was low in comparison to the great keel of modern flying birds.

The long tail would have been held out rigidly during flight, its vertebrae lashed together by bony tendons into an inflexible rod, which counterbalanced the animal's comparatively heavy forequarters. As in many other rhamphorhynchs, there was a vertical, diamond-shaped flap at the tip of the tail, which most probably functioned as a rudder during flight.

The short jaws of *Eudimorphodon* were armed with 2 kinds of teeth. There were long, peglike teeth at the front of the mouth, and short, broad teeth at the back. This pterosaur probably flew low over the sea, its large eyes trained on the surface to spot its fish prey.

NAME: *Dimorphodon*
TIME: **Early Jurassic**
LOCALITY: **Europe (England)**
SIZE: **4 ft/1.2 m wingspan**

Dimorphodon had the disproportionately large head typical of the rhamphorhynchs. It measured about 8in/20cm long, about a quarter of the total body length. But it had a remarkable puffin-like shape, deep and narrow, unlike that of its relatives. There seems to be no structural reason for this, since the teeth show that the jaws were simple. Perhaps the shape of the head represents some type of display structure for territorial or courtship behavior, like the showy heads of modern hornbills or toucans.

The walking method of pterosaurs has long been debated. Based on studies of *Dimorphodon*'s hips and legs, some paleontologists believe that they had an erect, birdlike stance, with the legs set directly under the body, so that they could run on their toes quite quickly.

But finds of other types of pterosaur in 1986 indicate that perhaps *Dimorphodon* was an exception. These recent finds show that the upper leg bones were splayed out sideways from the hips, which could only have resulted in a clumsy, sprawling, batlike gait. It is suggested that pterosaurs spent much of their time hanging from cliffs and branches, using their clawed fingers and toes to reach these vantage points, from which they could then launch themselves.

NAME: *Rhamphorhynchus*
TIME: **Late Jurassic**
LOCALITY: **Europe (Germany) and Africa (Tanzania)**
SIZE: **3 ft 3 in/1 m wingspan**

This pterosaur is particularly well known because it was preserved in the fine-grained limestones of Solnhofen in southern Germany. These limestones also yielded specimens of the earliest-

known bird, *Archaeopteryx*, complete with impressions of its feathers stamped into the rocks (*see p. 176*).

Similarly, the fine structure of *Rhamphorhynchus*' wings, made of membranous skin, has been preserved in these limestones. Microscopic study reveals that thin fibers ran from the front to the back of the wings, strengthening them — comparable to the radiating fingers that support the wings of a modern bat.

Rhamphorhynchus had long, narrow jaws filled with sharp teeth that pointed outward, like the barbs on a fishing spear. Fish remains have been found in the crop and stomach of some specimens; its habit was probably to skim over the water, its long tail held out for stability, snapping up fish in its jaws.

NAME: *Scaphognathus*
TIME: **Late Jurassic**
LOCALITY: **Europe (England)**
SIZE: **3 ft 3 in/1 m wingspan**

One specimen of this typical rhamphorhynch was preserved in such a way that its brain cavity could be studied. The size of this cavity revealed that *Scaphognathus* had a much larger brain relative to that of other similar-sized reptiles. It was almost as large as that of a modern bird.

Paleontologists have studied the relative sizes of the areas of the brain that controlled various senses. They conclude that *Scaphognathus*, and presumably all its relatives, had excellent eyesight, but a poor sense of smell. The cerebellum and associated lobes in the brain were highly developed, indicating agility of movement, which supports the theory that small pterosaurs were active flappers, like small modern birds.

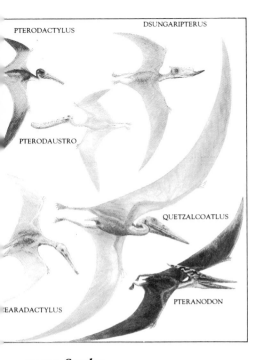

PTERODACTYLUS
DSUNGARIPTERUS
PTERODAUSTRO
QUETZALCOATLUS
CEARADACTYLUS
PTERANODON

NAME: Sordes
TIME: Late Jurassic
LOCALITY: Asia (Kazakhstan SSR)
SIZE: 1 ft 6 in/50 cm wingspan
For a long time, paleontologists have argued about whether carnivorous dinosaurs and pterosaurs were endothermic or warm-blooded. The active, predatory life of both these types of ruling reptile would suggest that they had a high metabolic rate, and could control their body temperature.

To support this theory, some paleontologists have suggested that both dinosaurs and pterosaurs were covered in an insulating layer of down or hair, as an aid to regulating their body temperature. In the case of dinosaurs, no such evidence has ever been found. But a find in 1971 seemed to confirm the theory for pterosaurs. A specimen of *Sordes pilosus* was discovered, southeast of the Urals. Its body appeared, from the impressions in the fine-grained deposits, to be covered in a pelt of dense fur. The tail and wings were naked.

Some paleontologists, however, have questioned this find, pointing out that the fine-grained limestones of southern Germany have yielded the best-preserved pterosaurs, and that no impressions of fur have ever been found in any of these specimens.

NAME: Anurognathus
TIME: Late Jurassic
LOCALITY: Europe (Germany)
SIZE: 1 ft/30 cm wingspan
This comparatively small rhamphorhynch had a deep, narrow head with short jaws, which were filled with strong, peglike teeth. This could suggest that it lived on a diet of insects. Unlike other rhamphorhynchs, it had a short tail, and this feature, combined with the small body size, would have made it highly maneuverable in flight after its fast-moving prey.

SUBORDER PTERODACTYLOIDEA

The pterodactyls are the most familiar of the flying reptiles. They were already an established group in Late Jurassic times, when their relatives, the rhamphorhynchs (*above*), became extinct. The pterodactyls continued through the Cretaceous, although only a few types survived to the end of that period.

These pterosaurs had the same general structure as the earlier rhamphorhynchs, but the tail was shorter, the neck longer and the skull more elongate. They ranged from some of the smallest-known pterosaurs to some of the largest flying vertebrates that ever lived.

NAME: Pterodactylus
TIME: Late Jurassic
LOCALITY: Africa (Tanzania) and Europe (England, France and Germany)
SIZE: up to 2 ft 5 in/75 cm wingspan
Pterodactylus shows the typical pterodactyl features — a short tail and long neck, and greatly elongated hand bones (metacarpals), which, with the long fourth fingers, supported the wings.

Many species of *Pterodactylus* are known, varying in the size and shape of the head. The species illustrated on p. 103, *P. kochi*, had long, narrow jaws, lined with sharp, fish-eating teeth.

NAME: Pterodaustro
TIME: Late Jurassic
LOCALITY: South America (Argentina)
SIZE: 4 ft/1.2 m wingspan
The remarkable feature of *Pterodaustro* was its jaws. They were elongated, slender and curved upward, accounting for most of the length of the small skull, which was about 9 in/23 cm long in total. The lower jaw bristled with long, fine, densely packed teeth. There were also tiny teeth in the upper jaw.

This pterosaur probably fed by skimming along the surface of the sea with its mouth open. As the water flowed through its jaws, the tiny animals of the plankton would have been enmeshed on the sievelike teeth — a feeding method comparable with that of a modern baleen whale.

NAME: Cearadactylus
TIME: Early Cretaceous
LOCALITY: South America (Brazil)
SIZE: 13 ft/4 m wingspan
Cearadactylus' jaws were expanded at the tip (rather like those of the modern gavial crocodile), and several large teeth protruded around the edges. These interlocked when the mouth was closed, forming a trap for slippery fish prey, which was then easily dealt with by the numerous conical teeth lining the jaws.

NAME: Dsungaripterus
TIME: Early Cretaceous
LOCALITY: Asia (China)
SIZE: 10 ft/3 m wingspan
Dsungaripterus had a peculiar bony crest running along its snout, and long, narrow jaws that curved upward to a fine point at the tip. These forcepslike jaws could have been used to prize shellfish off rocks or out of crannies on the seashore. The flattened teeth at the back of the jaws crushed the shells.

NAME: Pteranodon
TIME: Late Cretaceous
LOCALITY: Europe (England) and North America (Kansas)
SIZE: 23 ft/7 m wingspan
One of the longest-winged pterosaurs known, *Pteranodon* was most probably a glider. Its short, tailless body — relatively heavy, at about 37 lb/17 kg — would have been highly maneuverable in the air (like a modern, short-tailed fighter jet), and it probably relied on rising, hot-air currents to keep it aloft in soaring flight over the ocean.

The function of the great crest on the back of *Pteranodon*'s head, often as long as the skull itself, is unknown. It could have been an aid for flight, perhaps acting as a stabilizer, or being used for steering or braking; or it could simply have acted as an aerodynamic counterbalance to the heavy, elongated head.

The jaws were unusual for a pterosaur in being devoid of teeth. It is likely that *Pteranodon* fed like a modern pelican scooping up fish in its long, narrow jaws and swallowing them whole.

NAME: Quetzalcoatlus
TIME: Late Cretaceous
LOCALITY: North America (Texas)
SIZE: possibly up to 39 ft/12 m wingspan
Only fragments of this immense pterosaur have been found, in non-marine sediments, but they indicate a creature with enormously long, narrow wings and a weight of some 143 lb/65 kg. Should these findings prove correct, *Quetzalcoatlus* will be the largest flying vertebrate of all time.

Quetzalcoatlus was probably an accomplished glider. It lived far inland, unlike its marine pterodactyl relatives, and would have soared high above the ground on rising thermals. Like a modern vulture, its keen eyes would have spotted carrion from afar, and the long neck and toothless jaws could have probed far inside the carcass of a decaying dinosaur.

Small carnivorous dinosaurs

PROCOMPSOGNATHUS

SALTOPUS

COELOPHYSIS

COELURUS

COMPSOGNATHUS

ELAPHROSAURUS

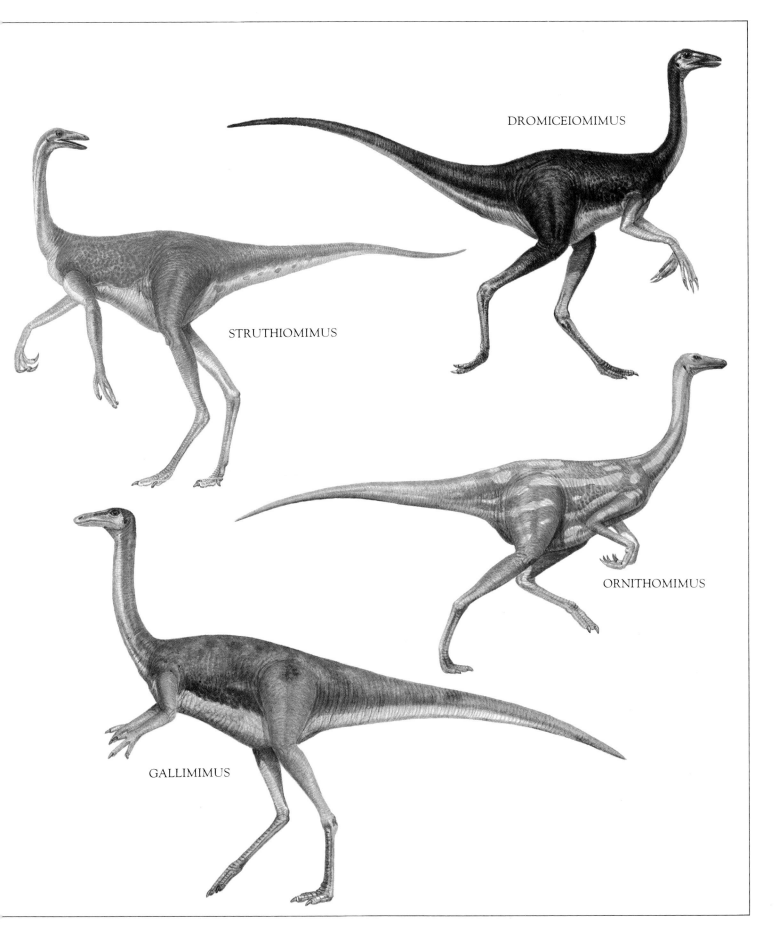

DROMICEIOMIMUS

STRUTHIOMIMUS

ORNITHOMIMUS

GALLIMIMUS

Small carnivorous dinosaurs

SUBORDER THEROPODA
The great reptilian order of "lizard-hipped" dinosaurs, the Saurischia, can be divided into 2 distinct groups (suborders) on the basis of what they ate. The flesh-eaters that walked upright on 2 legs belong to the Theropoda. The plant-eaters that moved about on all-fours belong to the Sauropodomorpha (see pp. 122–133). These differences in gait are reflected in the bones of the animals' feet.

INFRAORDER COELUROSAURIA
Traditionally, the carnivorous theropods are further subdivided (into infraorders) according to their size. There were large, massively built predators called carnosaurs (see pp. 114–121). There were medium-sized carnivores called deinonychosaurs, with a killing claw on each hind foot (see pp. 110–113). And there were small, lightweight hunters called coelurosaurs (below). Their name means "hollow-tailed lizards," and refers to the thin-walled, hollow bones that made up not only their tails, but most of their delicately built bodies.

FAMILY PODOKESAURIDAE
The earliest and most primitive of the small carnivorous theropods were the podokesaurs. As a family, they survived for some 50 million years — from the Late Triassic to the Early Jurassic.

Podokesaurids were little different from their immediate ancestors, the thecodontian reptiles (see pp. 94–97). They were fast, active predators, possibly hunting together in packs. They ran around on long legs, with slender necks and long tails outstretched to balance their bodies. The arms were shorter than the legs, and were used for grasping prey or transferring food to the mouth. The head was wedge-shaped, with many sharp, pointed teeth in the jaws.

NAME: *Procompsognathus*
TIME: **Late Triassic**
LOCALITY: **Europe (Germany)**
SIZE: **4 ft/1.2 m long**
This rapacious little beast was one of the earliest dinosaurs, and lived in the deserts that covered northern Europe during Triassic times. It would have chased after small lizards and insects on its long legs, running with only 3 of its 4 toes touching the ground. Each hand had 5 fingers; this is a primitive feature, since the trend in the more advanced dinosaurs was to have fewer fingers and toes.

NAME: *Saltopus*
TIME: **Late Triassic**
LOCALITY: **Europe (Scotland)**
SIZE: **2 ft/60 cm long**
Saltopus is one of the smallest and lightest dinosaurs discovered to date. In build, it was similar to its relative *Procompsognathus* (above), but much smaller and lighter. It was not as tall as a domestic cat, and probably weighed as little as 2 lb/1 kg.

Saltopus still had the primitive feature of 5 fingers on each hand, although the fourth and fifth were tiny. But it was more advanced than *Procompsognathus* in its hip/backbone arrangement. Four of the spine's sacral vertebrae were fused to its hips (rather than only the 3 of its relative), and this formed a fairly solid anchor for the long running legs.

NAME: *Coelophysis*
TIME: **Late Triassic**
LOCALITY: **North America (Connecticut and New Mexico)**
SIZE: **8–10 ft/2.4–3 m long**
The appearance of this comparatively large coelurosaur is well known from a find made in 1947 at Ghost Ranch in New Mexico. Here, a number of skeletons of different sizes were massed together, about a dozen of them complete. There were very young individuals (maybe just hatched) and adults, ranging in length from 3 to 10 ft/1 to 3 m. Finding all these animals together in one spot suggests that they lived as a group, and were all overcome at the same time.

This early dinosaur must have been a ferocious hunter — it was built for speed. Its slender, hollow-boned body probably weighed less than 50 lb/23 kg. The neck, tail and legs were long and slim, the tail making up about half the body length. The long, narrow head was armed with many sharp teeth, each with a cutting, serrated edge. The birdlike feet had 3 walking toes with sharp claws. There were 4 fingers on each hand, though only 3 were strong enough to grasp prey.

It is thought that *Coelophysis* roamed the upland forests, hunting in packs close to streams and lakes. Among their prey would have been the small, shrew-like mammals that had evolved towards the end of the Triassic period.

Two of the adult skeletons found in New Mexico contained the bones of tiny *Coelophysis* in their body cavities. Initially, paleontologists thought that this meant *Coelophysis* gave birth to live young, rather than laying eggs like most other reptiles. But the hip bones proved too narrow for this to be the case. The conclusion seems to be that this dinosaur was cannibalistic.

FAMILY COELURIDAE
The coelurids flourished worldwide from the Late Jurassic through to the Early Cretaceous. In lifestyle, they were similar to the podokesaurs — lightweight, active predators, running about on long legs, and grasping prey with their strong, clawed fingers. The number of fingers on each hand was reduced to 3.

NAME: *Coelurus*
TIME: **Late Jurassic**
LOCALITY: **North America (Wyoming)**
SIZE: **6 ft 6 in/2 m long**
Like all members of the coelurid family, *Coelurus* had a small, low head (only about 8 in/20 cm long), and the hollow, birdlike bones that characterized all the early dinosaurs.

This active predator lived in the forests and swamps of North America where prey was abundant. Its hands, with their 3 clawed fingers, were long and strong, designed for grasping the flesh of small animals like lizards, flying reptiles and mammals.

FAMILY COMPSOGNATHIDAE
To date, there is only one known member of this family. It was a contemporary of the coelurids, and closely resembled them in structure and lifestyle.

NAME: *Compsognathus*
TIME: **Late Jurassic**
LOCALITY: **Europe (Germany and France)**
SIZE: **2 ft/60 cm long**
This tiny, 2-legged creature, with the unlikely name of "pretty jaw," probably weighed no more than 8 lb/3.6 kg, and stood no taller than a chicken.

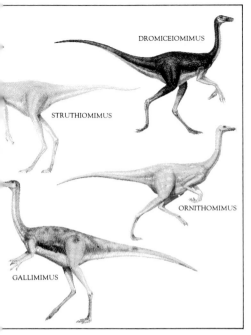

DROMICEIOMIMUS

STRUTHIOMIMUS

ORNITHOMIMUS

GALLIMIMUS

Compsognathus must have been a swift hunter, since the bones of a tiny lizard were found in the abdominal cavity of the specimen unearthed in Germany. The whole body was designed for speed. It had the typical hollow bones of a coelurosaur; a long neck for good stretch; an even longer tail for balance; short, grasping arms with only 2 pincer-like fingers; and slender legs with long shins, birdlike feet and 3 clawed toes on each. (A tiny fourth toe pointed backward.)

In fact, *Compsognathus* is similar in structure to the first known bird, *Archaeopteryx* (*see p. 176*). The two creatures were contemporaries, both living during Late Jurassic times among the wooded islands and lagoons of today's southern Germany.

FAMILY ORNITHOMIMIDAE

The so-called "bird mimics" were a specialized offshoot of the coelurosaurs. About the same height and proportions as a modern ostrich, they seem to have had a similar lifestyle to that bird, hence the popular name of the group — "ostrich dinosaurs." They were widespread in North America and East Asia in Mid-Cretaceous times, but seem to have died out before the end of that period.

All were large, long-legged sprinters. They probably traveled the open plains in groups, looking after their young while on the move, as do modern flightless birds.

Unlike most other dinosaurs, ornithomimids had no teeth. In place of the teeth, there was a horny, birdlike beak, which was used to snap up small animals and insects. Other special features were exceptionally large eyes and big brains. Both features would have made them well-coordinated, efficient and intelligent hunters.

NAME: *Elaphrosaurus*
TIME: **Late Jurassic**
LOCALITY: **Africa (Tanzania)**
SIZE: **11 ft 6 in/3.5 m long**
Only one skeleton of *Elaphrosaurus* has been found, and, unfortunately, the skull was missing. Since the characteristic feature of the ornithomimids was that they had no teeth, it is impossible to say whether *Elaphrosaurus* belonged to this family. Loose teeth have been found in the same sediments, and these may belong to this dinosaur.

The rest of *Elaphrosaurus'* skeleton, however, seems to be intermediate in structure between the earlier, Jurassic coelurids (*above*) and the later, Cretaceous ornithomimids (*below*). It may be that *Elaphrosaurus*, or some closely related animal, was the ancestor of the ostrich dinosaur group.

NAME: *Dromiceiomimus*
TIME: **Late Cretaceous**
LOCALITY: **North America (Alberta)**
SIZE: **11 ft 6 in/3.5 m long**
All ornithomimids had long, slender legs, with the shin bone (tibia) about 20 percent longer than the thigh bone (femur) — a sure sign of a sprinter. *Dromiceiomimus* had even longer shins than average, which indicates that it was a very fast runner indeed.

The size of the brain cavity and eye sockets in the skull of *Dromiceiomimus* show that it had an exceptionally large brain (proportionally larger than that of a modern ostrich), and huge eyes (proportionally larger than those of any modern land animal). So, like modern nocturnal or night-hunting creatures, *Dromiceiomimus* most probably hunted after dark, chasing small mammals and lizards through the gathering gloom of the deciduous woods in which it lived.

NAME: *Ornithomimus*
TIME: **Late Cretaceous**
LOCALITY: **North America (Colorado and Montana) and Asia (Tibet)**
SIZE: **11 ft 6 in/3.5 m long**
This ostrich dinosaur was the typical ornithomimid. It had a small, thin-boned head with a large brain cavity, no teeth and beaklike jaws.

Ornithomimus would have sprinted along with its body parallel to the ground, balanced by its extra-long, out-stretched tail. This was kept stiff by strong ligaments that lashed the vertebrae together, to form a rigid structure. Its neck would have curved upward in a long S-bend, holding the head high for good visibility through the large eyes. The arms would have dangled above the ground, with the dextrous, clawed fingers held ready to grasp potential food.

Like other ornithomimids, *Ornithomimus* was probably omnivorous, eating leaves, fruit, insects and small animals, such as lizards and mammals. It may even have raided the nests of other dinosaurs and eaten their eggs, pecking through the shells with its horny beak. If it were caught by an enraged parent, it would have employed its only means of defense — running away at a speed, it is estimated, of up to 30 mph/50 kmph.

NAME: *Struthiomimus*
TIME: **Late Cretaceous**
LOCALITY: **North America (Alberta and New Jersey)**
SIZE: **11 ft 6 in/3.5 m long**
For many years after its discovery in 1914, *Struthiomimus* was thought to be the same animal as *Ornithomimus* (*above*). But more detailed research in 1972 showed that they were indeed different, albeit in small ways. *Struthiomimus* had longer arms than its relative, and stronger, curved claws on its fingers. It also existed slightly earlier in the Late Cretaceous than *Ornithomimus*, and individuals probably hunted along riverbanks in open country.

NAME: *Gallimimus*
TIME: **Late Cretaceous**
LOCALITY: **Asia (Mongolia)**
SIZE: **13 ft/4 m long**
This is the largest ostrich dinosaur to be discovered to date. It differs from its close relatives, *Ornithomimus* and *Struthiomimus*, in 2 respects. It had a long snout ending in a broad, flat-tipped beak, and its hands seem poorly designed for grasping. Perhaps it was a specialist feeder; it could have dug out other dinosaurs' eggs buried in the soil with its spadelike hands, and cracked them open with its heavy beak.

An exciting discovery in 1965, from Late Cretaceous deposits in the Gobi Desert of Mongolia, has led paleontologists to believe that there were much larger birdlike dinosaurs around at the same time as *Gallimimus* (*above*). The fossil find consisted of a pair of shoulder bones and arms belonging to what must have been a gigantic creature. Each arm measured 8 ft/2.5 m in length, from the shoulder down to the tip of the 3 powerful, clawed fingers. Each claw bone alone was about 10 in/25 cm long, and would have carried an even longer nail.

No other parts of the skeleton have been found, so it is impossible to say whether this animal was an ornithomimid. It was certainly a very large theropod dinosaur. Predictably, it has been given the descriptive name of *Deinocheirus*, meaning "terrible hand," and is placed in a family of its own.

Carnivorous dinosaurs

OVIRAPTOR

DEINONYCHUS

DROMAEOSAURUS

VELOCIRAPTOR

SAURORNITHOLESTES

SAURORNITHOIDES

STENONYCHOSAURUS

BARYONYX

Carnivorous dinosaurs

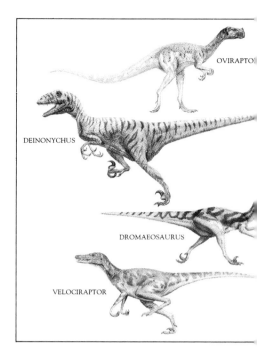

OVIRAPTOR

DEINONYCHUS

DROMAEOSAURUS

VELOCIRAPTOR

FAMILY OVIRAPTORIDAE

This small family of toothless thero-pods lived in Late Cretaceous times in eastern Asia, and were named the "egg thieves" because of their suspected eating habits. They had large heads and short, deep beaks — quite unlike the long, narrow skulls and pointed beaks of their relatives, the ornithomimids or "ostrich dinosaurs" (see p. 109).

NAME: *Oviraptor*
TIME: **Late Cretaceous**
LOCALITY: **Asia (Mongolia)**
SIZE: **6 ft/1.8 m long**

This "egg thief," for whom the family is named, had a distinctive skull, different from that of any other dinosaur. The head was almost parrotlike — short and deep, with a stumpy beak and no teeth. Powerful muscles operated the curved jaws, and gave the beak enough bite-power to crush objects as hard as bones. There was also a small, hornlike crest above the snout.

Oviraptor's body, however, was typical of the small, flesh-eating coelurosaurs. There were 3 grasping fingers on each hand, with strongly curved nails (each about 3 in/8 cm long). The animal walked upright on long, slender legs, each with 3 clawed toes. The body was balanced by the long, outstretched tail.

It seems likely that *Oviraptor* ate eggs. The first specimen discovered in 1924 was found preserved with a clutch of eggs laid by the horned dinosaur *Protoceratops* (see p. 165), the inference being that the "egg thief" was overcome, maybe in a sudden sandstorm, while raiding the nest.

FAMILY DROMAEOSAURIDAE

Members of this family must have been among the most fearsome predators of the Cretaceous period in North America and Asia. They are the only representatives of the Infraorder Deinonychosauria, the "terrible-clawed lizards," and structurally seem to have been an intermediate group of dinosaurs. They had the light, speedy body of a coelurosaur, and the large head of a carnosaur.

Although they were no larger than many of the other meat-eaters around at the time, dromaeosaurs were formidable predators. They had a lethal weapon in the form of a large, sickle-shaped claw on the second toe of each foot. They were also armed with sharp, pointed teeth and clawed, grasping hands. They had large brains, and were intelligent enough to have hunted in packs.

NAME: *Deinonychus*
TIME: **Early Cretaceous**
LOCALITY: **North America (Montana)**
SIZE: **10–13 ft/3–4 m long**

The discovery of *Deinonychus* in 1964 in the claystones of Montana is one of the most exciting finds in the recent history of paleontology. Well-preserved skeletons reveal a dinosaur built for the chase and the kill — a fast, agile, intelligent predator.

Deinonychus had the lightweight body characteristic of the coelurosaurs, from which it probably evolved. It was, on average, 10 ft/3 m long, stood about 6 ft/1.8 m tall, and weighed some 150 lbs/68 kg. The large head was equipped with many meat-shearing teeth, with serrated edges, which were curved backward to allow great chunks of flesh to be torn from the prey. The arms were quite long for a theropod (though still much shorter than the legs), and hung from sturdy shoulder girdles. Each hand had 3 grasping fingers with long, strongly curved claws.

The legs were slender, with long shin bones and 4 clawed toes on each foot. The first toe was tiny and non-functional, as in most of the later theropods; the third and fourth toes carried the whole weight of the body.

But it was the remarkable adaptation of the second toe that gave *Deinonychus* its most offensive weapon — and its name, which means "terrible claw." The second toe on each foot had a large, sickle-shaped claw, 5 in/13 cm long. This would have been used like a dagger, to slash through a victim's flesh as *Deinonychus* stood on one leg and kicked with its free foot.

When *Deinonychus* ran, the sickle-clawed toes were flicked back and held clear of the ground. The body was held horizontally and balanced by the long, outstretched tail. This was kept rigid by bundles of bony rods that grew out from the vertebrae themselves, and formed a supporting framework to stiffen the tail along most of its length. When *Deinonychus* was standing on one foot and attacking with the other, balance was essential and a tail like a ramrod would have made the pose easier to hold. The big brain (evident from the size of the skull's brain cavity) would have coordinated a finely tuned nervous system to control such complex movements.

One of the finds in Montana revealed 5 complete skeletons of *Deinonychus* lying by the body of a large, plant-eating dinosaur called *Tenontosaurus*, which measured some 24 ft/7.3 m long (see p. 141). This assemblage of bodies was most probably brought together by chance after death, washed down by a

flood into a hollow or river basin.

But one could perhaps reconstruct the scene that took place some 140 million years ago. A small pack of *Deinonychus* surrounded the plant-eater. Some may have leapt on its back, and held on with their clawed hands, while slashing through its thick hide by repeated kicks of the daggerlike, killing claws on their feet. The plant-eater may have wounded or even killed some of its attackers by lashing out with its long, heavy tail or rearing up on hindlegs to crash down on their bodies. But, perhaps in the end, it succumbed and bled to death, while the pack of carnivores waited nearby.

The active, predatory lifestyle suggested by the anatomy of *Deinonychus* is seen by some paleontologists as strong evidence that it was an endothermic ("warm-blooded") creature, and could control its body temperature, as do modern birds and mammals (see pp. 92–93).

NAME: *Dromaeosaurus*
TIME: **Late Cretaceous**
LOCALITY: **North America (Alberta)**
SIZE: **6 ft/1.8 m long**

This dromaeosaur was the first of the sickle-clawed dinosaurs to be discovered, in Canada in 1914, and gave its name to the whole family. However, it was not until *Deinonychus* (above) was unearthed in 1964 that the true nature and significance of *Dromaeosaurus* was assessed. Up until then, it was regarded as either a large coelurosaur or a small carnosaur; the new find made it apparent that the creature belonged to an intermediate group, and shared features with both types of theropod.

Dromaeosaurus is only known from its skull and some odd bones. But from such meager finds, paleontologists can piece together a picture of a dinosaur smaller than *Deinonychus*, intelligent

SAURORNITHOLESTES

SAURORNITHOIDES

STENONYCHOSAURUS

BARYONYX

and agile, a rapacious predator with large, killing claws on its toes, though not so large as those of *Deinonychus*.

NAME: *Velociraptor*
TIME: Late Cretaceous
LOCALITY: Asia (Mongolia and China)
SIZE: 6 ft/1.8 m long
A dramatic find in Mongolia during 1971 revealed two fossilized skeletons — *Velociraptor* locked in combat with the horned dinosaur *Protoceratops* (*see* p. 165). A great struggle had obviously taken place, since *Velociraptor* had died grasping the head shield of *Protoceratops* with its hands, while ripping into the belly with its sickle-clawed feet. *Protoceratops* had managed to cave in the chest of *Velociraptor*, possibly with its horny beak, before it, too, died. No scene could be more indicative of the ferocious lifestyle of the dromaeosaurs in general, and *Velociraptor* in particular.

The long, low, flat-snouted head of *Velociraptor* is the main feature that distinguishes it from other dromaeosaurs, which typically had short, deep heads. In other respects, it was similar to them, although its sickle claws were relatively small.

NAME: *Saurornitholestes*
TIME: Late Cretaceous
LOCALITY: North America (Alberta)
SIZE: 6 ft/1.8 m long
In 1978, the skull and some arm bones and teeth of this dinosaur were found. It is not clear whether it was a dromaeosaur or one of the "bird-lizards," the saurornithoidids (*below*).

The scanty remains suggest that *Saurornitholestes* had a larger brain than was usual among the dromaeosaurs (but not among the saurornithoidids), and that it possessed powerful hands adapted for grasping. The restoration on p. 111 is based on the evidence available, but remains highly speculative.

FAMILY SAURORNITHOIDIDAE
Like the dromaeosaurs, these "bird-lizards" were fast, intelligent, rapacious coelurosaurs, though smaller and lighter in build. They also had a sickle-shaped, killer claw on each foot.

But the skull of these saurornithoidids shows the greatest development. The brain cavity was large; relative to body weight, it was about 7 times the volume of the brain cavity of their modern relative, the crocodile. Combined with this well-developed nervous system, these dinosaurs had large eyes, very likely with binocular vision.

Thus, the saurornithoidids of Late Cretaceous times — living in North America, southern Europe and Mongolia — were among the most efficient hunters of the carnivorous dinosaurs.

NAME: *Saurornithoides*
TIME: Late Cretaceous
LOCALITY: Asia (Mongolia)
SIZE: 6 ft 6 in/2 m long
Although the skull was birdlike — long, low and light — it housed a large brain, giving its owner an intelligence far superior to that of most other dinosaurs around at the time. The eyes must have been huge relative to the head, judging from the size of their sockets. Moreover, their position suggests that these dinosaurs could have had binocular vision — all the better to judge distances between objects.

Such large eyes suggest nocturnal habits. *Saurornithoides*, together with other members of its family, was probably active after twilight, dodging through the woods to hunt down small mammals and reptiles.

NAME: *Stenonychosaurus*
TIME: Late Cretaceous
LOCALITY: North America (Alberta)
SIZE: 6 ft 6 in/2 m long
This was the "brainiest" dinosaur of them all — the brain cavity in the skull is, relative to its body size, the largest so far discovered. Its brain was larger than that of a modern emu. Comparing it to that of a mammal, scientists reckon that *Stenonychosaurus* was about as intelligent as one of the less-intelligent modern mammals, such as an opossum.

Only incomplete skeletons of this saurornithoidid have been found. It seems to differ little in structure from *Saurornithoides* (*above*), leading some paleontologists to think that it is actually the same animal. However, the clawed fingers of the *Stenonychosaurus* specimens seem longer and slimmer than those of *Saurornithoides*. Also

Stenonychosaurus was probably of a lighter overall build; it is estimated to have weighed between 60 and 100 lb/27 and 45 kg.

Like other members of its family, *Stenonychosaurus* possessed a large brain and large eyes — each eye was about 2 in/52 mm across, the same size as that of a modern ostrich. Combined with its slim build, these features would have made it an agile runner and a night-hunter, with fast reflexes and well-developed senses.

FAMILY BARYONYCHIDAE
This family was created in 1986 to cover one member — an oddity among theropods. A single skeleton was discovered in 1983 in Sussex, southern England; it had a peculiar skull and forelimbs, unlike those of any other dinosaur.

NAME: *Baryonyx*
TIME: Early Cretaceous
LOCALITY: Europe (England)
SIZE: 20 ft/6 m long
Two unusual features made this large, theropod dinosaur quite distinct from any other. First, it had a huge, curved claw, about 1 ft/30 cm long — hence its scientific name *Baryonyx*, meaning "heavy claw," and its popular nickname of "Claws." However, the claw was not attached to the skeleton, so it is not known whether it was part of the fore- or hindfeet.

Paleontologists assume that the claw belonged to one of the forefeet, since the forelimbs of this dinosaur were unusually thick and powerful for a theropod, and could therefore have carried such a weapon. In addition, the great size of the animal would have made the claw difficult to wield if it had been on one of the hindfeet.

The second peculiar feature of *Baryonyx* was its skull, which was long and narrow, rather like that of a crocodile. The jaws were armed with a great number of small, pointed teeth, twice as many as a theropod usually possessed. There was also a bony crest on top of the head. The neck was not so flexible as that of other theropods, and could not have been carried in their characteristic S-shaped curve.

The habits of this mysterious beast may be surmised from some fish remains that were found with the skeleton. It is possible that *Baryonyx* hunted on all-fours along riverbanks, hooking fish out of the water with its long, gafflike claws on the front legs — just as grizzly bears do today.

Large carnivorous dinosaurs

TERATOSAURUS

PROCERATOSAURUS

DILOPHOSAURUS

EUSTREPTOSPONDYLUS

YANGCHUANOSAURUS

CERATOSAURUS

ALLOSAURUS

MEGALOSAURUS

Large carnivorous dinosaurs

TERATOSAURUS

PROCERATOSAURUS

DILOPHOS

EUSTREPTOSPONDYLUS

INFRAORDER CARNOSAURIA

Some of the largest terrestrial carnivores that have ever existed belong to this group of theropod dinosaurs — the carnosaurs or "flesh lizards." *Tyrannosaurus* is the most familiar member of the group. They were massively built animals, and dominated life in Jurassic and Cretaceous times.

Their efficiency as predators is, however, debatable. In reality, the largest of them, such as *Tyrannosaurus* and *Tarbosaurus*, could have been part-time scavengers. They may have been the "hyenas" of the dinosaur world rather than the "lions." Their sheer bulk would, most likely, have precluded any sustained chase. But they could have ambushed prey, and attacked in short bursts of speed, like a modern tiger.

There were also other smaller carnosaurs, lighter and more agile than their giant contemporaries.

FAMILY MEGALOSAURIDAE

The earliest well-known carnosaurs belong to this family of "great lizards." Their remains have been found in North America, Africa and Europe, and as a group they span a period of 140 million years — from the Early Jurassic to the end of the Cretaceous.

All were massively built, big-boned creatures. The large head was high and narrow, equipped with powerful jaws and many sharp, saw-edged teeth. The arms were short but strong. The legs were long and massive enough to support the great body weight on the 3 spreading, clawed toes of each foot (a tiny fourth toe was also present), yet light enough to allow the creature to amble along quite quickly.

NAME: *Teratosaurus*
TIME: **Late Triassic**
LOCALITY: **Europe (Germany)**
SIZE: **20 ft/6 m long**
This is a puzzling beast among the dinosaurs. From fragments of its skeleton, mostly teeth, paleontologists have tentatively constructed a picture of *Teratosaurus* as a primitive carnosaur.

It was a large, 2-legged creature, with a heavy head and many sharp, curved teeth. Its body was also heavy, with a short neck and long, stiffened tail. Sturdy legs ended in 3 powerful, clawed toes, for walking and ripping flesh. (A fourth toe was present, but it was tiny.) The short, strong arms had grasping fingers with curved claws.

From the remains of *Teratosaurus*, and fragments of related beasts found in southern Africa, some paleontologists postulate that a group of large, meat-eating theropods may have existed some 60 million years before the main stock of carnosaurs appeared, in Early Jurassic times. *Teratosaurus* may, therefore, be the earliest-known relative of the megalosaur family.

However, other paleontologists reckon that it may be an early member of the prosauropod group of dinosaurs (*see pp. 122–125*) or even a large representative of the thecodontians, from which group arose the ancestors of the dinosaurs (*see pp. 94–97*).

NAME: *Proceratosaurus*
TIME: **Middle Jurassic**
LOCALITY: **Europe (England)**
SIZE: **16 ft/5 m long**
This early carnosaur is known only from a single skull. Although it is longer than average, the skull shows the same general features as other primitive carnosaurs. But there is one atypical feature — a small horn above the snout. This suggests that this creature may have been an ancestor, or even an early member, of the ceratosaurs — those carnosaurs characterized by a nose horn (*see p. 117*).

The restoration on p. 114 shows *Proceratosaurus* as a typical carnosaur — large head, short neck, heavy body, long tail, short arms with clawed fingers, and long running legs each with 3 toes.

NAME: *Dilophosaurus*
TIME: **Early Jurassic**
LOCALITY: **North America (Arizona)**
SIZE: **20 ft/6 m long**
First discovered in 1942 by an expedition from the University of California, *Dilophosaurus* seems to have been a lightly built carnosaur. This sounds like a contradiction, but it was intermediate in structure between the 2 groups. Its head was large (a typical carnosaur feature) but lightboned, while its neck, tail and arms were long and slender (typical coelurosaur features, *see pp. 106–113*).

The skull of *Dilophosaurus* was unusual for any group. A pair of semicircular, bony crests rose vertically on either side of the skull. Although wafer-thin in places, they were strengthened by vertical struts of bone. At the back of the head, the tip of each crest narrowed into a spike.

The function of these head crests remains a mystery. Some paleontologists think that they could have been sexual display structures, and that only the males had them — a theory supported by the fact that not all specimens found had the crests. Indeed, there were none on the first few skeletons unearthed, and the animals were thought to have been a species of *Megalosaurus* (*below*). The crests have never been found actually attached to the skull, but lying nearby, so there is a certain amount of educated guesswork about their position in life.

The jaws of *Dilophosaurus* give a clue to its lifestyle. The lower jaw was strong and full of long, sharp, thin teeth. The upper jaw had a cluster of teeth at the front, separate from the rest of the teeth — rather like the arrangement in the jaws of a modern crocodile.

So, although *Dilophosaurus* had a large head and strong jaws, it probably did not kill its victims by biting them; the thin teeth and delicate head crests would have been too vulnerable in a fight. More likely, this dinosaur caught and ripped its prey with the clawed feet and hands. Or, like many of its relatives, it could have fed on the corpses of creatures killed by stronger carnosaurs.

NAME: *Eustreptospondylus*
TIME: **Middle Jurassic to Late Cretaceous**
LOCALITY: **Europe (England)**
SIZE: **23 ft/7 m long**
A nearly complete skeleton of this early megalosaur was unearthed in southern England, and described in 1964. It is now mounted in the University Museum of Oxford, and although parts of its skull are missing, it remains the best-preserved specimen of any European carnosaur discovered to date.

In build, *Eustreptospondylus* was so similar to *Megalosaurus* that, until 1964, it was still thought to be that dinosaur.

NAME: *Megalosaurus*
TIME: **Early Jurassic to Late Jurassic**
LOCALITY: **Europe (England and France) and Africa (Morocco)**
SIZE: **30 ft/9 m long**
Megalosaurus, or "great lizard," may not be the biggest or heaviest dinosaur, but it can claim a number of other "firsts." The first dinosaur bone on record, dis-

YANGCHUANOSAURUS

...AURUS

...LOSAURUS

ALLOSAURUS

covered in England in 1676, probably belonged to *Megalosaurus*. It was the first dinosaur to be scientifically named and described, in the 1820s. And it was one of the 3 creatures that prompted the English paleontologist Richard Owen in 1841 to coin a name for the group; he chose "Dinosauria," meaning "terrible lizards."

With an overall length of 30 ft/9 m, a height of 10 ft/3 m, and an estimated weight in life of 1 US ton/900 kg, *Megalosaurus* was a massive creature, with the body of a typical carnosaur. A short, muscular neck carried the large head, with its powerful, hinged jaws armed with curved, saw-edged fangs. Its fingers and toes were strong and clawed. With such weapons, *Megalosaurus* was well equipped to attack and kill the large, long-necked, plant-eating dinosaurs of the day (*see pp. 126–133*).

Megalosaurus has left its mark clearly in southern England. Trackways of great footprints are found in the limestone rocks, and trace how these bulky bipeds walked upright on 2 legs, their toes pointing slightly inward, long tails maybe swinging from side to side at each step to balance their heavy bodies.

FAMILY ALLOSAURIDAE

Allosaurs were similar in build to megalosaurs, but even larger. They were the largest carnosaurs around during Late Jurassic times, and lumbered through every continent in the world. But they were soon to be rivaled by even bigger creatures — the tyrannosaurs of the Cretaceous (*see pp. 118–121*).

NAME: *Yangchuanosaurus*
TIME: **Late Jurassic**
LOCALITY: **Asia (China)**
SIZE: **up to 33 ft/10 m long**
The skeleton of this large carnosaur was discovered in Sichuan (Szechuan) Province of eastern China, and described in 1978. It is now on display in Beijing's (Peking) Natural History Museum.

It was a typical allosaur, with a huge head and powerful jaws, equipped with sharp fangs that curved backward and were serrated along their edges like steak knives. The neck was short, thick but flexible. The long tail made up about half the total body length. It was flattened from side to side and held out stiffly to balance the deep, narrow body of the animal as it strode along on its huge, pillarlike legs. Three great, clawed toes bore the whole weight of the body. (As usual, there was a small first toe that pointed backward.) Short arms ended in 3 powerful, clawed fingers.

The skull of *Yangchuanosaurus* differs from that of other allosaurs in having more teeth at the front of the jaws, and a bony hump above the snout.

NAME: *Allosaurus*
TIME: **Late Jurassic to Early Cretaceous**
LOCALITY: **North America (Colorado, Utah and Wyoming), Africa (Tanzania) and Australia**
SIZE: **up to 39 ft/12 m long**
This enormous carnosaur, the largest of the allosaurs, was the most fearsome predator of the Late Jurassic. It must have weighed between 1 and 2 US tons/1–2 tonnes, and stood some 15 ft/4.6 m tall.

In appearance, it was a bigger version of its close relative and contemporary *Megalosaurus* (*above*), although it had a few peculiarities of its own. The head, for example, had 2 bony bumps above the eyes, and a narrow bony ridge running from between the eyes down to the tip of the snout.

The skull was massive in size, but not in weight. This was due to several large openings ("windows" or *fenestrae*) between various bones of the skull that reduced its solid structure to an intricate network of bony struts, so lightening its weight. The bones themselves were only loosely articulated with one another (a feature also seen in the skulls of other large carnosaurs, such as *Ceratosaurus, below*). This resulted in a degree of flexibility, which added to the strength of the lightly built skull.

Allosaurus' efficiency as a hunter is a matter of debate. Some paleontologists think it was too heavy and clumsy to run down prey, and therefore probably fed on carrion. Others believe that it was

quite agile for its size, and may even have hunted in packs to bring down the giant, plant-eating dinosaurs of the day, such as *Apatosaurus* (=*Brontosaurus*) and *Diplodocus*. Bones of *Apatosaurus* have, in fact, been found in western North America with the marks of teeth similar to those of *Allosaurus* on them, and similar, broken teeth have also been found scattered around other specimens of this plant-eater.

FAMILY CERATOSAURIDAE
This family of megalosaur-type dinosaurs was characterized by a small horn on the snout. Contemporaries of the other large carnosaurs, they lived in North America and East Africa in Late Jurassic times. But their remains are rare in comparison to those of their relatives.

NAME: *Ceratosaurus*
TIME: **Late Jurassic**
LOCALITY: **North America (Colorado and Wyoming)**
SIZE: **20 ft/6 m long**
This "horned lizard" had a heavier skull than other carnosaurs because of the presence of a pair of bony ridges above its eyes, and a low crest, or horn, on its snout.

The function of the horn remains a mystery, although various suggestions have been put forward as to its use. It could have been used for defense, but it seems too small and not well placed for a fight. Or it could have been for sexual display, with only the males possessing it and using it in the ritualistic, head-butting battles probably engaged in to decide hierarchy among the group.

Ceratosaurus was evidently an active predator. It had massive jaws, armed with sharp, curved teeth. The short arms had 4 powerful, clawed fingers, and the long legs had 3 clawed toes on each foot. An unusual feature was a narrow row of bony plates running down the center of its back and tail, giving the appearance of a serrated crest. This could have been a device for losing heat from the body, similar to the back fin of *Spinosaurus* (*see p. 120*) or the plates of *Stegosaurus* (*see p. 156*).

Footprints thought to be those of *Ceratosaurus* have been preserved in the dinosaur-rich rocks of the Morrison Formation in the western USA. These ancient trackways suggest that these dinosaurs moved in groups, and maybe cooperated in packs to bring down the larger dinosaurs.

Large carnivorous dinosaurs

ACROCANTHOSAURUS

SPINOSAURUS

ALIORAMUS

ALBERTOSAURUS

DASPLETOSAURUS

TARBOSAURUS

TYRANNOSAURUS

Large carnivorous dinosaurs

FAMILY SPINOSAURIDAE

These dinosaurs were a specialized group of large theropods that may have evolved from the megalosaurs in Cretaceous times. Their special feature was an elongation of the back vertebrae, which produced a pronounced ridge down the center of the backbone. Some spinosaurs had an extreme development of this ridge into a tall crest or "sail," which may have been used to regulate body temperature in the same way as proposed for that of the "fin-backed" pelycosaurs (see pp. 186–189).

NAME: *Acrocanthosaurus*
TIME: **Early Cretaceous**
LOCALITY: **North America (Oklahoma)**
SIZE: **43 ft/13 m long**

In 1950, several skeletons of this enormous, flesh-eating dinosaur were found in North America. Its name means "top spiny lizard," and refers to the elongated spines (up to 1 ft/30 cm long) that grew up from its backbone. These would have been covered by a web of skin, to form a pronounced ridge or crest running down the length of the back.

The crest of *Acrocanthosaurus* was low in comparison to that of some of its relatives living in other parts of the world. For example, *Altispinax* of western Europe had spines that were 4 times the length of the vertebrae from which they grew, while *Spinosaurus* of Africa had a "sail" over 6 ft/1.8 m high on its back (below).

NAME: *Spinosaurus*
TIME: **Late Cretaceous**
LOCALITY: **Africa (Egypt and Niger)**
SIZE: **39 ft/12 m long**

The most spectacular member of the family, *Spinosaurus* was not only enormous — ranking with the largest of the carnosaurs — but also had an extravagant "sail" on its back, taller than a modern man. Broad, club-shaped spines, 6 ft 6 in/2 m long, projected upward from the backbone, and would have been covered over with skin. The whole arrangement was reminiscent of the tall fin on the back of the pelycosaur *Dimetrodon* (see p. 188).

The function of this strange, and highly vulnerable, structure is not known for certain. One theory is that the sail acted as a crude device to regulate body temperature. When the animal stood with the sail turned sideways-on to the sun's rays, its large surface area, amply supplied with blood vessels, would absorb heat rapidly; the warmed-up blood would then be carried all over the body. To cool down, the animal would angle its sail into the wind, so dissipating heat.

The advantage to *Spinosaurus* would be that it could warm up quickly in the early morning, and be prepared for hunting well in advance of its cold, sluggish prey, mostly other reptiles.

An alternative theory is that the sail was brightly colored, and was used for sexual display by the males to attract the attention of the females. Males could also have used their sails to threaten each other during the ritualistic fights engaged in to establish dominance.

There is no reason why both theories cannot apply, with the sail being used as a heat exchanger *and* as a sexual ploy.

At about the same time as *Spinosaurus* inhabited western Africa, a large, 2-legged, plant-eating dinosaur, *Ouranosaurus*, also lived in the region. It, too, had a high sail on its back (see p. 145). There is therefore good reason to believe that some environmental or climatic factor influenced the development of these structures.

The bony sail would have increased *Spinosaurus*' weight considerably. The total body weight is estimated to have been some 7 US tons/6 tonnes — close to that of *Tyrannosaurus*, the largest carnosaur of them all (below).

The arms of *Spinosaurus* were more massive than usual among large theropods, and it is possible that it spent some of its time on all-fours, which was an unusual posture among the 2-legged carnosaurs. Its teeth were also different from those of other carnosaurs; they were straight rather than curved.

FAMILY TYRANNOSAURIDAE

The largest terrestrial carnivores that ever lived belonged to this family of "tyrant lizards." It was a small, specialized group, with less than a dozen types (genera) identified to date. Yet its members have inspired the popular notion of what flesh-eating dinosaurs looked like and how they behaved.

The remains of tyrannosaurs have been found in Asia and western North America. As a group they were short-lived, appearing in Late Cretaceous times and disappearing at the end of that period in the mysterious mass-extinction of all the dinosaurs. Their existence, spanning less than 15 million years, was only a "moment" in terms of the evolution of life.

NAME: *Albertosaurus*
TIME: **Late Cretaceous**
LOCALITY: **North America (Alberta)**
SIZE: **26 ft/8 m long**

This "small" tyrannosaur shows all the features common to the family. It was massively built, with a big head and short body, balanced at the hips by a long, strong tail. Pillarlike legs, with 3-toed, spreading feet, supported the great body weight.

Albertosaurus and other members of its family were specialized theropods. Their arms were puny in comparison to the body size. They were so short that they could not have reached up to the mouth. There were only 2 fingers on each hand, which would not have been very effective for grasping prey. And although the jaws could be opened wide, the bones of the skull were rigidly fixed, without the same degree of flexibility as between those in the skulls of the allosaurs (see p. 117).

Tyrannosaurs had a well-developed second set of ribs on the underside of the body. A possible explanation for these extra ribs and the short arms could be that when a tyrannosaur rested, it lay on its belly. The innards would have been supported by the extra ribs, and not crushed by the great weight of the body. When the animal got up, its tiny arms stopped the bulky frame from sliding forward, and steadied it as it rose to its feet.

There is also a suggestion that the tiny arms were used by the males to hold onto the females while mating.

ETOSAURUS

TARBOSAURUS

NNOSAURUS

NAME: *Alioramus*
TIME: Late Cretaceous
LOCALITY: Asia (Mongolia)
SIZE: 20 ft/6 m long

A group of Asiatic tyrannosaurs, represented by *Alioramus*, differed from "typical" tyrannosaurs in the shape of their skulls. Whereas most members of the family had deep skulls with short snouts, *Alioramus* and its relatives had shallow skulls with long snouts. There were also some bony knobs or spikes on the face between the eyes and tip of the snout. These may have been display features to distinguish the sexes, perhaps with the males having larger structures than the females.

Alioramus and its tyrannosaur relatives lived in Asia and western North America during the Late Cretaceous period. At that time, the modern continents of Asia and North America were joined into one landmass; the Bering Strait that separates them today was then dry land (*see pp. 10–11*). But the North American part was divided in two by a shallow sea that ran north–south, and halved the land into "Asiamerica" to the west, and "Euramerica" to the east. Animals, including the great tyrannosaurs, could have migrated freely between Asia and western North America, but relatively few seem to have managed to cross the great divide over to the eastern half of the landmass. However, the remains of one tyrannosaur, similar to *Albertosaurus* (*above*), have been found in the eastern USA.

NAME: *Daspletosaurus*
TIME: Late Cretaceous
LOCALITY: North America (Alberta)
SIZE: 28 ft/8.5 m long

The short, deep jaws of this massive meat-eater held even larger teeth than other tyrannosaurs, though they were fewer in number. Each tooth was dagger-sharp, curved and saw-edged.

Formidable jaws, clawed feet and sheer bulk (with a body weight of up to 4 US tons/3.6 tonnes — these were the weapons used by *Daspletosaurus*. It was capable of killing the large, horned dinosaurs (ceratopians) that browsed in the forests of northern North America at the time.

NAME: *Tarbosaurus*
TIME: Late Cretaceous
LOCALITY: Asia (Mongolia)
SIZE: up to 46 ft/14 m long

This giant carnosaur lumbered around the lands of central Asia, eating anything it came across, whether dead or alive. Its skills as a hunter are suspect, because of its sheer bulk. It could have preyed on the herbivorous duckbilled and armored dinosaurs that lived in its environment. It could also have supplemented its diet with the kills of other carnosaurs. It was big enough to scare off even the most tenacious predator, with the exception of its larger relative *Tyrannosaurus* (*below*), which lived in central Asia at the same time.

Many skeletons of *Tarbosaurus* have been unearthed in Mongolia, some of them complete. In structure, it was almost identical to *Tyrannosaurus*, but it was more lightly built and had a longer skull. Because the specimens are so well preserved in the rock, it is possible to analyze the upright posture of this typical tyrannosaur. The back would have been held almost horizontal, with the body balanced at the hips; the long, flexible neck curved abruptly upward from the body, with the heavy head held almost at right angles to it — a birdlike pose.

In the fossil finds, *Tarbosaurus*' head was pulled right back, toward its shoulders. This often happens when an animal dies, because the ligaments of the neck dry out and shrink, pulling the head backward into an unnatural position.

NAME: *Tyrannosaurus*
TIME: Late Cretaceous
LOCALITY: North America (Alberta, Montana, Saskatchewan, Texas and Wyoming) and Asia (Mongolia)
SIZE: up to 49 ft/15 m long

"The most terrifying engine of destruction ever to walk the earth" sums up the popular notion of this awesome theropod. It was the largest of the carnosaur dinosaurs, and certainly the largest terrestrial carnivore yet known.

On average, *Tyrannosaurus* was 39 ft/12 m long, up to 20 ft/6 m tall, and weighed about 8 US tons/7 tonnes (heavier than a modern, adult African bull elephant). Its head alone was over 4 ft/1.25 m long, and was armed with numerous fangs, each measuring some 6 in/15 cm in length.

No complete skeleton of *Tyrannosaurus* has yet been found, although innumerable bones and teeth have surfaced since it was first discovered in the western USA in 1902. Early reconstructions were often inaccurate; mounted skeletons show the animal propped up on a whiplike tail, its body sloping backward at an angle of 45°. Since the discoveries of complete tyrannosaur skeletons, such as those of *Tarbosaurus* in Mongolia (*above*), paleontologists now have a more accurate idea of the stance of these dinosaurs.

The popular notion, that *Tyrannosaurus* was the most fearsome predator of the Cretaceous, was investigated during the 1960s, with particular attention paid to the structure of the animal's hips and legs. The indications were that *Tyrannosaurus* may have been no more than a slow-moving scavenger, only able to take small, mincing steps and commandeering the carcasses killed by other predators.

However, this view has since been revised by some paleontologists, who believe that the purpose of the unusually wide area of the skull behind the eyes was to anchor extremely powerful jaw muscles. Taken together with other features — such as the robust, saw-edged teeth; the strong, flexible neck; the large areas of the brain that were associated with the senses of sight and smell; and the possibility of binocular vision — the findings argue in favor of an active, predatory lifestyle.

It is surmised that *Tyrannosaurus*' diet could have consisted primarily of the duckbilled dinosaurs, or hadrosaurs, that browsed in the hardwood forests of North America (*see pp. 146–153*). These animals lived in herds, and were always on the alert, sprinting away on 2 legs when danger threatened. So it is likely that *Tyrannosaurus* hid among the trees, to ambush its prey. It would have leapt out on a passing victim in a short burst of speed. Charging with mouth open wide, the force of the impact would have been absorbed by its strong teeth, sturdy skull and powerful neck.

Early herbivorous dinosaurs

PLATEOSAURUS

ANCHISAURUS

EFRAASIA

MUSSAURUS

RIOJASAURUS

MASSOSPONDYLUS

THECODONTOSAURUS

Early herbivorous dinosaurs

SUBORDER SAUROPODOMORPHA

The lifestyle of the sauropodomorph dinosaurs was completely different from that of their contemporaries, the theropods. Although both were saurischians, or "lizard-hipped" dinosaurs, the theropods were 2-legged carnivores (*see pp. 106–121*), whereas the sauropodomorphs were, for the most part, 4-legged herbivores. Their lives were inextricably linked, however, since the sauropodomorphs were probably the chief prey of the larger theropods.

INFRAORDER PROSAUROPODA

Like the theropods, the sauropodomorphs can be grouped according to their size. There were gigantic types, with long necks and tails, placed in the Infraorder Sauropoda (*see pp. 126–133*). *Apatosaurus* (previously known as *Brontosaurus*) is the most famous sauropod (*see p. 132*). These gentle, plant-eating giants lived throughout the Jurassic and Cretaceous periods, and then met a similar fate to all other dinosaurs — mass-extinction.

There were also smaller sauropodomorphs (though some were still fairly large, at over 30 ft/9 m), which are grouped in the Infraorder Prosauropoda. As their name implies, they were "before the sauropods," and lived during Late Triassic times. Current theory rejects the once-held notion that the prosauropods were the direct ancestors of the sauropods. They are now regarded as a side branch of the sauropod family tree — a branch that got fatally pruned in the Early Jurassic period (*see pp. 90–93*).

Prosauropods themselves are thought to have evolved from theropod-type ancestors. The remains of 2 likely candidates have been found, both from South America. *Staurikosaurus* is the only known dinosaur from the Mid-Triassic period, and was about 6 ft 6 in/2 m long; *Herrerasaurus*, from the Late Triassic, was 10 ft/3 m long. Both seem to have been active, 2-legged flesh-eaters, with large heads and long tails.

FAMILY ANCHISAURIDAE

This family comprises the earliest prosauropods, which were among the first dinosaurs to appear. They were all fairly small (less than 10 ft/3 m in length), with long, lightly built bodies, slim limbs, small heads and long necks and tails.

Anchisaurs seem to represent an early experiment in plant-eating among dinosaurs. Their teeth were cylindrical and blunt, with filelike serrations along the edges — like the teeth of some modern herbivorous lizards. The arms were only slightly shorter than the legs, which suggests that the animal probably spent much of its time on all-fours. This stance would make it easier to reach plants growing at ground level. But the ankle joint was strong and well developed, too, indicating that the animal could also stand up on its hindlegs, and use its hands to pluck off higher vegetation.

Some paleontologists believe that anchisaur-type prosauropods may have been the ancestors of the bird-hipped dinosaurs, the ornithischians (*see pp. 134–169*). Certain features of *Anchisaurus* (*below*), in particular, seem similar. Its long, slender neck, the structure of its shoulders and forelimbs, and details of its hip bones and ankle joints — all these structures are similar to those of some of the early ornithopods, such as *Heterodontosaurus* (*see p. 136*).

NAME: *Anchisaurus*
TIME: **Early Jurassic**
LOCALITY: **North America (Connecticut) and southern Africa**
SIZE: **7 ft/2.1 m long**

This early dinosaur was probably typical of the small prosauropods. It had a small head, tall, flexible neck and long, slim body. The arms were shorter than the legs, by about a third. Each hand had 5 fingers, though the 2 outer ones were quite short. The first finger, or "thumb," had a large claw, which may have been used for rooting up plants or maybe for fighting.

The round, blunt teeth suggest that *Anchisaurus* ate plants. Ferns and horsetails flourished in damp places at the time, and conifers and palmlike cycads grew in drier, upland areas. But all plant-eaters, including modern ones, need a larger digestive system than meat-eaters, since tough, fibrous plant material takes longer to break down than flesh. So, a capacious stomach and long intestines would have been found in *Anchisaurus'* long body, accommodated in front of the hips. This mass of innards would have unbalanced a 2-legged animal, so, it is argued, *Anchisaurus* and its relatives had to take up a 4-legged stance most of the time for stability.

All the continents of today's world were fused together into one great landmass in Jurassic times, some 200 million years ago, when *Anchisaurus* was alive. To find its remains in such divergent places as the eastern seaboard of North America and in southern Africa is therefore not surprising, and is further evidence for the theory of plate tectonics (*see pp. 10–11*).

PLATEOSAURUS
ANCHISAURU
EFRAASIA

NAME: *Thecodontosaurus*
TIME: **Late Triassic to Early Jurassic**
LOCALITY: **Europe (England) and southern Africa**
SIZE: **7 ft/2.1 m long**

Thecodontosaurus was similar in build to *Anchisaurus*, but with a shorter neck and more teeth. It was first named in 1843 from remains discovered near Bristol in southwest England. The bones were found in Triassic deposits that had been laid down in gullies and caves eroded out of limestones that had been formed in earlier, Carboniferous times. During the desertlike climate that prevailed in Europe during Late Triassic times, when *Thecodontosaurus* was living, these limestones would have formed high, parched plateaus.

Piecing together such climatic and rock evidence suggests that *Thecodontosaurus* lived in dry, upland areas, possibly in or near the entrance to these caves; when it died, it was covered over by later, Triassic deposits. Alternatively, its bones could have been washed into the caves and gullies by torrents during the rainy seasons.

NAME: *Efraasia*
TIME: **Late Triassic**
LOCALITY: **Europe (Germany)**
SIZE: **8 ft/2.4 m long**

Discovered in 1909 by E. Fraas and named after him, *Efraasia* was slightly larger than its prosauropod relatives, but otherwise similar in build. Like them, it had multipurpose hands. Its long fingers could have grasped small plants and bundles of leaves, especially with the help of the mobile "thumbs." The wrist joint was also well developed, so the palm of the hand could be pressed to the ground easily, enabling the animal to walk on all-fours.

Efraasia had a primitive feature, however; only 2 sacral vertebrae joined the hips to the backbone, which made for a

MUSSAURUS

RIOJASAURUS

CODONTOSAURUS

MASSOSPONDYLUS

rather weak arrangement of the hind-quarters . All the other "lizard-hipped" dinosaurs had at least 3 vertebrae linking the hips to the spine.

FAMILY PLATEOSAURIDAE
These heavy, large, stout-limbed pro-sauropods were bigger versions of their contemporaries, the anchisaurs (above). The proportions of their bodies are reminiscent of the giant sauropods that thrived later, in the Jurassic and Cretaceous periods (see pp. 126–133).

NAME: *Massospondylus*
TIME: **Late Triassic**
LOCALITY: **Africa (South Africa and Zimbabwe) and North America (Arizona)**
SIZE: **13 ft/4 m long**
This was the most common pro-sauropod in southern Africa. It was named in 1854 by the English paleontologist Richard Owen from a few large vertebrae found in South Africa. On the basis of these bones, he called the dinosaur *Massospondylus*, which means "massive vertebra."

Massospondylus had a tiny head perched on a particularly long and flex-ible neck. Its 5-fingered hands were massive and had a great spread; they could have been used for walking or for grasping food. Each "thumb" had a large, curved claw.

Polished stones have been found in the stomach cavities of some skeletons. Rough stones would have been deliberately swallowed by *Massospondylus*, to help grind up the tough plant material that it ate. Many modern birds retain stones in their gizzards for just the same purpose. Since *Massospondylus* prob-ably spent most of its time eating, in order to maintain its great body, the surface of these stones would have been

polished smooth in a short time, and been of no further use. Then they would have been regurgitated, and replaced.

NAME: *Plateosaurus*
TIME: **Late Triassic**
LOCALITY: **Europe (England, France, Germany and Switzerland)**
SIZE: **up to 23 ft/7 m long**
Plateosaurus is the best known of the prosauropods. Dozens of well-preserved skeletons have been un-earthed in Triassic sandstones all over western Europe. In some places, groups of complete individuals have been found. Mass-burials of this kind suggest that the animals were gregarious, and traveled together in herds through the Triassic desert landscape of Europe, searching for new feeding grounds.

An alternative explanation is that solitary individuals lived in dry, upland areas. When they died, their bodies were washed away in the periodic flash floods that are typical of desert environ-ments even today. Many individuals could have piled up at the end of well-worn flood channels at the edge of desert basins.

Plateosaurus was a large animal, its tail making up about half its length. It had a stronger, deeper head than most pro-sauropods. Its many small, leaf-shaped teeth, and the low-slung hinge of its lower jaw (to give the muscles greater leverage) suggest that it fed exclusively on plants. It would have moved about on all-fours most of the time, occasion-ally rearing up and stretching out its long neck to browse at higher levels. The foliage of trees such as cycads and various conifers, which flourished at the time, would have featured in its diet.

Similar herbivorous dinosaurs to *Plateosaurus* lived in other parts of the world. In southern China there was the 20 ft/6 m-long *Lufengosaurus*, and in South America there was the smaller, 13 ft/4 m-long *Coloradia*. The presence of these animals, with similar builds and lifestyles, in such widely spaced parts of the globe is further evidence to support the theory that all continents were one in those days.

NAME: *Mussaurus*
TIME: **Late Triassic to Early Jurassic**
LOCALITY: **South America (Argentina)**
SIZE: **possibly 10 ft/3 m long**
The smallest known dinosaur was named "mouse lizard" in 1979 when a group of tiny, perfectly formed hatch-lings were found in a nest in southern Argentina. Two small, almost intact eggs lay nearby; each measured only 1 in/25 mm on the longest axis. The largest *Mussaurus* skeleton was only

8 in/20 cm long. It had a large head, with big eyes, and a short neck — features you would expect to find in a young animal, not yet fully developed.

Paleontologists think that the adult *Mussaurus* could have grown up to 10 ft/3 m in length, with the body pro-portions of a typical prosauropod.

FAMILY MELANOROSAURIDAE
Members of this family were the largest prosauropods. Some paleontologists think that they may even have been early representatives of the giant, plant-eating dinosaurs — the sauropods.

Melanorosaurs walked exclusively on 4 legs, unlike their smaller, more light-weight contemporaries, the anchisaurs (see p. 124), which could also walk up-right, on 2 legs.

NAME: *Riojasaurus*
TIME: **Late Triassic to Early Jurassic**
LOCALITY: **South America (Argentina)**
SIZE: **up to 33 ft/10 m long**
The limb bones, and the shoulder and hip girdles of this large prosauropod, were much more massive than those of its relatives, the plateosaurs (above). This indicates that it was an "obligatory quadruped" — that is, it had to walk on 4 legs in order to support its great weight.

The skeleton was modified accord-ingly. The limb bones were thick and solid, and held vertically beneath the body. The hips were fused to the back-bone by 3 vertebrae, giving a solid at-tachment for the heavy legs. The ver-tebrae themselves had extra articulating surfaces to help keep the backbone more rigid.

Riojasaurus was named after the northwestern Argentinian province of La Rioja where it was found. Other large prosauropods, similar in build and structure, lived in southern Africa at about the same time — *Roccosaurus* and *Thotobolosaurus* of the Late Triassic, and *Vulcanodon* of the Early Jurassic. This last animal shows a mixture of features. Some of them were "primitive" pro-sauropod, while others were "advan-ced" sauropod. *Vulcanodon* may, there-fore, have been close to the ancestry of the giant, long-necked browsers of the Mezozoic Era, the sauropods.

125

Long-necked browsing dinosaurs

OPISTHOCOELICAUDIA

CETIOSAURUS

EUHELOPUS

BARAPASAURUS

CAMARASAURUS

BRACHIOSAURUS

Long-necked browsing dinosaurs

INFRAORDER SAUROPODA

Between 65 and 200 million years ago, the largest herbivores — in fact, the largest land animals ever to have lived — were the giant, long-necked, 4-legged sauropods. As a group, they survived for some 50 million years. They evolved in the Late Triassic or Early Jurassic, reached their peak in the Late Jurassic, and became extinct by the end of the Cretaceous. Even in the early stages of their evolution, most sauropods were huge — well over 50 ft/15.2 m long.

The body plan of all sauropods was structurally similar. There was a small head on top of an extra-long neck; a long, deep body to accommodate an enormous gut; thick, pillarlike legs with 5-toed, spreading feet; and a long, thick tail tapering to a whiplash.

Two special adaptations of the skeleton were evident, even in the earliest sauropods. First, great cavities were hollowed out of the vertebrae; this helped to lighten the load of the animal considerably, while still retaining the structural strength of its skeleton. This hollowing-out became more extreme as the sauropods evolved. Bone was developed only along the lines of stress (comparable to the steel struts in a crane jib).

The second special feature was that the massive hip girdle was firmly fused to the backbone by 4 (and in later types, 5) sacral vertebrae, and formed a solid support for the heavy body and tail.

FAMILY CETIOSAURIDAE

The earliest sauropods lived worldwide during the Jurassic period and into the Cretaceous. Their name means "whale lizards," and refers to their great size, rather than to a water-dwelling lifestyle.

Two primitive features remained in members of the cetiosaur family. First, their vertebrae were only partially hollowed out, so the body weight would have been considerable. And second, the hips were attached to the backbone by only 4 sacral vertebrae, a weaker arrangement than in later sauropods.

NAME: *Barapasaurus*
TIME: **Early Jurassic**
LOCALITY: **Asia (India)**
SIZE: **49 ft/15 m long**
A field in central India yielded the only sauropod to be found on that subcontinent to date, and also the world's oldest-known sauropod.

In build, *Barapasaurus* followed the general sauropod plan (*above*). Only the neck and some of the back vertebrae were hollowed out, as a weight-saving adaptation. Its teeth were spoon-shaped and saw-edged, ideal for eating plants.

NAME: *Cetiosaurus*
TIME: **Middle Jurassic to Late Jurassic**
LOCALITY: **Europe (England) and Africa (Morocco)**
SIZE: **up to 60 ft/18.3 m long**
Bones of this huge sauropod were discovered in 1809 in Oxfordshire in southern England, 32 years before the word "dinosaur" had been coined. People thought the bones belonged to some great marine animal, hence the name *Cetiosaurus*, or "whale lizard." Others thought the bones came from some huge crocodile. It was not until the remains of a similar sauropod, *Haplocanthosaurus*, were found, in the Late Jurassic rocks of Colorado in western North America, that the true nature of the beast was appreciated.

Cetiosaurus was massively built, but with a shorter neck and tail than usual among sauropods. It may have weighed over 10 US tons/9 tonnes. The backbone was a solid mass, since the vertebrae were hardly hollowed out at all.

A skeleton unearthed in Morocco in 1979 revealed the size of the animal. The thigh bone alone was over 6 ft/1.8 m long, and one of the shoulder blades measured over 5 ft/1.5 m in length. The amount of plant food needed to power such great limbs must have been enormous.

FAMILY BRACHIOSAURIDAE

Members of this family were the giants of the sauropod group. They ranged through North America, Europe and eastern Africa during Mid-Jurassic to Early Cretaceous times. All had a similar structure — small heads perched on extra-long necks, deep bodies and shortish tails. They differed from all other sauropods in having their front legs longer than their hindlegs, so that the body sloped down from the shoulders, like that of a modern giraffe.

Until recently, the brachiosaurs could claim to have had among their members not only the most massive dinosaur ever to have lived, but also the largest creature ever to have walked on land. This was *Brachiosaurus* (*below*).

But recent finds in North America show that there were even larger sauropods than *Brachiosaurus*. In the 1970s, massive bones from 2 sauropods were found in Colorado, and unofficially called *Supersaurus* and *Ultrasaurus*. Then, in 1986, even larger bones were unearthed in New Mexico, and provisionally named *Seismosaurus*. Some of the remains are enormous, and suggest lengths of more than 100 ft/30 m. For example, there is a shoulder blade 8 ft/2.4 m long, and individual vertebrae 5 ft/1.5 m long.

The bones of these 3 finds have still to be scientifically studied, classified and reconstructed. Since no complete skeletons have been found, it remains to be seen whether the animals belong to the brachiosaur family or the diplodocid family (*see p. 132*), or even whether they belong to more than one new genus.

NAME: *Brachiosaurus*
TIME: **Late Jurassic**
LOCALITY: **North America (Colorado) and Africa (Tanzania and Algeria)**
SIZE: **75 ft/23 m long**
Of all the land animals for which a complete skeleton exists, *Brachiosaurus* is the largest and most massive. Larger sauropod bones have been unearthed recently in western North America (*above*), and preliminary findings indicate that these dinosaurs may have been 100–130 ft/30–40 m long. But the remains are incomplete, and await detailed scientific study.

In the meantime, a complete specimen of *Brachiosaurus* is displayed in the Paleontological Museum at Humboldt University in East Berlin. It is the largest mounted skeleton in existence. Its bones were found in Tanzania, East Africa, by an expedition from Humboldt University in 1908–12.

Brachiosaurus was, on average, 75 ft/23 m long, and 41 ft/12.6 m tall. Its shoulders were 21 ft/6.4 m off the ground; the upper arm bone, or humerus, alone accounted for 7 ft/2.1 m of this height. It weighed an incredible 89 US tons/80 tonnes — almost 3 times the weight of that other giant sauropod *Apatosaurus* (= *Brontosaurus*), or the equivalent of 12 modern, adult African bull elephants.

The secret of supporting such a massive body lay in the construction of *Brachiosaurus'* backbone. Great chunks of bone were hollowed out from the

CAMARASAURUS

BRACHIOSAURUS

sides of each vertebra, to leave a structure, anchor-shaped in cross-section, made of thin sheets and struts of bone. The resulting skeleton was a masterpiece of engineering — a lightweight framework, made of immensely strong, yet flexible, vertebrae, each angled and articulated to provide maximum strength along the lines of stress.

Brachiosaurus had a deep, domed head, with a broad, flat snout. The head was tiny in comparison with its body, and the brain cavity was equally small. Pointed, peglike teeth lined the jaws. Two great nasal openings (external "nostrils") were on top of the head above the eyes, as in all other sauropods. Their position originally led paleontologists to think that *Brachiosaurus* and its other massive relatives spent most of their time submerged in water, browsing on soft weeds, with their nostrils above the surface, breathing in air. But it is now recognized that the pressure exerted by the great depth of water needed to cover the animals would have made breathing difficult, if not impossible.

An animal's fleshy nostrils may not necessarily be close to its external nasal openings. Modern elephants, for example, have nasal openings on top of their heads, but they breathe through the fleshy nostrils at the tip of their trunks. This raises the question, did some sauropods have trunks (*below*)? Another possible function for the large nasal openings of sauropods involves heat regulation; the openings may have been lined with moist, blood-rich skin that helped to keep the animal's brain cool in hot weather.

Brachiosaurus' neck was extremely long, making up about half of its height. There were no more neck vertebrae than usual among sauropods (between 12 and 19), but each was elongated to 3 times the length of the back vertebrae.

An unusual feature among sauropods — but a characteristic of the brachiosaur family — was that the front legs were longer than the back legs. So, the whole body sloped down from its highest point at the shoulders, as in a modern giraffe, giving the animal's long neck an even greater reach, to tree-top foliage.

FAMILY CAMARASAURIDAE

Members of this family were much smaller than their contemporaries, the brachiosaurs and diplodocids. Their necks and tails were shorter, and their skulls were higher, with blunter snouts. The teeth, too, were quite different from those of other sauropods; they were long, spoon-shaped and forward-pointing.

All these features suggest that the camarasaurs ate different plants from the larger sauropods in the locality, and so did not compete with them for food.

NAME: *Camarasaurus*
TIME: **Late Jurassic**
LOCALITY: **North America (Colorado, Oklahoma, Utah and Wyoming)**
SIZE: **up to 59 ft/18 m long**

This ubiquitous sauropod probably roamed in herds over the moist, tropical plains that covered western North America during the Jurassic period. Its heavy, spoon-shaped teeth could have dealt with fibrous plants, such as ferns and horsetails. And it could have reached up to the lower branches of conifer trees, and torn away great mouthfuls of tough, needlelike leaves.

Camarasaurus had enormous nasal openings on top of its skull. Their size, together with the animal's short face, has led some paleontologists to speculate that this sauropod had a trunk, like that of a modern elephant, and used it in the same way. However, other scientists think that the large nasal openings acted as a cooling device for the brain (*see Brachiosaurus, above*).

The remains of juveniles have been found with adult *Camarasaurus* in the same sequence of rocks (known as the Morrison Formation) in the western USA. This suggests that the young traveled with the herd, maybe on long migrations if the animals were forced to find new feeding grounds. The periodic droughts typical of this tropical Jurassic land could have made such migrations necessary.

Another clue to lifestyle is found in the isolated heaps of polished pebbles preserved in the same rocks. These could be the regurgitated stomach stones that many sauropods, including *Camarasaurus*, swallowed as an aid to grinding up their tough plant food. Many modern birds also swallow stones for the same reason. When the stones have become so worn as to be of little use as digestive aids, they are regurgitated and new ones are found.

NAME: *Euhelopus*
TIME: **Late Jurassic or Early Cretaceous**
LOCALITY: **Asia (China)**
SIZE: **49 ft/15 m long**

Although *Euhelopus* and *Camarasaurus* lived on opposite sides of the world, the two sauropods were closely related and of similar build.

There were some differences, however. For example, *Euhelopus* had a much longer neck, made up of 17–19 elongated vertebrae (*Camarasaurus* had a short neck, with only about 12 vertebrae). Nor did *Euhelopus* have the "pug nose" of its relative; its head was longer, with a more pointed snout. But like *Camarasaurus*, it had the same heavy, spoon-shaped teeth, and large nasal openings on top of its head.

NAME: *Opisthocoelicaudia*
TIME: **Late Cretaceous**
LOCALITY: **Asia (Mongolia)**
SIZE: **possibly 40 ft/12.2 m long**

The exact size and appearance of this sauropod can only be guessed at, since the one skeleton unearthed in the Gobi Desert of Mongolia was missing the neck and head. However, the rest of the body was well preserved, and seems to be that of a typical, though relatively small and streamlined, camarasaur.

It is the way in which the tail vertebrae lock together that sets *Opisthocoelicaudia* apart from all other known sauropods. Usually, a sauropod's vertebrae are hollowed out on their front ends (ie concave toward the animal's head), and they lock together in a forward-pointing arrangement. The tail vertebrae of *Opisthocoelicaudia*, however, are concave on their rear faces, and lock together in a backward-pointing direction, toward the tip of the tail. This feature gives the animal its name, which means "tail bones hollow at the back."

The peculiar articulation of *Opisthocoelicaudia's* tail formed a powerful and rigid arrangement. Some paleontologists have suggested that the tail was used as a body prop, a "third leg," to steady the animal when it reared up on hindlegs to feed on the topmost branches of trees. Other sauropod dinosaurs, such as the diplodocids and the titanosaurs (*see pp. 132–133*), seem to have used their tails to prop themselves up in the same way.

Long-necked browsing dinosaurs

DIPLODOCUS

SALTASAURUS

MAMENCHISAURUS

DICRAEOSAURUS

APATOSAURUS
(=BRONTOSAURUS)

ALAMOSAURUS

Long-necked browsing dinosaurs

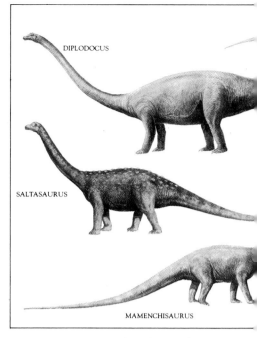

FAMILY DIPLODOCIDAE

Diplodocids were sauropod dinosaurs with enormously long necks and even longer tails. Their bodies and limbs were slender, and their heads tiny. But despite their great length, these giant plant-eaters were lightweights in comparison to their relatives, the bulky brachiosaurs (see pp. 128–129). This was because the vertebrae of diplodocids had been reduced to a complex latticework of bony struts, designed to save weight, yet take maximum stress.

The diplodocid family thrived worldwide during the Late Jurassic period and into the Cretaceous. But toward the end of that period, the group seems to have gone into decline, with only a few representatives restricted to eastern Asia.

NAME: *Diplodocus*
TIME: Late Jurassic
LOCALITY: North America (Colorado, Montana, Utah and Wyoming)
SIZE: 85 ft/26 m long

Diplodocus was a huge animal, some specimens reaching lengths of 100 ft/30 m, although the average individual was 85 ft/26 m long. Most of its length was accounted for by the long neck (about 24 ft/7.3 m), and the extra-long tail (about 46 ft/14 m). The high, narrow body was only about 13 ft/4 m long, and the tiny head measured just over 2 ft/60 cm in length.

Despite its great size, *Diplodocus* weighed only 11 US tons/10 tonnes — about one-eighth the weight of *Brachiosaurus* (see p. 128), and one-third that of *Apatosaurus* (= *Brontosaurus*, below), neither of which were as long as *Diplodocus*. The reason for this was in the lightweight structure of the animal's vertebrae, which were so hollowed out as to be almost cavernous. But the bony struts that remained were strong enough to support the animal's great frame.

The name *Diplodocus* means "double beam," and refers to a pair of anvil-shaped bones, or skids, that grew from the underside of each vertebra of the tail. These would have protected the delicate blood vessels and tissues on the underside of the tail as it was dragged over the rough ground.

A well-preserved skeleton of *Diplodocus* was found in Wyoming at the turn of the century by an expedition financed by the American steel millionaire, Andrew Carnegie. Several casts were made of this skeleton and distributed to 8 museums throughout the world. Unfortunately, the original Wyoming specimen was incomplete – the bones of the front feet were never found. But in order to complete the casts, the feet

were modeled — inaccurately, as it turned out — on the feet of *Camarasaurus*, a sauropod that lived in Wyoming at the same time as *Diplodocus* (see p. 129). The mistake can be seen in the front feet — *Diplodocus* had only one clawed toe on each foot, not 3 as portrayed.

The hindlegs of *Diplodocus* were longer than the front legs — as was usual among the sauropods (except for the brachiosaur family). The animal's body sloped down from the high hips. The vertebrae of the lower back, hips and upper tail had developed tall, vertical spines, which would have formed attachment points for strong muscles to operate the enormous neck and tail.

It was probably *Diplodocus*' habit to rear up on its hindlegs, bending the tail around to form a "third leg" for balance. Stretching up with its long neck, the animal could browse on the uppermost cones and leaves of the coniferous trees that dotted the Jurassic landscape. Just like today in parts of Africa where herds of giraffes gather, the trees of 150 million years ago would have had a "browsing line," below which level most of the leaves would have been stripped away. But instead of the modern browsing line at a height of about 20 ft/6 m, the Jurassic line would have been 49 ft/15 m above the ground.

The only predators big enough to attack *Diplodocus* would have been members of the allosaur family, such as *Allosaurus* which weighed up to 2 US tons/2 tonnes (see p. 117). *Diplodocus*' only weapons against such powerful carnivores were its tail and forelegs, combined with its bulk. The long, flexible tail, powered by great back muscles, could have swept clear a large area around the animal; its whiplash end could have stunned a predator. Another ploy could have been to rear up on hindlegs and bring the stout forelegs crashing down on its attacker.

NAME: *Apatosaurus* (= *Brontosaurus*)
TIME: Late Jurassic
LOCALITY: North America (Colorado, Oklahoma, Utah and Wyoming)
SIZE: up to 70 ft/21.3 m long

The giant, plant-eating dinosaur *Apatosaurus* was once known by the more familiar, and evocative, name of *Brontosaurus*. This means "thunder lizard," and could be a reference to the noise its 33 US tons/30 tonnes must have made as it walked through its homeland in today's western USA. But *Brontosaurus* was the second name allocated to remains of the beast. So, according to strict scientific convention, it is more properly called by the first name given to it — *Apatosaurus*.

Up until 1975, the skull of *Apatosaurus* was unknown, although the rest of its skeleton had been discovered about 100 years before. The head of this giant sauropod was tiny in comparison with its body — a mere 22 in/55 cm long out of a total body length of over 65 ft/20 m.

Although not as long as *Diplodocus*, *Apatosaurus* was simply a bulkier version of it. Both animals had long, slender teeth that grew only at the front of their jaws. As they became worn, they were replaced by new ones. Both animals could rear up on their hindlegs to crop the highest vegetation — though this would have been much more of an effort for *Apatosaurus* since it weighed 3 times as much as *Diplodocus*.

However, *Apatosaurus*' great weight could have been used effectively against a predator like *Allosaurus* — the plant-eater could have reared up and then brought its forelegs down to crush its enemy. Sometimes this ploy did not work; many bones of *Apatosaurus* have been found scored with tooth marks similar to those of *Allosaurus* (see p. 117). An alternative explanation is, of course, that the carnivore came across dead *Apatosaurus*, and fed off their corpses.

Apatosaurus had a longer tail than *Diplodocus*, made up of no less than 82 interlocking vertebrae (as compared with 73 in *Diplodocus*). Like *Diplodocus*, it had pairs of bony skids on the underside of the tail vertebrae, which protected the soft tissues of the tail.

Apatosaurus could have used its heavy tail as a great whiplash to deter attackers. The tail was powered by strong back muscles, which were anchored to tall spines projecting from the vertebrae of the lower body.

Like *Diplodocus*, *Apatosaurus* had 5 short toes on each foot, with one claw on the "big toe" of each front foot, and

DICRAEOSAURUS

APATOSAURUS
(=BRONTOSAURUS)

ALAMOSAURUS

3 claws on each back foot. There were thick wedges of weight-bearing cartilage in the ankle joints (as in those of modern elephants), for flexibility and to spread the body weight.

NAME: *Dicraeosaurus*
TIME: Late Jurassic
LOCALITY: Africa (Tanzania)
SIZE: 41 ft/12.6 m long
Not all diplodocids were giants. *Dicraeosaurus* was a relatively small member of the family. It was different in other ways, too — its neck was shorter, its head larger and its tail lacked the whiplash end.

The tall spines that projected from the vertebrae, and provided muscle-attachment points, were not straight as in *Diplodocus* and *Apatosaurus*. Each spine was forked at the top, like a "Y," and this feature gives *Dicraeosaurus* its name — "forked lizard." These tall spines were not confined to the lower back and upper tail as they were in other diplodocids. They ranged along the whole length of the back and even up into the neck. Perhaps they carried strong ligaments, which linked several vertebrae at a time to give extra strength to the backbone.

The remains of *Dicraeosaurus* were found in the fossil-rich rocks of Tendaguru Hill, in modern Tanzania. These Late Jurassic rocks yielded many other dinosaurs, including the giant sauropod *Brachiosaurus* (see p. 128) and the plated dinosaur *Kentrosaurus*, a relative of *Stegosaurus* (see p. 156). All these plant-eaters lived together peacefully on the tropical river plains of eastern Africa, browsing on different plants at different levels, and so avoiding competition with each other.

NAME: *Mamenchisaurus*
TIME: Late Jurassic
LOCALITY: Asia (Mongolia)
SIZE: 72 ft/22 m long
This animal had the longest neck of any known dinosaur, in fact of any known animal. Its neck is so unusual in structure that many paleontologists place *Mamenchisaurus* in a family of its own.

The neck accounted for almost half the animal's total length. It consisted of 19 vertebrae, each elongated to over twice the length of the 12 back vertebrae. Slender, bony struts grew out from each neck vertebra and overlapped the one behind, to provide greater strength.

As the animal walked, its stiff neck must have been held out almost horizontally from the body. All movement would have been restricted to the flexible joint between the neck and head, plus a swinging motion from the shoulders.

Presumably, this super-long neck gave *Mamenchisaurus* an advantage over other long-necked sauropods in the locality. When it reared up on hindlegs, it was able to reach a new food source — the fresh growth at the tips of the uppermost branches of conifers.

In 1986, the bones of a mighty sauropod were unearthed in Late Jurassic deposits in New Mexico. These have yet to be studied and formally described, but their owner has been tentatively given the name *Seismosaurus*, meaning "earthquake lizard" to reflect its possible weight. Initial calculations put this beast at 130 ft/40 m long. Its proportions seem to be like those of *Diplodocus*, but the forelegs were longer. If the preliminary findings prove correct, *Seismosaurus* will hold the record for the world's largest-ever land animal.

FAMILY TITANOSAURIDAE
This was the latest family of sauropods, surviving right to the end of the Cretaceous period. The group was widespread all over the world, especially in the southern continents, and survived for about 80 million years.

Not all members of this family were "titans" (the mythical giants of Greek legend), as their name implies. Most averaged 40–50 ft/12.2–15.2 m long, which was small in comparison to some of the brachiosaurs and diplodocids.

To date, only fragmentary remains of titanosaurs have been found, not complete skeletons. They seem to have been like *Diplodocus* in structure, but with a shorter neck and a high skull that sloped steeply down to the snout. But unlike *Diplodocus* and other large sauropods,

titanosaurs had solid vertebrae; their bones were not hollowed out as a weight-saving adaptation. In addition to this solid skeleton, some animals also had bony armor covering their backs — a unique feature among the sauropods.

NAME: *Saltasaurus*
TIME: Late Cretaceous
LOCALITY: South America (Argentina)
SIZE: 39 ft/12 m long
The remains of this medium-sized sauropod came as a surprise to paleontologists when discovered in Salta Province of northwest Argentina in 1970. Lying around a group of skeletons were thousands of bony plates. Most of these were tiny, about $\frac{1}{4}$ in/5 mm across; others were larger, about $4\frac{1}{2}$ in/11 cm across, and may have borne horny spikes.

In life, these bony plates would have studded the thick skin of the animal's broad back and sides, forming a protective armor for the otherwise defenseless plant-eater against the flesh-eating carnosaurs of the day (see pp. 120–121).

The fact that these unique armored sauropods were confined largely to South America indicates that the continent could have been separate, in Mid-Cretaceous times, from the great northern landmass that included North America and Eurasia. Present-day Central America was under water at the time. So the South American fauna would have developed in isolation, removed from evolutionary changes.

NAME: *Alamosaurus*
TIME: Late Cretaceous
LOCALITY: North America (Montana, New Mexico, Texas and Utah)
SIZE: 69 ft/21 m long
This was among the last sauropods to live before the mass-extinction of the dinosaurs at the end of the Cretaceous period, 65 million years ago.

During Late Cretaceous times, there had been a climatic change in many parts of the world. Much of lowland North America had turned into moist, swampy jungle, which was the domain of the ornithopod dinosaurs — 2-legged sprinters with birdlike feet (see pp. 135–153). But there were still some high, dry places where the sauropods could live.

It is appropriate that this section on the great saurischian dinosaurs should end with *Alamosaurus*. It was one of the last dinosaurs to survive, and, perhaps coincidentally, is named after the Alamo, that famous fortress in San Antonio where the Texans made their last stand in 1836 against the Mexicans.

Fabrosaurs, heterodontosaurs and pachycephalosaurs

LESOTHOSAURUS

SCUTELLOSAURUS

ECHINODON

HETERODONTOSAURUS

PISANOSAURUS

STEGOCERAS

PRENOCEPHALE

HOMALOCEPHALE

PACHYCEPHALOSAURUS

Fabrosaurs, heterodontosaurs and pachycephalosaurs

SUBORDER ORNITHOPODA

Members of the great reptilian order of "bird-hipped" dinosaurs, the Ornithischia, were exclusively plant-eaters. The other great order of dinosaurs, the Saurischia, had both carnivorous and herbivorous members (*see pp. 106–133*).

The cheek teeth of most ornithischian dinosaurs were set slightly in from the edges of the jaws. The space lateral to the teeth was probably enclosed by fleshy cheeks. (Evidence for these is seen in the slight depressions on either side of the skull in the cheek area.) The cheeks would have prevented food from falling out of the sides of the mouth while the plant-eater was engaged in the lengthy process of chewing up the material.

These cheeks were a useful development for herbivores, and may have been the reason for the great success of the small to medium-sized (up to 33 ft/10 m long) plant-eating dinosaurs of the Jurassic and Cretaceous periods. Linked to this success was the extinction of their early, cheekless rivals, the prosauropod saurischians of the Triassic period (*see pp. 122–125*).

Ornithischian dinosaurs can be divided into 4 distinct suborders, 3 of which consist of 4-legged creatures that were armed in one way or another. The stegosaurs had great bony plates down their backs (*see pp. 154–156*). The ankylosaurs had armor-plated skins and "clubs" at the end of their tails (*see pp. 157–161*). And the ceratopians had horns on their heads and bony neck frills (*see pp. 162–169*).

The fourth suborder consists of the ornithopods, or "bird feet" (*below*). They walked on 2 legs, and could have been the ancestral group from which the other ornithischian dinosaurs evolved. They were a mixed assemblage of animals in terms of their size, habits and distribution, but structurally, they were all similar. They were also a highly successful group, which survived for 148 million years, spanning the whole of the Jurassic and Cretaceous periods.

FAMILY FABROSAURIDAE

The earliest-known ornithopods belong to this family and date back to the Early Jurassic period, some 200 million years ago. This was the heyday of the fabrosaurs, and they spread throughout the world.

In appearance, they were small and lizardlike, but they ran upright on long, slender legs. Superficially, they looked like the small, carnivorous theropod dinosaurs — the coelurosaurs (*see pp. 106–109*).

NAME: *Lesothosaurus*
TIME: **Early Jurassic**
LOCALITY: **Africa (Lesotho)**
SIZE: **3 ft 3 in/1 m long**
This small animal was lightly built and fleet of foot, well able to sprint over the hot, dry plains of its home in southern Africa. Its long legs, short arms, flexible neck and slender tail were to set the general pattern which all subsequent ornithopods were to follow.

Lesothosaurus' skull was small, short and flat-faced, rather like that of a modern iguana. The pointed teeth were shaped like little arrowheads, with grooved edges; when the animal was chewing, its upper teeth fitted alternately between the lower ones, to produce a chopping motion which would have dealt with tough plant food.

A pair of *Lesothosaurus* skeletons were found preserved together in the rocks of southern Africa. Their bodies were curled up, and surrounded by worn, discarded teeth, although the skulls of both animals contained a full set of teeth. On the basis of this find, some paleontologists think that these little dinosaurs may have slept away the hottest, driest months of the year underground, as do many modern desert creatures. The worn teeth scattered around the bodies could have been shed during sleep, while new ones grew.

Another find in Lesotho consisted of a jaw bone and some teeth. These scanty remains were called *Fabrosaurus*. It is possible that this animal and *Lesothosaurus* were the same creature.

NAME: *Scutellosaurus*
TIME: **Early Jurassic**
LOCALITY: **North America (Arizona)**
SIZE: **4 ft/1.2 m long**
Scutellosaurus was an armored fabrosaur — the only one known. Rows of bony studs covered its back and flanks, forming a kind of skin armor. Perhaps to compensate for this extra weight, the animal's tail was particularly long, about half the total body length. It would have been held out stiffly behind the body to balance the animal on 2 legs when it needed to run away from an attacker.

The arms, too, were longer than those of other fabrosaurs, so that *Scutellosaurus* probably browsed and rested on all-fours, relying on its protective armor as its first means of defense.

NAME: *Echinodon*
TIME: **Late Jurassic or Early Cretaceous**
LOCALITY: **Europe (England)**
SIZE: **2 ft/60 cm long**
Only the jaw bones of this small fabrosaur have been found. But they are

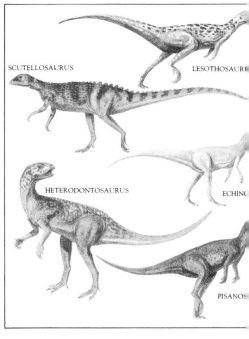

SCUTELLOSAURUS · LESOTHOSAUR[US] · HETERODONTOSAURUS · ECHIN[ODON] · PISANOS[AURUS]

enough to tell paleontologists that *Echinodon* had a shorter head than *Lesothosaurus*, and that it also possessed unusual teeth at the front of its jaws. These were paired canine-type teeth, long and sharp, like the "eyeteeth" of modern cats and dogs. Such teeth were a feature of a group of contemporary ornithopods — the heterodontosaurs.

FAMILY HETERODONTOSAURIDAE

Members of this family looked like fabrosaurs, but their teeth were quite different. In fact, the dental arrangement was unique among dinosaurs, and indeed among most other reptiles.

Heterodontosaurs were among the first dinosaurs to have developed cheeks, to retain food within the mouth (*above*). They also had 3 kinds of teeth in their jaws, and each performed a different function (*see Heterodontosaurus, below*). The family's name reflects this feature — "varied-toothed lizards."

NAME: *Heterodontosaurus*
TIME: **Early Jurassic**
LOCALITY: **Africa (South Africa)**
SIZE: **3 ft/90 cm long**
The rabbit-sized skull of *Heterodontosaurus* was discovered in 1962 in South Africa's Cape Province, and a complete skeleton has since been found. In build, it was like a fabrosaur (*above*) — a small, lightweight, 2-legged plant-eater.

Heterodontosaurus was, however, remarkable because of its teeth. They were unlike those of any other dinosaur and most other reptiles. Usually, a reptile's teeth are all the same size and shape. But *Heterodontosaurus* had 3 kinds of teeth — a dental pattern that is reminiscent of a mammal's, although *Heterodontosaurus* had no connection with the mammalian line of evolution.

STEGOCERAS

PHALE

HOMALOCEPHALE

PACHYCEPHALOSAURUS

At the front of the upper jaw, there were some small, pointed teeth (like a mammal's incisors). There were no opposing teeth at the front of the lower jaw; instead, the chin bone carried a horny beak. This bone (known as the predentary) was unique to the ornithischian dinosaurs. No other reptile, or indeed any backboned animal, has this bone; usually, the 2 dentary bones that make up the lower jaw meet in the center to form the chin.

Behind the upper teeth and the lower beak, *Heterodontosaurus* had 2 pairs of large, canine-type teeth (like the canines of a mammal). The lower pair fitted into a socket in the upper jaw. Behind these canines were the back teeth — tall, chisel-like teeth with cutting edges (comparable to a mammal's molars).

Each type of tooth performed a different job. The pointed ones at the front combined with the beak to nip off leaves; the back teeth cut the leaves up with a scissorlike motion and ground them into small pieces.

Nobody knows the function of this animal's canine teeth. Carnivorous mammals have canines for tearing apart flesh, but *Heterodontosaurus* was a planteater. Some skulls have been found that had no canines, or even sockets that would have contained them. This has led some paleontologists to suggest that only the males had canines, and that they used them for fighting each other. On the basis of this theory, those skulls without canines would have belonged to females.

NAME: *Pisanosaurus*
TIME: **Late Triassic**
LOCALITY: **South America (Argentina)**
SIZE: **3 ft/90 cm long**
Pisanosaurus has the distinction of being the oldest-known ornithischian dinosaur. It lived during Late Triassic times,

several million years before any other "bird-hipped" dinosaur appeared.

Although its remains are scanty, paleontologists think that *Pisanosaurus* belongs to the heterodontosaur family. The fact that all members of this family discovered to date lived in southern Africa or South America is taken as strong evidence that these southern continents were still joined together during Late Triassic times.

FAMILY PACHYCEPHALOSAURIDAE

The skulls of the so-called "thick-headed lizards," or boneheads, were dome-shaped, giving their owners a bizarre appearance. They had high foreheads and thick skull caps, made up of enormously thickened bones. Some species also had bony frills, knobs and spikes on the back and sides of their heads, and sometimes on their snouts.

Most paleontologists believe that these boneheaded dinosaurs had a similar lifestyle to that of modern mountain goats. Like these mammals, they would have lived together in herds, and the males would most likely have engaged in competitive, head-butting fights to establish a pecking order.

In other respects, pachycephalosaurs were like other ornithopods — 2-legged plant-eaters, with 5-fingered hands, 3-toed feet (with a tiny first toe), and a long, heavy tail. As a group they were rare, known mainly from Late Cretaceous times in North America and central Asia. But one bonehead, called *Yaverlandia*, has been found earlier than this — dating from Early Cretaceous rocks in southern England.

Some paleontologists think that the anatomy of the boneheads (especially their skull structure) is sufficiently different from that of the ornithopods to justify placing them in a separate group.

NAME: *Stegoceras*
TIME: **Late Cretaceous**
LOCALITY: **North America (Alberta)**
SIZE: **6 ft 6 in/2 m long**
The whole body of this boneheaded dinosaur seems designed to provide the power behind the ramming head. When an animal charged a rival, its head would have been lowered at right angles, and its neck, body and tail held out stiffly in a horizontal line, balanced at the hips. The skull cap was thickened into a high dome of solid bone, and the small brain was well protected inside. This domed area would have absorbed the main impact as the animal crashed head-on against its opponent. A full-grown *Stegoceras* could have weighed 120 lb/54.4 kg.

The "grain" of the bone in the dome was angled perpendicularly to the surface, indicating that it was built to withstand great impact.

NAME: *Prenocephale*
TIME: **Late Cretaceous**
LOCALITY: **Asia (Mongolia)**
SIZE: **8 ft/2.4 m long**
A truly bulbous dome surmounted the head of *Prenocephale*, and a row of bony spikes and bumps surrounded the solid skull, back and sides. The females probably had smaller, thinner skulls than the males, just like the modern, female big-horned sheep of the Rocky Mountains in the USA have smaller horns than the males.

Like other boneheads, *Prenocephale* probably had large eyes and a keen sense of smell. It lived in upland forests, browsing on leaves and fruits.

NAME: *Homalocephale*
TIME: **Late Cretaceous**
LOCALITY: **Asia (Mongolia)**
SIZE: **10 ft/3 m long**
Homalocephale means "even head," and refers to the fact that this pachycephalosaur did not have a dome on top of its skull. It had a rather flat, wedge-shaped head, although the bones of the skull cap were greatly thickened. There were numerous pits and bony knobs scattered all over the head. This has led some paleontologists to think that rival male *Homalocephale* fought the same kinds of ritualistic, head-butting battles as do the modern marine iguanas of the Galapagos Islands.

Homalocephale had particularly broad hips, and paleontologists interpret this feature in different ways. Some say that the hips could have been part of the impact-absorbing system when rival males fought together. Others postulate that the broad hips could indicate that this bonehead gave birth to live young.

NAME: *Pachycephalosaurus*
TIME: **Late Cretaceous**
LOCALITY: **North America (Alberta)**
SIZE: **15 ft/4.6 m long**
This was a giant among boneheads. Although it is known only from its skull, this measured 2 ft/60 cm in length. The enormous dome on top of the head was made of solid bone, some 10 in/25 cm thick. Like a great crash helmet, the thick skull could have absorbed tremendous impact as rival males butted each other, head-on.

Pachycephalosaurus was not only the biggest member of the bonehead family; it was also the last member to exist before all its plant-eating relatives and its carnivorous cousins became extinct at the end of the Cretaceous period.

Hypsilophodonts

DRYOSAURUS

HYPSILOPHODON

PARKSOSAURUS

OTHNIELIA

THESCELOSAURUS

TENONTOSAURUS

Hypsilophodonts

FAMILY HYPSILOPHODONTIDAE

Hypsilophodonts were the "gazelles" of the dinosaur world. They probably lived in social herds, like modern deer, and would have been continually alert. When danger threatened — and there were many carnivorous dinosaurs around to attack them — they sprinted off at high speed, their lightweight bodies and long, running legs facilitating a fast retreat.

Hypsilophodonts were among the most successful of the dinosaurs. As a group they flourished for about 100 million years, from the Late Jurassic to the end of the Cretaceous, and spread to every continent in the world except Asia.

They are also an important group in the evolution of the dinosaurs. Paleontologists believe that the hypsilophodonts gave rise to 2 other major groups of ornithopods — the iguanodonts (see pp. 142–145) and the "duck-bills" or hadrosaurs (see pp. 146–153).

The herbivorous lifestyle of hypsilophodonts was similar to that of the fabrosaurs, the group of earlier Jurassic ornithopods that became extinct at about the time the hypsilophodonts began their rise (see p. 136). In fact, some paleontologists believe that the fabrosaurs were the direct ancestors of the hypsilophodonts.

Structurally, the fabrosaurs and hypsilophodonts were also similar. But the hypsilophodonts had several anatomical modifications. For example, they had developed the retaining cheeks that prevented the food from falling out of the sides of the mouth. And their upper and lower teeth met, or occluded, as regular rows, rather than interlocking alternately as those of fabrosaurs. This arrangement would have given a better chewing and grinding surface.

The hips of hypsilophodonts were also more advanced than those of the fabrosaurs. Part of the pubis bone (known as the prepubic process) projected forward, and provided an extra area to which the leg muscles could attach (see pp. 104–105). This resulted in greater running power. But this extra bone was small enough to leave room for the plant-eater's capacious gut, which was accommodated, as usual, in front of its hips.

From the Late Cretaceous rocks of Montana comes possible evidence of how hypsilophodonts lived. Ten dinosaur nests were unearthed there in 1979. Each nest contained about 24 small, ellipsoidal eggs, arranged in a circular pattern, all with the pointed ends downward. The remains of young hypsilophodonts were found in the same area. From this indirect evidence, paleontologists surmise that the young left the nest immediately on hatching, but remained in the same area for a time, being cared for by their parent or parents. The fact that the eggs were so precisely arranged in the nests suggests that there was certainly some parental care, at least before birth. Modern turtles and alligators lay their eggs carefully in well-concealed nests in a similar manner, though both species then vacate the nesting site.

In contrast, when the eggs of sauropod dinosaurs have been found, they are always laid out in lines, as though the female dropped them while on the move, rather than collecting them together in a nest. This suggests that the young of sauropods were on their own after they hatched out.

NAME: *Dryosaurus*
TIME: **Late Jurassic to Early Cretaceous**
LOCALITY: **North America (Colorado, Utah and Wyoming), Africa (Tanzania). Possibly Australia and Europe (England and Romania)**
SIZE: **up to 10 ft/3 m long**

Dryosaurus (also known as *Dysalotosaurus*) was one of the largest of the hypsilophodonts. Although it was also one of the earliest, its anatomy was advanced in several ways. For example, each long, slender leg had only 3 toes. And there were no teeth in the front part of the upper jaw; the horny beak at the front of the lower jaw met with a tough, toothless pad opposite on the upper jaw — an efficient arrangement for cropping vegetation.

Like other members of this family of long-legged sprinters, *Dryosaurus'* shin bones were much longer than its thigh bones. The heavy leg muscles were concentrated around the short thigh bones, and the lower leg and long feet were operated by light but powerful tendons. This arrangement gave *Dryosaurus* extra speed, and is exactly the same pattern possessed by modern deer and gazelle.

Dryosaurus was obviously a wide-ranging ornithopod, living as far apart as western North America and East Africa. In Jurassic times, these continents were only separated by a fledgling North Atlantic Ocean, and animals could still migrate across land by way of Europe and via the Siberia/Alaska link. This is why the dinosaurs found in the fossil-rich beds of the Morrison Formation in the western USA are so similar to those found in Tendaguru Hill of Tanzania.

Dryosaurus would, therefore, have shared its world with giant plant-eating dinosaurs such as *Apatosaurus* (=*Brontosaurus*), *Diplodocus* and *Brachiosaurus*; small, rapacious carnivores like the coelurosaurs *Coelurus* and *Elaphrosaurus*; and large carnosaurs like *Allosaurus* and the horned *Ceratosaurus*.

NAME: *Othnielia*
TIME: **Late Jurassic**
LOCALITY: **North America (Utah and Wyoming)**
SIZE: **4 ft 6 in/1.4 m long**

This dinosaur is named after the famous 19th-century American fossil-hunter and Yale professor, Othniel Charles Marsh (see pp. 104–105). He had originally called it *Nanosaurus* in 1877, but it was renamed exactly 100 years later, in 1977, to commemorate his pioneering fieldwork in the study of dinosaurs.

Othnielia was a typical hypsilophodont, with long legs and tail, a lightweight body, and short arms with 5-fingered hands. Only its teeth differed. They were proportionally smaller than those of other hypsilophodonts, and were completely covered in enamel, not just on their grinding faces.

Maybe *Othnielia* ate tougher plants than usual, hence the protective tooth enamel to avoid excessive wear. A tough, fibrous diet would also have meant that *Othnielia* had to grind its food down more finely before it could be digested. As an aid to this, *Othnielia*, like all its relatives, had cheeks that retained the food in the mouth while it was being chewed.

PARKSOSAURUS

ELIA

THESCELOSAURUS

TENONTOSAURUS

NAME: *Hypsilophodon*
TIME: **Early Cretaceous**
LOCALITY: **Europe (England and Portugal) and North America (South Dakota)**
SIZE: **5 ft/1.5 m long**
About 20 perfect skeletons of this small hypsilophodont were found in one particular bed of Lower Cretaceous rocks in the Isle of Wight, off southern England. This find probably represents a herd of animals that lived and died together, perhaps overwhelmed by the rising tide of the shallow seas that lay over northern Europe some 120 million years ago.

Hypsilophodon is the classic representative of the family, and has given its name to the whole group. Its name means "high ridge tooth," and refers to the tall, grooved cheek teeth typical of all hypsilophodonts. The upper and lower teeth met to form a flat surface for grinding up plant food.

Oddly enough, in comparison with its earlier relatives of the Late Jurassic (*see Dryosaurus, p. 140*), *Hypsilophodon* had certain primitive features. For example, it had 4 toes on each foot, and there were incisor-type teeth at the front of the upper jaw. When these were closed on the toothless, horny beak of the lower jaw, they formed an effective device for cropping vegetation.

Hypsilophodon may also have been armored, with 2 rows of thin, bony scales running down either side of its back. But paleontologists are uncertain about this feature.

The study of *Hypsilophodon* since its discovery in the 19th century is a classic story of paleontological research. When it was first described, by Thomas H. Huxley in 1870, paleontologists of the day were struck by the similarity of its build to that of a modern tree kangaroo. For almost a century, classic illustrations of *Hypsilophodon* showed it

perched in a tree, 3 of its 4 toes gripping the branch, birdlike, and the fourth toe directed backward. This reconstruction neatly filled an ecological niche not yet occupied by any dinosaur, and so, the idea of a tree-dwelling, plant-eating ornithopod was conceived.

It was not until 1974 that the skeleton of *Hypsilophodon* was reassessed. Paleontologists concluded that there was no evidence to show that this dinosaur lived in trees. In fact, it was a perfectly adapted terrestrial animal, capable of running rapidly on 2 legs.

NAME: *Tenontosaurus*
TIME: **Early Cretaceous**
LOCALITY: **North America (Arizona, Montana, Oklahoma and Texas)**
SIZE: **24 ft/7.3 m long**
This dinosaur is so uncharacteristically large compared with other hypsilophodonts that some paleontologists class it with the iguanodonts (*see pp. 142–145*). Indeed, its skull is very similar in shape to that of an iguanodont, but its teeth and their arrangement in the jaws place it firmly in the hypsilophodont family.

Over half the total length of *Tenontosaurus* was made up of tail, which was enormously thick and heavy. The animal is estimated to have weighed about 1 US ton/900 kg, and probably spent much of its time on all-fours. Its arms were much longer and stouter than those of other hypsilophodonts.

A remarkable find in the rocks of Montana consisted of a skeleton of *Tenontosaurus* surrounded by 5 complete specimens of *Deinonychus*, a ferocious predator of the day (*see p. 112*). Although these bodies were most likely brought together by chance after death, perhaps in a flash flood, it is interesting to speculate that this mass-burial could have been the outcome of an encounter between the bulky plant-eater and a pack of predators.

Although *Deinonychus* was only about 10 ft/3 m long, it had sharp, meat-shearing fangs, and great, daggerlike claws on its feet. The bulky *Tenontosaurus* could have put up a good fight, kicking out with its heavy-clawed feet or using its great tail as a whiplash. But these were paltry defenses when compared with the lethal weapons of the agile carnivores.

NAME: *Parksosaurus*
TIME: **Late Cretaceous**
LOCALITY: **North America (Alberta)**
SIZE: **8 ft/2.4 m long**
Parksosaurus was one of the last of the long-lived hypsilophodont family to survive before the mass-extinction of the dinosaurs at the end of the Cretaceous period. It was similar in build to all other hypsilophodonts, but there were minor differences in the skull, notably its large eyes.

Parksosaurus probably foraged close to the ground, snuffling about among the low-growing undergrowth, and selectively nipping off its preferred food with its narrow, beaked jaws.

NAME: *Thescelosaurus*
TIME: **Late Cretaceous**
LOCALITY: **North America (Alberta, Montana, Saskatchewan and Wyoming)**
SIZE: **11 ft 6 in/3.5 m long**
Thescelosaurus was discovered in the topmost rocks of the Late Cretaceous period in western North America. It seems to have been bulkier and bigger-boned than its closest relatives, the typically small, lightweight hypsilophodonts. In fact, *Thescelosaurus* could be a member of the iguanodont family.

Several features distinguish *Thescelosaurus* from other hypsilophodonts. It had teeth in the front of its upper jaw. It had 5 toes on each foot (in contrast to the hypsilophodonts, which had 3 or 4). And its thigh bones were as long as its shin bones (the shins of the agile hypsilophodonts were always longer than the thighs).

The structure of the legs suggests that *Thescelosaurus* was not a gazelle-type sprinter like its relatives, but rather a slower-moving creature. Perhaps to compensate for this, there were rows of bony studs set in the skin of its back, which would have offered some measure of protection against the carnivorous dinosaurs that preyed on it.

Iguanodonts

CALLOVOSAURUS

CAMPTOSAURUS

IGUANODON

VECTISAURUS

OURANOSAURUS

MUTTABURRASAURUS

PROBACTROSAURUS

Iguanodonts

FAMILY IGUANODONTIDAE

Iguanodon is the most popular and familiar member of this family of large, plant-eating ornithopod dinosaurs. The iguanodonts evolved in the Mid-Jurassic, about 170 million years ago, and spread throughout the world. They have even been found within what is now the Arctic Circle, although these lands would have been ice-free all those millennia ago. Iguanodonts reached their peak of diversity and abundance by the end of the Early Cretaceous. Thereafter they declined, and finally died out at the end of that period.

Unlike their ancestors — the gazelle-like hypsilophodonts (*see pp. 138–141*) — iguanodonts did not evolve as running animals. Their bodies were bulky and big-boned; the thigh bones were longer than the shin bones (the relative lengths are reversed in sprinting animals); and both the fore- and hind-feet had heavy, hooflike nails. Iguanodonts, therefore, were probably fairly slow-moving animals that spent most of their time on all-fours, browsing on low-growing plants, such as horsetails. The beaklike jaws would nip off the leaves, and the rows of high, ridged cheek teeth grind them down to a pulp. These dinosaurs could also rear up on hind-legs, to reach higher vegetation, and to escape from predators.

NAME: *Callovosaurus*
TIME: **Middle Jurassic**
LOCALITY: **Europe (England)**
SIZE: **11 ft 6 in/3.5 m long**

Although this dinosaur is known only from a single thigh bone, this bone shows that *Callovosaurus* was unlike its contemporary relatives, the hypsilophodonts. It was, in fact, the earliest-known member of the iguanodonts, and presumably was similar in structure and appearance to the later *Camptosaurus* (*below*).

NAME: *Camptosaurus*
TIME: **Late Jurassic**
LOCALITY: **Europe (England and Portugal) and North America (Colorado, South Dakota, Utah and Wyoming)**
SIZE: **20 ft/6 m long**

Like *Callovosaurus* (*above*), *Camptosaurus* was a primitive member of the iguanodont family. From the many skeletons of different sizes found — particularly in the dinosaur-rich beds of the Morrison Formation in the western USA — *Camptosaurus* was evidently an abundant dinosaur. Finding it on both sides of today's Atlantic Ocean supports the theory that the continents of North America and Europe were still joined together some 120 million years ago.

The skull of *Camptosaurus* was very different from that of its hypsilophodont ancestors. It was long, low and broad; it was also fairly heavy, since some of the "windows" or gaps between the bones had been closed up. The snout was greatly elongated, and the jaws formed a pronounced toothless beak at the tip.

As in many other plant-eating dinosaurs, there was a bony palate that separated the air-breathing passages from the eating area of the mouth. This allowed the animal to breathe and chew at the same time — an important development for all herbivores, since they had to spend most of their time eating in order to fuel their massive bodies.

The legs were long and powerful, each with 3 hoofed toes. The thigh bones were massive and slightly curved. The arms were much shorter than the legs, but also equipped with small hooflike nails, so that the animal could use its hands as feet.

NAME: *Iguanodon*
TIME: **Early Cretaceous**
LOCALITY: **Europe (eg England, Belgium and Germany), North America (Utah), Africa (Tunisia) and Asia (Mongolia)**
SIZE: **30 ft/9 m long**

Iguanodon rightly deserves its place in dinosaur lore. It was the second dinosaur to be discovered, although the word "dinosaur" had yet to be invented (*see p. 117*). Part of its great shin bone was found in southern England in 1809, and then some teeth and other bones were discovered in 1819. Scientists of the day regarded the teeth as belonging to some giant mammal, like a rhinoceros. But Gideon Mantell, a geologist and keen fossil collector, saw that the teeth were reptilian, and that they resembled those of the modern iguana of Central and South America. So he named the animal *Iguanodon*, and described it in 1825 to the scientific community.

Mantell attempted a restoration, but with the sparse information he had to hand, it was speculative. He reconstructed *Iguanodon* as a 4-legged, dragonlike beast, with a heavy tail and small, lizard-like head. He placed a short horn on the animal's snout — this was actually one of the animal's "thumbs" (*below*).

It was not until 1877 that the true nature of *Iguanodon* became apparent. During that year, in the small town of Bernissart in Belgium, the massive bones of what turned out to be 31 *Iguanodon* were found by workers tunneling through a coalmine. These spectacular skeletons are now restored and on display in the Royal National Institute of Natural Sciences in Brussels.

Iguanodon stood 16 ft/5 m tall, measured 30 ft/9 m in length, and probably weighed about 5 US tons/4.5 tonnes. Herds of *Iguanodon* would have roamed the warm, tropical Cretaceous landscape, browsing on low-growing ferns and horsetails near rivers and streams. They would have spent much of their time on 4 legs; they could also walk upright, and reach higher vegetation, using their long outstretched tails to prop up or balance their bodies.

The head of this great dinosaur ended in a prominent snout and powerful, beaklike jaws. The cheek teeth would have provided a strong, grinding action, because the bones of the upper jaw could move apart when the lower jaw was raised up between them. Then, the banks of cheek teeth moved past each other, pulverizing the plant food.

The legs were long and pillarlike, each with 3 stout toes, ending in heavy, hooflike nails. Each short arm had a 5-fingered hand, which could be splayed wide, and used for walking when the animal was on all-fours. Three of the

fingers had hooflike nails. The fifth, or "little," finger was flexible enough to have been used for grasping or hooking down leaves to the mouth. The first finger, or "thumb," was developed into a prominent spike, which stuck out sideways from the hand. In 1825, Mantell had found only one of these thumb spikes, and, not knowing which part of the animal it came from, placed it, incorrectly, on the snout as a horn.

The function of these thumb spikes is not known. They could have been used to tear down foliage. Or they could have been used to defend itself against attacks from contemporary predators like *Megalosaurus* (see p. 117). Or, perhaps, the spikes were sexual display structures, used in courtship and mating.

Like *Megalosaurus*, *Iguanodon* has left its footprints in the rocks of southern England. Great trackways suggest that the animals were walking upright at the time they passed, and were traveling in a herd. Similar footprints, though no actual bones, have also been found in South America and in Spitzbergen, north of today's Arctic Circle, which shows how widespread *Iguanodon* must have been 100 million years ago.

NAME: *Vectisaurus*
TIME: **Early Cretaceous**
LOCALITY: **Europe (England)**
SIZE: **13 ft/4 m long**
Vectisaurus was a close relative of *Iguanodon*, living in the same place at the same time. Indeed, some paleontologists think it was a species of *Iguanodon*.

Only scanty remains have been found of *Vectisaurus* on the Isle of Wight, off the southern English coast. The only difference to *Iguanodon* was the height of the spines that grew upward from its backbone. These spines were long enough to have formed a prominent ridge down the animal's back. Some paleontologists think that *Vectisaurus*

may have been a forerunner in the evolution of the "fin-backed" ornithischian dinosaurs, such as *Ouranosaurus* (below).

NAME: *Ouranosaurus*
TIME: **Early Cretaceous**
LOCALITY: **Africa (Niger)**
SIZE: **23 ft/7 m long**
Two complete skeletons of *Ouranosaurus* were found in 1965, in the southern Sahara of northeastern Niger. Although identified as an iguanodont, it was an unusual-looking member of the family. It had a tall wall of spines running down the center of its back, from the shoulders to halfway along the tail. These spines were outgrowths from the vertebrae of the back, and would have been covered with skin to form a prominent "fin" or "sail."

Another group of dinosaurs, the saurischian spinosaurs, also sported such a fin on the back (see p. 120). In fact, one of their members — the large, carnivorous *Spinosaurus* — lived in Niger at about the same time as *Ouranosaurus*.

The function of the fin in both saurischian and ornithischian dinosaurs is not known for certain, but many researchers believe that it was used by these dinosaurs to regulate their body temperature. Such large, bulky animals as *Spinosaurus* and *Ouranosaurus* could easily have become overheated in the hot conditions that prevailed in West Africa during Cretaceous times. When the fin was turned toward the sun's rays, its large surface area absorbed heat; when it was turned away from the sun, it lost heat.

Such tall, vertebral spines would have made the body and tail of *Ouranosaurus* quite rigid. But this was compensated for by the extreme flexibility of the neck.

Some paleontologists have proposed that the tall spines actually supported a muscular hump on the back of *Ouranosaurus*, rather like that of a modern American bison.

Ouranosaurus also had an unusual skull, unlike that of other iguanodonts. It was long and low, and sloped gently down to a wide, flat snout. The overall appearance is reminiscent of a later group of ornithischian dinosaurs, the "duckbills" or hadrosaurs, that evolved in Late Cretaceous times (see pp. 146–153). A pair of bony bumps on the skull of *Ouranosaurus* increased its likeness to those hadrosaurs that had low crests on their heads.

In other respects, *Ouranosaurus* was like *Iguanodon*. It had 5-fingered hands, although they were much smaller and the fingers much shorter than those of

Iguanodon, and only the second and third fingers had "walking hooves." The 3-toed feet had heavy, hooflike nails, as in *Iguanodon*, and the neck was short but flexible. All in all, *Ouranosaurus* lived like other members of its family — a slow-moving browser that spent most of its time on all-fours, cropping leaves, fruits and seeds with its horny, ducklike beak.

NAME: *Muttaburrasaurus*
TIME: **Early Cretaceous**
LOCALITY: **Australia (Queensland)**
SIZE: **24 ft/7.3 m long**
One of the few dinosaurs to be found so far in Australia, *Muttaburrasaurus* was unearthed in 1981 from what are now the grasslands of central Queensland. In structure, it was similar to *Iguanodon*. Only the skull showed minor differences. There was a bony bump on the snout in front of the eyes. This could have been a sexual display structure, and was similar in appearance to the crests possessed by some of the later hadrosaurs, such as *Kritosaurus* (see p. 148).

NAME: *Probactrosaurus*
TIME: **Early Cretaceous**
LOCALITY: **Asia (China)**
SIZE: **20 ft/6 m long**
By the end of the Early Cretaceous period, about 100 million years ago, iguanodonts had reached their peak in abundance and diversity, and had spread all over the world. They began to decline from the Mid-Cretaceous onward, and very few are found in the Late Cretaceous. *Probactrosaurus* of eastern Asia and *Muttaburrasaurus* of Australia were among the few to survive to the end of the Mesozoic Era.

The demise of the iguanodonts was probably linked with the rise of a most successful group of plant-eating ornithopods. These were the duckbilled dinosaurs, or hadrosaurs, that were already common by Late Cretaceous times (see pp. 146–153). Like the West African *Ouranosaurus* (above), the anatomy of *Probactrosaurus* has several features akin to the hadrosaurs. It could, therefore, have been close to the ancestry of that group, or even been an early member of it.

Duckbilled dinosaurs

HADROSAURUS

BACTROSAURUS

ANATOSAURUS

MAIASAURA

SHANTUNGOSAURUS

KRITOSAURUS

EDMONTOSAURUS

Duckbilled dinosaurs

HADROSAURUS

BACTROSAURUS

ANATOSAURUS

MAIASAURA

FAMILY HADROSAURIDAE

The hadrosaurs were the most common, varied and well-adapted group of ornithopod dinosaurs — a real success story in the history of the ruling reptiles. The group probably evolved in central Asia, and by Late Cretaceous times had spread all over the lands of the northern hemisphere — migrating eastward into North America across the land bridge that existed at the time, and from there eastward again, into Europe.

The southern landmass of Gondwanaland had, however, broken up by Late Cretaceous times, and the continents were drifting apart. No hadrosaurs have been found in Africa, India or Australia. But some obviously managed to reach South America, because the remains of a primitive, flat-headed hadrosaur, called *Secernosaurus*, were discovered in Late Cretaceous rocks in southern Argentina. These animals probably crossed over from North America via the chain of volcanic islands that existed where Central America now lies.

Superficially, hadrosaurs looked quite different — with many variations of crests and bumps on their heads. But structurally, they were all the same. The most obvious feature that unites them as a group was the way the front of the face was elongated into a broad, flattened snout with a toothless beak. This beak looked rather like the bill of a modern duck, and it is this feature that has given the group its popular name of "duckbilled" dinosaurs.

Although there were no teeth in the front of a hadrosaur's mouth, there were batteries of cheek teeth arranged in rows in the upper and lower jaws, with new teeth continually replacing old, worn ones (*see Edmontosaurus, p. 149*). This was a unique development among dinosaurs, and was probably a major factor in the success of the group.

Another likely reason for the hadrosaurs' success was that the flowering plants (angiosperms) had evolved during Cretaceous times, and toward the end of that period had multiplied over all the earth's surface. So, besides plant foods such as ferns, horsetails, cycads and conifers, hadrosaurs could now add to their menus a profusion of flowering plants. The success of the hadrosaurs could well have been the reason for the decline of the other types of plant-eating dinosaurs — the iguanodonts and giant sauropods — which could not compete with the versatile newcomers.

All hadrosaurs had long hindlegs and shorter forelegs, both equipped with hooflike nails for walking. They probably spent most of their time browsing on all-fours, but when they had to run away from predators, they would have reared up on hindlegs and sprinted away, balanced by their long tails.

The hadrosaur family is divided into 2 distinct groups (subfamilies), according to the type of crest that grew on the head. Some animals had flat heads surmounted with solid, bony crests, while others had no crests at all. This group is called the hadrosaurine duckbills. They were the most successful, long-lived and wide-ranging members of the family, being among the last dinosaurs to survive.

The second group of hadrosaurs had high, domed heads, surmounted by flamboyant, hollow crests. These are called the lambeosaurine duckbills (*see pp. 151, 153*). They seem to have evolved in North America, and been largely confined to that continent.

NAME: *Bactrosaurus*
TIME: **Late Cretaceous**
LOCALITY: **Asia (Mongolia and China)**
SIZE: **13 ft/4 m long**
This is the earliest known hadrosaur, and seems to have been intermediate in structure between the 2 types of duckbills. It had a low, flat head with no crest, and a narrow bill (features of the hadrosaurine duckbills), but in build it was like a lambeosaurine duckbill. It most probably represents an ancestral stage in the development of the group. It could have evolved from one of the iguanodont family, such as *Probactrosaurus* of China (*see p. 145*).

NAME: *Kritosaurus*
TIME: **Late Cretaceous**
LOCALITY: **North America (Alberta, Montana and New Mexico)**
SIZE: **30 ft/9 m long**
Kritosaurus was a typical flat-headed duckbill. Although it had no crest on its head, there was the beginnings of one, developed as a large, bony hump on the snout in front of the eyes.

The function of this hump of solid bone is unknown. It could have been a sexual display structure possessed by the males only, and used in courtship and mating. Alternatively, it could have served the same purpose as the thickened skull caps of the pachycephalosaurs (*see p. 137*) — to absorb the impact when rival males crashed head-on in their ritualistic, head-butting battles, which took place at the beginning of each season to decide leadership of the herd, and control of the harem.

Some paleontologists think that *Kritosaurus* and *Hadrosaurus (below)* are different species of the same animal.

NAME: *Hadrosaurus*
TIME: **Late Cretaceous**
LOCALITY: **North America (Montana, New Jersey, New Mexico and South Dakota)**
SIZE: **30 ft/9 m long**
Hadrosaurus, meaning "big lizard," has the distinction of being the first dinosaur to be discovered in North America. Its bones were found in New Jersey, and it was reconstructed and named in 1858 by the American professor of anatomy, Joseph Leidy, of the University of Pennsylvania. He recognized that *Hadrosaurus* was structurally related to *Iguanodon*, whose remains had first been found in southern England, and described in 1825 (*see p. 144*).

But unlike the early, inaccurate reconstructions of *Iguanodon* by Mantell, the geologist — as a 4-legged, dragonlike creature — Leidy, the anatomist, knew from the structure of *Hadrosaurus* that it could also rise up on its hindlegs. He showed it in a running pose as a bipedal animal — standing upright on 2 legs, its short arms dangling and its body bent horizontal to the ground, balanced by the long, outstretched tail.

Hadrosaurus was the typical member of the duckbill family. Like *Kritosaurus (above)*, it had no crest on its long, low head, but there was a large hump on its snout, made of solid bone, and probably covered with thick, hard skin. Its bill, at the front of the jaws, had no teeth, but there were hundreds of teeth at the back of the jaws, in a continual state of replacement.

Hadrosaurs could move their upper and lower jaws against each other vertically *and* horizontally. This produced strong chewing and grinding actions, which would have thoroughly pulverized the food before it was swallowed.

SHANTUNGOSAURUS

KRITOSAURUS

EDMONTOSAURUS

NAME: *Maiasaura*
TIME: Late Cretaceous
LOCALITY: North America (Montana)
SIZE: 30 ft/9 m long
The discovery of *Maiasaura* in 1978 has given paleontologists a new insight into the family life of dinosaurs. In that year, a complete nesting site was found in Montana — the remains of an ancient nursery, some 75 million years old, where duckbills laid their eggs, and the young developed in safety.

This exciting find consisted of the skeleton of an adult (the mother, presumably); several youngsters (each about 3 ft 3 in/1 m long); a group of hatchlings (each about 20 in/50 cm long) together in a fossilized nest; and several other nests complete with intact eggs, and pieces of broken shell lying around.

The nests themselves had been made of heaped-up mounds of mud, now of course solid rock. Each nest was about 10 ft/3 m in diameter and 5 ft/1.5 m high. There was a craterlike depression in the center of each mound, about 6 ft 6 in/2 m in diameter and 2 ft 5 in/ 0.75 m deep. Spacing between the nests was about 23 ft/7 m, which meant that the mothers nested fairly close to each other, since the average length of *Maiasaura* was some 26 ft/8 m.

The fossilized eggs found in the nests were obviously laid with care. They were arranged in circles within the crater, layer upon layer. The mother probably covered over each layer with earth or sand as she went, and then covered the whole nest with earth when she was finished. This would have kept the eggs warm while they hatched, and well concealed from predators.

These duckbilled hadrosaurs were obviously social animals, as seen by this nursery site. The females nested in groups, probably even returning to the same site each year, as do some modern animals — seabirds, turtles and fish.

The youngsters stayed with their mothers until they were mature enough to fend for themselves — also seen in many modern groups.

NAME: *Shantungosaurus*
TIME: Late Cretaceous
LOCALITY: Asia (China)
SIZE: 43 ft/13 m long
This massive, flat-headed duckbill was among the biggest of the hadrosaurs. An almost complete specimen was discovered in Shandong (formerly Shantung) Province of eastern China during the 1970s, and its reconstructed skeleton is now on display in Beijing's (Peking) Natural History Museum.

Shantungosaurus had an extra-long tail, accounting for almost half the total length of its body. This was necessary to counterbalance the animal's greatweight — probably over 5 US tons/4.5 tonnes; when *Shantungosaurus* walked upright, the tail was held out stiffly behind, to balance the body at the hips.

Like that of other hadrosaurs, this duckbill's tail was deep, and flattened from side to side — rather like the tail of a modern crocodile. Because of this, paleontologists originally thought that duckbills spent most of their time in water, and used their tails for swimming. However, bony tendons lashed together all the vertebrae of the tail, making it much too rigid to have acted as a paddle. Also, the spines above and below the tail vertebrae sloped backward; in true aquatic animals, these spines are vertical, to provide attachment points for strong swimming muscles.

This does not mean that *Shantungosaurus* and its relatives did not venture into water. Most likely they did, to escape the attentions of contemporary predators such as *Tarbosaurus* and *Alioramus* in Asia, or *Albertosaurus* and *Tyrannosaurus* in North America.

NAME: *Anatosaurus*
TIME: Late Cretaceous
LOCALITY: North America (Alberta)
SIZE: 33 ft/10 m long
The popular name for this group of dinosaurs, the "duckbills," was coined after the discovery of the broad, flat skull of this hadrosaur in western North America. The name *Anatosaurus*, in fact, means "duck lizard," and refers to its horny, toothless bill or beak.

Several well-preserved skeletons of *Anatosaurus* have been found. From these, paleontologists can tell that this duckbill was over 30 ft/9 m long, stood some 13 ft/4 m tall, and probably weighed about 4 US tons/3.6 tonnes. Two "mummified" specimens were also

found — a rare discovery — with dried-up tendons and the contents of their stomachs intact. The last meal eaten by these 2 individuals consisted of pine needles, twigs, seeds and fruits.

Impressions of the animals' skin were also preserved, stamped into the surrounding rocks. Though all the skin had long since rotted, these impressions show that *Anatosaurus* was covered in a thick, leathery hide.

The same mummified specimens appeared to have had webs of skin between the 3 main fingers of each hand. At first, this seemed to reinforce the theory that duckbills were aquatic animals, using their webbed hands and flattened tails for swimming. But closer examination indicated that the hands could not be stretched widely, and the webs of skin were more likely to be the shriveled-up remains of weight-bearing walking pads, calloused with wear — like those on the feet of modern camels. Such pads tie in with the presence of hooflike nails on 2 of the main fingers of each hand, and support the current theory that duckbills were true land-dwellers that walked mainly on all-fours.

NAME: *Edmontosaurus*
TIME: Late Cretaceous
LOCALITY: North America (Alberta and Montana)
SIZE: 43 ft/13 m long
Many skulls of this large, flat-headed duckbill have been found. The teeth are particularly well preserved, and show the typical hadrosaur pattern. Behind the toothless beak, banks of tightly packed teeth formed a veritable grinding pavement in both the upper and lower jaws. As those at the top were worn down and discarded, new teeth replaced them from the bottom. At any one time, there may have been over 1000 teeth in *Edmontosaurus*' mouth.

The outer edge of each tooth was coated with hard enamel, which wore away more slowly than the dentine that made up the rest of the tooth. The result was that each tooth had a cutting ridge of hard, upstanding enamel. Packed so closely together in each jaw, the batteries of teeth presented a coarse, abrasive surface for pulverizing plant food.

The jaw structure was rather like that of *Iguanodon* (see p. 144) in the way that the upper jaw could move over the lower jaw, so that the teeth ground against each other when the mouth was closed. This produced a shearing, grinding action between the tooth rows, capable of shredding the toughest of plant material. Indeed, *Edmontosaurus* and its relatives lived on coarse food, as the fossilized stomach contents of *Anatosaurus* (*above*) showed.

Duckbilled dinosaurs

PROSAUROLOPHUS

SAUROLOPHUS

TSINTAOSAURUS

HYPACROSAURUS

LAMBEOSAURUS

CORYTHOSAURUS

PARASAUROLOPHUS

Duckbilled dinosaurs

NAME: *Prosaurolophus*
TIME: **Late Cretaceous**
LOCALITY: **North America (Alberta)**
SIZE: **26 ft/8 m long**

Prosaurolophus was a typical member of the hadrosaurine group of hadrosaurs — those duckbills with solid, bony crests on their heads. Its skull was similar to that of one of the flat-headed duckbills, such as *Anatosaurus* (*see p. 149*). But the nasal bones were extended into a low crest of bone that ran from the tip of the broad, flat snout up to the top of the head, where it was developed into a small, bony knob.

Since this crest became more pronounced in relatives of *Prosaurolophus*, this duckbill may have been ancestral to later members of the family, such as *Saurolophus* (*below*).

NAME: *Saurolophus*
TIME: **Late Cretaceous**
LOCALITY: **North America (Alberta and California) and Asia (Mongolia)**
SIZE: **30 ft/9 m long**

The face of this large duckbill swept upward in a graceful curve, from the broad, flattened snout to the tip of a solid, bony, hornlike crest that sloped backward from the top of its head. The size of the crest varied between species of *Saurolophus*. The Asian species had a larger crest than its North American relative and a correspondingly larger body size, of about 39 ft/12 m long.

The crest was an extension of the nasal bones, and the nasal passages would have run through it. This has led some paleontologists to think that there was a mass of nasal tissue which could have been inflated, and used to produce bellowing or honking sounds through the nose. The bony crest would have acted as a support for this inflatable sac, so increasing its area and, hence, its efficiency. Since hadrosaurs lived in herds, such sounds would have been an effective means of communicating with each other, especially over a distance.

NAME: *Tsintaosaurus*
TIME: **Late Cretaceous**
LOCALITY: **Asia (China)**
SIZE: **33 ft/10 m long**

A unicorn-type horn grew from the top of this Chinese duckbill's head, giving it a bizarre appearance quite unlike that of any of its relatives. The tall column of bone pointed straight up from between the eyes. Its tip was expanded and notched. And there was a connection between the base of the crest and the nostrils.

These facts have led some paleontologists to believe that there may have been a flap of skin attached to the horn, or

maybe even stretched between the tip of the horn and the beak. This flap could have been inflated like a balloon, and used as a signaling device between members of the herd, either for courtship or for threatening rivals. It may even have been brightly colored, in which case it would have made a spectacular display for either purpose — attracting or repelling.

Other paleontologists, however, think that the horn from the original specimen of *Tsintaosaurus* found in China was wrongly mounted on the reconstruction of the animal, and that it should point backward, as in *Saurolophus* (*above*).

NAME: *Corythosaurus*
TIME: **Late Cretaceous**
LOCALITY: **North America (Alberta and Montana)**
SIZE: **30 ft/9 m long**

A spectacular semicircular crest decorated the head of this large, North American duckbill, which weighed almost 5 US tons/4.5 tonnes. The crest rose steeply from just in front of the animal's eyes into a tall, narrow fan shape (about 1 ft/30 cm high) that curved down to the back of the head.

Several sizes of crest have been found in different specimens of *Corythosaurus*. This could reflect different species of this duckbill, or more likely, it could show different growth stages of the same species, with juvenile specimens having much smaller crests than adults. There may even have been a size difference between the sexes, with full-grown males having the largest crests.

Corythosaurus was a typical member of the lambeosaurine group of hadrosaurs — those duckbills with hollow crests on their heads. (Solid head crests characterized the hadrosaurine duckbills, *see pp. 146–149, 150, 152*.) As a group, the hollow-crested types seem to have evolved in North America, and been largely confined to the western part of that continent. Some species have also been found in eastern Asia, which fact lends support to the theory that western North America and eastern Asia were joined together in Late Cretaceous times as one landmass, "Asiamerica," and surrounded by shallow continental seas (*see pp. 12–13*).

The domed crest was made up of the greatly expanded nasal bones. The hollows inside the crest were the actual nasal passages, which ran up into the crest and looped back down into the snout. Several theories have been proposed for such an arrangement, some of them more likely than others. The old notion, for example, that hadrosaurs were aquatic animals, led to the belief

that the crest, with its series of hollow tubes, was some kind of snorkel, which allowed the animal to breathe air while its mouth and nostrils were submerged. Another theory stated that the crest acted as an air reservoir, so that the duckbill could draw on its supply while swimming or feeding underwater.

It is now known that the duckbills were well-adapted land animals. They were also gregarious and lived in herds, browsing in the forests on tough pine needles, magnolia leaves, seeds and fruits of all kinds. When threatened by predators such as *Tyrannosaurus*, they could sprint away on 2 legs; they may even have taken to water to escape.

Several more likely explanations exist for the hollow crest, and it is quite possible that it served some or all of the proposed functions. First, the hollow crest with its convoluted tube system could have been used as a vocal resonator — like the pipe of a trombone — to produce sounds for communication with the rest of the herd. These sounds could have been made for a variety of purposes — to warn other members of the herd of danger, to win a mate or discourage a rival, and for species-recognition between groups.

The results of recent research in the USA seem to support this theory. An exact model of a lambeosaur's crest was constructed, and experiments show that these duckbills could have produced a kind of foghorn sound from such a structure. These booming, resonant notes would have been heard over wide distances, and provided these forest-dwellers with an effective means of communicating between themselves and other herds. The postulated inflatable nasal sacs on the faces of the flat-headed, solid-crested duckbills (in the hadrosaurine subfamily) probably served the same purpose.

Another theory proposes that the

HYPACROSAURUS

CORYTHOSAURUS

LAMBEOSAURUS

PARASAUROLOPHUS

long air passage within the hollow crest could have served as a cooling system. Its surface may have been lined with a moist membrane, evaporation from which would have reduced the temperature of the surrounding tissue. This would have helped to cool down the animal when it was browsing in the open under the hot sun, or after a strenuous flight from a predator.

A third theory suggests that the hollow crest somehow enhanced the animal's sense of smell, so helping it to find food, detect the approach of danger and keep with the herd.

A primitive-looking crested duckbill was found in Montana after the discovery of *Corythosaurus*, and named *Procheneosaurus*. Its crest was much smaller than that of *Corythosaurus*, but it contained the same, typical S-shaped air passage. Some paleontologists think that this creature is possibly the most primitive of the hollow-crested duckbills. Others, however, believe it to be simply a juvenile specimen of *Corythosaurus* itself.

NAME: *Hypacrosaurus*
TIME: Late Cretaceous
LOCALITY: North America (Alberta and Montana)
SIZE: 30 ft/9 m long
Another duckbill with a prominent semicircular crest on its head was *Hypacrosaurus*. The crest was similar to that of *Corythosaurus*, but not so tall or narrow. Nor did it rise so steeply from the animal's face, but rather sloped upward in a gentle curve. Since *Hypacrosaurus* is found in slightly later rock deposits than *Corythosaurus*, it is possible that it evolved from that duckbill.

Another difference between these 2 similar-sized duckbills was that the back vertebrae of *Hypacrosaurus* were extended upward into tall spines, which would have formed a prominent, skin-

covered ridge down the animal's back. The function of this ridge may have been to regulate body temperature, operating in the same way as that proposed for other reptiles, such as the fin-backed pelycosaurs (*see pp. 186–189*) or the carnivorous spinosaurs (*see p. 120*).

NAME: *Lambeosaurus*
TIME: Late Cretaceous
LOCALITY: North America (Baja California, Montana and Saskatchewan)
SIZE: 30 ft/9 m long
This lambeosaur duckbill was unusual in having 2 distinct structures on its head. A tall, rectangular, hollow crest grew upward from the front of the head and pointed forward, while a solid, bony spike grew from the crown of the head and pointed backward. This V-shaped arrangement must have looked quite ungainly, mounted as it was on the long, flexible neck.

Like all members of the duckbill family, *Lambeosaurus* moved about on all-fours while browsing on vegetation. Its flexible neck seems to have been an adaptation to allow the animal to reach around its body and gather low-growing plants from a wide area, without having to shift its position.

The Californian specimen of *Lambeosaurus* seems to have been a giant among duckbills. The remains are fragmentary, but the size and weight of the bones found indicate that their owner may well have reached a length of 54 ft/16.5m, making it the largest hadrosaur known.

NAME: *Parasaurolophus*
TIME: Late Cretaceous
LOCALITY: North America (Alberta, New Mexico and Utah)
SIZE: 33 ft/10 m long
Like *Saurolophus* (*see p. 152*), this duckbill had a shorter snout than other hadrosaurs, and a single backward-pointing, hornlike crest mounted on the top of its head. But there the resemblance ends, since the crest of the lambeosaurine *Parasaurolophus* was not solid like that of its hadrosaurine relative; it was a hollow tube, and many times longer than that of *Saurolophus*. In fact, the great crest was up to 6 ft/1.8 m long. Inside, the paired nasal passages ran from the nostrils right up to the tip of the crest, and then curved back down to the snout.

A skull with a much shorter crest and more tightly curved nasal passages was originally identified as a separate species of *Parasaurolophus*. But it is now regarded as belonging to a female of the long-crested type, supporting the theory that the sexes had crests of different sizes.

There was a unique notch in the backbone of *Parasaurolophus*. It was placed behind the shoulders, just at the point where the tip of the crest would abut the back when the duckbill's neck was held in its natural, S-shaped pose. Some paleontologists have suggested that the crest fitted into this notch while the animal was running through dense undergrowth. Then, the crest may have acted like a deflector, sweeping low-hanging branches upward, away from the body. The head crest of the modern cassowary is often used to break a path in the same way.

The tail of *Parasaurolophus* was also unusual, in that it was particularly deep. This has led some researchers to think that it may have been brightly patterned, and was used as a signaling device, perhaps during courtship or maybe for keeping the herd together as it moved through the forest. In addition, there could have been a frill of skin at the back of the head, loosely connecting the crest with the neck. This frill could also have been brightly colored, and may have served a similar display function.

If the theory is correct, that the hollow crest was used as a vocal resonating chamber, then one might suppose that the sounds produced through the long crest of *Parasaurolophus* were different from those produced, for example, by the high, semicircular crest of *Lambeosaurus*. Indeed, the head-dresses of the lambeosaurine duckbills show such a variety in size and shape that it seems likely that different species had quite different calls.

The forests of North America in Late Cretaceous times must have reverberated with sounds — from the fog-horn bellowings of the hollow-crested duckbills, to the honking and trumpeting that came from the nasal sacs of their neighbors, the solid-crested duckbills.

Armored dinosaurs

STEGOSAURUS

KENTROSAURUS

TUOJIANGOSAURUS

WUERHOSAURUS

POLACANTHUS

HYLAEOSAURUS

SCELIDOSAURUS

Armored dinosaurs

SUBORDER STEGOSAURIA

The stegosaurs were a distinctive group of ornithischian, or "bird-hipped," dinosaurs. Their small-headed, massive bodies were characterized by double rows of great, bony plates that extended down either side of the backbone. Their heavy tails were armed with pairs of long, sharp spikes.

Like their ornithopod relatives, such as the iguanodonts (*see pp. 142–145*) and the duckbills (*see pp. 146–153*), the stegosaurs were plant-eaters, and probably lived in herds. But unlike the more agile ornithopods, they were not capable of running on 2 legs to escape predators. Stegosaurs moved about exclusively on 4 legs. When attacked, they would most likely have stood their ground, lashing out with the spiked tail, and protected to a certain extent by the bony plates on the back.

FAMILY STEGOSAURIDAE

All the familiar stegosaurs belong to this family, including *Stegosaurus* itself. They evolved in Mid-Jurassic times, some 170 million years ago, and reached their peak of diversity by the end of that period. They spread through western North America, western Europe, East Asia and East Africa. By Early Cretaceous times, the group had started to decline, although some species may well have survived in isolated pockets until the end of the Cretaceous.

NAME: *Stegosaurus*
TIME: **Late Jurassic**
LOCALITY: **North America (Colorado, Oklahoma, Utah and Wyoming)**
SIZE: **up to 30 ft/9 m long**
This armored dinosaur is the state fossil of Colorado and the largest and most familiar of the stegosaurs. It had a double row of broad, bony plates, shaped like huge arrowheads, embedded in the skin of its back. They ran down either side of the backbone, from just behind its head to halfway along its tail. Some of the plates were over 2 ft/60 cm high.

The heavy tail was armed with pairs of vicious spikes, each about 3 ft 3 in/ 1 m long. The number of spikes varied between species; for example, *Stegosaurus ungulatus* had 4 pairs, while *S. stenops* had only 2 pairs.

No-one is certain exactly how the bony plates were arranged on the back of *Stegosaurus*. Although many well-preserved specimens have been found — one of the best is mounted in Colorado's Denver Museum of Natural History — the plates have never been found actually attached to the skeleton.

Some paleontologists maintain that they lay flat in or on the skin, and formed a defensive armor over the back and upper flanks.

Most paleontologists, however, believe that the plates stood up almost vertically, and were arranged either in a zigzag pattern down the back or opposite each other in pairs. They would have formed a spiky fence of high armor, protecting *Stegosaurus* from attack by such predators as the contemporary carnosaur *Allosaurus* (*see p. 117*). Most likely, the plates were covered in tough horn, like the horns of modern cattle.

Alternatively, a thin layer of blood-rich skin could have covered the plates. This theory has led some paleontologists to propose an entirely different function for the plates — that of heat exchangers, a crude but effective means of regulating body temperature. The near-vertical plates could have been arranged alternately down the back. Their large surface area and rich supply of blood would have enabled them to absorb heat rapidly when oriented toward the sun (thus raising the body's internal temperature), and to lose heat when turned away.

The long, sturdy spikes on the tail of *Stegosaurus* were probably covered in horn, and were undoubtedly used for defense. *Stegosaurus* could have swung its long, heavy tail from side to side, and inflicted great damage on an attacker.

On average, *Stegosaurus* was 20 ft/6 m long, and weighed up to 2 US tons/ 2 tonnes. The massive hindlegs, with their heavy hooves, were over twice the length of the forelegs — a striking feature in this 4-legged animal, since it meant that the body sloped forward from its highest point at the hips.

Tall spines projected upward from the vertebrae of the hips and base of the tail, probably acting as anchor points for strong back muscles. This arrangement suggests that *Stegosaurus* could have lifted its forelegs off the ground without much effort, allowing it to feed off the lower branches of trees.

The skull of this huge dinosaur was low, narrow and tiny — only about 16 in/40 cm long. The brain was correspondingly small, about the size of a walnut. *Stegosaurus* was not particularly well equipped for chewing plant food; it had a toothless beak at the front of the jaws, and the cheek teeth were small and weak. In order to digest its food, it is likely that *Stegosaurus* swallowed stones (as did many of the herbivorous dinosaurs), and held them in its stomach, where they helped to grind down the tough plant material.

An intriguing cavity in the hip vertebrae of *Stegosaurus*, above the hindlegs and just at the point where the spinal cord would have passed in life, has led paleontologists to speculate that this site housed a "second brain" that controlled the movements of the animal's massive hindquarters. This "brain" would really have been a conglomeration of nervous tissue, situated where the nerves of the hips and hindlegs met.

In fact, all backboned animals have this extra "brain," but its size is related to the size of the hips; in big-hipped animals, such as many of the dinosaurs, the hip's "brain" was larger than that of the skull.

An alternative theory for this cavity in the hip vertebrae proposes that it housed a gland that produced glycogen. Doses of this sugary substance could have been released to provide the animal's hindquarters with an extra boost of energy in times of stress.

NAME: *Kentrosaurus*
TIME: **Late Jurassic**
LOCALITY: **Africa (Tanzania)**
SIZE: **16 ft/5 m long**
Well-preserved remains of this East African stegosaur — a contemporary of the North American *Stegosaurus* — have been found in modern Tanzania among the fossil-rich deposits of Tendaguru Hill.

Kentrosaurus was not as large as its American relative, but it was at least as well armored. A double row of narrow, triangular, bony plates rose on either side of the backbone, grouped in pairs along the neck, shoulders and front part of the back. The plates were then replaced by pairs of sharp spikes (some of them about 2 ft/60 cm long) that ran down the lower back right to the tip of the tail. In addition, a pair of extra-long spikes stuck out at hip-level on each side, affording good protection should a predator attack from the side.

WUERHOSAURUS

POLACANTHUS

SCELIDOSAURUS

NAME: *Tuojiangosaurus*
TIME: Late Jurassic
LOCALITY: Asia (China)
SIZE: 23 ft/7 m long
Tuojiangosaurus is one of several armored dinosaurs found in China. It was the first stegosaur to be discovered in Asia, and is known from an almost complete specimen. Structurally similar to *Stegosaurus*, it had a small, narrow head with low teeth and a heavily built body. Fifteen pairs of bony plates surmounted its back, becoming taller and more spikelike over the hips and down the tail. As in *Stegosaurus stenops*, there were 2 pairs of long spikes on the tail.

It seems that *Tuojiangosaurus* was not able to rear up on its hindlegs, as was *Stegosaurus*. This is deduced from the fact that the tall spines that projected upward from the back vertebrae of *Stegosaurus* (to provide muscle-attachment points) are not present in either *Tuojiangosaurus* or *Kentrosaurus* (above). This suggests that they were ground-feeding animals.

NAME: *Wuerhosaurus*
TIME: Early Cretaceous
LOCALITY: Asia (China)
SIZE: 20 ft/6 m long
This Chinese stegosaur is known only from a few fragmentary remains of bones and scattered plates. The restoration on p. 155 is therefore tentative.

The stegosaur group began to decline toward the end of the Jurassic period. *Wuerhosaurus* is one of the few to have survived into Early Cretaceous times. However, another possible stegosaur, *Dravidosaurus*, has been found in India in beds of Late Cretaceous age. It is possible that India was an island-continent at that time, isolated from the other landmasses, and may have acted as a kind of "lost world" for the stegosaurs. A few species may have survived there, while the rest died out.

SUBORDER ANKYLOSAURIA

The decline of the stegosaurs toward the end of the Jurassic period may be linked to the rise of another group of armored dinosaurs, the ankylosaurs. They spread throughout the northern continents during Cretaceous times, and were particularly abundant in Asiamerica toward the end of that period (*see pp. 10–11*).

Like the stegosaurs, ankylosaurs were heavily built, 4-legged plant-eaters. They were also armored, but with a different, and more effective, kind of defensive plating than that of the stegosaurs. The neck, back, flanks and tail were entirely covered in a mosaic of flat, bony plates, which were embedded in the thick, leathery skin, and covered in horn. Spikes and knobs of various sizes studded the bony armor.

There were 2 distinct families of ankylosaur. The nodosaurs had narrow skulls, armored backs and long spikes projecting from their flanks (*below and pp. 158, 160*). The ankylosaurs themselves had broad skulls and a heavy "club" of solid bone at the end of their tails (*see pp. 159, 161*). A third family, the scelidosaurs (*below*), are thought to be primitive representatives of the group.

FAMILY SCELIDOSAURIDAE

The position of the scelidosaurs in the dinosaur array is controversial. Some paleontologists maintain that they were the ancestors of the stegosaurs, while others believe them to be ancestral ankylosaurs. Here, they are regarded as primitive members of the ankylosaurs.

NAME: *Scelidosaurus*
TIME: Early Jurassic
LOCALITY: Europe (England)
SIZE: 13 ft/4 m long
Only 2 skeletons of *Scelidosaurus* have been found to date, both from the Early Jurassic of Dorset in southern England. The first specimen was discovered in about 1860 and the second in 1955.

Scelidosaurus seems to be one of the earliest and most primitive of the ornithischian dinosaurs. It had a small head (only about 8 in/20 cm long), a toothless beak and small, leaf-shaped teeth in its weak jaws. The body, however, was massive and well armored; the back was covered in bony plates, which were studded with parallel rows of spikes running from the neck to the tip of the tail and over the upper flanks. The arrangement of the bony armor suggests that *Scelidosaurus* was a primitive type of ankylosaur.

FAMILY NODOSAURIDAE

The nodosaurs were the earlier and more primitive of the 2 families of ankylosaur, and ranged throughout the Cretaceous period. Some paleontologists think that they may have evolved in Europe during the Late Jurassic, and then spread to the other northern continents. Some types at least also reached the southern hemisphere — *Minmi* is a recent discovery from Australia.

Nodosaurs had narrow skulls, longer than they were wide. Solid, bony plates covered the body from neck to tail, and long spikes guarded the flanks.

NAME: *Hylaeosaurus*
TIME: Early Cretaceous
LOCALITY: Europe (England)
SIZE: 20 ft/6 m long
This is the earliest creature that can definitely be identified as a nodosaur. It was first found in Sussex in southern England in the late 1820s, and named by that English pioneer of paleontology, Gideon Mantell, in 1832. To this day, its bones are still imprisoned in the slab of rock in which they were fossilized, but there are now plans to extract the skeleton with the use of acetic acid. This dissolves away the mineral calcite, which cements together the particles of rock, so releasing the fossilized bones.

Until new evidence is available, the restoration of *Hylaeosaurus* on p. 155 must remain speculative. The narrow head, armor-plated body and tail, and the outwardly projecting spikes on the flanks were typical nodosaur features.

NAME: *Polacanthus*
TIME: Early Cretaceous
LOCALITY: Europe (England)
SIZE: 13 ft/4 m long
This "many-spined" nodosaur was a contemporary of *Hylaeosaurus* (*above*); indeed, some paleontologists reckon that the 2 animals are the same. The remains of *Polacanthus* consist of the bones of the sturdy hindlegs and some solid armor plates and spines.

It is not known exactly how the armor was arranged on the body. The restoration on p. 155 is the traditional view of the animal. Pairs of heavy, vertical spines protected the shoulders and upper back; a shield of fused bone covered the hips; and 2 lines of small, vertical spines ran down to the tip of the deep, heavy tail.

Armored dinosaurs

SAUROPELTA

EUOPLOCEPHALUS

SILVISAURUS

TALARURUS

SAICHANIA

STRUTHIOSAURUS

PANOPLOSAURUS

NODOSAURUS

ANKYLOSAURUS

Armored dinosaurs

SAUROPELTA

EUOPLOCEPHALUS

SILVISAURUS

TALARURUS

NAME: *Sauropelta*
TIME: Early Cretaceous
LOCALITY: North America (Montana)
SIZE: 25 ft/7.6 m long

Sauropelta, from the western USA, is the largest known member of the nodosaur family of ankylosaurs, the armored dinosaurs of Cretaceous times. It is estimated to have weighed over 3 US tons/3 tonnes.

Its massive body was encased in a bony armor. This consisted of bands of horn-covered plates with raised keels, which ran transversely over the body from the neck to the end of the long, tapering tail. The plates were embedded in the skin to form a strong, but flexible, covering all over the animal's back. Attacks from the side were deterred by a row of sharp spikes that stuck out sideways from each flank.

This slow-moving herbivore would have needed such protection against the attacks of the carnivorous dinosaurs of the day.

NAME: *Silvisaurus*
TIME: Early Cretaceous
LOCALITY: North America (Kansas)
SIZE: 11 ft/3.4 m long

Silvisaurus was covered in the heavy bony armor characteristic of the nodosaurs. Thick plates encased the neck, a more open arrangement of plates lay across the back and tail, and heavy spikes flanked the body.

Silvisaurus is, however, considered to be a primitive member of the family. Most nodosaurs had toothless beaks at the front of their jaws, but *Silvisaurus* retained teeth in its upper jaw. For this reason, some paleontologists believe that *Silvisaurus* may be ancestral to some of the later members of its family.

As in most of the nodosaurs and later ankylosaurs, the amount of bone in the skull of *Silvisaurus* was much reduced, so that it was lightweight and full of cavities and air passages. These could have been used to produce sounds for communicating with other members of the species. Such vocalization was not unknown among dinosaurs; for example, the gregarious duckbills had inflatable nasal sacs or hollow crests on their heads, through which the animals probably produced sounds for social communications among the herd (*see pp. 146–153*).

NAME: *Nodosaurus*
TIME: Late Cretaceous
LOCALITY: North America (Kansas and Wyoming)
SIZE: 18 ft/5.5 m long

Nodosaurus is the typical nodosaur, and has given its name to the whole family (*see also p. 157*). Its body armor was arranged from neck to tail in transverse bands. These consisted of narrow, rectangular plates that covered the ribs, alternating with broad plates that occupied the spaces in between. Hundreds of bony bosses or nodes studded the broad plates, hence the animal's name — *Nodosaurus*, meaning "node lizard."

The skull of *Nodosaurus* was small, long and narrow, with weak teeth — typical features of the family. The shoulders and hips were powerfully developed to carry the great weight of the body armor, as were the strong, stout legs with their broad, hoofed feet. The bones of the hips were so modified as weight-bearing structures that they no longer resembled the typical ornithischian, or "bird-hipped," pattern (*see pp. 92–93*).

An unusual find in Kansas consisted of the skeletons of several nodosaurs, all lying on their backs. They were found in marine sediments of Late Cretaceous age. This could represent a small herd of animals that were overcome at the same time, and were washed down to the sea; alternatively, these individuals could have come together after death by chance.

In either case, as they were swept along in the river, the decaying organs would have generated gases that bloated the body. This, combined with the weight of the armor on the back, would have made them top-heavy, and so they would have flipped over, and floated downstream on their backs. Eventually, they would have sunk into the mud of the seabed, belly-side up, in which position they were preserved.

NAME: *Struthiosaurus*
TIME: Late Cretaceous
LOCALITY: Europe (Austria, France, Hungary and Romania)
SIZE: 6 ft 6 in/2 m long

Struthiosaurus is remarkable since it is the smallest-known member of the nodosaur family — in fact, the smallest of the whole ankylosaur group. This has led paleontologists to speculate that it may have lived and evolved on islands. Many large types of animal tend to develop dwarf species when confined to such isolated habitats — an adaptation to the limited food resources found there. In Tertiary times, for example, species of dwarf elephant and hippopotamus evolved on the islands of the Mediterranean. A modern example is provided by the ponies of the Shetland Islands off northern Scotland.

In Late Cretaceous times, some 80 million years ago, most of modern Europe was covered by shallow seas. Dry land was only present in the form of islands. Perhaps groups of *Struthiosaurus* got marooned on various of these islands, and gradually evolved a smaller species, maybe several species on different islands, in the same way as the fauna of today's Galapagos Islands is thought to have developed.

Despite this theory of isolated development, *Struthiosaurus* retained its protective body armor. A variety of armor covered its back. There were plates around the neck; small bony studs covered the back and tail; and a fringe of spikes guarded each flank.

NAME: *Panoplosaurus*
TIME: Late Cretaceous
LOCALITY: North America (Alberta, Montana, South Dakota and Texas)
SIZE: 15 ft/4.4 m long

The latest of the nodosaurs, and the last known, *Panoplosaurus* was a medium-sized animal in comparison to some of its relatives. But it was massively built, and encased in a heavy body armor. It could have weighed as much as 4 US tons/3.6 tonnes.

The armor consisted of broad, square plates with keels, arranged in wide bands across the neck and shoulders. The rest of the back was covered in smaller, bony studs. Massive spikes, angled to the side and front, guarded each flank, especially on the shoulders.

Even *Panoplosaurus*' head was protected with thick, bony plates, so solidly fused to the underlying skull bones that their boundaries cannot be seen. But inside, this solid, bony box was full of cavities and air passages, with a bony palate separating the nasal system from the mouth. This would have enabled the animal to eat and breathe at the same time. The snout was narrow, which could suggest that *Panoplosaurus* rooted about among the ground vegetation to find the plants that it preferred.

SAICHANIA

TRUTHIOSAURUS

PANOPLOSAURUS

ANKYLOSAURUS

ODOSAURUS

It is likely that *Panoplosaurus* actively defended itself against attack, unlike many of its relatives that would probably have squatted down on the ground and relied on their armor plating to protect them. *Panoplosaurus* could have charged, directing one of its spiked shoulders toward the attacker. Its forelegs were strongly built, and especially well endowed with muscles in the elbow area. This suggests that the animal was quite maneuverable, and could move its forequarters nimbly in reaction to its enemy's tactics. A charging rhinoceros is the most apt, modern equivalent.

FAMILY ANKYLOSAURIDAE

This family of armored dinosaurs became abundant toward the end of the Cretaceous period, and largely replaced their relatives, the nodosaurs, in western North America and East Asia. Like the nodosaurs, they were heavily armored on the back with thick plates and spikes. But the head armor was more extensively developed, and there was a unique weapon at the tip of their tails. This was a large ball of fused bone, which could be swung like a club from side to side with potentially lethal effect on an attacking carnosaur.

These ankylosaurs were built like military tanks, and some species were about the same size. They were shorter and stockier than the nodosaurs, with massive-boned hips and hindlegs to support the heavy, clubbed tail. The hips were fused to the backbone by at least 8 sacral vertebrae, forming a super-strong anchor for the hindquarters. The hip bones themselves had degenerated into a shapeless mass, with no obvious trace of the bird-like arrangement so characteristic of the ornithischian dinosaurs.

NAME: *Talarurus*
TIME: **Late Cretaceous**
LOCALITY: **Asia (Mongolia)**
SIZE: **16 ft/5 m long**
Talarurus shows the typical features of the family. The armor-plated skull broadened out at the back into a pair of bony spikes, which gave this dinosaur the appearance of having ears. Another pair of spikes projected from each cheek. There was a toothless beak at the front of the jaws and small weak teeth in the back.

The barrel-shaped body was armored with thick plates, and fringed with spikes on the flanks. The heavy club at the end of the tail was formed from 3 masses of fused bone, and welded to the tail vertebrae in 2 main lobes. Bony tendons lashed the vertebrae together, so that when the animal walked, its tail was held off the ground. The base of the tail, near the massive hips, was supple and well-endowed with muscles.

When *Talarurus* was threatened by, for example, a contemporary tyrannosaur like *Tarbosaurus* (*see p.121*), it would have swung its clubbed tail at the attacker. The ramrod stiffness of the tail would have increased the force of the bony mass at its tip.

NAME: *Euoplocephalus*
TIME: **Late Cretaceous**
LOCALITY: **North America (Alberta)**
SIZE: **18 ft/5.5 m long**
Most of what paleontologists know about ankylosaurs is based on studies of this animal, carried out in the 1970s and '80s. The bands of armor were embedded in the skin of the back, and dotted with huge bony studs. There were heavy plates over the neck, and large, triangular spines jutted up to protect the shoulders and base of the tail.

Externally, the head was a heavy box of bone, covered in plates that were fused to the skull bones. Inside was the complicated series of chambers and air passages that characterized both the ankylosaurs and nodosaurs. A pair of thick spines protected the sides of the face. Even the eyelids were armored, forming shutters that could descend to guard the eyes when danger threatened. These bony eyelids were only accessory structures; the real eyelids would have consisted of the usual delicate membranes.

There was a horny, toothless beak at the front of the broad face. It may be that *Euoplocephalus* was an indiscriminate plant-eater, cropping any and all vegetation that presented itself. In contrast, its nodosaur relatives had narrow snouts, and probably were more selective feeders.

NAME: *Saichania*
TIME: **Late Cretaceous**
LOCALITY: **Asia (Mongolia)**
SIZE: **23 ft/7 m long**
The massive head of *Saichania* was armored with great bony nodules that stuck out in high relief. Spikes swept outward from each flank, and the whole of the back was protected by rows of knobbly plates.

Inside the skull, the air passages were more complex than those of other ankylosaurs, and were probably more effective in cooling and moistening the air before it reached the lungs. The bony palate, separating the nasal tubes from the mouth, was also stronger, perhaps allowing the animal to eat tougher plants. And there is some evidence to show that there may have been a salt gland associated with its nostrils. All these features could suggest that *Saichania* lived in a hot, arid environment, unlike the cold climate that prevails in modern Mongolia's Gobi Desert where the remains of this ankylosaur were found.

NAME: *Ankylosaurus*
TIME: **Late Cretaceous**
LOCALITY: **North America (Alberta and Montana)**
SIZE: **up to 33 ft/10 m long**
This is the largest-known ankylosaur, and one of the last of the group to survive, right to the end of the Cretaceous period. It was massively built, and probably weighed a good 4 US tons/3.6 tonnes. Its skull was about 2 ft 5 in/76 cm long. Its body was broad (16 ft/5 m at the widest point) and squat, supported on strong, stumpy legs set directly beneath the body.

Thick bands of heavy armor ran across the animal's back, from the top of the head to near the tip of the tail, which ended in a great, bony club. The armor consisted of hundreds of oval-shaped plates set close together, and embedded in the leathery hide. This open arrangement would have given great flexibility to the armor plating.

Ankylosaurus had a blunt snout, broad face and toothless beak. Two spikes stuck out on either side at the back of the head, and 2 more projected from each cheek.

When attacked, *Ankylosaurus* would probably have stood its ground, well protected by its body armor. When the predator got within range, the heavy, clubbed tail was swung sideways, and if it hit its target, the attacker would have been severely wounded.

Horned dinosaurs

PSITTACOSAURUS

MICROCERATOPS

LEPTOCERATOPS

BAGACERATOPS

PROTOCERATOPS

MONTANOCERATOPS

CENTROSAURUS

PACHYRHINOSAURUS

Horned dinosaurs

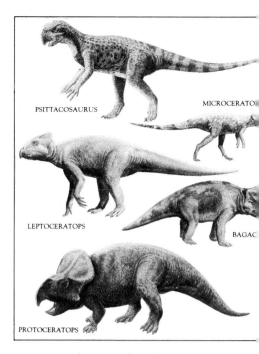

SUBORDER CERATOPIA

The horned ceratopians were the last group of ornithischian, or "bird-hipped," dinosaurs to evolve before the whole assemblage of these ruling reptiles suffered mass-extinction at the end of the Mesozoic Era.

The ceratopians (often incorrectly called ceratopsians) evolved late in the Cretaceous period. As a group, they existed for a mere 20 million years before becoming extinct, but in that short time, geologically speaking, they established themselves all over western North America and central Asia.

They were well-armored dinosaurs, although their weaponry was confined to the head, unlike the heavy armor plating that covered the backs of the ankylosaurs (see pp. 157–161). The advanced ceratopians had massive heads, armed with a sharp, parrotlike beak at the front; long, pointed horns on the brow or snout, sometimes both; and a great sheet of bone, the "frill," that grew from the back of the skull and curved upward, to protect the neck and often the shoulders, too.

The success of the ceratopians can be related to their efficient chopping teeth and powerful jaws. These dinosaurs could have eaten the toughest of plant foods, including a relatively new source — the shrubby flowering plants, similar to magnolia — that had begun to thrive worldwide in Late Cretaceous times. Ceratopians probably lived in herds in the upland forests, browsing on low-growing trees and ground vegetation.

FAMILY PSITTACOSAURIDAE

The "parrot" dinosaurs were a rare group of ornithischian dinosaurs, found only in the Early Cretaceous rocks of East Asia. Their skulls show many features that suggest that they were the ancestors of the horned dinosaurs, or ceratopians. Their bodies, however, were similar to those of the gazellelike hypsilophodonts, from which stock they probably arose (see pp. 138–141).

Like the hypsilophodonts, the parrot dinosaurs could rise up on 2 legs to run away from predators. The suggestion, therefore, is that the early ceratopians, descended from the parrot dinosaurs, were also bipedal, and only reverted to a 4-legged stance later in their evolution.

NAME: *Psittacosaurus*
TIME: **Early Cretaceous**
LOCALITY: **Asia (China, Mongolia and Siberia)**
SIZE: **up to 8 ft/2.5 m long**
A square skull and a horny, toothless beak are the features that have given this Asian dinosaur its name — *Psittacosaurus*, meaning "parrot lizard."

A thick ridge of bone on the top of the skull squared off the head at the back. This ridge served as an anchor point for the muscles of the powerful lower jaws. Over millions of years, it was to develop into the great, bony neck frill of the later ceratopians.

The cheek bones of *Psittacosaurus* were drawn out into a pair of hornlike projections. These were the forerunners of the horny spikes that grew out from each side of the head shield of later ceratopians.

The ancestor of the ceratopian group is believed to be among the parrot dinosaurs. But it is unlikely to be *Psittacosaurus* itself, since this animal had only 4 fingers on each hand, while the ceratopians had 5; also, *Psittacosaurus* had no teeth in its beak, while the early ceratopians, the protoceratopids (below), had teeth in the upper beak.

FAMILY PROTOCERATOPIDAE

The protoceratopids constitute the family of early, primitive horned dinosaurs, although only some of them had horns. They evolved in Asia, in the same region as the parrot dinosaurs (from which stock they probably evolved), but lived there many millions of years later, in the Late Cretaceous period. They also spread to western North America.

Like the parrot dinosaurs, the protoceratopids could walk upright, although they probably spent most of their time browsing on all-fours, and only rose up on 2 legs to run away from predators.

The protoceratopids were much smaller than their later relatives, the ceratopids. They had teeth in the upper beak, which is considered a primitive feature, lost in the more advanced ceratopids. They had no horns on their heads, or else only rudimentary ones. But they did have the beginnings of the neck frill that was to become so prominent in the later ceratopids.

NAME: *Microceratops*
TIME: **Late Cretaceous**
LOCALITY: **Asia (China and Mongolia)**
SIZE: **2 ft/60 cm long**
This creature is the smallest horned dinosaur known. It was probably not a direct ancestor of the later ceratopids, but rather an early, specialized offshoot of the main group.

Microceratops was a lightly built, 2-legged runner, as evidenced by the length of its shin bones — almost twice as long as the thigh bones, the sign of a sprinting animal. Its front legs, however, were also quite long in comparison to other bipedal dinosaurs, so it probably moved about mainly on 4 legs, only rising upright to escape from danger. Its lifestyle would have been similar to that of such ornithopods as the gazellelike hypsilophodonts of North America.

NAME: *Leptoceratops*
TIME: **Late Cretaceous**
LOCALITY: **North America (Alberta and Wyoming) and Asia (Mongolia)**
SIZE: **7 ft/2.1 m long**
This is one of the few protoceratopids known from North America; most of the family lived in Asia. In appearance, it was intermediate between the lightly built parrot dinosaurs and the heavier, early horned dinosaurs. It could probably walk on 2 legs as easily as on 4. Its hindlegs were built for running, as shown by the long shin bones, and the 5 clawed fingers of each hand could be used to grasp bundles of leaves, and pass them to the mouth.

The bones at the back of *Leptoceratops*' skull were expanded upward into a tall peak. This was an intermediate stage in development between the muscle-attachment ridge of the parrot dinosaurs and the neck frill of the horned dinosaurs.

NAME: *Bagaceratops*
TIME: **Late Cretaceous**
LOCALITY: **Asia (Mongolia)**
SIZE: **3 ft 3 in/1 m long**
This small protoceratopid represents another specialized offshoot from the main evolutionary branch of the horned dinosaurs. It had a squat, heavy body and long tail, supported on solid legs, 5-toed at the front and 4-toed at the back.

Bagaceratops possessed several of the features that were to be developed in the later horned dinosaurs. There was a prominent bony ridge at the back of its

MONTANOCERATOPS

CENTROSAURUS

PACHYRHINOSAURUS

skull (the precursor of the ceratopids' neck frill); a pair of leaf-shaped projections on either cheek (part of the ceratopids' head shield); and a definite, though short, horn halfway along its snout (anticipating the great horns of the ceratopids). In addition, it had lost its teeth in the upper beak; other members of its family retained these teeth, which is considered a primitive feature. But despite these advanced characteristics, *Bagaceratops* was probably not the direct ancestor of the horned dinosaurs.

NAME: *Protoceratops*
TIME: Late Cretaceous
LOCALITY: Asia (Mongolia)
SIZE: up to 9 ft/2.7 m long
The average adult of this early horned dinosaur measured about 6 ft 6 in/2 m long, and weighed almost 400 lbs/ 180 kg. It had a broad neck frill developed at the back of its large, heavy skull. This would have provided anchoring points for the powerful muscles of the toothed, beaked jaws.

Although *Protoceratops* had no horns, there was a prominent bump midway along its snout — more of a crest than a horn — that seems to have been larger in older male specimens, suggesting that it was used for ritual fights between rivals.

Protoceratops almost certainly spent most of its time on all-fours. But the hindlegs were still long in comparison to the forelegs, so this animal could probably also run upright, as did its likely ancestors, the parrot dinosaurs.

In the 1920s, the first dinosaur eggs and nests were discovered in Mongolia. They belonged to *Protoceratops*. The nests, dug in the sand over 70 million years ago, contained clutches of eggs, up to 18 in some nests. Each egg was sausage-shaped, about 8 in/20 cm long, with a thin, wrinkled shell, only a fraction of an inch thick. The eggs were carefully laid in 3-tiered spirals. Aston-

ishingly, some of the eggs were still intact, and inside were found fragments of fossilized bones from tiny embryos.

Another exciting find from Mongolia revealed *Oviraptor*, a small carnivorous dinosaur, preserved in the act of raiding a *Protoceratops* nest (*see p. 112*).

NAME: *Montanoceratops*
TIME: Late Cretaceous
LOCALITY: North America (Montana)
SIZE: 10 ft/3 m long
This North American dinosaur was similar in appearance to *Protoceratops* (*above*), with the notable exception of having a definite horn on its snout. This has led some paleontologists to regard it as an early member of the more advanced family of horned dinosaurs, the ceratopids (*below*). But *Montanoceratops* had the typical primitive features of the protoceratopid family — teeth in the upper beak, and claws on its feet, rather than hooves.

The tail of this medium-sized ceratopian was unusually deep due to the presence of tall spines that jutted upward from the vertebrae along its length. Evidently, the tail was also extremely flexible, and could be moved easily and rapidly from side to side. A possible explanation for these features could be that the tail was brightly colored, and used as a sexual signal during the mating season, or for recognition of its own species.

FAMILY CERATOPIDAE

The most abundant large herbivores of the Late Cretaceous period in western North America were the great horned dinosaurs of this family. They have been found nowhere else in the world.

Exclusively 4-legged, these herbivores were well protected from attack by contemporary, bipedal carnosaurs, such as *Tyrannosaurus* and *Albertosaurus* (*see pp. 118–121*). Long, sharp horns grew from their massive heads, and a bony frill, developed from the rear skull bones, guarded their necks. The pillar-like legs, with their heavy, hoofed feet, supported a stocky body that was covered in thick hide. There was also safety in numbers, and the horned dinosaurs moved in great, foraging herds through the upland forests, chopping off vegetation with their sharp, toothless beaks.

The family of horned dinosaurs is divided into 2 evolutionary lines. There were ceratopids with short neck frills and great horns on the snout. And there were ceratopids with long neck frills and great horns on the brow.

NAME: *Centrosaurus*
TIME: Late Cretaceous
LOCALITY: North America (Alberta and Montana)
SIZE: 20 ft/6 m long
This horned dinosaur was a typical member of the short-frilled group. (It used to be known by the name *Monoclonius*.) A long horn surmounted the snout of *Centrosaurus* (in some species, it curved forward), and two short horns rose above its eyes from the brow.

The neck frill stood up from behind the head, and was fringed with spines. There were 2 large openings on either side of the frill, which in life were covered over with skin, as was the rest of the frill. These holes reduced the weight of the bony structure, and their edges provided additional attachment points for the powerful jaw muscles.

A strong ball-and-socket joint connected the head to the neck. This was placed well forward in the skull, about under the eye region, so that the weight of the heavy frill at the back of the head was balanced by the great horn on the front. This mobile joint ensured that *Centrosaurus* could turn its massive head easily and quickly. This was important for such a slow-moving animal, since its head weapons were its only defense. Some of the neck vertebrae were fused together, to increase its strength, and the muscles of the forequarters were powerfully developed.

NAME: *Pachyrhinosaurus*
TIME: Late Cretaceous
LOCALITY: North America (Alberta)
SIZE: 18 ft/5.5 m long
This was an unusual horned dinosaur because it apparently had no horns. Instead, there was a large, thick pad of bone above the eyes in the place where the brow horns were usually found.

There are 2 theories to account for this strange bony pad. Some paleontologists equate its function with the thickened skull caps of the boneheaded dinosaurs — for in-fighting among male members of the herd. Other paleontologists, however, believe that the bony pad simply represents scar tissue, and marks the place where the brow horns had fallen off.

Only 2 skulls of *Pachyrhinosaurus* have been found, both without horns, so new finds will no doubt settle the argument.

Horned dinosaurs

STYRACOSAURUS

TRICERATOPS

CHASMOSAURUS

ARRHINOCERATOPS

ANCHICERATOPS

PENTACERATOPS

TOROSAURUS

Horned dinosaurs

STYRACOSAURUS

TRICERATOPS

CHASMOSAURUS

NAME: *Styracosaurus*
TIME: Late Cretaceous
LOCALITY: North America (Alberta and Montana)
SIZE: 17 ft/5.2 m long

One of the most spectacular of the short-frilled family of horned dinosaurs was the well-armed *Styracosaurus*. It had an enormous, straight horn on its snout, directed upward and forward. Two smaller horns grew above the eyes. The remarkable neck frill, like an oriental dancer's head-dress, had six main spikes arrayed around its top, some as large as the nose horn, and a number of smaller spikes made up a defensive fringe.

As in other short-frilled ceratopids, there were 2 large, skin-covered openings in the frill, which reduced the weight of this great bony structure considerably.

Styracosaurus could certainly have defended itself well. Charging head-down, rhinoceros-style, at an attacking *Tyrannosaurus*, for example, the herbivore's great nose horn could have ripped open the carnivore's soft belly, and the bony frill would have presented a formidable array of spikes to protect its neck from the carnivore's powerful jaws.

The spikes on the frill were probably also used for defensive display. If *Styracosaurus* stood head-on to an enemy, or even a rival male in its own herd, the spikes would have stood out from around its face, making the animal look sufficiently fearsome to deter most attackers. Modern African elephants hold their great ears out at the sides of the head to intimidate others in the same way.

NAME: *Triceratops*
TIME: Late Cretaceous
LOCALITY: North America (Alberta, Colorado, Montana, South Dakota, Saskatchewan and Wyoming)
SIZE: 30 ft/9 m long

Triceratops is the most familiar of the horned dinosaurs. It was also the most abundant of the group, the largest and the heaviest, weighing up to 11 US tons/10 tonnes — heavier than a modern, adult African bull elephant. Its skull alone, with the short neck frill, was over 6 ft 6 in/2 m long.

Great herds of these horned dinosaurs lived throughout western North America toward the very end of the Late Cretaceous period, some 70 to 65 million years ago. They were the most common ceratopids, and the last of the short-frilled group to survive.

The name *Triceratops* means "3-horned face." Although this dinosaur belonged to the short-frilled group — in which the nose horn was typically longer than the brow horns — the arrangement of horns on the face of *Triceratops* was more like that of the long-frilled types (*below*). It had a short, thick nose horn and 2 long brow horns, each over 3 ft 3 in/1 m long. In some species, the brow horns could have been even longer, reaching beyond the snout.

Also unlike other members of its group, *Triceratops*' neck frill was a solid sheet of bone. The fact that there were no openings in it suggests that its main function was to act as a defensive shield, rather than as an anchoring plate for the jaw muscles. In some species, there were pointed knobs, like great barnacles, set all around the edge of the frill, offering further protection.

Because of the massive structure of *Triceratops*' skull, it was more likely to be fossilized than other, less robust dinosaur skulls. Hundreds of well-preserved specimens have been found over the years in the western states of North America. Othniel C. Marsh, the famous American fossil hunter, first named the beast in 1889. By the turn of the century, another American fossil hunter, Barnum Brown, is supposed to have discovered over 500 skulls.

Today, more than 15 species of *Triceratops* are recognized, all based on differences in the structure of the skull. However, some of these may represent different sexes and growth stages in individuals of a much fewer number of species.

Many of the skulls, horns and neck frills were found to be damaged and scarred. This suggests that individual *Triceratops* often sparred with one another, possibly by locking horns and shoving with the head shield, rather than doing any actual damage with the sharp horns. These weapons were probably reserved for use against a real enemy, such as one of the large, contemporary tyrannosaurs — *Tyrannosaurus* or *Albertosaurus*.

NAME: *Chasmosaurus*
TIME: Late Cretaceous
LOCALITY: North America (Alberta)
SIZE: 17 ft/5.2 m long

Chasmosaurus was a typical long-frilled type of horned dinosaur. Its skull was quite long and narrow, with a pair of long, upwardly curved horns on the brow and a single, shorter horn on the snout. The bony frill, however, was enormous, stretching from the back of the skull to cover the neck and upper shoulders. Its margin was decorated with bony spikes and knobs. The 2 openings on either side of the frill were so large that the frill itself provided a mere framework surrounding these great holes. So, although the bony frill was a vast size, it was lightweight, and allowed the head to be moved easily.

This spectacular frill was undoubtedly a display structure. The great head area that it presented would have acted as a warning to attackers, whether predators or rival males, or as a sexual signal to females, especially when the head was moved about. It is possible that all the males in a herd would cooperate in a group-threat display, forming a ring around the young in times of danger, and shaking their great heads and neck frills at the enemy.

Some paleontologists think that these horned dinosaurs could run quite quickly when necessary. This is suggested by certain features of their anatomy. The shoulder blades, for example, were not firmly fixed to the rest of the skeleton, and there were no collar bones to keep them in place. So, the whole shoulder girdle would have moved back and forth with the forelegs, helping the animal to run quickly.

In contrast, the hips were firmly fixed in position, attached to the backbone by 8 sacral vertebrae, which provided a strong, solid anchor for the heavy hindquarters.

RRHINOCERATOPS

ANCHICERATOPS

PENTACERATOPS

TOROSAURUS

NAME: *Arrhinoceratops*
TIME: **Late Cretaceous**
LOCALITY: **North America (Alberta and Utah)**
SIZE: **18 ft/5.5 m long**

Arrhinoceratops was a close relative of the long-frilled *Chasmosaurus* (above). But it resembled the short-frilled *Triceratops* in having a short face, and well-developed brow horns that curved forward over the snout. There was also a modest-sized nose horn.

Round openings cut through the bone of *Arrhinoceratops'* neck frill, thereby reducing its weight. The frill itself had a deeply scalloped margin, set with great bony knobs at wide intervals.

The remains of this horned dinosaur are not as common as many others of its family. This may be due to the fact that the animal itself was not abundant, or perhaps it inhabited dry, upland areas where it was less likely to become fossilized.

NAME: *Anchiceratops*
TIME: **Late Cretaceous**
LOCALITY: **North America (Alberta)**
SIZE: **20 ft/6 m long**

The long-frilled *Anchiceratops* lived near the very end of the Late Cretaceous period, later than its relative *Chasmosaurus*. In fact, it may even have descended from that dinosaur.

Although it was larger than *Chasmosaurus*, *Anchiceratops* was somehow more streamlined. Its body was longer, with a shorter tail, and the tall neck frill was considerably narrower. Two long, narrow horns curved forward from the brow, and a shorter nose horn pointed directly ahead.

The frill was divided along its midline by a strong ridge, on either side of which were medium-sized openings in the bone. A pair of hornlike protuberances pointed forward at the top-rear edge of the frill.

The remains of *Anchiceratops* were found in delta deposits mixed with beds of coal, and dating from the topmost rocks of the Late Cretaceous. This suggests that it may have lived in or near swamps, feeding with its sharp beak and shearing cheek teeth on the abundant vegetation that grew in this waterlogged environment — plants such as swamp cypresses, ferns, giant redwoods and cycads.

NAME: *Pentaceratops*
TIME: **Late Cretaceous**
LOCALITY: **North America (New Mexico)**
SIZE: **20 ft/6 m long**

Like *Anchiceratops*, *Pentaceratops* may well have been a descendant of *Chasmosaurus*, which lived earlier in Late Cretaceous times. It, too, had a huge neck frill, its margin fringed with small spines. In some species, the frill stretched halfway along the back, and as many as 4 large openings punctured the broad, bony surface, to reduce the weight of the structure.

When *Pentaceratops* was discovered, the scientists reckoned that they had found an unusual dinosaur with 5 horns on its face, hence its name. In fact, *Pentaceratops* had the usual 3-horned face; there was a short, stout horn on its snout and a pair of long horns that curved forward from the brow. The 2 remaining "horns" projected outward from each cheek. But these were not true horns, merely outgrowths of the cheek bones, and were not unusual features among the long-frilled ceratopids.

NAME: *Torosaurus*
TIME: **Late Cretaceous**
LOCALITY: **North America (Montana, South Dakota, Texas, Utah and Wyoming)**
SIZE: **25 ft/7.6 m long**

This horned dinosaur, whose name means "bull lizard," is found in the topmost beds of the Late Cretaceous. It was the largest, and the last, of the long-frilled group. Its contemporary, *Triceratops*, was the largest of *all* the horned dinosaurs, and the last of the short-frilled group. Herds of both types of horned dinosaur would probably have roamed together through the North American landscape some 70 million years ago.

The skull of *Torosaurus* is the largest known from any land-living animal, either modern or extinct, with a length of 8 ft 5 in/2.6 m. The enormous neck frill accounted for more than half this length. It rose from the back of the head in a great hollowed-out sheet, with the usual pair of large openings on either side of its midline. The margin of the frill was smooth — not decorated with the typical array of bony knobs.

Two great horns surmounted the brow of *Torosaurus*, and a shorter horn grew from its snout, above the massive, sharp beak. All 3 horns were straight and pointed forward.

Like the rhinoceros or elephant today, few predators would have risked attacking such a formidable animal as *Torosaurus*. Weighing some 9 US tons/8 tonnes and moving at a fair pace on its stout legs, its head armed with sharp horns, its neck and upper back protected by the great, bony neck frill and the rest of its body covered in thick hide — this horned dinosaur could have done battle with the largest of carnivorous dinosaurs.

However, the days of the plant-eating dinosaurs and their flesh-eating cousins were numbered at the end of the Cretaceous period. The "Age of Dinosaurs" ended some 65 million years ago, with the mass-extinction of these ruling reptiles worldwide. Several other major groups disappeared at about the same time — the plesiosaurs, ichthyosaurs and ammonites in the sea, and the pterosaurs in the air. Not a single trace of any of these groups has been found in the rocks of the subsequent Tertiary period.

Dozens of theories have been put forward to account for this mysterious mass-extinction at the end of the Mesozoic Era. Earth movements, starvation, parasites, poisons, changes in climate, meteorites, extraterrestrial hunters — none of these theories satisfactorily explains why so many different animals, in such different habitats, all suffered the same fate (*see pp. 92–93*).

Birds: Masters of the air

Just as the conquest of space was the last great challenge for humankind, so the conquest of the air was the last great opportunity for the vertebrates. And, just as space travel required new engineering and new fuels, so flight demanded dramatic modifications of both structure and physiology.

Flight engineering

The birds are the acknowledged masters of the air. Their abundance and diversity, both past and present (with some 166 families of living birds), exceeds that of any other flying creature. Their success lies in the development of a structure unique in the animal world — feathers. These aerodynamic structures, developed from reptilian scales, were the ideal innovation for flight. They are lightweight and easily replaced if damaged, in contrast to the vulnerable skin-wings of pterosaurs and bats.

By transforming the forelimbs of their reptilian ancestors into feathered wings, birds acquired the enlarged surface area needed to support the body in the air. The wings could be folded away into a compact shape when the bird landed. The modified forelimbs could therefore be wholly devoted to the needs of flight, leaving the hindlimbs free to become adapted for walking upright.

The power for active, flapping flight comes from large muscles that make up 15 to 30 percent of a bird's total body weight. They stretch downward from the wings and attach to the pectoral, or shoulder, girdle. The sternum, or breast bone, is greatly enlarged, and bears a prominent keel (carina) down the middle; both surfaces provide a large area to which the wing muscles can attach (*see p. 173*). They also attach to the fused clavicles, or collar bones, which form the wishbone (furcula), and to a membrane that connects the wishbone to the sternum.

Archaeopteryx, the earliest-known bird, appeared in the Late Jurassic. The Cretaceous period saw an explosive evolution of the birds, and most modern groups had appeared by the end of that period or by the Eocene.

Since birds are rarely fossilized, this evolution chart is based on recent studies, carried out in the USA by Sibley and his colleagues, on the genetic material of modern birds. Only a proportion of the 27 or so orders of modern birds are shown here. Relatively few groups have become extinct over their 140 million years of evolution. (*For key to silhouettes, see p. 312.*)

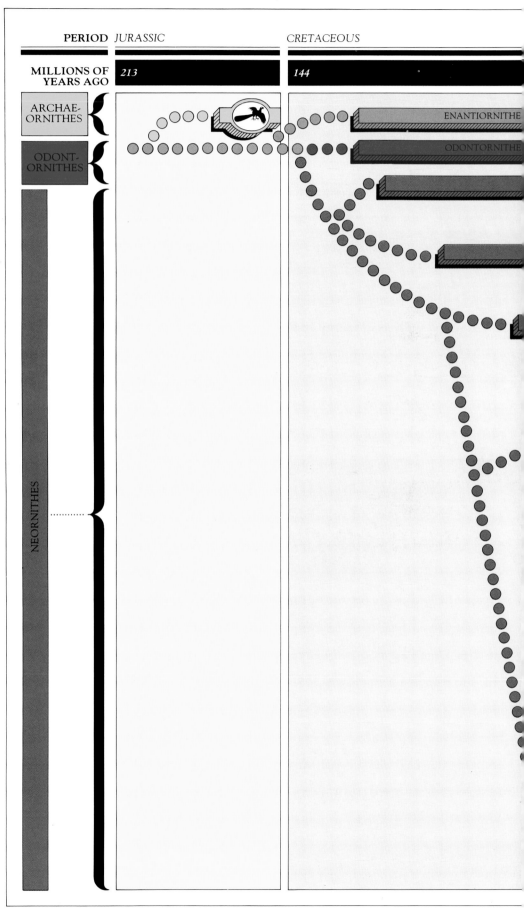

Solid bars show the known fossil record of a group. Dotted lines denote the possible evolutionary relationships between groups.

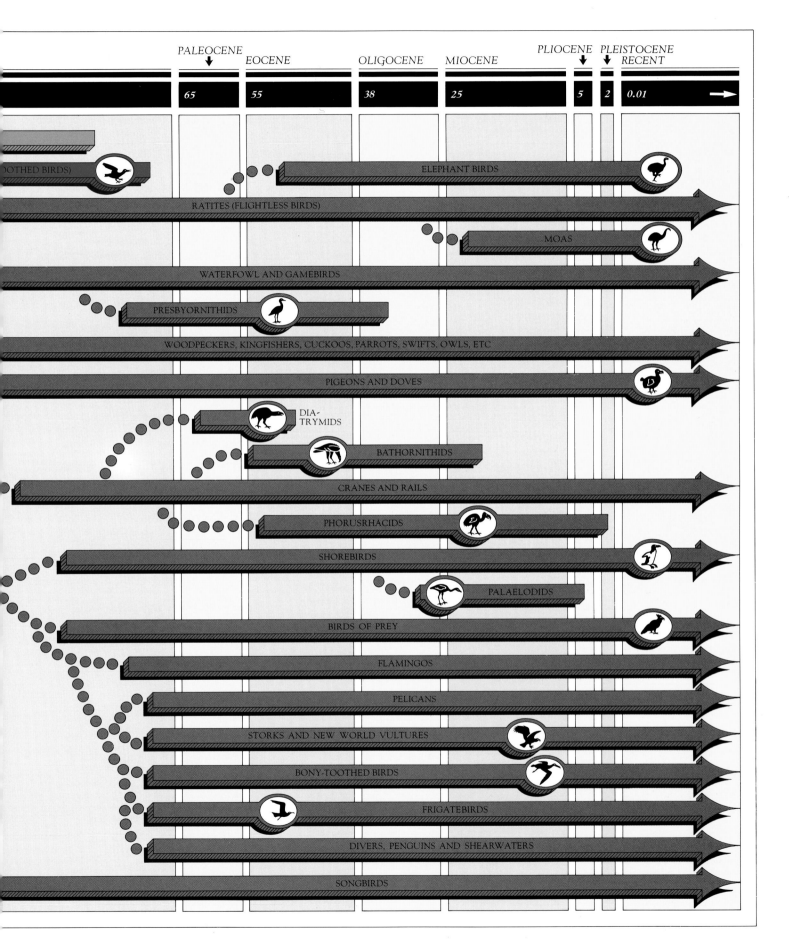

OOTHED BIRDS)

ELEPHANT BIRDS

RATITES (FLIGHTLESS BIRDS)

MOAS

WATERFOWL AND GAMEBIRDS

PRESBYORNITHIDS

WOODPECKERS, KINGFISHERS, CUCKOOS, PARROTS, SWIFTS, OWLS, ETC

PIGEONS AND DOVES

DIA-TRYMIDS

BATHORNITHIDS

CRANES AND RAILS

PHORUSRHACIDS

SHOREBIRDS

PALAELODIDS

BIRDS OF PREY

FLAMINGOS

PELICANS

STORKS AND NEW WORLD VULTURES

BONY-TOOTHED BIRDS

FRIGATEBIRDS

DIVERS, PENGUINS AND SHEARWATERS

SONGBIRDS

Birds: Masters of the air

To provide enough length and space for these muscles, the shoulder joint on each side has moved upward, to a position level with the backbone. And to resist the powerful forces produced when the flight muscles contract, the sternum is braced away from the shoulder joints by enlarged coracoid bones, and away from the backbone by strong bony ribs.

For a bird to run on 2 legs and to launch itself into the air from the ground, the hindlegs must be long and powerful. This has been achieved by elongating the bones of the lower leg, and by adding a new section to the ankle (the tarso-metatarsus), formed by elongating some of its bones.

The powerful muscles needed to swing the legs forward and backward are attached to the modified pelvic, or hip, girdle, the various bones of which have become elongated. The ilium projects far forward from the hip joint, and is strongly attached to the backbone by between 11 and 23 vertebrae (compared with only 2 or 3 in most reptiles). The pubis and ischium both project backward from the hip joint.

To prevent itself falling forward while walking, a bird's body has been shortened, and also moved backward between the legs to bring the center of gravity to a point above the feet. The enlarged sternum, therefore, ends up lying between the knees.

Because the powerful, flexible wings can both propel and guide the bird, a long tail is no longer needed for stability. It has been reduced to a short "pygostyle," the feathers of which can be erected to form a fan that acts as an air-brake when the bird alights.

Fueling the changes
As well as all these structural modifications to the skeleton, internal changes were necessary in a bird's physiology to cope with the heavy energy demands of flight. For example, the respiratory system became more efficient. The unique arrangement of numerous air sacs off the main respiratory passage ensures that air passes through a bird's lungs in a continual stream, rather than circulating solely within the blind-ending sacs that make up the lungs of other vertebrates.

More fundamentally, birds — like mammals — are warm-blooded (see p. 60), so that their levels of available energy do not vary as the temperature of the environment changes. This type of physiology requires some form of insulation, and this is provided by the fluffy down feathers, which lie beneath the larger, wider contour feathers that give a bird its streamlined shape.

***Archaeopteryx*, the first bird**
A modern bird's skeleton is very different from that of any reptile, and the origins of birds could not be deduced with certainty until, by great good luck, *Archaeopteryx* was discovered. This creature was preserved in Late Jurassic limestones, and provides an ideal intermediate, in both time and structure, between the reptiles and the birds.

The surprising, fortunate feature is that *Archaeopteryx* was fossilized in such fine-grained sediments that the clear impression of its feathers can be seen, spread around the skeleton. Both the individual feathers, and the shape of the wings that they formed, are exactly like those found in living, actively flying birds. So there is little doubt that *Archaeopteryx* was not merely a passive, gliding animal. This conclusion is supported by the fact that it possessed a wishbone, which in living birds forms one of the attachment sites for the flight muscles.

Archaeopteryx shows some primitive features that later birds have lost (see p. 173). For example, it had small, sharp teeth in its jaws, replaced in later birds by a horny, toothless beak. It had 3 clawed fingers on each forelimb, each finger separate and distinct from the others (unlike their partly fused arrangement in modern birds). Finally, *Archaeopteryx* had a long, bony tail, and the impressions in the rocks show that this was fringed on either side by a series of long feathers. These would have provided this early flyer with a source of uplift from behind to balance the uplift produced by the wings in front.

Paleontologists suggest that *Archaeopteryx* probably lived in trees, eating insects that it found there, and using both flapping and gliding flight to get from tree to tree. Inevitably, from time to time it would have landed on the ground, and then its sharp, clawed fingers would have helped it to climb back up into the trees.

Apart from the proportions of its wings, the skeleton of *Archaeopteryx* is strikingly similar to that of a small, lightly built, running dinosaur, such as the coelurosaur *Compsognathus* (right). This animal lived in Europe in Late Jurassic times, too (see pp. 106, 108).

Most paleontologists believe that *Archaeopteryx* evolved from just such a small, bipedal dinosaur, whose young may have fed on a more insectivorous diet than the adults. The young may have climbed into trees and bushes, using their clawed hands, in search of their prey. Perhaps even the feathers of birds evolved from a covering that kept warm the tiny bodies of these juvenile dinosaurs.

An alternative theory is that *Archaeopteryx* may have evolved from a reptile similar to early crocodiles. However, it is difficult to find strong specializations that *Archaeopteryx* shares with these crocodiles, and there are no fossils linking it to these Triassic forms.

The "missing link" controversy
Archaeopteryx makes an ideal link between the reptiles and the birds, and it is therefore a major piece of evidence for the theory of evolution. Its importance was recognized when the first specimen was discovered, in 1861, only a few years after Darwin had published his theory of evolution by natural selection.

Archaeopteryx has, therefore, always been a particular target of attack for those who do not favor the theory that living organisms have undergone gradual evolutionary change. For example, in 1985, the British astronomers Fred Hoyle and N.C. Wickramasinghe developed the idea that many evolutionary innovations were the result of the arrival on earth of a shower of viruses, which infected terrestrial organisms with new characteristics. They suggested that both birds and mammals had evolved as a result of just such a virus shower, at the end of the Cretaceous period, and that this was the cause of the extinction of the dinosaurs.

However, *Archaeopteryx*, found in Late Jurassic rocks, over 80 million years before the Late Cretaceous, is a fatal weakness in this virus-shower theory. So Hoyle and Wickramasinghe suggested that the specimens of *Archaeopteryx* were fakes, consisting of impressions of the feathers of living birds that had been pressed into a cement added around the genuine skeleton of a small dinosaur. However, it has been convincingly shown that identical tiny cracks and markings are present on both faces of the slabs of limestone that sandwich the *Archaeopteryx* skeletons — an impossibility if parts of the rocks had later been covered with a cement to take the impressions of the feathers.

The evolution of birds
Between *Archaeopteryx* and the great variety of living birds, 2 unusual groups (subclasses) existed in the Cretaceous period (see pp. 170–171). One group, the Enantiornithes, were discovered in Argentina, and described in 1981. Still only poorly known, certain features of their legs, upper arm bones and shoulder girdles distinguish them from all other birds.

Another group of Cretaceous birds, the Odontornithes or "toothed birds," provide the next major window on bird evolution. Like their ancestors, these

FROM REPTILE TO BIRD

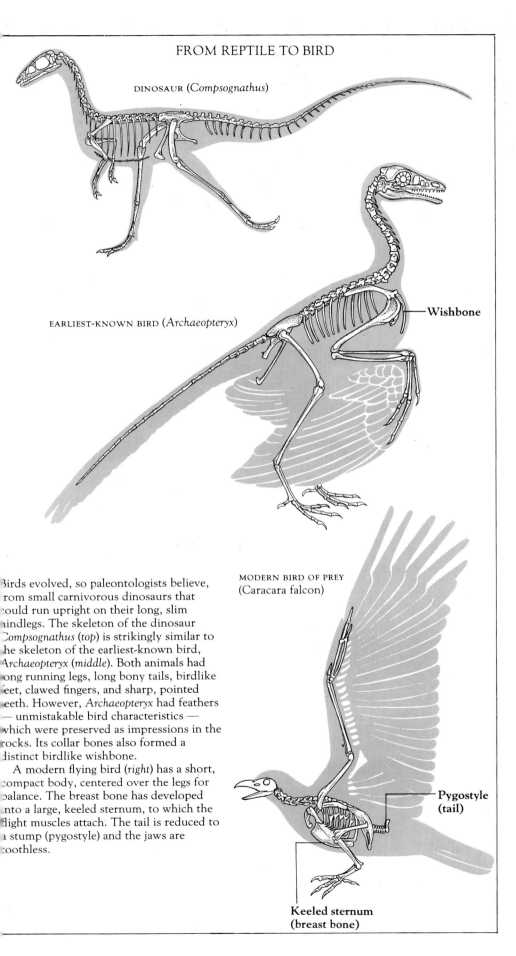

DINOSAUR (*Compsognathus*)

EARLIEST-KNOWN BIRD (*Archaeopteryx*)

Wishbone

MODERN BIRD OF PREY
(Caracara falcon)

Pygostyle
(tail)

Keeled sternum
(breast bone)

Birds evolved, so paleontologists believe, from small carnivorous dinosaurs that could run upright on their long, slim hindlegs. The skeleton of the dinosaur *Compsognathus* (top) is strikingly similar to the skeleton of the earliest-known bird, *Archaeopteryx* (middle). Both animals had long running legs, long bony tails, birdlike feet, clawed fingers, and sharp, pointed teeth. However, *Archaeopteryx* had feathers — unmistakable bird characteristics — which were preserved as impressions in the rocks. Its collar bones also formed a distinct birdlike wishbone.

A modern flying bird (*right*) has a short, compact body, centered over the legs for balance. The breast bone has developed into a large, keeled sternum, to which the flight muscles attach. The tail is reduced to a stump (pygostyle) and the jaws are toothless.

early seabirds had teeth in their jaws, to help catch slippery fish prey. Some, such as the loonlike hesperornithids, had lost the powers of flight, while others, such as the ichthyornithids, still had wings, and were probably more like modern terns.

Several types of bird have lost the ability to fly. This seems to happen particularly when there are no active predators in the birds' environment, and the energy-expensive power of flight is no longer necessary. Such was the case at the end of the Cretaceous period, when the predatory dinosaurs had disappeared, and new mammalian carnivores had not yet appeared — or had not yet reached certain areas. Many types of flightless bird evolved at that time, in the relative safety and isolation of, for example, South America, Australia and New Zealand.

The modern flightless birds (the ostrich, emu, kiwi, cassowary and rhea), together with the extinct moas and elephant birds, are placed in a group called the Ratites. These great flightless birds all share some features of the bony palate and shoulder girdle, which may suggest that they have descended from an original stock of birds that had become flightless.

Living birds and their fossil representatives are grouped in the subclass Neornithes. They all share a common, complicated structure of the bony palate, and this fact leads paleontologists to believe that they have descended from a common ancestor.

Throughout their evolutionary history, birds have retained essentially the same skeletal structure. Because of this similarity, together with the fact that the fragile bones of birds are rarely well preserved in the rocks, the fossil record reveals comparatively little about the interrelationships of the 166 families of modern birds. The relationships shown in the evolutionary chart on pp. 170–171 are based on recent studies by Sibley and his colleagues in the USA on the compatibility of DNA strands from the cells of living birds.

Since the fossil record for bird bones is so incomplete, and since the impressions of feathers are rarely fossilized (and feathers, of course, give birds their shape, as well as their plumed accessories, such as a peacock's tail and headdress), no-one can state with any certainty what prehistoric birds looked like. The reconstructions on the following pages are mainly the traditional view of these birds, based on the known fossil names and a degree of educated guesswork from studies of modern, related species.

Early and flightless birds

ARCHAEOPTERYX LITHOGRAPHICA

ICHTHYORNIS
DISPAR

AEPYORNIS
TITAN

HESPERORNIS REGALIS

DINORNIS
MAXIMUS

EMEUS CRASSUS

RAPHUS
CUCULLATUS

HARPAGORNIS MOOREI

Early and flightless birds

ARCHAEOPTERYX LITHOGRAPHICA

ICHTHYORNIS DISPAR

HESPERORNIS REGALIS

SUBCLASS ARCHAEORNITHES

This group of "ancient birds" currently contains one genus — Archaeopteryx — and perhaps only one species. This is the earliest-known bird, and it occupies a special place in evolutionary history, since it shows in its structure the link between 2 major groups — the reptiles and the birds.

NAME: **Archaeopteryx lithographica**
TIME: **Late Jurassic**
LOCALITY: **Europe (Germany)**
SIZE: **14 in/35 cm long**

The discovery of Archaeopteryx is a classic in the history of paleontology. In 1861, blocks of fine-grained limestone were being cut in a quarry at Solnhofen, southern Germany. These rocks are of Late Jurassic age, some 150 million years old; one split slab revealed the almost-perfect skeleton of Archaeopteryx, the first-known bird. Not only were most of its delicate bones intact, but the impression of its feathers was stamped in the rocks, preserved in their natural positions on the wings and tail. A glass-fiber cast of this specimen is displayed in London's Natural History Museum.

A second, more complete specimen was discovered from the same site in 1877, and this slab of rock, together with its priceless occupant, is now housed in East Berlin's Humboldt University Museum. Four more specimens are now known.

These fossil finds reveal a creature about the size of a modern pigeon, with a small head and large eyes, pointed teeth in its jaws and a long bony tail. Its limbs were long and slender, with 3 clawed digits on each elongated hand, and with typical bird feet. The lower-leg bones were long, and indicate a running animal (see p. 173).

This description does not wholly fit in with the picture of most modern birds, but Archaeopteryx had 2 unmistakeable features, unique to birds. It had a well-developed wishbone (formed by the union of the 2 collar bones) and the typical feathers of a bird, attached to its long arms and tail.

Were it not for these birdlike characters, Archaeopteryx could easily be mistaken for one of the coelurosaurs — small, 2-legged, carnivorous dinosaurs (see pp. 106–109). Indeed, one of the most recent Archaeopteryx specimens, discovered in Germany in 1951, was attributed to the coelurosaur Compsognathus until the early 1970s, when impressions of its feathers were noticed.

Most paleontologists believe that Archaeopteryx was an insectivorous creature that lived in open forests, and could fly or glide from tree to tree. It may have caught insects on the wing as it flew, or perhaps it swooped down in surprise attacks on ground-living invertebrates. Its clawed hands and feet could have been used to climb trees, in order to launch itself on the next flight.

The sternum, or breast bone, of Archaeopteryx appears to have been tiny, unlike the great, keeled sternum of modern birds, which provides the main site for the attachment of powerful wing muscles. Some paleontologists have suggested that the feathers of Archaeopteryx were merely for insulation, rather than for flight. This ancestral bird was almost certainly warm-blooded, like its modern relatives. By controlling its body temperature, it could have led a more active, predatory life.

However, Archaeopteryx's feathers are so similar in structure and arrangement on the wings to those of modern birds that it is almost certain they were used for flying, even if this was less powerful than the flight of modern birds.

SUBCLASS ODONTORNITHES

This group of "toothed birds" lived throughout the Cretaceous period. They were similar to modern birds, except that they possessed small, pointed teeth set in sockets in their jaws.

They had developed (though some had already lost) the main structural feature necessary for sustained flight — a broad, keeled sternum to which the powerful wing muscles could attach. They had lost the long bony tail of their ancestors.

ORDER ICHTHYORNITHIFORMES

Members of this group of primitive, probably fish-eating, seabirds are common in marine deposits of Late Cretaceous age in North America. They were good flyers, to judge from the strong, keeled sternum.

NAME: **Ichthyornis dispar**
TIME: **Late Cretaceous**
LOCALITY: **North America (Kansas and Texas)**
SIZE: **8 in/20 cm tall**

First discovered in the 1870s, the toothed jaws of this ancient bird were originally thought to belong to a mosasaur — a contemporary, fish-eating marine lizard (see p. 88). This reptile was preserved in the same rocks, and had similar jaws and teeth to those of Ichthyornis.

Ichthyornis dispar and others of its genus had a general structure like that of a large, modern sea tern, but with a proportionally bigger head and bill. The large sternum suggests strong flight.

ORDER HESPERORNITHIFORMES

This Cretaceous group of toothed birds were specialized diving seabirds that had lost the power of flight. Although they had a well-developed sternum, the keel was reduced, and the wings had degenerated. These birds seem to have fished the shallow waters that covered much of central North America during Cretaceous times, and would have nested on low shores.

NAME: **Hesperornis regalis**
TIME: **Late Cretaceous**
LOCALITY: **North America (Kansas)**
SIZE: **6 ft/1.8 m tall**

This large, flightless bird differed from other toothed seabirds in having lost its wings almost completely. It swam with powerful kicks of its large, webbed feet, set well back on the body, propelling itself along in the manner of a modern loon or grebe.

Hesperornis regalis could have chased fast-moving fish and squid underwater, holding such slippery prey in its long bill, equipped with sharp, pointed teeth. It probably nested at the water's edge, like a modern loon, and it would have been clumsy and vulnerable while on land.

SUBCLASS NEORNITHES

This group of "new birds" encompasses all recent species. They began to adapt to varied environments in the Early Cretaceous, and representatives of most of the modern groups had appeared by the Early Eocene, some 50 million years ago (see pp. 170–171).

A number of extinct groups and species are known, of which the following are some of the more striking.

EMEUS CRASSUS

HARPAGORNIS MOOREI

ORDER STRUTHIORNITHIFORMES

The typically large, long-legged flightless birds, collectively known as the Ratites, belong to this order. They all have small or tiny wings, and the sternum has lost the keel that provides the attachment site for the wing muscles of flying birds.

The Ratites first appeared during the Cretaceous or Early Tertiary, and different types evolved on the separating continents. Today, the only survivors of the group are the emus and cassowaries of Australia and New Guinea, the kiwis of New Zealand, the rheas of South America, and the ostriches of Africa (formerly also in Eurasia).

Two spectacular groups have become extinct only recently — the elephant birds of Madagascar and the moas of New Zealand (below).

NAME: *Aepyornis titan*
TIME: **Pleistocene to Recent**
LOCALITY: **Madagascar**
SIZE: **up to 10 ft/3 m tall**
The extinct, flightless birds of the genus *Aepyornis*, of which this species is the largest, were heavily built creatures, probably weighing up to $\frac{1}{2}$ US ton/ 500 kg. Their common name — elephant birds — stems from old Arabian tales of a giant creature the "rukhkh," that could pounce on an elephant and carry it up into the air. *Aepyornis* may be the legendary "roc" bird encountered by Sinbad in *The Book of a Thousand and One Nights*.

Each of *Aepyornis'* elephantine legs ended in 3 stumpy toes, which were spread wide to carry the body weight. The thick thigh bones were greatly elongated, evidence that this bird was not a runner, unlike its relative, the ostrich — the fastest creature on 2 legs.

Aepyornis laid huge eggs — more than 1 ft/30 cm long, with a capacity of some 19 US pints/9 liters, and when fresh they may have weighed 20 lb/10 kg.

Apart from size and strength, the elephant bird had no special defenses — no teeth in its beak, no talons on its feet, no wings for flying. But the only large predators in its island home were crocodiles, easily avoided. When man arrived in Madagascar, less than 1500 years ago, species of *Aepyornis* were still alive. This bird may have become extinct only in the 17th century.

NAME: *Dinornis maximus*
TIME: **Pleistocene to Recent**
LOCALITY: **New Zealand**
SIZE: **up to 11 ft 6 in/3.5 m tall**
Dinornis maximus was the tallest bird that ever existed — taller than the great elephant bird of Madagascar (*above*), but of a much lighter build. It was one of about a dozen types of flightless moa that survived in New Zealand until Recent times.

Man came to the islands in about the 10th century, and over the next 800 years destroyed most of the forests by burning, and hunted the moas relentlessly, causing their extinction by 1800.

All moas were bulky, heavy-legged, long-necked birds. In the absence of large carnivores and herbivores in their island home, these slow-moving birds had taken the place usually occupied by browsing mammals, feeding off the rich supplies of seeds and fruits.

NAME: *Emeus crassus*
TIME: **Pleistocene to Recent**
LOCALITY: **New Zealand**
SIZE: **5 ft/1.5 m tall**
This moa, only half the height of *Dinornis*, was peculiar in having massive lower legs, which were out of all proportion to its body size. Its feet were also enormously broad. It must have been a painfully slow-moving animal, providing easy prey for the moa-hunters.

The modern kiwi, the emblem of New Zealand, is regarded by some paleontologists as a highly specialized moa. The 3 living species are tiny in comparison to their extinct relatives. being less than 2 ft/60 cm tall.

ORDER COLUMBIFORMES

Modern pigeons have changed little since their first appearance in the Late Cretaceous or Early Tertiary. Larger types evolved on warm islands, free of predators, especially during the Pleistocene when several large, and often flightless, forms lived on the Mascarene Islands of the Indian Ocean.

NAME: *Raphus cucullatus*
TIME: **Pleistocene to Recent**
LOCALITY: **Mauritius**
SIZE: **3 ft 3 in/1 m tall**
The dodo was a giant, terrestrial pigeon that became another casualty of man's destruction. Flightless and slow-moving, it fell prey to sailors who stopped off on islands in the Indian Ocean to restock their larders.

The dodo was about the size of a modern turkey, covered in soft, downy feathers, and with a fat body (weighing some 50 lb/23 kg), large head and bald face. It had a massively strong, hooked bill and a curly, tufted tail. Its wings were tiny and useless, and it waddled about on stout, 3-toed feet, feeding on low-growing plants, seeds and fallen fruits.

There were no natural predators on the island to disturb its slow progress. But man and his introductions — pigs and dogs — exterminated the dodo by the 17th century — less than 200 years after it had been discovered.

ORDER CICONIIFORMES

This large order includes the modern shorebirds — the wading water birds (other than waterfowl, *see p. 181*), the seabirds and the typical birds of prey. Most of them evolved and diverged to occupy different habitats toward the end of the Cretaceous period. Birds of prey, such as the eagles, were widespread from the Eocene onward (*below*).

NAME: *Harpagornis moorei*
TIME: **Pleistocene to Recent**
LOCALITY: **New Zealand**
SIZE: **possibly 3 ft 6 in/1.1 m tall**
This eagle may not have been much larger than many of its modern relatives, the eagles and Old World vultures, but it was stronger and more heavily built. The legs were stout and equipped with heavy talons, the beak was deep and sharply hooked, and the powerful wings spanned some 7 ft/2.1 m.

Harpagornis moorei coexisted with the moas in New Zealand, and became extinct at about the same time — perhaps as recently as the 17th century. Since there were no other large predators on the islands, it may have fed on the smaller moas, such as *Emeus crassus* (*above*), and on other birds, such as the now-extinct flightless goose.

Moas would have been bulky prey to attack, but their probable slowness, together with their relatively small heads and long necks, could have made them vulnerable to aerial attack. Certainly, their chicks would have provided easy prey for these powerful raptors.

Water and land birds

PHORUSRHACUS INFLATUS

NEOCATHARTES GRALLATOR

PRESBYORNIS PERVETUS

DIATRYMA GIGANTEA

PALAELODUS AMBIGUUS

PINGUINUS
IMPENNIS

ARGENTAVIS
MAGNIFICENS

OSTEODONTORNIS ORRI

LIMNOFREGATA AZYGOSTERNUM

Water and land birds

PHORUSRHACUS INFLATUS

NEOCATHARTES GR

PRESE
PERVE

DIATRYMA GIGANTEA

PALAELODUS AMBIC

NAME: *Palaelodus ambiguus*
TIME: Late Oligocene to Early Miocene
LOCALITY: Europe (France)
SIZE: 2 ft/60 cm tall

This medium-sized, long-legged shorebird is related to the modern wading and water birds, seabirds and birds of prey (grouped in the Order Ciconiiformes, *see p. 177*).

It is often suggested that *Palaelodus* and its relatives represented early flamingos. But recent assessment suggests that they were more likely to be of shorebird origin; they branched off fairly late from the main shorebird assemblage, and lived from the Late Oligocene to the Early Pliocene in Europe, North Africa and North America (*see pp. 170–171*).

Paleontologists really know very little about what the head and bill of *Palaelodus* looked like; the reconstruction on p. 180 is the traditional view of the bird. However, the structure of its legs suggests that it may have dived and swum underwater to feed, behaving like a modern diving duck.

NAME: *Pinguinus impennis*
TIME: Pleistocene to Recent
LOCALITY: Small islands off western Europe (British Isles), Greenland, Iceland and North America (Maine to Labrador)
SIZE: 20 in/50 cm tall

Another member of the ciconiiformes, the great auk, *Pinguinus impennis*, lost its final battle for survival on a small island off Iceland in 1844. For years, it had been relentlessly hunted by sailors for its flesh, its eggs and the layer of insulating fat beneath its skin, which provided oil for lamps.

Despite its name, it was not a large bird, about half as tall again as the razorbill, the modern auk that it most resembled. It differed only in that it had become flightless. It was a well-adapted seabird, like all modern auks, propelled by its webbed feet when on the surface, and using its small wings for swimming underwater after its fish prey.

The legs of the great auk were set well back on its body, allowing it to walk upright on land, although in a slow and awkward way. It nested in colonies on islands where it could get ashore easily, and incubated its single egg on bare ground. These nesting colonies were highly vulnerable, and the birds were either killed on the spot by sailors or herded live into boats, like sheep.

The great auk evolved in the Pleistocene epoch, some 2 million years ago. Other members of the auk family, however, date back to Miocene times, and probably even earlier. During the ice-ages of the Pleistocene, great auks swam southward, and they are known from the Mediterranean and Florida.

Although unrelated to the modern penguins of the southern hemisphere, the greak auk was their northern counterpart in lifestyle and appearance. In fact, this bird was the original "penguin," being given this name by early mariners. Today's penguins are called after it.

NAME: *Argentavis magnificens*
TIME: Late Miocene
LOCALITY: South America (Argentina)
SIZE: 5 ft/1.5 m tall

Argentavis magnificens was a vulture with an enormous pair of wings compared with its body size. Although only some of its bones have been found, estimates place this bird's wingspan at about 24 ft/7.3 m — twice the wingspan of the longest-winged living bird, the wandering albatross.

A bird of this size did not fly by flapping its wings. Like modern vultures, it would have conserved its energy by gliding from one food source to another, using as few wingbeats as possible. Launching itself from high places, it used the rising thermal currents of warm air during the day to keep it aloft. As with the modern albatross, its initial take-off technique was probably awkward, especially when running over uneven ground.

Argentavis was most probably a scavenger, like its modern relatives. Its deep, hooked beak would have been used to tear through the tough hide of dead animals, rather than used to attack live prey. The large, herbivorous mammals that grazed the open plains of Argentina during the Miocene provided a rich food source. But such a large bird was vulnerable to changes in food supply or climate. *Argentavis*' fate would, therefore, have been closely linked to that of the early mammals of South America (*see pp. 202–205*).

Argentavis and other New World vultures are more closely related to storks than to other birds of prey; in fact, these vultures share a common origin with the storks, diverging from them very early in the Tertiary period.

NAME: *Limnofregata azygosternum*
TIME: Early Eocene
LOCALITY: North America (Wyoming)
SIZE: up to 1 ft/30 cm tall

Limnofregata azygosternum appears to have been an ancestral form of the modern frigatebirds. Today, these are specialized marine birds, related to pelicans, and almost wholly adapted to an aerial existence over the sea. But 50 million years ago, they were only just evolving, and *Limnofregata* may be a halfway stage in their development.

Limnofregata's general structure was similar, though less extreme, to that of modern frigatebirds. Its legs and feet, although reduced in size, were larger and longer than those of modern species. Its wings, too, were proportionally shorter, with a span of about 3 ft 3 in/1 m (compared with the long wings of the modern frigatebirds, up to 8 ft/2.5 m span in the largest species). Its bill was shorter, more tapering and less hooked than that of living species.

However, unlike the modern frigatebirds, *Limnofregata azygosternum* did not glide on thermals over the ocean — it flew by flapping its wings, and its habitat was large, freshwater lakes, far inland. It was probably more like a gull in appearance and feeding method, and more likely to land on water than its modern relatives, which snatch up fish and squid without alighting on the water surface.

NAME: *Osteodontornis orri*
TIME: Late Miocene
LOCALITY: North America (California)
SIZE: 4 ft/1.2 m tall

Osteodontornis orri is one of the larger and more completely known of the "bony-toothed" group of gliding seabirds. They seem to combine characteristics of the pelican family and the petrel/albatross family, and they probably arose from a common ancestor in the Late Cretaceous.

By the Late Paleocene, they were already highly developed, and were the largest seabirds throughout the Tertiary period, perhaps preventing the evolution of larger albatrosses.

Osteodontornis' body was heavily built, with legs and feet like those of a huge petrel. The long, narrow wings,

PINGUINUS IMPENNIS

RGENTAVIS
AGNIFICENS

LIMNOFREGATA
AZYGOSTERNUM

OSTEODONTORNIS ORRI

designed for gliding flight, had a wing-span in some of the larger species, such as O. orri, of up to 20 ft/6 m. The great wings would have been held out stiffly from the body for constant gliding. They were probably not much use for strong or rapid maneuvers. The head, made heavy by the long, pelicanlike bill, probably rested back on the shoulders during flight, in the manner of a modern heron or pelican.

The bill of these bony-toothed birds was unique. It was as long as that of a modern pelican, but stouter and more rounded, with a distinct hook at its tip. Toothlike outgrowths projected along the edges of both jaw bones, large and small ones interspersed. When the bill was closed, those of the lower jaw fitted into deep grooves on the palate inside the upper jaw.

The exact feeding method used by Osteodontornis is difficult to guess, but the wing structure suggests that it may have snatched prey from at, or just below, the surface of the water. The bony spikes along the bill would have been ideal for gripping slippery fish or squid. The slanting roof of the throat suggests that there was an elastic pouch along the neck, used as a temporary fish larder — another pelicanlike feature.

The fossil record tells nothing about the nesting habits of these birds. They are likely to have chosen level-topped islands, which would have provided a good runway for easy take-off. Constant, but not violent, breezes were essential for their gliding flight. Perhaps the demise of these birds occurred when stormier and more varied weather conditions were ushered in at the beginning of the Pleistocene epoch, some 2 million years ago.

ORDER GRUIFORMES

The gruiformes evolved in Late Cretaceous times, some 90 million years ago, and rapidly diversified into a great assemblage, ranging from small, strong flyers to giant, flightless forms.

Most of today's gruiformes are aquatic birds, such as the long-legged cranes and rails, moorhens and coots. There are also some ground-living species, such as the bustards and trumpeters.

NAME: *Phorusrhacus inflatus*
TIME: **Early to Middle Miocene**
LOCALITY: **South America (Patagonia)**
SIZE: **5 ft/1.5 m tall**

Phorusrhacus inflatus was a medium-sized member of a family of flightless birds that became the dominant predators in South America during the Tertiary period. All these phorusrhacids had strong running legs, small, useless wings and large heads, equipped with great, eaglelike beaks. Some species were giants, and stood 10 ft/3 m tall; the head of one species was more than 1 ft 6 in/50 cm long.

In the Early Tertiary, South America had become an island continent. The flesh-eating dinosaurs had died out, and no large carnivores had yet evolved to take their place. Herbivorous mammals grazed the plains, undisturbed by predators, until *Phorusrhacus* and its relatives filled this vacant niche.

Some paleontologists have suggested that phorusrhacids were also carrion-eaters. Their deep, hooked beaks could have been used for tearing at the flesh of dead animals, as well as for seizing prey.

These formidable birds were extinct by the Early Pleistocene. But their nearest modern relatives may be the 2 species of seriema that live in the grasslands of South America today. These small, ground-living birds can fly, but prefer to run about on their long legs.

NAME: *Neocathartes grallator*
TIME: **Late Eocene to Early Miocene**
LOCALITY: **North America (Wyoming)**
SIZE: **18 in/45 cm tall**

Originally thought to be a New World vulture modified for running, *Neocathartes* appears to be a flesh-eating member of another group of gruiform ground birds, the bathornithids. It was a slimly built bird, capable of flight, although from its structure it is likely that it spent most of its time hunting on the ground.

Chasing after prey on its long legs, in the manner of a modern secretary bird, *Neocathartes*' clawed feet and hawklike beak would have coped easily with small rodents and reptiles.

NAME: *Diatryma gigantea*
TIME: **Early Eocene**
LOCALITY: **Europe (Belgium, England and France) and North America (New Jersey, New Mexico and Wyoming)**
SIZE: **7 ft/2.1 m tall**

Diatryma gigantea belongs to a family of giant flightless birds that lived in North America and western Europe during the Paleocene and Eocene when these continents were still joined together.

Like other members of its family, *Diatryma gigantea* was a heavily built bird with tiny wings, incapable of flight. Its stout legs were armed with strong, clawed feet, and the large head, with its massive, hooked beak, was almost the size of that of a modern horse.

Some paleontologists suggest that diatrymids were the carnivores of the day in the northern hemisphere. This is deduced from the fact that there were no other large predators around at the time. So, like the later phorusrhacids in South America (*above*), the diatrymids may have been the dominant predators.

Other paleontologists, however, have suggested that diatrymids were herbivorous creatures that used their heavy, sharp-edged beaks to shear through vegetation, such as tussocks of grass or rushlike growth.

ORDER ANSERIFORMES

The ancestors of today's waterfowl — the ducks, geese and swans — belong to this order. They diverged from other birds early in the Cretaceous. One family, the presbyornithids, evolved into long-legged wading birds (*below*).

NAME: *Presbyornis pervetus*
TIME: **Late Cretaceous to Early Eocene**
LOCALITY: **Europe (England), North America (Utah and Wyoming) and South America (Patagonia)**
SIZE: **3 ft 3 in/1 m tall**

Presbyornis was a typical member of its family — a long-legged, long-necked bird, so slenderly built that paleontologists originally thought it was a flamingo, until it was discovered that its head and bill were strikingly similar to those of modern ducks.

From the abundant remains of both bones and eggs, it seems that *Presbyornis pervetus* flocked together on the shallow margins of lakes. They nested there in great, open colonies, and would have waded in the shallows, sifting the water with their broad, flattened bills to remove tiny animals and plants — the same filter-feeding method used by modern dabbling ducks.

Ancestors of the mammals

In the warm, moist, tropical forests that covered Nova Scotia more than 300 million years ago, there lived 2 types of reptile. Both looked much the same — small and lizardlike, with legs and feet that sprawled out to the sides of their bodies. One, *Hylonomus*, scuttled about after insects, and tried to avoid being eaten by the other — the larger, predatory *Archaeothyris*, with its powerful, snapping jaws.

Archaeothyris was the first of a long line of reptiles that were to dominate the land for the next 80 million years, throughout the Permian and much of the Triassic. These were the mammal-like reptiles, so-called because their evolutionary history culminated in the mammals — the most varied and successful group of vertebrates alive today (*see pp. 194–297*).

At first, the mammal-like reptiles gave no hint of unusual potential. Only their skulls betray their ultimate affinities with the mammals. A pair of openings, set low behind each eye socket, distinguishes them from all other reptiles. The same "synapsid" structure is seen in mammals, although the design is modified (*see p. 61*). Other reptiles fit into the anapsid or diapsid groups, their living descendants being, respectively, the turtles and tortoises, and the lizards, snakes and crocodiles (*see pp. 58–59*).

The development of stronger jaws among the mammal-like reptiles and their descendants, the mammals, may have been the direct result of the evolution of the synapsid type of skull. Related to this was the development of a new type of dentition — the typical mammalian pattern, with teeth of different sizes and shapes for cutting (incisors), tearing (canines) and chewing (cheek teeth).

The mammal-like reptiles appeared during the Late Carboniferous in the form of the pelycosaurs, all of which were well-adapted land animals. Some of them, including the edaphosaurs, could probably control their body temperature by means of a large, heat-regulating "sail" on their backs.

The sphenacodonts were the ancestors of the advanced mammal-like reptiles, the therapsids. Many of these were ferocious carnivores, which dominated land life during the Late Permian. Others, such as the dicynodonts, were large plant-eaters.

From among the cynodonts arose the ancestor of the mammals during the Triassic period. (*For key to silhouettes, see p. 312.*)

Solid bars show the known fossil record of a group. Dotted lines denote the possible evolutionary relationships between groups.

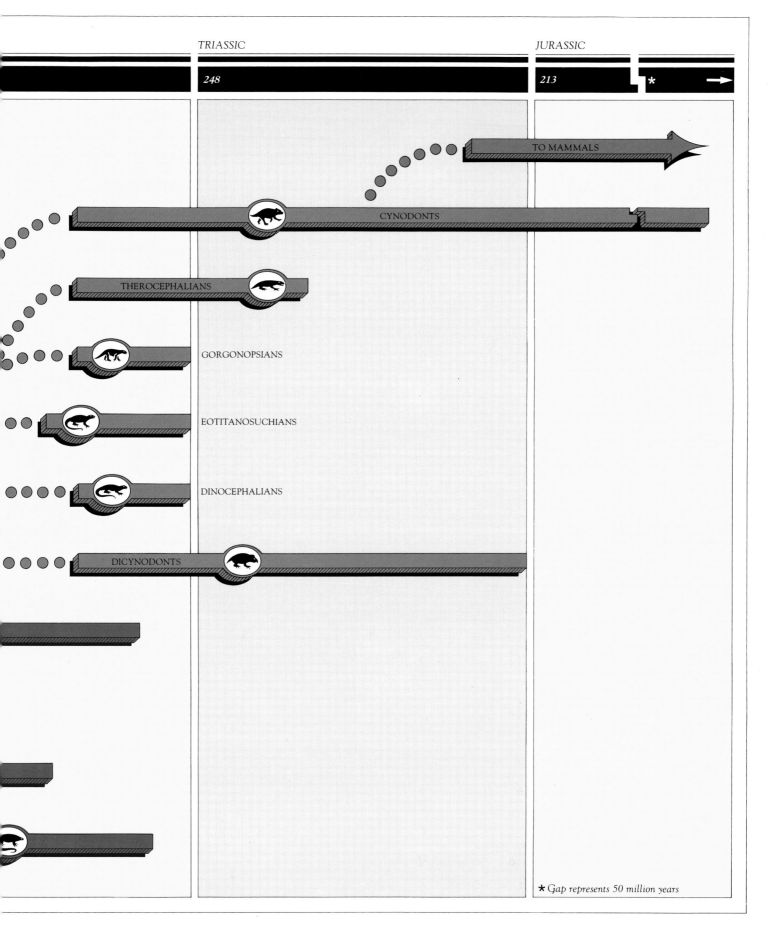

TRIASSIC

JURASSIC

248

213

*

TO MAMMALS

CYNODONTS

THEROCEPHALIANS

GORGONOPSIANS

EOTITANOSUCHIANS

DINOCEPHALIANS

DICYNODONTS

★ Gap represents 50 million years

Ancestors of the mammals

Rise of the mammal-like reptiles
The earliest synapsid reptiles to evolve were the pelycosaurs (*see pp. 186, 188*). From little creatures like *Archaeothyris* a variety of large reptiles evolved, both carnivores and herbivores. Their heyday was during the early part of the Permian period, when they made up some 70 percent of the terrestrial fauna. Their remains are particularly common in Texas. Some 280 million years ago, the warm, humid, delta floodplains of this region would have swarmed with a variety of early amphibians and fishes, all prey to the powerful jaws of the dominant predators of the day, the pelycosaurs.

Toward the middle of the Permian, another group of mammal-like reptiles arose from the pelycosaurs, and replaced them. These were the therapsids, the direct ancestors of the mammals. They are first found in the rocks of European Russia; their sudden appearance in the fossil record suggests that they may have evolved in more upland areas (where fossilization is less likely).

During the Late Permian, these therapsids spread to the great southern landmass of Gondwanaland. Many types are found in the Karroo rocks, laid down in the lowland basin of southern Africa. Others are found in European Russia, in the sediments eroded from the newly formed Ural Mountains. Later still, in the Early Triassic, they spread to Asia, South America, India and even Antarctica, all of which were joined together at the time into the supercontinent Pangaea (*see pp. 10–11*).

The therapsids dominated the land until the middle of the Triassic period, and successfully adopted the lifestyles of carnivores, herbivores and insectivores. Then, 2 new groups of terrestrial reptile surged into their niches — the early, carnivorous ruling reptiles (*see pp. 94–97*) and the herbivorous rhynchosaurs (*see p. 89*).

Thereafter, the therapsids began their slow decline; 55 million years later, by Mid-Jurassic times, the last group (the tritylodont cynodonts, *see p. 193*) became extinct. But not before its members had given rise to the first mammals — tiny, shrewlike creatures that were to wait for more than 150 million years before they entered the limelight of vertebrate history.

Through them, the synapsid reptiles had the last ghostly laugh over their dinosaur usurpers, when those great creatures lay dead at the end of the Cretaceous, and the mammal-like reptiles lived on to inherit the earth in the form of their mammalian descendants.

AN ADVANCED MAMMAL-LIKE REPTILE (*Thrinaxodon*)

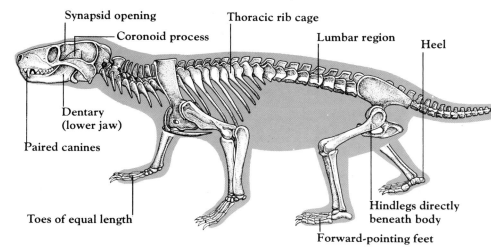

Thrinaxodon walked like a mammal, with its legs directly beneath its body. Its teeth and jaws were powerful, with a high coronoid process on the lower jaw for strong muscle attachment. The rib cage was probably closed off by a muscular diaphragm, which allowed the lungs to expand and contract for efficient breathing.

Vital steps toward warm-bloodedness
The main advance of mammals over reptiles is their ability to control their body temperature. Mammals are warm-blooded endotherms; reptiles are cold-blooded ectotherms (*see p. 93*). But there is little doubt that the early mammal-like reptiles were still cold-blooded, relying on the sun as their prime source of body heat. This is strongly suggested in early synapsids, such as the sphenacodont pelycosaurs. Some of these animals had great skin-covered sails on their backs, the function of which must have been to control body temperature — to absorb heat when cold, and radiate it when warm (*see Dimetrodon, p. 188*).

Pelycosaurs without such obvious devices, and early therapsids such as the dinocephalians, probably controlled their body temperature simply by increasing their body size. A larger, bulk-

FROM MAMMAL-LIKE REPTILE TO MAMMAL

PELYCOSAUR (*Varanosaurus*)

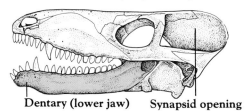

PRIMITIVE THERAPSID (*Procynosuchus*)

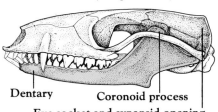

EARLIEST MAMMAL (*Morganucodon*)

A mammal's strong, biting jaws resulted from progressive changes in the skull and lower jaws of their ancestors. In the earliest mammal-like reptiles, the pelycosaurs, the lower jaw was made of several bones, the dentary being the largest. In the more advanced therapsids, the skull was higher and the synapsid opening larger, for longer jaw muscles. The dentary bone was also larger. In the mammals, the eye socket and synapsid opening merged, and the lower jaw was formed entirely of the dentary. This had a high coronoid process which formed an extra site for muscle attachment. The small bones at the rear of the therapsid's lower jaw had moved into the mammal's middle ear, to form part of a chain along which sound was transmitted.

ier body retains a greater amount of heat than a small one, providing a thermal reservoir that reduces the effects of fluctuating environmental temperature.

However, the later therapsids possessed other features that would finally end their dependence on the sun as a source of energy. By eating more food more frequently, and by digesting and metabolizing it more quickly, they could rely on food as their source of energy.

This new method of controlling body temperature required many changes, including better jaws and teeth, better locomotion, better breathing control, and better external insulation to maintain the body's internal temperature.

Dental developments

An innovation among the mammal-like reptiles was the evolution of teeth of different sizes and shapes (called a "heterodont" dentition). Even the earliest pelycosaurs had 3 kinds of teeth in their jaws. The food-grasping incisors at the front were separated from the biting cheek teeth at the back by several long, stabbing canines. In normal reptilian fashion, all these teeth were renewed periodically by waves of replacement along each jaw; the even-numbered teeth were replaced in one wave, and the odd-numbered teeth in the next.

The more advanced therapsids had departed from this reptilian "all-change" method of tooth replacement. Instead, teeth were replaced only a few times during the aninmal's life. This was a major development because it allowed each tooth to remain in the jaws for a longer period, so that the opposing crowns of the upper and lower teeth could develop a complex pattern of crests and valleys. These could then meet in a precision bite, and present a rough pavement on which food could be cut, crushed and ground to a pulp before being swallowed. Well-chewed food could be digested more quickly, which resulted in a more rapid release of the vital nutrients needed to fuel the body.

The jaws and skull also changed. First, the size of the synapsid openings increased, allowing longer jaw muscles to develop. Second, the back of the skull became longer, and the sides bowed out, to produce more space for the muscles.

Third, there was an improvement in the structure of the lower jaw. Previously, some of the jaw muscles were attached to the large dentary bone at the front of the jaw, while others were attached to a number of smaller bones at the back. These smaller bones were progressively reduced in size among the therapsids (and lost completely from

the jaws of mammals, *below*), so removing the potentially weak junction between the bones of the lower jaws. The dentary itself also developed a high flange (the coronoid process) at the back, which provided an attachment point for larger, more powerful jaw muscles (see p. 184).

Another small, but spectacular, change in connection with the jaw bones of mammal-like reptiles provided better hearing in mammals. The 2 bones that had formed the joint between the skull and the lower jaw in mammal-like reptiles retreated into the middle ear of mammals. Here, they linked up with the already present stapes ("stirrup") bone, to form a chain of 3 bones (called the hammer, anvil and stirrup because of their shapes). Sound is transmitted along this chain from the outer eardrum to the fluid-filled canals of the inner ear.

The progressive integration of these 3 small bones into the ear can be traced in therapsids of the Triassic. In fact, these changes can still be seen, telescoped in time, during the development of a modern mammal embryo. They provide as good a proof of evolutionary change as the *Archaeopteryx*-link between reptiles and birds (see p. 173).

Mammals also developed a pair of fleshy ear-flaps on either side of their heads. It is not certain precisely when these external ears evolved, but they have been shown on some of the later therapsids illustrated on p. 191.

Limb improvements

While all these changes were occurring in the jaws and teeth of mammal-like reptiles, other skeletal changes were making the limbs of these creatures more efficient. The primitive pelycosaurs of the Late Carboniferous, such as *Archaeothyris*, moved in the old reptilian style — bending the body from side to side, with the limbs sprawled out horizontally. By the Early Permian, sphenacodonts, such as *Dimetrodon*, had evolved a new type of locomotion. The shape of the bones in the hips and hindlimbs, and of the joints between the vertebrae, show that the stride of the hindlimbs was accompanied by an up-and-down flexure of the backbone (see p. 185).

From *Dimetrodon* onward, the evolutionary story of the mammal-like reptiles is of a steady and rapid increase in this flexing of the limbs and body in the vertical, rather than the old-fashioned horizontal, plane. In addition, the feet changed position, from projecting to the sides to pointing forward, and the toes became shorter and of similar lengths.

This whole system had far more po-

tential for fast movement, since a longer stride and a faster swing of the legs could be achieved simply by elongating various bones of the limbs and feet.

Better breathing

Other features of the advanced therapsid reptiles strongly suggest that they were warm-blooded, like their descendants, the mammals. For example, the abrupt reduction in the extent of the ribs in such cynodonts as *Thrinaxodon* suggests that the whole front part of the body cavity, which houses the lungs and heart, had been closed off by a muscular sheet of tissue, the diaphragm. This development set off a chain of events. It allowed larger lungs to be filled and emptied more rapidly and more frequently, which, in turn, resulted in more oxygen entering the bloodstream. This permitted the tissues to use the oxygen faster — to speed up digestion or to increase muscular exertion, when, for example, chasing prey or avoiding predators.

Because the tissues of a warm-blooded animal require a constant supply of oxygen, it cannot stop breathing for more than a short time. This need conflicts with the need to keep food in the mouth while it is being chewed up. This problem was solved by some of the advanced therapsids (the therocephalians and the cynodonts) by the development of a secondary palate — a shelf of bone that separated the air passage from the mouth. This structure is yet another pointer to support the theory that the advanced mammal-like reptiles were already warm-blooded.

Insulation for survival

There is no way of knowing whether the mammal-like reptiles were covered in hair or fur. Such insulation is not necessary in larger animals (and many of the therapsids were large), since they have a proportionately smaller surface area through which heat may be lost.

It is significant, however, that the final transition between the mammal-like reptiles and the mammals, at the end of the Triassic, was accompanied by a marked reduction in size.

The first mammals, such as *Megazostrodon* (see pp. 198, 200) were tiny, shrewlike creatures. There is no doubt that, as they watched from the trees through the long millennia of the reign of the dinosaurs, they were kept warm during that vigil by a covering of fur. And this simple, furry pelt may have been the vital feature that enabled the mammals to survive the catastrophe that exterminated the dinosaurs (see p. 93), and left these tiny creatures free to inherit the Cenozoic world.

185

Mammal-like reptiles

OPHIACODON

ARCHAEOTHYRIS

CASEA

VARANOSAURUS

EDAPHOSAURUS

SPHENACODON

DIMETRODON

TITANOSUCHUS

MOSCHOPS

PHTHINOSUCHUS

LYCAENOPS

GALECHIRUS

Pelycosaurs and therapsids

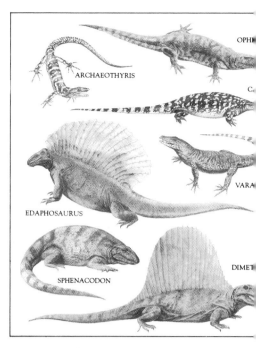

SUBCLASS SYNAPSIDA

The reptilian ancestors of the mammals — the pelycosaurs and therapsids (below) — and the mammals themselves all share the same type of synapsid skull (see p. 61) The single, large opening behind each eye socket allowed the development of longer jaw muscles, which resulted in stronger jaws that could be opened wide and closed forcefully, to deal with large prey.

ORDER PELYCOSAURIA

Pelycosaurs were the earliest of the synapsid, or mammal-like, reptiles to evolve. They appeared during the Late Carboniferous period, some 300 million years ago, soon after the very first reptiles colonized the land (see pp. 62–65). Like these early reptiles, the pelycosaurs started out as small, lizardlike creatures. But they rapidly evolved into many different types, of a much heavier build and with strong jaws and teeth of different sizes and shapes.

There are 4 families of pelycosaur (see pp. 58–59). The ophiacodonts were the earliest and most primitive, and were the ancestors of the other 3 families.

From an evolutionary point of view, the carnivorous sphenacodonts were the most important group, since they were the direct ancestors of the therapsid reptiles, and therefore, indirectly, of the mammals.

The third family, the edaphosaurs, were large plant-eaters, related to the sphenacodonts, but with a very different skull and dentition. The caseids were also herbivorous, and the latest, and last, of the pelycosaurs to evolve.

NAME: *Archaeothyris*
TIME: **Late Carboniferous**
LOCALITY: **North America (Nova Scotia)**
SIZE: **20 in/50 cm long**
This small, lizardlike creature is the earliest-known pelycosaur, a member of the ophiacodont family. Its remains were found in the same Late Carboniferous (Pennsylvanian) locality as those of the first-known reptile, the anapsid *Hylonomus* (see p. 64). These rocks indicate a warm, tropical, humid climate, with great forests of conifers and a rich undergrowth of ferns and club mosses. In the lowland swamps, masses of decaying vegetation accumulated (the coal beds of today), providing food and breeding grounds for insects and other invertebrates. They, in turn, attracted insectivorous reptiles, such as *Hylonomus*, which were probably preyed upon by the larger, newly evolved synapsid reptiles, such as *Archaeothyris*.

Archaeothyris was already more advanced than the other early anapsid reptiles. Its jaws were strong, and could be opened wide and snapped shut. Although its teeth were all the same shape — sharp and pointed — they were of different sizes, including a large pair of canines at the front of the jaws. Such teeth suggest a varied, carnivorous diet.

NAME: *Ophiacodon*
TIME: **Early Permian**
LOCALITY: **North America (Texas)**
SIZE: **up to 12 ft/3.6 m long**
Ophiacodon shows the rapid evolution of features within the pelycosaur group. Its skull had changed from the small, low shape of its earlier relative *Archaeothyris* (above) to a deep, narrow shape, allowing more space for longer jaw muscles to develop. Its hindlimbs were longer than the forelimbs, and set somewhat more directly beneath the body. So, although it still sprawled like a typical reptile, *Ophiacodon* was probably a better runner than *Archaeothyris*.

Ophiacodon was considerably larger than earlier pelycosaurs, a factor that may have helped it to control its body temperature (see p. 184). It is estimated to have weighed between 66 and 110 lb/30 and 50 kg. To support its weight, it may have spent some of its time in water, scuttling about floodplains or swamps, catching fish and amphibians in its elongated jaws, and despatching them with its sharp teeth.

NAME: *Varanosaurus*
TIME: **Early Permian**
LOCALITY: **North America (Texas)**
SIZE: **5 ft/1.5 m long**
Varanosaurus may have been a member of the ophiacodont family. It certainly lived in the same place at the same time as *Ophiacodon* (above), and probably competed with it for fish in the same swamps. Its skull was also deep and narrow, the jaws somewhat elongated and armed with small, spiky teeth. It had the build of a modern monitor lizard.

NAME: *Sphenacodon*
TIME: **Early Permian**
LOCALITY: **North America (New Mexico)**
SIZE: **10 ft/3 m long**
This large sphenacodont shows the characteristic features of its family — a deep, narrow skull with massive jaws and a formidable array of teeth — long canines, daggerlike incisors and small, cutting cheek teeth. The sphenacodonts were the first animals to develop such a specialized set of teeth, and were, in fact, the first large terrestrial carnivores to exist.

The vertebral spines of *Sphenacodon's* backbone were long, and acted as attachment points for massive back muscles, which allowed the animal to lunge powerfully at its prey. In other members of the family (below), these spines were greatly elongated, and supported a huge fin or "sail," the function of which was probably to regulate body temperature.

NAME: *Dimetrodon*
TIME: **Early Permian**
LOCALITY: **North America (Oklahoma and Texas)**
SIZE: **10 ft/3 m long**
The spectacular "sail" on the back of the sphenacodont *Dimetrodon* has earned it the popular name of the "finback." This structure is believed to be an early experiment in controlling body temperature.

The framework for the sail was provided by the elongated spines of the back vertebrae, up to 3 ft 3 in/1 m long in the center. In life, a sheet of skin covered the spines, and it was probably richly supplied with blood vessels.

Dimetrodon's suggested routine would have been to stand with its sail oriented toward the sun in the early morning. Like a solar heater, the sail would have absorbed heat and warmed the blood, which then coursed through the body, raising the reptile's temperature so it could begin its daily hunt for food. To cool down, after a strenuous chase, for example, *Dimetrodon* simply angled its sail away from the sun and into the wind, dissipating heat.

An interesting example of convergent evolution is seen between these synapsid sphenacodonts and the unrelated diapsid reptiles, the dinosaurs. Two dinosaurs, *Spinosaurus* (see pp. 118, 120) and *Ouranosaurus* (see pp. 143, 145) — both living in West Africa during the Cretaceous — had also developed solar-heating sails on their backs.

TITANOSUCHUS

CHOPS

PHTHINOSUCHUS

GALECHIRUS

CAENOPS

According to calculations, a *Dimetrodon* weighing about 440 lb/200 kg would have taken about an hour and a half to raise its body temperature from 79°F to 90°F (26°C to 32°C). Without its sail, the same animal would have needed to bask in the sun for more than three and a half hours to achieve the same rise in temperature.

The massive canines and well-developed shearing teeth of *Dimetrodon* confirm that it was a formidable predator; its name means "2 kinds of teeth." Its prey would have included other pelycosaurs, which without the advantage of a sail would have remained slow and sluggish until the sun warmed them sufficiently to allow activity.

NAME: *Edaphosaurus*
TIME: **Late Carboniferous to Early Permian**
LOCALITY: **Europe (Czechoslovakia) and North America (Texas)**
SIZE: **10 ft/3 m long**
Edaphosaurus was a member of the earliest-known herbivorous edaphosaurs. It had a great sail on its back, presumably with a similar function to that of *Dimetrodon* (*above*). The only difference between the sails of these 2 large reptiles was that the vertebral spines of *Edaphosaurus* had cross-pieces of bone along their length.

Edaphosaurus' sail could also have been for display purposes. It may have been brightly colored, and used in courtship rituals, or even to recognize members of its own species.

Certainly, this bulky pelycosaur was not an active creature, nor was it built for speed. Its body was long and barrel-shaped to accommodate the large gut, its limbs were short and stocky, and it had a sprawling gait. Its teeth were those of a well-adapted plant-eater. As well as the closely packed, peglike teeth lining

the jaws, there were also batteries of teeth on the palate, which formed a broad, chewing pavement, ideal for chopping up plant material.

NAME: *Casea*
TIME: **Early Permian**
LOCALITY: **Europe (France) and North America (Texas)**
SIZE: **4 ft/1.2 m long**
The caseids, represented by *Casea*, were the last family of pelycosaurs to evolve, in Early Permian times. They became the most abundant of the plant-eating pelycosaurs, and thrived almost to the end of the Permian.

Casea was small in comparison with some of its relatives, which reached lengths of 10 ft/3 m and weights of more than 1320 lb/600 kg. They all had deep, bulky bodies, in which the rib cage was enormously expanded to accommodate the long, plant-digesting gut. Their square-shaped heads were tiny, with huge synapsid openings at the back and large nasal openings at the front.

Caseids were unique among pelycosaurs in having no teeth in the lower jaw. Those in the upper jaw were thick, blunt pegs with wavy edges, like those of modern herbivorous lizards. In addition, numerous small teeth studded the palate. Such a dentition suggests a diet of tough plants, such as ferns and horsetails.

ORDER THERAPSIDA
The therapsids were advanced synapsid reptiles, and the direct ancestors of the mammals. Although the remains of the first therapsids are found at the base of the Late Permian, they had diverged from the sphenacodont pelycosaurs more than 20 million years before, probably during the Early Permian. They spread rapidly to all parts of the world, including Antarctica.

The therapsids are grouped into several suborders (*see pp. 58–59*), only one of which, the cynodonts, survived into the Jurassic (*see pp. 190–193*).

NAME: *Phthinosuchus*
TIME: **Base of Late Permian**
LOCALITY: **Europe (USSR)**
SIZE: **5 ft/1.5 m long**
Only the skull of this primitive therapsid is known. It is strikingly similar to that of a sphenacodont, but with larger synapsid openings behind the eyes and more prominent canine teeth. Paleontologists believe it to be intermediate in structure between the pelycosaurs and the therapsids.

NAME: *Titanosuchus*
TIME: **Late Permian**
LOCALITY: **Africa (South Africa)**
SIZE: **8 ft/2.5 m long**
Titanosuchus was a member of the dinocephalians or "terrible heads" — a reference to the large size of their skulls. Its sharp incisors and fanglike canines at the front of the jaws, together with the meat-shearing teeth at the back, testify to its carnivorous diet. Its main prey would have been its herbivorous relatives, such as *Moschops* (*below*).

NAME: *Moschops*
TIME: **Late Permian**
LOCALITY: **Africa (South Africa)**
SIZE: **16 ft/5 m long**
The Karroo Beds of South Africa have yielded many therapsids, among them this large, plant-eating dinocephalian, with a massive skull and deep body. The bones of *Moschops'* forehead were greatly thickened, which suggests that it engaged in head-butting battles with its rivals for dominance within the herd. The boneheaded dinosaurs (pachycephalosaurs) practised the same rituals (*see p. 137*), as do modern goats and bighorn sheep.

Moschops had sturdy forelegs that sprawled out to the sides, while the longer hindlegs were placed directly under the hips. Its short jaws had numerous chisel-edged teeth for cropping vegetation.

NAME: *Lycaenops*
TIME: **Late Permian**
LOCALITY: **Africa (South Africa)**
SIZE: **3 ft 3 in/1 m long**
Lycaenops, or "wolf face," was a small, lightly built carnivore, with long running legs. It was a member of the gorgonopsians, the dominant predators of the Late Permian in southern Africa and European Russia. It may have hunted in packs, and probably preyed on large, plant-eating therapsids, such as *Moschops* (*above*). The canines were particularly long, and the front part of the skull was deeper than normal to accommodate their roots.

NAME: *Galechirus*
TIME: **Late Permian**
LOCALITY: **Africa (South Africa)**
SIZE: **1 ft/30 cm long**
This tiny lizardlike reptile is thought to be an early member of the dicynodonts — the most abundant and successful group of the plant-eating therapsids (*see pp. 190–193*). But *Galechirus'* teeth seem to be those of an insectivore. Many paleontologists think that *Galechirus* simply represents the juvenile form of an adult therapsid.

Mammal-like reptiles

CISTECEPHALUS

ROBERTIA

DICYNODON

KANNEMEYERIA

LYSTROSAURUS

ERICIOLACERTA

PROCYNOSUCHUS

THRINAXODON

MASSETOGNATHUS

CYNOGNATHUS

OLIGOKYPHUS

Therapsids

SUBORDER DICYNODONTIA

The dicynodonts were the most successful and wide-ranging group of plant-eating therapsids, or mammal-like reptiles. They evolved in the Late Permian, and survived to the end of the Triassic — a span of almost 50 million years. The only group of therapsids to outlive them were the cynodonts — the direct ancestors of the mammals (see p. 193).

The advanced development of their skulls and jaws was the main factor in their success. The synapsid openings at the back of the skull (see p. 61) were greatly enlarged, to allow for longer, stronger muscles to operate the jaws. The hinge between the lower jaw and the skull permitted the jaws to move forward and backward, with a strong, shearing action. And the dentition of these reptiles was unique (below).

NAME: *Robertia*
TIME: **Late Permian**
LOCALITY: **Africa (South Africa)**
SIZE: **18 in/45 cm long**
Although *Robertia* was among the first dicynodonts to evolve, it already possessed the specialized dentition of its later relatives. There was a horny, turtle-like beak at the front of its jaws, and the only teeth that remained were a pair of tusklike canines in the upper jaw (reflecting the name *dicynodont*, which means "2 dog teeth").

In the case of *Robertia*, there was a notch in the jaw immediately in front of the canines, into which tough stems, twigs and roots were presumably inserted, then severed by the sharp beak.

NAME: *Cistecephalus*
TIME: **Late Permian**
LOCALITY: **Africa (South Africa)**
SIZE: **13 in/33 cm long**
Dicynodonts adapted to many life-styles. Some were semi-aquatic, while others browsed in the coniferous forests. Some, such as *Cistecephalus*, lived underground.

This creature had a wedge-shaped, flattened head, a short body and strong, stumpy forelimbs with broad toes, like those of a modern mole. It probably used its powerful limbs to dig into the soil to find worms, snails and insects.

NAME: *Dicynodon*
TIME: **Late Permian**
LOCALITY: **Africa (South Africa and Tanzania)**
SIZE: **4 ft/1.2 m long**
Dicynodon had the characteristic pair of canine tusks in its upper jaw, which gives the dicynodont group its name, "2 dog teeth." It may have used these

strong tusks to root up plants.

Another group of herbivorous reptiles, the pareiasaurs, were contemporaries of *Dicynodon* (see pp. 62–65). Some of these were elephantine beasts, heavily armored and with a full set of leaf-shaped teeth in their jaws. This was quite a different dentition to that of the horny-beaked, virtually toothless dicynodonts. These 2 types of unrelated reptile avoided competition with each other by eating different plants.

NAME: *Kannemeyeria*
TIME: **Early Triassic**
LOCALITY: **Africa (South Africa), Asia (India) and South America (Argentina)**
SIZE: **up to 10 ft/3 m long**
This ox-sized dicynodont was a well-adapted land-living herbivore. Its limb girdles formed massive plates of bone, to support the bulky body.

Kannemeyeria's head was massive, but lightweight, due to the great size of the openings for the eyes, nostrils and jaw muscles. The powerful, horny beak would have torn up great mouthfuls of leaves and roots, to be ground down by the shearing action of the toothless jaws.

A skull bone of *Kannemeyeria*, or a close relative, was found in Australia in 1985, adding to the mass of biological evidence for Gondwanaland (below).

NAME: *Lystrosaurus*
TIME: **Early Triassic**
LOCALITY: **Africa (South Africa), Antarctica, Asia (China and India) and Europe (USSR)**
SIZE: **3 ft 3 in/1 m long**
The remains of *Lystrosaurus* were found in Antarctica in the late 1960s. The wide distribution of this sturdy, herbivorous dicynodont provides further evidence that, during Late Permian and Triassic times, India and all the southern continents were united as one landmass, Gondwanaland (see p. 11).

Lystrosaurus was a kind of reptilian "hippopotamus." It probably wallowed in the shallows, browsing on water weeds uprooted with its single pair of tusks. Its nostrils were placed far back on the skull, near the eyes, where they would clear the water while the rest of the body remained submerged.

SUBORDER THEROCEPHALIA

The Late Permian rocks of European Russia and southern Africa reveal the remains of advanced mammal-like reptiles, the therocephalians. Also known from eastern Asia and southern and eastern Africa, they survived until the middle of the Triassic.

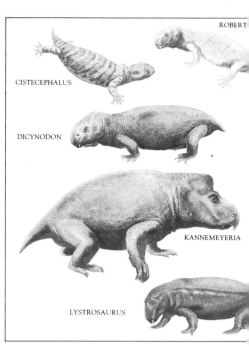

NAME: *Ericiolacerta*
TIME: **Early Triassic**
LOCALITY: **Africa (South Africa)**
SIZE: **8 in/20 cm long**
The abundant plant life — horsetails, ferns, conifers and early cycads — that supported the great populations of dicynodonts (above) also provided home and food for many insects and other invertebrates. These, in turn, were suitable prey for small therocephalians such as *Ericiolacerta*. This lizardlike creature was an active insectivore, judging from its small teeth and long, slim limbs.

SUBORDER CYNODONTIA

The cynodonts, or "dog teeth," were the most successful group of therapsid reptiles. Not only were they the longest-lived group, surviving for some 80 million years, from Late Permian times to about the middle of the Jurassic. They were also the direct ancestors of the world's most successful modern group of animals — the mammals.

The first fossil cynodonts are found in the Late Permian rocks of European Russia and southern Africa. They show many advanced mammalian characteristics. For example, they had fewer bones in the lower jaw, a secondary bony palate and a complex pattern on the crowns of their cheek teeth.

Such advanced features suggest that these reptiles had evolved much earlier, probably during the early part of the Permian. Their ancestors were most probably among the carnivorous sphenacodont pelycosaurs, which had already evolved a crude method of temperature control (see p. 188).

Although there is no trace in the fossil record, the cynodonts may well have been covered with hair, which would have insulated them and helped to maintain a high body temperature.

ERICIOLACERTA

PROCYNOSUCHUS

XODON

MASSETOGNATHUS

ATHUS

OLIGOKYPHUS

NAME: *Procynosuchus*
TIME: **Late Permian**
LOCALITY: **Africa (South Africa)**
SIZE: **2 ft/60 cm long**

Although not a typical cynodont, *Procynosuchus* is interesting because, although it is one of the earliest and most primitive members of the group, it was already specialized for living in water.

The rear of its body and tail were more flexible than was usual among cynodonts, and could obviously be flexed from side to side, in a crocodile-style swimming motion. The tail vertebrae were flattened, to increase the surface area, making the tail a more efficient swimming organ. And the limbs were paddlelike, like those of a modern otter.

Despite these specialized features, *Procynosuchus* is thought to be close to the ancestor of all the cynodonts.

NAME: *Thrinaxodon*
TIME: **Early Triassic**
LOCALITY: **Africa (South Africa) and Antarctica**
SIZE: **20 in/50 cm long**

Thrinaxodon was much more mammal-like than its earlier relative, *Procynosuchus* (above). It was a small, solidly built carnivore, capable of running quite fast to judge by the erect posture of its strong hindlegs. The body was long and distinctly divided, for the first time among vertebrates, into a chest (thoracic) and lower back (lumbar) region. The division was marked by the extent of the ribs; only the thoracic vertebrae bore ribs, and these formed a distinct cage, which housed the vital organs — the heart and lungs (*see p. 184*).

As in living mammals, there was probably a sheet of muscular tissue, the diaphragm, that closed off the rib cage in *Thrinaxodon*. As the animal breathed, the movement of the diaphragm would have filled and emptied its lungs efficiently — an essential development in the evolution of body temperature control (*see p. 185*).

Another indication that *Thrinaxodon* could control its body temperature is the presence of a secondary bony palate, which completely separated the breathing passage from the mouth. This development allowed the animal to breathe at the same time as retaining food in its mouth for longer periods, chewing it up into small pieces for quicker digestion.

Many other structural changes had occurred in *Thrinaxodon*'s skeleton. For example, one of the foot bones had developed a heel which, with the help of strong tendons, would have acted as a lever to lift the foot clear of the ground with each step. The toes were all of equal length, allowing the body weight to be evenly distributed over them.

Another mammalian trend is seen in the lower jaw of *Thrinaxodon*. The teeth on either side were set into a single bone, the dentary, which had become larger at the expense of the smaller bones at the back of the jaw. The effect of this trend among cynodonts, toward a single lower jaw bone, was to make the jaws stronger (*below*).

NAME: *Cynognathus*
TIME: **Early Triassic**
LOCALITY: **Africa (South Africa) and South America (Argentina)**
SIZE: **3 ft 3 in/1 m long**

The jaws of *Cynognathus* show without a doubt that it was a ferocious predator. It was one of the largest cynodonts, strongly built, with its hindlimbs placed directly beneath its body. Its head was more than 1 ft/30 cm long.

Practically the whole of the lower jaw on each side was made up of a single bone, the dentary, into which were set the teeth — the cutting incisors, stabbing canines and shearing cheek teeth. A great bony flange (the coronoid process) at the back of the dentary articulated with the skull, and enabled the jaws to be opened wide. This flange also provided a large area to which extra jaw muscles could attach, giving the jaws tremendous bite-power.

NAME: *Massetognathus*
TIME: **Middle Triassic**
LOCALITY: **South America (Argentina)**
SIZE: **19 in/48 cm long**

Of the dozen or so families of cynodonts, only 3 had herbivorous members. The traversodonts, represented by *Massetognathus*, were plant-eaters, with a distinctive dentition compared with their carnivorous relatives.

The cheek teeth were greatly expanded and their crowns were patterned with a series of crests and valleys. Those of the lower jaw fitted into those of the upper jaw. There was also a gap between the cheek teeth and the small canines toward the front of the jaws. This space probably had the same function as in living rodents (such as rats and beavers) and rabbits. These animals can nip in their cheeks to keep the food in the back of the mouth while it is being chewed.

The precise matching of the cheek teeth, and the advantage of concentrating chewing in the back of the mouth, would have made *Massetognathus* and its relatives efficient plant processors.

NAME: *Oligokyphus*
TIME: **Early Jurassic**
LOCALITY: **Europe (England)**
SIZE: **20 in/50 cm long**

Small and insignificant though *Oligokyphus* may have been, it and other members of its herbivorous family, the tritylodonts, were the last group of cynodonts to appear, in Late Triassic times. They were also the longest-lived group of all the therapsids, and the only mammal-like reptiles to endure into the Jurassic.

Oligokyphus was like a modern weasel in appearance, with a long, slim body and tail. Its forelegs, as well as its hindlegs, were placed directly beneath the body, as they are in mammals. This little cynodont had at last achieved a fully upright, 4-legged posture, unlike all other therapsids, which had sprawling forelimbs.

The dentition of the plant-eating *Oligokyphus* was also significantly different from that of other cynodonts. It had no canines, and the front pair of incisors were greatly enlarged, like those of a gnawing mammal such as a beaver. Like *Massetognathus* (*above*), a large gap separated the incisors from the square-shaped cheek teeth.

Each of the cheek teeth in the upper jaw had 3 rows of cusps, or projections, running along its length, with grooves in between; the lower teeth had 2 rows of cusps which fitted into the grooves in the upper teeth. This matching of the cusps allowed the teeth to occlude, or meet, in a precision bite.

Oligokyphus is so like a mammal that for years paleontologists believed it to be a member of that group. But the small bones at the back of the lower jaw betray its reptilian affinities.

Mammals: The evolution of versatility

The word mammal comes from the most important and unique characteristic of all species in this class of vertebrates, including humans: the presence in females of mammary glands, which produce milk to feed the young. Even the egg-laying mammals — the echidnas and platypus — have mammary glands.

The evolutionary implications of this milk-feeding strategy are enormous. The mother can leave her offspring in a den or nest while she goes foraging or hunting; she is then able to produce milk and so provide her young with a regular supply of this highly nutritious food. With nothing to do but sleep and suckle, the infants can grow fast.

The second most important mammalian characteristic is the presence of hairs, which usually form a dense fur coat. The prime purpose of the fur is to retain body heat, for mammals are warm-blooded. Most mammals keep their bodies at a constant temperature, which is usually well above that of the environment. Humans, for example, have a body temperature of about 98.6°F/37°C; if the air temperature is lower, then we shiver and must put on clothes to keep warm; if it is higher, then we sweat to lose heat.

By maintaining this regular temperature, mammals can be very active for long periods, regardless of external conditions. But they pay a high price for this benefit; mammals must eat a great deal of food to produce the energy needed for such a high level of activity.

The mammals arose during the Late Triassic period. Primitive members, represented today by the echidna and platypus, betray their reptilian ancestry by laying eggs. The ancestor of all the later mammals was probably one of the pantotheres. Two great groups arose, the marsupials, or pouched mammals, and the placental mammals.

Various groups of mammals are closely related, as shown by the colors in the chart. For example, the bats evolved from the insectivores; the carnivorous creodonts and true carnivores shared a common ancestor; and the dugongs are related to the elephant group. The primates date back to the Late Cretaceous, with prehistoric humans appearing in Africa some 4 million years ago. (For key to silhouettes, see p. 312.)

194

PERIOD *TRIASSIC* *JURASSIC* *CRETACEOUS*

MILLIONS OF YEARS AGO   248   213   *   144   **

EGG-LAYING MAMMALS {

MAR-SUPIALS {

PANTOTHERES

PLACENTAL MAMMALS

TRUE CARNIVORES {

PERISSODACTYLS {

ARTIODACTYLS {

GLIRES {

* Gap represents 50 million years

** Gap represents 60 millio[n]

Solid bars show the known fossil record of a group. Dotted lines denote possible evolutionary relationships between groups.

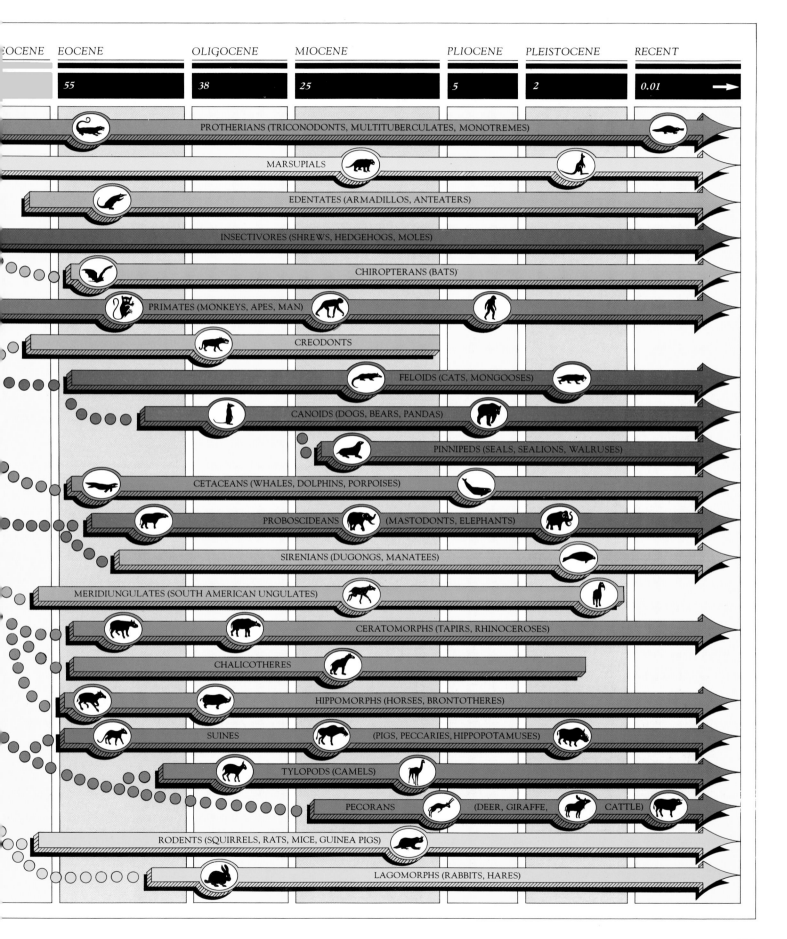

Mammals: The evolution of versatility

The earliest known mammals appeared in Late Triassic times, about 220 million years ago. Throughout the Jurassic and Cretaceous, mammals remained only minor elements in the world land faunas, which were dominated by reptiles, and in particular by dinosaurs. Mesozoic mammals were all small shrew- or vole-sized creatures. They lived by scavenging small animals such as insect pupae, caterpillars and beetles. Other early mammals, such as multituberculates, probably exploited plant matter, as do the voles today.

With the close of the Mesozoic Era, the world changed. On land, the major development was the disappearance of the dinosaurs. The succeeding Cenozoic Era began 65 million years ago, and the dominant forms of life on land since then have been flowering plants, insects, birds and mammals.

The rise of the mammals
The emergence of tropical rainforests, of temperate woodlands, of savannah and prairie grasslands, all provided new habitats for mammals to exploit. Mammals have inhabited all continents, most large islands and the oceans worldwide. Today, Antarctica is the only large landmass without resident mammals, save for the sealions that frequent its shores. However, back in Eocene times, some 50 million years ago, Antarctica had a wooded landscape in which lived marsupial mammals.

Mammals enjoyed their maximum diversity about 15 million years ago, during the Miocene. Since then, world climates have deteriorated, culminating in the Great Ice Ages of the Pleistocene, which began about 2 million years ago. Animal diversity is always greatest in the tropics, and the shrinkage of tropical habitats is largely responsible for the decline in the total number of mammal species. The alternating cold and warm periods of the Ice Age did, however, encourage the evolution of many remarkable large mammals, such as the wooly mammoth, giant deer and ground sloths — all of which have disappeared within the last 12,000 years.

An active lifestyle calls for a high degree of control over the nervous system, so mammals have a large and complex brain capable of rapidly processing information fed to it from the eyes, nose and ears.

Limb adaptations
As the small, scurrying, shrewlike early mammals evolved into large forms, they extended their range from the undergrowth up into the trees and out into the scrublands; some took to the water and others took to the air.

All these exploitations of different environments required the evolving mammals to develop adaptations in their limbs. Shrews have basically primitive 5-toed, or pentadactyl, feet. Those of fast-running predators, such as domestic cats, are essentially large-scale versions of this plan, with the loss of the inner toe. Mammals that climb and brachiate (swing from branch to branch) evolved elongated arms and legs with long fingers.

Mammals that graze the prairies and tropical savannahs have long slender legs with hoofed feet; in these "ungulate" mammals, the legs have only one purpose — to move the animal, slowly or rapidly, across the ground. The ability to turn the feet sideways is lost, and the lateral digits also disappear until only 2 toes (as in cattle) or a single toe (as in horses) remain. Carnivores cannot pursue this economical course, since they must use their limbs for a variety of purposes — for walking, running, crawling, digging, climbing and swimming, as well as for seizing, holding and tearing into their victims. Their limbs retain essentially the primitive structure for a multipurpose life.

Seals and sealions swim using highly modified limbs; the upper part of the limb is short, and the foot elongated and webbed to form a paddle. In whales, by contrast, the main power is provided by up-and-down movements of the tail fin. The forelimbs, modified into fins, are used mainly to control direction, and the hindlimbs are totally absent.

Bats make use of another sort of modification of their forelimbs as "wings," by elongating 3 fingers which radiate out like the spokes of an umbrella to provide support for the flight membrane, or patagium, made of a thin layer of skin.

Mammals basically have 3 different types of horny outgrowths at the end of their digits: nails, claws and hoofs. Nails are found in primates, elephants and rhinoceroses. Claws are best developed in carnivores, but also occur in digging animals such as anteaters and sloths. Hoofs characterize those mammals, such as horses and antelopes, which live on grass-covered plains and scrublands, but they are also found in mountain goats and desert camels.

So, by elongating or shortening parts of the primitive pentadactyl limb, and sometimes by losing bones and digits, the basic catlike leg has become modified to enable mammals to move in virtually all types of environments — on and under the ground, high in the trees, in and under fresh and salt water, and in the air.

Mammal teeth
Their ability to move efficiently through this great range of different habitats enables mammals to exploit a very wide range of food sources. This, in turn, requires a dentition adapted for obtaining the food in the first place, and then reducing it to an easily swallowed mass, or bolus. A mammal also needs an efficient digestive system, which can process the food to extract the maximum amount of the nutrients the creature needs.

Mammals are classified primarily on the basis of the structure and arrangement of their teeth and their limbs: that is, on how they feed and how they move. Since they have to move to obtain their food, these 2 functions are intimately related.

Teeth are made of very tough calcium phosphate, so they fossilize well and outlast every other part of a mammal's body, even the bones. It might be considered ironic that most of us spend so much time in dental surgeries in an attempt to preserve our teeth, yet after death it is our teeth which are most likely to endure the centuries and even millennia.

During its lifetime, a mammal has 2 sets of teeth: the first, or milk, dentition erupts after weaning and lasts only a short time, allowing the animal to feed while growing rapidly. The second, or permanent, set erupts to replace this. In an unspecialized, primitive mammal it comprises 44 teeth. These teeth are arranged in a distinct series, with different shapes and functions: 3 incisors, 1 canine, 4 premolars and 3 molars make up a total of 11 teeth in each half of each jaw. Few mammals exhibit this "primitive" pattern without modification; Some teeth have been lost, and those that remain are further specialized.

The incisor teeth are situated at the front of the jaws; they usually have a chisel edge, and are used for holding and tearing. Specializations include the loss of 2 incisors, with the remaining 1 becoming a tusk in elephants or a cutting tool in gnawing rodents.

The canine (or dogtooth) is a small tusklike tooth used by carnivores to pierce and hold their prey; in some it becomes greatly enlarged to form a sabertooth. In most herbivores, such as rabbits, cattle and horses, the canine is lost or is at most vestigial.

The incisors and canines are often separated, especially in herbivores, by a gap (the diastema) from the premolars and molars — the "cheek teeth." This allows their different functions to proceed simultaneously.

Like the incisors and canines, the premolars are often simple in shape,

ADAPTATIONS OF MAMMALS

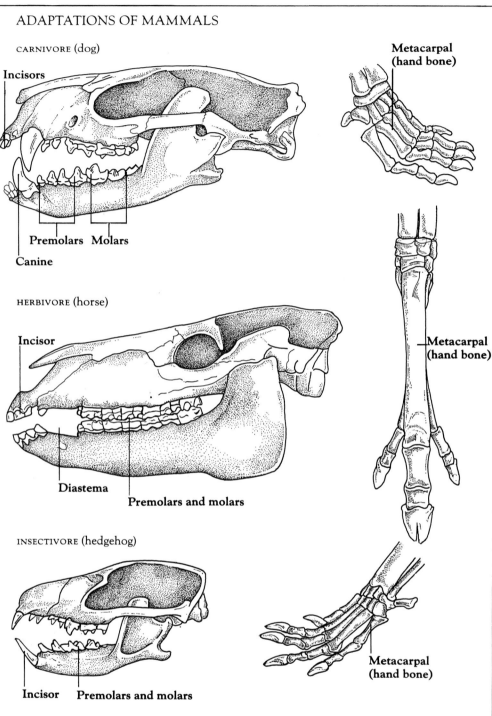

CARNIVORE (dog)

Incisors

Premolars **Molars**

Canine

Metacarpal (hand bone)

HERBIVORE (horse)

Incisor

Metacarpal (hand bone)

Diastema

Premolars and molars

INSECTIVORE (hedgehog)

Metacarpal (hand bone)

Incisor **Premolars and molars**

Mammal teeth and feet are well adapted for particular lifestyles. Most mammals have 4 kinds of teeth — incisors, canines, premolars and molars – whose functions vary with diet. In a carnivore, such as a dog, prey is killed with the canines and skinned with the incisors. Molars and premolars cut flesh. A herbivore such as a horse crops grass with strong incisors and grinds it with molars and premolars. The canines have been lost or are reduced. The gap (diastema) between the front and back teeth separates cropping and grinding

actions of the jaws. An insectivore like a hedgehog seizes prey with its incisors; molars pierce and cut soft food.

Carnivore limbs are used for capturing prey and for movement. They are essentially primitive and unspecialized. Herbivore feet are, by contrast, specialized for movement over the ground, with the lateral toes reduced as in *Parahippus* (*above*). Insectivores have 5-toed, lightly built unspecialized feet which perform a variety of functions — digging, grasping, climbing, swimming and running.

with only a single "cusp" (projection) on their biting surface, but they have 2 roots instead of 1. The premolars are often reduced in number, and may be specialized. In the hyenas, for example, premolars are thick, low cones used to crush bones, while they have become "molarized" in many herbivores, taking on the form and grinding function of the molar teeth.

The molar teeth are usually the most complex of all the teeth. They have no precursors in the milk dentition, and erupt last. The molars are usually multi-cusped and multirooted. The cusp patterns are constant for each mammal family and genus, and are of enormous value in identification and classification.

In primitive mammals, the cusps on the molar teeth are arranged in reverse triangles. These interlocked as the jaws close to produce a series of zigzag cutting edges capable of piercing soft food, such as worms or insects, while full closure of the jaw ensured the cutting up of the prey.

Carnivores have refined the cutting action, and evolved scissorlike blades — "carnassial teeth" for slicing meat. In herbivores, the addition of a fourth cusp changed the triangle into a square. This provides a solid platform, so that when the upper and lower teeth meet as the jaws close, the food is crushed. Sideways, front-to-back or circular movements can then break up the food ready for swallowing.

Reproduction and classification

The mammals are also reproductively highly sophisticated, and this forms the basis for classification into their major groups. There are 2 subclasses: the egg-laying Prototheria and the live-bearing Theria.

The Prototheria, the more primitive group, include the extinct multituberculates and the triconodonts, together with the monotremes. Monotremes survive today only in Australasia as the echidnas (spiny anteaters) and a single species of platypus.

The Theria are divided into 3 groups: the extinct Trituberculata, the Metatheria, and the Eutheria — a group which includes most living species.

The metatherians, also known as pouched-mammals or marsupials, have little or no placenta. The young are born in a far less advanced state than in eutherian mammals, but continue their development by crawling into their mother's pouch and attaching themselves to a nipple.

In the eutherian mammals, the fetus develops within a uterus, or womb, where it is nourished through a placenta by its mother's bloodstream.

Primitive mammals

MEGAZOSTRODON

PTILODUS

ALPHADON

CRUSAFONTIA

ZALAMBDALESTES

HARAMIYA

PURGATORIUS

Primitive mammals

SUBCLASS PROTOTHERIA

The most primitive mammals belong to this group of "first mammals." They evolved from the cynodonts, a group of synapsid reptiles (*see p. 192*), during the late Triassic, some 220 million years ago.

The only surviving prototherians are the monotremes — the echidnas, or spiny anteaters, and the duck-billed platypus, all of which are found only in Australasia.

The reproductive method of the monotremes reflects their reptilian ancestry — they all lay eggs. However, the newly hatched young then suckle milk from their mothers, as all other mammals do.

ORDER TRICONODONTA

The earliest-known mammals belong to this order. They lived in the desert environments of the Late Triassic, and among the lush undergrowths of the Jurassic forests. A few species survived until the Early Cretaceous. All were small, furry creatures, only about 5 in/12 cm long — as tiny as some of the smallest living mammals. They looked like modern shrews, but in many respects they still resembled the ancestral group of advanced mammal-like reptiles, the therapsids (*see pp. 190–193*).

The teeth of tricodonts had the basic mammalian pattern, consisting of simple biting incisors at the front, followed by piercing canines, with cutting premolars and molars at the back. The crowns of the back teeth had three main cusps, or projections — hence the name of the group Triconodonta, meaning "three-coned teeth." There was a complex chewing motion in which the jaws moved sideways to some extent as they closed, enabling the upper and lower teeth along one side to slice food, followed by the teeth along the other side.

This method of eating meant that food could be digested more quickly, to release the vital energy needed to maintain a high rate of metabolism and, in turn, a predatory lifestyle. Like small modern mammals, triconodonts would have spent most of their lives eating — chasing after insects and small reptiles.

These early mammals may have reproduced like modern monotremes, with immature young hatched from leathery-shelled eggs.

The best-known family is the Morganucodontidae, fossils of which have been found in Europe, southern Africa and eastern Asia.

NAME: *Megazostrodon*
TIME: Late Triassic to Early Jurassic
LOCALITY: Africa (Lesotho)
SIZE: 5 in/12 cm long

The morganucodont *Megazostrodon* looked like a modern shrew, and may have behaved like one too. It probably hunted for insects and other small invertebrates among the leaf litter and undergrowth, probably during the night, when it was less likely to fall prey to carnivorous dinosaurs.

Its body shape is well known from an almost complete skeleton found in Lesotho, while remains of closely related animals have been found in China and Britain. The skeleton is very similar to that of primitive mammals.

ORDER MULTITUBERCULATA

The multituberculates were the earliest of the plant-eating mammals, evolving during the Late Jurassic and Early Cretaceous, with some groups surviving into the Eocene. They ranged from mouse-sized creatures to animals the size of a modern beaver (very large for a primitive mammal), and were distinctly rodentlike in appearance, although they were in no way related to these animals. The similarity, especially of the tooth arrangement, is simply an adaptation to the same lifestyle and feeding habits.

Like rodents, the multituberculates had gnawing incisor teeth at the front of their jaws and grinding premolar and molar teeth at the back. The two types of teeth were separated by a gap called a diastema, which enabled them to be used independently. The array of grinding cheek teeth had many cusps (projections) to break up tough vegetation, as in many rodents. The jaws worked with an up-and-down action, without the sideways movement of the early insectivorous mammals, such as *Megazostrodon* (*above*).

The multituberculates show no close affinity with any of the other mammal groups, and it is possible that they evolved independently from the mammal-like reptiles.

The family Haramiyidae is a little-known Early Jurassic group of mammals with broad cheek teeth. Its members may be related to the ancestors of the multituberculates.

The family Ptilodontidae consists of animals with long tails that were prehensile, serving as a fifth limb for grasping branches of the trees in which they probably lived. Their feet, too, show adaptations for climbing: like squirrels, ptilodonts could point their toes backward, due to a highly mobile ankle joint, which enabled them to run down a tree trunk headfirst. They could also spread their big toes wide, to give a sure grip, aided by sharp claws. Their remains have been found mainly in North America.

NAME: *Haramiya*
TIME: Late Triassic to Early Jurassic
LOCALITY: Europe (England and Germany)
SIZE: 5 in/12 cm long

Haramiya is known from only a few isolated teeth. This fragmentary evidence suggests that it was somewhat like a miniature vole, and crushed its food with its broad cheek teeth. It may have lived on low-growing vegetation, possibly on the fruits of cycad-like plants.

NAME: *Ptilodus*
TIME: Early to Late Paleocene
LOCALITY: North America (the Rockies, New Mexico to Saskatchewan)
SIZE: 20 in/50 cm long

Apart from its long, prehensile tail, *Ptilodus* was similar to a modern squirrel in appearance, and may have lived in the same way — scampering about in the branches of trees. The lower premolar teeth were very large and bladelike, and *Ptilodus* may have used them to strip the husks from tough nuts and seeds.

CRUSAFONTIA

HARAMIYA

...AMBDALESTES

PURGATORIUS

SUBCLASS THERIA

This great group includes the majority of fossil mammals and their living relatives. It is subdivided into three major orders — the pantotheres, restricted to the Mesozoic; the marsupials, or pouched mammals, which still survive in Australasia and America; and the eutherians, or placental mammals, which include all other living mammals and many extinct ones, too.

ORDER PANTOTHERIA

The pantotheres are most probably the common ancestors of all modern mammals, except the monotremes (*see pp. 194–195*). They had quite complicated molar teeth with a triangular pattern of cusps similar to that in many modern mammals. These teeth were adapted for shearing and crushing, and would have dealt equally well with insects or fruit.

The family Dryolestidae probably represents an offshoot of the pantotheres, which branched away from the evolutionary line that led to the modern mammals. Dryolestids are known only from a few teeth and jaw bones, which show that the mammalian jaw hinge had fully evolved in this group (*see p. 184*). Three bones that had been part of the jaw in their reptilian ancestors were now incorporated into the middle ear, as the hammer, anvil and stirrup bones. These form part of a chain along which sound is transmitted to the inner ear (*see p. 185*).

NAME: *Crusafontia*
TIME: Early Cretaceous
LOCALITY: Europe (Portugal)
SIZE: 4 in/10 cm long

The dryolestid *Crusafontia* is known only from a few teeth. The reconstruction on p. 199 is based on a relatively complete skeleton of another member of the family from the Late Jurassic of Portugal. It probably resembled a tiny squirrel, living in trees and feeding on fruit, nuts and seeds. The long tail may have been prehensile, and the bones of its hip girdle suggest that it may have reproduced the way a marsupial does — giving birth to very immature young and suckling them in a pouch for the first few weeks of life.

INFRACLASS METATHERIA

The two major subgroups of the subclass Theria — the Metatheria and Eutheria — diverged from a common ancestor early in the Cretaceous. The Metatheria contains only one order, the Marsupialia, or pouched mammals. This group is dealt with in detail on pp. 202–205, but a primitive member is described here as a comparison with other primitive mammals.

NAME: *Alphadon*
TIME: Late Cretaceous
LOCALITY: North America (Alberta to New Mexico)
SIZE: 1 ft/30 cm long

Primitive marsupials such as *Alphadon* were probably very similar to modern opossums. They were omnivores, and ate a wide range of foods, including insects, small vertebrates and fruit. They were probably also tree-dwellers, able to climb well, using feet equipped with opposable toes, which could be brought together to give a good grip, and prehensile tails. Their small size and tree-dwelling habits would have meant that they did not compete directly for food with the Late Cretaceous dinosaurs, and so were able to survive alongside them.

INFRACLASS EUTHERIA

The placental mammals, or eutherians, give birth to well-developed young after nurturing them for some time inside a womb. They make up the vast majority of modern mammals, and are grouped in about 24 orders (*see pp. 194–195*).

One of the earliest families known, the Zalambdalestidae (*below*), may represent a side-branch from the main evolutionary line rather than a direct stage in the evolution of later placentals.

NAME: *Zalambdalestes*
TIME: Late Cretaceous
LOCALITY: Asia (Mongolia)
SIZE: 8 in/20 cm long

Zalambdalestes looked very much like the modern elephant shrew. It had a long upturned snout and powerful little legs, the back pair being longer than the front. The legs had greatly elongated foot bones. The fingers could not be brought to meet each other (were not opposable), so it is unlikely to have been a tree climber. The brain was quite small and the eyes large. *Zalambdalestes* may well have lived like the modern elephant shrews, running and jumping through the undergrowth after insects, and catching them with its long incisor teeth.

ORDER PRIMATES

The primates are a very ancient group of mammals, known from Late Cretaceous times, as long as 70 million years ago. The more advanced members are dealt with on pp. 286–297, but a primitive form is described here for comparison with contemporary mammals.

The family Paromomyidae consisted of small creatures like tree shrews, which may have been the ancestors of the later lemurs, monkeys and apes. However, some paleontologists do not regard them as members of the primate order at all, but place them in an order of their own.

NAME: *Purgatorius*
TIME: Late Cretaceous and Early Paleocene
LOCALITY: North America (Montana)
SIZE: possibly 4 in/10 cm long

Little is known about this small animal except for what can be deduced from a single molar tooth found in Late Cretaceous rocks. This one tooth is important because it belonged to the earliest-known primate. It resembles the molars of a modern lemur.

More complete sets of teeth from a slightly later, but related, creature from the Early Paleocene indicate that *Purgatorius* may have been omnivorous, but the small size — it probably weighed no more than about $\frac{3}{4}$ oz/20 g — suggests that it was primarily an insect-eater.

Marsupials

CLADOSICTIS

NECROLESTES

BORHYAENA

THYLACOSMILUS

ARGYROLAGUS

THYLACOLEO

DIPROTODON

PALORCHESTES

PROCOPTODON

Marsupials

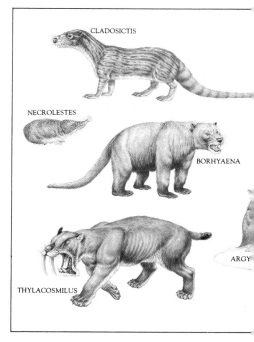

ORDER MARSUPIALIA

The marsupials—including the familiar kangaroos and koalas of Australia, and the opossums of America—are among the most ancient of all the orders of mammals. They evolved during the Late Cretaceous, between 100 and 75 million years ago.

The unique feature of marsupials is their method of reproduction. Placentals (the vast majority of mammals, including humans) nurture their young via a placenta within a womb, and do not give birth until the young have reached a relatively advanced stage. But marsupials give birth to very small and immature young — little more than embryos. These are then suckled, usually in a pouch on the belly, and grow to maturity outside the mother's body.

The marsupials seem to have evolved in North or South America, and one group migrated via Antarctica (then much warmer than it is today) to Australia. A further group of marsupials moved via North America into Europe. The closeness of the drifting continents to one another in Late Cretaceous times enabled them to do this (see p. 11). The marsupials flourished in isolation in South America during the Tertiary, where they developed before the placental mammals, and in Australia, where they have their stronghold today.

Another group of marsupials moved into Europe via North America during the Early Eocene, and in the Oligocene reached North Africa and central Asia. These were the didelphids, represented today by the opossums. They are thought of as the most primitive of the marsupials, and are the group to which the earliest-known marsupials belong.

By the Early Miocene, didelphid marsupials had become extinct in North America, and they disappeared from Europe, too, by Middle Miocene times. Although they never returned to Europe, the modern genus *Didelphis* (the Virginia opossum) reentered North America from South America some 3 million years ago, via the newly-formed Panama land bridge.

However, the South American marsupials are nearly all gone, wiped out by invasions of placental mammals from North America. This happened when, during the Pliocene, a Central American land bridge was formed between these 2 great continents. This bridge was a tenuous one, however, and was not "permanent" until the Panama connection was created.

The Australian marsupials still flourish today, despite competition from placentals. The reason may be that Australia had been moving northward by the slow process of continental drift during the Tertiary. This drift was relatively rapid, and the Australian climate changed from temperate conditions to tropical rainforest in a few tens of millions of years. The marsupial animal life there had to evolve continually to keep up with this change, and as a result the stock is genetically strong. This has not prevented some of them from being much reduced in numbers (such as koala bears) or maybe even extinct (such as the Tasmanian "wolf," or thylacine) as a result of human activities.

In contrast to Australia, South America has remained stationary during the same period of time. The animals did not need to evolve so much. Thus the placental invaders found a relatively primitive and genetically weak fauna there, which was easy to replace.

FAMILY BORHYAENIDAE

This family evolved from didelphid ancestors, and consists entirely of extinct carnivorous South American marsupials. Although completely unrelated to placental mammals of other continents, the borhyaenids evolved body shapes and lifestyles similar to those of cats, dogs, bears and other placental carnivores. This is a superb example of convergent evolution.

NAME: *Cladosictis*
TIME: **Late Oligocene to Early Miocene**
LOCALITY: **South America (Patagonia)**
SIZE: **2 ft 6 in/80 cm long**
Cladosictis was a primitive carnivorous marsupial which may have resembled an otter in shape and size, with a long body and tail and short limbs. It probably scampered through the undergrowth, seeking out, chasing and catching small mammals and reptiles, and swam in rivers after fish. It may even have eaten reptiles' or birds' eggs and insects. The tooth pattern was similar to that of carnivorous placental mammals. The teeth consisted of incisors at the front for holding prey, followed by pointed canines for killing it, and meat-shearing (carnassial) premolars and molars at the back.

NAME: *Borhyaena*
TIME: **Late Oligocene to Early Miocene**
LOCALITY: **South America (Patagonia)**
SIZE: **5 ft/1.5 m long**
Some borhyaenids were rather bear-like, with heavy bodies and flat feet. The wolf-sized *Borhyaena* was typical of this group, but other closely related types ranged from fox-sized creatures to animals as big as bears.

These were the main predators of the day. Their prey would have included the plant-eating ungulates (see pp. 246–253) that were restricted to South America. The short limbs suggest that *Borhyaena* was not much of a runner, but probably ambushed its prey. It may also have been a scavenger.

FAMILY THYLACOSMILIDAE

In this group of large predatory marsupials, the incisor teeth were lost, and very long upper canine teeth developed, which grew continually. These served as formidable weapons for killing prey.

NAME: *Thylacosmilus*
TIME: **Late Miocene to Early Pliocene**
LOCALITY: **South America (Argentina)**
SIZE: **4 ft/1.2 m long**
Thylacosmilus, like the sabertooth cats of North America and Europe (see pp. 222–225), sported a pair of upper canine teeth that had evolved into long, stabbing sabers projecting down well below the mouth-line. In both these unrelated creatures, the musculature of the neck and jaws allowed the saber-teeth to be driven downward with a tremendous killing force. And the jaws were capable of a gape that would leave the teeth clear to do their work.

Unlike the sabertooth cats, *Thylacosmilus* had no incisor teeth or scabbard-like tooth-guards on its lower jaw. Also the saber-teeth grew continuously throughout life, rather like the incisors of rodents.

The victims of *Thylacosmilus* may have been large, slow-moving hoofed mammals that could not be killed rapidly with a quick bite to the neck. The saber-teeth would have inflicted deep wounds and the prey presumably bled to death.

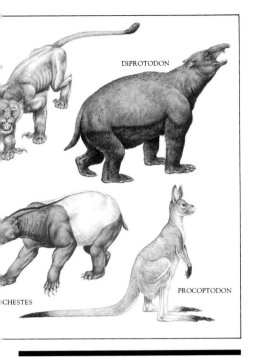

DIPROTODON

CHESTES

PROCOPTODON

FAMILY ARGYROLAGIDAE
This family consists of animals very similar to the kangaroo rats and jerboas of today, but are completely unrelated to them. Like such rodents they may have lived in deserts and been mostly nocturnal animals. They would have moved swiftly over the open ground by a series of prodigious leaps, and fed on the shoots and roots of desert plants.

NAME: *Argyrolagus*
TIME: **Late Miocene to Late Pliocene**
LOCALITY: **South America (Patagonia)**
SIZE: **16 in/40 cm long**
Just like modern kangaroo rats and other desert rodents (of which it is no relation), *Argyrolagus* moved quickly over open country on its slim 2-toed hindlegs, balanced by its long heavy tail. The head was somewhat rodentlike, but it had a pointed snout. Enormous eye sockets, which suggest that the animal foraged only at night, were situated far back in the skull. The teeth suggest that it ate desert plants.

FAMILY NECROLESTIDAE
This family has a single member, the extinct *Necrolestes* (below), so specialized that it can be classed with no other animal. However, its jaws and teeth do show some resemblance to those of the living golden moles of Africa.

NAME: *Necrolestes*
TIME: **Early Miocene**
LOCALITY: **South America (Patagonia)**
SIZE: **possibly 6 in/15 cm long**
All that is known of this little creature is a single specimen of the tip of the jaws with an oddly upturned snout. This may have ended in fleshy folds, possibly serving as sensitive organs of touch helping the animal to find its food, like the complex fringe of tentacles surrounding the nostrils of the living star-nosed mole.

From its many fine teeth, paleontologists think that *Necrolestes* was an insect- or worm-eater. It may have lived as a burrower, hence its ghoulish name, which means "grave-robber."

FAMILY THYLACOLEONIDAE
A family of lionlike marsupials lived in Australia in Pliocene and Pleistocene times. They probably hunted across the Australian grasslands.

NAME: *Thylacoleo*
TIME: **Pleistocene**
LOCALITY: **Australia (New South Wales, Queensland, Western and South Australia)**
SIZE: **5 ft 6 in/1.7 m long**
This "marsupial lion" had a short cat-like face. Projecting front incisors were modified into killing teeth, and looked rather like the canines in the placental carnivores — the canines themselves were insignificant. The back teeth formed powerful meat-shearing blades.

Thylacoleo was once believed to have used its unusual front teeth to break open nuts and fruit. However, recent studies have shown that wear on the teeth is consistent with a meat-eating diet, and it probably preyed on the giant kangaroos and wombats of the time.

FAMILY DIPROTODONTIDAE
This major group of Australian marsupials includes mostly herbivorous animals. Diprotodonts have a single pair of lower incisors, which point forward. They have between 1 and 3 pairs of upper incisors, no canines, and a long gap (diastema) between their incisors and cheek teeth, as in rodents. The second and third toes of their hindfeet are greatly reduced in size and are bound within a single sheath of tissue — a specialization used for grooming.

Living relatives of the diprotodonts include the familiar koalas and kangaroos, as well as the phalangers (Australian opossums) and wombats.

NAME: *Diprotodon*
TIME: **Pleistocene**
LOCALITY: **Australia (South Australia)**
SIZE: **10 ft/3 m long**
The grazing marsupials reached their greatest size in *Diprotodon* and its relatives. In appearance *Diprotodon* was rather like a rhinoceros-sized wombat. It probably fed on a particular species of salt-bush which it could scrape out of the ground with its paws. Remains of this bush have been found in the stomach cavities of several fossil specimens.

The body, head and neck were massive, and the limbs strong. The feet were plantigrade, or flat-footed, and the weight was borne on the palms and the soles, as in a bear, rather than on the toes. Unlike that of other mammals, the outer ("little") toe of this animal was the longest — a peculiar feature with no apparent function.

Complete *Diprotodon* skeletons have been found preserved in lake muds. In the dry climates in which these animals lived, salt crusts may have formed over the local lakes of the open landscape. The heavy *Diprotodon* would easily have fallen through and become entombed in the mud beneath.

FAMILY PALORCHESTIDAE
This family of large herbivores lived in Australia from Miocene to Pleistocene times. They may have been the marsupial equivalents of the ground sloths (*see pp. 206–209*).

NAME: *Palorchestes*
TIME: **Miocene to Pleistocene**
LOCALITY: **Australia**
SIZE: **8 ft/2.5 m long**
The arrangement of the nasal bones in the skull of this animal suggests that it had some sort of trunk. In that case it would have looked like a giant marsupial tapir. However, its front legs were strong, and had 5 toes with huge claws. The creature may have fed by pulling down branches to reach the leaves.

FAMILY MACROPODIDAE
The most familiar of the modern marsupials, the kangaroos and wallabies, are included in the family Macropodidae.

NAME: *Procoptodon*
TIME: **Pleistocene**
LOCALITY: **Australia**
SIZE: **10 ft/3 m long**
Extinct kangaroos tended to be larger than modern forms, and had some different features. *Procoptodon* was the largest of these, and was distinctive because of the short face and the fact that each hindfoot had only a single long, functional toe (the fourth), with mere nailless stumps on either side.

Procoptodon was a grazing kangaroo, which fed on grass and low vegetation, like most modern forms. Other extinct kangaroos were browsers, using their great height to reach up into trees.

Glyptodonts, sloths, armadillos and anteaters

METACHEIROMYS

HAPALOPS

GLOSSOTHERIUM

MEGATHERIUM

DOEDICURUS

PELTEPHILUS

EUROTAMANDUA

EOMANIS

Glyptodonts, sloths, armadillos and anteaters

COHORT EDENTATA

The edentates are represented today by the anteaters, tree sloths and armadillos. The name of the cohort (a grouping of many orders) means "without teeth," but in fact only the anteaters are completely toothless. The other members have teeth, although these are reduced to a few rudimentary pegs, often without roots or an enamel covering.

The edentates comprise some of the world's most bizarre mammals. As well as the living anteaters with their greatly elongated snouts, the armadillos with their flexibly suits of armor, and the proverbially slow sloths, the edentates include several strange, extinct groups. There were the tanklike glyptodonts with solid, immovable body armor, and the giant ground sloths, up to 6 ft/1·8 m high. Both these prehistoric animals ranged widely in North and South America during the Pleistocene.

The anteaters and armadillos became highly adapted for feeding on ants and termites. Glyptodonts, ground sloths and tree sloths are vegetarian.

The origin of the edentates, and their relationships with other mammals, is at present unknown. Whether they all evolved from a single ancestor or arose from several different groups is a matter of debate. The current uncertainty is reflected in the isolated location of the edentate line in the evolutionary chart on pp. 194–195.

FAMILY METACHEIROMYIDAE

These earliest and most primitive of the edentates, have uncertain relationships with other edentate groups. They may be the ancestors of the scaly anteaters or pangolins (below).

NAME: *Metacheiromys*
TIME: **Middle Eocene**
LOCALITY: **North America (Wyoming)**
SIZE: **18 in/45 cm long**

With its short legs, sharp claws and long, heavy tail, *Metacheiromys* may have resembled a modern mongoose. However, it had a long, narrow, armadillo-type head. It had strong canines, but had lost almost all of its cheek teeth. Horny pads grew in their place, which the animal doubtless used to crush its prey.

Metacheiromys' habitat was the dense, subtropical forests that covered parts of the western USA during the Eocene. The claws on its forefeet were much larger than those on its hindfeet, so *Metacheiromys* probably dug for its food, rooting out ants, beetles and grubs buried in the soil.

ORDER XENARTHRA

The name Xenarthra refers to the extra joints between the vertebrae which are a characteristic of the group. Their presence may have enabled animals as diverse as glyptodonts and armadillos to support the weight of a heavy suit of armor, or the giant ground sloths to haul their huge bodies into a near-vertical position in order to feed on leaves at considerable heights.

The xenarthrans evolved in South America during the Paleocene, some 60 million years ago. They flourished on their island continent, isolated from predators and evolutionary changes. Then, in the Early Pliocene, about 5 million years ago, the land bridge that had once connected the 2 Americas during Early Tertiary times was reestablished, and glyptodonts, ground sloths and armadillos lumbered across it, heading north.

FAMILIES MYLODONTIDAE, MEGATHERIIDAE AND MEGALONYCHIDAE

Today's tree sloths of Central and South America look and behave quite differently from their ancestors, the extinct ground sloths. Many of these creatures were so large that they could never have climbed trees, and so were permanently grounded. One of the largest, *Megatherium*, was some 10 times bigger than its living relatives.

Ground sloths were slow-moving creatures and strict vegetarians. They appeared in the Early Oligocene, some 35 million years ago, and survived up to recent times.

NAME: *Hapalops*
TIME: **Early to Middle Miocene**
LOCALITY: **South America (Patagonia)**
SIZE: **30 cm/1 m long**

By Miocene times, some 20 million years ago, ground sloths were well established in South America. *Hapalops* was an early Miocene member of the group, and small in comparison with its later relatives. Its short head, stout body and long tail were supported on long, slender forelegs and even longer, heavier hindlegs. The long, curved claws on all its toes must have forced this sloth to walk on the knuckles of its front feet, rather like a modern gorilla. But being of fairly light build, *Hapalops* could have spent some of its time in trees, clinging on with its sharp-clawed feet and using its long legs to hook down succulent leaves and fruit.

Like all the edentates, *Hapalops* had very few teeth, only 4 or 5 pairs of cheek teeth remaining in its jaws.

NAME: *Megatherium*
TIME: **Pleistocene**
LOCALITY: **South America (Patagonia, Bolivia and Peru)**
SIZE: **20 ft/6 m long**

This gigantic creature is the largest-known ground sloth. It probably weighed as much as 3 US tons/3 tonnes. Its head was deep and bearlike, and its jaws were equipped with strong muscles for grinding up its plant food between the few remaining, pegshaped cheek teeth.

Although this giant ground sloth was as large as a modern elephant, it could rear up on its sturdy hindlegs, supported on its thick tail. (Such a 2-legged pose is reminiscent of the great herbivorous dinosaurs, such as *Apatosaurus*, *see pp. 131, 132*.) In this position, *Megatherium* could browse near the treetops, hooking down branches with its 3-clawed forefeet.

NAME: *Glossotherium*
TIME: **Pliocene to Pleistocene**
LOCALITY: **North America (California)**
SIZE: **13 ft/4 m long**

The Rancho La Brea tar pits in Los Angeles have yielded excellent specimens of this great ground sloth, which traveled up from South America, some 3 million years ago, over the newly reformed land bridge. There it met its fate in the sticky pools of crude oil that had seeped up to the surface and lay innocently covered by water.

Glossotherium was a bulky creature, with a large head and heavy tail. Its long, clawed feet were turned inward, as they are in its relatives, so it walked on its knuckles, gorilla-style. *Glossotherium* could rear up on its hindlegs, and used the long claws to bring food to its mouth. It seems to have lived on desert shrubs, to judge by the plant remains preserved in its fossil droppings.

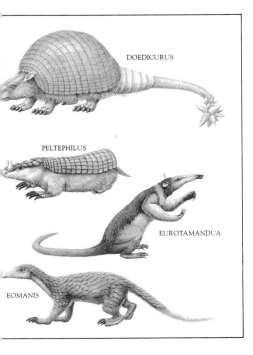

DOEDICURUS

PELTEPHILUS

EUROTAMANDUA

EOMANIS

FAMILY GLYPTODONTIDAE

The glyptodonts were gigantic, arma-dillolike creatures, which can be thought of as the mammalian equivalent of the heavily armored dinosaurs called ankylosaurs (*see pp. 155–161*). Some 50 genera evolved from the Early Miocene, about 20 million years ago, reaching their peak of success on the grasslands of South America and southern North America during the Pliocene and Pleis-tocene, between about 5 million and 3 million years ago. They survived until historical times, and feature in the legends of Patagonian Indians.

Glyptodonts were grazing animals, lacking teeth in the front of their mouths but having powerful grinding teeth at the back. They had massive, deep jaws with downward-pointing pro-jections of their cheekbones, which pro-vided a site for the attachment of the powerful muscles they needed to chew grasses and other tough vegetation.

Some glyptodonts became very large: one of the biggest, *Glyptodon*, which lived in Argentina during the Pleisto-cene, between 2 million and 15,000 years ago, was the size of a small auto-mobile and as formidably armored as a military tank (5 ft/1.5 m tall and 10 ft 6 in/3.3 m long). The glyptodonts evolved from armadillolike animals with armor arranged in rings.

By the end of the Pliocene, about 2 million years ago, the armor had become fused to form a rigid bony dome-shaped "shell" made up of a mosaic of polygonal bony plates that enclosed the animal's back, a helmet above its skull, and a series of rings or a solid tube of bone around the tail. This armor accounted for 20 percent of the animal's weight (the tusks of an elephant account for 3 percent).

NAME: *Doedicurus*
TIME: **Pleistocene**
LOCALITY: **South America (Patagonia)**
SIZE: **13 ft/4 m long**
As well as being protected by an armored suit, *Doedicurus* possessed a powerful defensive weapon at the end of its tail — a bony club covered in spikes and borne at the end of a stiff shaft. This remarkable structure bore a striking re-semblance to the maces carried by medieval knights, and like them, was probably used by its owner to flail out at enemies — such as the carnivorous borhyaenids (*see pp. 218–221*).

FAMILY DASYPODIDAE

The armadillos first appeared in Argen-tina in Late Paleocene times, about 60 million years ago. By the Late Oligocene, some 30 million years ago, several forms had evolved the character-istic articulated armor seen in the armadillos, which are essentially very similar and are included in the same family. Armadillos have always re-mained restricted to the Americas: the 20 modern species are almost all found in South and Central America, though 1 has recently extended its range into the southern part of the United States.

NAME: *Peltephilus*
TIME: **Oligocene to Miocene**
LOCALITY: **South America (Patagonia)**
SIZE: **20 ft/6 m long**
The armor of *Peltephilus*, like that of other armadillos, developed from its skin, and consisted of tough bony plates, or "scutes," covered with horn. These were arranged in bands around the armadillo's body, and were connec-ted to the underlying skin, making for a flexible protective "shell."

On the snout of *Peltephilus* a pair of long scutes was modified into a pair of horn cores, covered in life with horn. Unlike the true horns of cattle, sheep or antelope, the bony core was not an outgrowth of the skull bones. *Peltephilus* may also have borne a second, smaller pair of horns farther forward on its snout. Peculiar among the edentates in having large caninelike teeth, *Peltephilus* may possibly have been a carnivore or carrion-eater.

FAMILY MYRMECOPHAGIDAE

The myrmecophagids, or "true ant-eaters" (to distinguish them from the completely unrelated marsupial ant-eaters such as the modern numbat *Myr-mecobius*) are highly specialized for ex-ploiting a diet of ants and termites. Their evolution is little known: an early

form, *Protamandua*, from the Early Miocene about 20 million years ago, was already a typical anteater.

NAME: *Eurotamandua*
TIME: **Middle Eocene**
LOCALITY: **Europe (Germany)**
SIZE: **3 ft/90 cm long**
Until recently, when a fossil anteater was discovered in deposits of oil shale near Frankfurt in Germany, and named *Eurotamandua*, paleontologists thought that anteaters were confined to South America. With its long tubular snout, weak toothless jaws and powerful fore-limbs armed with huge claws, this was undoubtedly an anteater, and seems to have been very similar to the modern collared anteater *Tamandua*. The fossil record of anteaters is poor, so it is not known how this exciting European find fits into the overall evolutionary history of the group. Evidence of *Eurotamandua*'s typical anteater diet is provided by the fossilized ants found at the German site.

FAMILY MANIDAE

The sole family in the Order Pholidota, these are the pangolins — curious mammals covered in scales made of densely fused hairs, which give them the appearance of giant animated pine cones. They have stout limbs adapted for digging. Pangolins are often grouped together with the anteaters and armadil-los because of their similar lifestyle: they feed largely on ants and termites. However, this is probably an arrange-ment of convenience rather than a re-flection of any close relationship.

The extreme specializations of all these creatures make it difficult to deter-mine their true relationships. All 7 liv-ing species of pangolins are placed in the single genus *Manis*. They are found in tropical Africa and Southeast Asia.

NAME: *Eomanis*
TIME: **Middle Eocene**
LOCALITY: **Europe (Germany)**
SIZE: **20 in/50 cm long**
The earliest known pangolin, *Eomanis* is represented by a well-preserved fossil from the same oil shale deposits that yielded the skeleton of *Eurotamandua*. Even the scales were preserved, and it is quite obvious that *Eomanis* looked very much like the pangolins of today. The animal may have been able to close its eyes, ears and nostrils as a protection against ant stings, as the modern species can do. From the remains of *Eomanis*' stomach, it is clear that its diet consisted of both plant matter and insects.

Insectivores and creodonts

ANAGALE

LEPTICTIDIUM

PLANETETHERIUM

ICARONYCTERIS

PALAEORYCTES

SARKASTODON

HYAENODON

Insectivores and creodonts

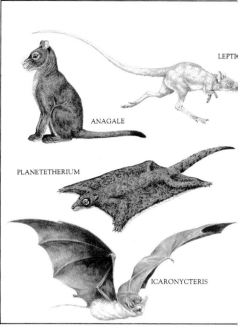

Insectivores include animals from a wide range of orders. The anagalids, for example, are believed to be more closely related to rabbits and rodents (Superorder Anagalida) than to members of the Superorder Insectivora (hedgehogs, shrews and moles). And both are quite distinct from the dermopterans (flying lemurs) and chiropterans (bats) in the Superorder Archonta.

ORDER ANAGALIDA
The anagalids were rabbitlike, digging mammals, known from the Early Tertiary of eastern Asia. They were once thought to be related to the elephant shrews, but they are now considered to have more in common with the rodents and rabbits.

NAME: *Anagale*
TIME: Early Oligocene
LOCALITY: Asia (Mongolia)
SIZE: 1 ft/30 cm long
Anagale may have looked like a modern rabbit, but it had a long tail and, probably, short ears. It also ran about, rather than jumping rabbit-style. This is conjectured from the proportions of the bones in its hindlegs.

Anagale's hindlegs were a little longer than the forelegs, and they were equipped with spadelike claws on the feet. *Anagale* probably searched through the soil for beetles, grubs, worms and the like. The fact that the teeth in many specimens found are thoroughly worn down suggests that it also ate the soil — perhaps the easiest way of extracting food from it.

ORDER DERMOPTERA
The dermopterans constitute the group of "flying lemurs" — a confusing name since they are neither lemurs, nor do they fly. Only 2 species survive today — the colugos (*Cynocephalus*) of Southeast Asia, both strict vegetarians.

These modern animals, less than 1 ft/30 cm long, can glide as far as 450 ft/137 m from tree to tree on outstretched skin membranes. It is assumed, though there is no direct evidence for this, that Mid-Paleocene and Early Eocene dermopterans could do likewise. There is some evidence that dermopterans are closely related to bats, tree shrews and primates, and that they all share a common ancestry with insectivores, but this is by no means certain: the similarities may be a result of convergent evolution of unrelated groups.

NAME: *Planetetherium*
TIME: Late Paleocene
LOCALITY: North America (Montana)
SIZE: 10 in/25 cm long
Planetetherium's remains have been found in beds of coal formed over many millions of years from dense lakeside forests of Cypress trees. As in the colugos, each incisor was divided to make a forward-pointing comb, with about 5 "teeth" arising from each root. Their function is unknown — they may have been used for grooming, or for scraping and straining food.

ORDER CHIROPTERA
These are the bats — the only mammals to have evolved true, powered flight. They have achieved this by modifying their forelimbs into flapping wings, made of a thin membrane (the patagium) supported by 4 greatly elongated fingers.

Most modern bats use echolocation to detect obstacles, prey and predators in the darkness of night and the gloom of their roosting haunts. The bat emits high-frequency sounds which bounce off objects in its path and are picked up by the sensitive ears of the bat, which then analyzes and acts on the information it receives.

The development of this extraordinary natural radar system involved great modification of the bat's larynx, nose, ears and brain, but it is impossible to trace the course of this evolution because the parts of the body concerned do not fossilize.

There are 2 distinct suborders of living bats. The Microchiroptera (or microbats) are by far the most numerous, with some 780 species alive today. They are found the world over, except for the Arctic and Antarctic regions and on the highest mountains. Most are small nocturnal animals with tiny eyes and large, often complex, extremely sensitive ears. Many also have specialized outgrowths of the nose which are used for echolocation.

The nature and arrangement of their teeth depends largely on their diet, but the great majority catch insects on the wing and have shearing ridges on their upper molars arranged in a W-shaped pattern. A few species are carnivorous.

The second suborder is the Megachiroptera (or megabats), with about 170 species alive today. These are the fruit bats and are restricted to the Old World tropics. They are large animals with foxlike faces, hence their alternative name of flying foxes. They lack the large, complex ears and elaborate noses of the microbats.

NAME: *Icaronycteris*
TIME: Early Eocene
LOCALITY: North America (Wyoming)
SIZE: 5½ in/14 cm long, 14 in/37 cm wingspan
Icaronycteris must have been almost identical to a modern microbat, but still had a few very primitive features. Its wings were relatively short and broad, and its mouth contained a large number of teeth, arranged like those of an insectivore (*see p. 196*). The body was not quite as rigid as that of a modern bat, and the tail was long and not connected to the hind legs by a web of skin. The thumb and first finger each bore a claw — modern bats have a claw only on the thumb — for hanging vertically from cave walls or other supports. Even at this early stage in their evolution, bats roosted upside down.

Icaronycteris undoubtedly lived like the modern microbats, catching insects on the wing, probably while flying low over water in the evening when there were few birds around.

Some remarkably well-preserved bats are known from the Middle Eocene oil shale deposits of Messel near Frankfurt-am-Mein in Germany. Even the wing membranes are still visible, and remains found in the area of the bat's stomach confirm it was an insect-eater.

SUPERORDER INSECTIVORA
Fossil forms of the Insectivora are known from the Mid-Cretaceous period, about 100 million years ago, which makes them the earliest known placental mammals (*see pp. 198–201*).

Although patchy, the fossil record includes about 150 genera and, like modern forms, these are found throughout the northern hemisphere, in Africa, Southeast Asia and Central America. There is also a single species of living shrew in South America.

YCTES

SARKASTODON

HYAENODON

Almost all insectivores are very small, and nocturnal or crepuscular (active at dusk or dawn). They usually have only poor vision but a good sense of smell and hearing. Like bats, many species of shrews use echolocation to find their way around and track down their prey. Because of their small size and high metabolic rate, they must feed more or less constantly.

Insectivores are a successful group of animals: they have colonized an impressive range of habitats and adopted a variety of lifestyles, from burrowing underground to a semi-aquatic existence. Their diet is equally varied. As well as insects, they eat worms, mollusks and other invertebrates, plus small fish, amphibians, reptiles, birds and even mammals, along with small amounts of plant matter.

To deal with this varied diet, the dentition in both fossil and living forms is usually quite complete (see pp. 195). The skeleton is generally little modified from the basic mammalian plan, with 5 digits on each foot and platigrade locomotion (palms and soles touching the ground), except for moles and golden moles, which have greatly shortened and strengthened forelimbs for digging.

ORDER LEPTICTIDA
The leptictids were one of many primitive groups of shrewlike mammals known from the Late Cretaceous, about 70 million years ago. They became prolific during the early part of the Tertiary and were widespread animals, appearing in North America, Asia, Africa and Europe.

NAME: *Leptictidium*
TIME: **Middle Eocene**
LOCALITY: **Europe (Germany)**
SIZE: **2 ft 6 in/75 cm long**
Leptictidium probably resembled the modern elephant shrew, except for its longer hind legs and tail. It was a bipedal runner, like humans and some of the smaller flesh-eating dinosaurs. The hind legs were long, light and birdlike, with most of the muscles concentrated around the thigh. The forelimbs were less than half the length of the hindlimbs and were adapted for holding food. The body was very short and the long tail served as a balancing organ.

Leptictidium ate more than just insects: some good skeletons show the remains of small mammal bones, lizard bones and plant matter, as well as fragments of insect shells.

ORDER LIPOTYPHLA
The Lipotyphla includes 5 fossil and 7 living families. The latter include hedgehogs, shrews and moles, as well as solenodons of the West Indies, golden moles of Africa, tenrecs of Madagascar and otter shrews of Central Africa.

NAME: *Palaeoryctes*
TIME: **Early Paleocene to Early Eocene**
LOCALITY: **North America (New Mexico)**
SIZE: **5 in/12.5 cm long**
A well-preserved skull shows *Palaeoryctes* must have closely resembled a modern shrew in appearance, with a small sleek body and a pointed snout armed with little insect-crushing teeth. Although it ate mostly insects, probably beetles and caterpillars, it may have taken a wide range of foods, including small vertebrates. Such a generalized feeder would have been in a good position to evolve into more specialized types, and, surprising though it might seem, *Palaeoryctes* or a close relative may have evolved into the great flesh-eating mammals of the Early Tertiary — the creodonts.

ORDER CREODONTA
The creodonts were the dominant flesh-eating mammals worldwide throughout the early part of the Tertiary, between about 60 and 30 million years ago, except in South America and Australia. Yet they had all disappeared by the Late Miocene, some 7 million years ago. Before doing so, they evolved a great number of forms, anticipating the equivalent members of the Order Carnivora — the "modern" flesh-eaters.

The main differences between the creodonts and the carnivores proper are the smaller brains of the creodonts, their lack of a bone enclosing the middle ear, their different foot bones (the wrist bones are not fused together and the claw bones have a groove in them) and differences in the teeth, especially in those teeth which perform a carnassial function (those pairs of teeth, one from the upper and the other from the lower jaws, which are formed like scissor-blades to shear meat).

The 50 or so genera of creodonts are classified in 2 families — the Oxyaenidae and Hyaenodontidae.

NAME: *Sarkastodon*
TIME: **Late Eocene**
LOCALITY: **Asia (Mongolia)**
SIZE: **10 ft/3 m long**
Around 35 million years ago, during the Late Eocene, Central Asia boasted some huge mammals, notably brontotheres, chalicotheres, and rhinoceroses (see pp. 258–264). To exploit such massive prey, the creodonts grew to a great size, too. *Sarkastodon* was one of the largest, bigger than the biggest bear. The teeth were large and heavy, and thick like those of a modern grizzly bear. Also like modern bears, *Sarkastodon* probably ate a wide range of foods.

Other oxyaenids living in the northern hemisphere during the Paleocene and Eocene periods, between about 55 million and 40 million years ago, included animals that resembled wolverines and cats.

NAME: *Hyaenodon*
TIME: **Late Eocene to Early Miocene**
LOCALITY: **Widespread over North America, Europe (France), Asia (China) and Africa (Kenya)**
SIZE: **Up to 4 ft/1.2 m long**
The hyaenodonts, the later of the 2 families of creodonts, were a much larger group than the oxyaenids. They evolved in the Eocene and persisted to the Late Miocene. They ranged from North America, to Asia, Europe and Africa.

Hyaenodon was a widespread and long-lived genus. There were many species, from animals the size of a stoat to species as large as a hyena. It probably evolved in Europe or Asia and later migrated into North America and Africa. Its long, slim legs and digitigrade feet (in which only the toes touched the ground) indicate that *Hyaenodon* could run, though its spreading toes suggest that it would not have been very fast.

Hyaenodon may have been hyenalike in habits, actively hunting down other animals but also scavenging dead ones.

Mustelids and bears

MIACIS

POTAMOTHERIUM

PLESICTIS

AMPHICYON

CHAPALMALANIA

HEMICYON

AGRIOTHERIUM

URSUS SPELAEUS

Mustelids and bears

ORDER CARNIVORA

Cats, civets and mongooses, dogs, bears and pandas, stoats, weasels and otters, seals, sealions and walruses — all these mammals belong to the order Carnivora (*see pp. 194–195*). They are all carnivores, meaning "meat-eaters," and they all share a common feature relating to their teeth. Living carnivores have (or their ancestors had) a pair of meat-shearing teeth, called carnassial teeth, which are specialized for slicing flesh. Some members of the Carnivora, such as seals, have lost these teeth, since they feed mainly on fish, and therefore no longer need them.

However, not all animals that eat meat are members of the Carnivora. The toothed whales, for example, are not "true carnivores," although one of their members, the killer whale, is a formidable predator. An extinct group of ferocious carnivores, the creodonts (*see pp. 211, 213*), were not members of the order, nor were the insatiable carnivorous dinosaurs. Conversely, not all members of the Carnivora only eat meat. Bears and badgers, for example, are omnivores, and eat a wide range of animal and plant food.

Besides the meat-shearing blades of the carnassial teeth, true carnivores also have small, sharp incisor teeth at the front of their jaws for holding prey and large, pointed canine teeth for delivering the killing bite (*see p. 196*).

The order Carnivora is divided into 2 major suborders. The first is the Fissipeda, meaning "split feet," which includes the extinct miacids, and the living mustelids (weasels and relatives) and bears (*below*), as well as dogs and hyenas (*see pp. 218–221*) and the cats and mongooses (*see pp. 222–225*). The second suborder is the Pinnipedia, meaning "fin feet," and consists of the seals, sealions and walruses (*see pp. 226–229*).

Carnivores appeared during the Late Cretaceous or Early Paleocene, about 70–65 million years ago. They evolved from the same ancestors as did the insectivores (*see pp. 210–213*). But the carnivores remained relatively insignificant until the Oligocene, some 35 million years ago, when they began to replace the creodonts, which had been the dominant carnivorous land mammals up to that time.

FAMILY MIACIDAE

The miacids were the earliest true carnivores to appear, during the Paleocene, some 60 million years ago. This is an "artificial" group, since it contains animals that were not closely related. However, it is a convenient classification that distinguishes these early carnivores from the more modern types.

Miacids were mostly small mammals that lived in woodlands, where they were unlikely to become fossilized. The scant remains they have left indicate that they resembled the creodonts in many ways, although they were possibly more intelligent and had better developed meat-shearing teeth.

NAME: *Miacis*
TIME: **Paleocene to Middle Eocene**
LOCALITY: **Europe (Germany)**
SIZE: **8 in/20 cm long**

Scampering through the branches and leaping from tree to tree, this little animal must have looked similar to a modern pine marten (*Martes martes*). The shape of its limbs and its flexible shoulder and elbow joints indicate that it was well adapted for ensuring a secure foothold in the trees of the tropical swamp forest in which it lived.

As well as looking like a pine marten, *Miacis* probably lived in much the same manner, hunting small mammals and birds on the ground and in the trees. It may also have eaten insects, birds' eggs and fruit. A primitive feature of *Miacis* was its full set of 44 teeth. This is the basic number of mammalian teeth, but the more advanced carnivores lost many of them during their evolution into more specialized forms.

FAMILY MUSTELIDAE

The mustelids probably evolved from the miacids (*above*) during the Early Tertiary. Modern members of this family include the weasel, stoat, badger, skunk and otter. They are all slim, long-bodied hunters, living mainly in temperate latitudes throughout the world. In the tropics, their place is taken by the civets, genets and mongooses (the viverrids, *see p. 225*).

NAME: *Potamotherium*
TIME: **Early Miocene**
LOCALITY: **Europe (France)**
SIZE: **5 ft/1.5 m long**

Potamotherium is the earliest-known otter, and like its modern counterpart it had a long, sinuous body and short legs. It probably ran through the riverside undergrowth in a series of leaps, its back arched and its head close to the ground. Its sense of smell was not well developed, but its hearing and sight seem to have been acute, helping it to hunt its fish prey in the water.

Potamotherium was without a doubt an excellent swimmer — its sleek, streamlined shape would have cut through the water, and its flexible back-

bone enabled it to dive and dart about easily underwater.

The otters are the only mustelids that are well represented in the fossil record. This is probably because they lived near water, and so were more likely to become buried in sediments and subsequently fossilized. Paleontologists believe that the true seals, or phocids, evolved from a mustelid ancestor (*see p. 228*).

FAMILY PROCYONIDAE

The procyonids, including the modern raccoons, pandas and coatis, first appeared in the Early Oligocene, about 35 million years ago. They had the typical meat-shearing blades on their premolar and molar teeth, the characteristic feature of the true carnivores. But this design has been lost in modern members, and their premolars and molars have reverted to a purely grinding and crushing function.

This dentition suits the omnivorous diet of most modern procyonids. However, the diet of the giant panda, *Ailuropoda melanoleura*, consists almost exclusively of bamboo shoots, and it is probable that this animal is more closely related to the bears than to the raccoons.

NAME: *Plesictis*
TIME: **Early Oligocene to Early Miocene**
LOCALITY: **Asia (China), Europe (France) and North America (USA)**
SIZE: **2 ft 5 in/75 cm long**

This tree-living hunter had big eyes, perhaps for nocturnal hunting, and a long tail for balance. It was similar to the modern cacomistle (*Bassaricus sumichrasti*), and may have been its direct ancestor. It probably led the same life-

style, scampering up and down tree trunks, leaping from tree to tree and sprinting along branches.

Like those of the other procyonids, the cusps of its teeth were blunt and the molars were square in cross-section, indicating that it probably had an omnivorous diet, devouring birds' eggs, insects and plant matter, as well as hunting for small mammals and birds.

NAME: **Chapalmalania**
TIME: **Late Pliocene**
LOCALITY: **South America (Argentina)**
SIZE: **5 ft/1.5 m long**

The procyonids were among the mammals that traveled south from North America via the Central American land bridge. Once in South America, they evolved into a number of specialized forms.

Chapalmalania was a gigantic raccoon that must have looked rather like the modern giant panda. It was so large that its remains were at first thought to be those of a bear. Like the panda, it doubtless had a very specialized diet, probably relying on some local plant on the mountainsides for much of its food. Its similarity to a giant panda is an example of convergent evolution.

FAMILY AMPHICYONIDAE

The amphicyonids were a family of "bear-dogs" that existed from Eocene to Miocene times, between about 50 million and 5 million years ago. A varied and successful group of large hunters, they spread throughout Europe, Asia, Africa and North America. They replaced the creodonts when they declined, and were themselves replaced by the true dogs during the Pliocene.

Their common name "bear-dogs" refers to their similarity to both creatures. The body was bearlike in shape and

bulk, and they walked with the whole foot on the ground ("plantigrade," like bears and humans), rather than just the toes ("digitigrade," like cats). The shape of the head and the arrangement of the teeth, however, were doglike.

NAME: **Amphicyon**
TIME: **Middle Oligocene to Early Miocene**
LOCALITY: **Europe (France and Germany) and North America (Nebraska)**
SIZE: **6 ft 6 in/2 m long**

Amphicyon was a typical "bear-dog." It probably looked like a large bear with the strong, sharp teeth of a wolf. It had a thick neck, strong legs and a heavy tail. It may have led a similar life to that of a modern brown, or grizzly, bear, eating a wide range of plant and animal foods, and killing its prey with powerful blows from its strong forefeet.

Amphicyon must have been a fearsome adversary for any other creature living on the plains of the northern hemisphere in Mid-Tertiary times, about 30 million years ago. One fossil species, *Amphicyon giganteus*, from the Miocene of Europe, was the size of a modern tiger.

FAMILY URSIDAE

The bears surface later in the fossil record than many other carnivores. They first appeared in Europe during the Oligocene, and since then have spread throughout most of the world. However, there are no bears native to Africa today, although there are 2 separate records of bears in that continent in the past. The primitive *Agriotherium* (*below*) lived in southwestern Africa during the Pliocene, some 5 million years ago, and brown bears are known to have lived in the Atlas Mountains of northern Africa during the Pleistocene, even surviving into Recent times.

Bears are omnivorous, eating anything from small mammals, fish and insects to eggs, nuts and, of course, honey. Their tooth pattern reflects this catholic diet, with unspecialized incisors, long canines, reduced or absent premolars (with no meat-shearing blades) and broad, flat molars with rounded cusps. The molars probably get used the most, to crush up the tough plant food that makes up the major part of a bear's diet.

The modern Kodiak bear (*Ursus arctos middendorffi*) is the world's largest living land carnivore.

NAME: **Agriotherium**
TIME: **Late Miocene to Pleistocene**
LOCALITY: **Africa (Namibia), Asia (China) and Europe (France)**
SIZE: **6 ft 6 in/2 m long**

Although bears are not found in Africa today, they lived there in the past. *Agriotherium* lived in southwestern Africa, a whole continent away from its usual haunts of Europe and Asia.

Agriotherium was a very large bear, even larger than the Kodiak bear (*above*). It was also very primitive, and looked rather like a dog in some ways. However, its teeth had developed the typical bear pattern. It is therefore safe to assume that was omnivorous.

NAME: **Hemicyon**
TIME: **Early to Late Miocene**
LOCALITY: **Asia (Mongolia), Europe (France and Spain) and North America (USA)**
SIZE: **5 ft/1.5 m long**

Despite its great size, *Hemicyon* was lightly built for a bear. Indeed, it was more like a heavy dog, and its name means "half-dog."

It was probably more carnivorous than most other bears, and so was likely to have been an active hunter. It had powerful legs, and the structure of its feet indicate that it ran on its toes — an adaptation for fast running — rather than with the whole foot pressed to the ground as in modern bears. These features suggest that *Hemicyon* was a hunter of the open plains, possibly roaming about in packs.

NAME: **Ursus spelaeus**
TIME: **Pleistocene to Recent**
LOCALITY: **Europe (Austria, Germany, Netherlands, Spain, UK and USSR)**
SIZE: **6 ft 6 in/2 m long**

The genus *Ursus* is represented today by the brown, or grizzly, bear, the polar bear and the American black bear. But in Pleistocene times, the cave bear, *Ursus spelaeus*, was a particularly numerous and impressive species.

It lived in Europe during the height of the Ice Age, and often escaped the worst of the winters by hibernating in Alpine caves. Many bears seem to have congregated together for this long, annual sleep, to judge from the heaps of fossil bones found together. One cave, the Drachenhohle, or "Dragon's Cave," in Austria, contains the remains of more than 30,000 cave bears. And many of them seem to have died in their sleep.

Despite its great size and fearsome appearance, the cave bear was probably a vegetarian. It was hunted by Neandertal people, and its bones were important in their rituals (*see pp. 295, 297*).

Dogs and hyenas

HESPEROCYON

PHLAOCYON

CYNODESMUS

CERDOCYON

OSTEOBORUS

CANIS DIRUS

ICTITHERIUM

PERCROCUTA

Dogs and hyenas

FAMILY CANIDAE

The canids — including the modern foxes, jackals, coyotes, wolves and dogs — are a successful group of "all-rounders." With an evolutionary history of some 40 million years, they have become adapted to a great range of habitats and a variety of diets. As members of the order Carnivora (*see p. 216*), they are related to the otters and weasels, cats and mongooses, and to the seals, sealions and walruses.

First known from Late Eocene times, about 40 million years ago, the earliest canids were relatively short-legged animals that resembled mongooses and civets more than dogs. They were almost entirely restricted to North America, the center of canid evolution; the family did not colonize other continents until the end of the Miocene, as recently as 6 million years ago.

From a mere 5 genera in the Early Oligocene (35 million years ago), the canids had diversified to 42 genera by the Late Miocene (10 to 6 million years ago), and have since declined to the 12 modern genera alive today, which includes the domestic dog.

The teeth of canids have contributed much to their versatility of habitat and diet. As well as the large, pointed canines (the word canine simply means "doglike") and well-developed meat-shearing (carnassial) teeth, they also possess powerful crushing molars at the back of the jaws. So they are omnivorous — eating anything from bones and flesh, to insects and fruit (*see p. 196*).

Canids also evolved a superb sense of smell, good vision and acute hearing. Their long limbs and great stamina, combined with their style of running on the tips of their toes (called digitigrade locomotion), allow them to chase swift-moving prey for considerable distances. Intelligence and social living, as seen today in hyenas and wolves, also enhance their ability to catch prey, avoid predators, rear young successfully and colonize new habitats.

NAME: *Hesperocyon*
TIME: **Early Oligocene to Early Miocene**
LOCALITY: **North America (Nebraska)**
SIZE: **2 ft 6 in/80 cm long**
An active little animal, looking like a mongoose or civet, *Hesperocyon* was one of the earliest members of the canid family to appear. With its long flexible body and tail, and its short, weak legs and spreading 5-toed feet, it may not have looked much like a dog. However, the structure of its ear bones and the arrangement of its teeth show without a doubt that it was a primitive canid.

Fossils of the creature's skull show that parts of the inner ear were enclosed in bone rather than in cartilage (gristle) — a doglike feature that distinguishes *Hesperocyon* from more primitive carnivores, such as *Miacis* (*see p. 214, 216*).

The teeth of *Hesperocyon* show that the last molar tooth was missing from each side of the upper jaw, giving a set of 42 teeth rather than the usual complement of 44. The last upper premolar tooth and the first lower molar tooth on each side were modified into meat-cutting (carnassial) blades, typical of dogs and most other true carnivores (that is, those grouped in the order Carnivora).

NAME: *Phlaocyon*
TIME: **Early Miocene**
LOCALITY: **North America (Nebraska)**
SIZE: **2 ft 6 in/80 cm long**
Just as *Hesperocyon* superficially resembled a member of the cat family (felids), so *Phlaocyon* looked more like a member of the raccoon family (procyonids, *see p. 216*). However, several features of its skull suggest it did belong to the dog family (canids), though it was a very primitive member.

Phlaocyon probably lived much like a modern raccoon. Although its feet were distinctly doglike, its limbs were adapted for climbing trees rather than for running. It had a short, broad head with the eyes set well forward.

The lower jaw of the creature was curved, like that of a raccoon, and the premolars and molars were all grinding teeth, rather than including the meat-cutting blades so typical of dogs. Such teeth suggest that *Phlaocyon* was omnivorous, feeding on a mixed diet of seeds, fruit, insects and birds' eggs, as well as small mammals and birds.

NAME: *Cynodesmus*
TIME: **Late Oligocene to Early Miocene**
LOCALITY: **North America (Nebraska)**
SIZE: **3 ft 3 in/1 m long**
Cynodesmus was one of the first canids that actually looked like a modern dog. It was roughly the size and shape of the coyote, *Canis latrans*, of today's North and Central America. Its face, however, was shorter (the long snout of typical dogs was to come much later in their evolution), and its body was still quite long, with a heavy tail.

Cynodesmus' legs were quite doglike, but they were not yet as efficient for running as those of modern dogs. The open grasslands of North America had not formed at this time; their development encouraged the evolution of fast-moving grazing mammals, which in turn led to the rapid evolution of swift-footed hunters such as dogs.

There were still 5 toes on each of *Cynodesmus'* feet, although the first toes were smaller than the rest. Its claws were narrow and partially retractable, like those of a cat, rather than the thick, blunt, weight-bearing structures that developed in later dogs. It was probably *Cynodesmus'* habit to ambush its prey, cat-style, rather than running it down, dog-style.

NAME: *Cerdocyon*
TIME: **Pleistocene**
LOCALITY: **South America (Argentina)**
SIZE: **2 ft 6 in/80 cm long**
The dog family evolved in North America throughout the Tertiary period. The animals that belonged to this group could not reach South America because the 2 continents were separated by a sea. Then, toward the end of the Tertiary, in Pliocene times (about 5 million years ago), the Central American land bridge was reestablished, and animals could migrate southward. The dogs crossed into South America in the Early Pleistocene, some 2 million years ago, and the early fox *Cerdocyon* was among the invaders in this trek southward.

Two million years later, *Cerdocyon* lives on in the form of the common zorro or crab-eating fox, *Cerdocyon thous*, found from Colombia to northern Argentina. Crabs are only part of the diet of this omnivorous night-hunter. It also eats rats and mice, frogs and insects, fruit and carrion, and any creature's eggs it can find. Its Pleistocene relative probably pursued the same opportunistic lifestyle.

BORUS

ICTITHERIUM

CANIS DIRUS

PERCROCUTA

NAME: *Osteoborus*
TIME: **Late Miocene to Early Pleistocene**
LOCALITY: **North America (Nebraska)**
SIZE: **2 ft 6 in/80 cm long**

Osteoborus was a member of the borophagines, a group of scavenging dogs that first appeared in the Late Miocene, about 8 million years ago. Its heavy build and swollen forehead made it look rather bearlike, but its hyenalike habits were partly reflected in the huge, bone-crushing premolar teeth lining its jaws. Its skull was shortened to accommodate the massive muscles needed to work the powerful jaws, which enabled it to splinter the bones of carcases and reach the nutritious marrow inside.

Osteoborus was widespread in North America, where it occupied the same niche as the contemporary hyenas in Europe, Asia and Africa, scavenging from dead animals or robbing other predators of their kills. Its scavenging role was eventually taken over in North America by more typical dogs, such as *Canis dirus* (below).

NAME: *Canis dirus*
TIME: **Pleistocene to Recent**
LOCALITY: **North America (California)**
SIZE: **6 ft 6 in/2 m long**

The genus of dogs called *Canis* includes the 9 living species of wolves, coyotes, jackals and dogs — both wild dogs and every domestic breed, from Great Dane to Chihuahua. Many more species existed in the past, one of the best known being *C. dirus*, the dire wolf.

In appearance, this prehistoric wolf was much like its modern counterpart, but it was more heavily built. It was probably a scavenger rather than a hunter, taking over the niche of borophagines, such as *Osteoborus* (above), after their extinction in the Early Pleistocene.

The remains of more than 2000 dire wolves have been excavated from the tar pits of Rancho La Brea, where the city of Los Angeles stands today. About 25,000 years ago, crude oil seeped to the surface here, and its volatile components evaporated away, leaving behind pools of sticky tar. These pools, disguised by innocent-looking puddles of water on top, trapped unwary animals, such as ground sloths and elephants, as they ventured in to drink. In turn, the panic of the dying animals attracted carnivores, such as the dire wolf and sabertooth cat, *Smilodon*, and these predators also became enmired.

The conditions under which fossilization took place have left a detailed record of life in Pleistocene times. Evidently, the dire wolves and sabertooths engaged in fierce fights, since their bones are often covered with scars inflicted by each other's formidable teeth.

More active hunters, such as the contemporary lions and dogs, were rarely trapped in the tar. It seems that these more intelligent animals could appreciate the danger of following their prey into the pools.

FAMILY HYAENIDAE

The hyenas, also members of the order Carnivora, appeared only relatively recently, in Mid-Miocene times, about 15 million years ago. They probably evolved on the African continent, and then spread throughout the Old World.

The only hyena known from the New World is *Chasmaporthetes*, which lived in North America during the Pleistocene. It also lived throughout Africa, Asia and Europe. It was a fast-running hunter rather than a scavenger, and its legs and teeth were similar to those of the modern cheetah. Indeed, in Africa it had to compete with the true cheetahs, which also lived there during Pleistocene times.

The role of "mammalian scavenger" in North America was played chiefly by the heavy-toothed borophagine dogs, such as *Osteoborus* (above). Their diet and lifestyle mirrored that of the hyenas elsewhere in the world.

Today, hyenas are restricted to the warmer areas of Africa and Asia. Although they are chiefly scavengers, they are also agile and intelligent hunters, running in packs to bring down swift-footed grazing mammals. They have heavy bone-crushing teeth, and their remarkably tough digestive system enables them to absorb the organic matter in bone, while indigestible bone fragments, hooves, horns, ligaments and hair are regurgitated as pellets.

NAME: *Ictitherium*
TIME: **Middle Miocene to Early Pliocene**
LOCALITY: **Africa (Morocco) and Europe (Greece)**
SIZE: **4 ft/1.2 m**

Ictitherium was one of the earliest hyenas, and probably looked more like a civet (a relative of the mongooses and genets, *see p. 225*) in build and appearance. It also had teeth like those of a civet, suited to an insectivorous diet, rather than the formidable bone-crunching teeth of hyenas.

Along with its primitive relatives, *Ictitherium* was among the most widespread hunters of its time. Indeed, at one stage during the Pliocene its fossil remains outnumber those of all other carnivores put together.

Groups of animals are often found fossilized together, which suggests that a flood swept them away at the same time. It is likely that this early hyena had already evolved a relatively advanced social order and hunted in packs, as hyenas do today.

NAME: *Percocruta*
TIME: **Middle to Late Miocene**
LOCALITY: **Widespread in Africa, Asia and Europe**
SIZE: **5 ft/1.5 m long**

Hyenas of the genus *Percocruta* were the largest hyenas that ever lived. One species, *P. gigantea* of China, was as large as a modern lion.

Despite its great size, *Percocruta* was very similar to the present-day spotted hyena, *Crocuta crocuta*, of Africa. This creature was much more widespread in Pleistocene times than it is today; fossils have been found throughout Africa, Europe and Asia).

Like its modern relative, *Percocruta* had a large head and extraordinarily powerful jaws, armed with great bone-crushing teeth. It had the typical sloping stance of its modern relatives, with forelegs that were longer than the hindlegs.

Cats and mongooses

NIMRAVUS

EUSMILUS

SMILODON

MEGANTEREON

HOMOTHERIUM

PANTHERA

DINOFELIS

KANUITES

Cats and mongooses

NIMRAVUS

EUSMILUS

SMILODON

FAMILY NIMRAVIDAE

The nimravids were the earliest cats to evolve, in the Early Oligocene, about 35 million years ago. They survived until Late Miocene times, about 8 million years ago. They are sometimes called false sabertooths to distinguish them from the true sabertooths, grouped in the family Felidae (*below*).

Nimravids had long, low bodies and long tails. Their prominent upper canine teeth (the "sabers") were longer than those of modern cats, but shorter than those of the true sabertooths, whereas their lower canines were proportionally longer.

NAME: *Nimravus*
TIME: **Early Oligocene to Early Miocene**
RANGE: **Europe (France) and North America (Colorado, Nebraska, North and South Dakota and Wyoming)**
SIZE: **4 ft/1.2 m long**

Even as long ago as the Early Oligocene, this false sabertooth was a contemporary of, and a competitor with, other sabertooths, such as *Eusmilus*. *Nimravus*, with its sleek body, was probably not unlike the modern caracal (*Felis caracal*) of Africa and Asia, although it had a longer back and more doglike feet. The head was short and the eyes positioned so that they could be directed forward, providing the stereoscopic vision so important to a hunting animal. The claws were thin and very sharp, and could be partially retracted to keep them from becoming damaged while the animal was running.

Nimravus probably hunted small mammals and birds; these it caught by ambush, like most cats, rather than by swift pursuit, the typical method used by dogs.

FAMILY FELIDAE

The modern cat family contains such familiar creatures as the lion, tiger, leopard, cheetah and domestic cat. Felids are the most highly specialized of all mammalian hunters. When the grasslands developed during the Mid Tertiary, some 15 millions years ago, the cats and dogs evolved to hunt on the great plains. In these open landscapes, any prey animal could see danger coming from a long way off, and a predator had to be either a skilled stalker or a very fast runner. Cats have adopted the first approach, while dogs employ the second.

Some cats, such as tigers, evolved as solitary hunters that killed by stalking and ambushing their prey, while others, such as lions, adopted a social lifestyle and stalked their prey in well coordinated groups, called prides.

Cats developed 2 chief methods of killing prey. The biting cats, including all the modern types, killed their victims by breaking their necks with one swift, powerful bite from the sharp canine teeth. The sabertooth cats, all now extinct, inflicted deep wounds and then waited for their prey to bleed to death.

In addition to the true sabertooths, another group of felids also developed saberlike teeth, just as the primitive nimravid cats had done (*above*). Sabertooth cats are often misnamed "sabertooth tigers," but they are not closely related to those big cats.

NAME: *Eusmilus*
TIME: **Oligocene**
LOCALITY: **Europe (France) and North America (Colorado, Nebraska, North and South Dakota and Wyoming)**
SIZE: **8 ft/2.5 m**

This leopard-sized cat was rather long-bodied and short-legged compared with a modern cat. It first appeared in Europe toward the very end of the Eocene, some 40 million years ago, and spread eastwards across the Bering land bridge into North America during the Oligocene.

Eusmilus was typical of the group of false sabertooth felids. The pair of upper canine teeth were enlarged into well-developed, stabbing "sabers." The lower canines were insignificant, and many of the other teeth had been lost. *Eusmilus* had only 26 teeth in its jaws, compared with the maximum of 44 found in some carnivores.

The jaw hinge was modified to open to an angle of 90°, which allowed the great saber teeth to do their work. The lower jaw had bony guards that lay along the length of the sabers, protecting them from damage when the mouth was closed. In this it resembled the marsupial sabertooth *Thylacosmilus* (*see pp. 202, 204*), although these mammals were not related. Their similarity is an example of convergent evolution (*see p. 16*).

Eusmilus and other false sabertooth cats inhabited the same parts of the world at the same time, and there is fossil evidence that their paths crossed. A skull of *Nimravus* (*above*) found in North America is pierced in the forehead region, the hole exactly matching the dimensions of *Eusmilus'* saber tooth. The wound was not fatal, however, for *Nimravus* survived the fight long enough to allow it to heal.

NAME: *Megantereon*
TIME: **Late Miocene to Early Pleistocene**
LOCALITY: **Africa (South Africa), Asia (India), Europe (France) and North America (Texas)**
SIZE: **4 ft/1.2 m long**

Megantereon was an early true sabertooth cat, and it was probably ancestral to other forms. Its teeth were not quite long enough to be really saberlike; they were more like daggers in size and shape, so *Megantereon* and its immediate relatives are often known as the dirktooth cats (from the Scottish word for dagger, "dirk"). The development of long canines enabled these powerful predators to kill the large, thick-skinned grazing mammals that shared their habitat.

Megantereon flourished in the Mediterranean region during the Late Pliocene and Early Pleistocene, between about 3 and 2 million years ago. It also spread across Africa and North America from its center of origin in northern India in Late Miocene times.

NAME: *Smilodon*
TIME: **Late Pleistocene**
LOCALITY: **North America (California) and South America (Argentina)**
SIZE: **4 ft/1.2 m long**

Smilodon was the classic sabertooth cat. Unlike most other cats, it had a short tail, like that of a modern bobcat. Its whole body was powerfully built, with the muscles of its shoulders and neck so arranged as to produce a powerful downward lunge of its massive head. The jaw opened to an angle of over 120°, to allow the huge pair of saber teeth in its upper jaws to be driven into its victim.

The sabers were oval in cross-section to retain strength, but also to ensure minimum resistance as they were sunk into the prey. They were also serrated

MEGANTEREON HOMOTHERIUM

PANTHERA

KANUITES

like steak-knives along their rear edges, so they pierced the victim's flesh more easily.

Smilodon probably preyed on large, slow-moving, thick-skinned animals, such as mammoths and bison. Unable to kill its prey with a quick bite to the neck, this sabertooth cat probably inflicted deep wounds in the victim's flanks or hindquarters, and then simply waited for it to bleed to death.

More than 2000 skeletons of *Smilodon* have been recovered from the Pleistocene tar pits of Rancho La Brea in Los Angeles, along with similar numbers of other carnivores, such as the dire wolf, *Canis dirus* (see pp. 219, 221). These animals had not yet developed the cunning of modern carnivores, and were lured into the tar by large animals already trapped there. The species of *Smilodon* found is *S. californicus*, and it has been adopted as the state fossil of California.

Another species of *Smilodon*, *S. neogaeus*, has been found in Argentina. It migrated from North America in Pleistocene times, once the land bridge between the 2 continents had been reestablished at the beginning of the Pliocene, about 5 million years ago.

NAME: *Homotherium*
TIME: **Early to Late Pleistocene**
LOCALITY: **Africa (Ethiopia), Asia (China and Java), Europe (UK) and North America (Tennessee and Texas)**
SIZE: **4 ft/1.2 m**
Besides sabertooth and dirktooth cats, there were also scimitartooth cats, so called because their death-dealing canines were shorter and flatter than those of the sabertooths. They also curved backward, like a scimitar's blade. The back teeth consisted of powerful, meat-shearing (carnassial) blades for slicing up flesh.

In profile, *Homotherium* must have had the sloping look of a hyena, since its forelegs were longer than its hindlegs. When it walked, the whole foot was placed firmly on the ground, as in a bear or a human. This is called "plantigrade" locomotion, and contrasts with most other cats, which walk on their toes (called "digitigrade" locomotion).

Homotherium survived until the end of the last ice age in the Pleistocene, about 14,000 years ago. Scimitartooth cats probably preyed on mammoths, since in Texas the remains of young mammoths have been preserved alongside the bones of a family group of scimitartooths. *Homotherium* may have become extinct when its prey died out in the northern continents at the end of the Pleistocene ice age (see pp. 242–245).

NAME: *Dinofelis*
TIME: **Late Pliocene to Middle Pleistocene**
LOCALITY: **Africa (South Africa), Asia (China and India), Europe (France) and North America (Texas)**
SIZE: **4 ft/1.2 m long**
Dinofelis was a panther-sized cat, with flattened canines that were considerably shorter than those of the sabertooths, scimitartooths or even the dirktooths. But they were longer than those of the biting cats (those that kill their prey with a single, well-placed bite). It is therefore a matter of debate among paleontologists as to which subfamily of the felids *Dinofelis* belongs.

Dinofelis became extinct in Eurasia and North America during the Early Pleistocene, but survived in Africa until Mid-Pleistocene times. The Chinese species, *D. abeli*, is the largest-known form. The name *Dinofelis* means "giant cat," and the species name honours Professor Abel, an Austrian paleontologist.

NAME: *Panthera*
TIME: **Pleistocene to Recent**
LOCALITY: **Africa (South Africa), Asia (India), Europe (England) and North America (California)**
SIZE: **up to 11 ft 6 in/3.5 m long**
Panthera leo, the modern lion, is found today in parts of Africa and in the Gir Forest of western India. A typical biting cat, its canine teeth are short compared with most extinct cats, and they are used to kill prey by biting through the bones and sinews of its neck and throttling it. The claws are long and sharp, and can be fully retracted into the foot by means of tendons. Each claw is tucked away neatly beneath a sheath of skin, and so is prevented from becoming blunt.

There are two notable extinct subspecies of lion. *Panthera leo spelaea* was the cave lion of Europe. It was probably the largest cat that ever lived, being about 25 percent larger than the modern lion, and even bigger than the largest living cat, the Siberian subspecies of the tiger, *Panthera tigris altaica*. Cave paintings and other archeological discoveries indicate that the cave lion existed until historical times in southeastern Europe; its last stronghold seems to have been in the Balkans, up to about 2000 years ago.

The other subspecies of extinct lion was *Panthera leo atrox*, which ranged throughout North America and was also found in northern South America. This subspecies evidently crossed to North America by way of the Bering Strait during the last ice age, about 35,000 to 20,000 years ago. At that time, the sea-level had fallen, and the Strait was dry land.

Remains of this lion have been found in Alaska. But the most famous fossils come from the tar pits of Rancho La Brea in Los Angeles, although they are scarcer than the remains of other carnivores. It seems this lion may have been intelligent enough to avoid the natural traps.

FAMILY VIVERRIDAE
This family of small carnivores contains the modern civets, genets and mongooses. The viverrids are among the oldest of the carnivores, with an ancestry dating back as far as the Middle Paleocene, about 60 million years ago. They are also among the most adaptable and least specialized of all carnivores.

Viverrids are mostly long-bodied, short-legged animals. Many of them are opportunistic omnivores, eating a great variety of food — from earthworms, mollusks, crabs, fish, birds and reptiles (including snakes in the case of mongooses), to eggs, carrion and fruit.

Despite the wide range of the group today — they are found throughout much of the Old World tropics (viverrids are the only group of carnivores to have colonized Madagascar) — the fossil record of the viverrids is poor.

NAME: *Kanuites*
TIME: **Miocene**
LOCALITY: **Africa (Kenya)**
SIZE: **3 ft/90 cm long**
The viverrids have changed remarkably little during their long evolution, and *Kanuites* doutless appeared very similar to the existing genets (*Genetta*). It had a long tail and perhaps retractable claws like those of a cat. It was probably omnivorous, feeding on fruit, insects, small mammals and reptiles, and may have lived in trees as well as on the ground.

Seals, sealions and walruses

ENALIARCTOS

IMAGOTARIA

ACROPHOCA

DESMATOPHOCA

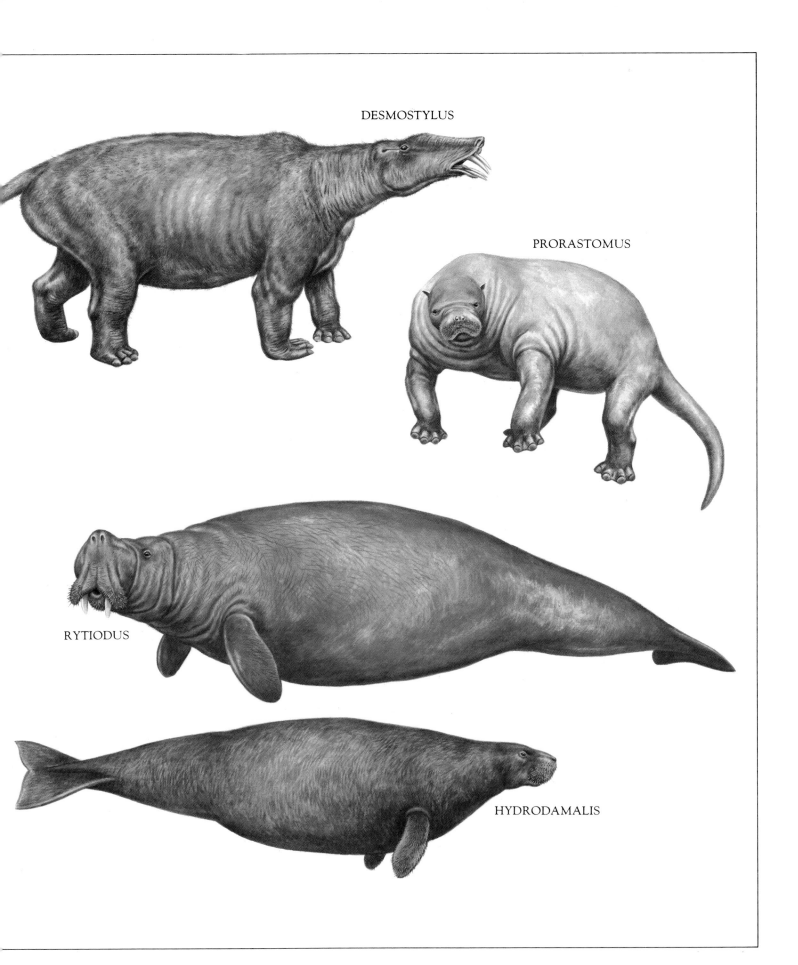

DESMOSTYLUS

PRORASTOMUS

RYTIODUS

HYDRODAMALIS

Seals, sealions and walruses

SUBORDER PINNIPEDIA

The order Carnivora includes not only the dominant carnivores of the land, the cats, dogs and bears, but also a successful group of marine carnivores, grouped together as the pinnipeds. They include the familiar modern sealions and fur seals (Otariidae), walruses (Odobenidae) and the true seals (Phocidae). All have their feet modified into flippers, or pinnae, hence their name.

The pinnipeds probably evolved in the northern hemisphere during the Late Oligocene, about 30 million years ago. They do not seem to have spread south of the equator until the Miocene, some 10 million years later. Although sealions and walruses were thought to have evolved from bearlike ancestors, and the true seals from otterlike carnivores, current opinion favors a single origin for the whole group from an ancestor among the mustelids (weasels, otters and their relatives, *see pp. 214, 216*).

FAMILY PHOCIDAE

Seals may not look much like dogs or cats, but they are nonetheless members of the order Carnivora. Grouped as phocids, they probably evolved from an otterlike mustelid, such as *Potamotherium* (*see p. 214, 216*), in the Late Oligocene, some 30 million years ago. They first appeared in European waters, and then spread north and south to the Arctic and Antarctic Oceans, and west to the Pacific, adapting rapidly to a marine, fish-eating lifestyle. However, they must still leave the sea to breed on land.

The phocids are often called the "true seals," to distinguish them from the otariids, or "eared seals" (the sealions and fur seals). They are more abundant and varied today than the sealions, fur seals and walruses, but their fossil record is sparse.

NAME: *Acrophoca*
TIME: **Early Pliocene**
LOCALITY: **South America (Peru)**
SIZE: **5 ft/1.5 m long**
Acrophoca may have been the ancestor of the modern leopard seal, *Hydrurga leptonyx*. Like that species, it was a fisheater, but it seems to have been less adapted to an aquatic life, and spent much of its time on or near the shore. Its flippers were not so well developed, its neck was longer and less streamlined than that of a modern seal (more like that of its otterlike ancestor), and its snout was quite pointed.

FAMILY ENALIARCTIDAE

The enaliarctids were the earliest members of the otarioids to evolve, and were the ancestors of the modern sealions, fur seals and walruses. They lived during the Early Miocene, about 23 million years ago, and like the phocids (*above*), probably evolved from among the mustelids.

Later in the Miocene, about 18 million years ago, enaliarctids gave rise to another extinct family of early seals, the desmatophocids (*below*). Later still, about 15 million years ago, some of the enaliarctids evolved into the odobenids, or walruses. Another branch, which evolved in the Middle Miocene about 13 million years ago, led to the otariids, the sealions and fur seals.

NAME: *Enaliarctos*
TIME: **Early Miocene**
LOCALITY: **North America (Pacific coast)**
SIZE: **5 ft/1.5 m long**
This primitive-looking sea mammal represents an early stage in the adaptation of a land-dwelling carnivore to a marine lifestyle. *Enaliarctos* is almost half-way between an otter and a sealion. Its cheek teeth still bore meat-shearing (carnassial) blades like those of a land-living dog. Its body was streamlined and rather otterlike, with distinct legs and a tail, although the feet were already modified into paddles.

Enaliarctos probably lived rather like the modern sea otter, spending time on land as well as in the water, and eating a variety of marine animals, including both fish and shellfish. However, some sealion characteristics had already evolved, such as the large eyes, sophisticated senses associated with the whiskers, and the specialization of the inner ears for detecting the direction of sound underwater. All these senses helped *Enaliarctos* to locate its prey. Smell probably played a minor role in hunting, as in living pinnipeds.

FAMILY DESMATOPHOCIDAE

The desmatophocids were a family of primitive sealions. These carnivores are superficially similar to the seals of the family Phocidae (*above*), and show the same adaptations to the same way of life. The most obvious difference between the 2 groups is in the structure of their hindlimbs. Sealions, fur seals and walruses can turn the hind flippers forward to help them move on land — something the true seals cannot do.

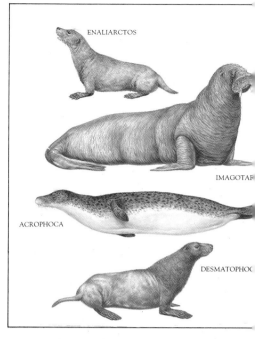

NAME: *Desmatophoca*
TIME: **Middle Miocene**
LOCALITY: **Asia (Japan) and North America (California and Oregon)**
SIZE: **5 ft 6 in/1.7 m long**
The typical streamlined shape of the modern sealion had begun to appear with *Desmatophoca*. As in its living relatives, its forelimbs were stronger than the hindlimbs, and the feet were modified to form paddles, with the fingers elongated, splayed out and held together by webs of skin to produce a large surface area for swimming. All the bones in the limbs were shortened to make them stronger.

Although *Desmatophoca* still had a tail, in contrast to the sealions, this was greatly reduced, being only about the length of the animal's skull. Like its ancestor *Enaliarctos* (*above*), its eyes were enormous, which suggests that sight was its most important sense for hunting. Its hearing may not have been fully adapted for underwater sounds, but no doubt served the animal well on land.

FAMILY ODOBENIDAE

The walruses, or odobenids, differ from the sealions and fur seals in that they are adapted to feed on shellfish rather than on fish. Their upper canine teeth are enlarged into a pair of heavy tusks, in both sexes, and used to prise and probe their mollusk prey from the seabed.

By the Early Pliocene, about 5 million years ago, at least 5 genera of walrus, many of them looking rather like sealions, lived on the North Pacific coast. Some of the early walruses swam across the seaway that separated North America from South America in the Late Miocene, about 8 million years ago. By the Early Pliocene, about 3 million years later, they had moved northward to American and European

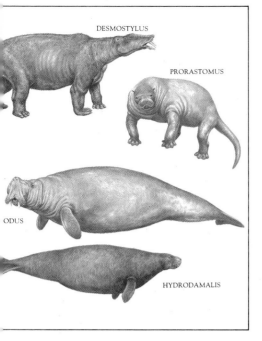

North Atlantic coastal waters.

Later in the Pliocene, walruses became extinct in the Pacific, where they had originated. The North Atlantic populations flourished in the meantime, and groups eventually made their way back to the North Pacific by way of the Arctic Ocean about 1 million years ago.

NAME: *Imagotaria*
TIME: **Late Miocene**
LOCALITY: **North America (Pacific coast)**
SIZE: **6 ft/1.8 m long**
Although *Imagotaria* is classed as a walrus, it probably looked and behaved like a sealion. It may represent a transitional stage in the evolution of the sealions and walruses.

The canine teeth, which are used by sealions to catch fish, had begun to enlarge, but not to the extent of forming the distinctive tusks used by walruses to dig up shellfish. Nor had the back teeth evolved into the broad shell-crushers of modern walruses. It therefore probably fed on both fish and shellfish.

ORDER DESMOSTYLA

The desmostylians were a group of strange aquatic mammals that have been aptly described as "seahorses." About the size of a pony, and superficially similar in appearance, they lived along the coasts of the North Pacific in Miocene times, between about 25 and 5 million years ago. The single record of a fossil from coastal Florida suggests that desmostylians found their way from the Pacific into the Atlantic via the narrow seaway that separated North and South America until the Pliocene, about 5 million years ago. But the origin, relationships and diet of desmostylian remain a mystery.

NAME: *Desmostylus*
TIME: **Miocene**
LOCALITY: **Asia (Japan) and North America (Pacific coast)**
SIZE: **6 ft/1.8 m long**
Desmostylus was a typical member of the group. Built like a hippopotamus, and perhaps behaving like one too, it had a thickset body and stout legs with broad feet, each with 4 hooved toes. The bones of the lower foreleg were fused into a solid pillar, which meant that the foot could not be turned without turning the whole limb. Underwater, the animal probably poled itself along, in the same manner as a modern hippo "walks" over the riverbed. On land, *Desmostylus* must have been quite clumsy.

The front parts of both the upper and lower jaws were elongated and carried an array of forward-pointing tusks, formed by the elongated incisors and canines. The animal's head must have looked similar to that of some of the shovel-tusked elephants that lived at the time (*see pp. 238–241*). The unusual back teeth formed clusters of upright cylinders.

Desmostylus must have had an amphibious lifestyle, paddling around in the coastal shallows, prising shellfish off rocks with its front tusks. It may also have sunk to the seabed in search of food. Some paleontologists suggest that it grazed on the seaweeds between the tides.

ORDER SIRENIA

The sirenians, or sea cows, are the only group of mammals to have become fully adapted, aquatic herbivores. Today, they are represented by 3 species of manatee (*Trichechus*) and a single species of dugong (*Dugong dugon*). They all have bulbous bodies, forelimbs modified into flippers, no hindlimbs and a horizontally flattened tail, like that of a whale, which they use to propel themselves through the water at a leisurely pace.

Sirenians are known from the Early Eocene of Hungary. Their evolution is something of a mystery, but many paleontologists believe they may share a common ancestry with the elephants. Throughout the Eocene, the climate was relatively warm, and vast meadows of seagrasses — the main food of the marine sirenians — grew in the shallow tropical waters of the Mediterranean and Caribbean.

NAME: *Prorastomus*
TIME: **Middle Eocene**
LOCALITY: **West Indies (Jamaica)**
SIZE: **possibly 5 ft/1.5 m long**
Prorastomus is the most primitive sirenian known. Only its skull and parts of its backbone and ribs have so far been discovered, and the restoration on p. 227 is therefore speculative. The appearance of its skull indicates that it was not specialized for an aquatic lifestyle, and it is likely that *Prorastomus* was still essentially a land-dweller. Its thick snout and double-crested cheek teeth suggest a diet of soft vegetation.

NAME: *Rytiodus*
TIME: **Miocene**
LOCALITY: **Europe (France)**
SIZE: **20 ft/6 m long**
By the Late Eocene, some 40 million years ago, dugongs were well established and resembled present-day forms. *Rytiodus* was an enormous beast — twice the size of the single modern marine species. It possessed all the typical sirenian features. Its body was fat and smooth, its hindlimbs had disappeared and its forelimbs had developed into flippers. The bones, particularly the ribs, were thick and dense, and acted as ballast, helping to give *Rytiodus* just the right buoyancy for its submerged existence.

Its snout was downturned, allowing the animal to graze on shallow coastal seabeds, and the pair of saberlike tusks in its upper jaw enabled it to root up seagrasses or seaweeds.

NAME: *Hydrodamalis gigas*
TIME: **Pliocene to Recent**
LOCALITY: **Arctic and North Pacific oceans**
SIZE: **26 ft/8 m long**
This enormous sirenian, only recently extinct, was known as Steller's sea cow, for Georg Steller, the German naturalist, who discovered it in 1741. A former member of the dugong family, *Hydrodamalis gigas* evolved toward the end of the Pleistocene, about 200,000 years ago, but became extinct (due to hunting) as recently as 1768. Its large size was probably an adaptation to the very cold waters of its northern range. (A large animal retains heat better than a smaller one, which has a greater surface area relative to its size.)

Steller's sea cow had lost the thickened ribs of other sirenians, and had developed great layers of blubber, covered by a thick, barklike skin, to serve as insulation against the cold. As a result, the animal was probably too buoyant to dive. Lacking teeth entirely, it fed on floating seaweed — a diet unique among mammals.

Whales, dolphins and porpoises

PROTOCETUS

PAKICETUS

ZYGORHIZA

BASILOSAURUS

PROSQUALODON

EURHINODELPHIS

CETOTHERIUM

Whales, dolphins and porpoises

ORDER CETACEA

The whales, dolphins and porpoises, sea creatures of magnificence and intelligence, are members of the only mammal order that have become thoroughly adapted to living their whole lives in the open oceans. The most specialized of all mammals, their sleek, streamlined bodies and fishlike shape allow them to swim with ease, but deny them any kind of life on land. However, they have retained the basic mammalian features of warm-bloodedness, the ability to suckle their young and the necessity to breathe air.

There are about 140 known genera of fossil cetacean. The 40 living genera are found throughout the oceans of the world, and there are also freshwater dolphins living in the rivers of South America, India and China. Many modern species are, however, threatened with extinction.

Cetaceans probably evolved from land-living early ungulates (*see pp. 234–237*) at the very beginning of the Tertiary, about 65 million years ago. There are 3 suborders of whales: the primitive archaeocetes, all now extinct; the modern odontocetes, or "toothed whales," including the great sperm whale and all the dolphins and porpoises; and the modern mysticetes, or "baleen whales." The baleen group includes the largest animal that has ever lived — the mighty blue whale, *Balaenoptera musculus*, which reached a length of 100 ft/30 m and a weight of some 144 US tons/130 tonnes.

SUBORDER ARCHAEOCETI

The archaeocetes were the first cetaceans to appear, in the seas of the Early Eocene, about 54 million years ago. They evolved from amphibious mammals, and at first were small (never more than 10 ft/3 m long), 4-legged, seal-like creatures with few specializations for life in water. But by the end of the Eocene, some 15 million years later, they had developed into enormous, serpentlike animals, highly adapted for a marine life.

NAME: *Pakicetus*
TIME: **Early Eocene**
LOCALITY: **Asia (Pakistan)**
SIZE: **6 ft/1.8 m long**
Pakicetus is the earliest-known whale. Although only part of its skull has been found, this has such primitive features that it is safe to assume that the rest of its body had few adaptations to a marine existence.

Pakicetus probably looked quite different from the modern whales. Its teeth were similar to those of the mesonychids, such as *Andrewsarchus* (*see p. 236*), and the cheek teeth had the same triangular arrangement of cusps. This suggests that *Pakicetus* had evolved from flesh-eating terrestrial ungulates only a short time previously.

Its ears were not particularly well adapted for functioning underwater, so *Pakicetus* probably spent much of its time on land. Discoveries of other land-living animals in the same deposits as this early whale seem to confirm this.

Pakicetus was probably rather seal-like in general appearance. Its limbs were probably paddle-shaped, allowing it to move about awkwardly on land, but making it completely at home in the rivers and estuaries along the eastern shores of the Tethys Sea. This expanse of water still existed along the southern edge of Asia in Early Tertiary times, about 50 million years ago.

NAME: *Protocetus*
TIME: **Middle Eocene**
LOCALITY: **Africa and Asia (Mediterranean area)**
SIZE: **8 ft/2.5 m long**
Protocetus, which lived only some 8 million years after *Pakicetus* (*above*), had become much more whalelike in appearance. Its body was more streamlined, approaching the shape of modern whales. Its forelegs were flat and paddle-like, but the hindlegs were greatly reduced, and while they may still have protruded outside the body, they would have been of little use in swimming.

A pair of horizontal lobes, called flukes, had probably developed on *Protocetus*' tail, to judge by the structure of the vertebrae in this area. Their up-and-down motion provided the propulsive force to drive the animal steadily through the sea.

The skull of *Protocetus* had become quite long, with a narrow snout. Its teeth were pointed and arranged in a zig-zag pattern at the front of the jaws. These teeth held the prey, while the back teeth cut it up. *Protocetus* and other early whales doubtless hunted for fish in shallow coastal waters.

This whale's nostrils had begun to move back on the head, away from their position in earliest whales at the tip of the snout. *Protocetus* still has a good sense of smell, but vision was probably its most important sense for hunting prey. In contrast to *Pakicetus*, its ears were adapted for underwater hearing, but it is unlikely that it had yet developed the sophisticated echolocation system used by modern whales.

NAME: *Zygorhiza*
TIME: **Late Eocene**
LOCALITY: **North America (Atlantic coast)**
SIZE: **20 ft/6 m long**
Zygorhiza belonged to a family of early whales which developed extremely elongated, eel-like bodies. *Zygorhiza* itself, however, was more conventionally whalelike than most of its relatives. Its body was about 6 times the length of its skull — the same proportion as in a modern whale. But, unlike modern whales, its head was attached to the body by a distinct, though short, neck, made up of the usual mammalian complement of 7 vertebrae.

Its forelimbs were paddle-shaped, and could probably have been moved from the elbow, unlike those of modern whales, which have their forearm bones fused rigidly to the upper arm. It is possible that these early whales still mated and bred on land, as their amphibious ancestors had done. Flexible joints in their forelimbs would have helped to haul their serpentlike bodies from the water and over the rocks.

NAME: *Basilosaurus*
TIME: **Late Eocene**
LOCALITY: **North America (Atlantic coast)**
SIZE: **up to 82 ft/25 m long**
When the remains of this remarkable early whale were first found in the 1830s, they were thought to belong to some kind of dinosaur. This creature, belonging to the same family as *Zygorhiza* (*above*), must have looked like a great sea-serpent. Indeed its bones were used in a famous sea-serpent hoax about a century ago.

Basilosaurus' snakelike body was supported by a backbone of enormously elongated vertebrae. The ribs were short and confined to the front part of the body. The hip bones were still present,

about two-thirds of the way down the animal, and the bones of the hindlegs could still articulate with them. However, the limb bones were so small that it is difficult to imagine what use they would have been, or indeed if they showed outside the body at all.

Basilosaurus must have swum in the Eocene oceans by undulating its long body and tail. For the cylindrical body to have worked efficiently as a swimming organ, this whale most probably had tail flukes.

The head was typical of the early whales, although it was small in proportion to the body. The nostrils were high up on the snout, and the teeth were of different shapes and sizes. The front teeth were pointed and conical, while the back teeth were saw-edged. (An obsolete name for this animal is *Zeuglodon*, which means "saw toothed.") These large early whales must have hunted fish and squid in deep waters, as do the larger species of modern toothed whale, such as the sperm whale.

SUBORDER ODONTOCETI

The odontocetes — the toothed whales — probably evolved from the archaeocetes in the Late Eocene, about 40 million years ago. Odontocetes make up the majority of the modern whales, including the sperm, beaked, pilot and killer whales, the belugas and narwhals, the dolphins and porpoises. All these modern species had appeared by Late Miocene times, some 10 million years ago.

The teeth of odontocetes tended to be simpler than those of the archaeocetes, losing their cusps and becoming rounded pegs or cones. Some odontocetes had several hundred teeth in their jaws, while others were almost toothless.

NAME: *Prosqualodon*
TIME: **Oligocene to Early Miocene**
LOCALITY: **Australia, New Zealand and South America**
SIZE: **7 ft 5 in/2.3 m long**

Prosqualodon and its immediate family may have been ancestral to all the other toothed whales. It probably looked like a small modern dolphin, with a long, narrow snout armed with pointed, fish-catching teeth. But the teeth were primitive, since there were still triangular teeth at the back of the jaws, as there had been in the earlier whales, the archaeocetes (*above*).

Prosqualodon's skull had become lightweight as a result of several modifications to the animal's front end. First, the neck had become very short, and the back of the head blended in with the body and needed less support and protection. Second, the complex jaw structure of earlier whales had been greatly simplified, due to the purely fish diet. And thirdly, since the sense of smell was no longer the primary sense used in locating prey (sound having taken over), the complex olfactory apparatus was reduced.

In *Prosqualodon*, the nostrils were positioned on the roof of the head, between the eye sockets, where they formed a blowhole (as found in modern whales). The spent air which had accumulated during a dive was expelled explosively through the blowhole when the animal surfaced.

NAME: *Eurhinodelphis*
TIME: **Middle to Late Miocene**
LOCALITY: **Asia and North America (Pacific coasts)**
SIZE: **6 ft 6 in/2 m long**

The odontocetes diverged into a number of groups during the Oligocene, about 30 million years ago. *Eurhinodelphis* was a typical member of the rhabdosteid family of long-snouted porpoises. The structure of its ears had become much more complex than in earlier odontocetes, so it is likely that this whale had developed the complex echolocation system seen in modern toothed whales.

Living whales use a form of ultrasonic sonar; they emit high-frequency clicking sounds which bounce off objects, and the echoes are analyzed by their large brains to determine — with astonishing accuracy — the size, shape, distance and speed of the object and, of course, its edibility.

Like that of a modern dolphin, the skull of *Eurhinodelphis* had become somewhat assymmetrical, with structures on one side different from those on the other. This arrangement might have been associated with the development of new abilities, such as chasing fast-moving prey and navigating with increasing accuracy.

The most distinctive feature of *Eurhinodelphis*, however, was its elongated snout. It was toothless at the tip, and may have been used like the "sword" of the modern swordfish, to strike at and stun its prey, which was then seized in the animal's jaws.

SUBORDER MYSTICETI

The mysticetes, or baleen whales, are first known from marine rocks in New Zealand dating from Early Oligocene times, some 35 million years ago. Only 8 genera survive today, and most are under severe threat from hunting.

Baleen whales have evolved a unique method of feeding on the tiny, shrimp-like animals in the plankton. They have no teeth in their jaws. Instead, great plates of a fibrous, horny substance, known as whalebone or baleen, hang from their upper jaws on either side.

These baleen plates form a huge natural sieve through which the whale can strain the abundant planktonic organisms found in the surface waters, especially in the southern oceans, where it is called krill.

The evolution of the baleen whales may have been triggered by the overall cooling of the southern oceans during the Early Oligocene, which encouraged the growth of the microscopic plants in the plankton and, in turn, the tiny, free-floating animals that feed on them.

NAME: *Cetotherium*
TIME: **Middle to Late Miocene**
LOCALITY: **Europe (Belgium and USSR)**
SIZE: **13 ft/4 m long**

Cetotherium belonged to a family of early baleen whales which evolved in the Late Oligocene and reached their peak during the Miocene, some 15 million years ago. It looked strikingly similar to the modern gray whale of the North Pacific, although it was less than a third of its length.

Its baleen plates were probably quite short, although this is difficult to determine, since baleen, like horn and hair, does not fossilize. However, the skulls retain the marks of blood vessels which supplied the baleen during life, and much can be told from their traces.

Cetotherium and its relatives were probably preyed upon by a species of great white shark *Carcharodon* which, judging by the size of the teeth that are often found fossilized, reached a size approaching that of a small whale.

Early rooters and browsers

CHRIACUS

ANDREWSARCHUS

EOBASILEUS

CORYPHODON

STYLINODON

TROGOSUS

ARSINOITHERIUM

KVABEBIHYRAX

Early rooters and browsers

Most ungulates (the word means "hoofed animals") are large plant-eaters which either root and browse among vegetation or crop grass. Early rooters and browsers (below) were a diverse group of ungulates most of which ate leaves, shoots and roots, though some evolved into scavengers.

It was from these early ungulates that more specialized grazers evolved, among them hoofed runners such as horses, cattle and deer (see pp. 254–281). They rose to dominance during the Miocene period, moving out of the forest to exploit the new feeding opportunities in the developing grasslands.

Some early ungulates were for many years regarded as members of the primitive order of carnivorous mammals, the creodonts (see pp. 210–213). This confusion is an indication of the very generalized nature of the mammals at the end of the Cenozoic era.

ORDER ARCTOCYONIA

The extremely successful, abundant and varied group known as the arctocyonids were mostly small mammals, little bigger than today's domestic dogs. They had long, low skulls, and a complete set of rather uniform teeth (evolved for crushing rather than biting).

FAMILY ARCTOCYONIDAE

This is the earliest and most primitive family of the order, and may be close to the ancestors of the later hoofed animals. Arctocyonids were mostly short-limbed, rather clumsily-built animals, up to the size of small bears.

NAME: *Chriacus*
TIME: **Early Paleocene to Early Eocene**
LOCALITY: **North America (Wyoming)**
SIZE: **3 ft/1 m long**
This agile climbing animal may have scampered about in the tropical forests of Early Tertiary North America, sniffing out and eating insects, small animals and fruit. It had powerful limbs, versatile joints and a semi-prehensile tail.

Chriacus had plantigrade feet — the full foot was placed on the ground rather than just the toes — and there were long claws. The forelimbs may have been used for digging, but the hind limbs were definitely those of a climbing animal.

FAMILY MESONYCHIDAE

When plant-eating mammals (excluding multituberculates) first flourished at the beginning of the Paleocene, there were no carnivores to prey on them. By the mid-Paleocene, however, above 60 million years ago, some primitive and generalized stock had developed into a new order, the Acreodi. Among them were mesonychids: wolflike, hyenalike or bearlike omnivores able to take advantage of this new source of food. They varied from the size of foxes to the immense *Andrewsarchus*.

The mesonychids flourished until the Early Oligocene, some 35 million years ago, by which time the creodonts and then the true carnivores had become the dominant flesh-eaters.

Similarities in the arrangement of bones in the base of the skull and in the teeth suggest that, despite their radically different habitats and lifestyles, the mesonychids may have given rise to the whales and dolphins (see pp. 230–233).

NAME: *Andrewsarchus*
TIME: **Late Eocene**
LOCALITY: **Asia (Mongolia)**
SIZE: **13 ft/4 m long**
With a gigantic skull nearly 3 ft/1 m in length, *Andrewsarchus* was the largest known terrestrial carnivorous mammal. The teeth were very large and adapted for crushing and tearing food.

Andrewsarchus' lifestyle is still something of a mystery since complete skeletons have never been found. Comparison with its relatives suggests it was not a hunter that actively pursued its prey but a carrion-eater, like most hyenas are today.

FAMILY CORYPHODONTIDAE

Coryphodonts are found within the Pantodonta, a diverse order of browsing animals that thrived in Paleocene and Eocene times from 60 million to 40 million years ago. In Asia, a few pantodonts did not become extinct until the Early Oligocene, some 35 million years ago. Though some were as small as rats, they were mostly bulky animals, some as large as rhinoceroses. They led a semi-aquatic lifestyle, feeding by rooting up tubers, roots and other vegetation.

NAME: *Coryphodon*
TIME: **Late Paleocene to Middle Eocene**
LOCALITY: **Widespread in North America, Europe and eastern Asia**
SIZE: **7 ft 6 in/2.25 m long**
Coryphodon was a large animal with canine tusks rather like those of a hippopotamus. These were especially well-developed in the male. Like a hippopotamus, too, *Coryphodon* probably

CHRIACUS

ANDREWSARCHUS

EOBASILEUS

lived in swamps and marshes, where it may have uprooted plants with its tusks. The 2 prominent cross crests on its molar teeth suggest that *Coryphodon* browsed on jungle vegetation.

The upper section of the leg was longer than the lower, which would have provided the strength needed to support a massive body but could not have been suited to fast running.

Coryphodon's brain was very small and, at 3¼ oz/90 gm per 1100 lb/500 kg, probably represented the smallest ratio of brain to body weight in any mammal.

ORDER DINOCERATA

The name Dinocerata means "terrifying horns," and refers to the 3 pairs of bony protuberances that adorned the skulls of these animals. Males in particular were armed with a pair of long, saberlike upper canine teeth.

Dinocerates were large, rhinoceroslike mammals from the late Paleocene and Eocene of North America and Asia, about 55 million years ago. However, their ancestry and evolution is something of a mystery.

FAMILY UINTATHERIIDAE

Except for 1 Mongolian genus, which had no skull protuberances or saberlike canines, all members of the order Dinocerata are included in this family.

The uintatheres were the largest land mammals of their time, with massive bones, heavy limbs and broad, spreading feet. But their brains were very small — no larger in relation to body size than the brains of many of the dinosaurs. Uintatheres died out in the Oligocene, about 35 million years ago, and were replaced in their ecological niche as massive herbivores by the brontotheres (see pp. 258–261).

NAME: *Eobasilus*
TIME: **Late Eocene**
LOCALITY: **North America (Wyoming)**
SIZE: **10 ft/3 m long; 5 ft/1.5 m high at the shoulder**

The grotesque *Eobasilus* looked rather like a rhinoceros with a pair of saberlike canine tusks in its upper jaw and 6 bony protuberances on its head. These "horns" were blunt and probably covered with skin. It is also likely that only the foremost pair on top of the nose were sheathed in "horn" formed of matted hair, as in rhinoceroses (*see pp. 262–265*). They may have been used by the males in head-butting contests to determine herd-leadership.

The incisor teeth were very small in the lower jaw and missing entirely from the upper, which suggest that the tongue and tusks were the most important food-gathering organs.

FAMILY ESTHONYCHIDAE

Esthonychids are the sole family in the Order Tillodontia. They were once widespread across Paleocene and Eocene North America, eastern Asia and Europe. Tillodonts may have been related to the pantodonts or to arctocyonids, but their evolutionary relationships, and even their lifestyles, are unclear.

NAME: *Trogosus*
TIME: **Early to Middle Eocene**
LOCALITY: **North America (Wyoming)**
SIZE: **4 ft/1.2 m long**

From a distance, the squat body, short head and flat feet of this large animal would have given it the appearance of a modern bear. However, as soon as it opened its mouth, its huge chisel-like incisors would have made it look more like a gigantic rat or rabbit. As among rodents, the incisors were adapted for gnawing: the front surfaces were coated with enamel and grew continuously throughout the animal's life. The grinding teeth to the rear of the jaw were constantly being worn away, which suggests that *Trogosus* ate abrasive plant material, perhaps roots and tubers clawed out of the ground.

FAMILY STYLINODONTIDAE

Stylinodontids form the only family within the Order Taeniodonta. They varied in size from that of a rat to that of a bear. Taeniodonts evolved quickly — in fact, faster than any other mammal group is known to have done — during Paleocene times, and became quite specialized as digging animals.

NAME: *Stylinodon*
TIME: **Early to Late Eocene**
LOCALITY: **North America (Wyoming, Colorado and Utah)**
SIZE: **4 ft 3 in/1.3 m long**

With its short powerful digging forelimbs and strong claws, *Stylinodon* was probably bear-sized, with a body like an aardvark and a piglike face. There were no incisor teeth in its massive jaws, but the canines had developed into huge, rootless, gnawing chisels. The peglike cheek teeth had the enamel on their surfaces arranged in a narrow band (taeniodont means "banded teeth"). They grew continuously throughout the animal's life, which suggests that *Stylinodon* had a diet of abrasive roots and tubers.

ORDER HYRACOIDEA

This order of herbivorous mammals was very diverse and abundant during the Early Oligocene period, about 35 million years ago, having radiated from its origins in the Eocene into many ecological niches. Some hyracoids looked like tapirs, some were similar to horses, while others resembled rabbits, as do modern hyraxes. Some grew as large as pigs, but most were smaller. They seem to have declined as grazing animals expanded, and are represented today by only 7 species living in Africa and parts of the Middle East. The most notable of these is the rock hyrax.

FAMILY PLIOHYRACIDAE

All the extinct forms of early Tertiary hyraxes are placed in this family. The later fossil hyraxes and all the living representatives of the order are placed in the Family Procaviidae.

NAME: *Kvabebihyrax*
TIME: **Late Pliocene**
LOCALITY: **Europe (Caucasus)**
SIZE: **5 ft 3 in/1.6 m long**

The great difference between the fossil types of hyrax and the modern animals can be seen in *Kvabebihyrax*. With its stout body and small eyes set high upon the skull, *Kvabebihyrax* must have looked more like a small hippopotamus than a hyrax. The snout was short, and a pair of very large incisor teeth projected downwards. The 2 pairs of lower incisors were flattened and horizontal, the upper pair fitting between their points when the jaw was closed.

FAMILY ARSINOITHERIIDAE

The rhinoceroslike arsinoitheres are the sole family in the Order Embrithopoda. Embrithopods do not fit neatly anywhere in the evolutionary scheme and have no obvious fossil ancestors or descendants. They may be distantly related to the elephants (*see pp. 238–245*), hyraxes (*see above*) or even the sea cows (*see pp. 228–229*), with whom their simple, small brains show affinities.

NAME: *Arsinoitherium*
TIME: **Early Oligocene**
LOCALITY: **Africa (Egypt)**
SIZE: **11 ft 6 in/3.5 m long; 6 ft/1.8 m high at the shoulder**

Arsinoitherium's most memorable features were the 2 massive cone-shaped projections, fused at their bases, which covered the area from the nostrils to midway up its skull. In spite of its appearance, *Arsinoitherium* was only superficially like a rhinoceros. Its "horns" were in fact hollow, and traces of blood vessels on their surface suggest that they were covered in skin, at least when the animal was young. There were 2 smaller knoblike projections higher on the head that must have looked like a giraffe's skin-covered ossicones.

With its complete set of 44 unspecialized teeth forming a continuous series from incisors to last molars, *Arsinoitherium* was obviously a plant-eater, and probably browsed in the riverside forests. However, the high cross crowns of its cheek teeth suggests it may also have been able to chew tougher vegetation. From an ecological point of view, *Arsinoitherium* may well have been the African equivalent of the North American uintatheres (*above*) and brontotheres (*see pp. 258–261*).

Early elephants and mastodonts

PHIOMIA

MOERITHERIUM

GOMPHOTHERIUM

PLATYBELODON

AMEBELODON

DEINOTHERIUM

ANANCUS

CUVIERONIUS

Early elephants and mastodonts

ORDER PROBOSCIDEA

The African and Indian elephants are the only 2 surviving species of a once diverse and widespread group.

Proboscids evolved from a basal stock of primitive hoofed animals that also gave rise to the modern hyraxes (*see pp. 262–265*) and the aquatic sirenians (the dugongs and manatees; *see pp. 226–229*). From their origins in northern India in the Eocene as pig-sized creatures without tusks or trunks, proboscids had evolved by Pliocene times, 50 million years later, into giants that had spread over all continents except for Australia and Antarctica.

Their evolution involved a progressive increase in size, the development of long pillarlike legs to support the immense weight, the extension of a proboscis or trunk, the massive enlargement of the head, and a shortening of the neck. Also, there was a reduction of the teeth to a few grinding molars — except for 1 or 2 pairs which were modified into specialized tusks. The trunk and tusks were originally adaptations that enabled a tall, short-necked animal to reach food on the ground or in the trees, but they also function in display.

By Pleistocene times, about 2 million years ago, mammoths and mastodonts flourished over the northern continents, only to suffer mass extinction in the encroaching ice. In Siberia, some have been found frozen in ice, their flesh and fur perfectly preserved. Meanwhile, the Elephantidae, the only family of the order to survive, had already undergone rapid evolution in warmer climates to the south. Four suborders are known.

SUBORDER MOERITHERIOIDEA

The name "moerothere" is derived from the word *Moeris* — an ancient Greek name for the lake in Egypt's Fayum province where its remains were found. In Eocene and Oligocene times, this area would have consisted of fertile, forested coastal plains.

NAME: *Moeritherium*
TIME: **Late Eocene to Early Oligocene**
LOCALITY: **Africa (Egypt, Mali and Senegal)**
SIZE: **2 ft/60 cm high**
This pig-sized, low-slung animal resembled a tapir or a pygmy hippopotamus more than an elephant. The external nostrils were at the front of the skull, which implies that it did not even possess a trunk, though it may have had a broad thick upper lip that helped it to root about among swamp vegetation.

Moeritherium would have weighed about 450 lb/200 kg. It was probably partly aquatic in its habits, like the modern hippopotamus. As with the hippopotamus, its eyes and ears were high up on the skull so that it could keep watch at the water's surface while wallowing in the swamps.

But *Moeritherium* also displays several features that clearly indicate the development of an elephantlike lifestyle. Its skull was long and low, with a large area at the back for the attachment of strong neck muscles, and the lower jaw was deep. The teeth were primitive — small and almost complete — yet there were no lower canines. Even at this early stage in the evolution of elephants, 2 of the incisors were already tusklike.

Although it showed many primitive features, *Moeritherium* itself was probably not the ancestor of the rest of the proboscideans. It was a long-lived genus, surviving into the Oligocene when several more advanced elephants were also around.

SUBORDER DEINOTHEROIDEA

Deinotheres were very large elephants with down-curving tusks in the lower jaw. They probably evolved in the Early Miocene in Africa but soon spread into central and southern Europe and southern Asia.

They thrived almost unchanged throughout the Pliocene but then retreated back to Africa. They vanished altogether about 2 million years ago.

NAME: *Deinotherium*
TIME: **Miocene to Pleistocene**
LOCALITY: **Europe (Germany and Bohemia), Asia (India) and Africa (Kenya)**
SIZE: **13 ft/4 m high**
The most remarkable feature of this elephant was its tusks, the purpose of which is still debatable. There were no tusks in the upper jaw, but the lower jaw was curved downward at a right angle and gave rise to two huge curved tusks. Such a shape seemed so unlikely that when scientists in the 1820s attempted the first reconstructions of *Deinotherium*, they attached the jaw upside down. The animal may have used the tusks for stripping the bark from trees or digging up tubers.

Surviving almost unchanged for 20 million years, *Deinotherium* was clearly a very successful animal.

SUBORDER ELEPHANTOIDEA

This suborder contains 3 families: 2 are families of browsing mastodonts (Gomphotheriidae and Mammutidae) and the other is the family which contains the mammoths and true elephants (Elephantidae).

Gomphotheres are the more primitive of the 2 families of mastodonts — the term refers to the paired domed cusps which occur along the length of the teeth. They appeared in the Early Oligocene about 35 million years ago.

In these early forms, both upper and lower jaws were quite long. More advanced forms, however, show 1 of 2 developments. Some exhibit a shortening of the upper jaw and an extreme elongation of the lower jaw into extraordinary "shovel tusks." In others, the lower jaw is so greatly reduced that they resemble modern elephants.

Gomphotheres were the dominant large mammals of the Miocene, with several different species in any region at any one time (a fact which greatly complicates specific identification). They had spread from Africa into southern Europe and the Indian subcontinent by Early Miocene times, reaching North America by the Mid Miocene, around 15 million years ago. They only invaded South America just before their extinction in the Pleistocene about 2 million years ago. They were gradually replaced by elephants from about 5 million years ago.

DEINOTHERIUM

ANANCUS

CUVIERONIUS

NAME: *Phiomia*
TIME: Early Oligocene
LOCALITY: Africa (Egypt)
SIZE: 8 ft/2.5 m high

Phiomia evolved alongside its smaller, distant cousin *Moeritherium*, yet it is unlikely that they competed for the same food. *Phiomia* probably browsed in forests, while its contemporary wallowed in the swamps. Its name means "creature of the lake province," referring to the Fayum area of Egypt in which its remains were found.

Both the upper and lower jaws were long, the flattened tusks of the lower jaw forming a spoon-shaped extension used for gathering food. It is likely that the upper lip was extended to form a primitive trunk which worked in conjunction with this strange lower jaw apparatus. Shorter tusks in the upper jaw may have been used as defensive weapons.

NAME: *Gomphotherium*
**TIME: Early Miocene to Early
 Pliocene**
**LOCALITY: Europe (France), Africa
 (Kenya), Asia (Pakistan) and
 North America (Nebraska)**
SIZE: 10 ft/3 m high

This 4-tusked mastodont was wide-ranging, cropping up as fossils on 4 continents. As a result, the same fossil animal has been given a variety of names, including *Trilophodon* and *Tetrabelodon*.

The lower jaw, with its parallel tusks, was very long. It was probably used in conjunction with an equally long trunk on the upper jaw.

There was a progressive reduction in the number of teeth, but those that remained developed a number of high ridges or cusps to increase the grinding area. This was necessary to cope with the large amounts of plant food required to satisfy the animal's immense bulk.

Most members of the genus *Gomphotherium* ate the leaves from bushes, but one species was a swamp dweller and ate soft water-plants.

NAME: *Amebelodon*
TIME: Late Miocene
**RANGE: North America (Colorado,
 Nebraska)**
SIZE: 10 ft/3 m high

Amebelodon was a typical, tall "shovel-tusker" of the gomphothere family, which roamed the prairies of North America during the Late Miocene. By around 10 million years ago, the forests had given way to vast dry grasslands, an environment best suited to hoofed running animals such as the horses (*see pp. 254–257*). But the plains were also crossed by many winding rivers in which luxuriant water plants flourished. This was the niche into which *Amebelodon* was able to evolve.

In body size and general appearance, *Amebelodon* was similar to the modern elephants, but its skull and tusks were quite different. The flattened tusks of the elongated lower jaw lay side by side, forming a shovel or trough which projected more than 3 ft/1 m to a spadelike cutting edge.

The water plants on which *Amebelodon* fed would have been gripped between the flattened trunk and tusks and ripped from the mud of the river bottom, then pulled up the trough to the mouth by the trunk.

NAME: *Platybelodon*
TIME: Late Miocene
**RANGE: Europe (Caucasus
 Mountains), Asia (Mongolia) and
 Africa (Kenya)**
SIZE: 10 ft/3 m high

Platybelodon was another shovel-tusker, similar to *Amebelodon*, which lived in Europe and Asia. Its shovel arrangement was shorter and broader, and was indented at each side to make room for the tusks of the upper jaw.

Platybelodon evidently enjoyed much the same lifestyle as *Amebelodon*, wading in shallow rivers and dredging water weeds.

The fact that related types of proboscidean lived in Eurasia and North America at this time suggests there was a migration route between the two landmasses — across a land bridge where the Bering Straits now lie.

The shovel-tuskers show an extreme specialization for a particular style of feeding. As with other highly specialized creatures, they were extremely vulnerable to environmental change and were not a very long-lived group.

NAME: *Anancus*
**TIME: Late Miocene to Early
 Pleistocene**
**LOCALITY: Widespread in Europe and
 Asia**
SIZE: 10 ft/3 m high

With its short lower jaw and long, prehensile trunk, *Anancus* looked much like a modern elephant; but it had shorter legs, and an extremely long pair of tusks. These tusks in the upper jaw were straight and, at 10–13 ft/3–4 m in length, were nearly as long as the rest of the animal.

Anancus seems to have been perfectly adapted to woodland life, being able both to browse from high branches and to root about among the leaf litter of the forest floor. *Anancus* became extinct when grasslands replaced the woodlands in which it lived.

NAME: *Cuvieronius*
TIME: Pliocene to Recent
**LOCALITY: North America (Arizona,
 Florida) and South America
 (Argentina)**
SIZE: 9 ft/2.7 m high

Cuvieronius was named for the great French comparative anatomist and founder of paleontology, Baron George Cuvier (1769–1832). A fairly small gomphothere, *Cuvieronius'* most remarkable feature was its tusks, which were spirally twisted like those of a narwhal.

We do not usually associate the South American continent with elephants. However, remains of *Cuvieronius* have been found in mountainous areas of both North and South America, a fact reflected in its synonym *Cordillerion* — "the one from the mountain range."

Cuvieronius evolved in western North America at the end of the Miocene, and migrated to South America during Pleistocene times, around 2 million years ago. It spread from the grassy pampas in the east to the heights of the Andes in the west, reaching as far south as Argentina. It was hunted to extinction, probably as recently as AD 400.

Mastodonts, mammoths and modern elephants

STEGOMASTODON

MAMMUT AMERICANUM

ELEPHAS ANTIQUUS

ELEPHAS FALCONERI

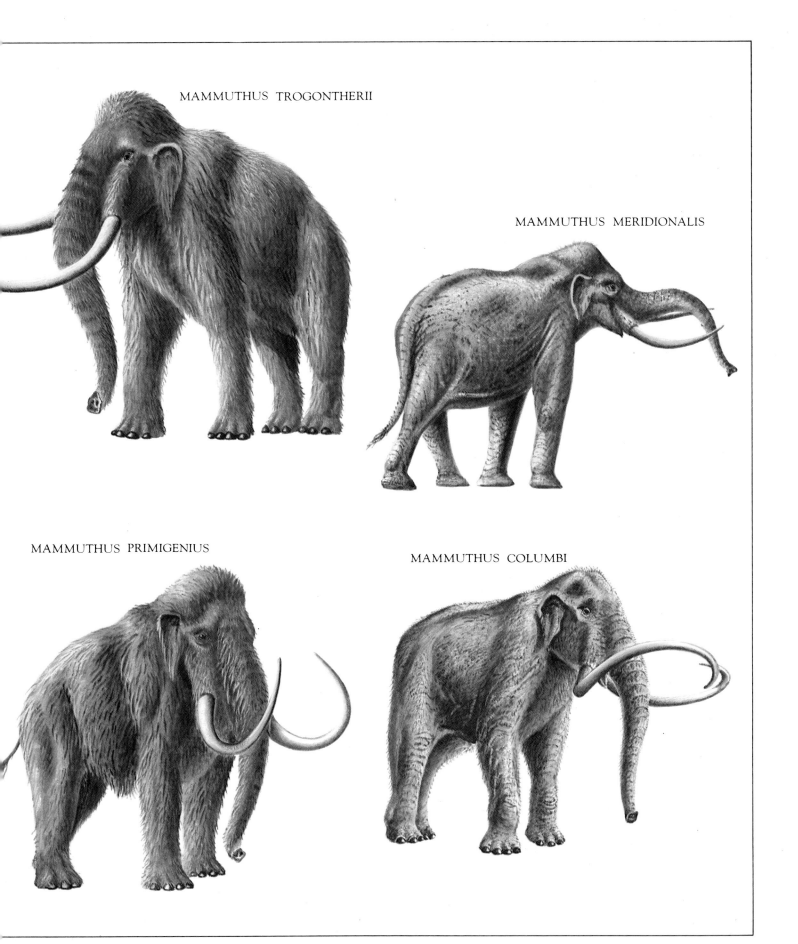

MAMMUTHUS TROGONTHERII

MAMMUTHUS MERIDIONALIS

MAMMUTHUS PRIMIGENIUS

MAMMUTHUS COLUMBI

Mastodonts, mammoths and modern elephants

NAME: *Stegomastodon*
TIME: Late Pliocene to Pleistocene
LOCALITY: North America (Nebraska) and South America (Venezuela)
SIZE: 9 ft/2.7 m high

Stegomastodon must have looked like a shorter, stockier version of a modern elephant. It had a short lower jaw, no lower tusks, and the upper tasks curved upward.

Stegomastodon's cheek teeth were even more elaborate than those of its forebears. With their convoluted pattern of enamel, which provided a wide abrasive surface and an efficient grinding action, it is possible that these teeth enabled *Stegomastodon* to eat grass.

Stegomastodon was one of the few proboscideans to reach South America, having migrated there around 3 million years ago once the Central American land bridge was established. This bridge was formed and broken several times during the Pleistocene before it reached its present proportions. Each time the continuous chain of volcanoes and fold mountains appeared above the ocean, the way was opened for a new influx of animals.

Stegomastodon became extinct in North America about 1 million years ago, but survived in Venezuela in association with early humans.

FAMILY MAMMUTIDAE

Despite their names, these were not mammoths but mastodonts. Their cheek teeth are characterized by having a simple pattern of low, flattish-sided cusps arranged to form transverse ridges with open valleys between. This contrasts with gomphotherid teeth, which have much more complex cusps in transverse rows, and many smaller cusps filling the valleys between.

NAME: *Mammut*
TIME: Late Miocene to Late Pleistocene
LOCALITY: North America (Alaska, New York, Missouri)
SIZE: 10 ft/3 m high

The American mastodont, *Mammut americanum*, was one of the commonest of the North American proboscideans. Like the wooly mammoth, it was a cold-climate animal, covered with a coat of long shaggy hair. Some of the hairy skin is sometimes found with the skeletons. Its remains have been found as far north as Alaska, and south to Florida.

The head was quite long and held low, with a pair of massive upward-curving tusks. It browsed in herds in spruce woodlands, and may have been a contemporary of modern humans, but no definite association has been demonstrated for mastodonts and humans on the same site at the same time. Like the wooly mammoth, *Mammut* became extinct only about 10,000 years ago.

Other mastodonts are known from Africa, Europe and Asia, but these were not covered in hair.

FAMILY ELEPHANTIDAE

This is the family to which the modern elephants belong. They differ from their earlier relatives, the mastodonts, principally in the form of the teeth. True elephants have lost the tusks of the lower jaw, and this has enabled them to modify their method of mastication. Mastodonts ground their food in a complex rotary motion, whereas elephants cut or shear it.

The change of action has also affected the teeth, which are taller, with longer, more complex enameled surfaces. In many species, there is only one grinding tooth at a time in each side, top and bottom.

Each of these 4 teeth has a series of up to 20 transverse loops of wrinkled enamel, infilled with softer dentine and separated from each other by thin bands of cement. The whole grinding surface thus forms a large, nearly flat area of very hard phosphate which resists the wear from grinding siliceous grasses. Another tooth appears only when the earlier teeth have worn down.

Several members of the family survived the end of the Ice Age but became extinct shortly after, some possibly as the result of being hunted by early humans. These extinct species include the Eurasian woodland elephant, *Elephas antiquus*; the dwarf forms, such as *E. falconeri*, which lived on the Mediterranean islands; and 2 mammoths, *Mammuthus primigenius* and *M. jeffersoni*. Their cousin, the American mastodont *Mammut americanum*, joined them in extinction at this time.

Only 2 species survive today, the African and the Indian elephants.

NAME: *Elephas antiquus*
TIME: Middle to Late Pleistocene
LOCALITY: Europe
SIZE: 12 ft/3.7 m high

E. antiquus was a very large, long-legged and straight-tusked elephant, whose bones are relatively common in European Pleistocene deposits.

During the Pleistocene Ice Age, the ice sheet came and went over large areas of the Northern Hemisphere. During the glacial retreats — the interglacials — the climate became much warmer. These interglacials tended to be warmer even than present-day climates, and subtropical conditions prevailed in places as far north as England.

E. antiquus was one of the warm-climate animals that frequented the lush woodlands that existed in these places at that time. The tusks were long and straight, and slightly curved at the tip. As each interglacial came to an end and the ice sheets advanced southward again, *E. antiquus* moved away southward as well. Its place in the northern lands was taken by the elephant group that was well adapted to cold conditions — the mammoths (*below*).

NAME: *Elephas falconeri*
TIME: Late Pleistocene
LOCALITY: Mediterranean islands (Cyprus, Crete, Malta, Sicily, southern Calabria and some of the smaller Greek islands)
SIZE: 3 ft/90 cm high

The genus Elephas includes the modern Indian elephant, *E. maximus*. The earliest members of the genus arose in Africa early in the Pliocene, about 5 million years ago, and radiated into Europe and Asia. There are a number of interesting extinct dwarf elephants which may be separate species but were possibly varieties of their parent stock.

E. falconeri stood less than 3 ft/1 m in height and lived on the Mediterranean

MAMMUTHUS TROGONTHERII

MAMMUTHUS MERIDIONALIS

...MUTHUS PRIMIGENIUS   MAMMUTHUS COLUMBI

islands. Its ancestors, probably the European elephant *E. namadicus*, migrated out of Africa in the Early Pleistocene and spread west into central Europe and east to India and China, and even reached Japan.

During the lower sea-levels of the glacial periods, this elephant was able to reach Malta, Cyprus, Crete and Sardinia. With the rise of sea level as the glaciers melted in the interglacial periods, these areas became isolated as islands in the Mediterranean sea. In this isolation arose the dwarf form *E. falconeri*. Similar dwarf elephants arose on the Celebes Islands in Southeast Asia.

On islands such as these, natural selection would favor animals that made best use of smaller quantities of food, and dwarf varieties and species would evolve. A modern equivalent is the small Shetland ponies that have developed on the northern Scottish islands. There is a possible dinosaurian example, also, in the dwarf ankylosaur *Struthiosaurus* (*pp. 158–163*). The experience of very small animals such as rodents, however, is the exact opposite: rodents on the Mediterranean islands were often larger than elsewhere. In the absence of natural predators, there was little need to maintain a small and slender structure that could swiftly take refuge in holes and crevices (*see pp. 282–285*).

NAME: *Mammuthus meridionalis*
TIME: **Early Pleistocene**
LOCALITY: **Europe (Spain)**
SIZE: **Up to 15 ft/4.5 m high**
The mammoths were a wide-ranging group of largely cold-adapted animals that radiated from Africa to Eurasia and North America in the Early Pleistocene.

M. *meridionalis* was one of the first of the mammoths, evolving in open woodlands in southern Europe, where the climates were not severe, around 2 mil-

lion years ago. Its ancestors probably came from farther east, or from Africa.

M. *meridionalis* resembled the modern Indian elephant but had much larger tusks. It may have been the ancestor of a number of more-specialized mammoths, including the European M. *primigenius* (*below*) and the North American M. *imperator*.

NAME: *Mammuthus trogontherii*
TIME: **Middle Pleistocene**
LOCALITY: **Europe (England, Germany)**
SIZE: **15 ft/4.5 m high**
M. *trogontherii* was the steppe mammoth. It lived in the middle Pleistocene in central Europe, in much colder conditions than its ancestors, and was probably the first to develop the hairy coat that is the familiar feature of the mammoth group. It probably roamed in herds across the cold grasslands and ate the coarse grasses that grew there.

M. *trogontherii* was one of the largest of the mammoths. The spiral tusks, which were thicker in the males than in the females, were very long, some measuring about 17 ft/5.2 m.

NAME: *Mammuthus columbi*
TIME: **Late Pleistocene**
LOCALITY: **North America (Carolina, Georgia, Louisiana, Florida)**
SIZE: **12 ft/3.7 m high**
M. *columbi* was one of the American mammoths which migrated from Asia to North America, late in the Pleistocene, during a mild period, when it was possible to walk dryshod across the Bering Straits. Such intervals occurred at the begining and end of an interglacial, when sufficient water was held up in ice sheets to lower the sea level and create a chain of islands across Beringia. During the peak of a glaciation the sea level would be still lower, but the temperatures would also have been much lower, thus making travel difficult and food hard to find.

M. *columbi* lived in warm grasslands in the south-eastern part of the continent, and may even have moved as far south as Mexico.

M. *columbi* had twisted tusks, which perhaps distinguish it from the other American mammoth M. *imperator*, whose long tusks curled backward in an even curve. This latter species or subspecies had a more westerly range and its remains have been found in the tar deposits of Rancho La Brea in Los Angeles.

NAME: *Mammuthus primigenius*
TIME: **Late Pleistocene**
LOCALITY: **Europe, Asia and North America**
SIZE: **9 ft/2.7 high**
M. *primigenius*, the wooly mammoth, is what most people think of as the typical mammoth. Relatively small for a mammoth, it was a cold-climate tundra-dweller, with a thick shaggy coat and a fatty hump.

Paleontologists are quite familiar with the animal's soft anatomy and appearance in life, since several well-preserved remains have been found buried in frozen mud in Siberia and Alaska. There are also the eye-witness reports of early people who painted and engraved the animal on cave walls in France and Spain.

The coat consisted of long black hair — not red as in most restorations. The red coloration, seen in specimens in which the hair is preserved, was due to a chemical reaction in the hair after death.

There was an undercoat of fine hair and a thick layer of fat to help the insulation. Behind the domed head was a hump of fat, evidently used as a source of nutrition when times were hardest during the winter.

Scratches on the ivory suggest that the characteristic curving tusks were used for scraping away snow and ice from the low tundra vegetation on which it fed.

M. *primigenius* survived until about 10,000 years ago. The warming of the climate that accompanied the end of the last glaciation may have reduced its numbers. Overhunting by early humans probably hastened its extinction.

South American hoofed mammals

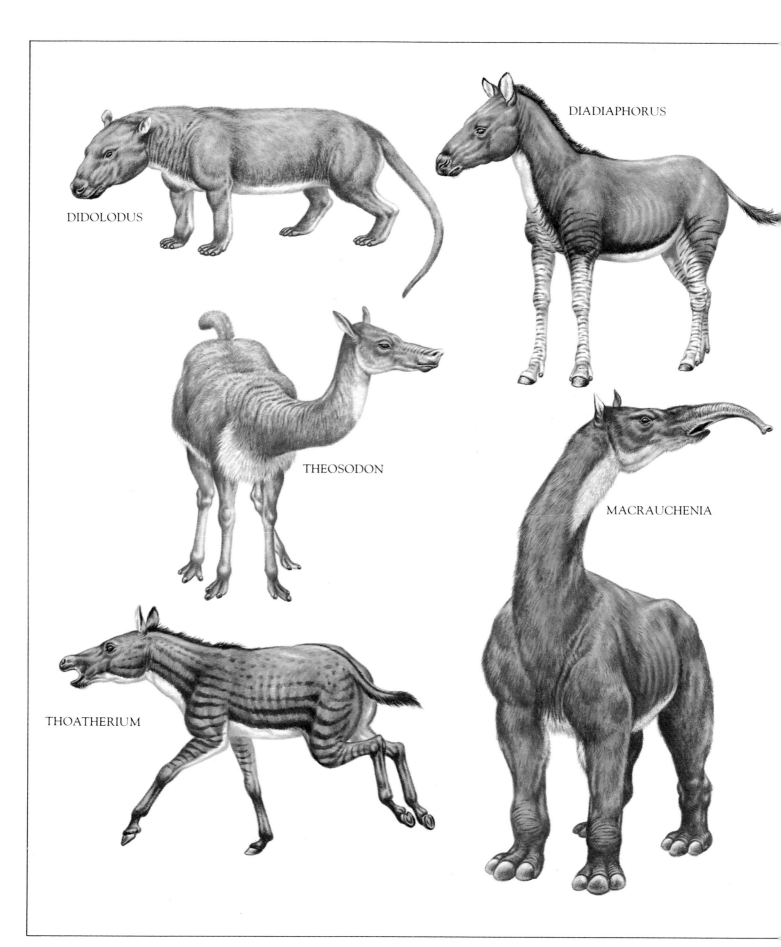

DIADIAPHORUS

DIDOLODUS

THEOSODON

MACRAUCHENIA

THOATHERIUM

ASTRAPOTHERIUM

TRIGONOSTYLOPS

PYROTHERIUM

South American hoofed mammals

During the Tertiary period, South America supported as strange and unique a collection of mammals as Australia does today, and for many of the same reasons (*see pp. 202–205*). Having once been part of a more or less unified landmass, a combination of continental drift and rising sea levels caused South America to become detached from North America and then from Africa and Antarctica. By early Tertiary times, roughly 50 to 60 million years ago, there was open sea, or possibly nothing more than a sporadic island chain, between North and South America.

At that time South America possessed 3 stocks of mammals on which evolution could act: marsupials (*see pp. 202–205*), primitive edentates (anteaters, sloths and hairy armadillos; *see pp. 206–209*), and some early rooting and browsing ungulates (*see pp. 234–237*). But whereas North America subsequently acquired virtually all of the other evolving mammal stocks, due to its land connections with the Old World (*see p. 11*), South America gained only the rodents and primates.

For about 50 or more million years, then, from Paleocene until Pliocene times when the land bridge was reestablished, the ocean marooned the South American mammals on an island continent that contained no placental carnivores. As a result, the original stocks were given the opportunity to diversify into a variety of ecological niches which were filled elsewhere by other groups.

The animals described in the following pages are meridiungulates: the descendants of those stranded early rooters and browsers.

ORDER LITOPTERNA

Litopterns are mostly horselike and camel-like animals. Their teeth are generally simpler than those of ungulates elsewhere; their dentition remained more or less complete, and the gap (diastema) between front and cheek teeth was never as highly developed.

The legs and feet are sometimes strikingly like those of the perissodactyls (the odd-toed ungulates, such as horses, tapirs and rhinoceroses; *see pp. 245–265*). There is the same tendency to a reduction in the length of the upper limb and an elongation of the lower limb. The hoofed toes, too, are reduced to 3 or 1, with the weight of the body being carried on the third digit.

There are differences, though. The radius/ulna and tibia/fibula bones of the fore- and hindlimbs did not fuse, as they have done in the horse, and the ankle bones are less complex (their name means "simple ankles").

FAMILY DIDOLODONTIDAE

It is not clear how this long-lived family should be classified. Some authorities place it with early rooting and browsing ungulates in the order Arctocyonia (*pp. 234–237*); others regard it as a litoptern. It is perhaps best considered as transitional between the two.

The earliest fossils are found from the Paleocene, around 60 million years ago, with examples still being found in the Mid-Miocene, 50 million years later.

NAME: *Didolodus*
TIME: **Early Eocene**
LOCALITY: **South America (Argentina)**
SIZE: **Possibly 2 ft/60 cm long**
The teeth of this creature were so much like those of the earliest hoofed animals (*see pp. 234–237*) that in life *Didolodus* may have resembled one closely.

A fleet-footed browser, which scampered through the undergrowth of the forests and eating the leaves of low-growing trees and bushes, *Didolodus* — or something closely related to it — may have been ancestral to most of the other hoofed South American mammals.

FAMILY PROTEROTHERIIDAE

The spread of the open plains over the South American continent helped induce the evolution of lightly-build running animals.

The proterotheres ("first creatures") were horselike animals ranging from late Paleocene to late Pliocene times. Protootheres appear to have undergone many of the same adaptive changes as the early horses in North America, sometimes in advance of developments elsewhere. It is unlikely that they were able to graze, though, since their dentition remains that of browsing animals.

NAME: *Diadiaphorus*
TIME: **Early Miocene**
LOCALITY: **South American (Argentina)**
SIZE: **4 ft/1.2 m**
The graceful *Diadiaphorus* would have been very much like a short-necked antelope or pony in appearance. It was about the size of a sheep, but with the feet of a 3-toed horse.

Although the paired bones of the lower limbs (ulna/radius and tibia/fibula) never fused as they did in the later true horses, the legs were long and slender. The middle toe (the third) was very large and bore the animal's entire weight, while the toes to each side

DIADIAPHOR
DIDOLODUS
THEOSODON
MACRAUC
THOATHERIUM

(the second and fourth) had atrophied.

The head was relatively short and deep, and the brain case was quite large. The low-crowned teeth, however, were quite different from a horse's and suggest that *Diadiaphorus* probably lived by browsing on the softer vegetation, bushes and trees of Patagonia's plains.

NAME: *Thoatherium*
TIME: **Early Miocene**
LOCALITY: **South America (Argentina)**
SIZE: **2 ft 4 in/70 cm long**
The smallest of the known litopterns, *Thoatherium* probably resembled a small gazelle. The feet and legs were very long for the size of the body, and it must have been a graceful runner.

Although the paired bones of the lower limbs were reduced, they did not fuse. But the reduction of lateral toes which can be seen in both the true horses and in *Diadiaphorus* is here taken to an extreme. Indeed, the vestiges of its other 2 toes were even smaller than those of the single-toed horse of today. The teeth, too, remained primitive, so it can be assumed that *Thoatherium* ate foliage rather than grasses.

Having achieved their greatest diversity in the early Miocene, the proterotheres became extinct in the Late Pliocene, about 3 million years ago.

FAMILY MACRAUCHENIIDAE

These curious camel-like litopterns, with rhinoceroslike feet, long necks and a proboscis, were once assumed to be extinct camels. This was not unreasonable because today the llamas and their close relatives in the camel family live in the same area (*see pp. 274–277*). They are, however, quite distinct; any similarities between the families are the result of evolutionary convergence.

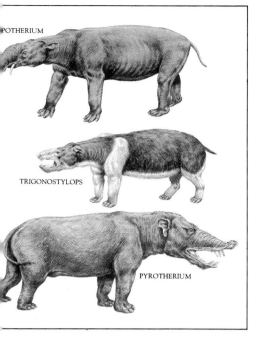

POTHERIUM

TRIGONOSTYLOPS

PYROTHERIUM

NAME: *Thesodon*
TIME: Early Miocene
LOCALITY: South America
(Argentina)
SIZE: 6 ft 6 in/2 m long

Trotting across the Pampas plains, this browsing and grazing long-necked creature would have looked much like a modern guanaco. The main difference would have been in the feet, which in *Thesodon* were 3-toed and hence rather heavier. The position of the nostrils in the skull suggests that a trunk was also present, but this may have been no more prominent than the one carried by the living saiga antelope.

The lower jaw was very slim and the mouth had a full set of 44 teeth — the maximum for a placental mammal — which is unusual for a plant-eater at such a late date in the Tertiary.

NAME: *Macrauchenia*
TIME: Pleistocene
LOCALITY: South America
(Argentina)
SIZE: 10 ft/3 m long

Macrauchenia was a later and larger version of *Thesodon*, from which it may have evolved. The lifestyle of *Macrauchenia* ("large neck") is an enigma. As its name implies, it had certain camel-like features — including size, posture, small head and long neck. But its 3-toed, hoofed feet were rhinoceroslike, and it probably bore a substantial trunk, too, since the nostrils enter the skull high up between the eyes.

Some paleontologists have suggested that signs of a trunk imply a semi-aquatic lifestyle. Others regard it as evidence that the nostrils were simply surrounded by lips which could be closed to keep dust out. The presence of a trunk allied to high-crowned cheek teeth also suggests that *Macrauchenia* may have been able both to browse and to graze.

The legs were long, and the front legs were much longer below the knee than above it — a common feature of running animals. However, *Macrauchenia* would probably not have been able to run fast since the proportions of the hind limbs were reversed, as in non-running animals.

ORDER ASTRAPOTHERIA

A small but well-represented order, the astrapotheres were low-bodied herbivores which survived from the Late Paleocene through to the Middle Miocene. Some were as large as rhinoceroses, and had tusks and a small trunk.

FAMILY ASTRAPOTHERIIDAE

Because they were engulfed in volcanic ash, it has been possible to reconstruct many complete astrapotheriid skeletons. Yet their lifestyle and their relationship to the rest of the South America ungulates remains puzzling.

NAME: *Astrapotherium*
TIME: Late Oligocene to Middle
Miocene
LOCALITY: South America
(Argentina)
SIZE: 8 ft/2.5 m long

Except for its greater size, *Astrapotherium* was typical of the family as a whole. The head was quite short, with a dome over the forehead created by enlarged air sinuses.

The canine teeth continued to grow throughout life and formed 4 tusks. As in a hippopotamus, the larger top pair of tusks sheared against the lower pair. The broad lower incisors protruded, and probably worked against a horny pad in the upper jaw to crop plants.

Evidence for a trunk is somewhat contradictory. The nose bones were certainly very short, and opened high on the forehead, which suggest a trunk. Yet there seems to have been no clear reason for a proboscis: *Astrapotherium's* neck was not particularly short, and its head could easily have reached the ground. It is possible that the "trunk" was really an inflated nose.

Astrapotherium had a long, low body with a weak back and legs, the hind legs feebler than the front ones. The feet were small and plantigrade — the weight was borne on the flat of the foot.

Taken together, the features seem to indicate that the animal was largely aquatic, wallowing in shallow water and rooting about with its tusks and trunk for water plants. Such a lifestyle and physical structure is reminiscent of the amyndont rhinoceroses found in the northern hemisphere (*see pp. 262–265*).

FAMILY TRIGONOSTYLOPIDAE

The trigonostylopids may comprise a family of the astrapotherioids, or they may represent an order of their own. Their principal resemblance to the astrapotheres lies in their prominent canine tusks, but the remainder of the teeth suggest that they are more closely related to the litopterns (*above*).

NAME: *Trigonostylops*
TIME: Late Paleocene to Early Eocene
LOCALITY: South America
(Argentina)
SIZE: Possibly 5 ft/1.5 m long

There are no relics of *Trigonostylops* other than its skull, so it is difficult to make any deductions about its appearance or its lifestyle. The teeth are very primitive, but if *Trigonostylops* is an astrapothere — a deduction based on the large size of the lower canines — then the remainder of the body was probably like *Astrapotherium's*.

ORDER PYROTHERIA

The mammals of South America are excellent examples of convergent evolution — the development of similar structures and features among unrelated animals in response to similar environmental pressures. The pyrotheres were the South American "equivalents" of the elephants, but it is not known from which group they evolved.

FAMILY PYROTHERIIDAE

This was the principal family of the order. They ranged from Argentina to Brazil, Venezuela and Colombia, and are found from the Eocene to the early Oligocene.

NAME: *Pyrotherium*
TIME: Early Oligocene
LOCALITY: South America
(Argentina)
SIZE: 10 ft/3 m long

The remains of *Pyrotherium* were first found in the volcanic ash deposits of Deseado, Argentina: hence their name, which means "fire animal." Since that time, specimens have been discovered in many other parts of South America.

In life, *Pyrotherium* probably looked like the early elephant *Barytherium*, its African contemporary (*see pp. 238–241*). *Pyrotherium* had a massive body supported on pillarlike legs, short broad toes, short thick neck, and a head equipped with a trunk and incisors enlarged to form tusks. There were 2 short, flattened tusks in the upper jaw and a single tusk in the lower jaw.

South American hoofed mammals

NOTOSTYLOPS

PROTYPOTHERIUM

PACHYRUKHOS

RHYNCHIPPUS

THOMASHUXLEYA

SCARRITTIA

TOXODON

HOMALODOTHERIUM

ADINOTHERIUM

South American hoofed mammals

ORDER NOTOUNGULATA

The notoungulates—literally "southern hoofed animals"—were the largest order of South American ungulates. There are about 100 genera grouped into 4 suborders. The suborders may already have diverged by the time South America was detached from North America at the end of the Paleocene.

The isolation of South America allowed the separate evolution of its mammal groups, many of which diversified into ecological niches taken, elsewhere in the world, by other groups.

Many notoungulates were small animals which looked and lived much like rabbits or beavers. Other, larger species came to resemble sheep, warthogs, horses, rhinoceroses and hippopotamuses. That they were related is confirmed both by the arrangement of cusps on the teeth and by ear bones, which are unique to the order.

Although most specimens are of South American origin, a few are also known from late Paleocene and Early Eocene deposits in North America. The latter groups quickly died out, and from then onward the order existed only in South America.

The notoungulates achieved their greatest success as a group in the Oligocene, but they were still abundant early in the Miocene. Thereafter they declined. They have no surviving members. The last notoungulates became extinct in South America in the Pleistocene, about 1 million years ago, shortly after the emergence of the Panamanian isthmus opened the way to the invasion of mammal groups from the north.

SUBORDER NOTIOPROGONIA

These are the most primitive of all notoungulates. When they first appear in the fossil record, members of all the suborders had primitive features. These include a complete dentition of all 44 teeth, low crowns to the teeth with little specialization, and no gap (diastema) between the front and cheek teeth.

The Notoprogonia were restricted to the Paleocene and Eocene; all its members were extinct by about 45 million years ago.

FAMILY NOTOSTYLOPIDAE

Notostylopid teeth show early specialization. They were somewhat rodentlike, with prominent incisors at the front separated by a diastema from grinding premolars and molars at the back. However, the chisel-shaped incisors, which had roots and did not grow continually as those of a gnawing animal usually do, were adapted for nipping, not gnawing.

NAME: *Notostylops*
TIME: **Early Eocene**
LOCALITY: **South America (Argentina)**
SIZE: **Possibly 2 ft 6 in/75 cm long**

Notostylops was a rather rabbitlike animal which lived in the undergrowth, eating herbaceous plants and other low-growing vegetation. Its body was probably fairly generalized with few adaptations to fit it for any particular niche.

Notostylops would have had a short, deep face to accommodate the unusual rodentlike dentition that is characteristic of the family.

SUBORDER TYPOTHERIA

Typotheres have much in common with rodents. Even their teeth are similar: the incisors and cheek teeth of advanced members of both groups are adapted for gnawing, and grow throughout life to compensate for the high rate of wear. Some typotheres grew to the size of the modern black bear, but most were smaller.

FAMILY INTERATHERIIDAE

Most interatheriids were quite small, rodentlike mammals. They were a long-lived group, with fossil representatives dating from the Late Paleocene through to the Late Miocene.

NAME: *Protypotherium*
TIME: **Early Miocene**
LOCALITY: **South America (Argentina)**
SIZE: **16 in/40 cm long**

Protypotherium was the size of a modern rabbit, but with a long tail and legs, and a somewhat ratlike head which tapered to a pointed muzzle. All 44 teeth were present, and these did not show specializations for any particular food. The neck was short and the body long, and there was a long and quite thick tail. The long and slender legs ended in paws which bore claws.

Protypotherium probably ate leaves and scampered, rodentlike, over the Pampas.

SUBORDER HEGETOTHERIA

Like the typotheres (*above*), in whose suborder they are often placed, the hegetotheres include rabbitlike and rodentlike forms which became effective gnawers. Later representatives have a diastema between incisors and cheek teeth, and all teeth grew throughout life.

They emerged slightly later than the interatheriids, during the Middle Eocene, and did not become extinct until the Pliocene, about 3 million years ago.

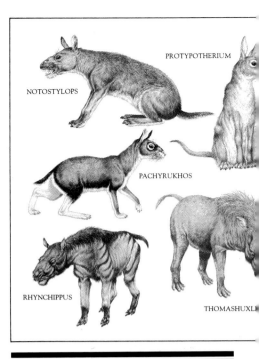

PROTYPOTHERIUM

NOTOSTYLOPS

PACHYRUKHOS

RHYNCHIPPUS

THOMASHUXL

FAMILY HEGETOTHERIIDAE

Hegetotheriids include animals which are rabbitlike in form, mode of locomotion, and lifestyle. Many had long hindlimbs which would have enabled them to lope in the characteristic way.

NAME: *Pachyrukhos*
TIME: **Late Oligocene to Middle Miocene**
LOCALITY: **South America (Argentina)**
SIZE: **1 ft/30 cm long**

Pachyrukhos shows certain similarities with the rabbits, whose ecological niche it filled in South America. It had a short tail, hindlimbs that were considerably longer than its front, and very long hind feet. It evidently moved about by hopping and leaping, just as a rabbit does.

The head was also rabbitlike, narrowing to a pointed muzzle. The teeth were adapted for a diet of nuts and tough plants. *Pachyrukhos* had a well-developed hearing apparatus, which probably means that the ears were long, and large eye sockets. These features suggest that the animal was nocturnal.

SUBORDER TOXODONTA

The suborder Toxodonta was widespread and varied during the Eocene, Oligocene and Miocene, when some reached the size of horses or even rhinoceroses. They did not become extinct until the Central American landbridge was established.

The term "toxodont" means "bow tooth," a reference to a sideways curve in the cheek teeth. As in other notoungulate suborders, the teeth were low-crowned and complete in early genera, but became specialized later. The cheek teeth became large, and were coated in tough cementum. A diastema also appeared in many species.

SCARRITTIA

TOXODON

ALODOTHERIUM   ADINOTHERIUM

FAMILY ISOTEMNIDAE

The isotemnids evolved early and represent the most primitive family of toxodonts.

NAME: *Thomashuxleya*
TIME: Early Eocene
LOCALITY: South America (Argentina)
SIZE: 4 ft 3 in/1.3 m long

Thomashuxleya was named for the 19th century British naturalist, paleontologist and stout defender of Charles Darwin, Thomas Huxley.

Robust and sheep-sized, *Thomashuxleya* appears to have been a very unspecialized animal, with few adaptations to any particular way of life. The head was quite large in relation to the body, and all 44 teeth were present in the jaws.

The canines, however, were enlarged into prominent tusks, so the animal may have rooted about in the undergrowth like a warthog.

The strong limbs were like those of any primitive ungulate, and the relatively short feet were digitigrade—the weight was borne on the toes, not the soles. It seems likely that *Thomashuxleya* was reasonably light on its feet, and perhaps not unlike a peccary (*see pp. 266–269*).

FAMILY NOTOHIPPIDAE

The term "notohippid" means "southern horse." Yet although it was once thought to be ancestral to the true horses, the similarities—which lie chiefly in the shape of the skull and the cropping incisors—are a result of convergent evolution. In fundamentals, everything is notoungulate.

NAME: *Rhynchippus*
TIME: Early Oligocene
LOCALITY: South America (Argentina)
SIZE: 3 ft 4 in/1 m long

Rhynchippus ("snout horse") presents a classic example of the convergence of South American ungulates with unrelated groups elsewhere in the world; in this case, with the horse. Its skeleton, with its deep body and its clawed toes, was not particularly horselike, but the teeth were similar to those of a grazing animal such as a horse or a rhinoceros.

The canine teeth did not form tusks, as they did in most other toxodonts, but were the same size and shape as the incisors. These were tall and ideal for cropping. The large cheek teeth had convoluted enamel for grinding tough vegetation, and were coated in a cement.

FAMILY LEONTINIIDAE

The relationship of this family to other groups is uncertain, but from the structure of the feet it seems reasonable to include it among the toxodonts. Leontiniids were powerfully-built animals, and some may have had a rhinoceroslike horn.

NAME: *Scarrittia*
TIME: Early Oligocene
LOCALITY: South America (Argentina)
SIZE: 6 ft 2 in/2 m long

Scarrittia is the only member of the Leontiniidae that we know from a well-preserved skeleton. In life, it probably looked much like a lumbering, flat-footed rhinoceros.

Scarrittia was a rather heavy animal with a long body and neck, stout legs, 3-toed hoofed feet, and a very short tail. The tibia and fibula were partly fused at the top, so the feet could not be turned sideways.

The face was quite short and the jaws contained the full complement of 44 low-crowned, fairly unspecialized teeth.

FAMILY HOMALODOTHERIIDAE

A characteristic feature of the homalodotheriids is the presence of clawed toes. This is highly reminiscent of the chalicotheres of the Old World and North America (*see pp. 258–261*).

NAME: *Homalodotherium*
TIME: Early and Middle Miocene
LOCALITY: South America (Argentina)
SIZE: 6 ft 6 in/2 m long

The llama-sized *Homalodotherium* is the only well-known genus of the family.

Unlike other notoungulates, *Homalodotherium* had a claw instead of a hoof on the four "fingers" of each "hand." The forelimbs were longer and heavier than the hindlimbs; and whereas the hind foot was plantigrade the forefoot was digitigrade. This made the animal higher at the shoulders than at the hips.

Such features made it likely that *Homalodotherium* was partly bipedal. It probably browsed on the leaves of low branches, rearing up on to its hind legs.

FAMILY TOXODONTIDAE

The toxodontids include animals whose teeth were exceptionally high-crowned and curved. They had open roots which grew all the time to compensate for the wear that resulted from feeding on the tough Pampas grasses. The animals themselves looked like rhinoceroses; some even had a horn on the snout.

NAME: *Toxodon*
TIME: Pliocene and Pleistocene
LOCALITY: South America (Argentina)
SIZE: 9 ft/2.7 m long

Toxodon was a rhinoceroslike animal, with a heavy barrel-shaped body supported on short stocky legs. The 3-toed, hoofed, plantigrade feet were rather small, however. Since the hind legs were longer than the front ones, the body sloped forward to the shoulders.

The front of the head was quite broad, and may have had a fleshy prehensile lip. Immediately behind the snout the skull narrowed, as in a rhinoceros, then widened again. Its teeth suggest that *Todoxon* was a mixed browser and grazer, chopping and chewing the hard Pampas grasses, but also taking foliage.

NAME: *Adinotherium*
TIME: Early to Middle Miocene
LOCALITY: South America (Argentina)
SIZE: 5 ft/1.5 m long

Adinotherium looked rather like a sheep-sized, and less ungainly, version of *Toxodon*. The front legs were relatively longer than in some toxodontids, so the shoulders were about the same height as the hips, and there was no hump.

Adinotherium also had a small horn on the skull. This was probably some kind of display structure.

Horses

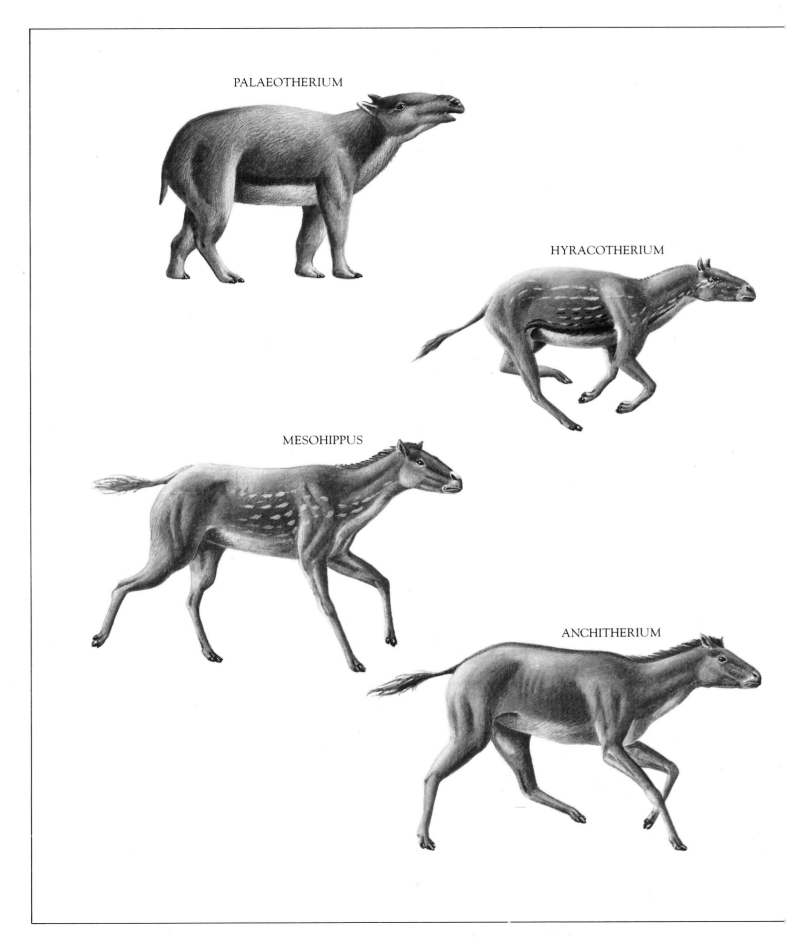

PALAEOTHERIUM

HYRACOTHERIUM

MESOHIPPUS

ANCHITHERIUM

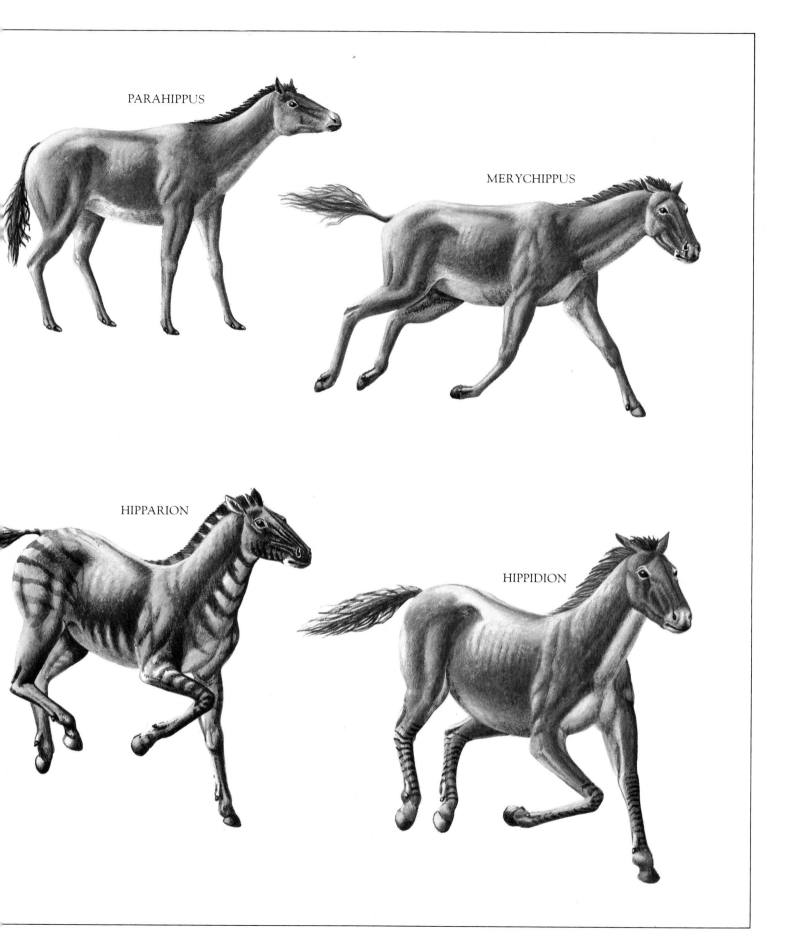

PARAHIPPUS

MERYCHIPPUS

HIPPARION

HIPPIDION

Horses

Ungulates — hoofed mammals — represent the main group of large plant-eating land animals living today. Their earliest representatives were early rooters and browsers (see pp. 234–237), which had been dominant during the Paleocene and Eocene periods, about 50–60 million years ago. Many evolved to take advantage of the new opportunities presented by the formation of open grassy plains during the drier Miocene period, about 20 million years ago.

Apart from the primitive rooters and browsers, ungulates can be divided into 2 great orders. The Perissodactyla or odd-toed ungulates (below) were represented by a large number of genera in the early Tertiary, but are now confined to horses, rhinoceroses and tapirs.

The other great group of modern ungulates, the even-toed Artiodactyla (see pp. 266–281), now have far more representatives, including deer, sheep, goats and cattle, pigs and peccaries, hippopotamuses, giraffes, and camels and llamas.

Unlike the early rooters and browsers, most of the advanced ungulates are adapted for fast running; a crucial advance for small and medium-sized animals threatened by swift predators. Hence the upper leg tends to be short, with long, thin, fused lower-leg and toe bones which enable the animal to gallop without risk of twisting its ankle or wrist joints. The muscles are concentrated around the upper bone and their power is transmitted to the rest of the leg by a series of tendons. The ankle joint tends to be rigid, and the animals walk up on their toes. The toes are generally elongated and reduced in number — another weight-saving feature — and the hoof itself is an enormously enlarged toe nail.

In the odd-toed Perissodactyla, where 1 or 3 toes are usual, most or all of the weight is taken on the middle digit. Among the even-toed Artiodactyla, the weight is divided between the toes, usually 2 or 4 in number.

Other ungulate developments associated with grazing include batteries of enlarged grinding teeth, a complex gut suited to the digestion of cellulose (the complex carbohydrate present in plant food), and living in large herds. Several groups have also developed skull outgrowths, made of horn, bone or even matted hair. The function of these growths varies, but includes defense and sexual display.

ORDER PERISSODACTYLA

The Perissodactyla probably originated in Late Paleocene times about 55 million years ago. There are 3 suborders. The Hippomorpha contain the horses and the brontotheres (see pp. 258–261), the Ancylopoda (see pp. 258–261), and the Ceratomorpha — the tapirs (see pp. 258–261) and rhinoceroses (see pp. 262–265).

NAME: *Palaeotherium*
TIME: Late Eocene to Early Oligocene
LOCALITY: Europe
SIZE: 2 ft 6 in/75 cm high at the shoulder

The tapir-shaped *Palaeotherium* lived in the tropical forests that covered Europe in early Tertiary times. Its build was well-suited to a forest-browsing lifestyle, and it is one that evolved several times in the evolutionary record among different mammal groups. The long head and short trunk enabled the animal to browse from low bushes, while the narrow body and long legs allowed it to run between close-growing trees.

Unlike the horses, the palaeotheres did not reduce the number of toes as they evolved; all palaeotheres have 4 toes on the front feet and 3 on the hind. These would have given the animal spreading feet suited to walking on boggy forest soil. Palaeotheres probably moved about in herds — evidence for this is that large numbers are often found fossilized together. Some palaeotheres grew as large as a rhinoceros.

FAMILY EQUIDAE

Equids have their origins in small, scampering animals, no larger than small terriers, which browsed in the forests of Early Eocene times. With the arrival of the generally drier climate of the Miocene, around 20 million years ago, humid forests began to give way to more open country, and in some parts of the world, notably in North America, to vast grassy plains. It is to such conditions that the modern equids — horses, zebras and asses — are so well adapted.

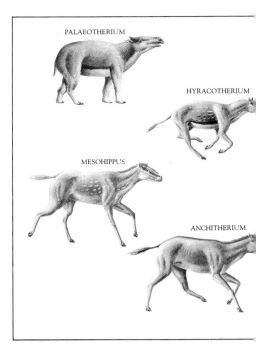

NAME: *Hyracotherium*
TIME: Early Eocene
LOCALITY: Widespread in Asia, Europe, and North America
SIZE: 8 in/20 cm high at the shoulder

In spite of its name, *Hyracotherium* is not a close relative of the hyraxes (see pp. 234–237) — this is the result of mistaken identification in the last century. A more evocative name, *Eohippus*, the "dawn horse," has been suggested, but science retains the earlier term.

Hyracotherium, the earliest known equid, is believed to be ancestral to the rest of the horse line, and possibly to the palaeotheres as well. It was tiny compared to modern horses, only about 2 ft/60 cm in length. Its skull was elongated and the mouth had a full complement of 44 teeth, indicating how primitive the animal was. The teeth were low-crowned and suitable only for chewing the soft leaves of tropical forest trees and shrubs.

As with *Palaeotherium*, there were 4 toes at the front and 3 at the back, making the feet large and unhorselike. Most of the weight was carried on the third toe, anticipating the evolutionary pattern to come. The body was long and arched, giving the animal a hunched appearance. The relative size and complexity of the brain suggests that *Hyracotherium* was alert and intelligent, and this may have been a factor in the survival of the horse line as a whole.

Hyracotherium was widespread in Eocene times, but when the horse line died out in Europe and Asia around during the Early Oligocene around 35 million years ago, further evolution took place on the North American continent.

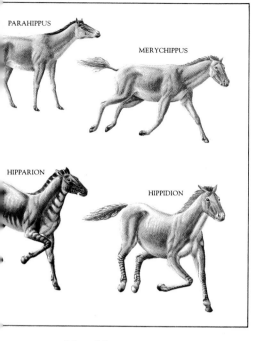

PARAHIPPUS
MERYCHIPPUS
HIPPARION
HIPPIDION

NAME: *Mesohippus*
TIME: **Middle Oligocene**
LOCALITY: **North America**
SIZE: **2 ft/60 cm high at the shoulder**

In areas where the forests were giving way to more open country, the horses were no longer confined to scampering among the undergrowth and began to develop the capacity to trot and run.

About the size of a greyhound, with a body some 4 ft/1.2 m long, *Mesohippus* was larger than its predecessors, but had rather lighter 3-toed feet. The central toe was larger than the others. The premolar teeth began to resemble the molars, which increased the chewing surface and hence their efficiency, but they were still low-crowned. Such teeth needed only a shallow jaw, so the head was quite long and pointed.

NAME: *Anchitherium*
TIME: **Early to Late Miocene**
LOCALITY: **North America and later Asia and Europe**
SIZE: **2 ft/60 cm high at the shoulder**

The evolution of the horse was not a simple "straight line" affair, and a number of side-branches developed which have left no descendants today. *Anchitherium* represents a very successful but conservative offshoot.

Anchitherium evolved in North America in the Early Miocene period, around 25 million years ago. A 3-toed browsing horse, much like *Mesohippus* in size and shape, *Anchitherium* browsed the tender vegetation of humid forests. Crossing the Bering land bridge that once joined modern Alaska to Siberia, it spread across Asia and Europe. There, it survived long after it had been replaced in North America by the first grazing horses during the Middle Miocene, some 15 million years ago. *Anchitherium* did not become extinct in China until the end of Miocene times, some 5 million years ago.

NAME: *Parahippus*
TIME: **Early Miocene**
LOCALITY: **North America**
SIZE: **3 ft 3 in/1 m high at the shoulder**

Parahippus represents an intermediate stage in the evolution of the horse. There were still 3 toes on the feet, and in appearance it was very similar to its ancestor *Mesohippus*. Its body was larger, though, as were its molars, which came to resemble millstones.

This latter change is highly significant. The newly evolved grasses contained abrasive silica in their cell walls, which made them difficult to crop and masticate. Teeth would have worn down even faster had it not been for the acquisition of hard-wearing "cement" that coated their enamel crests and outer sides. It seems likely, therefore, that *Parahippus* ventured out from the woodlands to take some advantage of the major new source of nutrition represented by the spreading grasslands.

NAME: *Merychippus*
TIME: **Middle to Late Miocene**
LOCALITY: **North America (Nebraska)**
SIZE: **3 ft 3 in/1 m high at the shoulder**

Herds of *Merychippus*, the earliest horse to feed exclusively on grass, once roamed the prairies of what is now Nebraska. Their teeth were tall-crowned — dental growth continuing for longer than hitherto — and interlined with cement. Continuing the development seen in *Mesohippus*, the premolars now had the same grass-grinding design as the molars. The tall teeth needed a deep jaw to contain them, so the head developed the heavy jawline of the modern horse.

Merychippus had a longer neck than its browsing ancestors, since it spent much of its time with its mouth down in the grass. It also developed a strong ligament along the neck from the skull to the shoulder. The springiness of this ligament enabled the heavy head to be raised with little effort, which meant that *Merychippus* could stay alert to threats from swift predators such as the early dogs and cats.

Merychippus still had 3 toes but now only the middle toe was used to bear the weight (the 2 side-toes did not reach the ground). In addition, an elastic tendon in the leg linking muscle to bone acted like a spring, further increasing the efficiency of movement and making possible a progressively lighter foot and lower leg. The compression of this tendon absorbed the shock of each step, thus saving the ankle from damage, then released the energy stored up in the process to spring the foot up into its next stride.

NAME: *Hipparion*
TIME: **Middle Miocene to Pleistocene**
LOCALITY: **Widespread in North America, Europe, Asia and Africa**
SIZE: **4 ft 6 in/1.4 m high at the shoulder**

Once the plains-living grazing horses had evolved they, too, radiated into many different types. Of these, all but the *Equus* species are now extinct.

Hipparion represents one of the many grazing horses that evolved during the Miocene, around 15 million years ago. It was particularly successful, spreading during the Miocene from North America into Asia, Europe and Africa. In Africa, it survived until the Pleistocene about 2 million years ago. This elegant creature resembled the modern horse, but like *Merychippus* had 3 toes, 2 of which were much reduced and did not touch the ground.

NAME: *Hippidion*
TIME: **Pleistocene**
LOCALITY: **South America**
SIZE: **4 ft 6 in/1·4 m high at the shoulder**

There seem to have been no horses in South America throughout the Tertiary. However, it cannot have been the environment that prevented their colonization, since conditions in South America were able to support the evolution of horselike litopterns such as *Diadiaphorus* (see pp. 246–249). When a land connection was re-established between North and South America during the Pliocene, 5 million years ago, horses were able to migrate and thrive there.

Hippidion, probably a descendant of *Merychippus*, was one of these South American horses. It probably resembled a small donkey, with a fairly large head. However, its long, delicate nasal bones were quite distinct from those of other horses, suggesting that *Hippidion* continued to evolve in isolation from the mainstream of horse evolution in North America until it became extinct around 8000 years ago.

The modern genus *Equus*, which includes the zebras and asses as well as the wild and domestic horses, seems to have evolved about 4 million years ago in North America, from where it migrated to Asia, Africa and Europe. Curiously, all the horses in the Americas died out about 8000 years ago, and did not reappear there until about 400 years ago — and then only as a result of deliberate introduction by humans. Some paleontologists have speculated that their demise was caused by some devastating epidemic disease, possibly like myxomatosis.

Tapirs and brontotheres

EOTITANOPS

DOLICHORHINUS

BRONTOPS

EMBOLOTHERIUM

BRONTOTHERIUM

MOROPUS

HEPTODON

MIOTAPIRUS

Tapirs and brontotheres

FAMILY BRONTOTHERIIDAE

The third family of the suborder Hippomorpha consists of the "thunder beasts." This group of rhinoceroslike creatures evolved in the Early Eocene, about 50 million years ago, in North America and eastern Asia from small animals similar to the first horses. Although they existed for only about 15 million years, about 40 different types have been described.

In some ways their evolutionary history parallels those of the uintatheres and arsinoitheres (*see pp. 234–237*). All the brontotheres browsed on soft forest vegetation. Some forms evolved massive horns and large canines, and there was a common tendency to hugely increased bulk. These animals are sometimes known as titanotheres, another allusion to their great size.

Although they are often referred to as "horns," brontothere head growths were not composed of, or even covered in, horn. Nor were they made of compacted hair, as are those of the rhinoceroses. In fact they were more like the ossicones of giraffes: bony structures with a covering of thick skin. Since these grotesque knobs were larger in the males than the females, they were possibly used for display, or perhaps as weapons during intra-species fights to determine the leadership of the herd.

Shortly after the brontotheres reached the peak of their monstrous development, climates became dryer and more open woodlands became plentiful. Evolution favored more lightly-built animals that could graze and live on the plains. Brontotheres became extinct in the middle Oligocene and were replaced by the rhinoceroses.

NAME: *Eotitanops*
TIME: **Early to Middle Eocene**
LOCALITY: **North America and Asia**
SIZE: **1 ft 6 in/45 cm high at the shoulder**

If you could travel back through time to watch a group of *Eotitanops* scampering through the undergrowth of an Early Eocene forest, it would be impossible to tell at a glance whether you were looking at *Eotitanops* or its distant cousin *Hyracotherium*. Both were small browsing mammals, with 4 toes on the front feet and 3 on the hind. But whereas *Hyracotherium* gave rise to the elegant and intelligent plains-dwelling horses of recent times, *Eotitanops* evolved into the huge, lumbering, small-brained brontotheres that failed to see out the Oligocene. It lived in North America in early Eocene times but survived into the middle Eocene in Asia.

NAME: *Dolichorhinus*
TIME: **Late Eocene**
LOCALITY: **North America**
SIZE: **4 ft/1.2 m high at the shoulder**

In appearance *Dolichorhinus* resembled a small hornless rhinoceros with a particularly long head. Indeed, with its low-crowned teeth, which were only suitable for chewing soft forest leaves, it probably lived very much like one of the modern rhinoceroses. The 4-toed front feet and 3-toed hind feet of its ancestors were retained, as they were through the whole brontothere line. The type of feet adapted for swift running, with reduced toes, as seen in the horses and antelopes, were never evolved in the brontotheres.

NAME: *Brontops*
TIME: **Early Oligocene**
LOCALITY: **North America**
SIZE: **8 ft/2.5 m high at the shoulder**

As the Eocene passed into the Oligocene, the brontotheres became very large indeed — larger than any living rhinoceros — and developed the distinctive bony knobs on the snout.

Skeletons of *Brontops* have been found with partly-healed breaks in the ribs, a fact which lends support to the theory that the skull outgrowths were used in fights among males for dominance. The breaks suggest that the animal had received a heavy blow in the flanks from a rival, since no other animals around at that time that could have inflicted such damage. The movement of the ribcage during breathing would have prevented broken bones from knitting together properly.

One of the most famous skeletons of *Brontops* was discovered in rocks that had formed in a bog. The animal had evidently lived in swampy woodland, and had died by becoming swallowed up in the mud.

NAME: *Embolotherium*
TIME: **Early Oligocene**
LOCALITY: **Asia (Mongolia)**
SIZE: **8 ft/2.5 m high at the shoulder**

The head of *Embolotherium* is typical of the grotesque shapes developed by the later brontotheres. From the back of the skull it swept forward in a deep hollow and then up to a massive single "horn" on the nose. The eyes were situated well forward, just behind the nostrils and at the horn's base. The shallow skull left little room for much of a brain — as in other large brontotheres, the brain was no bigger than a man's fist.

The occurrence of *Embolotherium* in the Gobi desert of Asia gives an indication of just how widespread and successful were the brontotheres in their heyday.

NAME: *Brontotherium*
TIME: **Early Oligocene**
LOCALITY: **North America**
SIZE: **8 ft/2.5 m high at the shoulder**

The bones of this giant mammal are quite common in the Badlands of South Dakota and Nebraska. The local Sioux Indians had always associated them with the creatures of mythology — the great horses that galloped across the sky producing storms — and so the term "brontothere," "thunder beast," was born. *Brontotherium* itself was one of the largest — larger than the living rhinoceroses. Its nasal horn was Y-shaped and swept upward higher than the back of the head.

The vertebrae at the shoulders had enormous upward-projecting spines. These were evidently used to anchor powerful neck muscles that must have been needed to support the heavy head with its huge, flamboyant ornamentation. There may have been fleshy lips and a prehensile tongue, enabling *Brontotherium* to select and nibble the juiciest twigs and leaves from the bushes; the teeth were of relatively simple design and were able to deal only with tender vegetation.

Brontotherium seems to have lived, like other brontotheres, in herds that wandered through open scrubby woodlands. They roamed along the foothills of the rising Rocky Mountains — an intensely volcanic area at that time. Every now and again an eruption would bury herds of *Brontotherium* in ash, and it is in these volcanic deposits that their skeletons are found today.

ONTOTHERIUM

JS

HEPTODON

MIOTAPIRUS

SUBORDER ANCYLOPODA

The second suborder of odd-toed ungulates includes some bizarre animals, which present paleontologists with many enigmas. There were 2 families. The eomoropids were the first to evolve and generally resembled other primative odd-toed ungulates. They lived in eastern Asia and North America during the Eocene and Early Oligocene, between 50 and 35 million years ago. The second and most important family of ancylopods are the chalicotheres. They probably evolved in Eurasia during the Eocene and spread into Africa and North America during the Miocene. They survived until about 2 million years ago in eastern Asia and central Africa with little evolutionary change.

FAMILY CHALICOTHERIIDAE

Whereas the rest of the ungulates have hooves on their toes, these animals evolved large claws instead and evidently could not run. The dentition and other features of some of the advanced chalicotheres, such as *Chalicotherium* from the Miocene of Europe, suggests that they were forest browsers, and may have been able to rear up on their hind legs while feeding on the succulent leaves of trees and shrubs.

Although fossil evidence is sparse, chalicotheres seem to have been a remarkably successful group, which flourished for almost 50 million years.

Animals resembling chalicotheres appear as decorations on Siberian tombs dating from the 5th century BC. Also sightings periodically recur in Kenyan forests of the so-called Nandi bear, a creature whose stance is alleged to be gorillalike, with forelimbs longer than its hindlimbs, large bearlike claws, and with a horselike face. It is little wonder, then, that claims are made that chalicotheres still survive!

NAME: *Moropus*
TIME: Early to Middle Miocene
LOCALITY: North America
SIZE: 10 ft/3 m long

The chalicotheres have often been described as "horses with claws." The comparison is not a very apt one, however: although the head and body may have been somewhat horselike, the limbs were heavy and not suited for running. The teeth were low-crowned, showing that it was a browser rather than a grazer, eating the soft leaves of trees rather than tough blades of grasses.

Moropus' back sloped upward toward the shoulders from heavy hips, while its forelimbs were long and armed with 3 long, cleft claws. The 3 toes of the hind foot had shorter claws. When the claws were first discovered, without the rest of the skeleton, they were thought to have belonged to some kind of anteater.

The function of the claws is something of a mystery. They may have been used for digging roots and tubers out of the ground, but the teeth do not show enough wear for a diet of this kind of food. Alternatively, *Moropus* may have stood on its hind legs and hooked branches down from the trees, but its elbow joints do not seem to have been flexible enough for this method to have been habitual. It is possible that *Moropus* could have fed either way, and the claws may also have been useful as defensive weapons.

SUBORDER CERATOMORPHA

The final suborder of odd-toed ungulates contains the tapirs and the rhinoceroses (see pp. 262–265).

The tapirs were among the first of the perissodactyls to evolve, appearing in the Early Eocene, about 55 million years ago, at the same time as the first chalicotheres (see above) and horses (see pp. 254–257). Bulky tropical browsers with short trunks, tapirs were widely distributed in Europe, Asia and North America, but were not found south of the equator until relatively recently. Tapirs survived in the warmer areas of Europe, Asia and North America until the Late Pleistocene era, about 10,000 years ago.

Tapirs are among the most "conservative" of mammals in terms of evolution: in 55 million years, they have changed remarkably little. Like the palaeotheres (see pp. 254–257), the tapirs evolved a body shape that is ideally suited to life in the dense tropical forests. Indeed, it was so successful an adaptation that it has evolved separately in several very different groups, such as the peccaries (see pp. 266–269) and capybaras (see pp. 282–285).

FAMILY HELALETIDAE

One of the earliest families of tapirs, the helaletids were much like today's species, but were smaller and more lightly built.

NAME: *Heptodon*
TIME: Early Eocene
LOCALITY: North America (Wyoming)
SIZE: 3 ft 4 in/1 m long

Heptodon, an early helaletid, had already evolved the characteristic tapir-shaped body but had no trunk. The short trunk that is such a distinctive feature of modern tapirs was just beginning to evolve as a fleshy outgrowth of the upper lip in *Helaletes*, a relative of *Heptodon* that lived during the Middle and Late Eocene in North America and Asia. The trunk is a valuable adaptation, which tapirs used as a sensitive tool for pulling within reach and handling the twigs and leaves on which they feed.

FAMILY TAPIRIDAE

The family to which the modern tapirs belong, the Tapiridae, can be traced back as far as the Early Oligocene, about 40 million years ago. The 4 species of living tapirs are all placed in the single genus *Tapirus*. Two species occur in Central America and northern South America and 2 in Southeast Asia: none remain in the group's original northern stronghold. This scattered "relict" distribution has often been cited as evidence for the existence of the southern supercontinent of Gondwanaland. It is supposed that the animals reached their present homes by migrating overland before the continents slowly drifted apart.

NAME: *Miotapirus*
TIME: Early Niocene
LOCALITY: North America
SIZE: 6 ft 6 in/2 m long

The characteristic tapir features — a heavy body, short legs and tail, a large head with a short flexible snout, and a short neck — appeared early in the evolution of perissodactyls and have remained unchanged ever since. *Miotapirus* was probably nocturnal, as are members of the living species *Tapirus*, and may have been just as versatile — fossils have been found from sea level up to heights of 15,000 ft/4,500 m.

Rhinoceroses

HYRACODON

HYRACHYUS

METAMYNODON

TRIGONIAS

TELEOCERAS

INDRICOTHERIUM

COELODONTA

ELASMOTHERIUM

Rhinoceroses

Rhinoceroses and their closest relatives are odd-toed ungulates, members of the Perissodactyla. Unlike the later horses, which have eliminated all the lateral digits and now have only 1 toe, most rhinoceroses have 3 toes, the axis of weight-bearing passing through the middle or third digit.

FAMILY HYRACHYIDAE
The hyrachyids mark the transition between tapirs (see pp. 258–261) and rhinoceroses, the latter evolved from a tapir similar to *Hyrachyus* in the Late Eocene, about 40 million years ago.

NAME: *Hyrachyus*
TIME: **Early to Late Eocene**
LOCALITY: **North America (Wyoming), Asia (China) and Europe (France)**
SIZE: **5 ft/1.5 m long**
Hyrachyus was generally very similar to *Heptodon* (see pp. 258–261), but a little larger and more heavily built. It was a common and widespread animal. Many species are known, ranging from the size of a modern tapir to that of a fox.

Hyrachus appears to be ancestral to both the later tapirs and the rhinoceroses. Indeed, its resemblance to a primitive form of the latter group is so pronounced that it is often classed as rhinoceros, albeit a lightweight one.

SUPERFAMILY RHINOCERATOIDEA
Rhinoceratoids — literally "nose horns," from the Greek — make up the largest superfamily of the suborder Ceratomorpha. In fact, only 1 family, the Rhinocerotidae, evolved "horns," and even these are not true horns but outgrowths composed of highly compacted hair.

Rhinoceratoids evolved in the Middle Eocene and adapted to the change in conditions as the worldwide forests gave way to grasslands. The inability of their cousins the brontotheres (see pp. 258–261) to do likewise soon led to extinction. Nevertheless the rhinoceroses have now passed their peak, with only 5 species surviving today. The evolutionary history of the rhinoceratoids is quite complex; they are grouped into 3 families.

FAMILY HYRACODONTIDAE
The hornless hyracodont rhinoceroses, of which there are about a dozen genera, were the earliest and most primitive family of the group. They probably evolved from a tapiroid close to *Hyrachyus*.

Their large, efficient cheek teeth were similar to those of the tapirs, but their incisors and canines were modified in various ways. Earlier hyracodonts were quite horselike in build, with slender, elongated limbs. Later members of the family developed a more robust build.

NAME: *Hyracodon*
TIME: **Early Oligocene to Early Miocene**
LOCALITY: **North America (Saskatchewan, Dakota, Nebraska)**
SIZE: **5 ft/1.5 m long**
Hyracodon was a lightly-built fast-running animal, not unlike a pony. As with the horses, the number of toes were reduced, so that the foot was lightened and could be moved quickly, and all the leg muscles were concentrated near the top. There were 3 toes on all feet.

The large and heavy head, however, seemed out of proportion to the body. No horns had evolved at this stage, and the only means of defense against such local meat-eaters as *Hyaenodon* (see pp. 210–213), the last of the creodonts, or the early dogs (see pp. 218–221) would have been to flee. The back teeth were of a typical rhinoceros pattern, low-crowned and adapted for chewing leaves.

NAME: *Indricotherium*
TIME: **Oligocene**
LOCALITY: **Asia (Pakistan and China)**
SIZE: **26 ft/8 m long**
It seems quite impossible that an animal as small, lightweight and fleet-of-foot as *Hyracodon* could have evolved into the largest land mammal known to have lived, but all of the evidence points in that direction.

Indricotherium — also known as *Baluchitherium* after the state in Pakistan in which major specimens were discovered — was an immense animal. With an estimated weight of 33 tons/30 tonnes, it was twice the weight of the largest known mammoth and more than 4 times that of the heaviest modern elephant. The skull itself was 4 ft 3 in/1.3 m long, but this was relatively small compared to the overall body size.

The vertebrae of the back and the long neck were sculpted into hollows and struts, like those of the largest dinosaurs, which kept weight down while retaining the strength. The legs were elephantine, but the entire weight would have been supported on only 3 toes — the normal rhinoceros pattern. Again, there was no horn; in fact, the nasal bones were quite weak.

The front teeth of the fossil rhinoceroses varied widely, but those of *Indrico-*

therium were very strange indeed. There were only 2 front teeth on top and 2 below: the upper pair pointing downward like tusks, while the lower pair pointed forward. Since there is some evidence that it had a large, flexible upper lip, such a construction would have enabled *Indricotherium* to browse giraffelike from the tops of trees more than 26 ft/8 m from the ground.

Indricotherium probably lived in small family groups, taking advantage of the scattered trees found in dry open woodlands.

One skeleton was discovered in rocks formed from swamp mud. It is easy to imagine the difficulties such a huge creature would have had in a bog.

FAMILY AMYNODONTIDAE
Amynodonts were a short-lived Eocene and Oligocene group of about 10 genera of hippopotamuslike, probably amphibious, animals with large bodies and short stout limbs.

Among the features which suggest a semi-aquatic lifestyle are the presence in some genera of prehensile lips and tusks. Canines were short or absent in the 2 other rhinoceros families, but in the amynodontids they were huge, curved, and continually-growing.

It seems likely then that amynodontids took the place in this habitat of the aquatic pantodonts such as *Coryphodon* (see pp. 234–237), and were themselves eventually replaced by the aquatic rhinoceroses of the more advanced rhinocerotid family, such as *Teleoceras* (below).

INDRICOTHERIUM

COELODONTA

HERIUM

NAME: *Metamynodon*
TIME: Late Eocene to Early Miocene
LOCALITY: North America (Nebraska, South Dakota) and Asia (Mongolia)
SIZE: 13 ft/4 m long

The remains of *Metamynodon* and its relatives are found in rocks that were formed from river sands and gravels, indicating that these beasts were mostly aquatic by nature.

Metamynodon was very much like a hippopotamus in appearance. It had a broad, flat head, a short neck, a massive barrel-shaped body, and short legs. The front feet were unique among rhinoceroses in having 4 toes.

Although there was a crest up the middle of the skull — something usually associated with meat-eating animals — *Metamynodon* was undoubtedly a plant-eater. It is possible that the crest anchored strong jaw muscles that evolved to cope with tough, woody food.

Also hippopotamuslike were the enlarged canine teeth. *Metamynodon* may have used its tusks for grubbing about in the mud at the bottom of a river. It is also likely that *Metamynodon* had prehensile lips.

Another adaptation to an aquatic lifestyle were the eyes. Set high up on the skull, they allowed the animal to see about itself while it was almost totally submerged.

FAMILY RHINOCEROTIDAE

This is the family to which modern rhinoceroses belong. They evolved in Late Eocene or Early Oligocene times and thrived throughout North America, Asia, Europe and Africa. However, rhinoceroses began to decline during the Pliocene, and they disappeared altogether from North America at the end of the Miocene, 5 million years ago.

Since this was about 2 million years before the Panama Isthmus reformed, rhinoceroses never colonized South America. Neither did the wooly rhinoceros *Coelodonta* (below), which was once widespread throughout northern Eurasia, migrate across the Bering land bridge to reach North America.

Rhinocerotids adapted to a wide range of diets and habitats. Many were browsers, but some became specialized grazers. Some developed thick coats which enabled them to survive in northern regions even during the Pleistocene Ice Ages. Some also acquired "horns" composed of matted hair, which have not fossilized.

It seems likely that the continued decline of these animals, now the largest land mammals after elephants, is associated with changing climate, but also with the rise of humans. Out of about 50 genera, only 5 species are still alive.

NAME: *Trigonias*
TIME: Early Oligocene
LOCALITY: North America (Montana) and Europe (France)
SIZE: 8 ft/2.5 m long

The earliest well-preserved example of a rhinocerotid is *Trigonias*. It was already similar to the modern rhinoceroses in general appearance, but there was no horn on the snout. There were also more teeth in the jaw than is found in any modern rhinoceros, though the actual number seems to have varied in different species.

Trigonias' front feet had 5 toes, although the fifth was small and could not reach the ground. This suggests that the evolutionary line split away from the other rhinoceroses before the lightweight 3-toed running forms developed.

NAME: *Teleoceras*
TIME: Middle to Late Miocene
LOCALITY: North America (Nebraska)
SIZE: 13 ft/4 m long

Like the amynodontids, the rhinocerotids developed hippopotamus-shaped forms as well. *Teleoceras* was typical of these. It had a long and massive body but short, stumpy legs. The legs were so short, in fact, that the body would at times have dragged on the ground. It is likely that they were used to "pole" the animal along underwater rather than for walking on dry land.

The most un-hippopotamuslike feature of this extraordinary animal was the short conical horn on the nose. It is possible that this feature was confined to males, and was used as a weapon of defense or for display.

NAME: *Elasmotherium*
TIME: Pleistocene
LOCALITY: Europe (southern Russia) and Asia (Siberia)
SIZE: 16 ft/5 m long

As the forests of the Early Tertiary gave way to the grasslands of the Late Tertiary, many animal families adapted accordingly. Among the rhinoceroses, *Elasmotherium* shows the result well.

Elasmotherium had no incisors, and would have used its lips to pluck grasses. The cheek teeth were like those of a huge horse — tall-crowned, covered in cement, and with wrinkled enamel. Such teeth are adapted to eating tough, abrasive grasses. As the teeth wore down, the wrinkled enamel produced ridges that provided additional grinding surfaces. The teeth had no roots but grew continually to counteract wear.

A grassland animal needs to be swift of foot to escape its predators, or so big and so well-armored that its predators are discouraged. As the largest known of the true rhinoceroses — almost as big as a modern elephant — *Elasmotherium* adopted the latter strategy.

Elasmotherium's "horn" was a truly remarkable structure, 6 ft 6 in/2 m long. Most rhinoceroses have their horns growing from the snout. In *Elasmotherium*, however, it grew from the forehead. There was a large dome of bone here, which presumably provided a more secure anchor for the massive structure than any foundation at the tip of the nose.

NAME: *Coelodonta*
TIME: Pleistocene
LOCALITY: Europe (Britain) and Asia (eastern Siberia)
SIZE: 11 ft/3.5 m long

Coelodonta had its origins in the Pliocene of eastern Asia, from where it migrated into Europe (but not into North America) and became the wooly rhinoceros of the Ice Age.

Coelodonta had a pair of huge horns on its snout, the front one growing to lengths of over 3 ft/1 m in old males.

Like the wooly mammoth (*see pp.242–245*), *Coelodonta's* massive body and shaggy coat allowed it to withstand the harsh conditions of the tundra and steppe that bordered the great glaciers of the Northern Hemisphere. Although normally hair does not fossilize, the presence of the shaggy coat is known because of corpses found preserved in frozen gravels in Siberia.

There are eye-witness accounts too. Early humans hunted this great beast, and depicted it on the walls of caves in southern France 30,000 years ago.

Swine and hippopotamuses

DIACODEXIS

ARCHAEOTHERIUM

DINOHYUS

ELOMERYX

HIPPOPOTAMUS GORGOPS

PLATYGONUS

METRIDIOCHOERUS

Swine and hippopotamuses

DIACODEXIS

ARCHAEOTHⅠ

DINOHYUS

ELOM

ORDER ARTIODACTYLA

The artiodactyls are the even-toed ungulates (from the Greek *artios*, "even," and *dactylos*, "fingers"), and are the most widespread and abundant of today's running, grazing animals. They differ from their distant relatives the perissodactyls (odd-toed ungulates such as the horses) in usually having 4 or 2, rather than 3 or 1, weight-bearing toes on each foot. Since the toes form a semicircular hoof, this gives rise to the typical "cloven hoof" seen in pigs, deer and cattle.

Artiodactyls first appeared in Eocene times, about 50 million years ago, and developed more slowly than the perissodactyls (see *pp. 254–265*). Most groups had emerged by the close of Eocene times about 37 million years ago, when they rapidly outstripped their rivals.

With the exception of the suines (pigs, peccaries and hippopotamuses; *below*), the artiodactyls all ruminate; that is, they "chew the cud" to improve the efficiency of digestion.

The ruminant stomach is divided into 3 or 4 chambers, the first of which is the rumen. Food is swallowed and passed into the first and second chambers, where it ferments until it is regurgitated for further chewing. It is only when this by-now fully masticated food is swallowed again that it makes the journey down the entire alimentary canal.

Such developments greatly increased the nutritional yield of the tougher plants that were evolving in the drier Miocene conditions. These, in turn, increased the range of habitats open to the artiodactyls.

The importance of the ungulates, particularly the artiodactyls, to human evolution and social development cannot be ignored. Artiodactyls were vital to our early ancestors to be hunted as a source of food, tools, and skin and fur clothing. More recently, several species were domesticated. This added greatly to the range of resources available, including milk, wool, transportation, and a new source of energy for powering machinery. Harnessed to plows, irrigation devices and mills, ungulates immeasurably enlarged the possibilities presented by the cultivation of plants. And, of course, humans are still deeply dependent on the ungulates today.

SUBORDER SUINA

The word "suina," like swine, comes from the Latin for "pig." The suborder includes the non-ruminant artiodactyls: the hippopotamuses, pigs, peccaries and a number of extinct groups.

These are generally considered the most primitive of the suborders of even-toed ungulates. Most have the simplest, almost complete teeth, and the least sophisticated digestive systems. Although the stomach may have 2 or 3 chambers, suines do not chew the cud.

FAMILY DICHOBUNIDAE

Dichobunids are a family of small, primitive animals which must have looked more like rabbits than ungulates. Also, their classification as even-toed ungulates might seem to be inappropriate, since many had 5 toes on each foot. However, features of the skeleton indicate that this was the group from which all the others evolved.

NAME: *Diacodexis*
TIME: **Early Eocene**
LOCALITY: **Europe (France), North America (Wyoming) and Asia (Pakistan)**
SIZE: **20 in/50 cm long including tail**
The earliest-known of the artiodactyls, *Diacodexis* had simple teeth, and all 5 toes were present (though as in most artiodactyls, the third and fourth were the longest). There may also have been small hooves on the toes. *Diacodexis* must have lived in forest undergrowth, browsing leaves from bushes.

Diacodexis had much the same shape and general appearance as a muntjac deer, but with short ears and a long tail. The legs, too, were relatively longer than a rabbit's, and forelimbs and hindlimbs were equal in length. This implies that *Diacodexis* ran rather than hopped and jumped. Indeed, it is the most highly-adapted running animal known from Eocene times — the joints restricted the feet to an up-and-down movement, and the foot and lower leg bones were longer than the upper.

FAMILY ANOPLOTHERIIDAE

This primitive group of artiodactyls has notoriously defied classification. It is possible its members are close to the camels.

NAME: *Anoplotherium*
TIME: **Late Eocene to Middle Oligocene**
LOCALITY: **Europe (France)**
SIZE: **3 ft 3 in/1 m high at the shoulder**
Anoplotherium was another of the tapir-shaped browsers so common in the forests of the Early Eocene. As in the other early forest-dwelling ungulates, the running habit had not developed very far. *Anoplotherium* was heavily built, with a long tail, and toenails which looked more like claws than hooves.

FAMILY ENTELODONTIDAE

These large piglike animals, which probably originated in Asia in the Late Eocene, became common in Europe and Asia, and spread into North America. They were most prolific in the Oligocene but some survived in North America until the early Miocene, about 20 million years ago. Some were massive, reaching the proportions of a hippopotamus.

A prominent feature of the entelodontids was the presence of two pairs of bony knobs protruding from the side of the lower jaw.

NAME: *Archaeotherium*
TIME: **Early Oligocene to Early Miocene**
LOCALITY: **North America (Colorado) and Asia (China, Mongolia)**
SIZE: **4 ft/1.2 m long**
Archaeotherium would have looked like a warthog with a narrow, crocodilelike head. Its skull was remarkably elongated, with long knobs of bone beneath the eyes and on the lower jaw. These protrusions may have been ornamental, or they may have anchored particularly powerful jaw muscles, used for grinding up tubers and tough roots. The arrangement of teeth suggests that, like a pig, *Archaeotherium* could eat just about anything, even scavenging on the corpses of animals.

The shoulders were high, owing to a series of long spines on the vertebrae which anchored the strong neck muscles needed to support the heavy head.

The brain itself was tiny, but it had large (olfactory) lobes associated with the sense of smell. *Archaeotherium* probably spent much of its time with its head down, snuffling and grubbing about in the soil of the Oligocene scrub for food.

HIPPOPOTAMUS GORGOPS

PLATYGONUS

RIDIOCHOERUS

NAME: **Dinohyus**
TIME: **Early to Late Miocene**
SIZE: **North America (Nebraska and South Dakota)**
SIZE: **10 ft/3 m long**

The entelodonts reached their maximum size in the omnivorous *Dinohyus* of North America. This animal was much like *Archaeotherium*, but about the size of a bull.

Although the bodily proportions were piglike, the face must have been quite different — for example, the nose was not flat, and the nostrils opened at the side of the muzzle rather than the front. Like *Archaeotherium*, *Dinohyus* fed close to the ground, its long muzzle making up for its short neck.

FAMILY ANTHRACOTHERIIDAE

The anthracotheres or "coal beasts," named for the deposits in which many have been found, may be related to the hippopotamus family. They were basically an Old World group, with many members appearing in Asia from the Eocene right up to the Pleistocene. They also migrated to North America, where they are mainly found in Oligocene deposits.

Like the hippopotamuses which many of them resemble, anthracotheres were probably chiefly aquatic animals. It is possible that one replaced the other in the same aquatic niche.

NAME: **Elomeryx**
TIME: **Late Eocene to Late Oligocene**
LOCALITY: **Europe (France) and North America (Dakota)**
SIZE: **5 ft/1.5 m long**

The hippopotamuslike *Elomeryx* had a long body and short stumpy legs, with a head which was long and superficially like that of a horse. Its teeth, however,

were quite different, with elongated canines to hook up the roots of water plants, and spoon-shaped incisors for digging in the mud.

Unlike other even-toed ungulates, in which the toes are usually reduced to 2, there were 5 toes (the first a "dew-claw") on the forefoot and 4 on the hind. Such broad feet would have been useful for walking on soft mud.

FAMILY HIPPOPOTAMIDAE

The hippopotamus family is a recent group dating from the Late Miocene. They may have evolved from the anthracotheres (*above*), whose niche as swamp-living rooters they probably took over, or possibly from fossil peccaries (*see below*).

The name of the family comes from the Greek for "river horse." Most were probably semi-aquatic, but some, like the living pygmy hippopotamus, were forest dwellers. The only other living species is the almost entirely aquatic *H. amphibius*.

NAME: **Hippopotamus**
TIME: **Late Miocene to Recent**
LOCALITY: **Asia, Africa and Europe**
SIZE: **14 ft/4.3 m long**

The only obvious differences between a *Hippopotamus gorgops* of Pleistocene East Africa and the living species *H. amphibius* were its huge size and particularly prominent eyes. These eyes probably stuck up above the skull on stalks like periscopes, which would have given the animal good panoramic vision even while its whole body was submerged.

Hippopotamus had the same familiar shape and heavy body which is more at home buoyed up in the water than it is on land, and equally broad feet for walking on mud. Its mouth, too, was wide, with characteristic huge tusks used for digging up water plants.

FAMILY TAYASSUIDAE

The tayassuids or peccaries resemble their close relatives the pigs in so many ways that it is difficult to distinguish them in the fossil record. They are readily identifiable among living suines, however, because a peccary's canines do not protrude when its mouth is closed. Their feet, too, are different, having only 2 toes (with laterals reduced) in the place of a pig's 4 toes (with little reduction in the laterals).

Living peccaries are confined to South America and the south-western states of North America, but most of the fossil forms are found in North

America, where the family evolved in the Oligocene. Fossil peccaries have also been discovered throughout Eurasia and Africa. They were, and are, versatile creatures, inhabiting a wide range of environments from virtual desert to tropical rain forest.

NAME: **Platygonus**
TIME: **Pliocene to Late Pleistocene**
LOCALITY: **North America (Great Plains) and South America**
SIZE: **3 ft 3 in/1 m long**

Platygonus was larger than modern peccaries, and had longer legs. Like them, it was basically a forest animal, yet it also inhabited the more open Great Plains region, a fact which may help to explain the elongated, running limbs.

The nose was piglike, as in modern forms, consisting of a flat disk in which the forward-pointing nostrils were set. Such a nose was ideal for snuffling about on the ground looking for food.

Platygonus was herbivorous, with a complex digestive system more like that of a cud-chewing animal than a pig's. Yet despite its diet, the canine teeth were almost those of a carnivore — long, straight and needle-sharp. It seems likely that these would have been used as weapons, perhaps chiefly for protection against big cats.

FAMILY SUIDAE

The suids, the pig family, evolved in the Old World, probably in Asia, in Oligocene times, and appeared in Europe in the Miocene. They never colonized the Americas.

Although pigs are omnivores rather than herbivores, they seem to have filled the same niches as were taken in the Americas by the peccaries. Fossil suids, like their living descendants, include animals which inhabited tropical rain forests, savannah woodlands, and even semi-aquatic environments.

NAME: **Metridiochoerus**
TIME: **Late Pliocene to Early Pleistocene**
LOCALITY: **Africa (Tanzania)**
SIZE: **5 ft/1.5 m long**

A contemporary of early humans, *Metridiochoerus* was a giant warthog of eastern Africa. Its head was heavy, and both its upper and lower canine teeth curled outward and upward to form great curved tusks. The cheek teeth were high, and had a complex pattern of cusps, indicating the omnivorous nature of its diet.

Oreodonts and early horned browsers

PROTOCERAS

BLASTOMERYX

SYNTHETOCERAS

SYNDYOCERAS

BRACHYCRUS

PROMERYCOCHOERUS

MERYCOIDODON

CAINOTHERIUM

Oreodonts and early horned browsers

SUBORDER TYLOPODA

Tylopods — the word means "padded foot" — are a broad grouping of artiodactyls (even-toad ungulates). These include Old World rabbitlike cainotheres, the New World piglike merycoidodonts and the camelids.

In many important respects, they stand midway between the suines (pigs, peccaries and hippopotamuses; *see pp. 266–269*) and the pecorans (giraffes, deer and cattle; *see pp. 278–281*). They first appeared in the Late Eocene, around 40 million years ago, and were common through the Oligocene and up to Late Miocene times, 5 million years ago. Only the camelids — the camels, llamas and their closest relatives — still survive (*see pp. 274–277*).

FAMILY CAINOTHERIIDAE

This is one of the most primitive families of the suborder. As in most primitive members of any group, the cainotheres were generalized animals, with few features to hint at the more specialized members to come. Most were rabbitlike in size, appearance and in their bounding or leaping style of locomotion.

NAME: *Cainotherium*
TIME: **Late Oligocene to Early Miocene**
LOCALITY: **Europe (Spain)**
SIZE: **1 ft/30 cm long**

Cainotherium was a small rabbitlike animal, with hind limbs longer than the front limbs. The parts of the brain associated with hearing and with smell were well developed, so it probably had long rabbitlike ears and a sensitive nose as well. It must have lived like a rabbit, too, scampering and hopping through the undergrowth, where it browsed on a variety of vegetation.

Yet it was clearly an even-toed ungulate. Even at this early stage in its evolution, the limbs were slender, with 2 toes and reduced lateral toes ending in hoofs.

Also, unlike the rabbit, it did not have particularly specialized teeth. The full number of mammalian teeth (44) were present. These formed a nearly continuous series with no gap (diastema) between front and cheek teeth. However, the back teeth were quite broad, with 5 cusps, and were well-adapted for chewing.

Cainotherium and its relatives may have competed with, and lost out to, the early rabbits and hares for the same ecological niches (*see pp. 282–285*). They were restricted to Europe and left no descendants after the early Miocene.

FAMILY MERYCOIDODONTIDAE

The suborder Tylopoda may well have evolved from the suborder Suina, as can be seen from this family which seems to combine features of pigs with those of camels. The merycoidodonts (the name means "ruminating tooth") are sometimes more euphoniously referred to as oreodonts — "mountain tooth," a reference to the terrain in which they were discovered.

A highly successful group of woodland and grassland browsers, merycoidodonts evolved in North America in the Late Eocene, around 35 million years ago; they were particularly abundant throughout the Oligocene and into the Miocene. They died out around 5 million years ago.

Members of the family may have diversified into a variety of habitats. Some fossil merycoidodonts have been found with long tails and clawed digits like those of tree-climbing animals; others have the hippopotamuslike high eyes and nostrils suited to semi-aquatic environments.

NAME: *Merycoidodon*
TIME: **Early to Late Oligocene**
LOCALITY: **North America (South Dakota)**
SIZE: **4 ft 6 in/1.4 m long**

Merycoidodon, a typical member of its family, probably looked something like a pig or peccary, but with a longer body and shorter legs. It could not have run particularly well since there was no fusion of the limb bones. Also, the lower limbs were about the same length as the upper limbs, and the feet had 4 toes.

The head, too, was piglike, but with a full complement of 44 teeth. A significant feature of the teeth is that the lower canines had taken on the appearance of incisors — a feature which would continue into the later camels and deer.

Another curious feature is a pit in the skull just in front of the eye which may have contained some kind of a gland. Modern deer have a gland here which they use to mark their territories with scent, so *Merycoidodon* may have been a similarly territorial animal.

Vast numbers of fossils of *Merycoidodon* lie in the Oligocene beds of the Badlands of South Dakota, so they probably roamed the woodlands and grasslands of the area in large herds.

NAME: *Brachycrus*
TIME: **Early and Middle Miocene**
LOCALITY: **North America (Great Plains)**
SIZE: **3 ft 3 in/1 m long**

Brachycrus was a merycoidodont that appeared quite late in North America. It was somewhat smaller than *Merycoidodon*, and considerably more specialized.

The skull and jaw were short — indeed, practically apelike — and the eye sockets faced forward. The nostrils were placed far back on the top of the skull, and this suggests that the animal had a short tapirlike trunk. *Brachycrus* may have used this trunk in sniffing out and manipulating food in the undergrowth.

NAME: *Promerycochoerus*
TIME: **Early Miocene**
LOCALITY: **North America (Oregon)**
SIZE: **3 ft 3 in/1 m long**

There are indications that some of the merycoidodonts were amphibious, pursuing a hippopotamuslike existence in the swamps and rivers of the time. *Promerycochoerus* may have been just such a semi-aquatic form since its body was particularly long and the limbs short and stumpy — features which often crop up in amphibious animals.

There were 2 principal species: *P. superbus*, which had a long tapirlike face, and *P. carrikeri*, with a short, almost piglike face.

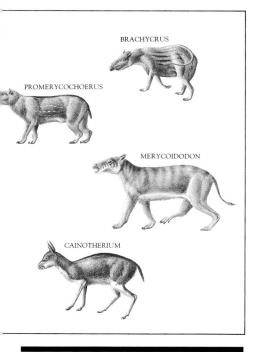

BRACHYCRUS

PROMERYCOCHOERUS

MERYCOIDODON

CAINOTHERIUM

FAMILY PROTOCERATIDAE

Protoceratids — "first horns" — were a family of about 10 genera of early animals that resembled deer but were more closely related to the camels. They inhabited the warmer, southern forests of North America for about 35 million years, from the Late Eocene to the Early Pliocene.

Their most extraordinary features are their "horns" (in fact, bony outgrowths rather than true horns), which were well-developed in males but reduced or absent in females. Some species simply manifested a variety of bumps and knobs, but others had complex forked structures. Such horns were probably organs of display rather than weapons, though later protoceratids doubtless "sparred" with their rivals.

The evolution of skull outgrowths in artiodactyls, whether horns, antlers or ossicones, relate to changes in body size, social behavior patterns and territorial structures.

Early ruminants were small, feeding on soft vegetation for which they had to range widely. They used their enlarged canine teeth for defense when necessary.

The ruminants moved out of the forests into the new scrublands that were developing, and adapted to feeding on the tougher vegetation there. With this change, the territory required to obtain food diminished in area. As territorial boundaries shrank, so the importance of defending them grew. Difference between the sexes became more pronounced, with larger, heavily armored males bearing antlers or horns defending a harem with many offspring.

Protoceratids show the beginning of these changes.

NAME: **Protoceras**
TIME: **Late Oligocene to Early Miocene**
LOCALITY: **North America (South Dakota)**
SIZE: **3 ft 3 in/1 m long**

This graceful little deerlike animal inhabited the upland woodlands of western North America. It was an early member of the family and was still quite primitive in having 4 toes on the fore feet and the hind feet.

The most remarkable and un-deerlike feature of Protoceras, and indeed all the protoceratids, was the arrangement of horns on the face. Unlike the ornamentation of deer, these were not antlers and were not shed annually. Nor could they be rightly termed "horns," since they were not covered in horn. They were actually bony outgrowths that were probably covered with skin, like the ossicones of giraffes.

Protoceras had 3 pairs of knobs — 1 just behind the nostrils, 1 above the eyes, and 1 at the top of the skull. This arrangement was only present in the males. The females possessed only the top pair, and these were somewhat smaller than in the male. This arrangement of horns was evidently some kind of display structure for use in mating or for warning away rivals. These knobs would have probably been more effective seen from the side, rather than front on.

The earliest protoceratids retained the upper incisor teeth at the front. However, by the time Protoceras evolved, these had been lost so that the lower cropping teeth worked against a bony pad in the upper jaw, just as in modern deer and cattle.

NAME: **Syndyoceras**
TIME: **Early Miocene**
LOCALITY: **North America (Nebraska)**
SIZE: **5 ft/1.5 m long**

Syndyoceras was more deerlike than its predecessor Protoceras in that the elegant running legs now had only 2 toes, each with a narrow pointed hoof.

The shape of the nasal bones suggests that the animal may have had an inflated muzzle like that of a saiga antelope. As in the other advanced proceratids there were no incisor teeth in the upper jaw. There was, however, a pair of canine tusks and these may well have been used for grubbing about on the ground in the search for food.

The head had a pair of horns at the snout and another long pair above the eyes. The snout horns were united at the base but grew forward, diverging and curling up and back. The rear pair of horns curved upward like those of cattle. These would not have been true horns and were probably covered in skin.

Whereas the horn arrangement of Protoceras would have been seen to best advantage from the side, that of Syndyoceras and the other advanced protoceratids would have been more spectacular when seen from the front. This suggests that they were used for sparring as well as for display.

NAME: **Synthetoceras**
TIME: **Late Miocene to Early Pliocene**
LOCALITY: **North America (Texas)**
SIZE: **6 ft 6 in/2 m long**

The head ornamentation of the protoceratids came to its climax in Synthetoceras, which was the latest and the largest of the family. The skull was long and shallow, and there was a pair of curving brow horns, as in Syndyoceras. However, the horn at the snout was long and Y-shaped, growing forward and upward in a strong thick shaft and forking into a pair of branches near the tip. As in the other members of the family, this flamboyant arrangement was only present in the males and was obviously used for sparring.

Like most other protoceratids, Synthetoceras browsed and grazed, probably in herds.

FAMILY TRAGULIDAE

This family seems to link the suborder Tylopoda with the pecorans — the cud-chewing family that contains the deer, the giraffes and the cattle (see pp. 278–281). Accordingly, there is much debate as to the true classification.

Always a rare group, it consists of small, hornless, deerlike animals. Only 2 species survive today, Hyemoschus, the African water chevrotain, and Tragulus, the chevrotain of south and east Asia.

NAME: **Blastomeryx**
TIME: **Early Miocene to Late Pliocene**
LOCALITY: **North America (Nebraska)**
SIZE: **2 ft 6 in/75 cm long**

This deerlike creature, not much bigger than a large rabbit, probably looked and lived like the modern chevrotains. Scampering, browsing forest animals, their canine teeth had evolved into long sharp saberlike tusks, useful for rooting up food or for defense.

Blastomeryx had no horns. However a late species from the end of the Miocene did have bony bumps on top of the skull, suggesting that horns were evolving; they also showed a reduction in the size of the tusks. This is consistent with the modern rule that deer with tusks have no horns, and vice versa.

Camels

POEBROTHERIUM

PROCAMELUS

PROTYLOPUS

STENOMYLUS

AEPYCAMELUS

CAMELOPS

OXYDACTYLUS

TITANOTYLOPUS

Camels

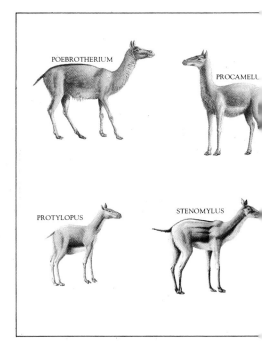

FAMILY CAMELIDAE

The modern camelids are found only where conditions are harsh. The camels are famed as "ships of the desert," capable of covering immense distances across difficult terrain in the most inhospitable of climates. Thanks to their extraordinary physiology, they can live for up to 2 months on rough grazing alone, without additional water, and can endure great changes of temperature. The South American camelids — the llamas and their relatives — are also found in challenging habitats, including that of the high Andes.

Modern camels have evolved a whole array of adaptations for coping with hot, dry environments. Most other animals, including humans, lose water steadily in hot, dry weather by sweating, panting and breathing. As a result, their blood thickens, until eventually it circulates too slowly to remove heat from the body processes via the skin, and the animal suffers a sudden and dramatic rise in temperature which soon kills it. Camels avoid this danger by having unique blood that does not thicken, and because they economize on water loss in a variety of ways.

Their thick coats protect them against becoming overheated and restrict water loss through evaporation from the skin. Their body temperature can fluctuate according to the outside temperature, so minimizing water loss through sweating. Camels also excrete very concentrated urine and dry feces, which contain very little water, and they store fat in their distinctive humps, drawing on this food reserve in times of scarcity. As they process it, the fat releases extra water. Finally, camels are able to drink remarkably quickly; they can take in as much as 25 gals/115 l of water at a single session.

It is easy, then, to think of camelids as very specialized animals that can exist only in these extreme environments. In fact the modern camels are merely the remnants of a formerly widespread and diverse group. They first evolved in Late Eocene times, about 40 million years ago, not in Asia or Africa but in North America, and reached their peak there in the Late Miocene, some 10 million years ago. It was not until the Pliocene, about 5 million years ago, that camels migrated into Eurasia and Africa, and llamas reached South America.

By the Pleistocene Ice Age, around 2 million years ago, the camelids ranged all over North America from Florida to Alaska. They had spread southward to South America across the Panama land bridge and eastward into Asia across the Bering land bridge.

Like some other animal groups that evolved chiefly in North America, such as the horses (see pp. 254–257), the camelids survive today only on other continents — they became extinct in North America toward the end of the Pleistocene, about 12,000 years ago.

There are living species of camel, the 2-humped Bactrian camel and the 1-humped Arabian camel or dromedary. Wild camels still inhabit the Gobi Desert, but the camels of Africa were introduced there by humans as recently as 2500 years ago. Camels that are now feral in Australia were brought there just over 100 years ago. In South America, the llama, alpaca, vicuña and guanaco are the only representatives of the second remaining group.

Camelids have no horns or tusks, and their jaws have a reduced number of upper incisors. The lower incisors are flattened and project forward horizontally. They have elongated facial bones, so there are wide spaces between the front teeth that are left, and a wide gap — the diastema — between the front and cheek teeth. The cheek teeth are formidably large and hypsodont — that is, they have short roots but high crowns, as in horses. Such spiky front teeth enable the camelids to rip and tear at tough vegetation, while their cheek teeth are well-suited to "chewing the cud."

Like many other artiodactyls, the camelids ruminate — a process which involves chewing the partly digested food (the "cud") before swallowing it so that it undergoes a second digestion. Unlike more advanced ruminants, such as deer or sheep, which have 4-chambered stomachs, those of camels are 3-chambered. The differences in the structure of their digestive systems suggest that they may have evolved the ruminant way of life independently from the other ruminants.

The camelids seem to have reduced the number of their toes much earlier than did most ungulate groups. Among the earliest camelids, the forelimbs had 4 toes, all of which touched the ground, but the second and fifth toes of the hind limbs were already vestigial (extremely reduced and insignificant). Indeed, the Late Miocene *Procamelus* (below) already had legs that were probably almost identical to those of a modern member of the family. The shanks were long and thin, there were 2 spreading toes on each foot, and the 2 metapodials had become elongated and fused at the top like an upside-down "Y" to form the cannon bone.

The later camelids thus walked in a characteristic way. Whereas other artiodactyls are unguligrade, walking on the tips of their hoofed digits, the later camelids are digitigrade: they have dropped down to walk on the entire underside of the splayed digits, and there is a tough pad beneath. Such developments have allowed modern camels to travel with ease across soft sand.

NAME: *Protylopus*
TIME: **Late Eocene**
LOCALITY: **North America (Utah and Colorado)**
SIZE: **20 in/50 cm long**

As in most groups of ungulates, the first camelids were small, rabbit-sized animals. The simple, low-crowned teeth were arranged along the jaw without any breaks — a primitive feature and one that indicates that the animal's diet was the soft leaves of the forest vegetation.

The forelimbs, which were shorter than the hindlimbs, had 4 toes, all of which touched the ground. The hind limbs also had 4 toes, but only the third and fourth were used to carry the animal's weight — the second and fifth toes were present as vestigial "dew claws." The functional toes were pointed, though, which indicates that the early camels had narrow hooves rather than broad pads.

It is unlikely the *Protylopus* was a direct ancestor of later camels, but it probably closely resembled, and was contemporary with, the earliest camels.

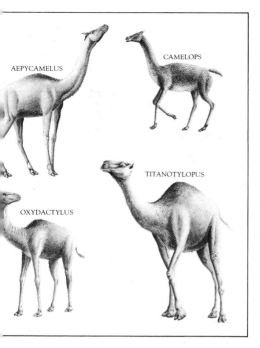

AEPYCAMELUS
CAMELOPS
TITANOTYLOPUS
OXYDACTYLUS

NAME: *Poebrotherium*
TIME: Oligocene
LOCALITY: North America (South Dakota)
SIZE: 3 ft/90 cm long

By Oligocene times, around 35 million years ago, the dense forests that once covered Dakota had given way to more open woodlands. Camelids became plentiful and began to look more like modern camels.

At about the size of a sheep, *Poebrotherium* was larger than *Protylopus*. Its head, with a distinctive narrow snout, was a smaller version of a llama's, and it may have had the llama's prominent ears as well.

Poebrotherium still had slightly longer hind legs than forelegs, and hoofed toes, yet its legs were clearly adapted for greater speed. These were relatively longer and more slender than those of *Protylopus*, they had lost their lateral toes, and the 2 central weight-bearing digits were beginning to diverge. *Poebrotherium*'s teeth, too, show an advance on *Protylopus*. Dentition is still complete but spaces were beginning to appear between the teeth. It seems likely that a number of different camelid lines radiated from *Poebrotherium*.

NAME: *Procamelus*
TIME: Late Miocene to Early Pliocene
LOCALITY: North America (Colorado)
SIZE: 5 ft/1·5 m long

Procamelus was either on the direct ancestral line to modern camels, or very close to it. It was much larger than any of the earlier camels, approaching the size of a modern llama. The head was very long but the braincase was quite small.

Procamelus still had incisors in the upper jaw, but only a single pair — and even these were reduced in size. Set in such a long jaw, the front teeth (1 pair each of incisors and canines, and the first pair of premolars) had long gaps between them — a dentition that is adapted for tearing at vegetation. Crowns on the cheek teeth had grown to such an extent that they were now hypsodont (*above*), like those of a horse, and well-adapted for dealing with tough vegetation.

With *Procamelus*, the structure of the leg had almost reached the modern camel condition. The metapodials had partially fused and elongated to form a cannon bone, the shanks were long and thin, and there were 2 spreading toes. This splaying out of the toes suggests that *Procamelus* may already have evolved a foot pad to spread the load when walking over soft terrain.

NAME: *Titanotylopus*
TIME: Pliocene to Pleistocene
LOCALITY: North America (Nebraska)
SIZE: 11 ft 6 in/3.5 m high at the shoulder

During the Pliocene, between 5 million and 2 million years ago, a number of very large camels evolved in North America. They were certainly closely related to *Procamelus* and may even have been derived from it. Among them was *Titanotylopus*, which must have been taller than the elephants of the time (*see pp. 238–245*). Otherwise, it was very similar to modern camels, with a narrow snout lacking upper incisors, a long neck and splayed 2-toed feet.

One distinctive feature of modern camels was almost certainly not present, though — their fatty hump. This is an adaptation to coping with the scarce supplies of food and water in particularly arid environments (*above*). Certainly the climate was cooling and drying throughout the Tertiary period in North America — changes which caused forests to give way to scattered woodland and then to grasslands — but it was still equable enough to support a large number of different mammals. As yet, there was no need for food-storage devices such as humps to evolve.

NAME: *Camelops*
TIME: Pleistocene
LOCALITY: North America (California and Utah)
SIZE: 6 ft 6 in/2 m high at the shoulder

Camelops, another giant of the late Cenozoic and a contemporary of early humans, appears to have been the last camel to have survived on the North American continent. It probably looked very much like the modern Asian camel, but certain parts of its anatomy indicate that it was more closely related to the South American llamas.

NAME: *Stenomylus*
TIME: Early Miocene
LOCALITY: North America (Nebraska)
SIZE: 3 ft/90 cm long

A number of side-branches of the camel family evolved in the Miocene, but became extinct soon afterward. *Stenomylus* and its relatives were small gazelle-like animals. They must have lived very much as African gazelles do today, browsing in herds on low vegetation and sprinting rapidly away from danger. The teeth of the lower jaw were unique in that the canines and the first premolars had taken the form of incisors, so the animal appeared to have 10 lower incisors. The neck was long and lightly-built, and the legs were slender. The 2 toes on each foot had small, deerlike hooves.

NAME: *Oxydactylus*
TIME: Early Miocene
LOCALITY: North America (South Dakota and Nebraska)
SIZE: 7 ft 6 in/2.3 m long

Another offshoot from *Poebrotherium* was the line of giraffelike camels with very long legs and necks — adaptations to browsing on high vegetation. The early Miocene landscape of central North America — grasslands with open scrub — must have been ideal for the evolution of such an animal. The toes were very narrow and bore slender antelopelike hooves, not the broad pads of the modern camels.

NAME: *Aepycamelus*
TIME: Middle and Late Miocene
LOCALITY: North America (Colorado)
SIZE: 10 ft/3 m high at the head

The giraffelike camel line reached its climax in *Aepycamelus*, formerly known as *Alticamelus* because of its extraordinary height. The legs were long and stiltlike, and the 2 toes had very small hooves. *Aepycamelus*, then, had lost the running hooves of its ancestors and put in their place the broad pads of modern camels.

The modern camel moves both legs on one side of the body in the same direction at the same time. This method of walking is known as pacing, and is confined to camels and giraffes. Pacing is a very efficient method of traveling great distances across open terrain. An extremely long-legged animal such as *Aepycamelus* must have moved with a similar gait. Indeed there is some direct evidence for this in camel-like footprints that have been discovered in Miocene deposits.

Giraffes, deer and cattle

PROLIBYTHERIUM

SIVATHERIUM

MEGALOCEROS

EUCLADOCEROS

ILINGOCEROS

HAYOCEROS

PELOROVIS

BOS PRIMIGENIUS

Giraffes, deer and cattle

FAMILY GIRAFFIDAE

Giraffes, like all other artiodactyls except the pigs and hippopotamuses (*see pp. 266–269*) are cud-chewers, or ruminants. There are no incisor teeth at the top of the jaw, instead the lower incisors work against a bony pad at the front of the mouth. Having ripped off foliage from bushes and trees, the animal chews and then swallows it for the first time. The food then passes into the rumen, the first chamber of a complex, 4-chambered stomach, where it is fermented by microorganisms. Once the food is partially digested, it is returned to the mouth and chewed again before its second journey back down the entire alimentary tract.

This method of digestion is very efficient at breaking down fibrous plant food, but the ruminant pays a price for this efficiency in that food takes a long time to pass through its gut, and it must spend a considerable proportion of each day chewing the cud.

There are two modern giraffes, both living in Africa south of the Sahara. The more familiar is the tall, long-necked, long-legged giraffe *Giraffa* of the African savannah, which feeds from the tops of thorn trees. The other is the smaller, darker okapi *Okapia*, at home in the gloom of the African tropical forest.

With the exception of the camels, the ruminants typically have paired head ornaments. In the case of the giraffes these take the form of hornlike growths, called ossicones, which are covered in skin.

Both the giraffe and the okapi are 2-toed browsers, the family having evolved before the grazing ungulates developed. The fossil record reveals a number of different forms, most of which were quite unlike the 2 modern representatives of the family.

NAME: ***Prolibytherium***
TIME: **Early Miocene**
LOCALITY: **North Africa (Libya)**
SIZE: **6 ft/1.8m long**
In contrast to the living giraffe and okapi, *Prolibytherium* sported broad, leaf-shaped ossicones that reached a span of about 14 in/35 cm. It probably used them for display and in sparring contests between rivals, and it is possible that their covering of skin was shed annually. Apart from its flamboyant head ornamentation, *Prolibytherium* probably resembled the modern okapi.

NAME: ***Sivatherium***
TIME: **Pliocene to Late Pleistocene**
LOCALITY: **India (sub-Himalayas) and North Africa (Libya)**
SIZE: **7 ft/2.2 m high at the shoulder**
Named for Siva, or the Lord of the Beasts, one of the principal Hindu Gods, this massive animal would have appeared more like a moose than a giraffe. The male, at least, had a pair of huge branched ossicones on the top of its skull, and a smaller pair of conical ones about the eyes. The body was quite stout, especially in the region of the shoulders, where strong muscles would have been needed to carry its huge, heavy head.

Libytherium, a close relative of *Sivatherium*, lived in North Africa at the same time. Prehistoric human rock paintings from the Sahara Desert depict an animal that looks very much like *Libytherium*, so it is possible that sivatheres coexisted with early humans until about 8000 years ago.

FAMILY CERVIDAE

Although the cervids, or true deer, were quite late to evolve they have become the principal browsing animals of the Northern Hemisphere and South America. Their diet includes leaves, grass, twigs, bark and moss.

A characteristic feature of all living cervids is the presence of antlers in the males (and in females of the reindeer *Rangifer*) of virtually all species. The exceptions are the hornless musk deer *Moschus* and Chinese water deer *Hydropotes*. Antlers are branched bony outgrowths of the head. They differ from the ornamentation of the other ruminants in that they are shed and regrown each year. They are readily distinguished from other head ornaments by the presence of a swollen "burr" at the point at which they are shed. Each year the antler develops with another branch until a maximum for each species is reached.

Cervids use their antlers chiefly in display or for ritual sparring rather than for actual fighting. The ultimate example of antler development is seen in the Pleistocene deer *Megaloceros* (*below*).

NAME: ***Eucladoceros***
TIME: **Pliocene to Pleistocene**
LOCALITY: **Europe (Italy)**
SIZE: **8 ft/2.5 m long**
Some of the deer evolved huge, flamboyant antlers. One of the most spectacular examples was *Eucladoceros*, whose antlers, each with a dozen points, or tines, had a total span of 5 ft

6 in/1.7 m. Such a spread must have been something of a disadvantage among the low branches of its forest home. As with *Megaloceros* (*below*), which had even bigger antlers, sexual selection probably sustained the development: the male that sported the most impressive antlers, and could spar most successfully in competitions for females during the breeding season, would have left the most offspring to continue his line.

NAME: ***Megaloceros***
TIME: **Late Pleistocene**
LOCALITY: **Widespread in Europe and Asia**
SIZE: **8 ft/2·5 m long**
Megaloceros is often called the giant Irish elk, but the name is doubly misleading. First, because it is not an elk (or moose) but is more akin to the fallow deer. Second, because *Megaloceros* was by no means confined to Ireland. Although many specimens have been unearthed in Ireland, with more than 80 found in a single bog near Dublin, *Megaloceros* ranged over the whole of the northern parts of the Old World, from the British Isles to Siberia and China.

The largest deer that ever lived, *Megaloceros* is chiefly known for its antlers. They were truly monumental, reaching a span of 12 ft/3.7 m and weighing over 100 lb/5 kg — about a seventh of the weight of the entire animal. Even more remarkable, perhaps, is that these horns were probably shed and regrown annually, as in all true deer. A male *Megaloceros* must have expended a great deal of energy growing such structures.

The *Megaloceros* herds reached their peak during the last interval between the cold spells of the Pleistocene Ice Age, and began to decline about 12,000 years ago. They died out in Ireland about 11,000 years ago, but may not have become extinct in Central Europe until

ILINGOCEROS

HAYOCEROS

BOS PRIMIGENIUS

PELOROVIS

about 2500 years ago.

Evidence that early humans knew and hunted *Megaloceros* is provided by cave paintings depicting animals very like *Megaloceros* in Europe. One French cave painting shows the great deer with a small triangular hump on its back, like that of modern zebu cattle. This may have been a fatty structure, like a camel's hump, which was used as a food store during the harshest periods of the Ice Age winter.

Dwarf species of *Megaloceros* are also known, from Malta.

FAMILY ANTILOCAPRIDAE

The pronghorn *Antilocapra* of North America is the only surviving genus of this family, but the Miocene and Pliocene saw the evolution of a large number of different types of antilocaprids. The other ungulates that evolved in North America — the camels and the horses — spread across to Asia and to South America and became extinct in their homeland. The antilocaprids, on the other hand, remained in North America and spread nowhere else, although they were a very successful and varied group during the Pliocene and Pleistocene periods.

Antilocaprid head ornamentation consisted of a horny sheath, usually branched, around an unbranched bony core. The sheath was shed annually but the core was retained. Most species had a single pair of horns, but others had as many as 5 or 6, and some were bizarre in shape. In the living pronghorn, males have longer horns, with forward-pointing prongs below backward-pointing hooked tips — hence the animal's common name.

Although most of the even-toed ungulates have only 2 functional toes, the others being greatly reduced and not touching the ground, it is only in the pronghorns that all vestiges of the other toes finally disappeared, not even bony splints remaining. Their evolution of long, pointed hooves at the end of long, slender legs has enabled them to be fast runners, reaching speeds of up to 55 mph (86 km/h) when escaping from predators. Their hooves are cushioned against the shock of leaping up to 26 ft/8 m in a single stride.

NAME: *Ilingoceros*
TIME: **Late Miocene**
LOCALITY: **North America (Nevada)**
SIZE: **6 ft/1.8 m long**
The various antilocaprids differ from one another in the shape and arrangement of the horns. *Ilingoceros*, which was slightly larger than the living pronghorn, had a pair of spirally-twisted horns which grew straight upward and ended in a slight fork. Other forms include *Osbornoceros*, with smooth, slightly curved horns; *Paracosoryx*, with flattened horns widening to a forked tip; *Ramoceros*, with extraordinary vertical fan-shaped horns, and the particularly well-endowed *Hayoceros* (below).

NAME: *Hayoceros*
TIME: **Middle Pleistocene**
LOCALITY: **Nebraska**
SIZE: **6 ft/1.8 m long**
Hayoceros had 4 horns: 1 pair of broad, forked horns over its eyes, as in the pronghorn, and another much longer, narrower pair farther back at the top of its skull. When 2 males competed for mating partners, they probably adopted a sparring technique similar to that of living pronghorns, which lock their forked horns and push until the weaker of the pair retires. These ritualistic bouts rarely seem to result in any permanent injury.

FAMILY BOVIDAE

These are the true antelopes and the cattle. The head ornamentation of both males and females consists of bony horn cores covered with true horn that is not shed annually.

The bovids evolved in the Old World in Miocene times about 20 million years ago. The earliest fossils, of gazellelike bovids, have been found in France, the Sahara and Mongolia. By the Late Miocene, about 10 million years ago, there was a huge increase in bovid variety, with 70 new genera appearing. By the Pleistocene, there were more than 100 genera, about twice as many as exist today.

Bovids are grazing animals, with high-crowned teeth adapted for chewing grass. Their lifestyle contrasts with most of the other even-toed ungulates, which feed on soft leaves. They were restricted to the Old World until as recently as the Mid Pleistocene, about 1 million years ago, when they migrated across the Bering land bridge that existed at the time to reach North America. There they survive today as bison, bighorn sheep and mountain goats. The vast majority of bovids, however, still live in the Old World, occupying a great range of habitats from forests and grasslands to swamps and even deserts.

NAME: *Pelorovis*
TIME: **Middle to Late Pleistocene**
LOCALITY: **East Africa**
SIZE: **10 ft/3 m long**
This massive animal was a close relative of the modern African buffalo. The main difference between it and its modern counterpart, apart from sheer size, was the enormous set of horns on its head. Since the bony cores alone had a span of 6 ft 6 in/2 m, in life the horns might have been twice that size. (This has to be an estimate since horn itself decays rapidly after death.) *Pelorovis* survived until about 12,000 years ago.

NAME: *Bos*
TIME: **Pleistocene to Recent**
LOCALITY: **Europe (Britain, Poland),**
Asia (India) and North Africa
SIZE: **10 ft/3 m long**
This is the genus to which our modern domesticated cattle belong. The ancestor of most of today's cattle was *Bos primigenius*, better known as the aurochs. It was somewhat larger than most of today's breeds and was first domesticated about 6000 years ago, although it was known to (and hunted by) humans much earlier: the famous cave paintings at Lascaux, in central France, include dramatic and beautiful representations of these great cattle.

The aurochs spread during the Pleistocene from its center of origin in Asia, and by the end of the last Ice Age it occupied a vast range in the Old World, from westernmost Europe to easternmost Asia, and from the Arctic tundras to North Africa and India.

Despite its success, however, the aurochs disappeared, succumbing to human hunting pressure. It became extinct in Britain by the 10th century AD, and the last surviving aurochsen died in Poland in 1627.

Rodents, rabbits and hares

ISCHYROMYS

EPIGAULUS

STENEOFIBER

BIRBALOMYS

EOCARDIA

TELICOMYS

PALAEOLAGUS

Rodents, rabbits and hares

Early classifications grouped together the rabbits and hares, which have 2 pairs of upper incisors, with the squirrels, rats and cavies, which have only 1. Certainly their lifestyles and anatomy are similar: all are vegetarian gnawers, and many species in both groups are adapted to life on or underneath the ground.

More recently, however, the 2 groups have been separated, in the belief that there is little relationship between them, and that any similarities are the result of an extraordinary degree of convergent evolution (*see p. 16*). However, our fossil record is still so meagre for the critical early stages of their radiation that we remain uncertain about the relationship between the two orders.

ORDER RODENTIA

The earliest-known rodents resembled small squirrels. They appeared in North America during the Late Paleocene, about 60 million years ago. Soon after, the rodents diversified, taking over niches abandoned by the disappearing multituberculates (*see pp. 198–201*). They have evolved into several major types, including squirrels, beavers, rats, guinea pigs and porcupines.

The rodents are by far the largest order of mammals today, with about 1600 species in 35 families, making up 40 percent of all known living mammals. There are almost as many fossil genera again, and another 12 families.

Rodents are a highly successful group. They have spread over every continent, except Antarctica, and conquered a huge range of habitats. Rodents can be found everywhere from tropical forests to freezing Arctic tundras, and from the hottest deserts to the mountain tops. Although they have not managed to invade the seas, there are some freshwater rodents. There are many tree-dwellers, too, notably the tree squirrels. Most rodents are, however, primarily terrestrial.

Given their versatility and impressive rate of reproduction, it is not surprising that rodents have had a major impact on human history. Some species are important crop-eating pests and carry diseases. The most notorious of these are the rats, which have probably accounted for more human deaths than all the wars in history. In the Middle Ages, plague borne by the black rat *Rattus rattus* killed around 25 million people — over a quarter of Europe's entire population.

Much of what is known about the evolution of rodents is the result of studying tiny fossil teeth. Rodents were abundant throughout the Tertiary, and their distinctive teeth can be used for dating and correlating continental sediments, just as fossils of invertebrate shells are used for dating and correlating marine sediments.

The chief distinguishing feature of rodents is their ability to gnaw using specially adapted front teeth. There is a single pair of large, curved incisors on the upper and lower jaws. These incisors are worn down with use but grow continuously from roots deep within the skull and mandible. Early members of the group had cylindrical gnawing teeth with enamel all round, but later forms had more triangular teeth with enamel confined to the front face. This keeps the edge sharp since the area behind wears down faster.

There are no canines, and even some of the premolars may be missing, so there is a large gap (diastema) between front and cheek teeth. The remaining cheek teeth form a battery of efficient grinding surfaces.

Most rodents are small, the harvest mice being among the smallest of all mammals at 1½ oz/5 g. There are exceptions, however. The largest living rodent is the 110 lb/50 kg capybara of South America, but some extinct forms reached the size of a rhinoceros.

An interesting case study of gigantism among the rodents is provided by the giant Pleistocene dormouse *Leithia*, an inhabitant of several Mediterranean islands, including Malta and Sardinia. Except for its much greater size (10 in/25 cm long without tail), *Leithia* was indistinguishable from the modern dormouse *Muscardinus*.

Having been marooned on the islands when sea levels rose (possibly the result of the influx of the Atlantic into the Mediterranean basin or changing world temperatures during the Pleistocene Ice Age), the inhabitants of Mediterranean islands showed some unusual trends in body size. But whereas elephants (*see pp. 242–245*) and hippopotamuses (*see pp. 266–269*) became smaller, to make better use of the limited amount of food that was available, rodents such as *Leithia* became larger. In the absence of potential predators, the rodents had no reason to run and hide in cracks and crannies, as their smaller counterparts had to do on the mainland.

The present classification divides the rodents into 2 suborders, differentiated by the arrangement of the bones and associated muscles of the lower jaw.

SUBORDER SCIUROGNATHI

The sciurognaths ("squirrel-jaws") have a deep lower jaw on which the chewing (masseter) muscles are attached. This is by far the larger of the 2 suborders of rodents, and possibly the more primitive. The suborder includes the present-day families of squirrels, beavers, pocket gophers, hamsters, rats and mice.

The sciurognath families seem to have diverged early in the evolutionary history of the rodents; apart from their jaw and tooth structure, they have little else in common. Most are wholly vegetarian, but some are scavenging omnivores, and a few eat insects.

A quarter of all mammal species today are rats, mice, and voles. Yet this immensely successful group only became ubiquitous at the beginning of the Pliocene, about 5 million years ago.

NAME: *Ischyromys*
TIME: **Early Eocene**
RANGE: **North America**
SIZE: **2 ft/60 cm long**

Ischyromys is among the earliest known true rodents. Mouselike in appearance, it had many typical rodent head features, including the characteristic pair of upper incisors. The rest of the body was that of a typical rodent as well, with versatile forelimbs, strong hindlimbs and 5 clawed toes on all feet.

While many of the other early Tertiary mammals were occupying the terrestrial niches, all the evidence suggests that *Ischyromys* and its more squirrel-like relative *Paramys* were taking advantage of the possibilities presented by trees. As the most advanced climbing animals of their time, they eventually displaced the primitive rodentlike primates which had existed there from Paleocene times (*see pp. 286–289*).

EOCARDIA

ELICOMYS

ALAEOLAGUS

NAME: *Epigaulus*
TIME: Miocene
RANGE: **North America (Great Basin)**
SIZE: **1 ft/30 cm long**

Epigaulus must have resembled a modern marmot, except for a pair of stout horns on the skull and long, powerful claws on the front feet. These claws are compressed from side to side — an adaptation to the digging habit.

No other known rodent had horns like these. Since it is so evidently a burrowing animal, the function of the horns is a mystery, but they may have been used for sexual display.

Epigaulus and its closest relatives died out when forests disappeared and were replaced by grassland in the Late Miocene, about 5 million years ago.

NAME: *Steneofiber*
TIME: Early Miocene
RANGE: **Europe (France, Germany)**
SIZE: **1 ft/30 cm long**

Beavers are well represented in the fossil record from as far back as the Early Oligocene, around 35 million years ago.

The early Miocene beaver *Steneofiber* was small, and lived on and near freshwater lakes, much as most living beavers do today. It is unlikely, however, that it could have felled large trees, as its modern counterparts do.

Many early species were more terrestrial, however, and some even burrowed. The Miocene deposits of Nebraska show strange vertical corkscrew-shaped burrows, 8 ft/2.5 m deep, which have been given the name "Daimonelix" or "Devil's corkscrews." These were excavated by the gopherlike beaver *Palaeocastor*, a close relative of *Steneofiber*.

Many beavers were giants, including the bear-sized *Castoroides* (7 ft 6 in/2.3 m long), found throughout North America in the Pleistocene.

SUBORDER HYSTRICOGNATHI

This is thought to be the more advanced suborder of rodents, despite the fact that the earliest known rodent probably belongs to this group. The hystricognaths or "porcupine-jaws" have their chewing (masseter) muscles anchored on a bony flange which has developed from the lower jaw.

Although hystricognaths include some Old World species — for example porcupines, and the gundis and cane rats — most are South American.

No rodents have been found in South America prior to the Early Oligocene, when they occur in the far south of Patagonia. South American hystricognaths include New World porcupines, cavies or guinea pigs, capybaras, pacaranas, chinchillas, agoutis and coypus.

NAME: *Birbalomys*
TIME: Early Eocene
RANGE: **Asia (Pakistan)**
SIZE: **1 ft/30 cm long**

Birbalomys is considered by some paleontologists to be the most primitive rodent, one which is probably close to the ancestry of the whole rodent group. So little is known about *Birbalomys* that the restoration given is highly speculative, but it may have resembled the North African gundis, creatures rather like guinea pigs which today inhabit desert or semi-desert habitats.

NAME: *Eocardia*
TIME: Miocene
LOCALITY: **South America**
SIZE: **1 ft/30 cm long**

Cavioids are the most typical South American rodents and are closely related to the guinea pigs and the capybara.

Some became quite large. *Protohydrochoerus*, for example, was about the size of a tapir, but *Eocardia* was more modest in size, and resembled the present day guinea pig in appearance.

NAME: *Telicomys*
TIME: Late Miocene to early Pliocene
RANGE: **South America**
SIZE: **7 ft/2 m long**

Closely related to the guinea pigs and capybaras were the stout-tailed burrowing dinomyids ("terrible mice"), the pacarana family. The largest of these — indeed, probably the largest rodent which has ever lived — was *Telicomys*

Telicomys reached the size of a small rhinoceros, and must have looked rather like a hairy hippopotamus or a giant capybara.

ORDER LAGOMORPHA

The lagomorphs — the pikas, rabbits, and hares — were once classed along with the rodents. Indeed, they seem to be very much like rodents, with their relatively small size and their continually growing, gnawing teeth.

The main difference between them lies in the fact that lagomorphs have 2 pairs of gnawing teeth in the front of the upper jaw, rather than the single pair possessed by the rodents. These teeth have enamel all the way around them, like the earliest but not the later rodents (which have enamel only on the front). Lagomorphs also tend to have more cheek teeth than rodents (5 or 6, as opposed to 5 or fewer), and these are usually less ridged.

The chewing action is different as well: lagomorph jaws work sideways, while those of rodents work backward and forward. The evidence that the lagomorphs are related to the rodents is ambiguous: their gnawing way of life might have developed through parallel evolution.

About 12 lagomorph genera survive today, although there have been 4 times that number since the order evolved. The earliest fossil representatives appeared, possibly in eastern Asia, in the Late Paleocene or Early Eocene.

Lagomorphs swiftly became a widespread vegetarian group, chiefly exploiting grassy plans and shrubs in rocky and desert areas. Having been deliberately introduced in the 19th century into Australasia, where there were no natural predators, the rabbits' prodigious rate of reproduction and immense appetite for leaves and grain made it a serious pest.

NAME: *Palaeolagus*
TIME: Oligocene
RANGE: **North America**
SIZE: **10 in/25 cm long**

The earliest lagomorph is *Eurymulus*, from the Late Paleocene of Mongolia. The separation of the group into the pikas on the one hand, and the rabbits and the hares on the other, had already taken place by the early Oligocene. The pikas became compact animals with short legs and short ears, while the rabbits and hares developed longer legs and a running, then finally a hopping, locomotion.

The skeleton of *Palaeolagus* is similar to that of a modern rabbit. However, the hind legs are a little shorter, suggesting that is was not yet the leaping animal so familiar today.

Lemurs and monkeys

PLESIADAPIS

NOTHARCTUS

MEGALADAPIS

NECROLEMUR

BRANISELLA

TREMACEBUS

MESOPITHECUS

THEROPITHECUS

Lemurs and monkeys

PLESIADAPIS

NOTHARCTUS

MEGALADAPIS

NECROLEMUR

ORDER PRIMATES

The term primates — from the Latin word *primus*, meaning "first" — groups together lemurs, monkeys, apes and humans, and their closest ancestors. Primates probably evolved in Paleocene times, some 60 million years ago, from an insectivore stock. Indeed, the earliest were so like insectivores that it is a matter of conjecture where the boundary is drawn (*see Purgatorius, p. 201*).

Primates seem to have developed in a predominantly forested environment. In fact, many specific adaptations can be traced to the exacting demands of tree-dwelling, and to daylight living rather than nocturnal activity. Among these were interrelated developments in the enlarged, complex brain, the senses, and the limbs and digits. There was also a tendency toward a bipedal gait: the body became more erect, the feet and legs were specialized for movement, and the hands were adapted for holding and manipulating. Balance, touch and grasp all improved, and there were 2 great developments in vision: the ability to see stereoscopically and in color.

Another critical development in such a precarious environment included a reproductive strategy that placed a premium on high parental involvement and a small number of offspring.

There are 2 suborders of primates — Prosimii and Anthropoidea.

SUBORDER PROSIMII

Prosimians form a varied group that encompasses early insectivorelike creatures, and the fossil and modern lemurs, lorises and tarsiers.

In living species, at least, the face is covered in hair, except for the nose, which extends down to the upper lip. The prosimian face is generally much less mobile and "expressive" than that of the monkeys and apes.

Another key feature of the group is the opposable thumb (or big toe). This allows greater dexterity, and in some species has greatly increased their mobility in trees. In humans, this has allowed the development of the "precision grip."

FAMILY PLESIADAPIDAE

These are the best-known of the 5 families of Plesiadapiformes. Examples are plentiful from the Paleocene and Eocene of North America and Europe (roughly 65 million to 40 million years ago), a fact which indicates both a land connection between the continents and a uniformity of conditions between these areas at this time. It is possible that plesiadapids spread from North America to Europe via Greenland, which was

at that time a warm, wooded "land bridge." Their features included a long tail, agile limbs with claws rather than nails, a long snout containing rodentlike jaws and teeth, and eyes at the sides of the head.

NAME: *Plesiadapis*
TIME: **Late Paleocene to Early Eocene**
LOCALITY: **North America (Rocky Mountains) and Europe (France)**
SIZE: **2 ft 6 in/80 cm long**
So many *Plesiadapis* remains have been found near Cernay in north-eastern France that it must have been a common animal at the time.

Plesiadapis was squirrel-like in build and about the size of a modern beaver. It may have spent much of its time on the ground, however it was also well-adapted for scrambling in trees, with hands and feet that could turn toward each other to grip branches, and long fingers and toes equipped with claws.

Nevertheless, the head was not that of a typical primate. The teeth resembled those of a rodent, with long gnawing incisors at the front, and a gap between them and the grinding molars in the cheek. This supports the notion that the rodents and primates evolved from a common stock early in the Tertiary, although there is little other evidence for this.

FAMILY ADAPIDAE

The lemurlike adapids were abundant in Eocene times, but then declined, becoming extinct in the Late Miocene about 10 million years ago. They were mostly European, but some lived in Asia and North America.

Adapids had several features that were a distinct advance on those of the plesiadapids. Their backs were more supple, which increased their mobility in trees, as did their longer, more flexible limbs (whose digits bore nails rather than claws) and grasping big toes and thumbs. They had shorter snouts, with eyes that had moved round closer to the front of the face. Their brains, too, were relatively larger. Although it is possible that adapids could only cling and leap, it seems likely that they were advanced enough to walk and run on top of branches.

The lemurlike adapids and lemurids (*below*) are sometimes grouped together as the strepsirhini ("twisted noses") becuase their moist noses are divided vertically and laterally by slits.

NAME: *Notharctus*
TIME: **Early to Middle Eocene**
LOCALITY: **North America (Wyoming)**
SIZE: **16 in/40 cm long**
This North American adapid was the last primate known from that continent. In appearance it was probably much like a modern lemur, and it was highly adapted for living in trees. It had eyes directed forward, which gave stereoscopic vision and enabled it to judge distances accurately, long hind legs that allowed it to jump from branch to branch, and a long heavy tail to balance it in its acrobatics.

The first digit in the hand and on the foot formed a kind of a thumb that enabled *Notharctus* to grasp both branches and food.

FAMILY LEMURIDAE

Lemurs are similar to the adapids, but have a long "comb" derived from the front teeth in the lower jaw, which is used for grooming.

About 50 million years ago, lemurs and their close relatives were found throughout Africa, Europe and North America. Today, the lemurs, the Indri lemurs and the aye-ayes survive only in Madagascar.

NAME: *Megaladapis*
TIME: **Recent**
LOCALITY: **Madagascar**
SIZE: **5 ft/1.5 m long**
The largest-known lemur, with a massive body and short limbs, *Megaladapis* must have weighed about 110 lb/50 kg. Unlike its smaller relatives, it would not have been able to swing and leap about in the trees. It was probably a slow climber, clambering about in the tropical forest in search of leaves to eat. It was possibly finally wiped out by humans.

FAMILY OMOMYIDAE

This is the largest family of the tarsiers, a group that still exists today (though in greatly depleted numbers) on some Southeast Asian islands such as Sumatra and Borneo. The omomyids were abundant in the Eocene but declined in the Oligocene and had virtually died out by the beginning of the Miocene.

Tarsiers are grouped together as the haplorhini (the "whole noses") because their noses are undivided.

Some paleontologists have considered that the tarsiers were the common ancestors of the monkeys and apes, though this seems unlikely given their extreme specialization.

NAME: *Necrolemur*
TIME: **Middle to Late Eocene**
LOCALITY: **Western Europe**
SIZE: **10 in/25 cm long**

Necrolemur is the best preserved fossil member of the tarsier group. It had large eyes and ears, which enabled the animal to hunt at night, and small sharp teeth which were ideal for dealing with tough-shelled insects — its main food. Its body, too, would have been similar to the living species, with gripping pads on its long fingers and toes, long agile arms and legs, and a long balancing tail.

SUBORDER ANTHROPOIDEA

The suborder Anthropoidea contains 2 infraorders — the platyrrhines ("flat noses") or New World monkeys, and the catarrhines ("downfacing noses") or Old World monkeys, apes and hominids. They evolved in North America or Eurasia around 40 million years ago. The 2 lines diverged soon after when a land bridge that linked North with South America once more disappeared.

NEW WORLD MONKEYS

The New World monkeys are distinguished from the Old World monkeys partly by their nostrils, which are placed wider apart and face outward rather than downward, and several other anatomical features, including distinctive skull joints or sutures, and the possession of one more pair of premolars. Some species have an additional "limb" in the form of a prehensile tail — one that is able to support the body by coiling around branches. Curiously, this feature never evolved in the Old World monkeys.

Modern representatives of this group include the delicate and often highly-colored marmosets and tamarins, and the spider and howler monkeys. Together they constitute about one third of modern anthropoid genera.

NAME: *Branisella*
TIME: **Early Oligocene**
LOCALITY: **South America (Bolivia)**
SIZE: **16 in/40 cm long**

This is the earliest-known monkey to have lived on the South American continent, but little can be said with confidence about *Branisella*'s lifestyle and relationships because the only fossil evidence of its existence are some fragments of jawbone. The teeth were quite primitive, with many tarsierlike features. This would suggest that it evolved from the omomyids farther north. However, some other attributes indicate that *Branisella* was quite close to the monkeys then living in Africa, so its ancestors may even have reached South America by drifting across the Atlantic from west Africa on floating islands of vegetation.

NAME: *Tremacebus*
TIME: **Late Oligocene**
LOCALITY: **South America (Argentina)**
SIZE: **3 ft 3 in/1 m long**

By the end of the Oligocene, the New World monkeys had become very much like the present day forms. *Tremacebus*, sometimes known as *Homunculus* because of its miniature humanoid form, must have resembled today's only truly nocturnal owl monkey, the douroucouli, a fruit and insect eater.

Tremacebus is known from only a few specimens, including a skull, from Patagonia. The paucity of remains in this area suggests that the plains of Patagonia were as treeless then as they are now, so there was too small a woodland environment to support any greater monkey diversity.

OLD WORLD MONKEYS

Old World monkeys, like apes and humans, differ from the New World monkeys in having nostrils that are close together and face downward, a bony canal leading from the exterior to the eardrum, and, in general, one fewer pair of premolar teeth.

Classed together in the Family Cercopithecidae, these monkeys form the largest and most primitive group of catarrhines, and include among their modern representatives guenons, baboons, macques, geladas, and the colobus monkey. Living species also have a thickened area of skin on the buttocks, which may also have been present in extinct forms.

The tail is never prehensile, and may be greatly reduced or even absent, especially in ground-living animals. The tail is still useful for tree-living monkeys, however, since it improves balance and may even allow a change of trajectory in mid-jump.

NAME: *Mesopithecus*
TIME: **Late Miocene to Late Pliocene**
LOCALITY: **Europe (Greece) and Asia (Asia Minor)**
SIZE: **16 in/40 cm long**

Mesopithecus, the "middle ape," was typical of the early cercopithecids. It was similar to the modern macaque and probably ancestral to the modern langur. It was slim, had long muscular arms and legs, and long, nimble fingers and toes. Its limbs, like those of the modern macaque, could be used both for walking on the ground and for climbing in trees, which suggests that its environment was quite open. *Mesopithecus* would have been active during the daytime rather than at night and would have eaten leaves and soft fruits.

NAME: *Theropithecus*
TIME: **Middle Pliocene to Recent**
LOCALITY: **South and East Africa**
SIZE: **4 ft/1.2 m long**

The baboons are largely ground-dwelling monkeys that travel across open plains in family groups. They generally have doglike faces and eat a wide range of foodstuffs. Although they tend to walk on all fours on the ground, they are still adept at climbing, especially among rocks. *Theropithecus* was a large baboon, remains of which have been found in the Olduvai Gorge in Tanzania. For a baboon it had a short face, and there was a large crest of bone along the top of its skull that must have held strong jaw muscles. It would have fed on tough dry-climate plant material.

Apes

OREOPITHECUS

PROPLIOPITHECUS

PLIOPITHECUS

DENDROPITHECUS

DRYOPITHECUS

SIVAPITHECUS

GIGANTOPITHECUS

RAMAPITHECUS

Apes

FAMILY OREOPITHECIDAE

The classification of the oreopithecids is problematical. Some paleontologists regard them as Old World monkeys related to *Mesopithecus* (*see p. 289*); others point to their apelike and even hominidlike attributes, such as their probable ability to brachiate (use their arms to swing from branch to branch) and even to walk upright. They are almost certainly an evolutionary blind alley, though, whose advanced features are a result of convergence. There is only 1 genus.

NAME: *Oreopithecus*
TIME: **Late Miocene**
LOCALITY: **Europe (Italy)**
SIZE: **4 ft/1.2 m tall**

Oreopithecus, the "mountain ape," has been jocularly referred to as "the abominable coalman." The name is apt for 2 reasons. First, because the remains of this animal were found in the brown coal (lignite) deposits of Tuscany in northern Italy, dated to about 14 million years ago. Second, because some of its features were almost human.

Oreopithecus had a monkey's snout, apelike brow ridges, and monkeylike ankle bones. The face was flat and small, the canines conical, and the patterns on the molar teeth resembled those of hominids. This mixture of monkey and human characteristics may be best explained by considering oreopithecines an independent lineage.

Since its remains were preserved in beds of soft brown coal, *Oreopithecus* probably lived in forested swamps by a riverside. It is likely that *Oreopithecus* survived on a diet of leaves, shoots and fruits of a wide variety of plants.

The arms were rather longer than the legs, which indicates that it spent much of its time in the trees and probably moved about by swinging under branches. The spine and hip bones suggest that it was also able to walk, or at least to lope, upright.

SUPERFAMILY HOMINOIDEA

The only living hominoids — the word means "resembling humans" — are the apes (pongids) and our own species, *Homo sapiens*. They differ from the Old World monkeys in having no tails, and arms and shoulder girdles that are designed for hanging and swinging from branches. In addition to pongids and hominids, the group includes an extinct family, the pliopithecids.

FAMILY PLIOPITHECIDAE

Although pliopithecids had some primitive features, including a long snout, a small brain case, and in some cases a tail, they are the earliest well-defined family of true apes. Advanced characteristics include apelike teeth, jaws and stereoscopic vision.

Pliopithecids almost certainly evolved in Africa, probably by the Early Oligocene, around 35 million years ago, and became extinct in the Miocene about 10 million years ago.

NAME: *Propliopithecus*
TIME: **Middle Oligocene**
LOCALITY: **Africa (Egypt)**
SIZE: **16 in/40 cm long**

In Mid-Oligocene times, about 27 million years ago, the Fayum region to the east of Cairo was not the dusty desert that it is today. The ancestral River Nile produced a swampy delta here, close to shoreline to the now-vanished Tethys sea. The forests of this delta supported a large number of tropical animal types, including several primitive apes such as *Propliopithecus* and *Aegyptopithecus*. (It is possible that both names apply to the same creature, in which case the former has priority.)

Propliopithecus was basically a quadrupedal animal, the size of a small gibbon, which ran on all fours along tree branches in much the same way as the macaques do today.

The eyes were set in well-developed sockets and pointed forward to give stereoscopic vision. The dentition was adapted for eating fruit and was apelike. *Propliopithecus* probably also ate insects and even small vertebrates.

NAME: *Pliopithecus*
TIME: **Middle to Late Miocene**
LOCALITY: **Europe (France and Czechoslovakia)**
SIZE: **1 ft/1.2 m tall**

Opinions vary among paleontologists, but it now seems unlikely that *Pliopithecus* gave rise to the gibbons, as was once thought. Nevertheless, there are distinct similarities between the 2 creatures. *Pliopithecus* was gibbon-sized, with a short face, large eyes and sharp canines. The body was long, and the limbs were equipped with long hands and feet. It may even have been able to brachiate.

On the other hand, arms and legs were much the same length (the arms are much longer in gibbons), and there is evidence of a short tail, with 10 or more vertebrae. Its stereoscopic vision may not have been perfect either, because the orbits of the eyes were not directed fully forward.

NAME: *Dendropithecus*
TIME: **Early to Middle Miocene**
LOCALITY: **East Africa (Kenya)**
SIZE: **2 ft/60 cm tall**

It is now widely thought that it was not *Pliopithecus* but its earlier relative, the slim-built *Dendropithecus* ("tree ape") that was ancestral to the gibbons. Remains of *Dendropithecus* have been dated to about 15 million to 20 million years ago.

Although it had shorter arms and a longer tail than *Pliopithecus*, and was probably no better at brachiating, *Dendropithecus* was more gibbonlike in other respects, including its diet. *Dendropithecus* almost certainly inhabited a densely-forested area and enjoyed fruit, leaves and flowers, just as the gibbon does today.

FAMILY PONGIDAE

The pongids are the fossil and living apes. They are semi-bipedal, sometimes walking on 4 feet and sometimes 2, and have no tail. Today, the pongids are restricted to tropical Africa and Southeast Asia, where 4 genera and 8 species survive. These are the gibbons, 2 species of chimpanzee, and a single species each of gorilla and orangutan.

Pongids were once much more diverse both in number of genera and in geographical distribution. The earliest members date from the Early Miocene, around 25 million years ago.

In the past, almost every new specimen of hominoid was treated as a separate genus, and given a new name. This became confusing, and certainly held back the understanding of the broad lines of hominoid evolution. It is now increasingly accepted that many of these near-people were in fact closely related, in spite of subtle differences in their anatomies, and should perhaps be thought of as members of the same

DRYOPITHECUS

SIVAPITHECUS

...OPITHECUS

RAMAPITHECUS

genus. (There are, after all, quite large anatomical differences among modern humans, too, yet we are 1 species.)

Until recent years, it was generally assumed that apes parted from the evolutionary line that resulted in australopithecines and humans (*see pp. 296–297*) around 15 to 20 million years ago. However, biochemical studies now suggest that this period may be much too long.

Detailed investigations have been carried out into our mutual immune responses, and structural differences in DNA (the genetic material incorporated in every living cell) and complex proteins such as the hemoglobin in blood corpuscles. Given certain reasonable assumptions about the spontaneous rate of change of these molecules, it would seem that gibbons only split away from the ancestral line about 10 million years ago, with the orangutan parting shortly after.

Perhaps the greatest surprise, though, lies in what these studies imply about the relationship between modern humans and chimpanzees and gorillas. Although superficially we seem so different from one another, our biochemistry is too similar for much more than 5 million to 8 million years to have elapsed since we separated.

This theory is still controversial, however, not least because fossil australopithecines have been discovered from as long ago as 3.5 million, and perhaps as long as 4 million to 5 million years ago. These seem too much like humans and too little like apes to be the product of only a few million years of evolution.

NAME: *Dryopithecus*
TIME: **Early to Late Miocene**
LOCALITY: **Europe (France and Greece), Asia (Caucasus) and Africa (Kenya)**
SIZE: **2 ft/60 cm long**

The evolutionary lines that developed into the modern apes and *Homo sapiens* may have begun with the widespread *Dryopithecus* ("tree ape") which lived about 12 million to 9 million years ago.

Dryopthecus evolved in East Africa, where the earliest remains have been found, and migrated to Europe and Asia (especially around the eastern end of the Mediterranean) when the continent of Africa fused with that of Eurasia.

The chimpanzeelike limbs show that it would have walked mostly on all fours but could also walk on 2 legs. Its wrist was more like a monkey's than an ape's, so it probably walked on the flat of its hand, rather than on its knuckles as chimpanzees do. Its head, too, was rather chimpanzeelike, but it lacked the heavy brow-ridges.

Dryopithecus was definitely a climbing, tree-living animal adapted to eating fruit, since its cheek teeth were too thinly enameled to chew tougher food such as roots or grasses. However, the environment of the time was developing into woodland mixed with open grassland, so it seems likely that *Dryopithecus* may also have moved about on the grasslands, probably in groups.

NAME: *Sivapithecus*
TIME: **Middle to Late Miocene**
LOCALITY: **Southeast Europe, Asia and Africa (Kenya)**
SIZE: **5 ft/1.5 m tall**

With its orangutanlike face, chimpanzeelike feet, and rotating wrists, *Sivapithecus* appears to be an ape in the transition period between life in the trees and life on the ground.

The evidence for this is principally found in the teeth. The canines were large and the molars had a thick covering of enamel — a dentition that is much more suited to the seeds, stems and roots that would be found on the savannah than to the leaves and fruits of the forest. It is clear that *Sivapithecus* ate drier, tougher foods than the dryopithecines could have managed. In fact, it is known that the climate was changing at that time, around 15 million to 7 million years ago. The forests were dwindling and the grasslands spreading, so it does seem likely that evolution would have promoted the animals that were adapting to these new conditions.

Since important finds were made in India, *Sivapithecus* was named for Siva, one of the principal Hindu gods, sometimes known as Lord of the Beasts.

NAME: *Gigantopithecus*
TIME: **Late Miocene to Middle Pleistocene**
LOCALITY: **Asia (China, Pakistan, India)**
SIZE: **10 ft/3 m tall**

This enormous creature, a veritable King Kong of the fossil apes, must have weighed something like 650 lb/300 kg. A close relative of *Sivapithecus*, it is known mostly from remains of jaw fragments and teeth, which were about twice the breadth of the teeth of a modern gorilla. They first came to the attention of scientists when a paleontologist saw 4 single molars in a Hong Kong drugstore in the 1930s. Some complete lower jaws were discovered in the 1950s.

Gigantopithecus was a ground-dwelling ape, something like a gorilla in appearance, but with a shorter jaw and relatively small incisors and canines. It probably ate roots, tubers and seeds, but also small vertebrates.

Gigantopithecus certainly lived until Pleistocene times, about 1 million years ago, and perhaps until more recently. Indeed, it has been surmised that *Gigantopithecus* is not extinct even now, but still survives in the foothills and passes of the Himalayas, where it is occasionally sighted and identified as the Yeti.

NAME: *Ramapithecus*
TIME: **Middle to Late Miocene**
LOCALITY: **Asia (Pakistan) and Africa (Kenya)**
SIZE: **4 ft/1.2 m tall**

Ramapithecus — named for Rama, the Hindu god of chivalry and virtue — was another close relative of *Sivapithecus*; indeed, some paleontologists believe they may have been synonymous. It was a little smaller in stature, and more definitely ground-dwelling, than *Sivapithecus*. The teeth were robust, with a large surface area, set in a deep, short jaw — features which indicate a diet of tough, grassland plants.

Like chimpanzees, *Ramapithecus* could have walked upright and so been able to see over tall grasses and wade across rivers. Bipedalism also freed its hands for other purposes. There is even evidence of tool-using and the formation of groups.

The teeth shared some features with those of modern apes, but have others which make them similar to those of modern humans. These findings have led to the widely-held belief that *Ramapithecus* was the common ancestor of both apes and humans, and that the 2 lines diverged about 15 million years ago. Genetic evidence, however, suggests that the point of divergence was in fact much more recent.

Humans

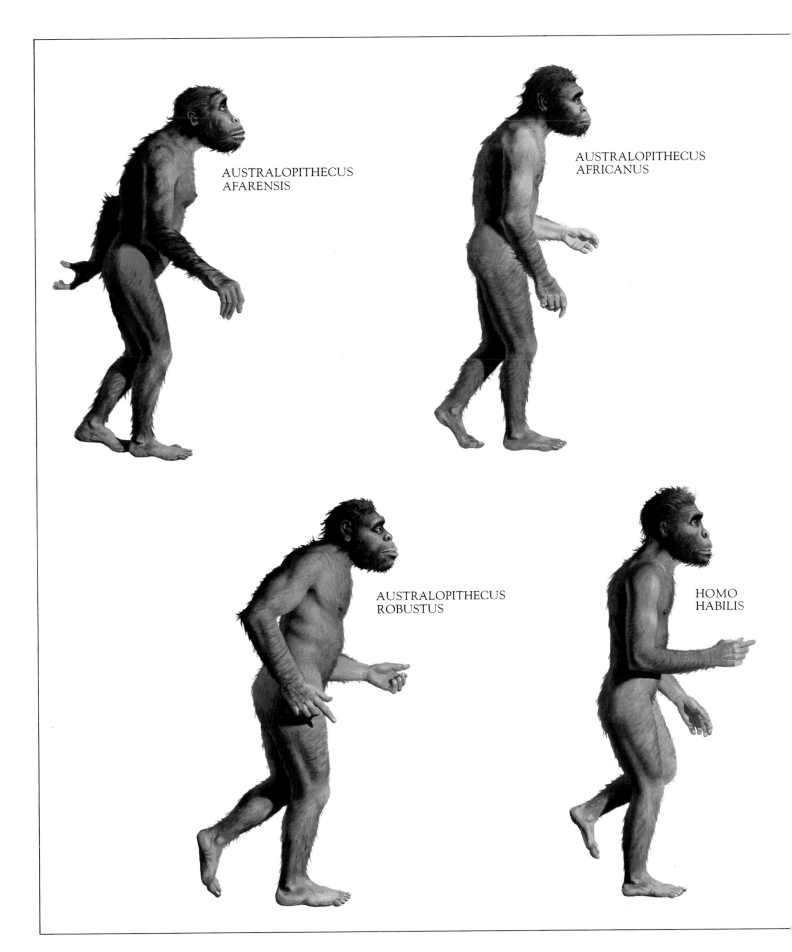

AUSTRALOPITHECUS
AFARENSIS

AUSTRALOPITHECUS
AFRICANUS

AUSTRALOPITHECUS
ROBUSTUS

HOMO
HABILIS

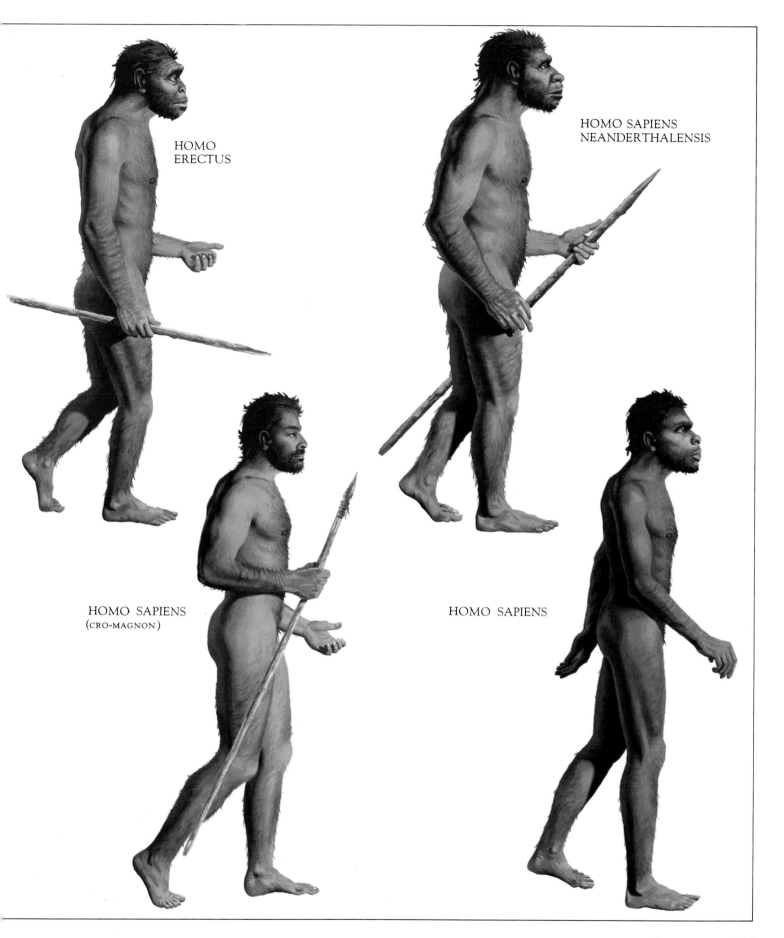

HOMO
ERECTUS

HOMO SAPIENS
NEANDERTHALENSIS

HOMO SAPIENS
(CRO-MAGNON)

HOMO SAPIENS

Humans

Although many different names have been coined in the last 100 years for the vast array of hominid fossils that have come to light, today only 2 genera of fossil hominids are recognized — *Australopithecus* ("southern ape") and *Homo* ("Man" or "human").

The key features of human evolution, or "hominization," on which attention has focused include physical but also cultural developments. In fact, as hominization has proceeded, differences in anatomy have been of less significance than changes in way of life, use of the environment, and interpersonal relations.

Physical developments have included changes in locomotion and posture, notably upright stance, bipedal locomotion, legs longer than arms, diminished big toes; the growth of the pelvis and of the birth canal to accommodate larger-headed (larger-brained) babies; increased manual dexterity, due to lengthened thumbs, and the "precision grip" — the ability to hold small objects delicately between thumb and forefinger; and modifications of the head.

Compared with less highly evolved primates, hominids have smaller jaws and teeth, flatter faces and more thickly enameled teeth. They have lost the ridges of bone over the eyes and the crest on the top of the skull, but their brains are larger relative to the rest of the body, and their brains are more complex.

Cultural developments have included the formation of groups, cooperative work, tool-making, the harnessing of fire, the making of sculpture and painting, and burial rites.

Each development should be seen not in isolation but as existing in a complex feedback relationship with the others. For example, the freeing of the hands from use in locomotion makes possible greater facility in the production of tools. This, in turn, encourages increased hand-eye coordination and the development of the brain.

But tool-use also puts a premium on improvements in child-rearing, social organization and communication. A long-term social group which prolongs infant care and supports its members throughout adulthood is more capable of acquiring, sharing and accumulating experience. Groups which cooperate intimately are also likely to use tools better, and to improve their design and manufacture.

Unfortunately, many crucial cultural developments — such as language and social structure — do not fossilize; we can only hazard guesses from those activities which leave traces, for example evidence of burial rites. And

precisely because we have such a selective record to go on, great caution must be exercised in interpretation.

It is easy to let prejudice color the picture of the past. On the whole, it is only hard objects which survive, so a lot is known about stone tools and almost nothing about tools made of animal and plant materials, such as leather and braided fiber bags and baby slings. This could lead to misunderstanding, not only of the nature of our ancestors' diet but even their social life — if hunting is emphasized, for instance, and the possible significance of foraging for plants ignored.

NAME: *Australopithecus afarensis*
TIME: **Mid Pliocene**
LOCALITY: **Africa (Ethiopia and Tanzania)**
SIZE: **around 4 ft/1.2 m tall**

The earliest known hominid, dating from around 3.5 million years ago, was *Australopithecus afarensis* — the "southern ape from Afar." The partial skeletons of this hominid, from the Afar Triangle in northern Ethiopia, match a slightly earlier series of footprints in volcanic ash near Laetoli in Tanzania. When it was excavated in 1974, the first skeleton was nicknamed "Lucy" after a song by the Beatles.

The adults were small — not much larger in height and weight than a 6-year-old child today. The skull and face were not unlike a chimpanzee's, with prominent brow ridges, but the brain was a little larger (about 400 cc). Lucy's teeth were chipped in front, probably the result of using them to grip with.

The hips were quite narrow — which implies that babies were born with relatively smaller heads and brains than modern ones — but otherwise quite humanlike. The legs, too, signify that Lucy was fully bipedal; she walked upright, albeit with a slight stoop, and with very little of the chimpanzee's lurching gait. The footprints confirm that the feet were essentially the same as modern human feet, but without a ball at the base of the big toe. Lucy would have walked flat-footed, with the toes slightly curled in.

The combination of ape and human features makes A. *afarensis* a likely ancestor of the later humans, but the absolute dating of the remains — an important part of the study of human evolution — has been something of a problem. Geological evidence suggests that they are about 3.5 million years old. Lucy and her closest relatives probably became extinct about 2.5 million years ago, having given rise to later australopithecines and modern humans.

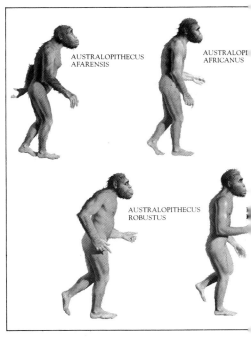

AUSTRALOPITHECUS AFARENSIS

AUSTRALOPI AFRICANUS

AUSTRALOPITHECUS ROBUSTUS

NAME: *Australopithecus africanus*
TIME: **Late Pliocene**
LOCALITY: **African (Ethiopia, Kenya, South Africa, Tanzania)**
SIZE: **4 ft 4 in/1.3 m tall**

The skull of an infant specimen of A. *africanus* — "southern ape of Africa" — was unearthed in the Transvaal in 1924. It was largely disregarded by anthropologists of the time, who thought that human origins lay with another fossil found some years earlier in Piltdown in southern England. This latter fossil, which appeared to possess a large brain, was later proved to be a fake.

A. *africanus* is now rightly regarded as a hominid; one which lived from about 3 million to about 1 million years ago. Even if A. *africanus* was not our direct ancestor, it was certainly very close. The brain was small by modern standards, being about the same size as a chimpanzee's (up to 400 cc), and the face still had heavy, apelike jaws. The canines were reasonably large, but in other respects the teeth were quite human.

Like A. *afarensis*, it was a slightly-built creature, weighing about 65 lb/30 kg, which walked upright. More important than its overall appearance, though, was its lifestyle. Some have claimed that it had moved from woodland to open savannah, and had already developed tools and cooperative hunting techniques, with a gang of individuals hunting down and killing a single animal or chasing away another hunting animal from its kill. Others argue that the evidence is equivocal. The bone "tools" are so ill-formed that they are probably nothing more than the remains of a hyena's meal.

Although hunting was probably significant in human evolution, it is likely that plants — including seeds, nuts, fruit, leaves, stems and roots — formed the major part of the diet.

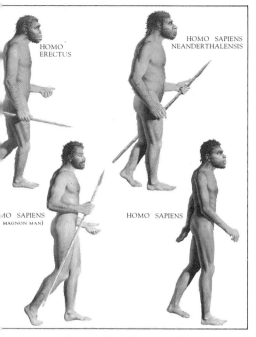

HOMO
ERECTUS

HOMO SAPIENS
NEANDERTHALENSIS

...O SAPIENS
...MAGNON MAN)

HOMO SAPIENS

NAME: _Australopithecus robustus_
TIME: Late Pliocene to Early
  Pleistocene
LOCALITY: Africa (South Africa and
  Tanzania)
SIZE: 5 ft 4 in/1.6 m tall
A probable sideline of human evolution, A. _robustus_ was a very large species of "southern ape" that emerged around 2.5 million years ago, and died out about a million years ago.

Apart from its relatively large build (it was still only about 110 lb/50 kg), the main difference between A. _robustus_ and the other species was its apelike face, massive jaws, and larger brain (about 500cc).

Like its relatives, A. _robustus_ seems to have left the forests and taken up a plains-dwelling existence. Almost certainly exclusively vegetarian, A. _robustus_ was the hunted rather than the hunter, since most of the best preserved skeletons come from carcasses that were killed by carnivores. A broken skull of A. _robustus_ has been found with teeth marks that match up exactly to the teeth of a leopard.

The very large jaws of A _robustus_ were powered by strong muscles anchored to a crest over the top of the skull, giving rise to one of the early vernacular names for this creature — "nutcracker".

NAME: _Homo habilis_
TIME: Early Plestocene
LOCALITY: Africa (Ethiopia, Kenya,
  Tanzania, possibly South Africa)
  and possibly Southeast Asia
SIZE: 4 to 5 ft/1·2 m to 1.5 m
By about 2 to 1.5 million years ago, several hominids existed alongside one another in East Africa. Some were close enough to modern humans to be classed in the genus _Homo._

Homo habilis was still quite short and light, with less massive jaws and brow

ridges. Its head too was larger than that of its predecessors, as was its brain (up to about 800 cc). The brain was also more complex — there is even some evidence from its structure that H. _habilis_ could speak.

However, the distinctive feature of H. _habilis_, or "handy human," is that it is the first hominid known to have fabricated tools. These mostly consisted of pebbles with a makeshift blade chipped out along one edge — other primates, for example _Ramapithecus_ (_pp._ 292–295), probably used unmodified pebbles. There is also evidence of simple shelters, scavenging and hunting of game.

NAME: _Homo erectus_
TIME: Early to Middle Pleistocene
LOCALITY: Africa (Tanzania, South
  Africa and Algeria), Europe
  (Germany, Spain, France, Greece
  and Hungary) and Asia (Java and
  China)
SIZE: about 5 ft 4 in/1.6 m tall
H. _erectus_, or "upright human," was an outstandingly successful creature. Having evolved around 1.6 million years ago, it saw the extinction of all other hominids, including its possible ancestors A. _afarensis_ or A. _africanus_, and survived until about 200,000 years ago.

In bodily appearance, posture and gait, H. _erectus_ must have been very similar to a modern human, although a little shorter. At 950 to 1200 cc, the brain volume, too, was approaching the modern size, and areas of the brain associated with speech are well-developed. The head, however, still had heavy apelike eyebrow ridges and protruding jaws.

H. _erectus_ was evidently a wandering gatherer and hunter, moving about in groups but also creating settlements; a site in the south of France provides evidence of huts with brushwood walls supported on a framework of poles and anchored by stones. Tools were sophisticated, and included spears, projectiles, blades, scrapers and choppers made from wood, stone, antler and bone. H. _erectus_ also used fire for cooking and for defense.

About half a million years ago, H. _erectus_ left its birthplace in Africa and spread throughout the tropical, subtropical and temperate parts of the Old World. Remains have been found in so many places that a multitude of confusing common and scientific names have been applied, including Java and Pekin (Beijing) people, _Pithecanthropus_ ('ape human") _Sinanthropus_ ("China human") and _Palaeanthropus_ ("old human"). All are now placed together in the same species.

NAME: _Homo sapiens neanderthalensis_
TIME: Late Pleistocene
LOCALITY: Europe (Mediterranean
  region) and Asia (Israel)
SIZE: up to 5 ft 7 in/1.7 m tall
H. _sapiens neanderthalensis_, the "wise person from the valley of the River Neander," is named for a site in Germany where skeletons were discovered in 1856. Many fossils have been discovered from Gibraltar and North Africa in the west, throughout the Near East, and east to central Asia.

Neandertal people evolved around 250,000 years ago. They were very successful during the warm periods toward the end of the Pleistocene Ice Age, but probably died out around 30,000 years ago. Although they may have interbred with later, more advanced migrants from Africa, it now seems more likely that they represent a side-branch of the human family.

Their bodies were short and powerfully built, they had large hands and joints, and a rather broad head, a flat or bulbous nose, and prominent eyebrows. The brain capacity, often in excess of 1400 cc, was in fact on average greater than that of modern humans.

Neandertal people were highly sophisticated, with a well-developed tool technology. They also show the beginnings of what has been thought of as a religious culture. For example, they buried the dead and clearly treated the cave bear, _Ursus spelaeus_ (see _p. 217_), with reverence.

NAME: _Homo sapiens "Cro-Magnon"_
TIME: Late Pleistocene to Recent
LOCALITY: Worldwide
SIZE: 5 ft to 6 ft/1.5 m to 1.8 m tall
The modern subspecies of H. _sapiens_ is well known throughout the world from about 35,000 years ago. Artefacts and cave paintings found in central France, dating from about 30,000 years ago, testify to their cultural sophistication.

These remains of "Cro-Magnon people" suggest that they had a strong tribal system, made tools, gathered plant materials, hunted, fished and possibly herded animals, and built shelters and manufactured clothing that enabled them to survive the last stages of the Pleistocene Ice Age.

Soon afterward, about 10,000 years ago, peoples in many different parts of the world independently developed a farming lifestyle. Animals were domesticated, crops planted, a more sedentary lifestyle developed, and populations grew. Thereafter the ability to modify the natural environment has led _Homo sapiens_ to the dominant position it currently enjoys.

Glossary

ADAPTATION: modification in the structure, physiology, development, behavior, etc of an organism which makes it better able to follow a particular way of life — eg to live in a particular environment, feed on a particular diet, etc.

ADAPTIVE RADIATION: the evolution of an ancestral stock into divergent forms (species, families etc) adapted to distinct lifestyles or *ecological niches*, eg primitive shrewlike mammals evolved into organisms as varied in structure and habitat as bats, whales and humans.

ADVANCED (of a feature of an animal): more modified, specialized, complex forms. Opposite of *primitive*.

ANAL: related to the anus, eg anal fin.

ATROPHY: to wither away; become a useless *vestige*.

BIPEDAL (locomotion): capable of standing, walking or running on 2 legs. See also *quadrupedal*.

BRACHIATE: to move through the trees by swinging from branch to branch using the hands.

CALCIFICATION: deposition of calcium phosphate and other salts, which stiffen *cartilage* and form *bone*.

CANINE ("dog" or "eye") tooth: conical mammal tooth between the *incisors* and *premolars*; well-developed and sharp for piercing prey among eg dogs, sabertooth cats, but absent or *vestigial* in many herbivores. There is a pair in each jaw in both the milk set of teeth and the adult set.

CARNASSIAL TEETH: upper and lower cheek teeth modified into meat-shearing blades in eg cats, dogs.

CARNIVOROUS: animal that eats the flesh of vertebrate animals, See also *scavenger*, *insectivorous*.

CARPAL: see *pentadactyl limb*.

CARTILAGE: gristly, flexible material that makes up the skeleton in many fish. It is also present in more advanced animals in the embryo and in bone joints. May become stiffened by *calcification*.

CAUDAL: related to the tail, eg caudal fin.

CERVICAL: related to the neck.

CHEEK TEETH: teeth lying in the cheek region of the jaw, eg mammalian *premolars* and *molars*.

CLASS: a level of grouping of similar organisms. A class contains 1 or more *orders*; similar classes form a *phylum*.

COLONIZATION: the "invasion" of a new habitat or *ecological niche*. May displace existing animals, eg North American mammals caused extinction of many South American species when Panama landbridge was established.

CONTINENTAL DRIFT: see *plate tectonics*.

CONVERGENT EVOLUTION: the phenomenon whereby 2 distantly-related animals evolve the similar structures in response to the same environmental pressures, eg the wings of bats, birds and pterosaurs. Compare with *parallel evolution*.

COPROLITE: fossilized animal droppings.

CRANIAL: related to the skull.

CROWN: the exposed part of a tooth, normally coated with *enamel*.

CUSP: high point on a mammalian tooth; the number and pattern of cusps is characteristic of a family, etc.

DENTICLE: pointed scales of many cartilaginous fishes; may be covered in *enamel*.

DENTITION: set of teeth.

DIAPHRAGM: sheetlike muscle and tendons separating the *thorax* from the abdomen; only found in mammals. Its movement helps draw air into the lungs and expel it.

DIASTEMA: a natural gap in a row of teeth; often seen in herbivores, such as that between the *incisors* and the *cheek teeth* of a rodent or horse, where it separates functions of biting from chewing.

DIGIT: see *pentadactyl limb*.

DIGITIGRADE: walking on the underside of fingers or toes, as in cat or dog, rather than flat of hand/foot. See also *plantigrade* and *unguligrade*.

DISTAL: away from point of attachment, usually away from body. Opposite of *proximal*.

DORSAL: related or near to the back or upper part of the body.

ECOLOGICAL NICHE: a particular "role" played, or position occupied, by an organism in its environment; determined by such factors as type of food, predators and tolerance of climatic conditions. Ecological niches tend to be exclusive, with no 2 closely-related species occupying the same niche in a particular area. However, the same niche in different areas may be filled by different species. See also *adaptation*.

ENAMEL: the hard layer that covers the crown of teeth and *denticles*; mostly calcium salts.

ENVIRONMENT: the sum total of all the factors — climatic, geological, biological, etc — in which a creature lives.

FAMILY: a level of grouping of similar organisms. A family contains 1 or more *genera*; similar families form an *order*.

FEMUR: see *pentadactyl limb*.

FIBULA: see *pentadactyl limb*.

GENERALIZED (of an organism): showing few specific *adaptations* to a particular *ecological niche*. A generalized organism tends to be similar to its remote ancestors. See also *primitive* and *advanced*.

GENUS (plural, genera): a level of grouping of similar organisms. A genus contains 1 or more *species*; similar genera form a *family*. The first of an organism's 2 scientific names refers to its genus, the second to its species. Eg the genus *Homo* includes species such as *Homo habilis* as well as the modern human *Homo sapiens*.

GONDWANALAND: see *plate tectonics*.

HERBIVOROUS: animal which eats plant matter only, vegetarian.

HOOF: massively-enlarged toenail adapted to take the weight of ungulates; made of *keratin*.

HORN: tough substance made of the protein *keratin*. A bony projection of the skull is properly called a horn if it is covered with horn (eg in cow), but those that lack a horny covering are called antlers (eg in deer) or *ossicones* (eg in giraffe). The "horn" of a rhinoceros is made of compacted hair.

HYPERDACTYLY: condition in which there are more than the usual number of digits, as in an ichthyosaur's paddle.

HYPERPHALANGY: condition in which there are more than the usual number of joints in the digit, as in a plesiosaur's paddle.

ICE AGE: a period of time in which climates are colder than usual and extensive areas of lowland are covered by permanent snow and glaciers. The last Ice Age took place during the Pleistocene — in the last 2 million years or so — but several others occurred throughout time. Often interrupted by relatively warmer periods called interglacials.

IGNEOUS: rock formed from molten material from deeper layers of the Earth.

INCISORS: the cutting teeth at the front of a mammal's mouth.

INSECTIVOROUS: animal which eats invertebrate animals, eg insects, worms.

KERATIN: strong fibrous protein occurring in outermost skin layers of vertebrates. Forms nails, claws, *hoofs*, feathers, hair and outer coating of *horn*.

LATERAL: related to the side of an organism.

LAURASIA: see *plate tectonics*.

LIGAMENT: An elastic fibrous tissue that joins bones together at a joint. Helps restrict their movement to prevent dislocation.

LITHOGRAPHIC LIMESTONE: fine-textured sedimentary rock from the Jurassic period found in southern Germany and formerly used in printing. Fossils preserved in it, eg *Archaeopteryx*, show a great deal of minute detail.

MAMMARY GLAND: a skin gland of female mammals specialized to produce milk.

MANDIBLE: lower jaw.

MAXILLA: the largest of the tooth-bearing bones of the upper jaw.

MEMBRANE: a thin sheet of tissue.

METACARPAL: see *pentadactyl limb*.

METAMORPHIC ROCK: rock transformed by heat and pressure.

METATARSAL: see *pentadactyl limb*.

MILK DENTITION: the first of a mammal's 2 sets of teeth. Includes no *molars*.

MOLARS: the back teeth of a mammal, usually adapted, eg for grinding, crushing or meat-shearing. Not present in *milk dentition*.

NATURAL SELECTION: according to Charles Darwin and most biologists today, the principal mechanism of evolution.

Emphasizes the importance of genetic mutation and hence variation in populations, and different rates of survival and reproduction consequent on possession of those variations. If a variation enables an organism to survive and leave more offspring, and the variation is inherited, the variation will tend to increase in the population.

OMNIVOROUS: animal able to eat material of plant or animal origin.

OPPOSABLE (of the thumb, etc): able to be brought up to meet or touch the tips of the rest of the digits; eg to grasp an object between big toe and other toes, as among chimps, or to grip an object between thumb and forefinger.

ORBIT: cavity in vertebrate skull which houses the eyeball.

ORDER: a level of grouping of similar organisms. An order contains 1 or more *families*; similar orders form a *class*.

OSSICONE: "horn" found among giraffes and possibly some fossil species, consisting of a bony core permanently covered in skin.

OSSIFICATION: formation of bone; involves *calcification*.

OVIPAROUS: animal which lays eggs. See also *viviparous*.

PALATE: the plate of bone at the roof of the mouth. See also *secondary palate*.

PALEONTOLOGIST: scientist who studies animal and plant life of the past.

PANGAEA: see *plate tectonics*.

PARALLEL EVOLUTION: the independent development of similar shapes or behavior in closely related organisms in response to similar environmental pressures. See also *convergent evolution*.

PECTORAL: related to the shoulders .

PELVIC: related to the hips.

PENTADACTYL LIMB: (literally "5 fingers"); basic structure of forelimb and hindlimb found among *tetrapods*. Consists of single bone in upper limb (humerus or femur), 2 bones in lower limb (radius and ulna, or tibia and fibula), 5 joint bones in wrist or ankle (carpals or tarsals), 5 rodlike bones in palm or sole (metacarpals and metatarsals) and digits (fingers or toes). Digits are made up of small bones arranged end-to-end, the phalanges. May be modified to fewer or more than 5 digits in course of *adaptive radiation*.

PHALANGES: see *pentadactyl limb*.

PHYLUM (plural, phyla): a level of grouping of similar organisms. A phylum contains one or more *classes*; similar phyla form a Kingdom.

PLACENTAL MAMMALS: the females of placental (eutherian) mammals nourish the fetus indirectly, through a placenta; the blood systems of mother and fetus never mix. All living mammals, except monotremes and some marsupials.

PLANTIGRADE: walking on the flat of the foot, as in humans. See also *digitigrade* and *unguligrade*.

PLATE TECTONICS ("continental drift"): the large-scale slow movements of the surface of the Earth resulting from convection currents circulating heat from its hot liquid core to the surface. Movement involves the generation and destruction of the floor of the oceans. It may also cause the fragmentation of landmasses.

250 million years ago there was probably a single "super continent" — Pangaea — which broke up into Laurasia and Gondwanaland. Laurasia, the northern landmass, further fragmented into North America, Europe and Asia (except India). Gondwanaland, the southern landmass, broke up into Africa, Antarctica, Australasia, South America and India.

Drifting landmasses may also collide and join up, throwing up mountain chains, eg the Himalayas were formed at the junction of the Indian subcontinent (from Gondwanaland) and Asia (from Laurasia).

PREMOLARS: mammalian teeth situated between the *molars* and the *canines*. May be enlarged or "molarized" for grinding, or simplified for meat-shearing. Unlike molars, they are present in the *milk teeth*.

PRIMITIVE (of a feature of an animal): having changed little from the condition in its ancestor. Opposite of *advanced*.

PROBOSCIS: a tubelike muscular extension of the nostrils, eg elephant's trunk, adapted to forage, grasp, suck water etc.

PROXIMAL: situated on the same side as the point of attachment; usually towards the body. Opposite of *distal*.

QUADRUPEDAL: habitually walking on 4 legs. See also *bipedal*.

RADIUS: see *pentadactyl limb*.

SACRAL VERTEBRAE: vertebrae attaching the backbone to the hips.

SCAPULA: bone in the shoulder girdle, the shoulder blade.

SCAVENGER: animal that eats the flesh of animals which it has not itself killed. See *carnivorous*.

SCUTE: a plate of bone or horn embedded in the skin.

SECONDARY PALATE: a sheet of bone that separates the mouth from the nasal passage.

SEDIMENTARY ROCK: rock laid down, usually in water, composed of particles that have been eroded from existing rocks. Sometimes incorporates material of organic origin, e.g. shells. See *lithographic limestone*.

SPECIALIZED, SPECIALIZATION: to become adapted to a particular lifestyle and habitat; to become restricted to a specific *ecological niche*.

SPECIES: a group of organisms which can interbreed and produce viable, fertile young. Similar species form a *genus*.

STEREOSCOPIC VISION: ability to judge depth and distance; having both eyes pointed forward and able to focus on an object.

STERNUM: breast bone of vertebrates, to which most ribs are attached.

STRATUM (plural, strata): layer of rock, etc. distinct from adjacent layers.

SUPERCONTINENT: see *plate tectonics*.

TARSUS: see *pentadactyl limb*.

TENDON: cord or band of strong tissue connecting muscle to bone or to other muscles.

TETRAPOD: 4-footed animal; characterized by *pentadactyl limbs*. Includes amphibians, reptiles, birds and mammals.

THORAX, THORACIC: region of vertebrate body containing heart, lungs, etc; the "chest."

ULNA: see *pentadactyl limb*.

UNGULIGRADE: walking on the tips of the toes, which bear thickened *hoof*, as in horses or cattles. See also *digitigrade* and *plantigrade*.

VENTRAL: related to the lower surface of an organism.

VERTEBRAL COLUMN, VERTEBRAE: chain of bones or cartilage surrounding spinal cord.

VESTIGIAL (of an organ): small, undeveloped, with little or no obvious function; diminished from its former state, as in the lateral toes of modern horses and the human appendix.

VIVIPAROUS: bearing live young that have been nourished by a placental connexion to the mother. See *placental mammal*.

Classification of vertebrates

The fossil vertebrate animals described in this book are grouped together in the following classification. The listings are not arranged in evolutionary sequence; the reader can refer to the evolutionary charts at the beginning of each main section in the book to see the relationships between groups.

This classification scheme is intended to show the reader to which group a particular animal belongs. In most cases, the animals are classified to family level, and arranged alphabetically for ease of reference.

The precise position of a few animals is as yet undecided. They are shown as, for example, "Order uncertain" or "Family uncertain."

FISHES *(see pp. 18–45)*

CLASS AGNATHA (jawless fishes)
SUBCLASS PTERASPIDOMORPHI
ORDER HETEROSTRACI: *Arandaspis, Drepanaspis, Doryaspis, Pteraspis*
ORDER THELODONTIDA: *Thelodus*
SUBCLASS CEPHALASPIDOMORPHI
ORDER OSTEOSTRACI: *Boreaspis, Dartmuthia, Hemicyclaspis, Tremataspis*
ORDER ANASPIDA: *Jamoytius, Pharyngolepis*

CLASS CHONDRICHTHYES (cartilaginous fishes)
SUBCLASS ELASMOBRANCHII (sharks, skates and rays)
ORDER CLADOSELACHIDA: *Cladoselache*
ORDER SYMMORIIDA: *Cobelodus, Stethacanthus*
ORDER XENACANTHIDA: *Xenacanthus*
ORDER EUSELACHII: *Hybodus, Tristychius*
ORDER NEOSELACHII: *Scapanorhynchus, Sclerorhynchus, Spathobathis*
SUBCLASS HOLOCEPHALI (chimaeras or ratfish)
ORDER CHIMAERIDA: *Deltoptychius, Ischyodus*

CLASS ACANTHODII (spiny sharks)
ORDER CLIMATIIFORMES: *Climatius*
ORDER ACANTHODIFORMES: *Acanthodes*

CLASS PLACODERMI (armored fishes)
ORDER RHENANIDA: *Gemuendina*
ORDER PTYCTODONTIDA: *Ctenurella*
ORDER ARTHRODIRA: *Coccosteus, Dunkleosteus, Groenlandaspis*
ORDER ANTIARCHI: *Bothriolepis*
ORDER UNCERTAIN: *Palaeospondylus*

CLASS OSTEICHTHYES (bony fishes)
SUBCLASS ACTINOPTERYGII (rayed-finned fishes)
ORDER PALAEONISCIFORMES: *Canobius, Cheirolepis, Moythomasia, Palaeoniscum, Platysomus, Saurichthys*
ORDER PERLEIDIFORMES: *Perleidus*
ORDER SEMIONOTIFORMES: *Dapedium, Lepidotes*
ORDER PYCNODONTIFORMES: *Pycnodus*
ORDER ASPIDORHYNCHIFORMES: *Aspidorhynchus*
ORDER TELEOSTEI: *Berycopsis, Enchodus, Eobothus, Hypsidoris, Hypsocormus, Leptolepis, Pholidophorus, Protobrama, Sphenocephalus, Thrissops*
SUBCLASS SARCOPTERYGII (lobe-finned fishes)
SUPERORDER CROSSOPTERYGII
ORDER ONYCHODONTIDA: *Strunius*
ORDER POROLEPIFORMES (rhipidistians): *Gyroptychius, Holoptychius*
ORDER OSTEOLEPIFORMES (rhipidistians): *Eusthenopteron, Osteolepis*
ORDER ACTINISTIA (coelacanths): *Macropoma*
SUPERORDER CHOANATA
ORDER DIPNOI (lungfishes): *Dipnorhynchus, Dipterus, Griphognathus*

AMPHIBIANS *(see pp. 46–57)*

CLASS AMPHIBIA
SUBCLASS LABYRINTHODONTIA
ORDER ICHTHYOSTEGALIA
  Family Ichthyostegidae: *Ichthyostega*
ORDER UNCERTAIN: *Crassigyrinus*
ORDER TEMNOSPONDYLI
  Family Colosteidae: *Greererpeton*
  Family Eryopidae: *Eryops*
  Family Dissorophidae: *Cacops, Platyhystrix*
  Family Peltobatrachidae: *Peltobatrachus*
  Family Capitosauridae: *Paracyclotosaurus*
  Family Plagiosauridae: *Gerrothorax*
ORDER ANTHRACOSAURIA
  Family Eogyrinidae: *Eogyrinus*
  Family Seymouridae: *Seymouria*

SUBCLASS LEPOSPONDYLI
ORDER AISTOPODA
  Family Ophiderpetontidae: *Ophiderpeton*
  Family Phlegethontiidae: *Phlegethontia*
ORDER NECTRIDEA
  Family Keraterpetontidae: *Diplocaulus, Keraterpeton*

ORDER MICROSAURIA
  Family Pantylidae: *Pantylus*
  Family Microbrachidae: *Microbrachis*

Modern amphibian orders
ORDER URODELA (newts and salamanders)
  Family Karauridae: *Karaurus*
ORDER PROANURA (early frogs and toads)
  Family Protobatrachidae: *Triadobatrachus*
ORDER ANURA (modern frogs and toads)
  Family Ascaphidae: *Vieraella*
  Family Palaeobatrachidae: *Palaeobatrachus*

CLASS AND ORDER UNCERTAIN
  Family Diadectidae: *Diadectes*

REPTILES *(see pp. 58–89)*

CLASS REPTILIA
SUBCLASS ANAPSIDA
ORDER CAPTORHINIDA
  Family Protorothyrididae: *Hylonomus*
  Family Captorhinidae: *Labidosaurus*
  Family Procolophonidae: *Hypsognathus*
  Family Pareiasauridae: *Elginia, Pareiasaurus, Scutosaurus*
  Family Millerettidae: *Milleretta*
ORDER MESOSAURIA
  Family Mesosauridae: *Mesosaurus*

SUBCLASS TESTUDINATA
ORDER CHELONIA (turtles, tortoises and terrapins)
SUBORDER PROGANOCHELYDIA
  Family Proganochelyidae: *Proganochelys*
SUBORDER PLEURODIRA
  Family Pelomedusidae: *Stupendemys*
SUBORDER CRYPTODIRA
  Family Meiolaniidae: *Meiolania*
  Family Testudinidae: *Testudo*
  Family Protostegidae: *Archelon*
  Family Trionychidae: *Paleotrionyx*

SUBCLASS UNCERTAIN
ORDER PLACODONTIA
  Family Placodontidae: *Placodus*
  Family Cyamodontidae: *Placochelys*
  Family Henodontidae: *Henodus*
ORDER PLESIOSAURIA
  Family Plesiosauridae: *Plesiosaurus*
  Family Cryptocleididae: *Cryptoclidus*
  Family Elasmosauridae: *Elasmosaurus, Muraenosaurus*
  Family Pliosauridae: *Kronosaurus, Liopleurodon, Macroplata, Peloneustes*

SUBCLASS DIAPSIDA
ORDER UNCERTAIN
Family Claudiosauridae: *Claudiosaurus*
ORDER NOTHOSAURIA
Family Nothosauridae: *Ceresiosaurus, Lariosaurus, Nothosaurus*
Family Pistosauridae: *Pistosaurus*
ORDER ICHTHYOSAURIA
Family Shastasauridae: *Cymbospondylus, Shonisaurus*
Family Mixosauridae: *Mixosaurus*
Family Ichthyosauridae: *Ichthyosaurus, Ophthalmosaurus*
Family Stenopterygiidae: *Stenopterygius*
Family Leptopterygiidae: *Eurhinosaurus, Temnodontosaurus*
ORDER ARAEOSCELIDA
Family Petrolacosauridae: *Petrolacosaurus*
Family Araeoscelididae: *Araeoscelis*
ORDER UNCERTAIN
Family Coelurosauravidae: *Coelurosauravus*
ORDER CHORISTODERA
Family Champsosauridae: *Champsosaurus*
ORDER THALATTOSAURIA
Family Thalattosauridae: *Thalattosaurus*
ORDER EOSUCHIA
Family Tangasauridae: *Hovasaurus, Thadeosaurus*

SUPERORDER LEPIDOSAURIA
ORDER SPHENODONTA (tuataras)
Family Sphenodontidae: *Planocephalosaurus*
Family Pleurosauridae: *Pleurosaurus*
ORDER SQUAMATA (snakes and lizards)
SUBORDER LACERTILIA (lizards)
Family Kuehneosauridae: *Kuehneosaurus*
Family Ardeosauridae: *Ardeosaurus*
Family Varanidae: *Megalania*
Family Mosasauridae: *Platecarpus, Plotosaurus*
Family Dolichosauridae: *Pachyrhachis*
SUBORDER SERPENTES (snakes)

RULING REPTILES (see pp. 90–169)

INFRACLASS ARCHOSAUROMORPHA
ORDER PROTOROSAURIA
Family Protorosauridae: *Protorosaurus*
Family Tanystropheidae: *Tanystropheus*
ORDER RHYNCHOSAURIA
Family Rhynchosauridae: *Hyperodapedon*

SUPERORDER ARCHOSAURIA
ORDER THECODONTIA (thecodontians)

SUBORDER PROTEROSUCHIA
Family Proterosuchidae: *Chasmatosaurus*
Family Erythrosuchidae: *Erythrosuchus*
SUBORDER RAUISUCHIA
Family Rauisuchidae: *Ticinosuchus*
SUBORDER PHYTOSAURIA
Family Phytosauridae: *Rutiodon*
SUBORDER AETOSAURIA
Family Stagonolepididae: *Stagonolepis*
SUBORDER ORNITHOSUCHIA
Family Euparkeriidae: *Euparkeria*
Family Ornithosuchidae: *Ornithosuchus*
Family Lagosuchidae: *Lagosuchus*
SUBORDER UNCERTAIN: *Longisquama*

ORDER CROCODYLIA (crocodiles)
SUBORDER SPHENOSUCHIA
Family Saltoposuchidae: *Terrestrisuchus*
Family Sphenosuchidae: *Gracilisuchus*
SUBORDER PROTOSUCHIA
Family Protosuchidae: *Protosuchus*
SUBORDER MESOSUCHIA
Family Teleosauridae: *Teleosaurus*
Family Metriorhynchidae: *Metriorhynchus*
Family Bernissartiidae: *Bernissartia*
SUBORDER EUSUCHIA
Family Crocodylidae: *Deinosuchus, Pristichampsus*

ORDER PTEROSAURIA (pterosaurs)
SUBORDER RHAMPHORHYNCHOIDEA
Family Dimorphodontidae: *Dimorphodon*
Family Eudimorphodontidae: *Eudimorphodon*
Family Rhamphorhynchidae: *Anurognathus, Rhamphorhynchus, Scaphognathus, Sordes*
SUBORDER PTERODACTYLOIDEA
Family Dsungaripteridae: *Dsungaripterus*
Family Pterodaustriidae: *Pterodaustro*
Family Pterodactylidae: *Cearadactylus, Pterodactylus*
Family Ornithocheiridae: *Pteranodon, Quetzalcoatlus*

ORDER SAURISCHIA ("lizard-hipped" dinosaurs)
SUBORDER THEROPODA
INFRAORDER COELUROSAURIA
Family Podokesauridae: *Coelophysis, Procompsognathus, Saltopus*
Family Coeluridae: *Coelurus*
Family Compsognathidae: *Compsognathus*
Family Ornithomimidae: *Dromiceiomimus, Elaphrosaurus, Gallimimus, Ornithomimus, Struthiomimus*
Family Deinocheiridae: *Deinocherius*
Family Oviraptoridae: *Oviraptor*
Family Saurornithoididae: *Saurornithoides, Stenonychosaurus*
Family Baryonychidae: *Baryonyx*
INFRAORDER DEINONYCHOSAURIA
Family Dromaeosauridae: *Deinonychus, Dromaeosaurus, Saurornitholestes, Velociraptor*

INFRAORDER CARNOSAURIA
Family Megalosauridae: *Dilophosaurus, Eustreptospondylus, Megalosaurus, Proceratosaurus, Teratosaurus*
Family Allosauridae: *Allosaurus, Yangchuanosaurus*
Family Ceratosauridae: *Ceratosaurus*
Family Spinosauridae: *Acrocanthosaurus, Spinosaurus*
Family Tyrannosauridae: *Albertosaurus, Alioramus, Daspletosaurus, Tarbosaurus, Tyrannosaurus*
SUBORDER SAUROPODOMORPHA
INFRAORDER PROSAUROPODA
Family Anchisauridae: *Anchisaurus, Efraasia, Thecodontosaurus*
Family Plateosauridae: *Massospondylus, Mussaurus, Plateosaurus*
Family Melanorosauridae: *Riojasaurus*
INFRAORDER SAUROPODA
Family Cetiosauridae: *Barapasaurus, Cetiosaurus*
Family Brachiosauridae: *Brachiosaurus*
Family Camarasauridae: *Camarasaurus, Euhelopus, Ophistocoelicaudia*
Family Diplodocidae: *Apatosaurus (=Brontosaurus), Dicraeosaurus, Diplodocus, Mamenchisaurus*
Family Titanosauridae: *Alamosaurus, Saltasaurus*

ORDER ORNITHISCHIA ("bird-hipped" dinosaurs)
SUBORDER ORNITHOPODA
Family Fabrosauridae: *Echinodon, Lesothosaurus, Scutellosaurus*
Family Heterodontosauridae: *Heterodontosaurus, Pisanosaurus*
Family Pachycephalosauridae: *Homalocephale, Pachycephalosaurus, Prenocephale, Stegoceras*
Family Hysilophodontidae: *Dryosaurus, Hypsilophodon, Othnielia, Parksosaurus, Tenontosaurus, Thescelosaurus*
Family Iguanodontidae: *Callovosaurus, Camptosaurus, Iguanodon, Muttaburrasaurus, Ouranosaurus, Probactrosaurus, Vectisaurus*
Family Hadrosauridae: *Anatosaurus, Bactrosaurus, Corythosaurus, Edmontosaurus, Hadrosaurus, Hypacrosaurus, Kritosaurus, Lambeosaurus, Maiasaura, Parasaurolophus, Prosaurolophus, Saurolophus, Shantungosaurus, Tsintaosaurus*
SUBORDER STEGOSAURIA
Family Stegosauridae: *Kentrosaurus, Stegosaurus, Tuojiangosaurus, Wuerhosaurus*
SUBORDER ANKYLOSAURIA
Family Scelidosauridae: *Scelidosaurus*
Family Nodosauridae: *Hylaeosaurus, Panoplosaurus, Nodosaurus, Polacanthus, Sauropelta, Silvisaurus, Struthiosaurus*
Family Ankylosauridae: *Ankylosaurus, Euoplocephalus, Saichania, Talarurus*

Classification of vertebrates

SUBORDER CERATOPIA
   Family Psittacosauridae: *Psittacosaurus*
   Family Protoceratopidae: *Bagaceratops,*
     Leptoceratops, Microceratops,
     Montanoceratops, Protoceratops
   Family Ceratopidae: *Anchiceratops,*
     Arrhinoceratops, Centrosaurus,
     Chasmosaurus, Pachyrhinosaurus,
     Pentaceratops, Styracosaurus, Torosaurus,
     Triceratops

MAMMAL-LIKE REPTILES
(see pp. 182–193)

SUBCLASS SYNAPSIDA
ORDER PELYCOSAURIA
   Family Ophiacodontidae: *Archaeothyris,*
     Ophiacodon
   Family Ceasidae: *Casea*
   Family Edaphosauridae: *Edaphosaurus*
   Family Sphenacodontidae: *Sphenacodon,*
     Dimetrodon
   Family uncertain: *Varanosaurus*

ORDER THERAPSIDA
SUBORDER EOTITANOSUCHIA
   Family Phthinosuchidae: *Phthinosuchus*
SUBORDER DINOCEPHALIA
   Family Titanosuchidae: *Titanosuchus*
   Family Tapinocephalidae: *Moschops*
SUBORDER GORGONOPSIA
   Family Gorgonopsidae: *Lycaenops*
SUBORDER DICYNODONTIA
   Family Galeopsidae: *Galechirus*
   Family Cistecephalidae: *Cistecephalus*
   Family Robertiidae: *Robertia*
   Family Dicynodontidae: *Dicynodon*
   Family Kannemeyeriidae: *Kannemeyeria*
   Family Lystrosauridae: *Lystrosaurus*
SUBORDER THEROCEPHALIA
   Family Ericiolacertidae: *Ericiolacerta*
SUBORDER CYNODONTIA
   Family Procynosuchidae: *Procynosuchus*
   Family Galesauridae: *Thrinaxodon*
   Family Cynognathidae: *Cynognathus*
   Family Traversodontidae: *Massetognathus*
   Family Tritylodontidae: *Oligokyphus*

BIRDS *(see pp. 170–181)*

CLASS AVES
SUBCLASS ARCHAEORNITHES
   Order Archaeopterygiformes:
     Archaeopteryx
SUBCLASS ENANTIORNITHES
SUBCLASS ODONTORNITHES
   Order Ichthyornithiformes: *Ichthyornis*
   Order Hesperornithiformes: *Hesperornis*
SUBCLASS NEORNITHES
   Order Struthiornithiformes: *Aepyornis,*
     Dinornis, Emeus
   Order Columbiformes: *Raphus*
   Order Ciconiformes: *Argentavis,*
     Harpagornis, Limnofregata,
     Osteodontornis, Palaelodus, Pinguinus

   Order Gruiformes: *Diatryma,*
     Neocathartes, Phorusrhacus
   Order Anseriformes: *Presbyornis*

MAMMALS *(see pp. 194–297)*

CLASS MAMMALIA
SUBCLASS PROTOTHERIA
ORDER TRICONODONTA
   Family Morganucodontidae:
     Megazostrodon
ORDER MULTITUBERCULATA
   Family Haramiyidae: *Haramiya*
   Family Ptilodontidae: *Ptilodus*
ORDER MONOTREMATA **(platypus, spiny
  anteaters)**

SUBCLASS THERIA
INFRACLASS TRITUBERCULATA
ORDER PANTOTHERIA
   Family Dryolestidae: *Crusafontia*

INFRACLASS METATHERIA
ORDER MARSUPIALIA **(marsupials)**
SUBORDER DIDELPHOIDEA
   Family Didelphidae: *Alphadon*
   Family Borhyaenidae: *Borhyaena,*
     Cladosictis
   Family Thylacosmilidae: *Thylacosmilus*
   Family Argyrolagidae: *Argyrolagus*
   Family Necrolestidae: Necrolestes
SUBORDER DIPROTODONTA
   Family Thylacoleonidae: *Thylacoleo*
   Family Macropodidae: *Procoptodon*
   Family Diprotodontidae: *Diprotodon*
   Family Palorchestidae: *Palorchestes*

INFRACLASS EUTHERIA
ORDER PROTEUTHERIA
   Family Zalambdalestidae: *Zalambdalestes*

COHORT EDENTATA
   Family Metacheiromyidae:
     Metacheiromys
ORDER XENARTHRA **(armadillos, sloths,
  anteaters)**
   Family Dasypodidae: *Peltephilus*
   Family Glyptodontidae: *Doedicurus*
   Family Megalonychidae: *Hapalops*
   Family Megatheriidae: *Megatherium*
   Family Mylodontidae: *Glossotherium*
   Family Myrmecophagidae: *Eurotamandua*
ORDER PHOLIDOTA
   Family Manidae: *Eomanis*

COHORT EPITHERIA
SUPERORDER INSECTIVORA **(hedgehogs,
shrews, moles)**
ORDER LEPTICTIDA
   Family Pseudorhyncocyonidae:
     Leptictidium
ORDER LIPOTYPHLA
   Family Palaeoryctidae: *Palaeoryctes*

SUPERORDER ANAGALIDA
ORDER ANAGALIDA
   Family Anagalidae: *Anagale*

SUPERORDER GLIRES
ORDER LAGOMORPHA **(rabbits, hares)**
   Family Leporidae: *Palaeologus*
ORDER RODENTIA **(squirrels, rats, beavers)**
SUBORDER SCIUROGNATHI
   Family Paramyidae: *Ischyromys*
   Family Mylagaulidae: *Epigaulus*
   Family Castoridae: *Steneofiber*
   Family Ctenodactylidae: *Birbalomys*
SUBORDER HYSTRICOGNATHI
   Family Dinomyidae: *Telicomys*
   Family Eocardiidae: *Eocardia*

SUPERORDER ARCHONTA
ORDER DERMOPTERA **(flying lemurs)**
   Family Plagiomenidae: *Planetetherium*
ORDER CHIROPTERA **(bats)**
   Family Icaronycteridae: *Icaronycteris*
ORDER PRIMATES **(lemurs, monkeys, apes
  and humans)**
SUBORDER PROSIMII
   Infraorder Plesiadapiformes
     Family Paromomyidae: *Purgatorius*
     Family Plesiadapidae: *Plesiadapis*
   Infraorder Strepsirhini
     Family Adapidae: *Notharctus*
     Family Lemuridae: *Megaladapis*
   Infraorder Haplorhini
     Family Omomyidae: *Necrolemur*
SUBORDER ANTHROPOIDEA
   Infraorder Platyrrhini
     Family Cebidae: *Branisella*
     Family Atelidae: *Tremacebus*
   Infraorder Catarrhini
     Superfamily Cercopithecoidea
     Family Cercopithecidae: *Mesopithecus,*
       Theropithecus
     Family Oreopithecidae: *Oreopithecus*
     Superfamily Hominoidea
     Family Pliopithecidae: *Dendropithecus,*
       Pliopithecus, Propliopithecus
     Family Pongidae **(great apes)**:
       Dryopithecus, Gigantopithecus,
       Ramapithecus, Sivapithecus
     Family Hominidae **(humans)**:
       Australopithecus, Homo

SUPERORDER FERAE
ORDER CREODONTA **(creodonts)**
   Family Hyaenodontidae: *Hyaenodon*
   Family Oxyaenidae: *Sarkastodon*
ORDER CARNIVORA **(true carnivores)**
SUBORDER FISSIPEDA
   Superfamily Miacoidea
     Family Miacidae: *Miacis*
   Superfamily Feloidea **(cats, mongooses)**
     Family Viverridae: *Kanuites*
     Family Hyaenidae: *Ictitherium,*
       Percrocuta
     Family Felidae: *Dinofelis, Eusmilus,*
       Homotherium, Megantereon,
       Nimravus, Panthera, Smilodon
   Superfamily Canoidea **(dogs, bears,
   pandas)**
     Family Mustelidae: *Potamotherium*
     Family Canidae: *Canis, Cerdocyon,*
       Cynodesmus, Hesperocyon, Osteoborus,
       Phlaocyon

Family Procyonidae: *Chapalmalania,*
  Plesictis
Family Amphicyonidae: *Amphicyon*
Family Ursidae: *Agriotherium,*
  Hemicyon, Ursus
SUBORDER PINNIPEDIA (seals, sealions, walruses)
  Superfamily Phocoidea (eared seals)
    Family Phocidae: *Acrophoca*
  Superfamily Otarioidea (fur seals and sealions)
    Family Enaliarctidae: *Enaliarctos*
    Family Desmatophocidae:
      Desmatophoca
    Family Odobenidae (walruses):
      Imagotaria
    Family Otariidae

SUPERORDER UNGULATA (hoofed mammals or ungulates)
ORDER ARCTOCYONIA (condylarths)
  Family Arctocyonidae: *Chriacus*
  Family Didolodontidae: *Didolodus*
ORDER TAENIODONTA
  Family Stylinodontidae: *Stylinodon*
ORDER PANTODONTA
  Family Coryphodontidae: *Coryphodon*
ORDER TILLODONTIA
  Family Esthonychidae: *Trogosus*
ORDER DINOCERATA
  Family Uintatheriidae: *Eobasileus*
ORDER EMBRITHOPODA
  Family Arsinoitheriidae: *Arsinoitherium*

ORDER ARTIODACTYLA (even-toed ungulates)
SUBORDER SUINA (pigs, peccaries, hippopotamuses)
  Family Dichobunidae: *Diacodexis*
  Family Entelodontidae: *Archaeotherium,*
    Dinohyus
  Family Suidae: *Metridiochoerus*
  Family Tayassuidae: *Platygonus*
  Family Anthracotheriidae: *Elomeryx*
  Family Hippopotamidae: *Hippopotamus*
SUBORDER TYLOPODA (oreodonts, camels)
  Family Merycoidodontidae: *Brachycrus,*
    Merycoidodon, Promerycochoerus
  Family Cainotheriidae: *Cainotherium*
  Family Protoceratidae: *Protoceras,*
    Syndyoceras, Synthetoceras
  Family Camelidae: *Aepycamelus,*
    Camelops, Oxydactylus, Poebrotherium,
    Procamelus, Protylopus, Stenomylus,
    Titanotylopus
SUBORDER RUMINANTIA (deer, giraffes, cattle)
  Family Moschidae: *Blastomeryx*
  Family Cervidae: *Eucladoceros,*
    Megaloceros
  Family Giraffidae: *Prolibytherium,*
    Sivatherium
  Family Antilocapridae: *Hayoceros,*
    Illingoceros
  Family Bovidae: *Bos, Pelorovis*

ORDER ACREODI
  Family Mesonychidae: *Andrewsarchus*

ORDER CETACEA (whales, dolphins, porpoises)
SUBORDER ARCHAEOCETI
  Family Protocetidae: *Pakicetus, Protocetus*
  Family Basilosauridae: *Basilosaurus,*
    Zygorhiza
SUBORDER ODONTOCETI (toothed whales)
  Family Squalodontidae: *Prosqualodon*
  Family Eurhinodelphidae: *Eurhinodelphis*
SUBORDER MYSTICETI (baleen whales)
  Family Cetotheriidae: *Cetotherium*

ORDER PERISSODACTYLA (odd-toed ungulates)
SUBORDER CERATOMORPHA (tapirs, rhinoceroses)
  Family Helaletidae: *Heptodon*
  Family Hyrachyidae: *Hyrachyus*
  Family Tapiridae: *Miotapirus*
  Family Hyracodontidae: *Hyracodon,*
    Indricotherium
  Family Amynodontidae: *Metamynodon*
  Family Rhinocerotidae: *Coelodonta,*
    Elasmotherium, Teleoceras, Trigonias
SUBORDER ANCYLOPODA
  Family Chalicotheriidae: *Moropus*
SUBORDER HIPPOMORPHA (horses, brontotheres)
  Family Palaeotheriidae: *Palaeotherium*
  Family Equidae: *Anchitherium,*
    Hipparion, Hippidion, Hyracotherium,
    Merychippus, Mesohippus, Parahippus
  Family Brontotheriidae: *Brontops,*
    Brontotherium, Dolichorhinus,
    Embolotherium, Eotitanops
ORDER HYRACOIDEA
  Family Pliohyracidae: *Kvabebihyrax*

SUPERORDER MERIDIUNGULATA (South American hoofed mammals)
ORDER LITOPTERNA
  Family Proterotheriidae: *Diadiaphorus,*
    Thoatherium
  Family Macraucheniidae: *Macrauchenia,*
    Theosodon
ORDER NOTOUNGULATA
SUBORDER NOTIOPROGONIA
  Family Notostylopidae: *Notostylops*
SUBORDER TOXODONTA
  Family Isotemnidae: *Thomashuxleya*
  Family Homalodotheriidae:
    Homalodotherium
  Family Leontiniidae: *Scarrittia*
  Family Notohippidae: *Rhynchippus*
  Family Toxodontidae: *Adinotherium,*
    Toxodon
SUBORDER TYPOTHERIA
  Family Interatheriidae: *Protypotherium*
SUBORDER HEGETOTHERIA
  Family Hegetotheriidae: *Pachyrukhos*
ORDER ASTRAPOTHERIA
  Family Astrapotheriidae: *Astrapotherium*
  Family Trigonostylopidae: *Trigonostylops*
ORDER PYROTHERIA
  Family Pyrotheriidae: *Pyrotherium*

SUPERORDER TETHYTHERIA
ORDER PROBOSCIDEA
SUBORDER MOERITHERIOIDEA
  Family Anthracobunidae: *Moeritherium*
SUBORDER DEINOTHERIOIDEA
  Family Deinotheriidae: *Deinotherium*
SUBORDER ELEPHANTOIDEA (elephants, mastodonts, mammoths)
  Family Gomphotheriidae: *Amebelodon,*
    Anancus, Cuvieronius, Gomphotherium,
    Phiomia, Platybelodon, Stegomastodon
  Family Mammutidae: *Mammut*
  Family Elephantidae: *Elephas,*
    Mammuthus
ORDER SIRENIA (dugongs, manatees)
  Family Prorastomidae: *Prorastomus*
  Family Dugongidae: *Rytiodus,*
    Hydrodamalis
ORDER DESMOSTYLIA
  Family Desmostylidae: *Desmostylus*

Bibliography

GENERAL

Augusta, J., Burian, Z. (1960) *Prehistoric Animals* Spring Books, UK

Carroll, R. L. (1988) *Vertebrate Paleontology and Evolution* Freeman, USA

Colbert, E. H. (1974) *Wandering Lands and Animals* Hutchinson, UK; (1973) E. P. Dutton, USA

Hublin, J. (1982) *The Hamlyn Encyclopaedia of Prehistoric Animals* Hamlyn, UK & USA

Hutchinson, P. (1974) *Evolution Explained* David & Charles, UK

Lambert, D. (1985) *The Cambridge Field Guide to Prehistoric Life* Cambridge University Press, UK

McFarland, W. N., Pough, F. H., Cade, T. J., Heiser, J. B. (1979) *Vertebrate Life* Collier Macmillan, UK; Macmillan, USA

Patterson, C. (1978) *Evolution* British Museum (Natural History), UK

Romer, A. S. (1974) *The Vertebrate Story* University of Chicago Press, USA

Spinar, Z. V., Burian, Z. (1962) *Life Before Man* Thames & Hudson, UK; McGraw-Hill, USA

Sprague de Camp, L. & C. C. (1985) *The Day of the Dinosaur* Bonanza Books, USA

Steel, R., Harvey, A. P. (Eds) (1979) *The Encyclopaedia of Prehistoric Life* Mitchell Beazley, UK; McGraw-Hill, USA

FISHES

Moy-Thomas, J. A., Miles, R. S. (1971) *Paleozoic Fishes* Chapman & Hall, UK

Saxon, J. *The Fossil Fishes of the North of Scotland* Caithness Books, UK

REPTILES

Colbert, E. H. (1965) *The Age of Reptiles* Weidenfeld & Nicolson, UK

Rowe, S. R., Sharpe, T., Torrens, H. S. (1981) *Ichthyosaurs: A History of Fossil Sea Dragons* National Museum of Wales, Cardiff, UK

RULING REPTILES

Bakker, R. T. (1986) *The Dinosaur Heresies* Morrow, USA; Penguin, UK

Charig, A. J. (1979) *A New Look at the Dinosaurs* Heinemann, UK

Colbert, E. H. (1986) *Dinosaurs: An Illustrated History* Hammond, USA

Desmond, A. J. (1975) *The Hot Blooded Dinosaurs* Blond & Briggs, UK

Edmonds, W. (1979) *The Iguanodon Mystery* Kestrel Books, UK

Glut, D. (1982) *The New Dinosaur Dictionary* Citadel, USA

Halstead, L. B. & J. (1981) *Dinosaurs* Blandford, UK

Kurtén, B. (1968) *The Age of Dinosaurs* Weidenfeld & Nicolson, UK; McGraw-Hill, USA

Lambert, D. (1983) *Collins Guide to Dinosaurs* Collins, UK; *A Field Guide to Dinosaurs* Avon Books, USA

Moody, R. T. J. (1977) *A Natural History of Dinosaurs* Hamlyn, UK

Norman, D. (1985) *The Illustrated Encyclopaedia of Dinosaurs* Salamander, UK

Swinton, W. E. (1967) *Dinosaurs* (3rd ed) British Museum (Natural History), UK (1970) *The Dinosaurs* Allen & Unwin, UK

Tweedie, M. (1977) *The World of Dinosaurs* Weidenfeld & Nicolson, UK

Wilford, J. N. (1985) *The Riddle of the Dinosaurs* Faber & Faber, UK

MAMMAL-LIKE REPTILES

Kemp, T. S. (1982) *Mammal-like Reptiles and the Origin of Mammals* Academic Press, UK & USA

BIRDS

Feduccia, A. (1980) *The Age of Birds* Harvard University Press, USA

MAMMALS

Aiello, L. (1982) *Discovering the Origins of Mankind* Longman, UK

Clutton-Brock, J. (1981) *Domesticated Animals from Early Times* Heinemann/British Museum (Natural History), UK

Colbert, E. H. (1980) *Evolution of Vertebrates* Wiley, USA

Halstead, L. B. (1978) *The Evolution of the Mammals* Peter Lowe, UK

Hamilton, W. R. (1972) *The History of Mammals* British Museum (Natural History), UK

Kurtén, B. (1971) *The Age of Mammals* Weidenfeld & Nicholson, UK; Columbia University Press, USA

Lambert, D. (1987) *The Cambridge Guide to Prehistoric Man* Cambridge University Press, UK

Leakey, R. E. (1981) *Human Origins* Hamish Hamilton, UK

(1981) *The Making of Mankind* Michael Joseph, UK

Leakey, R., Lewin, R. (1977) *Origins* E. P. Dutton, USA

Lewin, R. (1984) *Human Evolution: An Illustrated Introduction* Blackwell Scientific Publications, UK

Napier, J. R. & P. H. (1985) *The Natural History of the Primates* British Museum (Natural History), UK

Savage, R. J. G., Long, M. R. (1986) *Mammal Evolution: An Illustrated Guide* British Museum (Natural History), UK

Scott, W. G. (1967) *A History of Land Mammals in the Western Hemisphere* Macmillan, USA

Simpson, G. C. (1951) *Horses* Oxford University Press, UK

(1980) *Splendid Isolation: The Curious History of South American Mammals* Yale University Press, USA

Szalay, F. S., Delson, E. (1979) *Evolutionary History of the Primates* Academic Press, UK & USA

Wood, B. (1976) *The Evolution of Early Man* Peter Lowe, UK

International museums

The museums listed below are among those that contain outstanding collections of fossils of the prehistoric creatures described in this book.

ARGENTINA
La Plata: *Museum of La Plata University*

AUSTRALIA
Brisbane, Queensland: *Queensland Museum*
Sydney, New South Wales: *Australian Museum*

AUSTRIA
Vienna: *Natural History Museum*

BELGIUM
Brussels: *Royal Institute of Natural Sciences*

CANADA
Calgary, Alberta: *Zoological Gardens*
Drumheller, Alberta: *Tyrrell Museum of Paleontology*
Edmonton, Alberta: *Provincial Museum of Alberta*
Ottawa, Ontario: *National Museum of National Sciences*
Toronto, Ontario: *Royal Ontario Museum*

CHINA
Beijing (Peking): *Beijing Natural History Museum*

FRANCE
Paris: *National Museum of Natural History*

GERMANY (EAST)
East Berlin: *Natural History Museum, Humboldt University*

GERMANY (WEST)
Darmstadt: *Hesse State Museum*
Frankfurt-am-Main: *Senckenbert Natural History Museum*
Munich: *Bavarian State Institute for Paleontology and Historical Geography*
Stuttgart: *State Museum for Natural History*
Tubingen: *Institute and Museum of Geology and Paleontology*

GREECE
Athens: *Department of Geology and Paleontology, University of Athens*

INDIA
Calcutta: *Geology Museum, Indian Statistical Institute*

ITALY
Bologna: *G. Capellini Museum*
Genoa: *Civic Museum of Natural History*
Milan: *Civic Museum of Natural History*
Padua: *Museum of the Institute of Geology*
Rome: *Museum of Paleontology, Institute of Geology*

JAPAN
Osaka: *Museum of Natural History*
Tokyo: *National Science Museum*

KENYA
Nairobi: *Kenya National Museum*

MEXICO
Mexico City: *Natural History Museum*

MONGOLIA
Ulan-Bator: *State Central Museum*

MOROCCO
Rabat: *Museum of Earth Sciences*

NIGER
Niamey: *National Museum*

SOUTH AFRICA
Capetown: *South Africa Museum*

SWEDEN
Uppsala: *Paleontology Museum, Uppsala University*

UNITED KINGDOM
Cambridge: *Sedgwick Museum, Cambridge University*
Cardiff, Wales: *National Museum of Wales*
Edinburgh, Scotland: *Royal Scottish Museum*
Elgin, Scotland: *Elgin Museum*
London: *British Museum (Natural History); Crystal Palace Park*
Maidstone: *Maidstone Museum*
Oxford: *University Museum*

UNITED STATES OF AMERICA
Boulder, Colorado: *University Natural History Museum*
Buffalo, New York State: *Buffalo Museum of Science*
Cambridge, Massachusetts: *Museum of Comparative Zoology, Harvard University*
Chicago, Illinois: *Field Museum of Natural History*
Cleveland, Ohio: *Natural History Museum*
Denver, Colorado: *Denver Museum of Natural History*
Jensen, Utah: *Dinosaur National Monument*
Los Angeles, California: *Los Angeles County Museum of Natural History*
New Haven, Connecticut: *Peabody Museum of Natural History, Yale University*
New York, New York State: *American Museum of Natural History*
Pittsburg, Pennsylvania: *Carnegie Museum of Natural History*
Princeton, New Jersey: *Museum of Natural History, Princeton University*
Salt Lake City, Utah: *Utah Museum of Natural History*
Washington DC: *National Museum of Natural History, Smithsonian Institution*

USSR
Leningrad: *Central Geological and Prospecting Museum; Museum of Geology* Moscow: *Paleontology Museum*

Index

Index

Index

Key to evolution charts

FISHES (*see pp. 18–19*)
The fishes illustrated in silhouette to
represent the various evolutionary groups
are as follows, *from top to bottom, left to right:*
Heterostracans: *Pteraspis*
Thelodontids: *Thelodus*
Osteostracans: *Hemicyclaspis*
Anaspids: *Pharyngolepis*
Lampreys: modern lamprey
Elasmobranchs: *Cladoselache, Hybodus,
  Sclerorhynchus*
Holocephalians: *Deltoptychius, Ischyodus,*
  modern ratfish
Climatiiformes: *Climatius*
Acanthodiformes: *Acanthodes*
Rhenanids: *Gemuendina*
Ptyctodontids: *Ctenurella*
Arthrodires: *Coccosteus*
Antiarchs: *Bothriolepis*
Palaeonisciformes: *Moythomasia*
Semionotiformes: *Dapedium*
Pycnodontiformes: *Pycnodus*
Aspidorhynchiformes: *Aspidorhynchus*
Teleosts: *Thrissops, Eobothus*
Porolepiformes: *Gyroptychius*
Actinistians: *Macropoma,* modern coelacanth
Dipnoans: *Dipterus,* modern Australian
  lungfish
Osteolepiformes: *Eusthenopteron*
All the fossil fishes are described in the text
  (*see pp. 22–45*).

AMPHIBIANS (*see pp. 46–47*)
The amphibians illustrated in silhouette to
represent the various evolutionary groups
are as follows, *from top to bottom, left to right:*
Microsaurs: *Microbrachis*
Nectrideans: *Diplocaulus*
Aïstopods: *Dolichosoma*
Seymouriamorphs: *Seymouria*
Eogyrinids: *Eogyrinus*
Plagiosaurs: *Gerrothorax*
Dissorophids: *Platyhystrix*
Capitosaurs: *Paracyclotosaurus*
Eryopids: *Eryops*
Proanurans: *Triadobatrachus*
Colosteids: *Greererpeton*
Ichthyostegalians: *Ichthyostega*
All these animals are described in the text
  (*see pp. 50–57*).

REPTILES (*see pp. 58–59*)
The reptiles illustrated in silhouette to
represent the various evolutionary groups
are as follows, *from top to bottom, left to right:*
Mesosaurs: *Mesosaurus*
Pareiasaurs: *Pareiasaurus*
Protorothyridids: *Hylonomus*
Millerettids: *Milleretta*
Captorhinids: *Labidosaurus*
Chelonians: *Proganochelys*
Ichthyosaurs: *Ichthyosaurus*

Placodonts: *Placodus*
Araeoscelids: *Araeoscelis*
Choristoderans: *Champsosaurus*
Thalattosaurs: *Askeptosaurus*
Coelurosauravids: *Coelurosauravus*
Eosuchians: *Hovasaurus*
Nothosaurs: *Nothosaurus*
Plesiosaurs: *Elasmosaurus*
Sphenodonts: *Planocephalosaurus*
Lizards: *Ardeosaurus, Platecarpus*
Rhynchosaurs: *Hyperodapedon*
Snakes: *Pachyrhachis*
Protorosaurs: *Protorosaurus*
Tanystropheids: *Tanystropheus*
All these animals are described in the text
(*see pp. 62–89*).

RULING REPTILES (*see pp. 90–91*)
The ruling reptiles illustrated in silhouette
to represent the various evolutionary
groups are as follows, *from top to bottom,
left to right:*
Proterosuchians: *Erythrosuchus*
Rauisuchians: *Ticinosuchus*
Phytosaurs: *Rutiodon*
Aetosaurs: *Stagonolepis*
Ornithosuchians: *Lagosuchus*
Sphenosuchians: *Gracilisuchus*
Protosuchians: *Protosuchus*
Mesosuchians: *Metriorhynchus*
Eusuchians: *Deinosuchus*
Rhamphorhynchs: *Eudimorphodon,
  Rhamphorhynchus*
Pterodactyls: *Pteranodon*
Coelurosaurs: *Saltopus, Ornithomimus*
Carnosaurs: *Allosaurus, Tyrannosaurus*
Prosauropods: *Anchisaurus*
Sauropods: *Brachiosaurus, Alamosaurus*
Ceratopians: *Triceratops*
Ornithopods: *Heterodontosaurus, Iguanodon,
  Anatosaurus*
Stegosaurs: *Stegosaurus*
Ankylosaurs: *Polacanthus, Euoplocephalus*
All these animals are described in the text
(*see pp. 94–169*).

BIRDS (*see pp. 170–171*)
The birds illustrated in silhouette to
represent the various evolutionary groups,
both extinct and modern, are as follows,
from top to bottom, left to right:
Archaeornithes: *Archaeopteryx*
Odontornithes: *Ichthyornis*
Elephant birds: *Aepyornis*
Moas: *Dinornis*
Presbyornithids: *Presbyornis*
Pigeons: *Raphus*
Diatrymids: *Diatryma*
Bathornithids: *Neocathartes*
Phorusrhacids: *Phorusrhacus*
Shorebirds: *Pinguinus*
Palaelodids: *Palaelodus*

Birds of prey: *Harpagornis*
Storks and New World vultures: *Argentavis*
Bony-toothed birds: *Osteodontornis*
Frigatebirds: *Limnofregata*
All these birds are described in the text (*see
pp. 174–181*).

MAMMAL-LIKE REPTILES
  (*see pp. 182–183*)
The mammal-like reptiles illustrated in
silhouette to represent the various
evolutionary groups are as follows, *from top
to bottom, left to right:*
Cynodonts: *Cynognathus*
Therocephalians: *Ericiolacerta*
Gorgonopsians: *Lycaenops*
Eotitanosuchians: *Phthinosuchus*
Dinocephalians: *Titanosuchus*
Dicynodonts: *Kannemeyeria*
Sphenacodonts: *Sphenacodon*
Edaphosaurs: *Edaphosaurus*
Ophiacodonts: *Ophiacodon*
Caseids: *Casea*
All these animals are described in the text
(*see pp. 186–193*).

MAMMALS (*see pp. 194–195*)
The mammals illustrated in silhouette to
represent the various evolutionary groups
are as follows, *from top to bottom, left to right:*
Prototherians: *Megazostrodon, Ptilodus,*
  modern duckbilled platypus
Marsupials: *Borhyaena, Procoptodon*
Pantotheres: *Crusafontia*
Edentates: *Eurotamandua*
Insectivores: *Zalambdalestes*
Chiropterans: *Icaronycteris*
Primates: *Purgatorius, Necrolemur,
  Dryopithecus, Australopithecus africanus*
Creodonts: *Hyaenodon*
Feloids: *Kanuites, Smilodon*
Canoids: *Hesperocyon, Agriotherium*
Pinnipeds: *Desmatophoca*
Cetaceans: *Pakicetus, Cetotherium*
Proboscideans: *Moeritherium, Platybelodon,
  Mammuthus*
Sirenians: *Hydrodamalis*
Meridiungulates: *Thoatherium, Macrauchenia*
Ceratomorphs: *Hyrachus, Indricotherium*
Chalicotheres: *Moropus*
Hippomorphs: *Hyracotherium, Brontotherium*
Suines: *Diacodexis, Archaeotherium,
  Metridiochoerus*
Tylopods: *Cainotherium, Aepycamelus*
Pecorans: *Illingoceros, Sivatherium, Bos
  primigenius*
Rodents: *Epigaulus*
Lagomorphs: *Palaeolagus*
All these animals are described in the text
(*see pp. 198–297*).